GLOBAL POLITICS

fourth edition

GLOBAL POLITICS
Origins, Currents, Directions

Allen Sens
University of British Columbia

Peter Stoett
Concordia University

NELSON / EDUCATION

NELSON / EDUCATION

Global Politics, Fourth Edition

by Allen Sens and Peter Stoett

Associate Vice President, Editorial Director:
Evelyn Veitch

Editor-in-Chief, Higher Education:
Anne Williams

Senior Acquisitions Editor:
Anne-Marie Taylor

Marketing Manager:
Ann Byford

Developmental Editor:
Liisa Kelly

Photo Researcher/Permissions Coordinator:
Natalie Barrington

Senior Content Production Manager:
Imoinda Romain

Production Service:
Knowledgeworks Global Limited

Copy Editor:
Rodney Rawlings

Proofreader:
Saravanakumar Dharman

Indexer:
Nadia Digre

Manufacturing Manager:
Joanne McNeil

Design Director:
Ken Phipps

Managing Designer:
Franca Amore

Interior Design:
Nelson Gonzalez

Cover Design:
Jennifer Leung

Cover Image:
Lincoln Seligman/Getty Images

Compositor:
Knowledgeworks Global Limited

Printer:
Edwards Brothers

Sens, Allen G. (Allen Gregory), 1964-
    Global politics : origins, currents, directions / Allen Sens, Peter Stoett. — 4th ed.

Order of authors reversed on 1st ed.
Includes bibliographical references and index.
ISBN 978-0-17-650049-8

    1. World politics—1989-.
2. Canada–Politics and government. I. Title.

D860.S45 2009
909.82'9   C2009-903611-8

ISBN-13: 978-0-17-650049-8
ISBN-10: 0-17-650049-9

Brief Contents

Detailed Contents

PART TWO: CURRENTS

Preface

Teaching global politics is a challenging occupation. Few subjects are so interdisciplinary, requiring the level of command over history, geography, science, psychology, and politics that college and university courses demand. Many continuities and enduring concepts require elaboration, while political and social developments and theoretical innovations must be explained and put into context. To make matters even more challenging, global politics is anything but a static subject. The past quarter-century has been particularly tumultuous. The collapse of the communist regimes in Eastern Europe and the disintegration of the Soviet Union brought a remarkably swift and dramatic end to an ideological, geopolitical, and military struggle that defined the post–World War II era. The word *globalization* is often used to define the new era that emerged after the end of the Cold War, and although the word has its detractors, it does capture a sense of momentous change and uncertainty, and resonates with a generation of students grappling with the reality that their lives are increasingly affected by world events and global trends. The technological changes that characterized the 20th century have altered established patterns of economic activity, global communication, and military strategy. Furthermore, students today have a heightened awareness of the threats to human security presented by militarism, poverty, climate change, intolerance, pandemics, and economic recession (to name a few). Students do not want their comprehension of global issues stymied by traditional disciplinary barriers between the study of politics, economics, history, and culture, or between the social sciences and humanities and the physical and life sciences. Finally, major events such as the terrorist attacks of September 11, 2001, the Iraq War of 2003, and the onset of a global recession in 2008 challenge teacher and student alike to grasp the complexities of a subject that displays features of change as well as continuity, and trends of divergence as well as convergence.

An additional challenge facing Canadian teachers and students of global politics is the lack of textbooks that are Canadian in orientation. Most international relations textbooks are American, and their examples focus almost exclusively on American foreign policy issues. One crucial function of the first three editions of this text was to relate the academic study of global politics to the lives of students who reside outside the United States. The fourth edition retains this basic philosophy, and the rationale for this new edition is largely practical: things change. In fact, the second edition of *Global Politics* was printed and distributed in the summer of 2001, and only a few days after the edition reached store shelves, the terrorist attacks in the United States shook the world. Since the publication of the second edition, the world has witnessed not only those large-scale terrorist attacks and the subsequent wars in Afghanistan and Iraq, but also the launching of the troubled Doha Round of world trade talks. We also witnessed the establishment of an International Criminal Court; the intensification of violence between Israelis and Palestinians; the emergence of SARS, BSE, and avian flu and the continued spread of HIV/AIDS; the enlargement of NATO and the EU; debates over genetically modified organisms; a new commitment to the world's poor in the UN Millennium Development Goals; and an explosive growth in global wireless networks. Since the publication of the third edition, the war in Iraq has turned into a troubled postwar occupation, and the war in Afghanistan shows no sign of ending; additional conflicts have broken out in the Middle East and elsewhere; a global recession has hit with unprecedented speed; concerns over climate change and sustainability have increased dramatically; a swine flu pandemic has been declared by the World Health Organization; and the election of President Barack Obama has cast a new light on America's role in the world and Canada's foreign policy options. It was necessary to update significant portions of the book, and although it is impossible to cover everything, our intent was to make the book as comprehensive and contemporary as possible, while retaining our appreciation of the necessity for a solid grounding in theory and history.

It is important to remind both teachers and students how the study of global politics was conducted a little over two decades ago. The Cold War between East and West dominated international politics and the attention of policymakers for more than 45 years. Scholars and their students focused on issues such as the strategic nuclear and military balance, nuclear arms control, the shifting tides of superpower diplomacy, the politics of alliances such as NATO and the Warsaw Pact, and the extension of the Cold War rivalry into regional conflicts. The politics of the bipolar world also engaged many members of the public, as the superpower arms race sparked the development of a large peace and disarmament movement. However, it would be a mistake to argue that such Cold War issues excluded other global phenomena, since they occurred in a changing international context that included a growing and ever more integrated global economy; an increasing interdependence between societies and states; a growing divide between rich and poor societies, and between rich and poor within societies; the increasing activity of nonstate actors such as multinational corporations and nongovernmental organizations; rapid technological advances; and a growing concern over environmental degradation. Many of the issues that occupy our attention today have their origins in the Cold War. However, the politics of the superpower rivalry, attended by the threat of global nuclear war, was the primary subject of study in the realm of international affairs.

Today, the focus of global politics has been reoriented toward a much broader set of issues. These include efforts (often the object of vociferous protest) to manage the global economy, a vital subject to a trade-dependent state such as Canada. Of course, over 75 percent of Canadian trade is with the United States, and this relationship continues to dominate foreign policy considerations. The post–Cold War democratization process is also of great interest to Canadians, as other states embark on experiments similar to our own. Issues such as regional conflicts, human rights violations, gender issues, the proliferation of conventional weapons and weapons of mass destruction, threats to the global commons, refugee and population movements, terrorism, and the information and communications revolution are all on the agenda of the cosmopolitan, globally aware Canadian. And yet a cautionary voice must be raised here. Though it is tempting to speak of the end of the Cold War or the events of September 11, 2001 as the beginning of a new age of global politics, much remains the same. The world is still politically divided into a system of territorial states; conflict and cooperation between states and within states continues; and despite developments in economic interdependence and global communications, the world remains divided between rich and poor, between different religions and ethnicities, and between different forms of domestic governance. In this text we have tried to situate the immense change occurring around us within an understanding of these elements of continuity.

The central aim of *Global Politics: Origins, Currents, and Directions* is to introduce readers to the rich and diverse enterprise that is the study of contemporary international relations, encouraging an appreciation of the theoretical roots of divergent perspectives on how the international system operates. The text also establishes the vital historical context in which the modern world is embedded, and intends to stimulate thoughtful analysis and critical thinking while promoting a healthy skepticism for established wisdom and prevailing assumptions. *Global Politics* also reveals the human element of international relations by providing insights and biographies of individuals who have made an impact on the world in which we live. Finally, this text was conceived in a post–Cold War context and designed from the beginning to reflect the contemporary global environment and the issues faced by today's scholars, policymakers, students, and citizens. The Cold War is history (albeit important history), and this book is structured around this fact. To this end, *Global Politics* gives equal attention to the theoretical developments and historical events of the past, the key issues facing us today, and the emerging agenda that confronts us all. As the full title indicates, this book looks to the future as much as it looks to the past and the present. The book does not claim to be a crystal ball but it does identify trends and themes, and challenges the reader to think about the issues and theoretical approaches that loom on the horizon.

The Structure of the Book

As our subtitle suggests, *Global Politics* is organized into three parts: origins, currents, and directions. Part One, "Origins," examines the theoretical perspectives fundamental to any understanding of the debates and controversies in the discipline, and the historical evolution of the international system up to the end of the Cold War. The development of the key contending perspectives in international relations theory is discussed in historical context. Part One reveals how these contending perspectives tend to focus on different types of historical events or have different interpretations of history. For example, realists emphasize the history of empires, great powers, and wars, while liberals emphasize economic history and the development of interdependence. Critical theorists emphasize historical patterns of hierarchy and dominance and the processes that perpetuate poverty and disempowerment. In short, Part One looks at the history of war, the state, the Cold War, international political economy, international institutions, and law, and it gives us the theoretical background necessary to understand it.

In Part Two, "Currents," readers are introduced to some of the key issues on the contemporary security, economic, and ethical agendas. We look at today's varied conflict management efforts, the divisive impact of globalization on the world economy, and some principal human rights and human security questions. Part Two is designed to give the reader a snapshot of the contemporary international situation and an improved understanding of the issues that confront today's world. Key themes include armed conflict, weapons proliferation, terrorism, arms control, organized crime, humanitarian intervention, poverty and marginalization, relativist versus universalist conceptions of human rights, international criminal law, and many others.

In Part Three, "Directions," items of growing importance on the international agenda are explored. We begin with a discussion of contemporary global environmental problems. Next, we look at population growth and movements, global health issues, and the impact of the information revolution; and we look toward possible future trends in all of these areas of study. These admittedly selective subjects are discussed because, in the view of the authors, they will dominate the future agenda of global politics over the long term, and presumably have a direct impact upon the lives of many if not all of our students. Of course, all these issues are interlinked not only with each other, but with the security, economy, and human rights context established in Part Two. Not all of them will affect Canadians directly, but the connections between Canada's future and the complex trends outside the country are genuine.

We have made a special effort in this edition to make the conceptual links between issue-areas and theories of international relations more explicit throughout Parts Two and Three.

An overarching theme knits the subject matter of the book together. The past, present, and future of global politics can be characterized in terms of political *convergence* and *divergence*. Trends of convergence, or what some prefer to label *integration*, can be identified in economic globalization and interdependence; the development of international organizations and the expansion of international law; the growing volume of international communication and travel; the development of a global civil society of nongovernmental organizations; efforts to promote and strengthen democratization; and reduced friction between the great powers. Trends of divergence, often termed *fragmentation*, can be identified in the divide between rich and poor and the information haves and have-nots; the disintegration of states; interstate and intrastate conflict; ethnic, religious, and factional tension and violence; the development of regional trading blocs; friction between world cultures; and the impact of environmental degradation as a cause of social tension or conflict. The convergence/divergence theme is revisited throughout the book.

To the Student

It is an exciting, and no doubt anxious, time to be studying global politics. You are part of a growing generation of students who have been exposed to a global political environment quite different from that faced by students of international relations during the Cold War. However, as you look to the future of the world in which you live, it would be wrong to ignore the past. Despite changes in the global political scene and advancements in technology and communications, in some respects little has changed. Many of the issues and problems that have plagued the world for decades and even centuries persist today. Discovering that a hot topic today was also a hot topic a generation ago can be humbling, but much can be understood from past events and from how current issues are both similar to and different from those events.

Studying global politics is also a demanding undertaking, for the subject matter is broad, deep, and multidimensional, and many points of dispute and controversy exist. It is tempting for students to focus on certain issues (the environment, war, or technology, for example) to the exclusion of others. However, this is a mistake, for virtually all subjects in global politics are closely related, and it is impossible to understand any one issue in isolation. Furthermore, an appreciation of different perspectives is an absolute must. Part of the challenge of any scholarly pursuit is to understand perspectives that differ from your own. When you do this, you gain in two ways: first, you improve your understanding of the basis for disagreements between individuals, groups, and states; and second, you are forced to reexamine your own personal perspectives and beliefs. In some cases this process will cause you to change your mind, and in other cases it will not; but in any event, you will have gained a critical understanding of different views and ideas about the world.

This book is best treated as a guide through the interrelated subfields of global politics. It introduces the specialized terms and jargon international relations scholars use for different phenomena and contending perspectives. In each chapter we have put the significant terms, which are defined in the Glossary at the end of the book, in **bold** type. Of course, a large and rich literature exists on every subject discussed, and you may want to learn more about a certain topic or find materials for research papers. On the book's website, at http://www.globalpolitics4e.nelson.com, we supply a list of Suggested Readings and Internet resources to assist you in this task. Further, take care to read the Endnotes section at the end of each chapter, for they include some of the better-known and valuable sources, and we do not list them all again among the online Suggested Readings.

Since it is intended as a guide, *Global Politics* is only an introduction to the vast field of international relations. Your instructor may cover other issues, and you may find that you or your instructor do not agree with many of the points made in this book. However, we have tried to be as inclusive and balanced as possible in presenting the subject matter. As individuals, we differ on many aspects of our discipline and agree on many more. While it may be impossible to be completely balanced in such an undertaking (as we learned from preliminary reviews of the several editions), we have tried to incorporate as many diverse perspectives as possible while retaining the content traditionally expected in an international relations textbook. Ultimately, it is up to you to develop your own informed opinions and ideas. We would both be very interested in any comments regarding the present edition, and invite readers to write or e-mail us with them at

pstoett@alcor.concordia.ca

asens@politics.ubc.ca

We completed our bachelor's and master's degrees in the late 1980s and obtained our doctorates in the early-to-mid-1990s at Canadian universities. Our careers as students and professionals straddle the Cold War and post–Cold War eras. Our studies have taken us to Western and Eastern Europe, Africa, northern and southern Asia, Central and South America, and of course the United States. We have made our homes in Vancouver and Montreal, and we are both frequently involved with the foreign policy–making process in Ottawa. Our experience is one of change and flux, and we, like you, look to the future with excitement and deep concern. Though our views often differ, we have strived to achieve a workable and fair balance between them. We hope this experience and dedication gives us ample qualifications for authorship of a text on global politics, and we hope you are inspired to pursue similar paths of discovery and engagement after reading *Global Politics: Origins, Currents, and Directions*.

Acknowledgments

Many friends, colleagues, and scholars have contributed to the development, writing, and editing of this book. It would be impossible to list all those who have touched our lives and work in meaningful ways over the years, so any attempt that follows is necessarily partial.

We would like to thank the following colleagues whose expertise and assistance have been invaluable: Abbie Bakan, Robert Boardman, Max Cameron, Andrew Cooper, David Cox, Simon Dalby, Gerald Dirks, Bill Graf, David Haglund, Kal Holsti, Horst Hutter, Rosalind Irwin, Bob Jackson, Brian Job, Eric Laferrière, Jayent Lele, Don Munton, Jorge Nef, Kim Richard Nossal, Kwasi Obu-Fari, Angela O'Mahony, Charles Pentland, Richard Price, Norrin Ripsman, Patricia Romano, Doug Ross, Heather Smith, Lisa Sundstrom, Yves Tiberghien, Katharina Coleman, Claire Turenne Sjolander, Henry Wiseman, and Mark Zacher. Our apologies to the many we have left off our list.

We owe special thanks to the many reviewers commissioned by Nelson Education, including Paul Rousseau, University of Windsor; Paul S. Rowe, Trinity Western University; Elinor C. Sloan, Carleton University; Erika Simpson, University of Western Ontario; Jordi Diez, University of Guelph; Mary Goldie, Langara College; Derek Hall, Wilfrid Laurier University; and Arne Kislenko, University of Toronto and Ryerson University. Their comments not only enriched the text and filled gaping holes but also gave us a sense of the current state of the discipline across Canada. We would also like to thank the invaluable administrative assistance provided by staff in the Political Science departments at the University of British Columbia and Concordia University.

For the exhaustive editorial, production, and marketing effort at Nelson Education, we thank all those who worked on the fourth edition, including, but not limited to, Lenore

Taylor-Atkins, Liisa Kelly, and Susan Wong. Special thanks go to Rodney Rawlings and Saravanakumar Dharman for their comprehensive copyediting and proofreading, respectively. Most importantly of all, we would also like to express our appreciation for the comments offered by our students over the years. Students are the lifeblood of any scholarly enterprise, and ours have provided a wealth of critical insights and suggestions.

Special thanks go to Pam Baldwin and Cristina Romanelli, our better halves, life companions, and beacons of light during the dark early morning hours spent finishing this edition. As always, Peter thanks his children, Alexandra, Giuliana, and Gianluca, for their smiles and hope. We dedicate this book to these extraordinary sources of inspiration.

Any errors, of course, are our responsibility alone.

A Note on Maps and Names

In global politics, conflicts (especially territorial conflicts) are often symbolized by disputes over the name of a country or territory. For example, Macedonia is called "the Former Yugoslavian Republic of Macedonia" (FYROM), because the Greek government objects to the use of a name that distinguishes an area within Greece. In addition, the names of many countries change over time, often because of a change in government. For example, the Khmer Rouge changed the name of Cambodia to Kampuchea (today, Cambodia is the common usage once again); Burma has been renamed Myanmar by the military regime in power there (although it is still commonly referred to as Burma); and following a revolution in 1997 the African country of Zaire was renamed the Democratic Republic of Congo. Furthermore, separatist or nationalist movements that want to create or recreate their own states often refer to an area of land as their own. For example, the representatives of the Kurdish people claim parts of Turkey, Syria, and Iran as the territory of Kurdistan, while the leadership of the Palestinian people wants to reestablish an independent state of Palestine in an area now occupied by the state of Israel. The politically sensitive nature of names is compounded by the fact that the use of one name over another is often taken as an indication of political support. This book seeks to make the student aware of such disputes and changes, although space considerations often make this impractical. We have strived to be as balanced and respectful as possible.

PART ONE

Origins

This section of the book lays the foundation for subsequent discussions of contemporary and emerging themes in global politics. It begins with an introduction to the academic field of inquiry widely known as *international relations*, and the prevalent theoretical perspectives that guide researchers in the discipline. In Chapter 2, we turn to a brief history of the evolution of the international political system, including the rise and fall of empires, the prominent role of the state in the Westphalian system, and the impact of major wars on global politics. The next chapter discusses the Cold War and the study of how and why foreign policy decisions are made. Chapter 4 discusses the evolution of the world economy, with an emphasis on liberal economic theory and the origins of the historical process often referred to as *globalization*. Finally, Chapter 5 examines the evolution of international law and international institutions. This foundation will allow us to pursue more contemporary topics in Part Two.

Global Politics: The Discipline and Its Theoretical Foundations

Let us not imitate the historians who believe that the past has always been inevitable, and thus suppress the human dimension of events.

—Raymond Aron

If everyone's strategy depends upon everyone else's, then the Hitlers determine in part the action, or better, reaction, of those whose ends are worthy and whose means are fastidious.

—Kenneth Waltz

Breaking with the powerful bond among men, states and war in international relations theory ... feminist approaches [offer] a normative standpoint from which to construct alternative world orders.

—Jacqui True[1]

ON THE MENU: COMPLEXITY, INSECURITY, CONVERGENCE AND DIVERGENCE

For students interested in war and peace, **globalization**, climate change, poverty and inequality, human rights and gender discrimination, criminal acts and criminal inaction, and racial and religious divides, the study of global politics has it all—and more! Global politics is engaged with the eternal debates about human nature, the origins and development of societies, the interaction between economics, politics, and culture, and the causes and impacts of change. It is a subject replete with frustrating constraints and sobering limitations, as well as examples of breathtaking progress and unexpected opportunities. It is also a subject enriched with human stories of tragedy, despair, compassion, and hope. This textbook is designed to introduce you to this inherently broad and complex field of study. And because every student of global politics makes key decisions about how to proceed in his or her quest for greater understanding, we hope this textbook will help you make these decisions with a full awareness of the range of issues involved.

This first chapter is intended to introduce you to the discipline, and provide the theoretical foundations necessary for the further pursuit of the subjects we highlight in subsequent chapters.

As individuals, our relationship with global politics is an interactive one. At the most basic level, you are alive and reading this text because you have not been killed in a nuclear war. At the height of the Cold War such a fate seemed entirely plausible. It is possible that through a horrible accident or dramatic political change, nuclear war could become a predominant threat once again. There are concerns that deteriorating relations between Russia and the United States (and most European countries) might lead to a new Cold War, while tensions between India and Pakistan might result in war between these two nuclear-armed states. The rise of China and international crises over North Korean and Iranian nuclear weapons development also remind us that these weapons are far from irrelevant in global politics. Nevertheless, today we are more immediately concerned with climate change, the spread of infectious diseases, terrorist acts (and military responses to them), economic crises, access to safe food and water, and many other global issues that threaten lives on a daily basis. The impact of these issues might be felt differently depending on where we live. For example, changes in world oil or food prices have a different impact on people in Alberta and people in Haiti. On the other hand, other issues might threaten the **human security** of people regardless of location. For example, the SARS epidemic killed people in both East Asia and southern Ontario.

Of course, you need not be a professional diplomat, corporate executive, or social activist to interact with global politics: our everyday decisions impact the world economy, environment, and political landscape. This statement is as true for someone living in Canada as it is for someone living in Germany, Pakistan, Uganda, Peru, or Micronesia, although within and among these countries the range of choice available to any given individual (and the relative impact that choice may have) is remarkably varied. Furthermore, we are constantly absorbing impressions and images of global politics, and James Der Derian reminds us that many of these come "wrapped in representations, bundled in ideology, edited by the media, warped by official stories."[2] Anyone who has boarded an airplane since knows that the September 11, 2001 terrorist attacks on the United States changed the airport security environment in dramatic ways. However, for people of Arab origin the attacks have often also meant an increase in discrimination, ethnic stereotyping, and racial profiling. In short, we are all a part of global politics, although our lived experiences are often different.

Though some lament the passing of the good old bad days of the **Cold War** (the "bipolar" era—see Chapter 2), things were hardly simple then either, as Chapter 3 indicates. However, there is no doubt that the sheer volume of contemporary concerns (or perhaps the widespread awareness of them) makes the discipline a particularly challenging one today. Studying global politics can seem overwhelming because there is so much to learn, and so many issues to address. This places a great deal of importance on the theories, frameworks, and models used to analyze and understand developments and trends in global politics. We argue that two simultaneous trends have emerged as one of the central paradoxes of the last several decades: *convergence* and *divergence*. While economic, technological, and network integration (labelled *globalization* by many) is taking place, so is political fragmentation in the form of separatist movements, competition for scarce resources, religious animosity, and other sources of conflict. This concept is not a novel one, and many other authors have touched on these apparently contradictory trends.[3] It would be simpler for all of us if either convergence or divergence clearly prevailed, but we have to deal with the confusing fact that the two are happening simultaneously. While it is obvious that there are military conflicts under way in many parts of the world, the effort to encourage trade and expand telecommunications systems continues unabated. The horrors of genocide during World War II provided the impetus for the establishment of a universal human rights regime to protect individuals from persecution conducted by the state, yet massive crimes against humanity continue, and ethnic minorities within states (from the Québécois in Canada to the Kurds in Turkey, Iraq, and Syria) continue to feel insecure in political systems dominated by others. Their efforts to protect their culture and gain political influence can spark confrontation and conflict. As you read this text and follow world events, you might look for evidence of convergence and divergence, in order to decide for yourself which, if either, is prevailing.

STUDYING GLOBAL POLITICS

Global politics is a complex, and often surreal, congruence of physical and intellectual power, political structures and institutions, ideas, and personalities such as the Dalai Lama and U.S. President Barack Obama. Commonly, the study of international relations, or "IR," has been

---

PROFILE 1.1 Canada and Global Politics

Canada has a population of 33,441,277 (as of October 2008 according to Statistics Canada), the second-largest territory in the world (Russia has the largest), and the ninth-largest economy. Canada is in an enviable position in global politics. It faces no traditional military threats to its territory or political independence, possesses a virtually unequalled standard of living, and is largely free of the violent conflict that characterizes many states. However, this position is no excuse for complacency. Canada depends on a generally peaceful and stable international order for its physical security and its economic health. The Canadian economy is heavily dependent on trade (in particular, trade with the United States, the destination for approximately 80 percent of all Canadian **exports**), and Canada, along with the United States and Mexico, is a member of **North American Free Trade Agreement (NAFTA)**. Beyond trade, Canada's foreign policy emphasizes the maintenance of international peace and security and making contributions to international institutions, democracy promotion, human rights and human security, arms control, and development. September 11 had a considerable impact on Canadian troop commitments abroad in places such as Afghanistan, as well as the security of Canadian borders, coastal zones, and airspace. Canada is a significant diplomatic actor, and it belongs to many major international forums

and institutions, including the **Group of Eight (G-8)**, the **North Atlantic Treaty Organization (NATO)**, the **Commonwealth**, **La Francophonie**, and the United Nations, to name only a few. Successive Canadian governments have been strong supporters of **multilateralism**, because within international organizations and coalitions Canada can at least have a voice and some expectation of influence. And yet Canada's close proximity to the United States often overshadows these concerns. In 2003, Canada's decision not to play an active role in the Iraq War presented a serious challenge to Canadian–American relations. While changes in government do lead to changes in Canada's position on international issues, for the most part Canadian foreign policy has remained remarkably consistent. The three "pillars" of Canadian foreign policy—security, prosperity, and the promotion of Canadian values—have not been altered for many years.

FOR FURTHER READING ON CANADA IN GLOBAL POLITICS, SEE B. BOW AND P. LENNOX, *AN INDEPENDENT FOREIGN POLICY FOR CANADA? CHALLENGES AND CHOICES FOR THE FUTURE* (TORONTO: UNIVERSITY OF TORONTO PRESS, 2008); M. BYERS, *INTENT FOR A NATION: WHAT IS CANADA FOR?* (VANCOUVER: DOUGLAS AND MCINTYRE, 2007); A. COHEN, *WHILE CANADA SLEPT: HOW WE LOST OUR PLACE IN THE WORLD* (TORONTO: MCCLELLAND AND STEWART, 2003); S.K. HOLLOWAY, *CANADIAN FOREIGN POLICY: DEFINING THE NATIONAL INTEREST* (PETERBOROUGH, ON: BROADVIEW PRESS, 2006); T. KEATING, *CANADA AND WORLD ORDER: THE MULTILATERALIST TRADITION IN CANADIAN FOREIGN POLICY*, 2ND ED. (DON MILLS: OXFORD UNIVERSITY PRESS, 2002); C. S. SJOLANDER, H. A. SMITH, AND D. STIENSTRA, EDS., *FEMINIST PERSPECTIVES ON CANADIAN FOREIGN POLICY* (DON MILLS: OXFORD UNIVERSITY PRESS, 2003); AND J. WELSH, *AT HOME IN THE WORLD: CANADA'S GLOBAL VISION FOR THE 21ST CENTURY* (TORONTO: HARPERCOLLINS, 2004).

The U.S. presidency and global politics. Barack and Michelle Obama, with daughters Sasha and Malia, wave to the crowd at the election night rally in Chicago, Tuesday, November 4, 2008. The election of Obama was an important symbolic moment in American history, but it raised the question of how much of a difference even the President of the United States can make in global politics. (AP Photo/Jae C. Hong/CP Archive.)

considered part of the larger field of political science, and most political science departments have international relations specialists. However, many universities have moved toward a much more explicitly interdisciplinary approach by granting degrees in *international studies* or *international relations*. Students of business, medicine, law, geography, history, economics, and many other disciplines need a solid background in international relations to better understand their own disciplines. It is not necessary to label them political scientists to achieve this, though most of the theories advanced to explain the complex phenomena of IR are derived from political philosophy and political science. A basic education in IR can also reveal the extent to which global politics impacts on a wide range of occupations and human activities. Most large-scale businesses are engaged in some form of international activity. Many foreign firms hire domestic nationals to work in their branch companies. Increasingly, many young people are travelling to work or study abroad and are finding opportunities to learn (and teach) languages and establish careers in other countries. Still others are working with nongovernmental organizations (NGOs) such as humanitarian aid agencies, or as journalists or international lawyers. Regardless of one's eventual career path, it will likely involve contact with people in other countries.

Beyond the impact on occupations, there are other reasons for today's student to study global politics, not least of which—and here we reflect our personal bias without apology—is the sheer excitement of studying politics at the international level and learning more about how it affects a wide range of human activities. Every day, newspapers, television, and the Internet carry news items, features, and discussions on a bewildering array of events happening around the world. Indeed, knowledge may be power, but it must make sense to be of any use. Many Canadian students are from immigrant families, and they are concerned about the life circumstances of family and friends in other parts of the world. Many students travel to far-flung destinations, and need to have a solid educational foundation to help them adapt to new environments. While studying IR does not provide a student with comprehensive knowledge about the world, it does advance one's understanding of the context in which other states and peoples exist.

To some extent, all academic disciplines suffer from what we call the irrelevancy disease. In many cases, academics prefer to rely on highly abstract theoretical thinking, which many students find difficult to relate to their daily lives. While some of the theories found in the discipline seem rather abstract at first glance, they can reveal patterns of historical behaviour, raise interesting questions about current events, propose solutions to the world's problems, and challenge prevailing assumptions about the nature of global politics. Ideas and knowledge generated from theoretical thinking enables us to critically evaluate the position and rationales of governments, political leaders, and orthodox explanations of events. It helps that the application of IR theory has become more diverse than ever, as the study of the discipline itself has become increasingly global and scholars outside Europe and North America add their voices and perspectives to the literature.

Furthermore, ours is a dangerous world filled with a great deal of human suffering, and many people want to make a difference (see Profile 1.2), perhaps by working with intergovernmental organizations (IGOs) or nongovernmental organizations (NGOs). In many locales, civil wars, famines, harsh structural adjustment policies, chronic **malnutrition**, epidemics, pollution and environmental degradation, illiteracy, and many other hardships make life especially challenging. Though working on the ground in these areas can be very fulfilling, it comes with unique dangers. Nancy Malloy was a Canadian Red Cross nurse and a specialist in

PROFILE 1.2   Individual Actors on the Stage of World Politics

Members of the Brazilian Air Force, left, salute as Sérgio Vieira de Mello's coffin is loaded aboard a Brazilian presidential plane by UN officials at Baghdad International Airport, Iraq, August 22, 2003. Vieira de Mello, the top UN official in Iraq, was killed in a suicide truck bombing attack on UN headquarters on August 19, 2003, that killed at least 22 other people and left more than 100 injured. (AP Photo/Manish Swarup/CP Archive.)

SERGIO VIEIRA DE MELLO

Sérgio Vieira de Mello was born in Rio de Janeiro in 1948. He joined the United Nations in 1969 while studying at the University of Paris. In the course of his impressive career at the UN, Vieira de Mello served as United Nations Assistant High Commissioner for Refugees, Under-Secretary-General for Humanitarian Affairs, and Emergency Relief Coordinator. For a short time he was the Special Representative of the Secretary-General in Kosovo, and he also served as United Nations Transitional Administrator in East Timor. On September 12, 2002, Vieira de Mello was appointed United Nations High Commissioner for Human Rights.

In May 2003, he was asked by Secretary-General Kofi Annan to take a four-month leave of absence from his position as High Commissioner to serve in Iraq as Special Representative of the Secretary-General. It was there that Sergio Vieira de Mello was tragically killed on August 19, 2003, when the UN headquarters in Iraq fell victim to a terrorist attack. Following the tragedy, Kofi Annan appointed an Independent Panel on the Safety and Security of UN personnel in Iraq, and work continues to assure that UN personnel are protected in such circumstances. See S. Power, *Chasing the Flame: Sérgio Vieira de Mello and the Fight to Save the World* (New York: Penguin, 2007).

hospital administration. A resident of Vancouver, she joined the Red Cross in 1987 and took her first international assignment in 1990, motivated by a personal desire to help alleviate suffering in war-torn areas. She worked in five war zones over the next six years, in Ethiopia (1990), Kuwait (1991), the former Yugoslavia (1993), Zaire (1995), and Chechnya (1996). On December 17, 1996, gunmen broke into a Chechen hospital complex during the night and killed six Red Cross workers, including Ms. Malloy. A person need not be a ruling politician to be a hero in world politics, nor to be a victim of its vicissitudes.

THE INTERDISCIPLINARY, YET DIVIDED, DISCIPLINE

Formally, and according to academic convention, the field of IR is divided into several sub-fields, or what some prefer to term sub-disciplines. In this way, IR scholars can break an enormous amount of material and topics down into more digestible sections for investigation and analysis. For the sake of brevity, we will assume that the study of international relations has four major subfields.

International relations theory is a body of literature that seeks to explain the nature of the international system and the behaviour of the actors within it.[4] *International security* has traditionally involved the study of conflict and war and attempts to prevent or control it. Recently, international security specialists have also been examining ethnic and religious conflicts, the proliferation of weapons, and the link between the environment and security.[5] The study of *international political economy* grew in the 1960s and 1970s as issues such as trade, finance, foreign debt, and underdevelopment became increasingly prominent in international affairs.[6] Finally, the subfield that examines institutions such as the United Nations is generally referred to as *international organization*, and focuses on means of cooperation such as the establishment of regimes or agreements among states, groups, or individuals, including international law.[7] This division of the field into subfields is admittedly arbitrary. Some would argue that other subfields exist, such as gender studies in IR, foreign policy analysis, international ethics, development studies, or global ecopolitics. Yet others would argue that such a large overlap exists between the subfields that to separate them is parochial at best and misleading at worst. Provided that we are aware of these objections, however, the divisions allow us to conceptualize the overall project of the study of global politics.

Moreover—and this will become increasingly obvious as you read this text—those engaged in this project benefit from the collaboration of a large number of specialists from other well-established fields in the social sciences and humanities, including experts in comparative and domestic politics, world and local history, economics, geography, psychology, sociology, and anthropology. When we move beyond the descriptive and analytical into more prescriptive areas, we engage in normative work, in which writers are as interested in putting forth their vision of how the world should be as they are in telling us how it is. Normative projects reflect the moral and ethical judgments of the scholar or demonstrate how ethics are acted on by world leaders and diplomats.[8] Some scholars argue further that it is misleading to separate the analytic from the normative, since all investigators have their own biases, and all theories have their value-laden assumptions. Explicitly normative work borrows heavily from the vast literature on ethics and philosophy and ventures into questions concerning the just causes of war, the true meaning of human rights, religious differences, and environmental values. Finally, in this technological age, scholars and students also borrow knowledge and insights from the applied and natural sciences, such as physics, earth and ocean science, chemistry, biology, computer science, robotics, and genetics. In short, the student of global politics must become adept not only at taking a broad approach, but also at practising considerable **synthesis** as well.

The discipline is divided further by differences over what primary level of analysis should demand our attention. Three main levels of analysis exist—the *individual* level, the *state* or *group* level, and the *systemic* level—although this rough division is open to dispute.[9] The *individual* level of analysis focuses on the decisions of individuals, and the perceptions, values, and experiences that motivate those decisions. Generally, it emphasizes the role of political leaders, for it is often assumed (perhaps erroneously) that those individuals most influence the course of history.[10] While it is clear that powerful leaders such as Napoleon and Hitler changed the course of history, they could hardly have done so alone, or without the right conditions to aid them. The *state* or *group* level of analysis focuses on the behaviour of individual states, which is often attributed to the form of government one finds at a particular time. We will return to the debate over democratic peace theory later, but the argument here is that liberal democracies do not fight wars against each other, and thus the explanation for war may be found through analyzing different political modes of governance at the state level. Of course, it remains necessary to look within states as well to determine which groups are influencing foreign policy. For example, **free trade** agreements are supported by the industrial sectors within states that will benefit most from lowering restrictions on trade in their products, and opposed by labour groups and others fearful of the impact on jobs and competitiveness.

At the *systemic* level of analysis, the actions of states are seen as the result of external influences and pressures on them in relation to their attributes or position in world politics. In other words, the nature of the environment, or system, in which actors find themselves explains their behaviour. The capabilities and resources the actors have at their disposal establish the range of options they might have in any given situation. This leads us to an age-old debate within the social sciences concerning the relative causal weight assigned to systems and actors, otherwise known as structures and agents. Does the structure of the system predetermine the actions of actors? Or do humans shape events of their own accord? Many people today view this dichotomy as a false one, forcing us to reduce complex interactions to two essential forces. Rather, one can argue that continual interaction occurs between the individual and group or state units of action and the structures within which they operate. In the political world, each influences the other, although limitations exist as to how much influence can be projected by units into their environment, and by the environment onto units. For example, a state such as Canada cannot expect to be a dominant influence in the current international system, since it has a limited amount of power and is effectively overshadowed by the influence of its southern neighbour, the United States. However, in certain areas, such as peacekeeping and humanitarian assistance, certain Canadians have made extraordinary contributions to multilateral efforts. Though the modern state's extensive ties to the international system limit its ability to take autonomous action, they also provide opportunities (see Profile 1.3).

When we examine the behaviour of actors within a system, as political scientists we are often most interested in discerning their relative influence; we seek to identify the dominant actors, be they states, socioeconomic classes, organizations, corporations, or individuals. However, this identification is but half the story, for every form of dominance or control generates opposition. Thus, we seek also to identify and explain the motivations of counter-dominant actors, which could refer to the Ogoni resisting oppression by the Nigerian government, or antiglobalization activists protesting against the World Trade Organization. It could refer to ambitious entrepreneurs introducing innovative products to the global market, or it could refer to environmentalists chaining themselves to trees to prevent clearcut logging. However, it is too simple to say that dominant actors are conservative and support the status quo and counter-dominant actors are progressive and support positive change. After all,

PROFILE 1.3 — Canadian Political Leadership: Pierre Elliott Trudeau, 1919–2000

Searching for peace. Canadian Prime Minister Pierre Trudeau meets with China's Chairman Deng Xiaoping in the Great Hall of the People in Beijing in 1983. Trudeau met with Deng to discuss his peace proposals. (CP Picture Archive/Andy Clark.)

Pierre Elliott Trudeau was Canada's Prime Minister from 1968 to 1979, and again from 1980 to 1984. While he was always occupied with matters of national importance such as the separatist movement in Quebec and constitutional questions, he was also very visible on the international stage. Early in his term as prime minister, Trudeau halved Canada's commitment of troops to NATO. He became a friend of Fidel Castro, despite the American embargo on Cuba. His government recognized the People's Republic of China in 1970. At one point, and against widespread public opposition, Trudeau allowed the Americans to test cruise missiles over Canadian soil. Later, he undertook an international peace mission that saw him meet with world leaders to discuss disarmament. Although he was often controversial and his initiatives were frequently criticized, Trudeau was respected for his intellect and his commitment to peace and social justice. Abroad, Trudeau was known as a charming and novel statesman. Trudeau famously described Canada's relationship with the United States as "sleeping next to an elephant" and often worried about the threat America posed to Canadian sovereignty and independence. Thousands of Canadians paid tribute after his death in 2000 during a last train ride home, and at a large public funeral in Montreal. See J. L. Granatstein and R. Bothwell, *Pirouette: Pierre Trudeau and Canadian Foreign Policy* (University of Toronto Press, 1991).

neo-Nazi groups in Germany would certainly consider themselves counter-dominant actors. Each sphere of human activity differs, and since the political playing field is neither level nor stable, the question of just who is dominant and who is counter-dominant is not amenable to an eternal formula. To further confuse the issue, it might be argued that the influence of some actors will be greater than that of others in times of social upheaval.[11]

We also have to be careful regarding the nature of influence itself. It is impossible to define power—one of the most contested terms in all of political science—here, but power has both hard and soft dimensions.[12] Hard-power capability refers to the more obvious: military hardware, technological capabilities, and economic size. In many cases hard power is still put to the test today, as we saw with the American-led military assaults on Afghanistan and Iraq. Soft power refers to the role of ideas, persuasion, culture, and innovation, which possess less tangible qualities. However, the possession of more power does not guarantee a preferred outcome. Even the United States could not pressure the government of India to sign a new treaty banning nuclear weapons testing in 1996, or resolve conflict in the Middle East. Despite international pressure, the government of Burma (officially the Union of Myanmar) refused to allow the free movement of aid and humanitarian workers inside the country in the wake of Cyclone Nigris in the spring of 2008. But the agent–structure debate noted above continues: should we focus on the power of states per se or on the power of a larger structure, or system, such as the capitalist world economic system, where the soft power of prevailing ideas becomes even more important? Some scholars argue that hegemony is not just about military or economic power, but the gradual acceptance of orthodoxy in the realm of ideas. For example, globalization is often described as a powerful and inevitable force with no alternative. Is this true, or have most governments and populations simply accepted it as such? Ultimately, this is one of the many analytic questions students need to answer for themselves.

Below we discuss some of the more prevalent basic perspectives that have been generated by international relations theorists. However, keep firmly in mind the interdisciplinary contributions, and methodological divisions, discussed above. Some have even suggested that we have moved into a world of "post-international" politics, an age characterized by the "decline of long-standing patterns" leaving us uncertain about "where the changes may be leading."[13] However, an unmistakable continuity exists: the international system remains fundamentally competitive, as different states, economic players, and ideas battle to secure or advance their interests or their dominance. To gain even a cursory understanding of all this, we need to impose clarity, and this is done by referring to the various theoretical perspectives we have outlined below. Even to the well-initiated, global politics is a strange and heady conceptual brew, to be sipped with caution. However, if we proceed with a basic understanding of the main conceptual ingredients, we will drink with greater confidence.

IR THEORY: A BRIEF SURVEY

Charles Lindblom, in the introduction to his book on the purpose and effects of contemporary social science, readily admits that "classical nineteenth-century liberalism is my prison. It is not the most inhumane of prisons; its cells are by far larger than those of any other prison I know. Indeed, its construction is such that inmates often succeed in persuading themselves that they are wholly free."[14] This admission acknowledges an important point: we are all, to some degree, trapped within our own particular way of seeing and making sense of the world. As Kenneth Boulding warned us back in 1959, "It is what we think the world is like, not what it is really like, that determines our behaviour."[15] Textbook writers are hardly free of this circumstance; the perspectives of the authors, their origins, and the assumptions they make become part of the book, though we have made every effort to be as inclusive as possible. We might add also that our own perspectives differ sufficiently to add what we hope is a good measure of balance. However, we must keep in mind that all these perspectives are best viewed as fluid conceptions, subject to change, reinterpretation, and manipulation. Further, none of these theories emerged from an intellectual vacuum: they took shape in an historical context that informed their development. As the historian Arthur Schlesinger Jr. has observed, traumatic events (such as war, acts of terror, and environmental decay) often lead to "skeptical reassessments of supposedly sacred assumptions."[16] We might ask ourselves whether events such as the September 11, 2001 attacks, the Iraq War, or the global economic crisis of 2008–2009 have forced us to rethink things yet again.

IDEALISM

The death and destruction caused by World War I resulted in a condemnation of how international politics had been conducted in the past. The war also created a reaction against power politics, secret diplomacy, arms races, and what was seen as the abuse of unchecked power by the monarchs who led the Central Powers into war. For many, the horrors of World War I served as the final exhibit of the folly of war in human history. A change was required, a change that would alter the international environment in a way that would prevent future wars and eliminate the practices and policies that had made the history of humanity a history of conflict and war. This sentiment prompted the search for a theory of international politics that provided an explanation for all wars and offered directions and policies for preventing them in the future. What emerged from this search was the theoretical framework known as political idealism. An idealist perspective assumes the best of human nature: we are essentially cooperative beings who are occasionally led astray by evil influences into war and conflict, and we have a natural affinity toward the communal, as opposed to the individual, good. When people behave violently, or when states go to war, it is because of the institutional or structural setting in which they exist.

Political idealism has its origins in the philosophical tradition of liberalism, which emerged in Europe in the 16th century, although many of the moral principles of liberalism and idealism can be found in earlier works. This philosophical tradition emphasizes the liberty of the individual and the need to protect this liberty from the state. Liberalism, with its focus on individuals as the centre of moral virtue, regards the pursuit of power, authoritarian governance, and intolerance as obstacles to human progress. Some liberal philosophers put their emphasis on building a tolerant, liberal society as the only humane response to pluralism and diversity. Others put more emphasis on the development of capitalism, free trade, and republican democracy as the answer to global problems and the absence of global order. Liberal philosophers include John Locke, Immanuel Kant, Benjamin Constant, John Stuart Mill, Montesquieu, David Hume, Adam Smith, T.H. Green, L.T. Hobhouse, and Thomas Jefferson.

Postwar idealists such as G. Lowes Dickinson, Alfred Zimmern, **Norman Angell**, James T. Shotwell, and U.S. President **Woodrow Wilson** drew on the liberal philosophical tradition. Although idealists differed on many issues, they all shared a number of assumptions about the nature of humanity, the nature of world politics, the experience of World War I, and the road to the future. To varying degrees, idealists assumed the following:

- *Human nature is essentially good.* As a result, assistance and cooperation are possible and natural, motivated by the human qualities of altruism, philanthropy, and humanitarianism.

- *Evil is not innate to humanity.* Evil activity or harmful behaviour is the result of bad institutions, states, and structures that motivate individuals to act in a self-interested, distrustful, or aggressive fashion.

- *Social progress is possible.* Human society has developed and improved and will continue to do so.

- *The main problem in international relations is war.* International society must reform itself with the aim of preventing future wars.

- *War can be prevented.* Eliminating bad institutions, states, and structures will eliminate the root causes of war.

- *International cooperation will promote peace.* International organizations and international law will help prevent war.

The policy program of the idealists—their proposed solutions to the problem of war and the issues facing the international system—was expansive and ambitious. Idealists regarded the structure of international relations as a war-making imposition that promoted distrust, hostility, conflict, and confrontation. The history of international relations, idealists believed, proved their argument that war was endemic because of the nature of the international system. Idealists believed that by changing the latter it would be possible to reduce or eliminate war. Their answer was the **collective security** system. Within such a system, all states would agree that in the case of aggression by any state against any other state in the system, all other states would respond to defend the attacked state. In effect, a collective security system sought to make any aggression against any member of the system an act of aggression against all members. As a result, any potential aggressor, faced with the prospect of having so many enemies, would not engage in aggression in the first place. In this way, peace would be preserved. Idealists also believed that international peace could be encouraged through the development of international organizations, international law, and arms control.

The principles and hopes of political idealism did serve as a guide for postwar efforts to remake the international system, most famously in the creation of the League of Nations and in U.S. President Woodrow Wilson's famous **Fourteen Points**, which influenced the post–World War I settlement. The Covenant of the League of Nations was drafted at the Paris Peace Conference in 1919. The League comprised an assembly and a council of permanent members, which included Great Britain, France, Italy, and Japan, and later Germany (1926) and the Soviet Union (1934). We discuss the operations of the League in more detail in Chapter 5. Between 1920 and 1939, the League considered 66 disputes between states and contributed to peaceful outcomes in 35 of them. The League reflected the idealist perspective's assumption that international organizations would serve to maintain peace and promote cooperation among states on a wide variety of international issues and problems. Peace would be strengthened by the development of international law, including efforts to make war illegal, such as the 1928 **Kellogg–Briand Pact**. Peace would also be strengthened through **arms control**, such as the 1922 Washington Naval Treaty, which restricted the number and armament of battleships in the fleets of the great powers. However, the treaty is also an example of how states pursue their own interests in arms control negotiations; under the treaty some states could have more battleships than others, and naval competition continued in the aircraft carrier and cruiser classes of ships.

The principles of political idealism were neither universally shared nor admired, and the immediate postwar period was characterized by "power politics" as much as by idealist behaviour. The events of the interwar period and the erosion or failure of many of the key elements of the idealists' reform program removed much of the enthusiasm for idealist assumptions and solutions. Political idealism as a popular view of the world receded. However, it did not vanish. As we will see in later chapters, many of the key elements of the idealist program remained in place and were employed in the international system long after idealism's golden years had faded. Today, the legacy of political idealism lives on in the principles that form the foundation for arms control, international organizations, and international law.

REALISM

Not surprisingly, the realist perspective developed within IR as a discipline following World War II, which many felt provided clear evidence that idealist claims about the progressive inclination of human nature were hopelessly naïve. Classical realism, as it has come to be called, is less generous regarding human nature. People are generally viewed as self-interested creatures, and political power merely corrupts them further. Political relations are fundamentally about conflict, as unitary rational actors seek their own self-interest. In the case of global politics, the relevant actors are states, which seek their national interest at all times in an anarchic environment lacking a world government or police force. Military power is the most important expression and guarantor of survival, and the most important issue-area in the field is the threat or actual use of force (everything else is "low politics"). When it comes to foreign policy and security, states have to choose what to do in certain situations purely on the basis of their own self-interest, and we should not be surprised when they choose to go to war. The only way to change this situation would be to make the world system non-anarchic; but this would require a world government, and realists reject that prospect as a virtual impossibility.

The intellectual roots of realism lay in early writings about war and statecraft in the work of the ancient Greek historian Thucydides, in the writings of Kautilya, in the advice of Sun Tzu, in the philosophies and advice on statecraft of Niccolo Machiavelli, and in the reflections of the English theoretician Thomas Hobbes (see Chapter 2). These and other writings emphasized the importance of power and self-interest above all other considerations. The realist perspective was thus built on the intellectual heritage of **realpolitik**. As writes David Boucher in his excellent exposition on classical political philosophy and international relations, "Hobbes does not believe that there is any higher law ordained by a force outside of human will ... morality is equated with expediency.... In the international sphere, in the absence of a sovereign, there is no justice or injustice, but there are principles relating to honourable and dishonourable acts which serve to restrain excessive acts of cruelty or recklessness."[17]

Early exponents of political realism include E.H. Carr, Hans J. Morgenthau (see Profile 1.5), Kenneth W. Thompson, and Reinhold Niebuhr. As a group, realists made several assumptions about the character of international politics. States were the principal actors in international politics since no authority in international politics superseded the authority of the state. For the purposes of analysis, states were also taken to be rational, unitary actors, interested above all else in their security and in maximizing their power. The pursuit of power—the ability to make other actors do what they would not otherwise do—was the core aim of international politics. Although most realists would find the following to be an oversimplification of their world view, to varying degrees, realists assume that

- People are essentially selfish and acquisitive by nature.
- The desire for power is instinctive to all individuals and cannot be eliminated.

PROFILE 1.4	The Idealist Perspective and the Realist Perspective Compared	
ISSUE	**IDEALISM**	**REALISM**
Human nature	Good; altruistic	Evil; selfish
Central problem	War and the establishment of peace	War and security
Key actors	States and individuals	States
Motives of actors	Mutual assistance; collaboration	Power; national interest; security
Nature of international politics	Cooperation and community	Anarchy
Outlook on future	Optimism; human progress	Pessimism; stability at best
Policy prescriptions and solutions	Reform the system; develop institutions	Enhance power; protect national interests

PROFILE 1.5 Hans J. Morgenthau

Hans J. Morgenthau was born in Germany in 1904. He received his university education in Germany and practised law in Frankfurt before moving to the United States in 1937, where he was appointed to the University of Chicago in 1943. His most famous work was entitled *Politics Among Nations*, first published in 1948. Morgenthau presented a theory of international politics in the book, and his "six principles of political realism" became one of the foundations of the realist perspective:

1. Politics is governed by objective laws that have their roots in human nature, which has not changed since the time of classical China, India, and Greece.

2. States, and their leaders, think and act in terms of interest defined as power, and to understand their actions observers of international politics must think the same way.

3. The idea of interest is the essence of politics and is unaffected by time and place; efforts to transform politics without considering this basic law will fail.

4. Tension exists between moral command and the requirements of successful political action. Morality cannot be applied universally in the abstract but must be filtered through the circumstances of time and place.

5. The moral aspirations of a particular nation are not to be confused with the moral laws that govern the universe.

6. Intellectually, realism maintains the autonomy of the political sphere, as economists, lawyers, or doctors maintain theirs.

Morgenthau, then, argued that international relations is characterized by states pursuing their national interests defined in terms of power. The world is the result of forces inherent in human nature, and is characterized by opposing interests and conflicts among them. For Morgenthau, international politics was governed by universal principles or laws based on the pursuit of the national interest.

SOURCE: FROM *POLITICS AMONG NATIONS*, 4TH EDITION BY HANS J. MORGENTHAU, COPYRIGHT 1967 BY ALFRED A. KNOPF, A DIVISION OF RANDOM HOUSE, INC. USED WITH PERMISSION OF ALFRED A. KNOPF, A DIVISION OF RANDOM HOUSE, INC.

- International politics is a *zero-sum* (see Chapter 2) struggle for power, where relative gains in power by one state or group necessarily mean a relative loss in power for other states or groups.

- The international system is anarchic in nature as no central authority or world government exists that is capable of enforcing rules.

- In such an environment, the primary objective of all states is to follow their national interests, defined in terms of power.

- In such an environment, states must ultimately rely on their own efforts (self-help) to ensure their own security.

- Military power and preparedness is the most important factor in determining state power and security.

- Alliances can increase the security of a state, but the loyalty and reliability of allies should always be questioned.

- International organizations and international law cannot be relied on to guarantee security, as state actions are not bound by enforceable rules.

- Order can be achieved only by the balance of power system in which stability is maintained by flexible alliance systems.

If power is as important as realists suggest, we need to know how to measure it. This task is not easy, conceptually or empirically, since much emphasis has been placed on the tangible, measurable capabilities of states. Such factors include the base assets of a state, such as its territory, population, geography, natural resources, and **gross domestic product (GDP)**. These elements of power are long-term attributes that generally change slowly over time. They represent the foundation of state power, or what Canadian foreign policy analyst Kim Richard Nossal has termed "relative invariates."[18] Some states are more endowed with these elements than others by virtue of location or conquest. Frequently, though not exclusively, these states become great powers. Other states stand little or no chance of attaining such status.

For realists, the most important kind of power is **hard power**, which emphasizes the ability of a state to wage war. Military power is the principal means through which states exercise power in the short term. Military capabilities are the most important measure of state power in war when other power elements are not directly engaged. However, if a war is long, the states with the greater economic and social resources to mobilize and commit to military ends will have the advantage. Estimating the power—especially the military power—of others is a crucial element of international politics, realists argue. As Sun Tzu wrote: "Know the enemy and know yourself; in a hundred battles you will never be in peril." Realists acknowledge that tangible and measurable hard power factors are not the only considerations in power politics. Power also encompasses intangibles, elements that are not easily measured or compared. And a state must be able to deploy hard-power capabilities in an effective fashion. This ability depends on the unity of purpose within the state, which can be influenced by public opinion, religion, ideology, or nationalism (the conscription crisis in Canada during World War I is an example of such a difficulty, as was the American war effort in Vietnam). Nevertheless, for realists hard power is the most important currency of power in global politics.

Realism is not a monolithic theory, and has evolved considerably from its early origins. Classical realists such as Morgenthau and Niebuhr emphasize the role of human nature. **Structural realists** such as Kenneth Waltz emphasize the anarchic nature of the system as a determinant of state behaviour. The term *anarchy* implies not complete chaos or absence of law but rather the lack of a central authority or government capable of enforcing rules. Within states, governments can deter participants from breaking legal restrictions, can enforce contracts, and can use their monopoly on the use of coercion to compel citizens to obey the law. In contrast, no central authority exists to enforce and ensure state compliance with international rules or norms. Consequently, states must become self-reliant if they are to survive. All states must, therefore, be prepared to use force in their own defence, for in an anarchic environment, a state may use coercion or force at any time if the benefits to be gained outweigh potential costs (see the discussion of the stag hunt in Profile 1.6). So, in the absence of an effective security system, states arm themselves for protection against such an eventuality, following the advice of the Latin phrase *Si vis pacem, parabellum*—"If you want peace, prepare for war."

In doing so, however, states can find themselves in a situation that scholars have called the **security dilemma**. In this situation, when states take unilateral measures to ensure their own security (such as increasing the capabilities of their military forces), they decrease the security of neighbouring states, which will perceive these measures as threatening and will take countermeasures (increasing the capabilities of their armed forces) to enhance their own security. These military enhancements will provoke insecurity in other states, which will increase their military capabilities as well. This action–reaction cycle occurs when states increasingly spend resources on military capabilities but make no real gains in the way of security. This dynamic is the basis of the many arms races that have occurred between states. Characterized by periods of high tension and the rapid escalation of the military capabilities of the states engaged, they promote

PROFILE 1.6 The Trouble with Cooperation: The Stag Hunt

Jean-Jacques Rousseau. (© Bettman/Corbis.)

The stag hunt is an allegory that originated in the writings of the Geneva-born 18th-century philosopher *Jean-Jacques Rousseau*. Although Rousseau is best known for his enormous contributions to Western political thought that influenced conservative, liberal, and socialist theory and the idealism of the French Revolution, realists have borrowed and adapted his stag-hunt example to illustrate the power of self-interested motives in anarchic environments. In this allegory, five individual hunters exist in a state of nature, with no government or social structure to determine their behaviour. The hunters have a choice of cooperating to attain a mutually desired goal or defecting from such cooperation if their own individual short-term interests can be satisfied. They can collaborate to encircle and subsequently capture a stag, which will satisfy the food needs of all five hunters if they share it. However, in doing so, it is possible that one of the hunters will encounter a tempting hare, which will satisfy that individual hunter's food needs. That hunter then faces a choice: let the hare go and serve the common interest by continuing the effort to capture the stag, or take the hare and defect from the group, thus ruining the hunt for the other four hunters, who will not have their food needs satisfied.

The allegory raises several questions about incentives and disincentives for cooperation. If a hunter prefers to cooperate to capture the stag, can the other hunters be trusted to do the same? Is it not in the rational self-interest of a hunter to take the hare? If this is the case, how can the hunters trust each other to cooperate on a hunt for the stag? And if they cannot trust each other, is it not in their interests to take the hare before any of the other hunters do? Indeed, what is the incentive to cooperate at all? The allegory illustrates the difficulty of establishing cooperation in an anarchic environment and the corrosive effect short-term self-interest can have on collaborative efforts. On Rousseau see S. Hoffman and D. Fidler, eds., *Rousseau on International Relations* (Oxford: Clarendon, 1991) and the famous treatment in K. Waltz, *Man, the State and War: A Theoretical Analysis* (New York: Columbia University Press, 1954).

hostility and mistrust and create the conditions in which a crisis could easily lead to misunderstanding, miscalculation, and war. In Chapter 3, we will examine in detail the evolution of what was, arguably, the greatest security dilemma of all time, the Cold War.

For realists, the existence of an anarchic self-help system does not mean that the international system lacks order or cooperation. In fact many **English school realists** (or **liberal realists**) such as Hedley Bull argue that the international system is far from chaotic.[19] In an anarchic system, states can cooperate and do so all the time. For example, states reach trade agreements, create and join international institutions, and form alliances. However, realists argue that this cooperation occurs, not for altruistic reasons, but because it is in the interests of states to cooperate. Cooperation is simply another reflection of self-help. Nevertheless, when states interact they follow international norms and conventions most of the time. Norms are shared expectations about what constitutes appropriate behaviour in the international system. An example of such a norm is the concept of sovereignty, the principle that a state has control over affairs within its own territory, free from external interference by other states. In principle, states are therefore autonomous in that they answer to no higher authority in the international system. Another prominent norm is respect for internationally recognized borders. Despite the fact that most borders in the world today are the result of past wars and international agreements or the legacy of colonial occupation, the territorial integrity of states is regarded as one of the foundations of international stability. Attempts to revise these borders—through conquest or succession—are generally regarded as dangerous or destabilizing events, because a challenge to an existing border is in principle a challenge to borders everywhere. Other norms regulate the conduct of diplomatic relations between states. For example, embassies are considered to be the territory of their home states, rather than that of the host country, and are therefore not subject to interference or the laws of the host country. As we will see, governments obey a wide variety of international norms, procedures, regulations, and laws every day.

English school realists argue that since cooperation and norms do provide the basis for some order in the international system, anarchy does not mean the complete absence of order in global politics. As a result, an international society does exist, based on these shared norms and agreements that regulate relations between states. However, all realists emphasize that when it comes to security issues, or so-called high politics concerns, states rely on power to manage relations between them. This reliance has led to the development of the concept of the balance of power, discussed in greater detail in Chapter 2.

LIBERALISM

As mentioned in our description of idealism, liberalism has deep intellectual roots. Liberals emphasize the importance of values such as liberty, private property, the rule of law, free markets, democracy, and justice in the governance of domestic society. Liberals seek to project these values onto global politics. The aim is to remake the international system into a liberal society of states, governed by the same values that govern individuals in liberal democratic societies. Liberals are therefore champions of international trade, international law, the promotion of democracy around the world, and the development of international institutions to manage the affairs of states and regulate global politics. Liberals argue that individuals and states will rationally cooperate if given the opportunity to do so. They believe that cooperation is mutually beneficial, that what is good for one may be good for another (in contrast to a zero-sum world perspective in which a gain for one is a loss for another). Liberals place a great deal of importance on economic growth, both domestically and internationally, assuming prosperity will mean peace, and peace will mean prosperity. International trade is to be encouraged, because it will lead to greater wealth and human well-being, as well as fewer wars since trade promotes cooperation, trust, and mutual interest. In addition, so-called transnational avenues for international cooperation such as the creation of international organizations, advocacy groups, and cultural exchanges, can reduce the chances of war through dialogue and understanding. In general, liberals assume the following about global politics:

- States are not the only important actors in global politics. Non-state actors such as multinational corporations and advocacy groups are also significant sources of agency and change.

- The state is in decline. Borders are increasingly permeable and governments have less control over economic activity, information, and social activity.

- Global politics is characterized by interdependence, not by anarchy. Interdependence is growing, reflected in increased trade, financial, social, and communications flows around the world.

- International institutions matter. Institutions bind states into mutual commitments and obligations that are costly to break.

- War and failed efforts at cooperation are the result of bad decision making and bad policies by leaders and governments.

Liberals do not share the realist view of the primacy of hard power. For liberals, the effective deployment of power can also depend on **soft power**. Soft power includes the support a state has obtained in the international system, which may in turn depend on the moral legitimacy of its cause, the loyalty of its allies, and the diplomatic and political skills available to the state. Power can also be found in the ability of an actor to set agendas, establish norms of behaviour, and gain wider agreements on rules and regulations that others agree to obey. The less tangible elements of soft power reflect the appeal or attraction of ideas and values. If a state's ideas and values are seen as attractive, they will provide that state with opportunities to exert influence and leadership. For example, some have argued that the United States leads the world in terms of soft power because of its position as the world's leading capitalist marketplace and liberal democracy. Many have also argued that this soft power was damaged by the unpopular Iraq War, the conduct of the so-called War on Terror, and other policies of the George W. Bush administration. Repairing that damage is a stated goal of the Obama administration. Some Canadians (such as former Foreign Affairs Minister Lloyd Axworthy) have suggested that Canada has influence in the world beyond its capabilities (especially its military capabilities) because of its emphasis on international cooperation and institutions over the use of military force and coercion. In this view, soft power has enabled Canada to provide limited leadership on issues such as peacekeeping, the movement to ban land mines, and sanctions against South Africa during the **apartheid** era. This view of soft power rejects the hard-power perspective advanced by realists. For their part, realists argue that soft power flows from the ability to exert hard power.

Three popular variants of liberalism remain in circulation today: complex interdependence, liberal institutionalism, and democratic peace theory. If we blend realism's concern with power and state conflict with liberalism's optimism and emphasis on transnational phenomena, we get what Robert Keohane and Joseph Nye Jr. called **complex interdependence**.[20] In a prelude to our more current concerns with globalization, they argued that economic factors were fast becoming as important as military matters, and that nonstate actors such as **multinational corporations (MNCs)** and **nongovernmental organizations (NGOs)** play important roles alongside states. Further, states are not always rational, coherent actors, since they respond to internal discord. Keohane and Nye intended their theory to be a modification, not a refutation, of realism, but much of what they argued has been subsumed under the liberal banner.

Idealists and liberals have much in common, including the desire for stronger institutions to facilitate global cooperation. **Liberal institutionalism** focuses on the impact of formal international organizations in global politics. Other forms of cooperation, such as informal agreements or associations, are often called **regimes**, which can be defined as sets of principles, norms, rules, and decision-making procedures around which actors' expectations converge. According to liberals, institutions and regimes increase cooperation and understanding and reduce uncertainty and conflict in global politics. Institutions and regimes also facilitate the efforts of states and individuals to conduct trade, investment, communication, travel, and activism efforts such as strengthening protection for human rights. The essential argument here is that the anarchy so instrumental in a structural realist understanding of global politics need not prevent states and individuals from achieving a more harmonious world; in some cases international institutions and regimes could actually replace the state as a provider of goods to citizens. This gives rise to neo-functionalist theory, exemplified by the evolution of the European Union, a supranational institution that has substantial impact on the daily lives of citizens in states as diverse as Belgium and Greece. We return to these themes in Chapter 5.

Finally, democratic peace theory asserts that historically, liberal democracies rarely if ever go to war against each other. This view was an important component of the work of Immanuel Kant (see Profile 1.7). The key to global stability is not necessarily a balance of power, or even increased trade, but rather the spread of Western-style liberal democracies, whose executives are constrained in their autonomy and cannot get away with the hazardous act of starting wars against other democracies. People will throw expansionist politicians out

PROFILE 1.7　Immanuel Kant (1724–1804)

Immanuel Kant. (© Corbis.)

IMMANUEL KANT

Immanuel Kant was a German philosopher who wrote as the Enlightenment was sweeping through Germany in the 18th century. He wrote his most famous work, *Perpetual Peace*, in 1795. Based on the experience of the wars of the French Revolution, Kant argued that there were two possible futures for humanity: the end of all hostilities through international agreements, or the perpetual peace of the cemetery of humankind after an annihilating war. *Perpetual Peace*

is written as a contract similar to the diplomatic documents of the day; in this sense, it is a model for the establishment of international peace through international agreements between states. In it Kant proposes the following: the establishment of a system of conduct among states, including the principles of sovereignty, noninterference, and eventual disarmament; the conversion of authoritative states into republican states (which are less likely to go to war than the former); the development of an international federation of free states with a republican constitution that respects the sovereignty of its members; and the creation of conditions for universal hospitality and growing commerce across state borders. Kant believed that these measures would lead to peace among all peoples, a peace that would be reinforced by the natural tendency of states to engage in commerce rather than war with one another: "In connection with the life of the agriculturalist, salt and iron were discovered which were perhaps the first articles that were sought far and near, and which entered into the commercial intercourse of different peoples. Thereby they would be first brought into a peaceful relation to one another; and thus the most distant of them would come to mutual understanding, sociability and pacific intercourse."

SOURCE: "IMMANUEL KANT," IN M. FORSYTH ET AL., EDS., *THE THEORY OF INTERNATIONAL RELATIONS: SELECTED TEXTS FROM GENTILI TO TREITSCHKE* (LONDON: GEORGE ALLEN AND UNWIN, 1970), 220.

of office if their designs on international power exceed the willingness of the population to sacrifice. More to the point, there is little incentive for one liberal democracy to attack another, as neither will regard the other as a threat to its way of life. Democratic peace theory has come under considerable scrutiny for several reasons: it is based on a Western or Eurocentric definition of democracy; there are methodological problems with the measurement of war; and the fact that republics such as the United States are obviously quite willing to wage war is undeniable. The theory leads some to suggest the key to peace is the spread of not only democracy per se but the market institutions that often accompany it. More nuanced explorations of the theory ask questions about the relative autonomy of the executive decision-making units in democratic states, and take into account the abilities of even democratically elected leaders to deceive civilians into accepting the need for warfare.[21] Again, we return to this theory in later chapters.

CRITICAL PERSPECTIVES

There are two central ways critical theories challenge the more mainstream variations of realism and liberalism described above. The first involves a rejection of the central values, or lack of values, posited by the realist and liberal frameworks, emphasizing concerns with social justice that neither mainstream approach can adequately embrace. The second is an epistemological rejection of the orthodoxy of positivism, or the belief that we can take adequate stock of the world through empirical observation and the testing of hypotheses. This does not mean critical theorists are on a different page altogether: if Christian Reus-Smit is correct, the main debate animating IR theory today "revolves around the nature of social agency, the relative importance of normative versus material forces, the balance between continuity and transformation in world politics, and a range of other empirical-theoretical questions."[22] These same questions inspire theorists of all stripes; however, the different strands of critical theory discussed below are united by their common rejection of realism or liberalism as ideological justifications for an unjust status quo. In this view, global politics is not only about relations among states; nonstate actors and social forces, such as entrenched classes and popular movements, are also agents of change. History can be seen in terms of the domination, exploitation, and marginalization of one group over another: of the Southern Hemisphere by the northern European imperialist powers; of women by men; of some races by others.

MARXISM

The origins of Marxism lie in the writings of **Karl Marx** (1818–83), who studied law and philosophy and wrote about history. In league with Friedrich Engels (1820–95), Marx campaigned for a socialist Germany. Marxism itself is a branch of thought emerging from the French Revolution, the British Industrial Revolution, and German philosophy. Marx insisted on a materialist worldview, asserting that throughout history the political nature of society was determined by its economic structure. For Marx, the economic structure of society in his time was characterized by capitalism. As a result, society was divided into classes, on the basis of their relationship to the means of production in a capitalist system. The **bourgeoisie** owned the factories and the land, and governed society in their own interests. It is this class which controlled technology, invention, natural resources, and property systems and dominated religious, philosophical, governmental, legal, and moral values. In contrast, the **proletariat** did not own any means of production and were forced to sell their labour to the bourgeoisie in return for payment. For Marx, this social structure was inherently exploitative and unjust, and he envisioned a revolution of the proletariat which would overthrow the bourgeoisie and usher in a classless communist society of equality and justice. According to Marxism, classes are the social engines of history. The state is merely a vehicle of the ruling economic class; it exists primarily to serve their interests and not those of society as a whole. Although Marx did not write extensively on international affairs, Marxist thinkers such as **John Hobson**, **Rosa Luxemburg**, and **Vladimir Lenin** wrote about the international impact of capitalism, which they considered to be the primary cause of **imperialism** (see Profile 1.8). Luxemburg is a very significant figure, since she was a prototypical Marxist feminist intellectual. As the domestic economies of the European powers ran out of markets, it became necessary to expand into the colonial areas to find new markets, natural resources, and a place to export capital. This in turn brought about conflict between the capitalist empires over territory and resources, which ultimately (from a Marxist perspective) led to World War I.

In global politics today, the central assumption behind what are known as **neo-Marxist** perspectives is that economic classes are the primary units of analysis in world affairs and that the economic growth experienced by the rich Northern world has come at the expense of others, namely those in the poor Southern world. Economic relations are determined by geography and colonial history. Thus, states rich in natural resources, such as Canada, have

---

PROFILE 1.8 Lenin and Monopoly Capitalism

Revolutionary leader Vladimir Ilyich Lenin, St. Petersburg, February 1897. Russians listed Lenin as their number one choice for "man of the century" in their country, followed by dictator Josef Stalin, the Interfax news agency reported December 26, 2000. Lenin (1870–1924) founded Bolshevism and was the Soviet leader from 1917 until his death in 1924. (AP Photo/CP Archive.)

Though Lenin's place in history is well known, his role in the formation of an intellectual perspective on international political economy is less celebrated. In a treatise published at the end of World War I ("Imperialism: The Highest Stage of Capitalism"), Lenin argued that the war had resulted from competition among the major capitalist powers, which had reached the target of monopoly capitalism, "in which the division of all territories of the globe among the great capitalist powers has been completed." Imperialism resulted from the concentration of production in combines, cartels, syndicates, and trusts; the competitive quest for sources of raw materials; and the development of banking oligarchies. Under these conditions, imperialism was inevitable and not a matter of choice. The principal exporters of capital would be the dominant powers in the international system. Critics argue that this essentially economic explanation does not take into account other causes of imperialism, such as the search for glory and recognition. However, Lenin did explain nationalism as part of the false consciousness that guided the working classes to the battlefield and perpetuated their mutual slaughter; the sentiment of futility that eventually characterized participation in World War I worked in the Bolshevik's favour immediately prior to the Russian Revolution in 1917. Lenin's ultimate creation, the Soviet Union, is dead, but for many concerned with the plight of the Southern Hemisphere, his ideas still form the core of their thinking. For an engaging biography of Lenin, see R. Payne, *The Life and Death of Lenin* (New York: Simon and Schuster, 1964).

gained from exporting them abroad and in particular to large markets such as the United States. At the same time, however, this traps states such as Kenya, Argentina, Zambia, and Peru into dependencies based on staple exports such as tea, bauxite, coffee, tobacco, and wood. Reliance on staple products is exacerbated by relative political weakness. Within under-developed states, the upper classes participate in the North–South exploitative relationship, not only reinforcing global inequality but also benefiting from it. Thus, most neo-Marxist analysis in IR has focused on how global capitalism has created a world divided between a few rich and many poor, and how globalization is merely imperialism and colonialism in another guise.

International thinking along neo-Marxist lines has taken many paths. One of the more influential modern variants has been **dependency theory**, which argues that Southern states have become trapped in a system of exploitation, one that forces them to be dependent on the North for capital and locks them into an unfair trading relationship. Inspired largely by the Latin American states' relationship to the United States, dependency theory suggests that the world system evolved from European imperialism to the disadvantage of those in the periphery. The wealth of the North was derived in part from the poverty of the South. States in the South were complicit, because the ruling classes in the periphery also benefited from the system. An important link existed between local capitalists, the underdeveloped state apparatus, and multinational corporations (or, put another way, transnational capital). In addition, even the working classes in the North gained from this exploitative relationship. Thus, some theorists, such as Andre Gunder Frank, proclaimed that the real choice was between underdevelopment and revolution. The world was not interdependent; it was hierarchical and exploitative. We will explore dependency theory in more depth in Chapter 4.

Neo-Marxists and dependency theorists share several assumptions and views regarding global politics:

- The most important actors in global politics are dominant economic interests or socioeconomic classes.
- Both the state and war are largely (though not exclusively) instruments of the ruling economic classes.
- States (and their ruling elites) are bound into a hierarchical structural relationship characterized by patterns of dominance and dependence.
- A wide differential in power exists between the rich and the poor, and this is related to their relationship to the means of production in national and global economies.
- For the marginalized and dependent states and peoples everywhere, revolution and the overthrow of the world capitalist system are the only hope for change. However, since this prescription of "delinking" from the world economy has proven elusive, and stunted efforts have produced unwanted violence, many advocate major reform in both domestic and international systems instead.

Finally, many neo-Marxist scholars today are inspired by the work of the Italian Marxist scholar Antonio Gramsci. Gramsci argued that a form of hegemony exists within states and societies that serves to reinforce the social order controlled by rich elites. The instruments of this hegemony include the media, social organizations, and government propaganda designed to socialize the masses to convince them that their lives are better off under capitalism than could be otherwise, and that they should aspire to imitate the upper classes in order to live the good life—a life most will never achieve. Similarly, one can argue that the dominant states and elite capitalist centres of the world economy have also ensured that the development of global politics protects their wealth not only with guns and warships, but with the spread of capitalist ideology and aspirations, reflected perhaps most visibly in the idea that globalization will be good for all, and not just a select few. The neo-Marxist project calls for sustained attention to a critical reading of such ideology, and reform of the system that allows its perpetuation.[23]

FEMINISM

Feminism is a broad intellectual, political, and social movement that cuts across a wide variety of academic disciplines and social discourse. The primary focus of feminism is how gender matters. Feminists assert that gender has largely been ignored due to assumptions that a universal human experience exists, when in fact these assumptions have been based exclusively on the male experience. In particular, feminists seek to expose the ways in which inequality and injustice are gendered, and seek to describe the nature of the patriarchal (male dominated) systems that perpetuate the marginalization and oppression of women. Feminist scholarship is also directed toward the advancement of women, in the form of legal and political equality and economic and social inclusion.

Feminists who study global politics argue that a patriarchal system exists at the international level. They point to the relative lack of women in senior government positions, on the boards of major multinational corporations, and in the leadership of major international institutions as evidence. In addition, they observe that women own very little land worldwide, have lower pay and incomes, and a very small share of private wealth. Many countries and societies systematically discriminate against women. Women also face high levels of sexual violence worldwide and form a disproportionate share of refugee populations. In making these and many other observations, feminists reveal the gendered nature of global politics and the need for policy responses that must serve the specific needs of women as well as men if they are to be successful. Further, as J. Ann Tickner argues, dominant academic perspectives have served to reinforce patriarchy not only in research but in policy debates and decisions as well. In particular, realism has been criticized by feminists for its gender-specific language and the cult of masculinity surrounding realist concepts like sovereignty and anarchy. Realism has also served to diminish the importance of issues of special relevance to women, such as human rights, health care, family planning, education, and development.[24] All feminists also share a belief that the state has had an instrumental role in enforcing and perpetuating patriarchy. As Jean Bethke Elshtain writes, "received notions of sovereignty incorporated in their absolutist heart of hearts a demand for blood-sacrifice: *pro patria mori*. This sacrificial demand got encoded into modern identities, male and female, with the triumph—the very bloody triumph—of the modern nation-state."[25]

However, quite distinct versions of feminism exist. **Liberal feminists** argue that women's participation in world affairs has been silenced or marginalized and that this situation must be corrected. By bringing women into the halls of political and economic power, female experiences and perspectives will be included and contribute to more effective decisions and policies. **Radical feminists** submit that merely bringing women into existing institutions and structures would be insufficient and deeper changes are therefore necessary. There is a large divide here: while liberal feminists argue the central injustice is the lack of women in positions of authority, for radical feminists the entire state and international apparatus is based on patriarchal ideologies that perpetuate cycles of violence and environmental destruction. **Socialist or Marxist feminists** (recall the mention of Rosa Luxemburg, above) assert that the capitalist system is patriarchal in character and privileges men and marginalizes women. The solution is to alter the character of the economic system of society toward socialist theories emphasizing equality and redistributive justice. **Postcolonial feminists** offer perspectives based on the unique experiences of women in the developing or postcolonial world, experiences grounded in racism, class discrimination, and cultural exclusion. Postcolonial feminists often criticize liberal feminists for assuming a universality to the female experience and ignoring the unique characteristics and issues confronting women of different backgrounds, particularly in the non-Western world. **Ecofeminists** link violence against women with violence against nature, and argue we need to transcend both to achieve a more just and sustainable world.

The feminist perspective operates at two levels: First, the argument is made that the role women play in global politics and economics is essential and must be recognized in any salient analysis, whether the researcher is looking at structural adjustment programs, the international sex trade, the microelectronics production industry, the generation of intellectual capital, armed conflict, or any other topic. Similarly, the role women have played in historical developments, including the great ages of imperialism, should not be overlooked simply because history has not, by and large, been written by them. Second, there is a rejection of the dominant realist values and an emphasis on the values of self-worth, community development, cooperation, peace, and sustainable development. While it remains to be seen whether some of these values can infiltrate the halls of academia and become dominant in the field, there can be little doubt that the feminist critique of traditional international relations theory has had a profound impact on the thinking of a new generation of scholars and on policy debates in government and international institutions such as the UN. The larger question may well be whether, in an economic world still dominated by males and masculine discourse, feminist perspectives can have a serious impact on actual policy decisions. We return to feminist approaches to specific issue-areas throughout this book.

GLOBAL ECOPOLITICAL THEORY

Although environmental approaches are not unified in any coherent body of theory, environmentalists do agree that liberal economic theories do not adequately account for the ecological costs of global economic growth, while realism ignores the role played by the state in perpetuating environmental exploitation. The multitude of ecological crises afflicting the world at present did not appear without warning: the misuse of agricultural land, for example, has long been known to have dire consequences, and pollution was a prevalent theme in the 1960s in North America and Europe. The historic connection between industrial development and environmental decay has become for many the overwhelming theme of human history. In contemporary global politics the trend looks as problematic as ever. Although there have been improvements in certain areas, such as protection of the ozone layer, there remains great uncertainty about the eventual consequences of global warming, species extinctions, and the harmful effects of chemicals.

Again, many varieties of global ecopolitical theories exist, some of which stress dealing with overpopulation, overconsumption, pollution, or the threat to endangered species with an institutionalist, regime management approach. This line of thinking, with its liberal pedigree, dominates the policy process and much of mainstream political science. More radical approaches advocate reconceptualizing capitalism or redefining human relations. Again, ecofeminists link patriarchy with **ecocide**. Nonstate actors are often seen as the most important agents of change, although some radical environmentalists believe in direct action through protest or even acts of violence. Others argue that stronger states are necessary to preserve what is left of the natural world, even if it means limiting human personal freedoms in the process. We address this issue in greater detail in Chapter 10. In general, one can argue that all the forms of theory discussed here, including realism and liberalism, begin with certain

PROFILE 1.9	Realism, Liberalism, and Critical Theories Compared		
ISSUE	**REALISM**	**LIBERALISM**	**CRITICAL THEORIES**
Human nature	Evil, selfish	Good, willing to cooperate for mutual gain	Variable
Central problem	War and security	Encouraging cooperation on global issues	Marginalization and imperialism; gender inequality; ecocide
Key actors	States	Individuals; MNCs; "penetrated" states; international institutions; NGOs	Classes; groups; MNCs; NGOs
Motives of actors	Power; national interest; security	Rational self-interest; justice; peace; prosperity	Power; greed; liberation; justice
Nature of international politics	Anarchy; economic growth will not overcome state conflicts	Interdependent; economic growth will promote peace	Hierarchy; dominance; exploitation; resistance
Outlook on future	Pessimism; stability; states will pursue neomercantilist policies	Optimism; progress is possible; economic growth is good for all	Pessimism unless paradigmatic change is achieved
Policy prescriptions and solutions	Enhance power; protect national interests	Develop institutions and regimes to encourage cooperation	Engender revolution, transformation, and social change

premises about the relationship between humans and nature, though it is evident that radical ecological thought has the most in common with critical approaches.[26]

Some commentators suggest that the high oil prices experienced in 2008 and the economic recession which began in 2008–2009 will force those in high-consumption societies to rethink our priorities and reexamine the impact of our own behaviour on the environment and on global politics. For example, Western dependence on foreign oil supplies leads to the support of many "petro-tyrannies," which fail to foster democracy and encourage anti-Western sentiment. Some point to the failure of several Western oil companies to build a trans-Afghanistan pipeline as one of the causes of further Taliban–United States hostility. Those taking a critical international political economy perspective would stress the importance of American and Western efforts to secure oil access in the Middle East and elsewhere, and this may be viewed as all the more regrettable as renewable energy sources are available but underfunded. Even as oil prices fell in 2009 and recession placed an emphasis on encouraging economic activity and growth, analysts and many politicians (including U.S. President Obama) emphasized the importance of developing alternative energy sources and more energy-efficient products and processes. In Chapter 10 we return to this theme, which is highly relevant for people living in a resource-dependent state such as Canada.

THE POSITIVIST/POSTPOSITIVIST DISTINCTION AND CONSTRUCTIVISM

As mentioned above, critical theories are separated not only by more explicit concerns with social justice issues, but also by their tendency to reject the positivist foundations of liberalism and realism. We need to be cautious here, since many Marxists, for example, base their analyses in historical materialism, which claims empirical validity, and it would be improper to label all feminists or environmentalists postpositivist. Postmodernists are primarily concerned with how people interpret the world around them and how they act on this understanding; they are critical of the positivist aspirations of the traditional theories. Postmodernists reject the idea that realists, liberals, or Marxists (all positivist and materialist theories) can ever really know anything concrete about global politics (or build objective knowledge about the world), since their personal biases will invariably influence their conclusions. For postmodernists, we cannot truly understand reality because how we see the world is socially constructed by subjective images that have their origins in our formative experiences, our cultures, our educations, our languages, and our political perspectives. "Reality" is, therefore, inherently intangible and subjective and is dependent on the nature of the viewer, not on the existence of an objective world, and all viewers are ensconced in power relations previously socially constructed by others.

The more critically inclined postmodernists argue that individuals who have inherited the Western tradition have performed the bulk of research work in the sciences and humanities. This hegemonic intellectual tradition serves to marginalize other perspectives and non-Western thought. At the heart of the postmodern research agenda is an investigation into how power distribution in a relationship affects policy and scholarship. Every analysis, or policy, is constructed in such a way as to perpetuate or enhance a power relationship. As a result, the traditional approaches contribute to the present social injustice brought about by the development of modernity, the scientific revolution of the West. Postmodernist thought has many strands as well: deconstructionists emphasize the importance of breaking down popular texts or discourses to understand the power relations they perpetuate, while feminist postmodernists look for gender bias in traditional discourse. It is not fruitful to contrast these more interpretive approaches with the positivist orientations, since neither can claim to actually be "better" than the other. Their sets of assumptions and aims are fundamentally different. Where they do converge, however, is in the effort to contribute to the intellectual debate over the need and possibility of avoiding mass violence.

Another approach, broadly labelled **constructivism**, depicts global politics (or any social subject, for that matter) as intersubjective. That is, "material resources only acquire meaning for human action through the structure of shared knowledge in which they are embedded."[27] For constructivists, meaning is derived from collective understandings of the material world: it is on the basis of such collective understandings that human action, group action, and social action is based. Stefano Guzzini described the "common ground" of constructivist theory as the social construction of knowledge and the construction of social reality.[28] In other words, what we attempt to understand in global politics is not independent, or separate, from our interpretation of global politics and the language we use to describe it. Constructivism stresses the impact of intersubjective understandings among political actors on constituting their own identities. This social construction of the self, be it by national leaders (I am the leader of the free world), members of international organizations (I am a neutral international civil servant), environmental scientists (I am a citizen of the world), or others, determines the normative acceptability of practices and discourses within issue-areas. Some or all of the practices and discourses considered acceptable and even normatively positive in one social context (I will lead the free world in a war against terrorism) will be less positive in another (I believe only the UN can legitimize a "War on Terrorism") or unacceptable in others (I reject the "War on Terrorism" as short-sighted and counterproductive). In short, "it is collective meanings that constitute the structures which organize our actions."[29]

In this sense, constructivism builds on the work of theorists such as Michel Foucault, Anthony Giddens, and others. How is constructivism distinguished from other theories? Emanuel Adler puts it this way:

> Unlike positivism and materialism, which take the world as it is, constructivism sees the world as a project under construction, as becoming rather than being. Unlike idealism … and post-modernism, which take the world *only* as it can be imagined or talked about, constructivism accepts that not all statements have the same … value and that there is consequently some foundation for knowledge.[30]

Constructivists thus like to argue that there is much more room for actors to effect change in global politics. They are skeptical of the idea that enduring realities or continuities or structures determine the behaviour of actors. For example, take the realist concept of anarchy, which according to realists exerts pressure on decision makers to act in a certain way. For constructivists, this idea of anarchy is not a material condition of global politics, but a social construct. Anarchy does not make states act the way they do: anarchy is what states make of it.[31] We hesitate to include constructivism as a distinct theory since it is in essence a way of understanding change that borrows from postmodernism and can be applied by a wide range of analysts with roots in all the perspectives outlined above. In particular, constructivism can be applied by those interested in studying international institutions, many of whom come from the liberal institutional school.[32]

THE HISTORICAL PERSPECTIVE

Historians who study global politics approach the discipline from a different perspective. Historians argue that international relations scholarship has emphasized the development of theories and models, while deemphasizing the importance of historical research and knowledge. This has led to the development of theory based on historical generalizations that are at the very least highly contentious and at worse completely inaccurate. Historians studying global politics argue that a deeper understanding of history is needed if we are to truly comprehend the subject matter of international relations. Furthermore, in-depth examination of historical cases and examples can yield new information and insights that can challenge prevailing historical "truths" and "lessons" that inform not only theory but also policy practice. In other words, hindsight is seldom perfect and historical understanding is seldom static. Historians also remind students of international relations that much of what seems new may not be that new after historical reflection. For example, globalization is often described as a new phenomenon, one that has changed our world in ways never before experienced. Historians suggest that at least some of the patterns we associate with globalization are actually quite old, and previous eras experienced some of the same angst and wonder about the dawning of a new age as we do today. Globalization is a contested term and idea in the study of global politics, and historians have often been at the centre of the debate over whether globalization even exists or whether its supposed qualities and impacts are as new or profound as they have been portrayed. By examining history more closely, historians remind us of the need to use history more carefully. IR scholars are certainly indebted to the painstaking work conducted by historians, without which it would be impossible to present any sort of contextual understanding of contemporary issues (we borrow from history in the next chapter to do just that).

EMBRACING THEORETICAL DIVERSITY

At this point it would be inaccurate to say that any one perspective dominates the study of global politics. Realism certainly held sway in the United States for much of the Cold War era, but liberal perspectives are at least as prominent today and have often been so in the United Kingdom, Australia, and Canada. Critical perspectives are as popular as ever, especially among graduate students and in the Southern Hemisphere. There has certainly been a growing interest in constructivism in recent years. While the debates between theoreticians can be fascinating, and often quite overwhelming, we will not devote significant sections of this text to them, but attempt to integrate various perspectives in our own treatment of the subject matter. It will be clear to most readers, for example, that the next chapter, focusing mostly on historical conflicts and empire-building, has a realist context. Subsequent chapters will also demonstrate the relevance of liberal, Marxist, feminist, postmodern, and historical and environmentalist perspectives. There may be very good reasons to insist on your own perspective being the right one. At the same time, however, we would encourage you to proceed in this complex field with an open mind, and try to arrive at new conclusions regarding which perspective best suggests and explains global politics to you. There is no need to impose a rigid orthodoxy on the field; one of its attractions is the eclectic nature of the work it has inspired among generations of scholars and practitioners.

ONWARD!

This book intends to introduce students to the discipline of international relations (IR) in the 21st century, and from a distinctly non-American viewpoint. Put bluntly, most IR textbooks are written by Americans, from an American perspective, for American students. The key examples and foreign policy dilemmas offered are American ones, reflecting that state's obviously unique position in world affairs. However, students living in **middle powers** such as Canada appreciate an approach that takes the circumstances of their country (as well as their own values and interests) into account. The task before citizens of countries such as Canada, Norway, Australia, Brazil, South Africa, Thailand, and many others is to better understand the global political environment and all that it entails, rather than to maintain national preeminence within it. Some may think of themselves not as citizens of states at all, but as global citizens. None of this denies the significance of the question of American power and influence in today's global political theatre. Nevertheless, there are issues in the world beyond those that concern the United States, and these are central to both everyday life and the bigger picture of global politics but are often neglected or given peripheral treatment in other texts.

This chapter has introduced the field of global politics and has argued that an approach that escapes the American focus typical of most texts is needed. But the most central rationale for a new look at this topic is that, as the new century evolves, history is moving on. Though the older concepts that have shaped the field—such as state, war, and diplomacy—have retained their significance, we face an era when nonstate actors are often as important, when market forces are changing millions of lives on a daily basis, and when people are attempting to forge new definitions of human rights and dignity. This idea generates a lengthy set of questions—an agenda for study—that requires looking into both traditional and nonconventional areas. A partial list of such questions includes the following:

1. Which theoretical perspective best describes and explains the world? This question is a fundamental one, because different theoretical perspectives provide very different explanations of events and have different implications for policymakers. Does a postpositivist approach add to our understanding? Is constructivism a unifying approach?

Is the feminist critique of realism reasonable? Is a Marxist understanding of the evolution of world order more or less relevant today?

2. What are the lessons of the past? This is an enduring question in the field, but in the contemporary and future context it involves the examination of periods in history that more closely approximate our own. The hope is that we can avoid the repetition of mistakes.

3. Is the international system diverging or converging? Two phenomena seem to exist side by side in the international system: the breakup and collapse of empires and states, and increasing interdependence and political and economic amalgamation. Is there a discernable trend in one direction or another?

4. Are states becoming obsolete? One trend in international affairs has been the increased permeability and penetrability of state borders. Has the **sovereignty** of the state eroded to the point where we may speak of the imminent demise of the state in world politics?

5. What are the implications of terrorism and responses to terrorism for the international system and our understanding of it, including our conceptions of national security and individual liberty?

6. What are the causes of war, and how can conflicts be managed or prevented? This is also a question of enduring importance in international relations, but today efforts are concentrated on addressing the problem of wars within states, as well as the protection of civilians during armed conflict.

7. How can the proliferation of conventional weapons and weapons of mass destruction be stopped? The flow of weapons of mass destruction, sophisticated conventional weapons, and small arms to areas of tension and conflict is a pressing international concern.

8. What is the future of the international economy? Are we heading toward an increasingly liberalized world economy characterized by global free trade, or is the world economy heading toward the development of regional trading blocs or increased protectionism? Will the global economy be characterized by growth and stability or by crisis and recession?

9. Are international organizations getting stronger or weaker? International organizations are a key manifestation of cooperation in international affairs. Some would argue that they serve to enhance and reinforce cooperation. Yet the invasion of Iraq in 2003, and the bombing of Serbia in 1999, proceeded without United Nations approval.

10. How will environmental issues, especially climate change, affect global politics? Environmental degradation has emerged as a serious issue between states and within them. Will environmental pressures from climate change and resource scarcity contribute to increased cooperation or increased conflict among states and peoples?

11. What will be the impact of the information revolution on global politics? Does the information revolution promise a world of improved communication, understanding, and sharing of knowledge leading to a global community, or a world of the information rich and the information poor?

12. How will increasing migration of people affect global politics? People are on the move around the world, in the form of emigrants, refugees, and migrant workers. Increasing hardship and population pressures in the developing world suggest that even larger

population movements will occur in the future, posing hard questions for immigration and refugee policy. Human smuggling is a growing international organized-crime activity.

13. What will be the future impact of the power differential between the developing and developed world? An ever-widening gap in economic and political power exists between the richer countries of North America and Europe and the poorer countries of Latin America, Asia, and Africa. This question has given rise to the broader North–South debate.

14. What are the best strategies for development and aid? This issue has been a pressing one since the 1960s, and as the divide between the world's rich and the world's poor continues to widen, the debate over development strategies has taken on a new urgency. Placing more priority on the role of women in development has led to opportunities and new challenges.

Arguably, all these issues are linked by the pursuit of various forms of security. And, if global politics is largely about the pursuit of security (or the freedom from harm), security must be understood in terms of individual, community, national, and even global survival. Responding to this broad agenda is the greatest challenge we face in global politics. As one major study argued, "diverse kinds of new or revitalised international institutions will be key to meeting strategic challenges as varied as limiting climate change, countering terrorism, providing effective responses to humanitarian catastrophes, managing changing power dynamics in Asia, and preventing further nuclear proliferation."[33]

These are but a few of the many questions challenging students of global politics today as they embark on a journey of overwhelming complexity, frustration, and discovery. Above all, this text is designed to provide interested readers with a rough guide for that journey, one that encompasses origins, currents, and directions. Some aspects of the study of global politics are timeless. As one author contends, "diplomacy, in the sense of the ordered conduct of relations between one group of human beings and another group alien to themselves, is far older than history."[34] Some theorists argue that human nature has always been with us and will not change; others insist it can change for the better, or worse, according to circumstances. As our historical discussions in Part One of this book suggest, war and trade—two primary modes of human interaction—have both been around a very long time. We turn now to an historical account of the international system.

Endnotes

1. Raymond Aron, *Peace and War: A Theory of International Relations* (1966; Garden City, NY: Anchor, 1973), 9; Kenneth Waltz, *Man, the State, and War: A Theoretical Analysis* (New York: Columbia University Press, 1959), 238; Jacqui True, "Feminism," in S. Burchill et al., *Theories of International Relations*, 2nd ed. (London: Palgrave, 1996), 231.

2. J. Der Derian, "A Reinterpretation of Realism: Genealogy, Semiology and Dromology," in Der Derian, ed., *International Theory: Critical Investigations* (New York: New York University Press, 1995), 363–96, 366.

3. One of the most cited examples is Kal Holsti's article "Change in the International System: Interdependence, Integration, and Fragmentation," in O. Holsti, R. Siverson, and A. George, eds., *Change in the International System* (Boulder, CO: Westview Press, 1980), 23–53; more popularly, see B. Barber, "Jihad vs. McWorld," *Atlantic* 269 (March 1992), 53–63.

4. See, for example, J. Dougherty and R. Pfaltzgraff Jr., *Contending Theories of International Relations: A Comprehensive Survey*, 5th ed. (New York: Harper & Row, 2000); R. Keohane, ed., *Neorealism and Its Critics* (New York: Columbia University Press, 1986); O. Holsti, "Models of International Relations and Foreign Policy," *Diplomatic History* 13 (1989), 15–43; K.J. Holsti, *The Dividing Discipline: Hegemony and Diversity in International Theory* (Boston: Allen and Unwin, 1985); J. Der Derian, op. cit.; J. Sterling-Folker, ed., *Making*

Sense of IR Theory (Boulder, CO: Lynne Rienner, 2005); C. Weber, *IR Theory: A Critical Introduction*, 2nd ed. (London: Routledge, 2005); R. Jackson and G. Sorensen, *Introduction to IR: Theories and Approaches* (New York: Oxford, 2007).

5. See D. Dewitt and D. Leyton-Brown, eds., *Canada's International Security Policy* (Scarborough, ON: Prentice Hall, 1995). A classic text on conflict management is R. Matthews, A. Rubinoff, and J. Gross Stein, eds., *International Conflict and Conflict Management: Readings in World Politics* (Scarborough, ON: Prentice Hall, 1984). Another subfield, known formally as *peace studies*, has focused on theories related to cooperation. In fact, the study of peace has a technical name: *irenology*. See J. Starke, *An Introduction to the Study of Peace (Irenology)* (Leyden, Holland: A.W. Sijthoff, 1968).

6. See K. Stiles and T. Akaha, eds., *International Political Economy: A Reader* (New York: HarperCollins, 1991); and R. Stubbs and G. Underhill, eds., *Political Economy and the Changing Global Order*, 3rd ed. (Toronto: University of Oxford Press, 2005); for a Canadian perspective, see D. Drache and M. Gertler, eds., *The New Era of Global Competition: State Policy and Market Power* (Montreal/Kingston: McGill-Queen's University Press, 1991). See also K. Narinzny, *The Political Economy of Grand Strategy* (Ithaca: Cornell University Press, 2007).

7. See R. Riggs and J. Plano, *The United Nations: International Organization and World Politics* (Chicago: Dorsey Press, 1994); J. Ruggie and H. Milner, eds., *Multilateralism Matters: New Directions in World Politics* (New York: Columbia University Press, 1993); S. Krasner, ed., *International Regimes* (Ithaca, NY: Cornell University Press, 1983); and A. Cassese, *International Law* (Oxford: Oxford University Press, 2001). This subfield has been overtaken by the formal study of global governance: see Chapter 5, and the flagship journal *Global Governance: A Review of Multilateralism and International Organizations*; and S. Bernstein and L. Pauly, eds., *Global Governance: Towards a New Grand Compromise?* (Albany: State University of New York Press, 2007).

8. For example, see M. Walzer, *Just and Unjust Wars* (New York: Basic Books, 1992); F. Kratchvil, *Rules, Norms, and Decisions: On the Conditions of Practical and Legal Reasoning in International Relations and Domestic Affairs* (Cambridge, UK: Cambridge University Press, 1989); R. Jackson, *The Global Covenant: Human Conduct in a World of States* (Oxford: Oxford University Press, 2000); T. Pogge, ed., *Global Justice* (Oxford: Blackwell, 2001); and R. Friman, ed., *Challenges and Paths to Global Justice* (New York: Palgrave Macmillan, 2007).

9. See J.D. Singer, "The Level of Analysis Problem in International Relations," *World Politics* 14 (1961), 77–92; K. Waltz, op. cit.; and R.C. North, *War, Peace, Survival: Global Politics and Conceptual Synthesis* (Boulder, CO: Westview Press, 1990).

10. In fact, much of this work is termed *diplomatic history*, and continues today; for example, the Society for Historians of American Foreign Relations continues to publish its flagship journal, *Diplomatic History*.

11. For example, John Naisbitt argues that the larger the system, the more powerful and important its smaller parts. See his *Global Paradox: The Bigger the World Economy the More Powerful Its Smallest Players* (New York: William Morrow, 1994).

12. These two dimensions are outlined in more detail in Joseph S. Nye Jr., *Bound to Lead: The Changing Nature of American Power* (New York: Basic Books, 1990).

13. J. Rosenau, *Turbulence in World Politics: A Theory of Change and Continuity* (Princeton: Princeton University Press, 1990), 6.

14. C. Lindblom, *Inquiry and Change: The Troubled Attempt to Understand and Shape Society* (New Haven: Yale University Press, 1990), x.

15. K. Boulding, "National Images and International Systems," *Journal of Conflict Resolution* 3 (June 1959), 120–31.

16. See A. Schlesinger Jr., *The Cycles of American History* (Boston: Houghton Mifflin, 1986).

17. D. Boucher, *Political Theories of International Relations: From Thucydides to the Present* (Oxford: University Press, 1998), 162–63.

18. See K.R. Nossal, *The Politics of Canadian Foreign Policy*, 2nd ed. (Scarborough, ON: Prentice-Hall, 1989).

19. See H. Bull, *The Anarchical Society: A Study of Order in World Politics* (London: The Macmillan Press, 1977).

20. For the most recent edition of this work, see *Power and Interdependence*, 3rd ed. (New York: Longman, 2001).

21. A wealth of literature has emerged on this theoretical proposition; for an excellent overview and sophisticated application, see N. Ripsman, *Peacemaking by Democracies: The Effect of State Autonomy on the Post–World War Settlements* (University Park, PA: Pennsylvania State University Press, 2002). See also J. Owen, "How Liberalism Produces Democratic Peace," *International Security* 19, no. 2 (1994), 87–125.

22. C. Reus-Smit, "Constructivism," in S. Burchill et al., *Theories of International Relations* (London: Palgrave, 2000), 209–30, 221–22.

23. See M. Rupert and H. Smith, eds., *Historical Materialism and Globalization* (London: Routledge, 2002), for a series of sophisticated essays; and S. Gill, and J. Mittelman, eds., *Innovation and Transformation in International Studies* (Cambridge University Press, 1997). For a critical take on the "appropriation" of Gramsci for these purposes see J. Femia, "Gramsci, Machiavelli and International Relations," *The Political Quarterly* 76, no. 3 (2005), 341–349.

24. For a review of feminist approaches to IR, see J. Ann Tickner, "Feminist Perspectives on International Relations," in Walter Carlsnaes, Thomas Risse, and Beth A. Simmons, eds., *Handbook of International Relations* (London: Sage, 2002), 275–91. See also J. Steans, *Gender and International Relations: An Introduction* (New Brunswick, NJ: Rutgers University Press, 1998), C. Sylvester, *Feminist International Relations: An Unfinished Journey* (Cambridge, UK: Cambridge University Press, 2002); J. Goldstein, *War and Gender: How Gender Shapes the War System and Vice Versa* (Cambridge: Cambridge University Press, 2001); and J. Joachim, *Agenda Setting, the UN and NGOs: Gender Violence and Reproductive Rights* (Washington: Georgetown University Press, 2007).

25. "Feminist Themes and International Relations," in J. Der Derian, op. cit., 340–62, 353. On Luxemburg, see R. Dunayevskaya, *Rosa Luxemburg, Women's Liberation, and Marx's Philosophy of Revolution*, 2nd ed. (Chicago: University of Illinois Press, 1991).

26. See E. Laferrière and P. Stoett, *International Relations Theory and Ecological Thought: Towards a Synthesis* (London: Routledge, 1999); and same, eds., *International Ecopolitical Theory: Critical Approaches* (Vancouver: UBC Press, 2007); and R. Saunier and R. Meganck, *Dictionary and Introduction to Global Environmental Governance* (London: Earthscan, 2007).

27. A. Wendt, "Constructing International Politics," *International Security* 20 (Spring 1995), 73.

28. S. Guzzini, "A Reconstruction of Constructivism in International Relations," *European Journal of International Relations* 6 (Summer 2000), 149.

29. A. Wendt, "Anarchy Is What States Make of It: The Social Construction of Power Politics," *International Organization* 46, no. 2 (1992), 391–25.

30. E. Adler, "Constructivism and International Relations," in Walter Carlsnaes, Thomas Risse, and Beth A. Simmons, eds., *Handbook of International Relations*, 95.

31. Hence the title of Wendt's seminal article; see note 29.

32. For a spirited discussion and defence of this broad yet emergent thinking, see especially J. Der Derian, "Post-Theory: The Eternal Return of Ethics in International Relations," in M. Doyle and J. Ikenberry, eds., *New Thinking in International Relations Theory* (Boulder, CO: Westview, 1997), 54–76. For a general treatment of constructivism, see I. Hacking, *The Social Construction of What?* (Cambridge, MA: Harvard University Press, 1999); and see also P. Katzenstein, *The Culture of National Security: Norms and Identity in World Politics* (New York: Columbia University Press, 1996).

33. A. Nicoll and T. Huxley, "Introduction," in A. Nicoll and T. Huxley, eds., *Perspectives on International Security*, Adelphi Paper 400–401 (London: International Institute of Strategic Studies, 2008), 27.

34. Sir Harold Nicolson, *Diplomacy*, 3rd ed. (London: Oxford University Press, 1963), 5.

Suggested Websites

Note: The websites listed here are both general in nature (that is, are broad resources for the study of IR) and pertinent to IR theory in particular.

Libraries

Berkeley Sunsite Library Links Libweb
http://sunsite.berkeley.edu/Libweb

Carrie: A Full Text Electronic Library
http://kuhttp.cc.ukans.edu/carrie

Gabriel: Gateway to European Libraries
http://portico.bl.uk/gabriel/en/welcome.html

General Political Science and International Relations Resources

ACUNS home page
http://www.acuns.wlu.ca

Berkeley Institute of International Studies
http://globetrotter.berkeley.edu

Canadian Institute of International Affairs (CIIA)
http://www.ciia.org/index.htm

Foreign Affairs Canada (FAC)
http://www.fac-aec.gc.ca/menu-en.asp

Foreign Policy
http://www.foreignpolicy.com

International Affairs Resources Library
http://www.etown.edu/vl

International Relations and Security Issues

University of Oregon documentation centre
http://libweb.uoregon.edu/govdocs/cat-ir.html

International Trade Canada (ITC)
http://www.itcan-cican.gc.ca/menu-en.asp

Policy.ca: A Non-Partisan Resource for the Public Analysis of Canadian Policy Issues
http://www.policy.ca

SACIS International Relations Resources
http://www.library.ubc.ca/poli/international.html

Social Science WWW Virtual Library
http://www.clas.ufl.edu/users/gthursby/socsci

United Nations
http://www.un.org

The Virtual Library: International Affairs
http://vlib.org/InternationalAffairs.html

Weatherhead Center for International Affairs
http://www.wcfia.harvard.edu

Yale University, International Affairs: Internet Resources
http://www.library.yale.edu/ia-resources/resource.html

History and Global Politics: War and Peace

Even the ordinary, the "impartial" historiographer, who believes and professes that he maintains a simply receptive attitude; surrendering himself only to the data supplied him—is by no means passive as regards the existence of his thinking powers. He brings his categories with him, and sees the phenomena presented to his mental vision, exclusively through those media.

—*Georg Wilhelm Friederich Hegel[1]*

The twentieth century is hardly behind us but already its quarrels and its achievements, its ideals and its fears are slipping into the obscurity of mis-memory.

—*Tony Judt[2]*

AN INTRODUCTION TO THE ROLE OF HISTORY

History is crucial to our understanding of contemporary global politics, because we need to understand the past in order to even begin to comprehend the present. The study of history can help us identify examples of continuity and change, and patterns of divergence and convergence. History can provide case studies and examples for research into any number of topics, such as the origins of war, terrorism, and political tensions within states. For example, any attempt to understand or address the conflict in Afghanistan requires an awareness of the cultural evolution of the country as well as its past experiences with foreign occupation. The division of the Korean peninsula must be understood with reference to World War II and the **Korean War**. An understanding of the September 11, 2001 terrorist attacks against America is impossible without an awareness of the history of the Middle East or American foreign policy. It is impossible to understand the persistent national unity question or First Nations issues in Canada without some knowledge of the colonial legacy in North America. In short, history is all around us, and both scholars and decision makers ignore it at their peril.

As our opening quotes suggest, rarely is the importance of perspective more evident than when examining history, since many different interpretations of past events exist and compete for validity. States tend to have official versions of historical events, often glorifying the importance and righteousness of their country's actions, or perhaps minimizing the harm caused in their name. For example, Japanese textbooks still omit many of the facts about Japanese foreign policy during World War II (see Profile 2.1). Many states have suffered collective amnesia after particularly traumatic events, including war-related atrocities.[3] Groups of individuals unified by race, religion, or clan ties also have their own interpretations of history, which are frequently at odds with the interpretations of other groups or governments. Scholars of international relations also have divergent views of historical events, depending on their educational and social background, as well as their theoretical orientation. Furthermore, as feminists and postmodernists often argue, historical perspectives are inherently exclusionary. Many groups—including women and ethnic and religious minorities—make the accurate observation that they have been underrepresented in mainstream histories. Others insist that the legacy of human interaction with nature, or environmental history, is of fundamental importance.[4] Finally, history is vulnerable to radical revisions for political ends. For example, those who deny that the Holocaust ever took place are not interpreting history; they are trying to rewrite it for their own ends. Vigilance against this sort of manipulation is as important as respect for different perspectives (see Profile 2.1).

In this chapter, we will briefly examine world history with a view to highlighting three key themes in the relationship between history and global politics. First, history is most often presented, as it is here, as the history of war and conflict and the rise and fall of civilizations, states, and empires. This is the interpretation of the realist perspective on global politics, which emphasizes the historical continuity of balance of power politics, the importance of alliances, and the inevitability of war. Although this view of history is not necessarily inaccurate, as we will see in future chapters, it is incomplete. Second, developments in history have had a defining impact on the development of theories of war and peace. The two are inseparable, and the changing nature of global politics has stimulated the development of new theories and the adaptation of old ones. As we shall see, the theories we discussed in Chapter 1 are all grounded in historical developments and interpretations of those developments. Third, history reveals the importance of ideas as driving forces of change and conflict. Religious faiths and political ideologies have had an enormous impact on the evolution of human societies and how they interact. Of course, historical interpretations are always undergoing revision, often by theories that seek to challenge prevailing assumptions. Hindsight is seldom 20/20, and the lessons of history are always subject to critical reassessment.

THE ANCIENT LEGACY: THE RISE AND FALL OF CIVILIZATIONS AND EMPIRES

In the Middle East, civilization first developed around 3500 B.C.E., in the basins of three great river systems. The river basin of the Tigris and Euphrates was the cradle for the early Mesopotamian city-states and the Assyrian (1244–605 B.C.E.) and Persian (550–331 B.C.E.) empires. The Nile River basin sustained the great Egyptian empires of the Pharaohs, which rose to the heights of the age of the pyramids (c. 2590 B.C.E.) and the XII (1991–1786 B.C.E.) and XVIII (1570–1320 B.C.E.) dynasties. The Indus River basin and the plain of Ganges was the cradle of India's early Harappa and Mohenjo-Daro civilizations (c. 2550–1550 B.C.E.). These city-states, empires, and civilizations developed complex instruments of diplomacy and trade. However, they also developed complex systems for waging war. Civilization and war have a symbiotic relationship. Once individuals settle in a given area, and their survival becomes tied to the land around them, the idea of ownership and the protective instinct become very strong. As John Keegan suggests, "Pastoralism, and agriculture even more so,

PROFILE 2.1 Abusing History

CONTENT OMISSION IN JAPANESE SCHOOL TEXTBOOKS

In 1997, a Japanese historian named Saburo Ienaga won a landmark case before the Japanese Supreme Court. The court ruled that the Japanese Education Ministry broke the law when it removed certain material from a high school textbook written by Ienaga. Since the 1950s, the Education Ministry has screened Japanese textbooks, removing references to the atrocities committed by the Japanese military in World War II. As a result, generations of Japanese schoolchildren have gone through school with only a general or highly sanitized account of Japan's war record. One of the references removed from Ienaga's textbook concerned biological warfare experiments conducted by the Japanese military on Chinese subjects during the war. Opposition to such references comes from nationalists (who regard such references as an attack on Japanese pride) and widespread ignorance of Japan's war record (largely a result of the education policy). Japanese textbooks now include more information and facts concerning Japan's role in the war. For example, most textbooks now mention the infamous "comfort women" who were forced into prostitution to serve the soldiers of the Japanese military. However, references to Japan's share of the responsibility for World War II, and the atrocities committed by the Japanese military, remain brief and incomplete. Japan provides an important example of how states and governments can abuse history through censorship and the suppression of unpopular ideas or facts. Because of the court's decision, the material on biological warfare experiments was restored to Ienaga's textbook. However, other references in his book were not restored. The coverage of Japan's war record in school textbooks remains a controversial subject inside and outside the country: outrage over textbook coverage of Japan's war record led to protests in China and Korea in 2005 and on the Japanese island of Okinawa in 2007. See G. Hicks, *Japan's War Memories: Amnesia or Concealment?* (Aldershot: Ashgate, 1997).

JIM KEEGSTRA AND HOLOCAUST DENIAL

In 1985, an Alberta schoolteacher and town mayor named Jim Keegstra went on trial in Red Deer, Alberta. Keegstra was charged with willfully promoting hatred against an identifiable group—Jewish people—from 1978 to 1982 while he taught social studies at Eckville High School in Alberta. Keegstra taught his students that Judaism was an evil religion that perverted the laws of God and condoned the harsh treatment of non-Jewish peoples. He implicitly taught his students that the Holocaust was a hoax and that an international Jewish conspiracy—called the "hidden hand"—was working behind the scenes with the support of Jewish financiers to establish a new world order in which there would be one government. According to Keegstra, Jews had infiltrated every institution of society, and this demanded that non-Jews be aware and watchful. Keegstra taught his students that conventional history books had lies in them, and in his classes he used books and pamphlets from his own library. Class exams and essays were based on these readings and class notes. In most respects, Keegstra's teachings were typical of anti-Semitic views, full of conspiracy theories based on historical distortions and outright inaccuracies, suppression and denial of evidence and fact, and barely concealed hatred. He passed these views on to students in a high school social studies class as fact, one example among many of the abuse of history by individuals or groups. Jim Keegstra was found guilty, fined $5,000, and prohibited from teaching high school. The Supreme Court upheld this decision, although the Alberta Court of Appeal reduced his sentence. See W. Hare, "Limiting the Freedom of Expression: The Keegstra Case," *Canadian Journal of Education* 15, no. 4 (1990), 375–389.

make for war."[5] Furthermore, large-scale warfare can be conducted only by systems of government that possess the organizational capacity to marshal surplus resources for war. In ancient civilizations, revenues from taxes and rents tended to go to war, worship, or welfare.[6]

Civilization in the Mediterranean was dominated by successive waves of Greek peoples, who established control over much of the region (c. 1150–550 B.C.E.). In Asia Minor (present-day Turkey) the Greek advance clashed with the Persian Empire of Darius and Xerxes. Although Greece resisted conquest, the unity of the Greek city-states collapsed and the resulting Peloponnesian War (431–404 B.C.E.) between Athens and Sparta enabled Macedon, under Philip, to dominate the Greek peninsula. The Peloponnesian War is regarded as an important case study in global politics (see Profile 2.2). Philip's son, **Alexander the Great**, conquered a dominion that stretched from Macedon to the Indus River, but his empire collapsed after his death. A new power centre developed around Rome in central Italy, and soon expanded over the entire Italian peninsula (510–264 B.C.E.). Bolstered by an extremely effective military and administrative system, Roman rule (first as a republic and then as an empire) eventually stretched from present-day Spain to Mesopotamia. However, the Roman Empire declined due to internal decay, civil war, and "barbarian" invasions. Peter Heather suggests the fall of Rome was attributable to its thirst for conquest: "By virtue of its unbounded aggression, Roman imperialism was ultimately responsible for its own destruction."[7] The Roman Empire was divided in 330 C.E. when an Eastern Empire (known as the Byzantine Empire) was created under the control of Constantinople (Byzantium). The western half of the empire fell to invasion in the fifth century, but the Byzantine Empire survived another 1000 years until Constantinople (today called Istanbul) was conquered by the Ottoman Empire in 1453 C.E. When the power of Rome collapsed, most of the infrastructure, knowledge, and security its rule had provided disappeared as a Dark Age enveloped much of Europe and the Mediterranean. Many observers of our own time have argued that the United States exerts a greater hegemonic influence today than Rome at the height of its power: the decline and fall

---

PROFILE 2.2 Thucydides (460–400 B.C.E.)

Thucydides is regarded as the greatest of the classical Greek historians, because of his unfinished account of the Peloponnesian War between Athens and Sparta (Lacedaemon). Thucydides himself was an Athenian general who was exiled from Athens. While in exile he wrote a history of the war that was taking place all around him. His exhaustive and dramatic account can be read as a Greek tragedy, a story of human virtue and human deceit, and an exploration of the origins of war. Many contemporary students of global politics maintain that the themes in the book are applicable across time, culture, and place. Thucydides sought to draw themes and generalizations about the origin of all wars and to offer historical lessons for those who might read his work in the future. For Thucydides, "the growth in the power of Athens, and the alarm this inspired in Lacedaemon, made war inevitable." Thucydides thus identified the cause of war in the fear provoked by shifts in the distribution of power across the Greek city-states. His focus on the importance of power is most graphically illustrated in the famous Melian Dialogue, in which the powerful Athenians say to the less powerful Melians, "for you know as well as we do that right ... is in question only between equals in power, while the strong do what they can and the weak suffer what they must." Thucydides also reflected on the role of prominent individuals in the course of events, and he is considered one of the intellectual founders of political realism.

SOURCES: THUCYDIDES, *THE PELOPONNESIAN WAR*, THE CRAWLEY TRANSLATION (NEW YORK: THE MODERN LIBRARY, 1982), 14, 351. SEE ALSO J. MONTEN, "THUCYDIDES AND MODERN REALISM," *INTERNATIONAL STUDIES QUARTERLY* 50 (2006), 3–25.

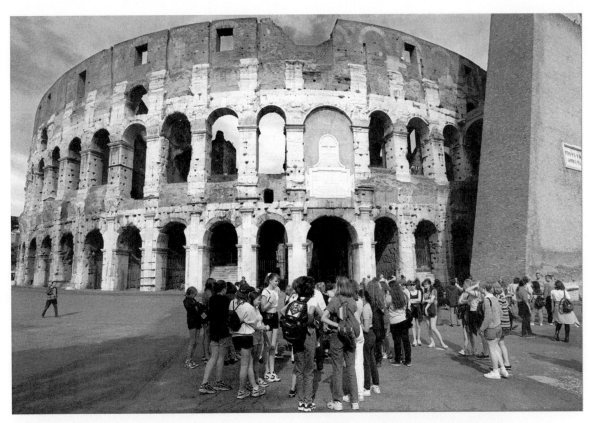

Remembering Rome. Will tourists of the future learn about the decline and fall of the American empire, as these tourists are learning about the decline and fall of the Roman Empire? (AP Photo/Plinio Lepri/CP Archive.)

of Rome is therefore studied with great interest. Is American power failing, as did Rome's, and if so what will be the consequences?

In northern Europe, distinct cultural groups had developed by 800 B.C.E. Much of northern Europe came under Celtic domination by 450 B.C.E. The Slavic peoples established a centre of civilization in what is today central Russia. The decline and fall of the Western Roman Empire in the fourth and fifth centuries exposed Europe to numerous invasions from nomadic peoples living in northern and southern Europe (Goths, Vikings, Vandals, and Magyars), and from larger incursions that originated in central Asia (Huns, Avars, and, later, Mongols). These nomadic peoples also invaded Mediterranean Europe, China, India, and Persia, throwing all of these centres of civilization into ruin or near-collapse. In the aftermath of the fall of Rome, power in Europe devolved to local nobles, ushering in the era of European feudalism and the Middle Ages. Political and economic life was highly localized and controlled by small numbers of nobles and knights who exerted a measure of political independence derived largely from their dominance over military affairs and the defensive strongholds of their castles. In feudal societies, concepts like nationalism and citizenship did not exist, and authority and loyalty were invested in lord, religion, town, and guild. For Karl Marx, the development of feudalism was an important step in the evolution of society toward capitalism, which in turn was a step toward communism. Feudal Europe continued to experience nomadic invasions: from 1206 to 1696 C.E. the Mongol empire launched repeated invasions into Europe, the Middle East, and Asia under Genghis Khan and his sons and grandsons. However, the unity of the Mongol empire broke down, and Mongol power receded in the face of an expanding Russia and China.[8]

Larger kingdoms ruled by dynastic monarchies began to establish themselves in Europe between the 10th and 13th centuries in what are today the British Isles, Germany, France, and eastern Europe. Wealth from trade and gunpowder facilitated this process of political consolidation: cannon blow could destroy castle or city walls, and with them went the ability of the knight or the town to resist a monarch with the wealth to purchase the new weapons. Indeed, commerce and cannons helped to make many kings. This process of political consolidation, as well as agricultural, industrial, and intellectual development, was slowed by famine, plague, and war (in particular, the Hundred Years' War between England and France). European recovery from these events began in 1450, as the empires of France, the **Hapsburgs**, Muscovy/Russia, Sweden, and Lithuania all grew through the 15th and 16th centuries. However, resistance to amalgamation was widespread. For example, the Scots and Irish resisted the expansion of English rule. This resistance left an enduring legacy in the independence movements of Scotland and the violence in Northern Ireland. Italy remained divided into city-states, and this period is often regarded as a case study in power politics (see Profile 2.3). Finally, the religious wars of the Reformation, culminating in the

PROFILE 2.3   Niccolo Machiavelli (1469–1527)

Niccolo Machiavelli. (© Bettman/Corbis.)

Machiavelli was a civil servant and diplomat in the republic of Florence during the Italian city-states period of the 15th and 16th centuries. These city-states vied for power and influence, and advising the rulers of Florence during this struggle was Machiavelli's profession. When Florence fell in 1512, Machiavelli was without a job, and he spent the final years of his life writing books, including his most famous works, *The Prince* and *The Discourses*. Drawing heavily on his examination of Greek and Roman writings as well as his own experience as a diplomat, he wrote of power, alliances, and the causes of conflict in the Italian city-state system. Much of

what he wrote was aimed at the leaders—or princes—of states, advising them on the principles of statecraft, the conduct of their affairs with other princes, the importance of military force, and the lessons of historical experience. For Machiavelli, the security and survival of the state was the paramount concern of the prince; all other concerns were subordinated to this objective. The ends—the security of the state—justified the means necessary to achieve that objective. This Machiavellian approach to politics has often been criticized as amoral. However, Machiavelli argued that rulers must do what is in the best interests of the state; to do otherwise would in fact be immoral. Machiavelli also stressed that his advice to princes was based not on ethical principles or visions of the world as it should be or ought to be, but rather on the way the world was, according to historical and contemporary evidence. To act based on how one felt the world ought to be, as opposed to how the world really was, would be a recipe for disaster. In the study of international relations, Machiavelli's emphasis on interests, power, and the conduct of statecraft is inseparable from the realpolitik tradition of political realism; he also engaged in the formal study of military strategy, which would have a lasting effect on security studies as well.

SOURCES: NICCOLO MACHIAVELLI, *THE PRINCE* AND *THE DISCOURSES* (NEW YORK: THE MODERN LIBRARY, 1950); SEE ALSO F. GILBERT, "MACHIAVELLI: THE RENAISSANCE OF THE ART OF WAR," IN P. PARET, ED., *MAKERS OF MODERN STRATEGY: FROM MACHIAVELLI TO THE NUCLEAR AGE* (NEW JERSEY: PRINCETON UNIVERSITY PRESS, 1986), 11–31.

devastating **Thirty Years' War** (1618–48), dominated political, intellectual, and religious affairs (see Profile 2.4).

Despite this instability, this era was one of European exploration and expansion. European exploration by Portugal and Spain, and then by France, England, and Holland, was originally motivated by a desire to circumvent the controlling influence of the commercial cities (primarily Venice and Genoa) that dominated the medieval trade routes to central Asia and the Middle East. This brought a European presence to virtually all the inhabited continents. These events produced several lasting outcomes. The focus of political and commercial activity shifted from the Mediterranean to the trading empires of western Europe. Trade and commerce became truly global in scope. The political and economic life of Europe was extended throughout the world, particularly in the form of growing rivalries between the trading empires, and the colonization of millions. Trade and political violence became inseparable. As Jeremy Black argues, "Violence was employed in order to influence or even dictate the terms of trade, in particular by excluding rivals, rather than to gain territory."[9] Slowly but steadily, the age of European empire was beginning.

In the Middle East, the spectacular rise and expansion of Islam dominated the period after the fall of Rome. Established by the prophet Muhammad (c. 570–632 C.E.), Islam expanded

PROFILE 2.4 Thomas Hobbes (1588–1679)

Thomas Hobbes. (© Bettman/Corbis.)

Hobbes was an English political philosopher who wrote in the turbulent years of the early 17th century, which were dominated by the Thirty Years' War in Europe. In England, Parliament was asserting its power against the monarchy, which would eventually lead to the English Civil War, and Hobbes, a royalist, was compelled to flee to France for eight years. In his writings, Hobbes's primary focus was politics within the state. In his most famous work, *Leviathan*, he depicted the condition of humanity in a hypothetical "state of nature" that would exist in the absence of governmental authority. This condition, he argued, would be characterized by anarchy, "a war of every one against every one," in which there would be "continual fear and danger of violent death; and the life of man, solitary, poor, nasty, brutish, and short." This condition could be avoided only by the creation of the "Leviathan," a state or ruler who would establish and maintain order. Without order, there could be no civilization. Realists often describe international relations as a Hobbesian state of nature that lacks a Leviathan in the form of a world government or a dominant power to impose order. Like individuals in a state of nature, states exist in an anarchic environment, in a war of everyone against everyone in which suspicion, distrust, conflict, and war are inevitable. In such a "self-help" world, states must pursue their individual self-interests.

SOURCE: THOMAS HOBBES, *LEVIATHAN*, ED. MICHAEL OAKESHOTT (NEW YORK: COLLIER MACMILLAN, 1974). FOR A CONTRARY VIEW ON HOBBES AND IR, SEE M. WILLIAMS, "HOBBES AND INTERNATIONAL RELATIONS: A RECONSIDERATION," *INTERNATIONAL ORGANIZATION* 50:2 (1996), 213–236

Map 2.1 The Extent of the Islamic World in 1500

Atlas of the Islamic World since 1500.

SOURCE: *ATLAS OF THE ISLAMIC WORLD SINCE 1500* (OXFORD: PHAIDON PRESS LTD., 1982), 88.

within a century from the Arabian Peninsula to include North Africa and southern Spain, and the western reaches of China and India. This extraordinary success was due to the weakness of the post-Roman world, military supremacy, and the vitality of the new religion of Islam.[10] After a period of great prosperity and cultural and intellectual development, internal dissension weakened the empire, which lost some of its territories in southern Europe and the Mediterranean to crusading Christians from Europe in the 10th century.[11] The Crusades remain a powerful source of resentment in the Arab world, and are often invoked (along with the colonial period of the 19th and 20th centuries) to contextualize and explain Western actions in the region. Islam experienced a resurgence between 1300 and 1639, led by the Ottoman Empire. By 1354 the Ottoman Empire expanded through the Balkans east of the Adriatic and south of the Danube, and all around the Black Sea. By the time of Suleiman the Magnificent (1520–66), the Ottoman Empire was one of the great empires of the world. In the East, Islam spread through Persia, expanding to central Asia, southern Asia and the outlying provinces of China, as well as present-day Indonesia (see Map 2.1). However, the Islamic world began to fracture politically (as the Mughal Empire in India and Safavid Persia clashed with each other and the Ottoman Empire) and religiously (as the **Sunni** and **Shiite** branches of Islam came into conflict). Although increasingly referred to as the "sick man of Europe," the Ottoman Empire remained a world power until World War I.[12]

In Asia, civilization began with the development of the first agricultural, hunting, and fishing communities around 4000 B.C.E., in what are today northern China, Southeast Asia, and India. The Shang Dynasty (1700–1100 B.C.E.) was the first historical dynasty in China, but

---

PROFILE 2.5 Kautilya (350–275 B.C.E.)

Also known as Chanakya or Vishnugupta, Kautilya was councillor and chief minister to Chandra-Gupta, the founder of the Mauryan Empire. His views survive in the form of the *Arthasastra (The Book of the State)*, a treatise on the science of politics, which is summarized in 6,000 verses. Written primarily for rulers, the *Arthasastra* is essentially a compendium of reflections on human nature and the conduct of political activity. The *Arthasastra* contains advice to rulers on the conduct of war, foreign policy, and empire building. Kautilya argued that war must serve political objectives. The purpose of war is to strengthen an empire, not merely to destroy an enemy. Weakening an enemy before fighting was the key to success in battle and was more important than the force of arms. He advised that rulers should fight weaker states and ally with stronger ones. Kautilya warned that the natural enemies of a ruler were the rulers of bordering empires. However, the rulers of the empires that bordered one's neighbours were natural friends, a piece of advice more commonly captured by the dictum "The enemy of my enemy is my friend." Kautilya also commented on the qualities of the ideal ruler, who, he argued, had to possess good character and a willingness to listen to advisors (like Kautilya). The character of the ruler affected the character of the ruled. Kautilya warned about the corrosive effects of injustice and advised the ruler that it was his responsibility to keep the people content if rebellion, chaos, and violence were to be avoided. Kautilya is sometimes called the "Indian Machiavelli," but it would be more accurate to call Machiavelli the Italian Kautilya. Many of the themes familiar to the power politics approach can be found in the *Arthasastra*, far removed from the time and context of Machiavelli's Italy.

SOURCE: A. PARMAR, *TECHNIQUES OF STATECRAFT: A STUDY OF KAUTILYA'S "ARTHASASTRA"* (DELHI: ATMA RAM AND SONS, 1987).

like the enormous Harappa and Mohenjo-Daro civilizations of India (c. 2550–1550 B.C.E.), it succumbed to foreign invasion. A period of consolidation and fragmentation of political units in both China and India followed. In India, Chandra-Gupta and his dynasty (297 B.C.E.–236 C.E.) succeeded in unifying most of the Indian peninsula under one ruler (see Profile 2.5). Invasion from the north fragmented the empire, which was reestablished under the Gupta empires (320–410 C.E.). In China, the Chou Dynasty (1122–221 B.C.E.) replaced the Shang Dynasty. Between 1122 and 771 B.C.E., this empire maintained stability and order based on a feudal system. However, after 771 B.C.E. the empire increasingly fragmented into independent kingdoms engaged in almost continual conflict, culminating in the Warring States period of 403–221 B.C.E. (see Profile 2.6 and Map 2.2). This period in Chinese history is often used to illustrate the themes of power politics, in much the same way as the Italian city-state period. The victorious Ch'in Empire in turn collapsed and was replaced by the Han Dynasty (206 B.C.E.–220 C.E.), which established a prosperous and well-administered empire. Invasions of nomadic peoples prompted both the Ch'in Empire and the Han dynasty to build the Great Wall of China. However, the Great Wall could not protect the Han Empire from internal dis-integration, and nomadic invaders breached the wall in 304. Recovery was slow, but under the Sui (581–617 C.E.), T'ang (618–907 C.E.), Sung (960–1279 C.E.) dynasties, China expanded and became prosperous, stable, and intellectually and scientifically advanced beyond any other civilization. Mongol invasion brought a period of decline, but under the Ming dynasty (1386–1644) Chinese power and prosperity were restored. In Japan, feudal warlords dominated politics until the Tokugawa shogunate unified Japan for 250 years before the forced opening of Japan by the European powers.

In Africa, civilization developed in the Nile tributaries and in eastern Africa, where the Kingdom of Kush dominated from c. 900 B.C.E. to 400 C.E. Settlers moved through present-day Ethiopia into southern Africa, and **Iron Age** civilizations developed in central

---

PROFILE 2.6 Sun Tzu

Sun Tzu was a warrior philosopher in fourth-century (B.C.E.) China. His *Art of War*, one of the greatest classical Chinese texts, is one of the most influential books on strategy ever written. *The Art of War* was evidently composed during the Warring States period in ancient China. The period was characterized by competition, shifting alliances, and warfare between the kings who struggled for power in the latter years of the Chou Dynasty. Sun Tzu drew heavily on Chinese philosophy—in particular, the Taoist works *I Ching (Book of Changes)* and the *Tao-te Ching (The Way and Its Power)*—and Chinese military practices in writing what is in essence a study of the conduct of competition and conflict on any level, from the interpersonal to the international. Most popularly known for its general advice that to win without fighting is best, *The Art of War* emphasizes shunning battle except when victory is assured,

avoiding risk, dominating an opponent through psychological means, and using time rather than force to wear an enemy down. The book also includes advice on preparations for war, battle tactics, sieges, manoeuvres, and the use of terrain. Much of the advice emphasizes the importance of achieving advantage over one's enemy before any military engagement. Today, military leaders, politicians, and business executives study *The Art of War* as a window on the political and business approaches of Asian countries and firms. For international relations scholars, and realists in particular, the themes in Sun Tzu's work reflect the nature of politics and power in anarchic environments. Along with Kautilya, Sun Tzu offers evidence of the existence of power politics themes across time, place, and culture.

SOURCE: SUN TZU, *THE ART OF WAR*, TRANS. THOMAS CLEARY (BOSTON: SHAMBALA, 1988).

Map 2.2 China and the Warring States Period (300 B.C.E.)

SOURCE: M. V. CREVELD, *THE ART OF WAR AND MILITARY THOUGHT* (LONDON: CASSELL AND CO., 2000).

and southern Africa by 100 C.E. Great trading empires developed in Africa over the next 1,000 years in what are today Zimbabwe, the Democratic Republic of Congo, and Ghana. The influence of Islamic expansion into North Africa contributed to the wealth of the Mali, Songhay, and the Kanem Borno empires, as Arab merchant colonies spread along Africa's north and east coasts (see Map 2.3). By the arrival of the first Europeans (the Portuguese in 1448), Africa had a thriving trading system based on gold, ivory, copper, and slaves. Portuguese, and later British and Dutch, trading stations spread rapidly in Africa. Trade with Europeans, at first based on gold, shifted to slaves, who were in demand for the colonial sugar plantations in South America and the West Indies and the tobacco and rice plantations of North America. Between 1450 and 1870, some 15 million Africans were shipped across the Atlantic, 90 percent of them to South America and the Caribbean. Some Africans suffered terribly from this trade; others profited. In 1800, most of Africa (except the northern areas held by the Ottoman Empire) remained independent.

In the Americas, the first large civilizations emerged in Mesoamerica (present-day southern Mexico) in the form of the Olmecs and Zapotecs and in the central Andes around 1000 B.C.E. In the fifth century C.E., the Olmecs and Zapotecs were conquered by the invading Maya (300–900 C.E.), who left an enduring cultural legacy in Mesoamerica. In North America, large trading and agricultural centres emerged in Hopewell territory (300 B.C.E.–550 C.E.) around the southern Great Lakes. In Central America, Mayan civilization

Map 2.3 African Empires in History

SOURCE: M. GLASSNER AND H. J. DE BLIJ, *SYSTEMATIC POLITICAL GEOGRAPHY*, 4TH ED. (NEW YORK: JOHN WILEY AND SONS, INC., 1989). REPRINTED WITH PERMISSION OF JOHN WILEY AND SONS, INC.

was followed first by the Toltecs in the 11th century, and then the Aztecs in the 13th century. Aztec expansion, conducted through a combination of alliance and conquest, reached its zenith under Montezuma II (1502–20). In South America, several diverse civilizations developed in the Andes and were unified under the Huari and Tiahuanaco empires (600–800 C.E.). These empires collapsed, and unity in the Andes was not achieved until the Inca civilization of the 15th century. The Inca Empire expanded between 1438 and 1525 to an area 4,000 kilometres long and more than 300 kilometres wide, with a hereditary dynasty and an advanced bureaucracy and infrastructure (see Map 2.4). However, the Spanish on their arrival in the beginning of the 16th century overthrew the Aztec and Inca civilizations. The defeat of such large, established empires by small bands of Spanish soldiers has been explained by a combination of superior military technology, different cultural approaches to war, the introduction of disease, the assistance of native allies, and Aztec and Incan political weakness.[13] Elsewhere, the Portuguese slowly expanded into Brazil, establishing an extensive sugar industry worked by slaves. In North America, colonization was slower, and economic and political activity was based on a wide range of cultural traditions (see Map 2.5).

So far, the principal actors in this narrative have been the mighty civilizations and empires. The fate of less powerful actors in the evolution of human society is often rather stark. In a history defined by power politics, the less powerful (whether groups, city-states, or small empires) have been at a disadvantage. The weak have indeed suffered what they must. The least powerful have often disappeared from history altogether,

Map 2.4 The Peoples and Civilizations of Central and South America

Gulf of Mexico

TARASCAN
1400–1522

TEOTIHUACAN
100 B.C.E.–750 C.E.

OLMEC
1200–100 B.C.E.

Chichén Itzá

Teotihuacán
Tenochtitlán

Uxmet

Mitla

MAYA
100–1542

Piedras Negras

TOLTEC
900–1200
AZTEC
1325–1521

Oopan

ZAPOTEC
and MIXTEC
300–1524

Atlantic

Ocean

CHIBCHA
1200–1538

Zipaquirá

Quito

CHIMU
1000–1471

MOCHICA
2000 B.C.E.–700 C.E.

Chan Chan

CHAVIN
1000–500 B.C.E.

Machu Picchu

Pachacamac

Cuzco

TIAHUANACO
600–1000

Pacific

Ocean

INCA
1200–1535

SOURCE: M. GLASSNER AND H. J. DE BLIJ, *SYSTEMATIC POLITICAL GEOGRAPHY*, 4TH ED. (NEW YORK: JOHN WILEY AND SONS, INC., 1989). REPRINTED WITH PERMISSION OF JOHN WILEY AND SONS, INC.

Map 2.5 The Peoples of North America (c. 1500)

SOURCE: "NATIVE AMERICAN PEOPLES" FROM *ATLAS OF WORLD HISTORY*, EDITED BY PATRICK K. O'BRIEN. REPRINTED WITH PERMISSION OF OCTOPUS PUBLISHING GROUP LTD.

having been assimilated into larger political units, forced to accept humiliating terms of surrender or tributary status, or had their populations killed, scattered, or sold into slavery. For realists, this history confirms the centrality of power in the world, and the importance of those who wield the greater share of it. Across time and place, say realists, history is "made" by the powerful. The other, weaker actors, far more numerous though they may be, are largely irrelevant to the course of history. However, many cultural groups survived, maintaining their language and traditions, only to reemerge later to find independence or some measure of autonomy. Furthermore, weaker actors have made an impact in history, and even shaken empires and mighty civilizations through resistance and revolution.

At this point in history, the rise and fall of civilizations and empires came to be dominated by the slow but steady rise of Europe to a position of global dominance. The legacy of this historical development (also referred to as the rise of the West) remains with us in many forms today, including the nature of the modern state, the formalities of diplomacy, the spread of Western legal principles, and the remnants of colonialism. The military and commercial power of Europe was to leave an indelible imprint on rest of the world.

THE MODERN STATE AND THE PEACE OF WESTPHALIA

The modern international system is often called the *Westphalian state system*. The Peace of Westphalia ended the Thirty Years' War in Europe in 1648 (see Map 2.6) and established a new

Map 2.6 Westphalian Europe, 1648

SOURCE: R. PALMER AND J. COLTON, *A HISTORY OF THE MODERN WORLD,* 8TH ED. (NEW YORK: MCGRAW-HILL, 1995). REPRINTED WITH PERMISSION OF THE MCGRAW-HILL COMPANIES.

order in Europe. From its origins in Europe, this system was extended throughout the world through the expansion of the European empires. With the virtual collapse of the European empires in the second half of the 20th century, what was left behind was a world of sovereign states that inherited the territorial, legal, and administrative structures and practices of the European tradition. However, it is important to recognize that the global expansion of the European state system does not provide a complete picture of the modern international system. After all, civilization flourished in other regions of the world long before it existed in Europe, and these historical and cultural traditions continue to exert a profound influence on contemporary international relations.[14] Nevertheless, the Peace of Westphalia is a significant benchmark, for it established the foundations of the modern state. Although the principles behind the sovereign state had begun to emerge before 1648, this date is a useful point of differentiation between medieval Europe and modern Europe, and "kingly states" and "territorial states."[15] In medieval Europe, kingly states were not fully autonomous or sovereign; they were under the authority (in spirit if not always in practice) of the Pope or the Holy Roman Emperor. Interference in the domestic politics of these states was commonplace, primarily in the form of efforts to convert the rulers or the people to one or another Christian denomination (a cause of the devastating Thirty Years' War). The Peace of Westphalia established the constitutional, legal status of states as territorial entities. The territorial state was sovereign, free to determine and practice its domestic affairs (meaning the religious denomination followed by the ruler and the people), and free from external interference. The year 1648 thus marked the beginning of the supremacy of the state in European affairs.

This change occurred for a number of reasons. First, the power of the church had been weakened by the splits in Christendom, in particular during the Reformation. The horrors of the Thirty Years' War (in what is today Germany, two-thirds of the population was killed or displaced) revealed the fragility of Christian Europe. The answer was the establishment of the sovereign state, which in principle was to be free from foreign interference in its domestic affairs. The hope was that devastating religious conflicts such as the Thirty Years' War might be prevented if the domestic affairs of territorial units were recognized as the exclusive reserve of the rulers of states. Second, some of the monarchs of medieval Europe had been slowly acquiring increased economic and military power, which enabled them to expand their territories through the amalgamation and conquest of less powerful political units. Furthermore, the establishment of hereditary monarchies promised increased stability with respect to leadership transition. The expansion of administrative and legal systems, with their power derived from the monarch, improved the capacity of rulers to exert control over their territories and subjects. For these reasons, the state emerged as the dominant political actor in international affairs and took on the distinctive characteristics that we recognize today (see Profile 2.7). As these developments occurred, European monarchies were embarking on the first period of European exploration and empire building. The world was entering the age of the European empires.

PROFILE 2.7 The Nature of the Modern State

Different theories abound in social science regarding the formation and present role of the state, but in typical international relations discourse, the term *state* refers to political entities with the following qualities:

- They occupy a defined territory.

- They possess a permanent population.

- They are sovereign with respect to other states (that is, they are, in principle, free from interference in their internal affairs).

- They are diplomatically recognized by other states.

- They possess a monopoly on the legitimate use of force within their territories.

The terms *nation* and *state* are often used interchangeably in discussions of global politics. However, they are not quite equivalent. "State" refers to an autonomous institutional and legal structure that governs a defined territory; it is a political and legal concept. "Nation," on the other hand, refers to a people who possess a shared sense of common descent and unifying ethnic, religious, or linguistic characteristics; it is an ethnic and cultural concept. A nation may exist without a state: two contemporary examples are the Kurdish and the Palestinian nations. A state that has essentially one nation living within its borders is called a nation-state. In this sense, very few nation-states exist, because most states in the world comprise many nations within their borders. Canada and the United States are examples of such multination-states.

The distinction between states and nations is becoming increasingly important in international politics, as in many cases disputes between the nations living within multination-states have led to domestic instability, turmoil, and, in extreme cases, violence. The formalities of statehood and the complex legal and ethical questions they raise were in evidence in 2008, when Kosovo declared its independence from Serbia (see Chapter 7)

THE RISE OF THE EUROPEAN EMPIRES

The defining feature of the 17th and 18th centuries was European imperialism, particularly the overseas expansion of the Spanish, Portuguese, Dutch, English, and French empires. Under Louis XIV, France was the most powerful state in Europe in the mid-to-late 1600s, but Louis's territorial ambitions provoked repeated alliances against France, which soon became weakened by almost continual warfare. Although formally in existence until 1806, the **Holy Roman Empire** had fragmented into some 300 small principalities and city-states, which were vulnerable to conquest. Prussia (largely through the conquests of Frederick the Great) and Austria under the Hapsburgs (largely through the conquests of Prince Eugene of Savoy) emerged as the dominant states in central Europe. Great Britain, protected from continental wars by the English Channel, carved out a global empire that was the envy of the rest of Europe. The Russian Empire (especially under **Peter the Great** and **Catherine the Great**) expanded to the borders of the Prussian and Austrian Empires in the west, the Ottoman Empire to the south, and China and the Pacific Ocean to the east.

However, revolts rocked the European empires in the second half of the 18th century. While the character of the revolts varied—from peasant unrest to a desire for independence in some regions—their origins lay in the spread of the Enlightenment, with its emphasis on the rights of individuals and its rejection of traditional authority. Enlightened monarchs, seeking reform, provoked a backlash of resistance from their aristocrats and provincial rulers. Provinces such as the Austrian Netherlands and Hungary rebelled against the centralization and reform policies imposed by enlightened monarchs. Overseas colonies, such as those in Spanish America and Haiti, rebelled against imperial rule and demanded more autonomy or outright independence. The most significant revolution occurred in the Thirteen Colonies in America, and the independence of the United States of America would later be recognized as one of the most significant developments in world history. Many European regions, such as Corsica, Sardinia, Ireland, Serbia, and Tyrol, also sought independence. However, the most significant revolution in Europe occurred in France.

The French Revolution (1789–94) changed the face of Europe. The revolution began as a middle-class phenomenon but spread to worker and peasant uprisings. When Austria and Prussia threatened invasion, combining external threat with internal chaos, the monarchy collapsed. A republic was established that ruthlessly suppressed its enemies at home and defeated its enemies abroad. The ideals of the French Revolution spread across Europe: equality before the law, the abolition of feudalism, and the "rights of man." The French Revolution sparked the beginning of the development of modern **nationalism**, and while nationalism was initially rejected by monarchs (and unknown to the poor) it was to become one of the driving forces behind events in Europe and around the world. Nationalism would be a motive force for soldiers in battle, would enable the establishment of the first true national armies of citizen soldiers, would prove to be the inspiration for revolution, and would become inextricably linked with the institutional and legal apparatus of the emerging nation-state.

However, the French Republic did not survive. In 1799 a 30-year-old general named **Napoleon Bonaparte** seized power. During the subsequent **Napoleonic Wars**, Napoleon was practically unbeatable, defeating the armies of Austria and Prussia (see Profile 2.8). By 1810 most of western Europe was controlled by France. However, Napoleon could not subdue England, nor could he completely conquer the Iberian Peninsula. His invasion of Russia

(1812) was a disaster, destroying most of the best formations in the Grand Army. Napoleon's final defeat at Waterloo in 1815 ended French dominance in Europe. The subsequent **Congress of Vienna** and the formation of the **Concert of Europe** were an attempt by the great powers to manage their relations and prevent a recurrence of the Napoleonic Wars. For almost 100 years, no continent-wide war occurred between the European great powers. The Concert of Europe is often studied by contemporary scholars interested in how great powers can successfully manage their affairs without resorting to major wars. However, it is inaccurate to say that peace prevailed, for several wars took place in this period, including the Wars of Italian Unification, the **Crimean War**, and the Franco-Prussian War (and colonial expansion abroad was hardly peaceful, either). Nationalism continued to be a driving force for change. In the 1830s Greece, Belgium, and Norway obtained independence. Italy was unified in 1861 and Germany (as the German Empire) in 1871. In both cases, the union was accomplished through a combination of war and the use of nationalism as a political instrument.

The European empires also continued to expand abroad. However, by the 19th century the nature of European imperialism was beginning to change. As the Industrial Revolution took hold in Europe, imperial expansion was driven less by the search for trade routes, precious metals and slaves and more by the search for raw materials and markets for products and territorial competition between the imperial powers. Between 1880 and 1914 the European empires added more than 13.6 million square kilometres (approximately one-fifth of the world's surface) to their colonial possessions (see Profile 2.9). Much of this was acquired in the so-called scramble for Africa, which began in earnest in 1882; by 1914, only Ethiopia and Liberia were independent. For peoples across the world, colonial rule meant the imposition of arbitrary political boundaries, a profound dislocation in local patterns of commerce, and the dominance of colonial administrations. These administrations ruled through a combination of political and economic coercion and reward, often co-opting local elites into the colonial system of governance. This period was the beginning of the expansion of capitalism, both in

---

PROFILE 2.8 **Karl von Clausewitz (1780–1831)**

Karl von Clausewitz was a Prussian military officer, instructor, and strategist who rose to the rank of general in the Prussian army and served on the Prussian general staff during the Napoleonic Wars. His famous work, *On War*, was written after the Napoleonic Wars and his recall to duty in East Prussia in 1830 (he died of cholera in 1831, leaving *On War* unfinished, although his wife completed the manuscript). Virtually unknown when he was alive, Clausewitz had a major influence on all subsequent intellectual thought on war. Clausewitz viewed war as a timeless phenomenon with its own elements and dynamics. Written in the dialectical and comparative style associated with German idealist philosophy, *On War* is often misunderstood or misinterpreted. For Clausewitz, war is distinguished from other social activity by its large-scale violence, which tends toward absolute war—the highest degree of violence. However, wars usually fall short of this level, because they are mitigated by political goals and the characteristics of societies and their economies and governments. Clausewitz believed that even military force had to be subordinate to the political aims and objectives of the state. War, Clausewitz argued, should not be regarded as separate and distinct from peacetime politics among states. Rather, war should be seen as "a continuation of political activity by other means." In international relations theory, realists regard *On War* as an illuminating treatise of the prominence of the military instrument in the conduct of statecraft.

SOURCE: KARL VON CLAUSEWITZ, *ON WAR*, ED. AND TRANS. MICHAEL HOWARD AND PETER PARET (PRINCETON: PRINCETON UNIVERSITY PRESS, 1976).

Europe and across the European empires around the world. For Marx, this was another key development in the social history of human society.

Because of the worldwide expansion of the European empires, wars in Europe quickly became global in scope. Wars in Europe between France, England, and Spain broke out in 1744 and 1754, and the supremacy of British naval power resulted in the loss of the French colonial empire in North America and the weakening of the Spanish empire. However, the rebellion of the 13 colonies in 1776 (aided by France) and the American War of Independence compelled Great Britain to recognize American independence in 1783. American expansion proceeded rapidly after independence (largely through the Louisiana Purchase, war with Mexico, the annexation of Texas, and war against indigenous peoples). The **American Civil**

PROFILE 2.9 The Colonial Legacy

Many of the states that we consider indepen-dent today were at one point colonized by imperial powers or listed as protectorates. Here we list just some of them. Note that some were colonized by more than one empire over time. For example, the Philippines, a Spanish colony from 1565, became a U.S. possession after 1898 (it was occupied by the Japanese during World War II, and then achieved independence in 1946). Note also that many names have changed over time. For example, what is now known as Zimbabwe was once called Rhodesia; while under British control, Sri Lanka was known as Ceylon. What follows is a partial list of the imperial powers and some of their possessions over the course of the past few hundred years.

BRITAIN

Anguilla, Antigua and Barbuda, Australia, Bahamas, Bahrain, Botswana, Brunei, Canada, Ceylon, Dominica, Fiji, Gambia, Ghana, Grenada, Hong Kong, India, Ireland, Kenya, Malawi, Malaysia, Maldives, Malta, Nigeria, Papua New Guinea, Sierra Leone, South Africa, Uganda, Zambia, Zimbabwe

FRANCE

Algeria, Benin, Burkina Faso, Cambodia, Chad, Comoros, Dakar, Djibouti, French Cameroon, French Congo, Gabon, Haiti, Ivory Coast, Laos, Madagascar, Mali, Mauritania, Morocco, Niger, Senegal, Vietnam

THE OTTOMAN EMPIRE

Albania, Algeria, Anatolia (Turkey), Armenia, Bosnia-Herzegovina, Bulgaria, Cyprus, Egypt, Iraq, Jordan, Lebanon, Libya, Qatar, Yemen

SPAIN

Argentina, Bolivia, Chile, Colombia, Cuba, Ecuador, El Salvador, Equatorial Guinea, Guam, Guatemala, Honduras, Mexico, Nicaragua, Paraguay, Peru, Philippines, Puerto Rico, Venezuela

PORTUGAL

Angola, Azores, Brazil, East Timor, Equatorial Guinea, Guinea-Bissau, parts of India, Macao, Mozambique

GERMANY

Burundi, Cameroon, Namibia, Rwanda, Tanganyika (Tanzania), Togo, Western Samoa, other occupations during World War II

ITALY

Ethiopia, Libya, Somalia

THE NETHERLANDS

Dutch Borneo, Dutch East Indies, Dutch West Indies, Suriname

BELGIUM

Burundi, Rwanda, Zaire

DENMARK

Faroe Islands, north Germany, Greenland, Iceland, parts of Norway, Sweden

JAPAN

Bonin Island, Korea, other occupations during World War II

THE UNITED STATES

Guam, Hawaii, Midway, Panama, Philippines, Puerto Rico, Samoa, Cuba

War interrupted the territorial expansion of the United States. After the war, the United States continued to expand with the purchase of Alaska from Russia, and territorial gains through annexation or conquest in the Pacific (Hawaii, Samoa, Midway, and the Philippines) and in Latin America (Cuba and Puerto Rico). The hope of some in the United States for expansion into British North America had been thwarted in the War of 1812, and subsequently with the formation of Canada in 1867 and its expansion to include western territories. Nevertheless, by 1914 the United States was one of the world's leading powers.

In South America, Napoleon's invasion of the Iberian Peninsula enabled the Spanish and Portuguese colonies to attain independence. These revolutions were carried out by a colonial aristocracy that sought independence, but with minimal social change. For the most part, colonial administrations were replaced by military dictatorships, which were to become an enduring feature of political life in Central and South America. In 1823, revolution created the Republic of Mexico. In South America, Spanish power was broken by revolt and military defeat at the hands of Simón Bolívar. Portugal agreed to Brazilian independence in 1822. In post-revolutionary Central and South America, territorial disputes between the newly independent countries were frequent and violent, and efforts to unite South America into a union failed at the Congress of Panama (1826). Export-driven economic growth and control of land increased the wealth of elites, but the bulk of the population lived in poverty (and still does).

In China, dominated by the Ch'ing (or Manchu) dynasty since 1644, trade with Europe—primarily in textiles, tea, porcelain, and opium—had flourished, although the empire was beset with rebellions and internal unrest. By the 1830s, China was the world's largest and most populous empire, but economic and political decay left China vulnerable to the Western powers, which sought to open the Chinese market to their products. The British exerted their power in China through the Opium War (1839–42), seized Hong Kong as an imperial possession, and opened five (later many more) treaty ports, where foreigners enjoyed exemption from Chinese law and rule. Other powers—especially Russia, France, and Japan—then expanded their authority in China, seizing territory and opening more treaty ports. The failure of the Manchu leadership to institute reform and resentment of foreign influence in China led to the Taiping Rebellion (1850–1864), the third-bloodiest war in human history. In 1900, the so-called Boxer Rebellion was inspired by growing anti-foreigner and anti-imperial sentiment in China. On the eve of World War I, China remained unstable and dominated by foreign colonial powers.

PATTERNS IN THE HISTORY OF WAR AND PEACE

Many themes and generalizations have been drawn from this conventional account of global history up to the world wars of the 20th century. As we will see, these themes formed the foundation of the realist approach to international relations.

- *The recurrence of war and conflict between civilizations, peoples, and empires.* The history of the world is a history of armed struggle. When cooperation does occur, it is in the form of alliances based on short-term need or convenience, or short-term trade and commercial interests. War is a historical inevitability, and the prudent are prepared for it, even in times of peace. The price for those who are not able or willing to prepare for war is political domination or outright conquest.

- *The rise and fall of civilizations and empires.* The explanations for the rise and fall of the great world civilizations and empires are many and varied. First, the fate of these empires is often linked to the emergence and the decline of a single great ruler. Second, empires have repeatedly been subject to conquest, either at the hands of other empires or from invasion by barbarian peoples. Third, many empires suffer from internal decline due to a combination of economic failure, social decay, and the costs associated with protecting a growing territory. The fortunes of civilizations, empires, and great powers are, therefore, historically fleeting; all eventually decline, to be superseded by others.[16]

- *The recorded political history of the world is primarily the history of the activities of great civilizations, empires, and states.* History is made by the powerful. For some, history can be described in terms of the machinations of hegemonic powers, civilizations, great powers, or empires that dominated all others. As a result, smaller or weaker civilizations, empires, and states have not been considered significant in history except as allies or pawns of the powerful.

- *The development of an intellectual tradition on statecraft, drawn from historical experience.* Advice to leaders—kings, princes, or emperors—was the privilege of only a very few individuals, but these individuals represent the beginning of thought on international relations, offering insights into the perspectives of those who lived hundreds and even thousands of years ago. What is revealing about these writings is the extent to which they display common themes about the nature of the conduct of international politics. Writers such as Sun Tzu, Kautilya, Thucydides, and Machiavelli established the intellectual foundation of the realist perspective in international relations.

- *The rise of political geography and geopolitics.* Before World War II, diplomatic historians conducted most of the research on international affairs. These historians studied historical patterns and the leaders and officials of empires and states. Political geographers developed theories that promoted the decisive influence of geography on state power in general and the calculations of decision makers in particular. The use of geographic explanations or arguments to characterize political decisions or advocate certain policies became known as political geography or geopolitics (see Profile 2.10). Geopolitical thought has had a profound influence on the conduct of many states and has served as the cornerstone for many national security strategies, including those of the European imperial powers, Nazi Germany, and the United States during the Cold War.

The beginning of the 20th century was a time of general peace—with a few exceptions, most notably the Russo–Japanese War (1904–05)—and growing prosperity. Long-term peace appeared to be in the offing: No major war had occurred in Europe since 1870, and international law on armaments and war had been strengthened at the Hague Peace Conferences of 1899 and 1907. The prevailing sentiment was that increasing trade and industrialization was making war more costly and less likely (an argument often made today). However, this sense of optimism began to erode as disputes between the European great powers and their alliances intensified. Nationalist rhetoric intensified, an arms race ensued, and war flared in the Balkans (1912–13). Nevertheless, few sensed the impending disaster that would soon befall Europe.

WORLD WAR I

The beginning of World War I is generally marked by the assassination of the heir to the throne of the Austro-Hungarian Empire, Austrian Archduke Franz Ferdinand, at Sarajevo,

PROFILE 2.10 | Geopolitical Thought: Sir Halford Mackinder and Alfred Thayer Mahan

SIR HALFORD MACKINDER (1861–1957)

Sir Halford Mackinder was a British geographer who wrote a famous paper on "the geographical pivot of history," which he presented to the Royal Geographical Society in 1904. Mackinder argued that the world could be divided into three regions: the Heartland (at the centre of Eurasia); the Interior or Marginal Ring (Europe, the Middle East, and southern and northern Asia); and the Ring of Islands or Outer Continents (North and South America, Africa, and Australia). For Mackinder, the geographic pivot in world politics was the Heartland. From this view he derived the following geopolitical calculation: whoever controls the Heartland controls the World Island (Europe, Asia, and Africa); whoever controls the World Island controls the world. He concluded that Russia must not be permitted to expand into the lands of the Interior Ring, as this would lead to Russian world domination. His theory was influential in Europe, particularly in Germany, where it contributed to the geopolitical views of Karl Hausofer, who advocated *Lebensraum*, German territorial expansion eastward. Mackinder's theory also influenced U.S. strategy to contain the Soviet Union, which already dominated the Heartland, during the Cold War. However, Mackinder's many critics have pointed out that his theory could not explain why tsarist Russia and the Soviet Union had not dominated the world despite controlling the Heartland. Nor could his theory explain the dominance of the United States for most of the 20th century. Others criticize his view as a thinly veiled rationale for the maintenance of the British Empire, which controlled territories in the Middle East and southern Asia and so served as the guardian of the Interior Ring against aggression from the Heartland.

ALFRED THAYER MAHAN (1840–1914)

Alfred Thayer Mahan was an American naval strategist. His most famous work, *The Influence of Sea Power on History 1660–1783*, influenced the naval doctrines of the United States and the European imperial powers. His central conclusion was that naval powers, rather than land powers, were dominant in history. For Mahan, the principles of naval strategy and naval warfare remained constant, and these principles pointed to one historical theme. Contrary to land power explanations of world politics, the key to state power lay in powerful naval forces supported by a network of overseas possessions and naval bases. From these possessions and bases, naval forces could dominate the seas, and that dominance would lead to control of the merchant traffic of the world. The influence of Mahan's views was felt in Europe in the struggle for naval mastery between Great Britain and Germany, and in the United States, where it provided a rationale for American imperial expansion during and after the Spanish–American War.

on June 28, 1914. The assassination of the archduke set in motion a series of actions and reactions that led the European powers to war. However, while this event may indeed have been the spark that set Europe ablaze, the fuel for the conflict had been accumulating for years. Europe had divided into two hostile alliances: the Triple Alliance of Germany, Austro-Hungary, and Italy; and the Triple Entente of Great Britain, France, and Russia. The latter was wary of the increasing power of Germany and its desire for a place in the sun with the other established imperial powers. The Triple Alliance feared encirclement and the expansion of Russian power in the Balkans. Commercial rivalry, disputes over colonial possessions, and a naval arms race between Great Britain and Germany intensified the antagonism between these two countries. The naval arms race would later become one of the most studied arms races in history, as analysts sought to learn lessons that could

Map 2.7 The World According to Mackinder

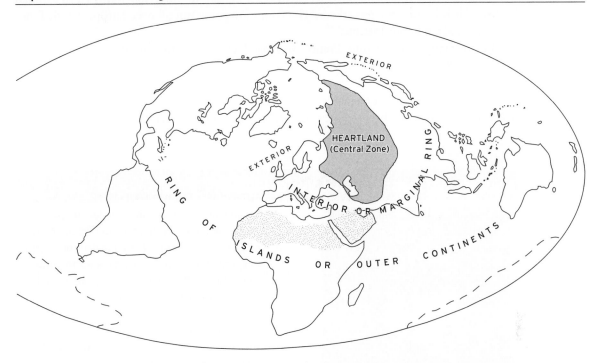

SOURCE: G. CHALIAND AND J. RAGEAU, "THE WORLD ACCORDING TO MACKINDER," *STRATEGIC ATLAS: COMPARATIVE GEOPOLITICS OF THE WORLD'S POWERS*, 3RD ED. (NEW YORK: HARPERCOLLINS, 1993), 21. © 1993 BY G. CHALIAND AND J. RAGEAU. REPRINTED BY PERMISSION OF HARPERCOLLINS PUBLISHERS. INC.

be applied to the nuclear arms race between the superpowers during the Cold War. In all countries, enormous national armies could be created rapidly through the mobilization of the citizenry, trained for war through **conscription**. Most European military establishments believed that success in a future war would go to the country that mobilized most rapidly and launched its offensive first. This "cult of the offensive" existed in most European countries.[17] In particular, German planning sought to avoid a two-front war by attacking and quickly defeating France before turning against Russia. The mood in most societies was one of extreme nationalism (which was often explicitly racist) and faith in the superiority of one's own country and people.

After the assassination of the Archduke, Europe began its slide toward war. The assassination, planned in Belgrade by Serbian nationalists, intensified Austro-Hungarian concerns about the threat Serbia posed to Austro-Hungarian power in the Balkans. Germany, hoping to deter Russian intervention in the Balkans in support of its Serbian ally, issued its famous "blank check" of support to Austria. Austria then delivered an ultimatum to Belgrade and declared war on July 28, 1914. Russia, fearing Austrian hegemony in the Balkans, mobilized to support Serbia, a fellow Slavic country. Germany then mobilized and, as called for in prewar planning, attacked France through neutral Belgium. Germany's violation of Belgian neutrality brought Great Britain into the war. The war assumed a global aspect with Japan's declaration of war on Germany, the outbreak of fighting between British and German colonial forces in Africa, and the entry into the war of the Ottoman Empire. For many, war was welcome, and nationalist fervour brought cheering crowds into the streets and long lines at recruiting stations. Throughout Europe, the war was expected to be short, with the recently mobilized soldiers home by Christmas. Some had more sombre thoughts. On August 3, following a speech to Parliament in which he confirmed British intentions to enter the war, British Foreign Minister Sir Edward Grey remarked: "The lamps are going out all over Europe; we shall not see them lit again in our lifetime."[18]

The German offensive into France was conducted according to the carefully crafted **Schlieffen Plan**, which saw Germany's armies in the west move through Belgium and northern France toward Paris. In doing so, Germany violated Belgian neutrality, another testament to the fate of weaker powers in great-power politics. However, Germany failed to defeat France quickly. The firepower of modern weapons soon created a stalemate, and by

---

PROFILE 2.11 | **Canada and World War I**

We will always remember. Lance Corporal Iden Herbert Baldwin when he was 22 years old and waiting to return to Canada after fighting in World War I. Iden Baldwin died on January 31, 2003, at the age of 105. (CP Photo/Globe and Mail.)

Canada entered World War I when Great Britain declared war on August 4, 1914. Canadian Prime Minister Robert Borden had promised Canadian support for the Empire's war effort. Little dissent existed in Parliament as the Liberals under Wilfrid Laurier supported Canada's entry into the war. However, dissent was expressed in French Canada, where many French Canadians opposed Canada's involvement in the war and the increasing sacrifices the war effort entailed. The First Canadian Division entered the battle lines in France in February 1915, although most of the senior

commanders were British. Canadian troops performed admirably in the field during the Battle of Ypres in April 1915. The Canadian contingent in Europe grew rapidly, and a Canadian Corps (composed of three divisions) was established in mid-1915. However, the war had settled into a costly stalemate, and losses at the front made conscription an issue in 1917. The conscription crisis was very divisive, generating strong opposition in French Canada and among workers and farmers. In April 1917, Canadian troops seized Vimy Ridge at a cost of 3,598 lives after repeated Allied efforts had failed. This success was followed by the Passchendaele offensive, a sobering experience in which the Canadian Corps occupied a few square kilometres of mud and water-filled craters at a cost of 8,134 lives. By this time Canadian officers under General Arthur Currie commanded the Canadians. By the end of the war, 56,634 Canadians had been killed and more than 150,000 wounded.

Some maintain that Canadian nationalism was born at Vimy Ridge in 1917—that Canada's service and sacrifice developed a sense of Canadian independence. Sir Robert L. Borden himself was to argue that the war had made Canada an international personality and entitled Canada to a certain independent status. Canada was a signatory to the Versailles Treaty, and it received a seat in the League of Nations. Others would point to the political and workplace advances of Canadian women during the war years. Others, however, caution that the conscription crisis and labour disputes divided the country and that, for many, the war meant lost loved ones and shattered lives.

October 1914 a front line of trenches, barbed wire, machine guns, and artillery extended from the Swiss border to the English Channel. Offensives designed to break the stalemate by punching through these defensive lines with long artillery bombardments and massive infantry attacks failed repeatedly, with great loss of life (see Profile 2.11 for Canada's experience). Germany embarked on a submarine warfare campaign against merchant ships at sea. With the exception of the Battle of Jutland, the massive battleship fleets that had been built during the Anglo–German naval arms race saw little action (the British battle fleet did impose a naval blockade against Germany, blocking German access to products and materials from abroad). The German decision to expand the submarine campaign also brought the United States into the war against Germany on April 6, 1917.

In the east, military defeat and economic chaos had led to the collapse of the Russian war effort and the Bolshevik Revolution of October 1917. The Romanov dynasty was overthrown, and the new **Bolshevik** government sued for peace. With the eastern front secured, Germany transferred its forces west for a final great offensive aimed at defeating Britain and France before the United States could mobilize. The offensive, launched on March 21, 1918, failed with heavy losses, and in July the French, British, and Americans began their counter-offensive, which was to be the decisive turning point of the war. By September, Germany was near defeat. Its armies were exhausted, and its economy was in shambles from the war effort and the British naval blockade. Austria was near collapse. Fearful of domestic unrest and the possibility of a Bolshevik revolution in Germany, the German government sued for an **armistice**, which went into effect on November 11, 1918. Seven months later, on June 28, 1919, Germany signed the Treaty of Versailles. Under its terms, Germany was prevented from possessing a large army or modern military equipment, the province of Alsace-Lorraine was returned to France, Germany's colonies were distributed to the victors, East Prussia was separated from the rest of Germany by the new Poland, the German government was forced to pay reparations, and war guilt was assigned to Germany. The legacy of Versailles would cause much bitterness in Germany, bitterness that would be deftly exploited by Adolf Hitler and the Nazi Party.

The consequences of World War I were enormous. More than 13 million people had died, and millions more were wounded (as many died in an influenza pandemic—named the "Spanish flu"—made possible by military demobilization). The state, nationalism, and the Industrial Revolution had combined to create a lethal mix. Large, conscripted armies, motivated by nationalism and equipped, transported, and supplied by the technologies of the Industrial Revolution, were guided by the unparalleled strategic planning capacities of the modern state into organized slaughter by the killing machines of modern war. Entire societies, and not just militaries, became targets in total war. As Richard Overy has remarked, "To be able to wage total war states would have to mobilize all the material, intellectual, and moral energies of their people; by implication the enemy community as a whole—its scientists, workers and farmers—became legitimate objects of war."[19] Four empires had collapsed—the German, Austro-Hungarian, Russian, and Ottoman—and new, independent nations emerged in Czechoslovakia, Poland, Yugoslavia, Finland, Estonia, Latvia, and Lithuania (see Map 2.8). The Russian Revolution had brought a change in government and ideology to Russia that would shape international politics in the years to come. Fear of the Russian Revolution was widespread, as was concern over the emergence of **fascism** as a major political movement. Nationalism remained a potent force, and the peace settlement left dissatisfied minorities across Europe seeking their own state and national independence. The United States emerged as a global power but slowly turned to **isolationism** with respect to European affairs. Finally, dissatisfied revisionist powers such as Germany, Japan, and Italy emerged from the ashes of the World War. The ambitions of these revisionist countries and their authoritarian

Map 2.8 Territorial Changes in Europe after World War I

SOURCE: GERARD CHALIAND AND JEAN-PIERRE RAGEAU, *STRATEGIC ATLAS: COMPARATIVE GEOPOLITICS OF THE WORLD'S POWERS*, 3RD ED. (NEW YORK: HARPERCOLLINS, 1993), 34. © 1993 BY GERARD CHALIAND AND JEAN-PIERRE RAGEAU. REPRINTED BY PERMISSION OF HARPERCOLLINS PUBLISHERS, INC.

ideologies would clash with democratic, antirevisionist countries that favoured the status quo. Ultimately, the war to end all wars had merely set the stage for World War II.

THE INTERWAR PERIOD

The horror of World War I inspired efforts to make that war "the war to end all wars." Pacifist sentiments were widespread after the war, and peace movements such as War Resisters' International grew in popularity. Feminists established the Women's International League for Peace and Freedom (WILPF) to pressure governments to pursue more peaceful policies (WILPF still exists today and gained consultative status at the UN in 1948). As we discussed in Chapter 1, idealism gained credence as an alternative to the realpolitik behaviour, balance of power machinations, and secret alliances that had led the world to such a disaster. For idealists, such as U.S. President Woodrow Wilson, the hope was to establish a new order, based on the League of Nations, collective security, the rule of law, and arms control. However, behind the outward unity displayed by the victorious powers after World War I were serious disagreements, particularly among Great Britain, France, and the United States, over the treatment of Germany. France was the most uncompromising. It had been devastated during the war: 1,355,800 French citizens had been killed and 4,260,000 wounded; almost 300,000 homes had been destroyed; and the country was heavily in debt due to the financial costs of the war effort.[20] The French were not willing to place their faith in Wilson's collective security concept (see Chapter 1), deciding instead that a system of alliances built against Germany would be the best guarantee of peace. Another matter of dispute was the issue of reparations. France and Great Britain wanted Germany to pay for the entire cost of the war, and Germany began to default on reparations payments as early as 1920. In response, the French government acted unilaterally and occupied the Ruhr Valley in 1923. Within Germany, popular resentment against the Versailles Treaty increased.

In the interwar period, Russia went through the throes of revolution to resurface as a major actor in Europe. Increased economic hardship, growing hunger, and the clear incompetence of the Russian political and military leadership in the war led to the overthrow of the tsar in February 1917. The Duma, or Parliament, assumed power, but its decision to continue the war alienated the people, leaving it vulnerable to revolutionary organizations of workers, called Soviets, and the return from exile of Vladimir Lenin, who promised peace, land, bread, and all power to the Soviets (see Chapter 1). The provisional government collapsed, and Lenin's Bolsheviks seized power in the October revolution. Lenin's first task was to obtain peace, and despite opposition he accepted unfavourable terms from Germany in return for peace in the Treaty of Brest–Litovsk (1918). After a civil war in which the Bolsheviks prevailed against a pro-monarchist White Russian movement supported by Britain, France, and the United States, the Union of Soviet Socialist Republics (U.S.S.R.), more commonly called the Soviet Union, was established in December 1922. Initially, many Marxists had seen the war as the culmination of the failures of the capitalist system and the beginning of the proletarian revolution that would sweep across the world. But as Marxist movements in other countries failed to attain power, there was a shift toward securing the revolution in Russia. By 1925 the Soviet Union had recovered economically and was reaching out internationally, even obtaining diplomatic recognition from France, Great Britain, and other European countries. Lenin's death in 1924 eventually brought Josef Stalin to power. With his doctrine of "socialism in one country," Stalin embarked on a massive program of industrialization and agricultural collectivization, as well as purges of the Communist Party and the Red Army that left millions dead. However, the Soviet Union was firmly established as a great power.

In the Middle East and Asia, the interwar period saw the fall of an empire, chaos in another, and the rise of a new great power. As one of the defeated powers, the Ottoman Empire was partitioned by the victorious states. These humiliations sparked a nationalist uprising led by Mustapha Kemal (Ataturk) that marked the beginning of a secular Turkish state, the heir to the Ottoman legacy. China experienced a period of chaos, instability, and invasion in the interwar period. Central rule broke down, and provincial warlords assumed local power. Under the leadership of Sun Yat-sen and then Chiang Kai-shek, the Nationalist (Koumintang) Party, allied with the Chinese Communists, attempted to suppress the warlords, end foreign power in China, and reunify the country. After initial success in the north of the country, the alliance between the Koumintang and the Communists broke down. However, Japan intervened in Manchuria in 1931, and Chiang now had to meet two threats simultaneously: the Japanese, and the Communist movement in the countryside, led by Mao Tse-tung. Chiang's efforts to crush Mao's Communists forced Mao and his supporters into the famous Long March of 1934–35. The Nationalist and Communist forces were to battle the Japanese until the end of World War II.

The interwar period saw the rise of a new power in Asia: Japan. The Meiji Restoration of 1868 reopened Japan to the world after 200 years of isolation. Japan embarked on a period of rapid industrialization and established an empire on the mainland. Japan was recognized as a victorious power at the Paris Peace Conference and was given great-power status and a permanent seat on the Council of the League of Nations. However, the Great Depression hit Japan hard as the rise of trade barriers around the world hurt the trade-dependent Japanese economy. The government fell, and was replaced by a military government. These changes, coupled with China's efforts to recover Manchuria (an important source of raw materials and industrial production) from Japan, led to the Japanese fabrication of an attack on a Japanese railway line, which provided the pretext for a Japanese military intervention in Manchuria in 1931. The League failed to respond forcefully, issuing a report in 1933 calling for Chinese control of Manchuria with protection of Japanese interests. The collective security provisions of the League were not invoked. In response to its report, Japan walked out of the League of Nations. In 1937, Japan invaded China, and tensions between Japan and the United States escalated over the invasion and trade issues.

The League also failed to respond effectively to European aggression. The fascist leader Benito Mussolini came to power in Italy in 1922. In 1935 Italy invaded and conquered Ethiopia. The League responded with an arms embargo, but all other products (including oil, coal, and steel) could still be traded to Italy, and the enforcement of the embargo was never effective. The collective security provisions of the League were not activated. In 1937, Italy withdrew from the League of Nations and annexed Albania in 1939. The League would also prove unable to stop German expansionism. The onset of the **Great Depression** in Europe devastated the German economy and inflation spiralled out of control, plunging most Germans into misery. It was in this economic and political context that the Nazi Party rose to prominence in Germany on a platform of resentment toward the Versailles Treaty, renewed German nationalism, and **anti-Semitism.** Under Hitler Germany began to rearm. In 1938 Germany annexed Austria into the Third Reich, and demanded a solution for the Sudetenland Germans, who lived in Czechoslovakia. At Munich, the British and French governments sought to appease Hitler and accepted the incorporation of the Sudetenland into the Third Reich. This region was also Czechoslovakia's main line of defence; when it was annexed, the country was in a hopeless position to resist any further German expansion. In April 1939, Hitler occupied the rest of Czechoslovakia, and once again a small state had fallen victim to the power politics of the great powers. The league was unable to respond. Subsequent German demands for territory around Danzig from Poland prompted the British and the French to become allies to protect Poland.

In the face of increasing international diplomatic and economic tensions, the League was increasingly unable to act effectively. For most of its history, the League counted only four of the seven great powers among its membership, and as a result it could not serve as the universal organization it was intended to be. The League was further damaged when it could not take effective action against Italian aggression in Ethiopia, Japanese aggression in Manchuria, and later German and Soviet aggression in Europe. The aims of the revisionist powers of the 1930s were fundamentally at odds with the principles of the Covenant. Although some League committees continued to operate during the war, the organization was irrelevant as an instrument of peace and security. In April 1946, it was formally disbanded. The experience of the League would be remembered after World War II, and the lessons of its shortcomings would play an important role in the design of the United Nations Charter.

The revisionist powers of the interwar period—Germany, Italy, and Japan—encountered limited resistance to their territorial gains and aggressive acts. Why? The experience of World War I was clearly a factor; no one wanted to risk another world war. The neutralist position of the United States also weakened the strength of non-revisionist states. Without U.S. support and active involvement in world affairs, countries such as Great Britain and France lacked the power to decisively respond to aggression, or so they believed. In addition, all countries in the world were grappling with enormous domestic economic problems, especially after the stock market crash of 1929. In the face of huge domestic economic hardships, international aggression in Manchuria and Ethiopia seemed very far away. Countries had turned inward: the United States had retreated into isolationism, the British behind the English Channel, and the French behind the supposedly impregnable fortifications of the Maginot Line. As a result, the policy toward revisionist countries, in particular toward Germany, became known as **appeasement:** giving in to the demands of revisionist states in the hope that they would soon be satisfied with their gains. Munich, and appeasement, would later be vilified as a naïve and idealistic failure. However, appeasement was not a policy of blind subjection to threats. The publics in Great Britain, France, and the United States were opposed to war, and all countries were unprepared for it. Appeasement might satisfy Hitler and Mussolini, and if not it would at least buy time to rearm.

WORLD WAR II: TOTAL WAR

In August 1939, Nazi Germany and the Soviet Union signed the Nazi–Soviet nonaggression pact. The pact was a surprise, since German National Socialism and Soviet Communism were self-declared ideological enemies. A month later, the motivation for the pact would become clear. Hitler invaded Poland on September 1, 1939, and would later split the gains with the Soviet Union, which would invade Poland and the Baltic States only a few weeks later. By then, Britain and France had honoured their pledge to Poland by declaring war on Germany on September 3, 1939. World War II had begun. The war rapidly expanded. Utilizing the new tactics of the *blitzkrieg* (lightning war), and seizing command of the air, German forces invaded and conquered Denmark, Norway, the Netherlands, and Belgium. France succumbed as German forces swept around the Maginot Line, circumventing the fortifications that had been built at great effort and cost. Paris fell in June 1940. The Battle of Britain then began, an air campaign in which the German Luftwaffe unsuccessfully attempted to bomb Britain into submission. In the Mediterranean, Mussolini's Italy had invaded Greece, but the failure of the campaign brought Germany into the conflict, and Germany conquered Yugoslavia and

Greece in early 1941. German and Italian troops in Africa moved toward Egypt, with the aim of wresting the Suez Canal from British control. In what we might with retrospect label the greatest strategic blunder of all time, in June 1941, Hitler invaded the Soviet Union. Having achieved total surprise, German forces swept through Russia, destroying much of the Red Army in the process. By December, German troops had advanced to within a few kilometres of Moscow. However, the German advance was halted by the Russian winter, lack of supplies, and stiffening Russian resistance around Moscow and Leningrad as Russia began to mobilize its superior resources and population.

In another notable strategic blunder, on December 7, 1941, Japan launched a surprise attack on the United States at Pearl Harbor, home of the American Pacific Fleet. Japan also mounted a swift campaign of conquest in the western Pacific, seizing the Philippines, French Indochina, the Dutch East Indies, Singapore, much of New Guinea, and the Bismarck and Solomon Islands in the South Pacific in the course of a few months. American isolationist sentiment collapsed in the face of the Pearl Harbor attack, and the democratic United States forged an alliance with democratic Great Britain and the Communist Soviet Union—the *Allied powers*—to oppose Nazi Germany, fascist Italy, and Imperial Japan—the *Axis powers*. In 1942 and 1943, the fortunes of war began to turn against the Axis powers. German and Italian forces were repulsed from Egypt. The 1942 German offensive in southern Russia ended in German defeat at Stalingrad. In the Atlantic, after heavy losses to German submarines, more and more merchant ships carrying supplies from Canada and the United States began to get through to Britain. In the Pacific, the Japanese Imperial Navy was defeated at the Battle of Midway and at the Battle of the Coral Sea. The United States then began to embark on a series of campaigns to retake the South Pacific from the Japanese. In May 1943, German and Italian forces in North Africa were defeated. At the decisive battle of Kursk in July 1943, the Red Army was victorious and forced the Germans onto the defensive on the entire eastern front. American and British strategic bombing raids against Germany began, damaging German industry and transportation, killing many civilians, and complicating the German war effort.

The decisive blows of the war were struck against the Axis powers in 1944. In June, British, Canadian, and U.S. troops landed in northern France, broke through German defences, and liberated France, Belgium, and the Netherlands. The Soviet Union launched an offensive on the eastern front a few weeks later and by late 1944 had pushed German forces back into eastern Europe. In 1945, after an unsuccessful German counteroffensive in the west, British and American forces advanced into Germany (see Map 2.9). In January 1945, the Red Army launched a final offensive aimed at Berlin.

Adolf Hitler committed suicide on April 30, and on May 7 Germany surrendered unconditionally. Thus would end the career of one of the most influential and darkly troubling politicians in modern history. Indeed, one might argue that World War II would not have occurred without the existence of this single man, lending credence to the value of the individual level of analysis discussed in Chapter 1.

In the Pacific, American forces began the reconquest of the Philippines, and the Japanese Imperial Navy was eliminated as an effective fighting force at the Battle of Leyte. British and Indian troops retook Burma, and Japan came under air attack from American bases in China and the Marianas Islands. In 1945, the American capture of Iwo Jima and Okinawa secured air bases closer to Japan, enabling the air offensive to be accelerated. Despite the devastation of most Japanese cities and Japan's industrial capacity, the Japanese still resisted, and preparations were made to invade the home islands of Japan (see Map 2.10). The war soon ended but not in a conventional manner. Throughout the war the United States had been engaged in top-secret research to develop an atomic weapon. Such a device had been successfully

Map 2.9 The War in Europe

Legend:
- Allied thrusts
- Lend-Lease supply lines
- Hitler's "empire"
- Occupied by Axis
- At war Against the Axis
- Allied with Germany

Map labels:
1. Hitler Invades Poland September 1, 1939
2. France Surrenders June 22, 1940
3. United States: Bases-Destroyer Deal, September 2, 1940 Enacts Lend Lease March 11, 1941 Enters the War December 8, 1941
4. Greatest Axis Expansion, December 1941—November 1942
5. Allies Invade: North Africa, November 8, 1942 Normandy Coast, June 6, 1944
6. Germany Surrenders, May 8, 1945

SOURCE: R. PALMER AND J. COLTON, *A HISTORY OF THE MODERN WORLD*, 8TH ED. (NEW YORK: MCGRAW-HILL, 1995). REPRINTED WITH PERMISSION OF THE MCGRAW-HILL COMPANIES.

tested near Alamogordo, New Mexico, in the spring of 1945. In a controversial decision, President Truman authorized the first military use of the **atomic bomb,** which was dropped on Hiroshima on August 6, 1945. A second bomb was dropped on Nagasaki on August 9. On September 2, 1945, Japan capitulated, and the war was over.

The use of the atomic bomb remains controversial even today. Was it necessary? Defenders of the decision cite the enormous casualties that American service personnel would have suffered in any invasion of Japan. Others suggest the atomic bomb was dropped primarily to demonstrate American military might to the Soviet Union. Many argue that the decision to use the bombs against densely populated civilian targets was inhumane, as well as unnecessary. However, the saturation bombing of cities had long been practised by both sides during the war. London, Rotterdam, Dresden, Hamburg, and many other cities suffered extensive bombing. The firebombing of Tokyo caused more casualties than those suffered at Hiroshima and Nagasaki. In this context, the atomic bomb did not seem very different. Nevertheless, to this day the bombings of Hiroshima

Map 2.10 The War in the Pacific

SOURCE: R. PALMER AND J. COLTON, *A HISTORY OF THE MODERN WORLD*, 8TH ED. (NEW YORK: MCGRAW-HILL, 1995). REPRINTED WITH PERMISSION OF THE MCGRAW-HILL COMPANIES.

and Nagasaki retain special symbolic importance, since the atomic era began with the destruction of those cities.

World War II was the most destructive conflict in history. Approximately 15 million combatants and 35 million civilians were killed. The Soviet Union alone suffered 20 million casualties—more than the entire population of Canada at the time (for Canada's role in the war, see Profile 2.12). Six million Jews and more than five million others were murdered in the concentration camps of Nazi-occupied Europe (see Chapter 9 on human rights for a discussion of genocide, the Holocaust, and the important **Nuremberg war crimes trials**). Cities

Canada and World War II

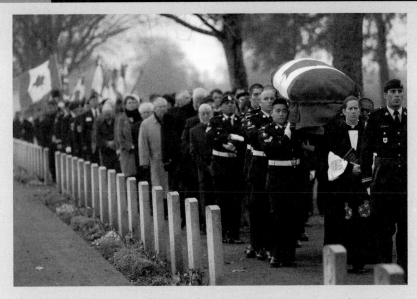

Finally laid to rest. The coffin of Private Ralph Tupper Ferns is carried during a funeral ceremony at the Canadian war cemetery at Bretteville-sur-Laize, 2008. Private Ferns went missing during the Normandy campaign in 1944 and his remains were discovered in 2005. Family members, World War II veterans, youth representatives, and parliamentarians attended his funeral. (AP/David Vincent/CP Archive.)

Canada declared war on Nazi Germany on September 10, 1939, seven days after Great Britain. The government of Mackenzie King had envisioned a limited overseas commitment when it entered the war. Opinion in Canada was not as deeply divided as it had been in World War I, and although conscription was once again an issue in 1944 due to battlefield losses, the divisive debates of 1917 were not repeated. By June 1940 only Great Britain, Canada, and the other Commonwealth countries stood against the Axis. Canada was now committed to a total war and produced vast amounts of ammunition and military equipment in cities such as Hamilton, Toronto, and Montreal. The Royal Canadian Navy bore most of the convoy escort duty early in the war, providing security for the vital merchant shipping lanes to Great Britain. More than 1,100,000 Canadians served during the war, and at its peak, the Canadian Army fielded nearly 500,000 soldiers; most students are surprised to learn that, at this time, the Canadian Air Force and the Navy were among the largest in the world after those of the great powers.

Canadians first fought together in large numbers in the disastrous Dieppe raid in August 1942. The circumstances of the raid are a subject of controversy to this day, since some suggest Allied commanders sent the Canadians to their slaughter. Canadians first saw mass service in the Italian campaign in 1943. Canada was assigned its own landing beach (along with the United States and Great Britain) in the Normandy invasion of 1944. The Canadian Army fought in the Normandy campaign and then liberated much of the Netherlands (to this day, the people of the Netherlands have a deep respect for the sacrifice made by Canadians in liberating their country in the war). More than 42,000 Canadians died in World War II. It may seem surprising now, but Canada ended the war as one of the most powerful countries in the world. This position was the foundation of Canada's postwar middle-power status and the basis for Canada's postwar internationalism. See D. Bercuson, *Maple Leaf Against the Axis: Canada's Second World War* (Toronto: Stoddart, 1995).

and industries across Europe and Asia had been reduced to rubble. A massive rebuilding task faced the survivors. Never before had war so fundamentally affected the lives of civilians. To an unprecedented degree, they had become targets of bombing campaigns and had participated in war production.[21] The concept of total war had reached its apogee: industrialization, nationalism, and the power of the state had combined with the increased firepower of new technologies to truly devastate whole societies.[22] World War II was the ultimate war of attrition: the societies that could bring the greatest human and material resources to bear were victorious, but at a terrible price.

World War II also had enormous political consequences. The victory of the Allied powers over the Axis powers altered the distribution of power in the world. Borders in Europe changed in accordance with agreements made between **Winston Churchill** and Josef Stalin in 1944 and at the "big three" conference of Roosevelt, Stalin, and Churchill at Yalta in February 1945. The Soviet Union absorbed some 600 square kilometres of territory, which included the Baltic States and land from Poland, Finland, Czechoslovakia, and Romania, recovering what had been lost under the Treaty of Brest–Litovsk. Poland was compensated with land from Germany, which was divided into four occupation zones. Austria was separated from Germany. In the Far East, Japan lost control over Manchuria, Taiwan, and Korea (which was divided into Soviet and U.S. zones) and suffered the loss of the Kurile Islands, which were seized by the Soviet Union. The war also ushered in the nuclear era. The European colonial powers were weakened, and a great wave of decolonization swept the world in the following decades, leading to an explosion in the number of independent states. Finally, the end of World War II saw the emergence of two powers—the United States and the Soviet Union—that possessed capabilities far greater than those of any other country. The emergence of these superpowers would define international politics in the postwar era, and suspicion and distrust between them grew rapidly. World War II had ended, but the Cold War, to which we will turn in Chapter 3, had just begun.

HISTORY, ALLIANCES, AND THE BALANCE OF POWER CONCEPT

For realists, war and the rise and fall of states and empires are a universal experience, and the writings of thinkers from Clausewitz to Kautilya confirm that political responses to this universal experience are common across time and culture. In essence, these responses champion the importance of military power and the utility of **alliances**. Military power and alliances are at the core of what realists argue is the ordering mechanism of international politics since the ancient world: the **balance of power.**

The term *balance of power* can be used in several ways. It can be used as a descriptive term to denote the state of the power balance between certain states or groups of states in a geographic region (it was not until the 20th century and the superpower confrontation that the concern with a global balance of power arose). The term can be used to describe a particular policy of states that may be seeking a balance of power. Most commonly, it refers to a historical phenomenon in which empires and states have repeatedly formed alliances against other states or groups of states. The balance of power is a system of order in an anarchic international system in which states act to ensure that no one state or group of states can come to dominate the system or conquer all other states in the system. This balancing behaviour preserves the system of sovereign states because no one state or group of states can acquire the power to control the entire region (or the world). This balancing behaviour can also preserve peace, by redistributing power in an effort to maintain an equilibrium, or balance, in the system. However, the balance of power does not necessarily mean the preservation of peace. In fact, the balance of power does not exist to ensure peace, but rather to ensure the survival of the state system. The preservation of the balance of power system often requires war to defeat the efforts of certain states to dominate the system.

The concept of the balance of power suggests that if the power of a state or a group of states grows, other states in the system will balance against this growing power. States can balance in one of two ways. They can increase their own power (generally through military spending) or they can engage in alliances with other states. Alliances are formal agreements between states that commit them to a common purpose, such as military security against a common threat. Alliances are often referred to as **collective defence** arrangements. Arrangements that are not formalized in treaties and that tend to be of shorter duration are often called *coalitions*. Alliances are a quick and relatively cheap method of supplementing one's own power with the power of another. Therefore, alliances are a form of self-interested cooperation (a "marriage of convenience"). Realists argue that the historical frequency of alliances reveals the universality of the balance of power concept.

Generally, alliances form when two or more states share a perceived threat and agree to coordinate their efforts to meet that threat.[23] This agreement may take the form of treaty obligations to assist the other state if it is attacked. In other cases, agreements may extend to high levels of cooperation on political and military issues, including the formation of joint institutions and joint military forces. Alliances are notoriously fluid and changing, and alliance commitments are often broken. However, a state might be reluctant to defect from an alliance relationship because of concerns that it would acquire a reputation as an unreliable ally. When the threat common to alliance members disappears alliances tend to collapse, although as our discussion of the North Atlantic Treaty Organization (NATO) in subsequent chapters suggests, some alliances have endured after the threat that led to their formation has disappeared. In such cases, alliances might survive because self-interested states want to maintain the advantages of the cooperative relationship they have built. Alliances vary with respect to the commitment of their members and their internal unity, often called **alliance cohesion**. Cohesive alliances (such as NATO) have a high degree of shared interests and coordination among their members, and tend to be formally institutionalized. Alliances that are less cohesive have lower levels of coordination and have more widely divergent interests among their membership. Cohesion is important because the ability to form a strong united effort against a threat is the key to a credible alliance.

For realists, because states will act to balance the power of other states, the distribution of power in the international system or in regional systems is extremely important. The distribution of power is defined by concentrations of power in a region or in the entire international system and by how many of these concentrations exist. These concentrations of power are called poles, and the distribution of power is often described in terms of **polarity** (a term borrowed from physics). Polarity describes the number of independent centres or concentrations of power in the system. These poles of power, and the relations between them, determine the polarity of the system. Other actors may exist, but they are not decisive in determining system polarity. Changes in the distribution of power may take place slowly, the result of different economic growth rates and technological innovation among states. Some changes in the distribution of power may be very dramatic, the result of a sudden shift in alliances across the states in the system or the sudden weakening of one or more of the powers in a system through internal collapse or defeat in war. When this happens, the polarity of the system may change, and a different kind of system may emerge. For the purposes of study, realist scholars have identified three different kinds of polarity in the history of international relations: multipolar systems, bipolar systems, and unipolar systems. Each system type has a certain distribution of power (polarity), and each is the subject of debate as to its relative advantages and disadvantages.

Multipolar systems consist of three to seven independent centres, or poles, that are relatively equal in power. These systems can be global in scope (the global balance of power), regional (such as the historical European balance of power systems), or localized (such as the Warring States period in China). The stability of multipolar systems is a major issue of debate among realists. Morgenthau argued that such a system is stable (and therefore more peaceful) because enough centres of power always exist to prevent a single power or group of powers from dominating. However, some realists, such as Kenneth Waltz, warn that multipolar systems are inherently unstable, precisely because they are so flexible.[24] In such a system, the actions of one centre of power (such as an attack on another centre of power or a decision to expand its military) can reverberate throughout the system and have unintended consequences (such as system-wide war or an arms race). A special kind of multipolar system is the tripolar system in which three centres of power exist. Tripolar systems are very unstable, as there is a tendency for two of the power centres to ally against the third, with no prospect of achieving a power balance to deter war. Historical examples of such power distributions are rare, although some of the characteristics of such systems can be found in the "strategic triangle" between the United States, the Soviet Union, and China during the Cold War.[25]

In **bipolar** systems, two centres of power, in the form of either two predominant states or two great rival alliance blocs, dominate the international system, such as in Greece during the height of the Athenian and Spartan empires, and during the early Cold War between the superpowers and their respective allies. As the Cold War wore on, however, other countries attained more flexibility, largely because of their recovery from the devastation of World War II. As a result, while the superpowers remained militarily and economically predominant, other states increasingly embarked on their own foreign policy agendas and relationships, although these rarely challenged the policy of the superpowers. (In practice, the major allies of the United States maintained more freedom of manoeuvre than the allies of the Soviet Union did.) This system is sometimes referred to as **bipolycentrism.** Realists also disagree on the stability of bipolar systems. Some, such as Kenneth Waltz, argue that bipolar systems are stable because the two centres of power deter each other from rash actions, and they can develop a familiarity that will reduce the chances of miscalculation. Others argue that such a system is inflexible because of the lack of balancing potential and because each state sees its position with respect to the other as a **zero-sum game.**[26] As a result, even small changes in the distribution of power between the two centres of power can have destabilizing effects that might lead to war. As we shall see in the next chapter, this became particularly dangerous in the nuclear age, when an all-out war between the two poles could have resulted in the destruction of most life on the planet.

The third configuration is a **unipolar** system, characterized by a single centre of power: a state or a powerful state and its allies dominate the forums, rules, and arrangements governing political and economic relations in the system. Such actors are often called *hegemons*. Most often, **hegemony** is a reflection of one state's preponderant power in traditional economic and military terms. However, hegemony can also refer to the dominance of certain ideas or certain cultures.[27] The theory of **hegemonic stability** holds that a hegemon can have a stabilizing or ordering influence on a regional system or the international system by performing some of the functions a central government would perform. It can deter aggression or use political and economic pressure to prevent or stop wars between smaller countries. It can provide hard currency for use as a world standard. Two prominent examples of hegemonies in history are Great Britain in the 19th century and the United States in the 20th century. Great Britain's period of dominance occurred after the defeat of France in the Napoleonic Wars. The United States' period of hegemony began with the defeat of Nazi Germany and Imperial Japan at the end of World War II, and, arguably, persists to this day.

It is important to note that scholars of international relations do not always agree on which states have achieved hegemonic status in the past and how long this position lasted. Some scholars would include 17th-century Netherlands and 16th-century Spain as examples of hegemony. It is also important to note that in practice a hegemon may exist in a multipolar setting (as did Great Britain in the 19th century) and in a bipolycentric setting (as did the United States during the Cold War). In such cases, the term *hegemony* merely describes the existence of a state that is more powerful than all others in the system but not so powerful that one can speak with empirical confidence of a unipolar system. For example, the Cold War is described as a period of bipolarity, as there were two clearly preeminent centres of power in the system. However, it was also clear that the United States was the more powerful in terms of the influence it exerted over international institutions, rules, and the world economy. As a result, the American role was often described as hegemonic, despite the broader bipolar context.

States that achieve hegemonic status do not retain this status indefinitely. Hegemonic decline will eventually occur over decades or centuries. A combination of domestic internal decay and costly military overextension weakens the hegemonic state. The hegemon will then face the efforts of a challenger to overthrow the hegemon's preeminent position. The transition from one hegemon to another may take the form of a hegemonic war or a peaceful transition in which the first hegemon will be compelled to pass on its status to a rising power.[28] Alternatively, the challenger may fail and the hegemon survive. As we shall see in Chapter 4, the status of the United States today is a point of debate among scholars, who disagree on whether the United States is a hegemon in decline.[29]

Realist concepts such as the balance of power and polarity have had an enduring impact on the study of global politics. However, other theoretical perspectives have challenged these concepts and their explanatory power. Liberals argue that the balance of power and polarity deemphasize the importance of economic interdependence and other forms of cooperation between states, as well as the influence exerted by international institutions, regimes, norms, and law. Constructivists suggest the balance of power concept serves to reinforce and perpetuate ways of thinking about global politics that create crisis and conflict. In other words, these concepts are part of the problem, not just descriptions of historical "patterns" or "truths." Feminists point out that the balance of power and polarity are inherently masculine frameworks, serving to marginalize issues such as economic development, social justice, human rights, and a variety of other concerns of import to people in general and women in particular. These perspectives remind us that much of what we know (or think we know) about history is reflective of a certain perspective, one that is contestable and subject to challenge in many different ways.

HISTORY AND ASYMMETRIES IN POWER

The historical record also reveals that across time and place most political units (whether they be groups or states) do not possess anything like the power wielded by the strongest political units. For the most part, history is characterized by a small number of very powerful political units and a large number of less powerful units. Realists tend to focus on the most powerful actors, or **great powers**, because these actors define the character of the system (the distribution of power and the polarity of the system), and therefore their actions are the most important. There is no question that great powers are tremendously influential. Few of them exist at any given point in history, and yet they possess most of the world's power resources at that time. Great powers possess the strongest military forces and the largest economies. Often these capabilities are based on natural endowments of large populations and plentiful resources, as in the case of the United States, Russia, and China. In other cases, these resources might be acquired through expansion, as was the case with the British Empire, or through economic growth and trade, as is the case with Japan. As a result, great powers tend to endure. Only great powers (or alliances of great powers) can decisively defeat other great powers militarily. They also tend to have global interests and commitments, and have a disproportionate influence on the spread of ideas, the rules and laws governing diplomatic affairs, and the regulations governing international trade and finance. And on occasion, great powers are formally recognized as such by international structures such as the Concert of Europe or the UN Security Council.

However, the bulk of state actors in the history of international politics have not been great powers. For the most part, historical systems have been composed of a small number of large (powerful) states and a large number of smaller (less powerful) states. The latter states vary widely in terms of their characteristics, resources, and capabilities, and, as a result, classifying them has been very difficult. The term *middle power* has been used to refer to a group of states that rank below the great powers in terms of power resources and influence in international politics. These states may exert influence within their respective regions, or they may have an international profile on certain specific issues, but for the most part their ability to influence the larger global setting is limited. Some middle powers may be geographically large, such as Canada or Australia, while others may be quite small, such as South Korea or Sweden. Small powers, or **small states** as they are more generally known, are countries that have less power capabilities than middle powers and little or no influence on international politics. Small states have smaller economies (although many small states are very wealthy on a per capita basis), tend to have small populations and territories, and tend to have limited power capabilities (such as small militaries) as a result. Small states are generally considered significant only to the extent that they become important in the schemes of the great powers. For example, Belgium has been a small state in Europe since its creation, but it has been important because of its status as a buffer state between Germany and France. Vietnam might be far less well known today but for the engagement of the United States in the Vietnam War and its historical conflicts with China. In addition, regional context is an important factor in judging the importance of states. Some small states in Europe or Asia would be among the most powerful states if they were relocated in different regions of the world. And Brazil, South Africa, and India all have a claim to great-power status in their respective regions.

Canada provides a good example of the difficulty inherent in classifying states according to their power. The country has been described variously as a small state, a satellite of the United States, a middle power, and even a "principal power."[30] Canada has one of the leading economies of the world but has a very small military. The country is rich in resources but has a small population. And yet, Canada consistently is ranked among the top 10 countries in the world in which to live, has one of the 10 largest economies in the world, and is a member of the G-8 group of countries. Classifying states according to their power therefore raises the question of how power is measured. For realists, military and economic indicators (hard power) best determine a state's power and its associated diplomatic status. However, power can also be measured in terms of the power to persuade without coercion, the power of ideas and values, and the power of social stability and a high quality of life. In this sense, small states can be significant actors in global politics, often serving as a source of ideas, as mediators, and as contributors to multilateral institutions. Furthermore, in an increasingly interdependent world, classifying states may become increasingly problematic in the face of the permeability of borders, the significance of multinational corporations, and the evident limitations on the use of force as experienced by the United States in Vietnam and the Soviet Union in Afghanistan. Nevertheless, the classification of states continues. The United States is invariably described as the world's only superpower. The United Kingdom, France, China, Russia, and sometimes Germany and Japan are frequently referred to as great powers. Some countries are described as *regional powers*, such as India, Israel, Indonesia, Australia, and Brazil. Almost all other states are called *small states*. And some states are so small (often literally) they are called *micro-states*. The symbolism of state equality is maintained in the principles of diplomatic formality (see Chapter 7) and in organizations such as the UN General Assembly (see Chapter 5), in which the United States has the same number of votes (one) as Nauru. However, that is where the equality ends, and the reality of power asymmetry begins.

CONCLUSIONS

In this chapter we have provided a necessarily brief (and of course incomplete) history of global politics, focusing on the rise and fall of civilizations and empires, the formation of the modern state system, and the enduring problem of war. This historical experience reminds us of the need to be aware of both continuities and changes in the course of human affairs, and to be careful when proclaiming the dawning of a new era or a transformation in the nature of world politics. We also explored some of the core themes related to war and peace up to 1945, and noted the seminal impact they had on the development of related ideas and theories, such as geopolitics, realism, collective security, and the balance of power. All of these ideas, derived from historical developments and interpretations of those developments, maintained their relevance into the Cold War period. The next chapter examines in detail the most protracted power struggle in recent history, one that affected all states, small and large: the epic confrontation between the West and the East during the Cold War.

Endnotes

1. Georg Wilhelm Friederich Hegel, "An Introduction to the Philosophy of History," in Jacob Loewenburg, ed., *Hegel Selections* (New York: Scribner's, 1929).
2. T. Judt, "What Have We Learned, If Anything?," *New York Review of Books*, May 1, 2008, 16.
3. For an engaging read on this topic, see E. Paris, *Long Shadows: Truth, Lies and History* (Toronto: Vintage Canada, 2001).
4. See, for example, J. R. McNeill, *Something New Under the Sun: An Environmental History of the Twentieth Century World* (New York: Norton, 2001); J. F. Richards, *The Unending Frontier: An Environmental History of the Early Modern World* (Berkeley: University of California Press, 2003); and B. Fagan, *The Great Warming: Climate Change and the Rise and Fall of Civilizations* (New York: Bloomsbury Press, 2008).
5. J. Keegan, *A History of Warfare* (New York: Alfred A. Knopf, 1993), 122.
6. See W. H. McNeill, *The Pursuit of Power: Technology, Armed Force, and Society since A.D. 1000* (Chicago: University of Chicago Press, 1982), 5.
7. P. Heather, *The Fall of the Roman Empire: A New History of Rome and the Barbarians* (Oxford: Oxford University Press, 2006), 458.
8. For a history of Mongol power, see R. Marshall, *Storm from the East: From Genghis Khan to Kublai Khan* (Berkeley: University of California Press, 1993).
9. J. Black, *War and the World: Military Power and the Fate of Continents, 1450–2000* (New Haven: Yale University Press, 1998), 32.
10. H. Kennedy, *The Great Arab Conquests: How the Spread of Islam Changed the World We Live In* (London, Phoenix, 2007), 376.
11. For an excellent account of the impact of Islamic expansion on Europe, see D. L. Lewis, *God's Crucible: Islam and the Making of Europe, 570–1215* (New York: W. W. Norton, 2008).
12. See A. Hourani, *A History of the Arab Peoples* (Cambridge, MA: Belknap Press, 1991).
13. See V. D. Hanson, *Carnage and Culture: Landmark Battles in the Rise of Western Power* (New York: Anchor Books, 2001), esp. 193–232; and Mark Cocker, *Rivers of Blood, Rivers of Gold: Europe's Conquest of Indigenous Peoples* (New York: Grove Press, 1998).

14. See A. B. Bozeman, *Politics and Culture in International History* (Princeton: Princeton University Press, 1960).

15. P. Bobbitt, *The Shield of Achilles: War, Peace, and the Course of History* (New York: Alfred A. Knopf, 2002), 118–43.

16. On the theme of the overextension and decline of empires, see the popular text by P. Kennedy, *The Rise and Fall of the Great Powers: Economic Change and Military Conflict from 1500 to 2000* (London: Unwin Hyman, 1988).

17. See S. Van Evera, "The Cult of the Offensive and the Origins of the First World War," *International Security* 9 (1984), 58–107; and J. L. Snyder, *The Ideology of the Offensive: Military Decision Making and the Disasters of 1914* (Ithaca, NY: Cornell University Press, 1984).

18. Quoted in B. W. Tuchman, *The Guns of August* (New York: Bantam Books, 1962), 146.

19. R. Overy, "Total War II: The Second World War," in C. Townshend, ed., *The Oxford History of Modern War* (Oxford: Oxford University Press, 2000), 139.

20. See W. L. Shirer, *The Collapse of the Third Republic* (New York: Simon and Schuster, 1969).

21. It is important to note that as Canadian and American men fought abroad, women were recruited into wartime production at home, continuing a fundamental shift in the economic role played by women in advanced capitalist economies that began under similar circumstances during World War I.

22. See G. Kolko, *Century of War: Politics, Conflicts, and Society Since 1914* (New York: The New Press, 1994).

23. See S. Walt, *The Origins of Alliances* (Ithaca, NY: Cornell University Press, 1987).

24. See K. Waltz, "The Stability of a Bipolar World," in D. Edwards, ed., *International Political Analysis* (New York: Rinehart and Winston, 1970), 340. See also J. Mearsheimer, "Why We Will Soon Miss the Cold War," *Atlantic Monthly*, August 1990, 37.

25. See A. N. Sabrosky, ed., *Polarity and War: The Changing Nature of International Conflict* (Boulder, CO: Westview Press, 1985).

26. See K. W. Deutsch and J. D. Singer, "Multipolar Power Systems and International Stability," in J. Rosenau, ed., *International Politics and Foreign Policy*, rev. ed. (New York: Free Press, 1969), 315–24. In a zero-sum game, one state's gain is automatically perceived as another's loss. Therefore, the outcome of the game is still zero (+1 for the winner, –1 for the loser = 0).

27. The Marxist (Gramscian) tradition in international political economy refers to hegemony as ideational domination by transnational class interests. See also S. Gill, *American Hegemony and the Trilateral Commission* (Cambridge, UK: Cambridge University Press, 1990).

28. The most famous treatment of this theory of hegemonic stability and transformation is probably R. Gilpin's *War and Change in World Politics* (Cambridge, UK: Cambridge University Press, 1981). See also R. Keohane, *After Hegemony: Cooperation and Discord in the World Political Economy* (Princeton: Princeton University Press, 1984).

29. This debate is crystallized in two popular works: P. Kennedy, *The Rise and Fall of the Great Powers, op. cit.*; and J. S. Nye Jr., *Bound to Lead: The Changing Nature of American Power* (New York: Basic Books, 1990).

30. See D. Dewitt and J. Kirton, *Canada as a Principal Power: A Study in Foreign Policy and International Relations* (Toronto: John Wiley and Sons, 1983). For further discussion, see K. R. Nossal, *The Politics of Canadian Foreign Policy*, 3rd ed. (Scarborough, ON: Prentice-Hall, 1997), 52–68; and A. Cooper, *Canadian Foreign Policy: Old Habits and New Directions* (Scarborough, ON: Prentice-Hall, 1997), 9–21.

Suggested Websites

Best of History Websites
     http://www.besthistorysites.net/index.shtml

The History Guide: Resources for Historians
     http://www.historyguide.org/resources.html

The History Net
     http://www.thehistorynet.com

Princeton University Library History Websites
     http://www.princeton.edu/~pressman/hiswebs.htm

The Cold War and Foreign Policy Analysis

To the extent that the nuclear threat has deterrent value, it is because it in fact increases the risk of nuclear war.

—*Robert S. McNamara*[1]

Restraint? Why are you so concerned with saving their damn lives? The whole idea is to kill the bastards. At the end of the war if there are two Americans and one Russian left alive, we win.

—*General Thomas Power, Commander of U.S. Strategic Air Command in the 1960s*[2]

THE COLD WAR: POWER POLITICS ASCENDANT

The Cold War dominated global politics for over 40 years.[3] Citizens of every state on earth were put at risk by the nuclear arms race. Canadians would have been caught in a horrific crossfire if nuclear war had occurred. A high level of animosity existed between East and West, between the ideologies of the communist command economies (the so-called Second World) and democratic liberal capitalism (the so-called First World), between the Red Scare and the American imperialists, between the "commies" and the "Yankees," between the "pinkos" and the "fascists"—the list of quaint phrases depicting the evils of each side seemed endless. The Cold War was a comprehensive ideological, geopolitical, military, and international rivalry between the two superpowers (and their respective allies and **client states**) that became increasingly global in scope as the postwar era evolved. Thankfully, the Cold War never became a global hot war. The vast military capabilities of the superpowers never directly fought each other. Instead, the Cold War was fought in the international arena through diplomacy, ideological rhetoric, arms races, regional **proxy wars** and interventions, and the competition for allies and military bases around the world. Although the Cold War was sometimes called the "long peace," this somewhat misleading label only applies to the absence of great-power war between 1946 and 1991.[4] Millions of people died in the regional wars and related human rights outrages of this period. The Cold War may have been a long peace for some, but it was certainly not so for others.

We can destroy you. The testing of nuclear weapons by the United States and the Soviet Union was the most visible expression of Cold War animosity. This was the U.S. test at the Bikini Atoll in the Marshall Islands on July 24, 1946. The dark spots in the foreground are old naval vessels placed near the blast to test the effects of nuclear explosions on ships. Such technology introduced a new possibility: omnicide. (AP Photo/CP Archive.)

The Cold War was not the only issue in post–World War II international relations. Decolonization greatly increased the official number of states, and development became a major international issue. There was growing interest in the protection and promotion of human rights. The global economy grew dramatically. Nonstate actors, especially multinational corporations and nongovernmental organizations, became more prominent. Nevertheless, the dominant characteristic of this era was the superpower rivalry; the international politics of this period cannot be addressed or examined in isolation from this fact. An examination of the history of the relationship between the superpowers reveals several themes that persisted until the collapse of the Soviet Union:

- *A cyclical pattern of confrontation and cooperation.* The Cold War was characterized by periods of high tension and crisis between the superpowers, alternating with periods of a relative relaxation of tensions and increased levels of cooperation. Good relations reached a high point between 1968 and 1978, a period sometimes called **détente**, in which both countries sought restraint and increased cooperation in their relations with each other.

- *The nuclear stalemate.* For most of the Cold War, especially after the late 1960s, each superpower was vulnerable to complete destruction by the nuclear arsenal of the other. Nuclear deterrence became the dominant military strategy of the Cold War.

- *The development of informal rules and mutual understandings.* Over time, the superpowers established formal and informal understandings and agreements that often guided relations between them. For example, it was generally understood that both sides possessed spheres of influence (such as Eastern Europe and Central America) within which the other side would not interfere. When these agreements or understandings were violated in the view of one of the superpowers, tensions between the countries increased.

- *Political pragmatism versus ideological rhetoric.* During the Cold War, both superpowers professed the superiority of their respective ideologies. However, both superpowers sacrificed the principles of their respective ideologies if geopolitical considerations demanded it. For example, both superpowers supported allies with political systems antithetical to their own.

- *Superpower involvement in regional wars.* Although the two superpowers avoided direct warfare, both used or supported allies and client states in wars directed against their opponent's allies and clients. These wars are referred to as *proxy wars*. For example, Cuba's involvement in the Angolan Civil War was a proxy for direct Soviet involvement.

For other countries in the international system, the Cold War was the context for much of their foreign policy decision making. Many countries voluntarily sought security arrangements and alliances with the superpowers. Most of the countries of Western Europe joined the

United States and Canada in the North Atlantic Treaty Organization (NATO), which bound its members to come to the assistance of any member should it be attacked. This alliance was built against the threat posed by the Soviet Union. The Warsaw Treaty Organization (WTO), more commonly called the **Warsaw Pact**, joined the countries of Eastern Europe with the Soviet Union in an alliance against NATO. However, the Warsaw Pact countries were much more tightly controlled from Moscow. The Soviet Union used force to keep puppet governments in power in Hungary in 1956 and Czechoslovakia in 1968.

Around the world, states established relationships with the superpowers based on a combination of ideological affinity and pure self-interest. Both superpowers established a network of client states. The United States gave large amounts of assistance to countries such as Israel, Iran (before the Iranian Revolution), Pakistan, and South Korea. The Soviet Union supported North Korea, Cuba, Vietnam, and Syria. A few countries succeeded in following a neutral path, such as Switzerland, Austria, and Sweden. Some countries such as India, Indonesia, and Egypt sought to distance themselves from the Cold War by forming the Nonaligned Movement (NAM) but never succeeded in becoming a major political force, since few if any countries could escape the fact that international issues were invariably affected by the behaviour of one or both superpowers. To varying degrees, all countries had to accommodate this fact when making foreign policy decisions.

The aim of this chapter is to explore the origins, character, and collapse of the Cold War. This task is a crucial one because our own time is often defined as the "post–Cold War era." The chapter also examines the formal study of decision making, or *foreign policy analysis*, which developed dramatically during the Cold War because the consequences of intentional or accidental nuclear war were so great. Today, decision-making theories are valuable tools in our search to understand how the decisions that shape global politics are made.

THE ORIGINS OF THE BIPOLAR ERA

The seeds of the Cold War were planted in the latter half of World War II, when distrust and friction began to develop between the Western Allies (primarily the United States and Great Britain) and the Soviet Union. Each side was suspicious of the other's ultimate intentions, although distrust was held in check by the larger interest in continued cooperation to defeat Nazi Germany and Imperial Japan. Was the Cold War inevitable? The Western Allies and the Soviet Union had cooperated during World War II despite their differences, and both had expressed a desire to maintain that cooperation in the postwar period. The membership of the United States and the U.S.S.R. in the newly created United Nations (UN), which was mandated to preserve world peace, offered hope that cooperation would continue. However, relations between "the West" and "the East" deteriorated into an open hostility and rivalry that largely paralyzed the UN Security Council. This hostility and rivalry had an ideological dimension, a geopolitical dimension, a strategic dimension, and an international dimension, which together established the character of the Cold War.

THE IDEOLOGICAL DIMENSION

The Cold War was a rivalry between two antagonistic political, economic, and social systems. It was a confrontation between two different ways of life, and a competition to determine which system performed best and which could build a better society. On the one hand, the majority of Western countries and their peoples perceived Marxism-Leninism as a fundamentally authoritarian political ideology that stifled the political and economic freedom of the individual. Communism threatened the overthrow of Western liberal democracy and the free market economic system. The imposition of communist rule in Eastern Europe after WWII was seen as evidence of the intentions of the Soviet leadership. On the other hand, the ideological pronouncements of the Soviet Union characterized the West as a bastion of capitalist interests that controlled the world economy and was bent on surrounding and then destroying the Marxist-Leninist revolution in Russia. Capitalism and communism could not coexist, and the Soviet Union had to do what it could to accelerate the historical inevitability of communist revolutions around the world. The efforts of Western states to overthrow the communist revolution in the Russian Civil War and the delay in the opening of a second front in Europe until 1944 was seen as evidence of the hostile intent of the West. U.S. Secretary of State James Byrnes once argued that "there is too much difference in the ideologies of the U.S. and Russia to work out a long term program of cooperation."[5] These ideological differences, reinforced by historical experiences, served to create a climate of suspicion and outright animosity between the Western allies and the Communist bloc.

During the Cold War, a persistent and intense debate raged in government and academic circles (as well as in the general public) about whether the U.S.S.R. was an expansionist power. For many, particularly early in the Cold War, the answer to this question was yes: the Soviet Union was a messianic state bent on expanding its power and influence in the world through direct aggression and the support of communist national liberation movements abroad. For these **hawks**, Marxist-Leninist ideology was a blueprint, a guide, for Soviet actions. Just as Hitler's book *Mein Kampf* had outlined the plans and worldview of that dictator, the ideological writings of Lenin and Stalin and the pronouncements of Soviet leaders outlined the plans and worldview of the Soviet leadership. However, many argued otherwise. These **doves** argued that the foreign policy of the Soviet Union was essentially defensive, concerned primarily with preserving and protecting the Soviet state. While the Soviet Union would take advantage of opportunities to increase its power or expand its influence, it would not take undue risks in the pursuit of such opportunities. Doves argued that ideology was not a guide to Soviet policy. At best, it was a perceptual lens through which the Soviet leaders saw the world. Soviet behaviour actually had more in common with the policies of Russia's tsars. It was power politics that drove Soviet policy, not ideology.

As the Cold War dragged on, the ideological intensity of the superpower competition receded, as did the hostility of the rhetoric between the two countries. However, ideology remained the cornerstone of the confrontation between the United States and the Soviet Union. The competition between the two systems manifested in extreme nationalism (or patriotism) in both countries. Even in periods of détente, it surfaced in sports, the arts, scientific achievement, and space travel. In the 1980s, the ideological rhetoric of the Cold War intensified when Ronald Reagan became president of the United States. He took a firmly hawkish view of the U.S.S.R., believing it was the root of all evil in the world. The ideological animosity of the Cold War also existed between allies of the United States and other communist countries; however, the ideological rivalry of the Cold War was not uniform. Canada, for example, had better relations with Romania and Cuba than did the United States. In fact, Canada's relatively friendly relations with (and financial investment in) Cuba remain a central point of contention in Canada–U.S. relations today.

THE GEOPOLITICAL DIMENSION

Ideological rivalry does not provide a complete characterization or explanation for the events of the Cold War. Just as important was the geopolitical rivalry between the superpowers. The preeminence of the United States and the Soviet Union at the end of World War II led them naturally to regard each other with suspicion. As Robert Tucker has observed, "The principal cause of the Cold War was the essential duopoly of power left by World War II."[6] In other words, the structure of the international system at the end of World War II led each super-power to regard the other as a rival. The ideological differences between the two countries only exacerbated this situation. As the Cold War intensified, geography played an important role in the strategic and foreign policy decisions of Washington and Moscow.

In the United States, the Soviet threat was cast in the geopolitical context of Halford Mackinder and his view of the world (see Chapter 2). The Soviet Union, after all, seemed to occupy the "heartland," and was poised to expand along the "interior ring" to dominate the "world island"—and thereafter the world. From this position, the Soviet Union had the tremendous geopolitical advantage of the interior lines of transport and was thus poised to expand anywhere along a wide perimeter (see Map 3.1). To contain the U.S.S.R., the United States and its allies were forced to defend this wide perimeter around the heartland of Eurasia. This prompted the U.S. to form multilateral and bilateral alliances with countries around the perimeter of Eurasia, and it found many willing partners. The governments of Western Europe saw the Soviet Union as a direct (and geographically close) threat. Common threat perceptions shared by most Western European countries and the United States led to the creation of **NATO** in 1949. Japan also felt threatened, not least because the U.S.S.R. had occupied several Japanese territories at the end of World War II. Japan and the U.S. would sign a bilateral security treaty in 1951. In Canada, concern arose about the threat the Soviet Union represented to the postwar order.[7] This would prompt the Canadian government to join NATO as a founding country and to establish a wide array of security agreements with the United States, most notably the North American Air Defence Agreement (**NORAD**) in 1958.

However, in its search for allies the United States also found willing partners that capital-ized on the anti-communist passions of U.S. foreign policy by accepting American aid and using it for their own purposes. In its desire to geographically contain the Soviet Union and prevent the spread of communism, the United States would assist not only democratic coun-tries that felt threatened by the U.S.S.R., but also dictatorial and military regimes which main-tained their power through repressive and systematic human rights violations. Realists would proclaim that such alliances were natural if unfortunate manifestations of power politics. For successive U.S. governments, the enemies of communism and the U.S.S.R. were automatically perceived as friends. However, for liberals, Marxists, and feminists, U.S. support for regimes in Chile, Guatemala, South Africa, Indonesia, Iran (and later Iraq), and the Philippines were perversions of American principles and values. By supporting such regimes diplomatically, financially, and militarily while ignoring the brutal treatment that many citizens of these countries endured at the hands of their governments, the United States was complicit in some of the worst human rights abuses perpetrated during the Cold War.

In the Soviet Union, the geopolitical position of the country was regarded in a rather dif-ferent fashion. We can simulate a Soviet geopolitical view of the world by using a polar projec-tion of the world (see Map 3.2). The difference is striking. No longer does the Soviet Union seem poised to strike out in any direction with the advantage of the interior lines. Instead, the Soviet Union is encircled, and the long border of the Soviet Union is threatened by enemies and security concerns. Any potential effort to break out of this encirclement or to conduct military operations from the U.S.S.R. would encounter some of these enemies or threats. In Europe are the NATO countries, backed by the power of the United States. In southern Europe are the NATO countries of Greece and Turkey, which dominate the straits between the Black Sea and the Mediterranean. In the Middle East lies the Muslim world, a security concern because of the fear that this region might have an influence in the Islamic republics of the

Map 3.1 The Western Geopolitical View of the World During the Cold War

				★

U.S.S.R.
Soviet annexations
U.S.S.R. allies
Yugoslavia
Communist aggression

1946–54	War in Indochina
1947–49	Greek civil war
1948	Yugoslavian crisis
1948	Coup in Prague
1948–57	Guerrillas in Malaysia
1948–49	Blockade of Berlin
1949–52	Huk guerrillas in the Philippines
1950	Invasion of Tibet
1950–53	Korean war

Korea (1950)

Philippines (1949)

Malaysia (1948)

Indochina (1946)

1949

Tibet (1950)

1945

Berlin (1949)

Czechoslovakia (1948)

1945

Greece (1947)

SOURCE: GERARD CHALIAND AND JEAN-PIERRE RAGEAU, *A STRATEGIC ATLAS: COMPARATIVE GEOPOLITICS OF THE WORLD'S POWERS*, 3RD ED. (NEW YORK: HARPERCOLLINS, 1993). © 1993 BY GERARD CHALIAND AND JEAN-PIERRE RAGEAU. REPRINTED BY PERMISSION OF HARPERCOLLINS PUBLISHERS, INC.

Map 3.2 The Soviet Geopolitical View of the World During the Cold War

The Soviet Union's
Perception of Its
Encirclement by the
United States and Its
Military Allies
(1950–55)

Communist world
U.S.A. and allies
American naval fleets
Conflicts, crises

Pacific Ocean

Atlantic Ocean

Indian Ocean

Arctic

USA

CANADA

WESTERN
EUROPE

JAPAN

S. KOREA

TAIWAN

PHILIPPINES

AUSTRALIA

N. ZEALAND

PAKISTAN

TURKEY

IRAQ

THAILAND

NATO

SEATO

SECOND FLEET

SIXTH FLEET

SEVENTH FLEET

Guatemala 1954

Korea 1950

Quemoy-Matsu 1950

Indochina 1946

Malaysia 1948

Berlin 1953

Yugoslavia 1948

Greece 1947

Azerbaijan 1945

BAGHDAD
PACT

Iran 1951

SOURCE: GERARD CHALIAND AND JEAN-PIERRE RAGEAU, A STRATEGIC ATLAS: COMPARATIVE GEOPOLITICS OF THE WORLD'S POWERS, 3RD ED. (NEW YORK: HARPERCOLLINS, 1993), 44. © 1993 BY GERARD CHALIAND AND JEAN-PIERRE RAGEAU. REPRINTED BY PERMISSION OF HARPERCOLLINS PUBLISHERS, INC.

Soviet Union. To the east is China, a great ideological competitor by the second half of the Cold War, and Japan, a close ally of the United States. From the perspective of Soviet planners, the geopolitical position of the U.S.S.R. was not an enviable one.

THE STRATEGIC DIMENSION

Both superpowers and their respective allies maintained large conventional military forces throughout the Cold War. An immense amount of time, money, and effort was devoted to the maintenance of these forces and their training, equipment modernization, and deployment around the world. By the late 1980s the size of these conventional military forces was immense. In particular, Europe was host to the large armies of NATO and the even larger armies of the Warsaw Pact. However, the strategic character of the Cold War was defined by nuclear weapons and the nuclear arms race between the United States and the Soviet Union. The nuclear weapon was a revolutionary development in the history of warfare, a fact dramatically punctuated by the two bombs dropped on Japan at the end of World War II.[8] Ironically, the weapons were so destructive, and the consequences of their use so enormous, that the military usefulness of such weapons came under question. But if nuclear weapons could not be usefully employed on the battlefield, what could they be used for? In short, they were useful only for preventing their use by others. In other words, nuclear weapons were instruments of **deterrence**, not warfighting.

Deterrence is a policy of preventing or discouraging an action by confronting an opponent or opponents with risks they are unwilling to take. The actor doing the deterring is a *deterrer*, and the actor being deterred is a *deterree*. A potential aggressor will likely be deterred when the probability of victory is low or the costs of a war (whatever the outcome) are high. Two broad types of deterrence strategies are:

- *Deterrence by denial.* A deterree will not start a war because it is convinced it cannot achieve its objectives. Deterrence by denial was a prenuclear phenomenon, based on the view that powerful military forces and high levels of military preparedness could discourage an attack by one country against another.
- *Deterrence by punishment.* A deterree will not start a war because of the threat that it will receive unacceptable damage in return. The enormous destructive power of nuclear weapons, coupled with advanced delivery systems, made deterrence by punishment feasible.

Nuclear deterrence defined the military relationship between the superpowers during the Cold War. Though the nuclear arsenal of the United States remained superior to that of the U.S.S.R. at least until the mid-1960s, the explosion of the Soviet atomic bomb in 1949 had ended America's nuclear monopoly, forcing both leaderships to contemplate the consequences of a nuclear war between them. By the mid-1960s, a rough parity, or equivalence, existed between the arsenals of the two superpowers, with each capable of inflicting **unacceptable damage** on the military forces and civilian populations of the other in the event of a nuclear war. The logic of deterrence by punishment suggested that if the two superpowers could inflict unacceptable damage on each other in a nuclear war, neither would start such a war by launching an attack, or **first strike**. The ability of both sides to essentially destroy the other was a signature feature of Cold War politics and came to be called **mutual assured destruction (MAD)**. During the Cold War both superpowers devoted massive resources to the development and maintenance of enormous nuclear forces so there could be no doubt that they were capable of devastating the other under any possible set of circumstances. The result was a nuclear arms race (see Figure 3.1).[9]

Figure 3.1 Nuclear Warhead Stockpiles of Permanent Security Council Members, 1945–2006

YEAR	UNITED STATES	U.S.S.R./RUSSIA (1949)	UNITED KINGDOM (1953)	FRANCE (1964)	CHINA (1964)	TOTAL
1945	6	—	—	—	—	6
1950	369	5	—	—	—	374
1955	3,057	200	10	—	—	3,267
1960	20,434	1,605	30	—	—	22,069
1965	31,982	6,129	310	32	5	38,458
1970	26,662	11,643	280	36	75	38,696
1975	27,826	19,055	350	188	185	47,604
1980	24,304	30,062	350	250	280	55,246
1985	24,237	39,197	300	360	425	64,519
1990	21,004	37,000	300	505	430	59,239
1995	12,144	27,000	300	500	400	40,344
2000	10,577	21,000	185	470	400	32,632
2005	10,295	17,000	200	350	400	28,245
2006	10,104	16,000	200	350	200	26,854

Note: Date In Brackets Is Year Of Acquisition. In 2010, Israel is believed to have a stockpile of some 200 warheads, the first of which may have been assembled as early as 1967. India is believed to have 50–60 nuclear warheads, and Pakistan about 60.

SOURCE: "GLOBAL NUCLEAR STOCKPILES, 1945–2006," *BULLETIN OF THE ATOMIC SCIENTISTS* 62 (JULY/AUGUST 2006), 66.

As the Cold War progressed, the size and destructive potential of the nuclear arsenals of both superpowers led to a growing realization that all-out nuclear war between the two countries would be devastating on a global level. Indeed, the known effects of nuclear radiation and the possibility of nuclear winter (the cooling of the global climate from the ejection of dust and debris into the atmosphere) raised the question of whether humanity itself would survive a nuclear war. This fear of **omnicide**, coupled with the enormous expenses of the nuclear arms race, fostered the development of large peace and antinuclear movements dedicated to stopping the nuclear arms race and promoting arms control and disarmament (see Chapter 7). The signing of arms control agreements often accompanied larger efforts to improve the relationship between the United States and the Soviet Union in periods of détente. In addition, some arrangements were made in an informal manner: U.S. President Jimmy Carter and Soviet Foreign Minister Andrei Gromyko promised each other that their countries would never be the first to use nuclear weapons. This pledge was never made formal in an agreement, despite the efforts of "no-first-use declaration" advocates.

Profile 3.1 reflects the impressive scope of bilateral arms control agreements between the United States and the Soviet Union/Russia (Russia has assumed the U.S.S.R.'s treaty obligations). Among the most important formal agreements were the **Strategic Arms Limitation Treaty (SALT)** and the **Strategic Arms Reduction Treaty (START)**. Signed in 1972, SALT I put limits on the number of **intercontinental ballistic missiles (ICBMs)** and **submarine-launched ballistic missiles (SLBMs)** deployable by both sides for five years. SALT I also put limits on the deployment of **antiballistic missiles (ABMs)** in the so-called ABM Treaty. In 1979, the more comprehensive SALT II agreement put a ceiling of 2,250 on the number of ICBMs, SLBMs, heavy bombers, and air-to-surface ballistic missiles (ASBMs) permitted to each side. After the 1979 Soviet invasion of Afghanistan, the U.S. Senate never ratified SALT II, although both countries continued to abide by the basic provisions of the treaty. The criticism of both SALT I and SALT II was that neither agreement actually reduced the number

PROFILE 3.1 — Major Bilateral Arms Control Agreements Between the United States and the Soviet Union/Russia

DATE	AGREEMENT	PRINCIPAL AIMS
1963	Hotline Agreement	Establishes a direct radio and telegraph communications link between Moscow and Washington (updated with a satellite communications link in 1971).
1971	Nuclear Accidents Agreement	Creates a procedure for notification of a nuclear accident or unauthorized detonation and establishes safeguards to prevent accidents.
1972	SALT I Interim Agreement	Limits number of ICBMs and SLBMs allowed to each side.
1972	Anti-Ballistic Missile Treaty	Limits deployment of antiballistic missile systems to two sites (later reduced to one in a protocol in 1974) and prohibits development of space-based ABM systems.
1973	Agreement on the Prevention of Nuclear War	Commits superpowers to consult in the event of the threat of nuclear war.
1974	Threshold Test Ban	Restricts underground testing of nuclear weapons over the yield of 150 kilotonnes; broadened in 1976.
1977	Convention of the Prohibition of Military or Any Other Hostile Use of Environmental Modification Techniques	Bans weapons that threaten alteration or modification of the environment.
1979	SALT II (not ratified)	Restricts number of strategic delivery vehicles permitted by both sides.
1987	Nuclear Risk Reduction Centers Agreement	Establishes facilities in both capitals to manage nuclear crisis.
1987	Intermediate-Range Nuclear Force Treaty (INF Treaty)	Eliminates U.S. and Soviet ground-launched intermediate-range nuclear weapons in Europe.
1990	Chemical Weapons Destruction Agreement	Bans further production of chemical weapons and calls for reduction in weapons stockpiles to 5,000 tonnes each by 2002.
1991	START (Strategic Arms Reduction Treaty)	Reduces nuclear arsenals by approximately 30 percent.
1992	START I Protocol	Commits Russia, Belarus, Ukraine, and Kazakhstan to strategic weapons reductions specified in START I.
1993	START II	Reduces strategic nuclear arsenals to 3,000 (Russia) and 3,500 (United States) by 2003; bans multiple-warhead land-based missiles.

of weapons held by the superpowers. The agreements simply introduced restrictions on the numbers of weapons that could be deployed in the future.

However, progress on nuclear arms control was quickly overshadowed when the Reagan administration embarked on a new course. In a speech on March 23, 1983, President Reagan announced a program to develop a defence against ballistic missiles. The idea was not a new one: by the 1960s both the United States and the U.S.S.R. had developed antiballistic missile systems. However, these systems were of doubtful reliability and effectiveness, and in a world of nuclear deterrence, defences could threaten the logic of MAD. Indeed, the 1972 ABM Treaty ensured the dominance of deterrence by banning the development and deployment of missile defences (with the exception of one installation of 100 interceptors). President Reagan proposed a much more ambitious scheme. His Strategic Defense Initiative (SDI) envisioned the deployment of ground and space-based missile and energy weapons of sufficient capability to shoot down incoming missiles and nuclear warheads. SDI would completely protect the United States and would render nuclear weapons, as Reagan put it, "impotent and obsolete."[10] Due to the high-technology aspects of the program, SDI became known popularly as "Star Wars" after the famous 1977 science fiction movie.

SDI had many supporters. As hard as it is to believe today, some analysts in the United States believed that the U.S.S.R. was surpassing the Americans in military power, and missile defences promised to restore U.S. dominance. Others hoped to escape the immorality of MAD and the prospect of a devastating nuclear war. U.S. defence contractors, and many scientific researchers, were naturally supportive of SDI and the billions of dollars in contracts the program promised. Others argued that SDI would strengthen deterrence: faced by both assured destruction and U.S. strategic defences, the U.S.S.R. would never contemplate war. However, there were also many critics of the program, who argued that SDI was technically infeasible, could never be 100 percent effective, was too costly, would start an arms race in space, and would violate the 1972 ABM Treaty.[11] Critics also argued that SDI was destabilizing and could increase the risk of nuclear war. If a U.S. shield were only partially effective (as it certainly would be) then both the United States and the U.S.S.R. would have an incentive to strike first in a crisis. The U.S.S.R. could strike first, firm in the knowledge that a U.S. shield could not stop a massive first attack. However, if the United States were to strike first and damage the Soviet nuclear arsenal, weakening its striking power, SDI might be able to protect the United States from this smaller, less coordinated retaliatory attack. The United States could thus "win" a nuclear war, unless the U.S.S.R. struck first! SDI thus undermined the logic of MAD and made nuclear war more likely.

By the mid-1980s, political developments began to undermine the SDI program. The possibility of a nuclear war receded as the diplomatic relationship between the Reagan Administration and the new Soviet government of Mikhail Gorbachev steadily improved. Arms control once again became a focus of bilateral relations, and in 1987 the superpowers signed the Intermediate-Range Nuclear Forces (INF) agreement, eliminating all U.S. and Soviet medium-range nuclear missile systems in Europe. SDI was quietly shelved, but some research continued, and as we shall see the debate over ballistic missile defences would reemerge in the late 1990s. In July 1991 the superpowers signed the START treaty, which committed both sides to reducing their nuclear arsenals by one-third. This dramatic agreement was made possible largely by the changing climate in the last years of the Cold War. Critics charged that the agreement would reduce the nuclear arsenals of the superpowers only to the levels that existed in 1982, the year the START negotiations began. However, by 1989–91 events were in motion that would dramatically alter the entire context of nuclear arms control.

THE INTERNATIONAL DIMENSION

The Cold War rapidly became a fixture of international politics. Not only was the Cold War an immediate concern in North America and the Soviet Union, it had a visible impact in Latin America, Europe, Africa, the Middle East, and in South and East Asia (for the impact of the Cold War on Canada, see Profile 3.2). Indeed, no region was uninfluenced by the superpower rivalry, and crises occurred with startling frequency. In the early years of the Cold War, tensions were high and confrontations were numerous, including the Soviet refusal to pull out of Iran in 1946 and reports of Soviet involvement in the Greek Civil War. These events

PROFILE 3.2 Canada and the Cold War

Canadian Prime Minister Lester Pearson and American President Lyndon Johnson. Though they had some differences over American foreign policy, particularly with regard to the war in Vietnam, Canada was for the most part a firm ally during the Cold War. (CP Photo.)

Canada was a close ally of the United States and a member of the "Western club" of countries. Some have argued that Canada was a close American ally because it was largely controlled by American interests and capital; essentially, a satellite economy with little real foreign policy autonomy. However, although the flexibility of Canadian governments was limited, Canada adopted the foreign policy it did during the Cold War largely on the basis of an appraisal of Canadian interests in the Cold War world. The reality was that Canada was strategic territory, and any attack on the continental United States would devastate Canada as well. As a result, Canada joined in efforts to deter or prevent war

by participating in NATO and the North American Air Defence (later Aerospace) Agreement. Canada's economy was heavily dependent on a stable international trading system (built by the United States) and on trade with the United States itself. Since Canada is a democratic country, Canadian governments and the majority of the Canadian people were suspicious and even hostile to communism as a political and economic system. In other words, Canada was a status quo state, comfortable with its position in the world under the *Pax Americana* and interested in the prevention of instability or war.

However, this comfort did not mean that Canada did not exert an independent foreign policy. Canada was a strong supporter of the United Nations throughout the Cold War and was a key contributor to UN peacekeeping (which contributed to efforts to prevent regional wars from becoming larger conflagrations that might draw in the superpowers). Canada consistently advocated multilateralism during the Cold War, largely because multilateralism gave it an opportunity to participate in cooperative efforts and institutions, giving Canada a voice in international affairs. Canada also took an independent stand toward Cuba, and established good diplomatic relationships and a positive reputation in much of the developing world. However, successive Canadian governments took care not to alienate the United States; Canadian criticisms of U.S. policy in Central and South America and Vietnam were muted as a result.

SEE R. WHITAKER AND S. HEWITT, *CANADA AND THE COLD WAR* (TORONTO: LORIMER, 2003) AND, FOR AN INTERESTING COLLECTION OF ESSAYS INCLUDING FEMINIST VIEWPOINTS, SEE R. CARELL, ED., *LOVE, HATE AND FEAR IN CANADA'S COLD WAR* (UNIVERSITY OF TORONTO PRESS, 2004).

prompted U.S. President Harry S. Truman to adopt the policy suggestions put forward by **George Kennan**. Kennan, a junior official in the United States' embassy in Moscow, decisively influenced postwar U.S. attitudes toward the Soviet Union. Instructed to analyze the postwar intentions of the Soviet Union, Kennan responded with a famous "long telegram," in which he argued that the U.S.S.R. regarded the United States as its foremost international opponent, and that as long as the United States remained strong, Soviet power could not be secure. In an anonymous published statement of his beliefs in the influential journal *Foreign Affairs* in

1947—the famous "X" article—Kennan argued that the Soviet Union represented a dangerous blend of an autocratic ruler (Stalin), a revisionist and messianic ideology (Marxism-Leninism), and a violent and expansionist history. Kennan recommended the political containment of the Soviet Union until the internal nature of the Soviet Union changed, and, along with it, its foreign policy.[12]

Truman soon declared "that it must be the policy of the United States to support free peoples who are resisting attempted subjugation by armed minorities or outside pressures."[13] This commitment came to be called the **Truman Doctrine**, and was the first articulation of what was to become America's grand strategy during the Cold War: the **containment** of the perceived expansionist and revisionist power of the Soviet Union. The aim of containment was to prevent the spread of communist ideology around the world, to prevent any direct aggression by the U.S.S.R., and to prevent the Soviet Union from expanding its influence in the world. Virtually all U.S. foreign policy action, from foreign assistance to military intervention to diplomacy, was directly related to or influenced by the objectives of containment. Kennan, however, did not support the emphasis placed on military containment. He felt that the Soviet threat was primarily political and that it could not be met entirely by military means.[14] As tensions between the United States and the Soviet Union escalated, further crises followed, including the American decision to establish the Federal Republic of Germany, a communist coup in Czechoslovakia in 1948, the Soviet blockade of West Berlin of June 1948, the communist victory in China in 1949, Chinese coercion against Tibet, numerous Taiwan Strait crises, and the Korean War in 1950. The Cold War era was also characterized by mass decolonization as the former European empires finally crumbled, and both superpowers competed for allies among newly independent countries.

Europe, which would be the focal point of the superpower competition for much of the Cold War, was divided. The concern of the United States and other Western governments was that the Soviet Union might gain control of Western Europe, either through direct conquest or by having Communist parties taking control in the war-devastated region. To prevent this, the United States launched the **Marshall Plan**, a program of U.S. financial assistance to rebuild the economies of Western Europe. The most prominent confrontations of the early Cold War were centred on the status of Berlin. Germany was split into what would become the Federal Republic of Germany (FRG) or West Germany and the German Democratic Republic (GDR) or East Germany. West Berlin, a small enclave of the city controlled by West Germany, was surrounded by East German territory. The Berlin crises of 1948 and 1961, in which the Soviet Union attempted to gain full control of the city, led to armed standoffs, but not to war. Across Germany, a fenced and guarded line—which Winston Churchill called the "iron curtain" in 1946—dramatically symbolized the division of Europe. In 1961, East Germany built the **Berlin Wall**, separating East and West Berlin, and forcibly preventing Berliners from communicating or travelling across this divide.[15]

In 1949, the United States, Canada, and several European allies established NATO, a formal alliance arrangement that solidified the American and Canadian commitment to Western Europe. Throughout the Cold War, half the world's total defence spending would be devoted to the superpower standoff in Europe. It was along the inter-German border that the military forces of NATO (including soldiers from European NATO countries and the United States and Canada) would face the military forces of the Warsaw Pact. In this respect, NATO was a classic alliance, a collective defence arrangement made to counter a common threat. However, NATO also served other functions. First, it guaranteed that U.S. forces would be involved immediately if the Soviet Union attacked Western Europe. NATO thus bound Western Europe and the United States together. Second, NATO also provided for the safe, albeit slow, reintegration

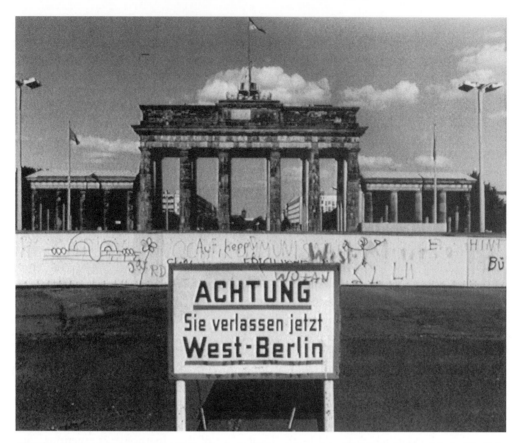

Attention. You are now leaving West Berlin. The Berlin Wall, seen here from West Berlin looking into East Berlin in the background, was a symbol of the Cold War division of Europe and the East–West confrontation. The Brandenburg Gate, at the centre of the picture, was in the zone dividing Berlin. (AP Photo/CP Archive.)

of West Germany back into European politics. West Germany would become a member of NATO in 1951. NATO thus served a collective security purpose, providing confidence that Germany did not pose a threat in Europe. And so, in the iconic (and today perhaps ironic) words of NATO's first Secretary-General, Lord Ismay, NATO was established to "keep the Russians out, the Americans in, and the Germans down."

In China, the nationalists under Chiang Kai-shek and the Communists under Mao Zedong (or Mao Tse-tung) had battled invading Japanese forces during World War II. However, the evacuation of the forces of the defeated Japanese left the nationalists and the communists to battle over control of China. Despite assistance from the United States, Chiang Kai-shek was defeated by the communists and forced to flee to the island of Formosa, which is today known as Taiwan. The United States extended political and security guarantees to Taiwan, and to this day U.S. support for Taiwan remains a source of tension between China and the United States. On October 1, 1949, the People's Republic of China (PRC) was proclaimed. To the capitalist West, the "loss" of China to communism was the first of what have been called the two shocks of 1949 (the second shock was the explosion of the first Soviet atomic bomb). However, ideological differences, distrust, and Chinese resentment of what they perceived as domineering Soviet attitudes led to the Sino–Soviet split of the early 1960s. Thereafter, the Soviet Union and China were geopolitical and ideological competitors in the world. During the rest of the Cold War, the Soviet Union devoted approximately one-third of its military resources to guarding the Sino–Soviet frontier. The two countries also engaged in rhetorical sparring matches, each claiming to represent the true path to communism. The threat posed by Soviet power even prompted China to establish a rapprochement with the United States, which culminated in a visit by U.S. President Nixon in 1972.

In June 1950 the Korean War broke out when communist North Korea attacked South Korea. In response, the United States and 15 allied countries sent military forces to South Korea. This deployment was achieved under the collective security provisions of the United Nations, although in practice the United States dominated both the political and military direction of the war. The U.S.S.R. had walked out of the Security Council over the issue of Chinese representation and so was absent (and could not cast a **veto**) when the decisive vote was taken to give UN authorization to the U.S.-led collective security operation. (The Soviet Union would never walk out of the Security Council again!) As the war progressed, allied forces pushed the North Koreans back toward the Chinese border, with the intent of unifying the country. China then intervened, sending more than 300,000 "volunteers" into North Korea, who pushed allied forces back in retreat. A stalemate followed near the original border along the 38th parallel, and the war ended in a truce in 1953 (see Profile 3.3). The Korean War heightened Western fears of communist expansionism and revealed that conventional wars could still occur in an era of nuclear weapons.

After this period of crisis and the death of Stalin in 1953, the Cold War thawed to some extent. Nikita Khrushchev emerged as the new General Secretary of the Communist Party of the Soviet Union. The first U.S.–Soviet Summit meeting was held at Geneva in 1955. However, the spirit of Geneva did not last long. In 1956, the Soviet Union crushed a rebellion in Hungary. In the Suez Crisis of the same year, Israel, France, and Great Britain invaded Egypt. The European states were clinging to imperial prestige and resented Egypt's **nationalization** of the Suez Canal. The Soviet Union threatened to intervene on behalf of Egypt, one of its allies in the region. The United States, which opposed the actions of its allies in Egypt, compelled them to accept a proposal forwarded by Canadian Foreign Minister Lester B. Pearson for a ceasefire and a UN interpositionary force in the region. Great Britain and France withdrew, and Israel pulled its forces back. Though peace in the region would be short-lived, the

---

PROFILE 3.3 **Canada and the Korean War**

On June 25, 1950, North Korea invaded South Korea. The next day, under U.S. request, the UN Security Council passed a **resolution** calling on member states to respond to halt North Korean aggression. The Canadian government agreed in principle with the U.S. position, but was noncommittal about sending troops. Initial Canadian contributions involved naval vessels and transport planes. Not until August 7 did the St. Laurent government, under criticism at home for its inaction, commit ground troops to Korea. Canada was anxious that the operation in Korea be controlled and managed by the UN. It was thought that multilateral management of the conflict would restrain American impulsiveness. However, the Korean War was fought largely by American and South Korean forces, and the political decision making was dominated by Washington. This situation led to some criticism in Canada that the Canadian government was too closely tied to that of the United States, a critical theme that persisted throughout the Cold War. Canadian troops joined the 27th Commonwealth Infantry Brigade in February 1951 and later formed the 25th Canadian Infantry Brigade Group operating as part of a Commonwealth Division. Canadian troops took part in a number of battles, and by the war's end on July 27, 1953, Canadian troops had suffered 312 killed and 1,577 wounded in what came to be known as Canada's "forgotten war."

SEE J. MELADY, *KOREA: CANADA'S FORGOTTEN WAR* (TORONTO: MACMILLAN, 1983); AND T. BARRIS, *DEADLOCK IN KOREA: CANADIANS AT WAR, 1950-1953* (TORONTO: MACMILLAN, 1999).

Suez Canal crisis signalled the end of European dominance in world affairs, the beginning of superpower management of crises, and the introduction of modern peacekeeping.

Cold War intrigue also spread to the Caribbean, where the United States attempted to overthrow Fidel Castro's revolution by supporting the **Bay of Pigs** invasion by Cuban exiles. The invasion failed, serving only to drive Castro further into the Soviet camp. In 1960, an American U-2 spy plane was shot down over the Soviet Union. These incidents culminated in the 1962 Cuban Missile Crisis in which the United States and the Soviet Union came closer to all-out nuclear conflict than they would at any time during the Cold War.[16] The crisis was precipitated by the construction of medium-range ballistic missile launch sites on the island of Cuba. These sites, built to offset Cuba's strategic inferiority and to help deter another invasion of the island, were detected by U.S. aerial reconnaissance. Soviet merchant vessels carrying missiles were also detected as they sailed to Cuba. U.S. President John F. Kennedy imposed a naval blockade of Cuba to prevent the landing of the missiles and to force the removal of the bases. The world seemed headed toward war when the U.S.S.R. agreed not to station missiles in Cuba in return for an American promise not to invade the island. The fear prompted by the Cuban Missile Crisis led both superpowers to establish closer ties, agreeing in 1963 to a Limited Test Ban Treaty that banned atmospheric nuclear tests, as well as to a Moscow–Washington hotline, and a variety of scientific, cultural, and space and aviation agreements.

However, Cold War competition continued around the world (see Profile 3.4). Both the United States and the Soviet Union supported insurgency movements in the allied and client

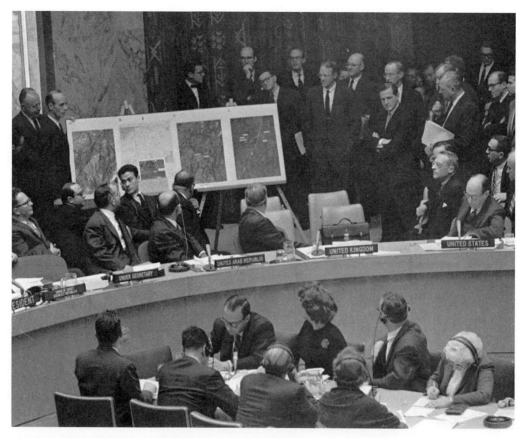

The visual evidence, 1962. The scene in the United Nations Security Council on October 25, 1962, as U.S. Ambassador Adlai Stevenson provides evidence of missile launch sites being built in Cuba. The launch sites were intended for Soviet ballistic missiles aimed at the United States. (AP Photo/CP Archive.)

PROFILE 3.4 The Domino Theory and Other Zero-Sum Views

During the Cold War, successive American administrations committed the United States to combating the spread of communism whenever and wherever it took place, a perspective that was shared to varying degrees in many other Western capitals. This commitment grew from the fear that if one country in a region fell under communist rule, the other countries in that region would also be at risk. Therefore, communism had to be prevented from taking root in even the smallest and remotest of countries. This concept came to be called the *domino theory*, by analogy with dominos stood up on end close together, tipping over one another until all have fallen. The domino theory suggested that communism might spread in the same way: once one country fell, its neighbours would inevitably fall as well. This fear contributed to American efforts to prevent the spread of communism around the world, most prominently in Korea and Vietnam. Another analogy was *salami tactics*, in which the world was represented as a salami. Communism was taking over the world slice by slice, country by country. Yet another instrument was the use of world maps that showed communist countries in red. As more countries fell to communism, more red appeared on the map. This method contributed to the fear that the Soviet Union was "painting the map red." All these conceptualizations were based on a zero-sum view of the Cold War, that a gain for one side was an equivalent loss for the other side, so both superpowers found themselves engaged in struggles for countries whose citizens often knew or cared little about the broader Cold War context.

states of the other superpower. The pattern of support did not necessarily reflect ideological positions. In many cases, the United States supported governments and movements that were authoritarian and undemocratic (though not opposed to the investment of American capitalists), while the Soviet Union often supported governments and movements that could scarcely be called communist. Proxy wars continued, the largest of which occurred in Vietnam, where warfare had persisted since World War II during the painful retreat of French colonialism. In the Vietnam War, the United States backed a succession of authoritarian governments in Saigon against an internal insurgency mounted by the Viet Cong and supported by communist North Vietnam (which in turn was supported by the Soviet Union and China). The United States, concerned with expanding communist influence in Asia, committed itself to preventing a communist takeover in Vietnam.

In the face of continued communist successes in South Vietnam, what was initially a small U.S. involvement (in the form of military advisors) soon escalated to the deployment of more than 540,000 U.S. troops by 1968. However, the U.S. military was designed to fight the Soviet military, not a counterinsurgency campaign against a lightly equipped enemy using the jungle for concealment. In an attempt to use superior firepower to win an insurgency war, the U.S. military conducted a massive saturation bombing campaign against North Vietnam and Cambodia, and made widespread use of chemical defoliants such as Agent Orange and other so-called "rainbow herbicides" to remove the jungle canopy in parts of Vietnam. This was a modern variation of a practice called ecocide: the deliberate destruction of the environment. The use of chemical defoliants in Vietnam also left a legacy of increased rates of disease, cancer, and birth defects for the U.S. soldiers and Vietnamese civilians exposed to these chemicals. However, despite superior technology and firepower, the United States failed to defeat the insurgency. The Vietnam War divided the American public and compelled the Nixon Administration to seek an end to the war. The Paris Peace accords of 1973 led to the withdrawal of all American troops from South Vietnam, which fell to the North in 1975. Approximately 58,000 Americans were killed in Vietnam, and more than one million

Vietnamese perished. The Vietnam War had a profound impact on the American psyche, as many questioned the rightness of the war and were hesitant to support the deployment of U.S. forces in the future. This "Vietnam syndrome" lasted for over a decade, and some suggest that a similar "Iraq syndrome" may be developing in America today.

In 1979 another Cold War crisis erupted when the Soviet Union invaded Afghanistan. U.S. President Jimmy Carter responded by enunciating the Carter Doctrine, which committed the United States to protecting its interests in the Persian Gulf by any means necessary, including military force. He also organized a **boycott** of the 1980 Moscow Olympics, suspended U.S. grain exports to the Soviet Union, and dramatically increased defence spending. The invasion of Afghanistan was to prove as much of a quagmire for the Soviet Union as Vietnam had been for the United States. The Soviet Union was unable to fully suppress Afghan resistance to the invasion, and the Soviet army was to suffer 13,000 dead and 35,000 wounded by the resistance fighters, who were given financial and weapons support from the U.S. through Pakistan. Some of this support would later come back to haunt the United States: among some of the benefactors of U.S. assistance were those who would later rule Afghanistan in the Taliban government. It was this government that provided sanctuary to terrorists, including Osama Bin Laden and Al-Qaeda, the group believed to be responsible for the September 11, 2001 terrorist attacks.

If the invasion of Afghanistan soured U.S.–Soviet relations, the election of President Ronald Reagan in 1980 ushered in a period sometimes referred to as Cold War II. President Reagan and his supporters came to power with a very hostile view of the Soviet Union, which was reflected not only in his public speeches and proclamations (most famously, he repeatedly referred to the U.S.S.R. as an "evil empire") but also in the policies of his administration. The Reagan Administration accelerated the military buildup initiated by President Carter, proposed the development of the Strategic Defense Initiative, and enhanced U.S. support to insurgency movements in Soviet client states (particularly in Nicaragua and Angola). Escalating tensions between Washington and Moscow fuelled increasing concerns about the possibility of war and growing opposition to the nuclear arms race in the form of a growing antinuclear movement.

THE END OF THE COLD WAR: POWER POLITICS DESCENDANT?

The combination of the superpower confrontation during the Cold War, the regional wars that broke out around the world, and the nuclear arms race all served to provide ample ammunition to realists. The Cold War seemed to confirm much of the premise and dynamics of the power politics approach to explaining the international system and international relations. However, as we will explore over the next few chapters, some significant new trends began to take shape in the Cold War world, including the development of an increasingly interdependent world economy, the growth of international institutions and organizations, heightened concern over the environment, increased international travel and communication, and the widening gap between the rich and the poor. These trends began to challenge the accuracy of the realist framework. Nevertheless, it was the end of the Cold War that removed the shadow of the superpower rivalry and brought these trends from the back burner of international relations to the front of the international agenda. Few international events have been as dramatic as the end of the Cold War. The revolutions against communist rule in Eastern Europe, the reunification of Germany, and the collapse of the Soviet Union itself took place within a startlingly short time—from mid-1989 to the end of 1991—and changed the face of global politics. The Cold War ended not with a hegemonic war (as many had feared and anticipated) but with the disintegration of one of the two poles of power. It is crucial to explore the question of why this occurred.

The Soviet Union experienced increased economic stagnation during the rule of Leonid Brezhnev. By the time Mikhail Gorbachev came to power in 1985, the problems facing the Soviet Union were enormous. The economy was performing poorly and in some sectors was actually shrinking. By the 1980s Japan had overtaken the U.S.S.R. as the world's second-largest economy. Soviet central planning had created an economic structure that was inefficient, obsolete, and incapable of meeting the demand for food and even basic consumer items. The Soviet Union's two vital energy resources, coal and oil, were becoming more difficult to extract. The U.S.S.R. had become the world's largest importer of grain, with a quarter of its own crops rotting in the fields because of a poor distribution system. The military budget was absorbing approximately 20 to 25 percent of the country's gross national product (GNP), as well as 33 percent of the country's industrial force, 80 percent of its research and development personnel, and 20 percent of its energy output. In addition, the Soviet Union subsidized its allies, spending more than US$20 billion a year. The workforce suffered from poor morale, with strikes and demonstrations taking place in many cities. Food rationing had to be reintroduced. Life expectancy and infant mortality compared unfavourably with those of the West. The closed nature of the Soviet system, which restricted access to information and controlled television, newspapers, and books, was unable to take advantage of the computer and information revolution.[17]

Gorbachev's solution to these problems was to implement a reform program based on three elements: **glasnost** (openness) to broaden the boundaries of acceptable political discussion; **perestroika** (restructuring) to reorganize the old economic system by introducing limited market incentives; and democratization to increase the involvement of the people in the political process. It was Gorbachev's hope that this program would revitalize the Soviet economy while the Communist Party remained in power. Gorbachev never envisioned that his reforms would fundamentally alter the nature of political power in the U.S.S.R.; he was a reformer, not a revolutionary (see Profile 3.5). To embark on this program of domestic reform, Gorbachev required a favourable international environment. He required good relations with the West to obtain Western aid so that resources could be diverted from military spending to the civilian economy. Gorbachev embarked on a foreign policy that saw him reach out to the West with arms control proposals and summits with Western leaders. He also withdrew Soviet forces from Afghanistan. In so doing, Gorbachev changed the tone of the East–West relationship, and even became something of a celebrity in the West. Gorbachev's arrival on the international scene marked the beginning of the end of the Cold War.

However, Gorbachev's domestic program did not yield the desired results. In fact, the opposite occurred, as the standard of living of the average Soviet citizen actually began to fall. By the end of the 1980s, the contradictions in the Gorbachev reform program were evident. In the attempt to reorganize the economy, the old system was dismantled, while no new legal or reformed banking system was put in place to allow market forces to operate. The result was economic decline, unemployment, and a drop in production. Glasnost served to expose the inefficiencies and corruption of the economic system and increasingly of the government and the Communist Party itself. Within the U.S.S.R., some wanted to slow reform and maintain many of the characteristics of the old economic system, while others wanted to accelerate reform and remove the old system entirely. Gorbachev was increasingly isolated politically between these two factions and his credibility and influence began to wane.

By the late 1980s the end was near. The last gasps of the Soviet Union began in 1989. In a series of revolutions in Eastern Europe—some peaceful, others violent—the ruling communist parties in those states were swept away with no response from Gorbachev. The Berlin Wall, the symbol of the Cold War division of Germany and the division of Europe, was officially opened up on November 7, 1989, although citizens of both countries had been singing

PROFILE 3.5 Mikhail Gorbachev

Hailed in Canada. Former Soviet Union President Mikhail Gorbachev presents the James S. Palmer Lecture at the University of Calgary, October 12, 2000. (CP Picture Archive/Adrian Wyld.)

The last leader of the Soviet Union (from March 11, 1985 to December 25, 1991), Mikhail Gorbachev was the architect of the reform program that initiated a chain of events that was to culminate in the collapse of the U.S.S.R. After studying law in Moscow (graduating in 1955), Gorbachev worked his way through the ranks of the Communist Party organization, eventually becoming responsible for agriculture. He became a full **Politburo** member in 1980, and after the deaths of Brezhnev's successors (Yuri Andropov and Konstantin Chernenko), Gorbachev became General Secretary of the Central Committee of the Communist Party of the Soviet Union. He embarked on an ambitious program of political and economic reform, what he called "the new political thinking" on domestic and foreign policy issues. This reform was dramatically displayed in Gorbachev's approach to arms control, a cooperative relationship with Europe, and a hands-off approach to the Eastern European countries (even when they were throwing off Communist rule).

While Gorbachev's international diplomacy earned him international acclaim and the Nobel Peace Prize in 1990, at home he was increasingly unpopular, and his reform program had unleashed forces that were soon spiralling out of control. Central control over the economy was lost, nationalism spread and intensified, the constituent republics of the U.S.S.R. began to agitate for more autonomy, and the political spectrum in the U.S.S.R. diverged into radical reformers and conservatives. Ultimately, the reform program was rendered obsolete by the political events surrounding the breakup of the Soviet Union.

In retrospect, Gorbachev was one of the great reformers in world history, but his efforts were inadequate in the face of a system that required transformation rather than mere reform. Outside contemporary Russia, Gorbachev is remembered as the Soviet leader who did more than any one individual to make the end of the Cold War peaceful by acquiescing to the freedom of Eastern Europe. However, within Russia, Gorbachev is vilified as the man who caused the collapse of the Soviet Union and increased the misery of the average citizen. The last leader of the Soviet Union remains far more popular abroad than in his own country.

SEE HIS BOOK *GORBACHEV: ON MY COUNTRY AND THE WORLD*, TRANS. GEORGE SHRIVER (NEW YORK: COLUMBIA UNIVERSITY PRESS, 1999).

and dancing on the wall and taking picks and hammers to the Cold War symbol for days. Germany, divided during the Cold War, was reunified on October 3, 1990. The Warsaw Pact, the Soviet Union's alliance system in Eastern Europe, was dissolved. Although Germany and Eastern European countries would now have to struggle with political and economic reform and the legacy of more than 40 years of Communist rule, the Europe of the Cold War had vanished.

People power defeats the Berlin Wall. Germans from East and West Berlin celebrate the fall of the Berlin Wall, November 10, 1989. The wall was removed and the Brandenburg Gate was restored. (AP Photo/CP Archive.)

Within the U.S.S.R., increasing disaffection with the central leadership in Moscow led to demands for an increased devolution of powers to the constituent republics. A new Union Treaty was to be signed on August 20, 1991, that would have weakened the power of the centre. However, on August 19, a coup attempt was mounted while Gorbachev was away on (an apparent) vacation, and an eight-person council took power.[18] The coup failed, largely because key elements of the internal security apparatus and the military refused to support it. Instead, many backed Boris Yeltsin, a former Communist Party official who had been elected Chairman of the Supreme Soviet of the Russian Republic in May 1990 and President of the Russian Republic (the largest of the 15 republics) in June 1991. Faced with public opposition and without control of the army, the coup plotters caved in, and Gorbachev was brought back to Moscow. However, the central government began to simply wither away as governments in the republics gathered increasing power in their own jurisdictions. Gorbachev was quite literally president of a federal bureaucracy detached from the republics and possessing little real authority. The final blow fell with the Ukrainian vote for independence on December 1, 1991, which effectively scuttled attempts to revive a Union Treaty. Declarations of independence from other republics followed. On December 8 the **Commonwealth of Independent States (CIS)** was formed as a coordinating framework for most of the former republics of the U.S.S.R. (only the Baltic States were nonmembers). In the last week of December 1991, the Soviet flag was taken down from the Kremlin in Moscow. The Soviet Union had disintegrated, and the Cold War was over.

PONDERING THE END OF THE COLD WAR

For almost half a century, the Cold War defined global politics. Virtually everything deemed internationally newsworthy was directly or indirectly related to the Cold War, whether it was the announcement of new defence spending projects, the negotiation of a new arms control agreement, or the outbreak of a war somewhere in the world. Everyone feared the ever-present threat of nuclear war and the unspeakable yet certain devastation such a war would bring. Indeed, it is possible to speak of a Cold War generation for whom nuclear annihilation was a constant possibility (it still is, but the threat is much less intense). The Cold War affected domestic politics as well. In the democratic industrialized world, the fear of communism led to suspicion and often suppression of domestic communist movements. In some countries, witch-hunts were conducted to purge government, the arts, and society of communist influences. The most famous of these efforts took place in the United States in 1952–53 under Senator Joseph McCarthy, whose use of accusation and innuendo with no substantial evidence gave rise to the term *McCarthyism*, an extreme example of the general tendency during the Cold War to regard with suspicion those who were sympathetic to or supportive of communism and the Soviet Union (or China). In other countries, anti-communism was used as an excuse to suppress dissident movements, communist or non-communist, often with the larger purpose of maintaining a political and military elite in power. For example, hundreds of thousands of people died in Indonesia as a result of a bloody anti-communist purge by the Suharto government in 1965. In communist countries, political freedoms were almost nonexistent, and state-controlled media emphasized the evils of the capitalist West. The brutal repression of dissent in the Soviet Union and China (and many of their client states) was a vivid illustration of the gulf between the theories and dreams of Karl Marx and the reality of life in most so-called communist states.

The Cold War was the foundation of the foreign policies of most states. Patterns of tension and conflict around the world either originated in the Cold War or were influenced by it. Events such as the Berlin Airlift and the Cuban Missile Crisis were a direct result of Cold War tensions between the superpowers. Conflicts in Africa, the Arab–Israeli wars, the conflicts between India and Pakistan, and wars such as those in Vietnam and Afghanistan had local or regional origins but took on a Cold War dimension through the direct or indirect involvement of the superpowers. At the same time, Cold War considerations also formed the basis for much cooperation among states. This cooperation took a variety of forms, including the creation of alliances aimed at a common enemy (such as NATO and the Warsaw Pact), the sale of arms to client countries, and arms control agreements between the principal antagonists, the United States and the Soviet Union.

Intellectually, the Cold War contributed to a sense of predictability and order in world affairs. The most predominant concern was maintaining a stable superpower relationship and keeping the Cold War cold. A consensus (although by no means universal) emerged in most countries with respect to foreign affairs and defence policy. Broadly supported by their publics, governments maintained their alliance commitments and a certain level of defence spending. In scholarly circles, the Cold War seemed to vindicate much of the realist perspective, and academic work concentrated on issues such as strategic stability, deterrence, and arms control. The Cold War fed an interest in the history and politics of the Soviet Union, and Kremlinology became an important area of study. This does not imply that scholarship during the Cold War was stale or uniform. On the contrary, major theoretical debates took place. An increased interest in economic interdependence fostered the rise of liberal perspectives, and a growing academic voice for and from the Southern Hemisphere pushed theories about imperialism and dependency to the fore.

The Cold War was characterized by periods of high tension, crises, proxy wars, and a conventional and nuclear arms race between the superpowers and their allies. Why did these differences and confrontations not lead to a global war between the United States and the Soviet Union? First among the reasons was the nuclear stalemate between the two countries. The leaders of both countries knew that if a conflict between them developed into a war, there was a very good chance that the war would escalate to the use of nuclear weapons, resulting in a strategic nuclear war that would at the very least devastate both societies. The Cuban Missile Crisis proved to be the catalyst for a growing realization that to avoid a nuclear war, the superpowers would have to manage their relationship more carefully. The superpowers established a hotline between Washington and Moscow to facilitate communication in a crisis. Over time, informal rules were established between the two countries, such as the acknowledgment of spheres of influence in which the other would not overtly interfere and consultation and communication during times of war or crises in regions such as the Middle East and Asia. The leaders of both countries met in summits, arrived at cooperative arrangements such as cultural exchanges and trade agreements, and signed several arms control treaties. All these efforts served to enhance the communication and cooperation between the United States and the Soviet Union and were a reflection of the awareness of both countries that the Cold War had to be kept cold.

Because the end of the Cold War meant the end of conditions that had been so pervasive and all-encompassing, it left a conceptual and intellectual aftershock. Political leaders, scholars, and the public began to ask fundamental questions about the nature of global politics, questions that were seldom asked during the Cold War. Little thought had been devoted to what a post–Cold War world would be like. No plans were made for such an eventuality, and some, like John Mearsheimer, suggested that we would come to miss the Cold War, with its familiarities and certainties.[19] In contrast Francis Fukuyama suggested that the end of the Cold War represented the final triumph of liberal democracy and market economics over authoritarianism and central planning. For Fukuyama, this meant the "end of history," the end of the historical ideological struggle over how human society would be organized.[20] However, in the former communist world, the end of the Cold War was much more traumatic. Economic hardship, social decay, and environmental problems afflicted most of the former Soviet Union and Warsaw Pact countries, and these problems have not been resolved in many of these regions even today.

The collapse of the Soviet Union left many people in Russia wondering what had happened. Post-Soviet Russia embarked on a rapid program of economic reform designed to bring capitalism to the country. The reforms, coupled with the resistance of powerful bureaucratic and industrial interests, caused massive disruptions in the economy. While a few new rich prospered, life for most Russians improved only slightly, and for many it became worse. The sense of pride associated with being citizens of one of only two superpowers vanished, replaced by the country's fragmentation and the humiliation of declining standards of living and an erosion of personal safety in the face of growing crime rates. The formerly well-funded sectors of Russian society and industry were also deeply troubled. A poorly led, poorly prepared, and cash-starved military performed poorly in the suppression of Chechnya, a small region in the Caucasus that sought independence. Scientists who worked in the huge Soviet military-industrial complex struggled to support their families. Some feared that the state of affairs in Russia were disturbingly similar to those that existed in 1920s **Weimar Germany**, and those conditions were instrumental in enabling Adolf Hitler to rise to power. Indeed, the government of the former Russian President Vladimir Putin (who came to power in March 2000) was characterized by an enthusiasm for centralized power, suppression of dissent, control of the media, and disregard for the rule of law. Fear that a new Cold War may be emerging between Russia and the West is discussed in Chapter 13.

WHY DID THE SOVIET UNION COLLAPSE?

Realism has been attacked for its failure to predict the end of the Cold War. However, none of the theoretical frameworks employed by international relations scholars can claim a better record in this regard. We can isolate several factors that offer possible explanations for the fall of the Soviet Union. In general, these factors point to a superpower that was in increasingly dire straits, a superpower that had become a "Potemkin Village" and was facing an unpromising future (see Profile 3.6).

In retrospect, many observers in the West were well aware of the problems facing the U.S.S.R. However, they underestimated the extent to which these forces were undermining the Communist Party of the Soviet Union, which after all could call on massive military forces, a large internal security apparatus, and state control of political and economic life to maintain its power and keep order in the country. The autopsy following the collapse of the U.S.S.R. has yielded the following perspectives and explanations for this dramatic event:

- *A victory for containment.* One explanation is that the grand strategy of containment by the United States worked. The cost of the nuclear arms race, the cost of maintaining a massive military establishment, and the cost of supporting allies in Eastern Europe and overseas bankrupted the Soviet Union. Unable to devote resources to the revitalization of its civilian economy and boost sagging consumer and agricultural production, the U.S.S.R. simply spent itself into its grave. Many realists in the West (particularly in the United States) take this position and argue that the policy of firm containment and high defence spending contributed to the end of the Cold War and a Western victory. In contrast, liberals argue that the containment policies of the West may have prolonged the Cold War. Soviet leaders could use the threat posed by the West as a rallying point for political support and as an excuse to maintain high levels of defence spending and centralized control over the economy. Without an external threat to distract attention from domestic hardships, the U.S.S.R. may have embarked on reform (or even collapsed) far earlier. George Kennan, the original author of containment, argued in 1992 that "the general effect of Cold War extremism was to delay rather than hasten the great change that overtook the Soviet Union at the end of the 1980s."[21]

- *Soviet imperial overstretch.* Another explanation can be found in the theories of power transition and imperial decline. Using the theories publicized by Yale historian Paul Kennedy, this explanation suggests that empires tend to expand until they overstretch

---

PROFILE 3.6 **The Potemkin Village Analogy**

The Potemkin Village analogy originates with the story of a Russian prince named Grigori Potemkin, a favourite of the famous tsarina of Russia, Catherine the Great. Potemkin had helped organize her imperial tour of the southern provinces of the Russian Empire in 1787, taking great efforts to make the tour as spectacular as possible. This effort included the construction of attractive false fronts, or façades, for many of the buildings and towns along the tsarina's route, to impress Catherine with the prosperity of the empire, a prosperity that was at least in part an illusion manufactured by Potemkin. This story is used as an analogy for the state of the Soviet Union by the 1980s, a superpower that was in truth a superpower in military terms only. This façade of strength, while significant, obscured the fact that the Soviet Union was sliding deeper into economic decline, with most of its citizens cynical about the political and economic system and struggling to maintain their meagre standard of living.

themselves. The costs of these commitments burden the economy at home, which undercuts the long-term capacity of the economy to sustain itself. By this explanation, the U.S.S.R. took on too many commitments in the world, which forced it to devote scarce resources to client states such as Cuba, Syria, and Vietnam. The war in Afghanistan burdened the economy even more in the early 1980s. The costs of these commitments drew already scarce resources out of the country, resources that could have been used to reinvigorate the Soviet economy.

- *The economic and social decline of the U.S.S.R.* The most widely accepted explanation of the collapse of the Soviet Union is that the communist system simply did not work very well. The command economy that had been so successful in guiding the rapid industrialization of the Soviet economy later served to hinder reform and innovation. Consumers suffered from shortages of even basic goods and endured long lineups for food items. Industries in the civilian sector turned out poorly manufactured goods developed and built not for the consumer but to fulfill production quotas set by the state. Agricultural techniques stagnated and led to poor distribution and massive waste. Worker morale declined, as exhibited in the famous Soviet workers' proverb: "They pretend to pay us, and we pretend to work." New technologies and techniques could not be absorbed into the Soviet economic system, which became increasingly entrenched in a heavily bureaucratized political system that favoured the elite few—the *nomenklatura*—but was resistant to change. The collapse of the Soviet Union was therefore the result of a failed economic system, one that could not sustain itself, let alone compete with the West, which was entering the electronic and information age.

- *The failure of Gorbachev's reforms.* Another explanation argues that the reform program of Mikhail Gorbachev was the most important reason behind the collapse of the U.S.S.R. Gorbachev sought a middle way to reform between the command economy and market forces. However, no middle way was to be had, and the poorly conceived reform program was doomed from the beginning. This misdirected reform effort made an already bad situation worse, creating such desperation and discontent that the centre lost its grip on power. A different reform program might have succeeded. The Soviet system was badly run down, but in trying to fix the system, Gorbachev broke it.

- *The triumph of democracy and the market.* Finally, liberals argue that the collapse of the Soviet Union represented a victory for democracy and the market as systems of governance. The virtues and advantages of an open political system, the efficiencies of a market economy, and the capacity to innovate and adapt to changing conditions and technology served as a standard against which all other systems were measured. Clearly, the communist system did not measure up. The average Soviet citizen was becoming increasingly aware of the living standards enjoyed in the West, and this was a source of increasing concern and embarrassment to the Soviet leadership. This explanation argues that soft power played an important role in the end of the Cold War.

It is tempting to argue that everything changed when the Cold War ended. However, as we saw in the previous chapter, major historical tidal waves leave both changes and continuities in their wake. From a global perspective, the end of the Cold War can be described as the third defining event of the 20th century, following the shocks of World War I and World War II. Just as the interwar period and the Cold War years saw changes and continuities, so have the post–Cold War years. We will turn to the issues of contemporary global politics in Part Two of this book, but turn now to examine one of the intellectual legacies of the Cold War, the development of foreign policy analysis as a subfield of international relations.

THE STUDY OF FOREIGN POLICY DECISION MAKING

During the Cold War, international relations scholars began to take an interest in how states (and, to a lesser extent, other actors) made foreign policy decisions. This growing interest created a distinct area of study in international relations that continues to fascinate.[22] Scholars had a natural interest in how governments reached decisions that might have devastating consequences, and how the breakdown of decision-making systems due to miscalculation and error might lead to crises or even wars. Scholars working in this area of study borrowed ideas and concepts from psychology (with its interest in motives and perception), economics (which examines the decisions of consumers in terms of tradeoffs and preferences), and business administration (with its interest in efficiency and organizational culture). The field was grounded in rational choice theory, which makes certain controversial assumptions about the decision maker.

In general terms, foreign policy is "the concrete steps that officials of a state take with respect to events and situations abroad … [it is] … what individuals representing the state do or do not do in their interactions involving individuals, groups, or officials elsewhere in the world."[23] Foreign policy can also be described as the public policy of a state implemented in the international environment. However, this definition excludes nonstate actors and the influence of domestic politics. We must remember that nonstate actors, such as terrorist groups, multinational corporations, and humanitarian relief organizations, can make decisions relevant to events and situations in global politics. We also have to be aware that domestic decisions can have foreign policy consequences. In fact, the boundary between domestic and international issues has been eroding steadily. In short, foreign policy decision making often involves more than just the consideration of the actions of governments.

As defined by James Dougherty and Robert Pfaltzgraff Jr., "decision making is simply the act of choosing among available alternatives about which uncertainty exists."[24] The primary concern of decision-making theory is process, rather than outputs or actual decisions. When actors make decisions, these decisions are made in a larger context, which influences the nature of the decision. This context includes:

- *The external environment.* The broader setting in which the decision must be made includes the kind of issue confronting the actor, the position and power of the actor with respect to others, and the influences and pressures that are being exerted on the actor by others.

- *The internal environment.* The domestic setting in which the decision must be made concerns the nature and structure of the political system, the role of key decision makers, the influence of public opinion or interest groups, the influence of domestic political factors (such as elections), and the role of certain bureaucracies in foreign policy decision making.

- *The perceptions of the decision makers.* The perceptual lenses of individual decision makers can have a major influence on decision making. How individuals in the process see the world and the actors in it is a key determinant of actor behaviour.

- *The decision-making process.* The rules governing how decisions are made can be a crucial influence. Is one individual making the decision? Is the decision made by majority vote or the achievement of consensus among a leadership group? Was the decision taken with wide consultation and democratic input?

- *The time constraints.* The temporal setting (the amount of time the decision makers have in which to reach a decision) is crucial. If a decision is required quickly, it will be made in a different way than if the decision involves long-term planning.

In order to analyze foreign policy decisions, students and scholars of global politics must account for this context if they are to have a complete picture of why a decision was made.

An important constraint on students of decision making is access to information. In many cases, vital documents may be held as state secrets, sometimes for decades. Interviews with key decision makers may yield self-serving interpretations of events. Incomplete media reports can lead to erroneous conclusions or the development of conspiracy theories. Propaganda and misinformation may lead analysts astray. As a result, the study of decision making often involves revisions to supposed facts and truths, and reassessments of explanations once thought to be above reproach. Of course, all of this makes it very difficult to engage in analysis of recent decisions. The more recent the decision under analysis, the less information will be available on how the decision was made.

In order to make sense of how decisions are made, a variety of different models have evolved. Two main models of decision making are used, and they offer alternative explanations of how decisions are made by actors in the international system (although they are primarily focused on states). The **rational actor model** argues that decision makers make decisions in a rational fashion. The **bureaucratic politics model** suggests that decision outputs are the result of competition and bargaining among different organizations within government. While many other models are treated in this textbook, including constructivist frameworks for the development of foreign policy, we expand on these two here, since they are most closely associated with the impact of the Cold War on theoretical developments.

THE RATIONAL ACTOR MODEL

Recall that the realist perspective, which dominated academic discourse on international relations during the Cold War, assumes that states are rational, unitary actors. Liberals make the same basic assumption about individuals. In the rational actor model of decision making (also called the *classical model*), decisions are regarded as the product of a largely unified and purposeful process based on considerations of available alternatives aimed at selecting the best option. In other words, decisions are the result of a rational process of choice designed to maximize outcomes. The rational choice process has four steps:

1. *Recognize and identify the problem.* Recognizing that a decision must be made, and identifying the nature of the problem, is the first step in any rational process of decision making.

2. *Establish objectives and aims.* The next step involves considerations of one's goals with respect to the issue at stake. These goals must be established on the basis of judgments about interests and preferences, in addition to expectations about prospects for success.

3. *Establish options.* Next, possible alternative decisions must be formulated and considered in the context of available resources, capabilities, and potential reactions by other actors.

4. *Select an option.* Finally, the best option available—in terms of satisfying the goals of the actor and having the best chance of success—will be selected.

As a result, this model contends that decisions are—or, certainly, should be—the product of a careful cost–benefit analysis process.

As an example, take the decision of the Canadian government under Brian Mulroney to pursue and then sign the Canada–U.S. Free Trade Agreement, which came into force on January 1, 1989. The rational actor model would explain this decision beginning with the belief of the Canadian government that it faced a problem. The problem was a looming crisis in the Canadian economy: the economy could not be competitive in the future or sustain a high living standard for Canadians by serving the small Canadian market. In fact, this was the conclusion of the Macdonald Royal Commission in 1985. With the problem established, the rational actor model suggests the Canadian government would then have developed its objectives, which included developing markets for Canadians products abroad (in order to expand the demand for Canadian products). The government would then have examined its options. Canada could have pursued increased trade liberalization through multilateral trade negotiations. However, multilateral negotiations were slow and cumbersome. Canada might have pursued bilateral trade agreements with Europe or Japan. However, the limited demand for Canadian products in Europe or Japan and the constraint of transportation costs reduced the viability of this option. Another option was to seek a free trade agreement with the United States, the largest market in the world and already the destination of the vast majority of Canadian products. A free trade agreement would secure Canada's access to the U.S. economy, and preempt economic nationalists in the United States from erecting protectionist trade barriers that would shut Canadian products out of the U.S. market. However, there was concern across Canada that signing a free trade agreement would threaten Canadian sovereignty and cultural distinctiveness, and compromise Canadian policies on health and environmental regulations. Finally, the rational actor model suggests that the Canadian government would have weighed the advantages and disadvantages of each option, and then selected the option that it considered best: that option was pursuing a free trade agreement with the United States. The rational actor model thus provides us with one possible explanation of the decision-making process. The next step for the analyst is to test the accuracy of the model, by conducting research to determine whether the Canadian government really did act in this "rational" manner.

However, decision making in the real world can seldom exist in such a pure or comprehensive theoretical form; it is impeded or constrained by a number of factors, a phenomenon is known as **bounded rationality**.[25] The ability of individuals to process information and operate effectively under pressure varies. The information decision makers receive may be incomplete or inaccurate. Decisions may also be made based on **satisficing**,[26] which occurs when decision makers examine their available alternatives until they encounter one that meets their minimum standards of acceptability. They then select that alternative without proceeding to examine any further options, even though better ones may be available. Other decision makers may choose to make small, incremental decisions and so avoid having to undertake a fundamental review of an existing policy or make a decisive decision on a current issue. Finally, decision makers will seldom select an option that carries a high level of risk. Instead, decision makers will bypass such options and decide on those that entail fewer prospects for gains but also fewer risks.[27]

Decision makers are risk-averse rather than risk-acceptant; even Saddam Hussein's decision to invade Kuwait in 1990 may be explained with reference to the idea that he did not realize he risked an American counteroffensive. Time constraints may also force decision makers to make choices under pressure without the advantages of careful deliberation. Indeed, during crises rational decision-making processes tend to break down.[28] Very little time is available to gather information and assess its accuracy, and communications between individuals and groups may be disrupted. Insufficient time may be available to formulate a comprehensive set of options and to consider their advantages and disadvantages. Decision makers tend to fall back on prevailing views or assumptions and ignore or dismiss contrary opinions or information. Stress and sleep deprivation may affect the ability of decision makers to make reasoned choices. Emotions become more intense and are a greater factor in decisions. Mistakes and errors are made with greater frequency, with fewer opportunities to catch and correct them. As a result, at a time when the issues at stake are very important and when the need for an effective decision is most urgent, the decision-making procedures and systems designed to make effective, reasoned outputs might break down. All of these factors suggest that human and organizational variables will compromise the extent to which decisions can be made in a perfectly rational manner. However, decision makers may still be acting rationally, in accordance with the four steps outlined above. The idea that rationality may be bounded does not challenge the rational actor model; it simply reminds us that there are limits to what decision makers can know and how perfectly rational they can be.[29]

Furthermore, government officials do not make decisions in a vacuum. In liberal democracies such as Canada, two variables often have immense influence: interest groups and public opinion. Interest groups comprise individuals who share common perspectives and goals on particular issues and seek to influence the decisions made on such issues. For the leaders of states, these societal interests must often be accommodated, although in practice the influence of various groups and the openness of the political system to such groups vary considerably. Interest groups can take a wide variety of shapes and forms, including political parties, professional associations, business coalitions, labour unions, churches, senior citizens, veterans' groups, and activist organizations such as human rights or environmental groups. These groups engage in two levels of activity: lobbying and public awareness campaigns.

Lobbying occurs when representatives of interest groups meet with decision makers in an attempt to change or influence their views on an issue. In some cases rewards might be offered to the decision maker in return for taking a particular stand on an issue. In countries where corruption is a serious problem, rewards might take the form of bribes or favours of various illicit kinds. In other cases, interest groups might take their case directly to the public in an effort to influence public attitudes and wishes about certain issues. In this way, interest groups can achieve their aim by compelling decision makers to respond to larger public pressure. Public awareness campaigns can take the form of written or electronically disseminated material, protest rallies and marches, Web-based awareness campaigns, and community or "town hall" seminars. For example, nongovernmental organizations raised international awareness of the global land mines problem by using all these techniques. The profile of this campaign encouraged the governments of states such as Canada to respond to the issue with the creation of a global land mines treaty. In practice, interest groups do not always reflect the views of a majority; in fact, many have goals or views that clash with the beliefs or values of broader society (however those might be defined), and wealthy clients can hire lobbyists who are more effective. To return to our example of Canada and free trade with the United States, during the private and public deliberations leading up to the Canada–U.S. Free Trade Agreement, interest groups lobbied the Canadian government in an effort to influence the outcome of the decision. Most (though not all) corporations, business associations, and provincial governments were prominent supporters of free trade, and lobbied the government to reach an agreement. On the other hand, most labour unions, social activist groups, and environmental nongovernmental organizations were opposed to a free trade agreement, or wanted it to address their key concerns (this would occur, to some extent, with NAFTA, signed several years later). And so, one interpretation of the Canadian government's decision to enter a free trade agreement with the United States is the superior lobbying power of Canadian business interests, a power derived from close connections in government and large monetary resources. The influence of interest groups has often been derided as counterproductive and a threat to representative decision making in a democratic society.

Public opinion is a general reference to the range of attitudes held by the people in society. Public opinion is especially important in democratic political systems, although it is not irrelevant in authoritarian systems. To win public support for their foreign policies, governments will launch information or propaganda campaigns. These campaigns can vary considerably, from efforts by governments to explain and justify their actions to blatant distortions and falsifications of evidence. In democratic political systems, public opinion can be gauged through polls, which can influence government action. In some cases, autocratic and democratic governments may embark on a foreign policy venture to increase their popularity or to distract the public from domestic problems. This has been called the "diversionary theory of war" or "wagging the dog," after a popular movie released in the 1990s.[30] An example of this phenomenon is the 1982 Falklands War, in which the military government of Argentina seized Las Malvinas (the Falklands) in an effort to revive its sagging popularity at home. It worked, but only for a short time, as Great Britain retook the islands by force. The Argentine government fell shortly thereafter. The same argument might be applied to the British government of Margaret Thatcher, which was low in the polls before the crisis and may have used the British military response to bolster its domestic popularity.

As any pollster knows, public opinion is rarely monolithic. Frequently, public opinion can be uninformed and tend toward simplistic views and beliefs, which can complicate the efforts of decision makers to explain their policies or the constraints facing the country on a certain issue. As a result, public opinion can send mixed or contradictory signals to government decision makers. Public opinion can also change and influence governments to act in haphazard and unpredictable ways. For example, in 1992 media coverage of the war and famine in Somalia created public opinion pressure on the U.S. government to lead a multinational force (which included Canada) to support the relief effort and end the war. Less than a year later, 18 U.S. soldiers were killed in an ambush and one soldier's body was dragged through the streets of Mogadishu. U.S. public opinion shifted dramatically against U.S. involvement in Somalia, and the U.S. withdrew shortly thereafter. However, it would be a mistake to assume that governments are always at the mercy of swings in domestic public opinion; governments can (and often do) pursue foreign policy actions that either lack a broad base of support or are deeply unpopular.[31] For example, the Spanish and Italian governments both supported the invasion of Iraq in 2003, despite widespread domestic protests. However, the Spanish government was voted out of office in March 2004, as public opposition to its domestic policies grew, especially in the wake of a series of bombings against commuter trains in Madrid, which left 191 people killed and over 1,800 injured.

Nevertheless, public opinion does not have the same level of influence over foreign policy issues that it does over domestic issues. Foreign policy decision makers generally have more autonomy from both public scrutiny and public input, because diplomacy tends to be both less visible and more secretive. Therefore, international affairs is often regarded as the exclusive reserve of a foreign policy elite, composed of elected and unelected government officials, some business elites, journalists, lobbyists, and experts. For this reason, advocates of the rational actor model argue that it remains the best explanation of how decisions get made.

THE BUREAUCRATIC POLITICS MODEL

The bureaucratic politics model makes very different assumptions about the nature of the decision-making process. This model suggests that decision-making outputs do not reflect a process of the rational consideration of alternatives by individuals but rather are the result of the process of competition or bargaining among bureaucratic units with divergent perspectives on the issues.[32] One of the most famous works on decision making was *Essence of Decision: Explaining the Cuban Missile Crisis*, written by Graham Allison in 1971.[33] In his discussion of the bureaucratic politics model, Allison argued that state decisions would be the result of "pulling and hauling" between government agencies. What bureaucratic interests are involved in this process? Governments have become increasingly dependent on foreign policy bureaucracies, which provide a source of expertise on the issues and have the staff and instruments at their disposal to execute the decisions of governments. Many of these bureaucratic units are engaged in the decision-making process. In Canada, for example, the Prime Minister's Office, the Department of Foreign Affairs and International Trade, the Department of National Defence, the Department of Finance, and parliamentary committees have input into foreign policy decision making.

The assumption of the bureaucratic politics model is that those who represent different bureaucratic interests within the decision-making structure will hold different views on the issue confronting the decision makers. This assumption is premised on the idea that where an individual stands on an issue depends on where that individual sits; individuals representing the Department of Foreign Affairs and International Trade may have a very different view of how the Canadian government should act than individuals from the Department of Finance or from the Canadian International Development Agency. Also at stake in this bureaucratic process—whether it involves struggling or bargaining—are the prestige, influence, and perhaps the budget, of the bureaucratic agency.

Another influence that organizations can exert on decision making is through the organizational process by which they implement or execute decisions. The organizational process model suggests that decisions are neither the result of a rational process of choice nor the result of competition or bargaining among bureaucracies. Instead, decision-making outcomes are the result of the constraints imposed on decision makers by the bureaucratic organizations that execute the decisions of policymakers. These constraints come in the form of standard practices or routines called standard operating procedures (SOPs). Because these SOPs reflect what an organization is prepared or equipped to do, they can limit the range of choices available to the decision maker. In other words, the organization responsible for executing a decision may not be capable of performing the desired tasks. In effect, the capabilities, preparedness, and contingency plans of an organization often determine the range of choice available to decision makers.

Returning to our example of the Canadian government's decision to pursue a free trade agreement with the United States, the bureaucratic politics model would explain the decision-making process very differently than the rational actor model. The decision of the Canadian government would have been the outcome of "pulling and hauling" between organizational units of the Canadian government. The Department of Foreign Affairs and International Trade, the Department of Finance, Industry Canada, Natural Resources Canada, the Prime Minister's Office, and myriad other departments and agencies of the Canadian government would have advanced their own positions on the issue of free trade depending on their bureaucratic interests. At the end of the day, the bureaucratic units in favour of a free trade agreement with the United States prevailed. This perspective thus challenges the notion that foreign policy decisions are the result of a process of rational deliberation. Instead, they are the result of bureaucratic and organizational interests engaged in a process characterized by a lack of unity among the key departments and agencies in state governments.

THE INDIVIDUAL, THE GROUP, AND THE ROLE OF PERCEPTION

Perception plays a crucial role in the decision-making process. Perception can have an impact on decision making on two levels: the level of the individual and the level of the group or organization. At the level of the individual, all decision makers have different and often unique life experiences, preconceptions, personal beliefs, value systems, prejudices, and fears that influence their perspective of the world and how they process information about it. As a result, considerable attention has been devoted to the perceptions of individual decision makers and the link between these perceptions and their decisions.[34] This study can be done through content analysis (the exploration of themes in speeches and writings), examinations of personal histories, or the discovery of operational codes in which routine and method act as an influence on personal beliefs.[35] In addition, leadership style can have an important influence on decisions, especially when a single leader dominates the decision-making process.[36]

In short, we all possess perceptual lenses through which we view the world. Individuals examine and process information through these perceptual lenses, which leads to some of the following tendencies in decision making:

- *Worst-case analysis.* Decision makers tend to regard their own decisions as objective responses, while attributing hostile motives to the decisions of others.

- *Mirror imaging.* Decision makers can form similar images of each other ("we are peaceful, they are warlike," etc.) that reinforce mutual hostility. Decision makers can also make the mistake of believing that other decision makers are mirror images of themselves and that they will act in the same manner.

- *Wishful thinking.* Decision makers may have a personal attachment to a certain outcome, and may overestimate the chances of achieving that outcome.

- *Historical analogy.* Frequently, decision makers will employ history as a guide to policy, a process that can be beneficial or counterproductive, depending on the appropriateness of the analogy and the similarities with the current issue.

- *Affective bias.* All decision makers have learned or intuitive preconceptions of issues or actors. Decision makers tend to be more accepting of information that confirms their predispositions and less accepting of information that challenges those preconceptions.

- *Grooved thinking.* Decision makers may categorize information or events into a few basic types, and in some cases information and events may be unsuitably categorized, which can lead to inappropriate foreign policy responses.

- *Uncommitted thinking.* Decision makers may have no opinions on certain issues and questions and may vacillate or flip-flop among different views of the issue and the different options available to respond to it.

- *Committed thinking.* Alternatively, decision makers may have a strong commitment to certain beliefs and views that remain consistent over time and are difficult to change.

At the group level, the dynamics that take place between individuals within a decision-making body (whether it be the foreign policy team of a state or the decision-making body of a nonstate actor) can also influence the decision-making process. In some circumstances, the influence of group dynamics can promote a rigorous and systematic approach to the problem by accounting for a number of individual differences expressed by those in the group. In effect, the group can promote rationality by encouraging deliberation and debate. However, group dynamics may also interfere with the rationality of a decision-making process. Groups can develop shared mindsets or belief systems—in essence, dominant views—that individuals within the group are afraid to challenge. Psychology experiments have shown that when a group of six people are shown two lines on a screen and five of the six people (who are accomplices to the experiment) say that the lines are of equal length when in fact they are not, the sixth individual is likely to agree with the group rather than make the correct assessment. This phenomenon is called **groupthink**.[37] In extreme cases, those who advocate policies at odds with the prevailing view may be ostracized or isolated from the group.

In addition, groups and organizations have their own cultures, perceptual lenses, and value systems, and information and ideas that are in accordance with these belief systems are passed up the organizational ladder. Those ideas that are not in accordance with prevailing views are discarded, subjected to intense scrutiny, and perhaps never passed up the organizational ladder by junior officials, who may try to anticipate what senior decision makers want to hear or read. This is called **anticipatory compliance**.[38] In the wake of the Iraq War, questions have arisen in both the United States and the United Kingdom concerning prewar intelligence reports on Iraqi weapons of mass destruction. Iraq did possess chemical weapons in the 1980s and in fact used them on numerous occasions, especially during the Iran–Iraq War. However, no evidence has yet come to light suggesting Iraq had possessed the vast stocks of chemical and biological weapons that U.S. and British intelligence dossiers claimed it did. This intelligence was a crucial component of the case for war presented by former U.S. President George Bush and former British Prime Minister Tony Blair. Some have accused the two leaders of engineering a deliberate deception in order to gain domestic and international support for the war. Others have suggested that political interference from senior government officials distorted the intelligence reports, and this distorted evidence was presented to the leaders as accurate information. It is also possible that decision makers in both governments experienced groupthink. It is also possible that intelligence officials engaged in anticipatory compliance when passing intelligence information up the ladder to senior government officials. In any case, this example is likely to occupy the attention of many analysts for a long time.

The development of constructivism as a theoretical framework in the study of global politics (see Chapter 1) has increased the attention paid to the role of constructed belief systems in decision making. As David Patrick Houghton points out, "A full appreciation of foreign policy decision making surely requires that we understand both individual construction (cognitive psychological approaches) and collective construction (social construction)."[39] When U.S. President John F. Kennedy and his advisors chose to establish a naval blockade of Cuba during the Cuban Missile Crisis, they did so for a combination of reasons informed by their own individual constructions about what was the best option as well as their wider social constructions about the superpower rivalry and the Soviet threat. When U.S. President George W. Bush and his advisors made the decision to go to war in Iraq, that decision was informed by their individual constructions about Iraq as well as their broader social constructions about the Middle East and America's role in the world. Constructivism thus promises to bring the study of social construction into the wider debate over foreign policy decision making.

The conceptual models of decision making introduced in this chapter can be valuable instruments for students of global politics, as the models can be used to derive alternative explanations for why decisions were made. To use another example, in May 1998, India tested a series of nuclear warheads, tests that established India as a declared nuclear power. Why did India conduct these tests? One explanation is derived from the rational actor model. From this perspective, India tested nuclear warheads because the government felt it was the best option in the face of India's security concerns about Pakistan and China. Furthermore, the tests would bolster India's power and prestige in the world. The tests could also be interpreted as a dramatic signal of India's antipathy toward the Nuclear Non-Proliferation Treaty, which India has long regarded as privileging the Western great powers. Another explanation can be derived from the bureaucratic politics model. From this perspective, the tests were the outcome of competing interests within the Indian state, with the pro-test factions led by the military and nuclear science establishments emerging victorious. Alternatively, the tests could have

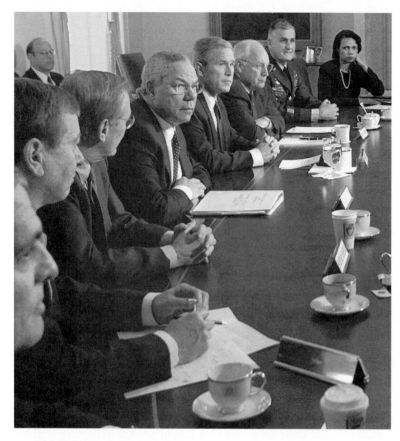

How did this group make decisions? Former U.S. President George W. Bush and his National Security Council meet the day after the September 11, 2001 terrorist attacks on America. From left to right, CIA Director George Tenet, Secretary of Defense Donald Rumsfeld, Secretary of State Colin Powell, President Bush, Vice-President Dick Cheney, Chairman of the Joint Chiefs of Staff General Henry Shelton, and National Security Advisor Condoleezza Rice. Were these individuals rational actors or bureaucratic actors? What were their views of the world, and their perceptions of the attacks that had taken place the day before? (AP Photo/Doug Mills/CP Archive.)

been an effort (and a successful one at that) to appeal to Indian pride and nationalism in order to rally public support behind the new Bharatiya Janata Party government. In other words, the tests might have been driven by domestic political considerations. The same models can be applied to the nuclear tests conducted by North Korea in October 2006 and May 2009. By using these decision-making models to analyze historical and contemporary events, we can gain a richer understanding of the nature of the decisions made in the arena of global politics.

PLAYING GAMES

Yet another instrument used to study the decisions of policy makers is **game theory**, which is further derived from a rational choice model. Game theory is a branch of mathematics concerned with modelling behaviour and outcomes under certain prescribed conditions. Two or more actors are provided with a set of alternative policy choices, and each is provided with a set of payoffs that are dependent on both their policy choice and the policy choices of others. In other words, the expected utility (the payoff or gain) is influenced by the decisions of others. Therefore, the policy choices of the players are influenced not only by their policy preferences but also by their expectations about the policy preferences of others. Game theory attempts to predict the outcomes of games by anticipating the preferences of the players. The outcomes of games can also be affected by altering the payoffs or gains that the actors receive. Some games are zero-sum games in which a loss by one actor is considered a gain for the other. Other games are non-zero-sum games in which it is possible for both players to gain (or to lose).[40]

Game theory is employed by some scholars in international relations to model the behaviour of states under certain conditions. It should not surprise us that realists often employ models that assume rationality and utility maximization. In particular, a game called **Prisoner's Dilemma** is used by realists to demonstrate how the character of an environment can lead actors to make rational, self-interested choices that will actually leave them worse off than if they were to cooperate with one another. The actors in the game do not cooperate because no basis for trust exists among them; this situation is roughly equivalent to the security dilemma discussed in the previous chapter.

Prisoner's Dilemma is the most commonly used game theory model. It is based on a story of two prisoners who have jointly committed a crime, such as armed robbery. The two prisoners are placed in their own cells and are unable to communicate with each other. The prosecutor knows that the two prisoners have committed the crime but requires a confession to get a conviction on the charge of armed robbery. Otherwise, the prosecutor has enough evidence only to get a conviction on the lesser charge of possession of a gun. The prosecutor offers the following deal to each prisoner:

> If you confess, and your partner does not, you will go free and your partner will go to jail for armed robbery for 10 years. If your partner confesses, and you do not, your partner will go free and you will go to jail for armed robbery for 10 years. If you both confess, you will split the penalty for armed robbery, and you will each go to jail for 5 years. If you both do not confess, you will both be convicted for gun possession and will serve a penalty of 1 year.

The game assumes there is no possibility for retaliation, that this is an isolated case, and that the prisoners care only about their own individual interests. Given these payoffs, the outcome of the game is clear: both prisoners will confess to the crime of armed robbery. The logic for such a decision is based on the following calculation of individual interest by each prisoner:

> I should confess, because if I confess and my partner does not, I will go free and my partner will go to jail. If I confess and my partner also confesses, I will still go to jail, but for a shorter term than I would if I didn't confess and my partner did. Under no circumstances should I not confess, for I cannot trust my partner to do the same.

Both prisoners will serve fairly long sentences when they could have served a short one by trusting each other to keep quiet. The Prisoner's Dilemma game can be represented by the following chart:

| | | PRISONER A | |
		Confess	Do not confess
PRISONER B	Confess	5, 5	0, 10
	Do not confess	10, 0	1, 1

This chart, called a *payoff matrix*, illustrates the choices and payoffs facing each prisoner. As you see, if both prisoners confess, they each get five years in prison. If prisoner B confesses and prisoner A does not, prisoner B goes free while prisoner A receives ten years in prison for armed robbery. If both prisoners do not confess, they receive one year in prison for gun possession charges. In international relations theory, this game has been used to illustrate how countries may find themselves in arms races. It is in the interest of both countries not to engage in an arms race, for they will expend vast sums of money and yet end up no more secure than they were before. However, neither country can afford to trust the other by not arming itself, for if one country armed and the other did not, then the country that did not arm would be at a disadvantage. So both countries arm, even though both states would do better to avoid an arms race altogether.

Another game often employed by international relations scholars is called Chicken, drawn from a practice allegedly popular among North American teenagers in the 1950s and immortalized by James Dean in the movie *Rebel Without a Cause*. Two cars are driven toward one another, on a collision course, at high speed on a narrow stretch of road. The first to swerve to avoid the imminent collision is "chicken" and suffers a corresponding drop in prestige. The driver who does not swerve wins an increase in prestige at the cost of the other driver's reputation. If both drivers swerve, they both lose prestige but not as much as they would have if they had swerved alone. If they both do not swerve, they will collide and be killed or seriously injured. As they approach each other, the two drivers may take actions designed to signal their commitment to stay on course, such as accelerating, raising their hands off the steering wheel, or removing the steering wheel and throwing it out the window (entirely removing the ability to swerve).[41] The following payoff matrix applies:

		DRIVER A	
		Swerve	Do not swerve
DRIVER B	Swerve	−2, −2	−5, 5
	Do not swerve	5, −5	−10, −10

This game is used to model international crises in which countries are on a collision course toward war; the country that blinks or backs down first "loses." If neither country backs down, the outcome may be a costly or devastating war.

As mentioned earlier, the study of decision making grew rapidly in popularity among scholars during the Cold War. This interest grew largely because the decisions made in Washington and in Moscow were so significant for the international system. Because decisions made in these capitals could have led to conflict or even nuclear war, a natural interest in the character and dynamics of decision making emerged. The study of foreign policy decision making remains of vital importance today, as analysts and students evaluate the Bush Administration's decision to go to war in Iraq in 2003 and launch the "war on terror," or the Canadian decision to send troops into Afghanistan, but not into Iraq. The foreign policy decisions of the Obama administration, and future Canadian governments, will face similar analytical scrutiny. More than ever, we seek to understand the causes and implications of foreign policy decisions in an uncertain world characterized by influential decisions on war, climate change, trade, poverty, human rights, and myriad other issues.

CONCLUSIONS

This chapter began with an examination of the various themes and dynamics of the Cold War, an omnipresent reality in global politics after World War II, which influenced virtually every aspect of international life. The tense relationship between the superpowers and the nature of the nuclear arms race fuelled the growth of decision-making analysis as a subfield of the study of international relations. However, as we will see in later chapters, the international system began to experience some significant changes in the latter half of the Cold War period, changes that served to challenge the accuracy and applicability of the power politics approach. We now turn to an examination of such changes, including the growth of economic interdependence, and increasing inequality, in the global economy.

Endnotes

1. R. S. McNamara, "The Military Role of Nuclear Weapons: Perceptions and Misperceptions," *Foreign Affairs* 62 (1983), 59–80.
2. J. Isaacs and T. Downing, *Cold War: An Illustrated History* (Toronto: Little, Brown, and Company, 1998), 232.
3. The term *Cold War* originates in the 14th century and refers to the long conflict between Muslims and Christians for the control of Spain.
4. See J. L. Gaddis, *The Long Peace* (New York: Oxford University Press, 1987); and J. L. Gaddis, "Great Illusions, the Long Peace, and the Future of the International System," in C. W. Kegley Jr., ed., *The Long Postwar Peace* (New York: Harper Collins, 1991), 25–55.
5. Quoted in C. W. Kegley Jr. and E. R. Wittkopf, *World Politics: Trend and Transformation*, 5th ed. (New York: St. Martin's Press, 1995).
6. R. W. Tucker, "1989 and All That," *Foreign Policy* 69 (Fall 1990), 94.
7. See D. Smith, *Diplomacy of Fear: Canada and the Cold War 1941–1948* (Toronto: University of Toronto Press, 1988).
8. L. Freedman, *The Evolution of Nuclear Strategy* (London: The Macmillan Press, 1983).
9. For excellent reading on the nuclear arms race see R. Rhodes, *Arsenals of Folly: The Making of the Nuclear Arms Race* (New York: Alfred A. Knopf, 2008).
10. R. Reagan, "Speech on Military Spending and a New Defense," in D. P. Lackey, ed., *Ethics and Strategic Defense* (Belmont, CA: Wadsworth, 1989), 36.
11. For a review of some of the contending perspectives on SDI, see Craig Snyder, ed., *The Strategic Defense Debate: Can "Star Wars" Make Us Safe?* (Philadelphia: University of Pennsylvania Press, 1986); and H. Binnendijk, ed., *Strategic Defense in the 21st Century* (Washington, DC: Center for the Study of Foreign Affairs, 1986).
12. X [George F. Kennan], "The Sources of Soviet Conduct," *Foreign Affairs* 25 (July 1947), 566–82.
13. Quoted in J. L. Gaddis, *Strategies of Containment: A Critical Appraisal of Postwar American National Security Policy* (New York: Oxford University Press, 1982), 64–65.
14. Ibid., 40.
15. For a history of the Berlin Wall, See F. Taylor, *The Berlin Wall: A World Divided 1961–1989* (New York: Harper Perennial, 2006).
16. See M. Dobbs, *One Minute to Midnight: Kennedy, Khrushchev, and Castro on the Brink of Nuclear War* (New York: Alfred A. Knopf, 2008), and L. V. Scott, *The Cuban Missile Crisis and the Threat of Nuclear War: Lessons from History* (London and New York: Continuum Publishing, 2007).
17. D. Mackenzie and M. W. Curran, *A History of the Soviet Union*, 2nd ed. (Belmont, CA: Wadsworth, 1991), 474–75.
18. In a rather embarrassing episode, Canadian government officials decided to reach out to the coup leaders, stating they would communicate with them in the near future.
19. J. Mearsheimer, "Why We Will Soon Miss the Cold War," *Atlantic Monthly*, August 1990, 35–50.
20. See F. Fukuyama, *The End of History and the Last Man* (New York: Free Press, 1992).
21. G. Kennan, "The G.O.P. Won the Cold War? Ridiculous," *New York Times*, October 21, 1992, A21.
22. For a discussion of the development of foreign policy analysis, see W. Carlsnaes, "Foreign Policy," in W. Carlsnaes, Thomas Risse, and B. A. Simmons, eds., *Handbook of International Relations* (London: Sage, 2002), 331–49. See also V. M. Hudson, *Foreign Policy Analysis: Classic and Contemporary Theory* (Lanham, MD: Rowman and Littlefield, 2007).

23. J. N. Rosenau, "The Study of Foreign Policy," in J. N. Rosenau, K. W. Thompson, and G. Boyd, eds., *World Politics: An Introduction* (New York: Free Press, 1976), 16.

24. J. E. Dougherty and R. L. Pfaltzgraff Jr., *Contending Theories of International Relations: A Comprehensive Survey*, 4th ed. (New York: Longman, 1996), 457.

25. H. A. Simon, *Models of Bounded Rationality* (Cambridge, MA: MIT Press, 1982).

26. See H. A. Simon, *Models of Man* (New York: Wiley, 1957).

27. J. S. Levy, "An Introduction to Prospect Theory," *Political Psychology* 13 (June 1992), 171–86. See also Y. Vertzberger, *Risk Taking and Decision-making: Foreign Military Intervention Decisions* (Stanford: Stanford University Press, 1998).

28. M. Brecher, *Crises in World Politics: Theory and Reality* (New York: Pergamon Press, 1993).

29. For a discussion of the role of individual psychology and judgment in decision making, see S. A. Renshon and D. W. Larson, *Good Judgment in Foreign Policy: Theory and Application* (Lanham, MD: Rowman and Littlefield, 2003).

30. See J. S. Levy, "The Diversionary Theory of War: A Critique," in M. I. Midlansky, ed., *Handbook of War Studies* (Boston: Unwin Hyman, 1989), 259–88.

31. For more on public opinion and U.S. foreign policy, see E. R. Wittkopf and J. M. McCormick, eds., *The Domestic Sources of American Foreign Policy* (Lanham, MD: Rowman and Littlefield, 2003).

32. For an overview, see M. H. Halperin, P. Clapp, and A. Kanter, *Bureaucratic Politics and Foreign Policy* (Washington, DC: The Brookings Institution, 2006), and D. A. Welch, "The Organizational Process and Bureaucratic Politics Paradigms: Retrospect and Prospect," *International Security* 17 (1992), 112–46.

33. G. T. Allison, *Essence of Decision: Explaining the Cuban Missile Crisis* (New York: Harper and Row, 1971). See also G. T. Allison and P. Zelikow, *Essence of Decision: Explaining the Cuban Missile Crisis*, 2nd ed. (New York: Longman, 1999); and J. Bendor and T. H. Hammond, "Rethinking Allison's Models," *American Political Science Review* 86 (1992), 301–22.

34. For a discussion of psychological factors in the study of decision making, see J.E.C. Hymans, *The Psychology of Nuclear Proliferation: Identity, Emotions, and Foreign Policy* (New York: Cambridge University Press, 2006), and J. G. Stein, "Psychological Explanations of International Conflict," in W. Carlsnaes, T. Risse, and B. A. Simmons, eds., *Handbook of International Relations* (London: Sage, 2002), 292–308.

35. See R.G.L. Waite, "Leadership Pathologies: The Kaiser and the Fuhrer and the Decisions for War in 1914 and 1939," in B. Glad, ed., *Psychological Dimensions of War* (Newbury Park: Sage, 1990), 143–68; and A. George, "The 'Operational Code': A Neglected Approach to the Study of Political Leaders and Decision-Making," *International Studies Quarterly* 13 (1969), 199–222.

36. See M. G. Hermann, T. Preston, B. Korany, and T. M. Shaw, "Who Leads Matters: The Effects of Powerful Individuals," *International Studies Review, Special Issue* 3 (Summer 2001), 83–131.

37. I. L. Janis, *Victims of Groupthink: A Psychological Study of Foreign-Policy Decisions and Fiascoes* (Boston: Houghton Mifflin, 1972). See also P. A. Kowert, *Groupthink or Deadlock: When Do Leaders Learn from Their Advisors?* (Albany, NY: State University of New York Press, 2002).

38. E. K. Stern and B. Sundelius, "Understanding Small Group Decisions in Foreign Policy: Process, Diagnosis, and Procedure," in P. t'Hart, E. K. Stern, and B. Sundelius, eds., *Beyond Groupthink: Political Dynamics and Foreign Policy Making* (Ann Arbor: University of Michigan Press, 1997), 123–50.

39. D. P. Houghton, "Reinvigorating the Study of Foreign Policy Decision Making: Toward a Constructivist Approach," *Foreign Policy Analysis* 3, no. 1 (January 2007), 42. See also V. Kubalkova, ed., *Foreign Policy in a Constructed World* (Armonk: M. E. Sharpe, 2001).

40. P. Allan and C. Schmidt, *Game Theory and International Relations: Preferences, Information, and Empirical Evidence* (Brookfield, VT: Edward Elgar Pub., 1994).

41. In the movie, James Dean and his opponent race toward a cliff in separate cars; the one who jumps out of the car first loses. The other driver is killed when his door jams and he goes over the cliff. This may be a more appropriate analogy.

Suggested Websites

The Cold War Museum
http://www.coldwar.org/index.html

Center for Defense Information: Nuclear Weapons
http://www.cdi.org/issues/nukef&f/database

The National Security Archive
http://www.gwu.edu/~nsarchiv

The U.S. Nuclear Weapons Cost Study Project
http://www.brookings.edu/projects/archive/nucweapons/weapons.aspx

Cold War International History Project
http://www.wilsoncenter.org/index.cfm?topic_id=1409&fuseaction=topics.home

Political Perspectives on the World Economy

The British taste for tea ... could not have been cultivated in that damp little island had it not been able to export its cheap textiles to Southern Asia, albeit to sell them in captive colonial markets, along with common law, cricket and railways.

—Malcolm Waters

Goodbye to the sovereignty of nation-states. The world dances to the music of money, and the only frontier that matters is the one that separates the gardens of the rich from the deserts of the poor.

—Lewis Lapham

... many people now take an integrated world economy for granted, regard it as the natural state of things, and expect it will last forever. Yet the bases on which global capitalism rests today are not much different from what they were in 1900, and the potential for their disruption is as present today as then. Globalization is still a choice, not a fact.

—Jeffry Frieden[1]

AN INTRODUCTION TO INTERNATIONAL POLITICAL ECONOMY

Historians, economists, and anthropologists alike remind us that long before the advent of the modern state era, the spread of ideas, technology, and culture was facilitated first and foremost by the growth of trade between people in groups ranging in size from small communities to nations and empires. The development of modern capitalism in Europe and its subsequent global expansion established European dominance in the global economy by the 17th century. Following the two world wars and the decline of European imperial power, the United States became the dominant state actor in the world economy, and the leading proponent of liberal economics. Today capitalism remains the primary socioeconomic system, and the principles of liberal economics guide the theory (if not always the practice) behind the economic policies of most states, **international financial institutions (IFIs)** and banks, and corporations. Trade agreements, financial flows, technology, IFIs, and increased communications traffic all suggest the world economy is a place of great convergence, and that increasingly open and competitive global markets are making room for vast improvements in the quality of life on this new "flat earth."[2]

For advocates of liberal economics, the spread of capitalism is seen as a positive phenomenon, bringing greater wealth and quality of life to the world's population and reducing the prospects for war as trade and investment promote international interdependence and cooperation. However, many analysts, students, and activists dispute this view. Critics argue that the world economy is unfair, unstable, and unsustainable. The growth of wealth in some highly protected locales has come at the expense of poverty, dislocation, and violence in other areas, and has uniformly damaged the natural ecosystems on which it is based. The world is increasingly polarized between the rich and poor, and this polarization is at the root of the North–South debate, reflected in different opinions about IFIs; and in diplomatic disputes at international conferences on environmental and development issues. An emergency conference on soaring food prices in June 2008 brought these differences to the fore once again. Many wonder whether there is any long-term hope for those people Paul Collier recently termed the "bottom billion" who live in **absolute poverty**.[3] For neo-Marxists and many other critical theorists, this polarization of wealth is seen as the inevitable outcome of the evolution of global capitalism.

These wildly different visions of the future are at opposite ends of the divide that exists within the field of International Political Economy (IPE). Those who study the vast field of IPE are interested in the relationship between economics and politics at the international level. For example, Robert A. Isaak defines IPE as "the study of the politics behind the economic relations among peoples and nations in order to assess their relative wealth and power."[4] Theodore H. Cohn suggests that IPE is "concerned with the interaction between 'the state' and 'the market.' The state and the market, in turn, are associated with the (political) pursuit of power and the (economic) pursuit of wealth."[5] The famous political economist, Karl Polanyi, once argued that states and markets are analytically inseparable.[6] Thomas Oatley defines IPE as "the study of how economic interests and global processes interact to shape government policies."[7] While many scholars and students of IPE explore the relationship between states and markets, others focus on specific but integral aspects of the world economy, such as the transformational role played by women, the position of trade dependent states such as Canada, or ecological economics. This chapter will begin with an examination of the ascendance of IPE in the study of global politics, followed by a discussion of both mainstream and alternative theories of IPE. We then present a condensed version of the evolution of the world economy, setting the stage for our examination of contemporary IPE issues and debates in Chapter 8. This chapter thus explores the conceptual and historical foundations of the modern world economy, and thus the origins of globalization and marginalization.

ECONOMIC POLITICS ASCENDANT?

We make no attempt here to educate the reader on pure microeconomics or macroeconomics. A wealth of literature written by economists is readily available.[8] Rather, our focus is on the interaction between political and economic forces, forces that are so interwoven that it is often difficult to discern between the two. In fact, any debate on whether politics drives economics or economics drives politics is at least partially artificial. The realm of politics and the realm of economics almost always overlap.[9] The United Nations, for example, is well known as a political institution. Yet, through the work of its development agencies, the World Bank, and the associated **International Monetary Fund (IMF)**, it is certainly an economic actor as well. When the Prime Minister of Canada personally promotes increased trade in the Pacific region, he or she is acting in the capacity of a political actor, although an economic agenda is being followed. At the same time, economic matters can transcend political matters and vice versa. A particularly dramatic example of the separation of commerce from politics occurred in the Crimean War of 1854–56. While England was at war with Russia, London banks floated loans for the Russian government! Today, despite ongoing tensions between the governments of Taiwan and China over the vexing issue of Taiwanese independence, high levels of mutual investment and business cooperation continue.

The study of IPE did not always have a high profile among students and scholars of global politics. Realists characterized IPE as a subject of "low politics" rather than "high politics." From a realist perspective, the two world wars illustrated the dominance of military security issues, and the subsequent Cold War was defined by the geopolitical, military, and ideological competition between the superpowers. Nuclear weapons were thought to have transformed international politics, and it was believed that both conventional weapons and economic dimensions of power would be less important as a result. For realists, international political economy in the postwar period was defined by American economic power, which offered a stable market for world production and provided the foundation for a system of international institutions, regimes, rules, and norms. However, by the latter half of the Cold War, the profile of international economic issues began to increase, and by the 1990s economic issues were arguably the leading priority for most states. The ascendance of political economy issues in global politics can be attributed to the following factors:

- *Increasing global interdependence.* It became visibly evident by the 1960s that economic activity in the form of trade, financial flows, and monetary policies, facilitated by advances in communications technology, was linking the economies of states to an unprecedented extent. This interdependence was reflected in the increased importance of the economic institutions, organizations, and agreements designed to promote economic transactions across states. These organizations became just as prominent as international institutions with military security objectives (and in some instances more so).

- *The decline of the U.S. economy.* For much of the early Cold War, the United States was the world's only economic superpower (the closest competitor was the Soviet Union, with an economy half the size of the U.S. economy). However, in the latter half of the Cold War, the U.S. economy entered a period of what some describe as decline, and many observers concluded that the era of U.S. economic dominance was over. The implications of this decline are still hotly debated, even as a general consensus emerged that the United States was no longer in as dominant an economic position as it had been when the postwar international economic system was established. In the 2000s, the American dollar continues its slide against the euro, the yen, and the Canadian dollar, prompted by concerns about American public debt; and the global financial crisis of 2009 leaves us with similar questions about the role of American leadership.

- *The rise of other state economies.* During the Cold War, other states recovered from the devastation of World War II and became increasingly important actors. The economies of Western Europe and Japan emerged as economic centres of power, and several countries in East Asia—led by the Four Tigers of Hong Kong, Taiwan, Singapore, and South Korea—experienced high levels of economic growth. China's emergence as an economic power in the late 1980s led to much speculation that the Chinese economy may one day rival that of the United States, with dramatic implications for global politics.

- *The rise of multinational corporations (MNCs).* The emergence of MNCs—corporations with operations in several countries—as major economic actors in the world challenged prevailing views about the dominance of states as economic actors. There are over 60,000 MNCs in the world economy, accounting for approximately one-third of world trade. As the size and resources of MNCs grew, so did debates about their impact on global trade and their role in the economic development of poor countries.

- *The oil shock.* In 1960, a group of oil producing states formed the **Organization of the Petroleum Exporting Countries (OPEC)** to coordinate their oil production. Their objective was to resist pressure from consuming countries for lower prices and to ensure steady oil revenues for producers. In 1973, OPEC had a profound influence on international politics through the imposition of an oil embargo against the U.S. and other countries in retaliation for their support of Israel in the 1973 Arab–Israeli War. The embargo caused economic chaos in the United States and other countries, raised the international significance of the oil-producing states, and increased the attention paid to the economic dimension of international relations. Oil remains an important subject in global politics today, with any increases in oil prices affecting all aspects of the global economy, and the issue of climate change raising questions about fossil fuel dependence.

- *European integration.* In 1951, France, West Germany, Italy, Belgium, the Netherlands, and Luxembourg formed the European Coal and Steel Community (ECSC) to coordinate their production and trade policy in these sectors. Buoyed by their success, and mindful of the ongoing need to reinforce cooperation to prevent Franco–German conflict and to strengthen Western Europe against the Soviet threat, in 1957 these six countries established the European Economic Community (EEC). In 1993, an expanded community of 15 states renamed itself the European Union (EU), and on May 1, 2004, ten new states joined the EU, continuing a process that remains the leading example of economic and political integration in the world.

- *Growing awareness of global disparities.* While poverty and wealth disparity predate the modern world economy, the wave of decolonization in the post–World War II period led to the creation of a large number of newly independent countries that for the most part were ill prepared to meet the economic challenges they faced. Beset by high levels of poverty, poor infrastructure, economies dislocated by colonialism, a lack of modern technology, and political instability, these countries were automatically at a disadvantage in the world economy. The wide disparity between the wealth and power of the rich industrialized countries of "the North" and the great majority of **less-developed countries (LDCs)** in "the South" emerged as one of the most serious challenges in global politics, and remains so today.

- *The collapse of the Soviet Union.* The fall of the Soviet Union dramatically illustrated the importance of economics as a foundation for state power. As discussed in Chapter 3, the U.S.S.R.'s decline and eventual collapse were due largely to the failure of its economic system. As well, the fall of the U.S.S.R. removed the military and ideological threat to the West, and as a result economic issues became more prominent on the global stage.

Chapters 2 and 3 focused on a historical and political perspective that emphasized the politics of war and peace. IPE scholars tend to see global history differently. They focus on the relationship between economics, politics, society, and power. However, while this focus unites all scholars of IPE, there are vast differences in their theoretical orientations and how they describe and explain events in the global economy. In Chapter 1, we explored the core differences between these theoretical perspectives, and we now turn to an explanation of how they approach the subject of IPE.

REALIST APPROACHES TO IPE: MERCANTILISM AND ECONOMIC NATIONALISM

In Chapter 1, we explored the foundations of realist thought, with its emphasis on the state and the survival and security of the state in an anarchic international environment. Realist approaches to IPE are consistent with this view of global politics. The state is the most important actor in international economic affairs, and states act to secure and advance their economic interests defined in terms of economic power. This is critical because economic power is regarded primarily as a foundation of state power. Realists argue that states are concerned with **relative gains** in economic strength across states. So, if country A and B both experience gains in wealth (that is, they both experience **absolute gains**) but state A experiences a greater gain in wealth than state B, it is this *relative* gain that matters in terms of the power relationship between these two states. Realists thus tend to see the world economy as a **zero-sum** competition: gains experienced by one state are a proportionate loss to another. Relative gains and economic competition are therefore crucial components of the struggle for survival and power among states.[10]

This focus on the state in IPE does not mean realists completely dismiss the relevance of nonstate actors such as MNCs or NGOs. However, since these actors must operate in an international system with regulations defined by states, nonstate actors do not possess the kind of power or significance that liberals would ascribe to them. Similarly, realists argue that international economic organizations are built and managed by states, especially the most powerful states, and as such are primarily forums for state action and arenas for state competition. Why then do states cooperate on trade and financial matters? For realists, states cooperate because of the need for self-help: when the interests of states converge, cooperation is possible. When the interests of states diverge, cooperation is not possible, and conflict is likely.

The origins of the contemporary realist perspective on IPE can be found in **mercantilism**. *Mercantilism* is a term derived from the writings of Adam Smith, who criticized the economic practices of the mercantile system that prevailed in Europe between 1500 and 1750. Mercantilists argued that the accumulation of gold and silver in a state treasury would provide the foundation for military strength and political influence. In order to accumulate such wealth, states sought not only to acquire more precious metals, but to export more goods than they imported. If they could achieve this, more money would flow into the state compared with that flowing out. Mercantilists were therefore early advocates of **balance of trade** surpluses. The desire to accumulate gold and silver to increase state power also drove European colonialism, as trade surpluses with colonial economies and the precious metals of the colonies helped fill the treasuries of the European imperial states. Today, states remain concerned about the status of their trade balance as well as their balance of payments (see Profile 4.1).

In the wake of the Industrial Revolution, when industrialization and the development of manufacturing capabilities were seen as crucial to state power, mercantilist practices evolved into what today are generally referred to as neomercantilist or economic nationalist practices. Neomercantilists and economic nationalists emphasize the building of state power not through the accumulation of precious metals, but almost entirely through economic practices aimed at generating balance of trade surpluses. This is achieved through the stimulation of

PROFILE 4.1 — The Balance of Payments

The **balance of payments** is an accounting system for recording a state's financial transactions with the outside world. The balance of payments comprises two accounts: the current account and the capital account. The first includes exports and imports of merchandise (cars, radios, CD-ROM drives), exports and imports of services (management consulting, information), investment income and payments (dividends and interest income earned from foreign investments along with payments to foreigners who have invested in the home country), and foreign aid and other transfers (humanitarian relief, loans and grants, the sale of military weapons). The capital account includes short-term and long-term investment inflows (foreign investment in the home state) and outflows (investment abroad). States with a highly troubled balance of payments may borrow money from the International Monetary Fund or sell bonds to make up the difference. One other account is important: a state's official reserves, which represent the foreign currencies, gold, and other financial assets accumulated by its central bank to pay for imports and meet other financial obligations. In 2007, Canada had a balance of payments surplus of $13,607,000,000, down from 20,231,000,000 in 2006. However, this surplus had declined by more than 50 percent through 2008 and early 2009 as the global economic recession hurt Canadian exports. See Statistics Canada, "Canada's Balance of International Payments," http://www40.statcan.ca/l01/estol/econ0la.htm.

domestic production and the promotion of exports.[11] However, a balance of trade surplus can come only at the expense of one's trading partners (who must then have a trade **deficit**). As a result, neomercantilism is often referred to as a **beggar-thy-neighbour** economic policy. Richard Rosecrance suggests that states have evolved into "trading states," intervening in economic affairs to secure trade surpluses and to ensure that national economic interests are protected and promoted.[12] Neomercantilists and economic nationalists also emphasize the importance of advanced industrial development and technological innovation. Put simply, there is a hierarchy of economic activity in the global economy: high-technology industries are preferable to steel or textile industries, which are in turn preferable to agricultural production and natural resource exports. Those states that position themselves as industrial and technological leaders in the world economy will be best placed to maintain and increase their power in global politics.

How do neomercantilists and economic nationalists translate these principles into government practice? In general, states pursuing this approach employ a combination of **protectionism** and export promotion. **Tariffs** are essentially taxes charged to goods as they enter a country, and the cost of the tariff is generally passed on to the consumer, thus making that product more expensive and therefore less desirable compared with a domestically produced alternative. Domestic producers thus benefit, and consumer money stays in the country rather than going to a foreign producer. Today, tariffs are still an instrument of protectionism, but international trade agreements between states have eliminated or lowered tariffs on most products as states try to derive greater economic benefits from trade. This has led to the use of nontariff barriers to trade, which include safety, health, labelling, or environmental standards that may serve to exclude foreign products and shield domestic firms from foreign competition. Nontariff barriers to trade have been a major issue in global trade negotiations, with champions of free trade arguing that international rules need to be put in place so government policies cannot be used as barriers to trade. However, critics of free trade have argued that international trade agreements restricting the use of nontariff barriers place excessive restrictions on government powers and threaten the ability of governments to set appropriate rules for safety, health, and other social standards.

States following neomercantilist practices also employ **subsidies**, government programs that provide direct financing, low-cost loans, or tax exemptions to particular high-value industries in order to encourage their development and their international competitiveness or to protect them from foreign competition. The extensive use of subsidies in the world economy today has led to the use of countervailing duties (taxes imposed on imports from a state accused of using illegal subsidies) and anti-dumping duties (taxes imposed on imports that are allegedly being exported into a foreign market and sold at a price below the cost of production). States can also impose **quotas** on imported products, which serve to limit the number of any given product that is imported into the country. A common practice is for states to negotiate "voluntary" export quotas, in which exporting states essentially agree to voluntarily restrict their exports to a particular country, usually in return for similar concessions from their negotiation partners. Taken together, all of these measures are tools (or weapons) employed by states as they seek economic survival and economic gain in an anarchic world. Of course, states with the greatest economic power will have a structural advantage when wielding these instruments, and will have a greater capacity to influence international organizations and use coercion and reward to further their economic objectives. In reality, most states in the global economy pursue some neomercantilist or economic nationalist policies some of the time. Some states, such as Japan, have been known as especially mercantilist, because they strongly protect their domestic markets, allowing limited goods and services in, while they actively promote their products abroad. Even less mercantile countries such as Canada have maintained high levels of protectionism on some products while promoting exports abroad.

Despite the limited success of the **General Agreement on Tariffs and Trade (GATT)** negotiations in reducing tariffs, the 1970s ushered in a new era of protectionism, which resulted from several events. The boom in oil prices brought on by the OPEC cartel, the shift from fixed to flexible **exchange rates** that occurred as the United States finally gave up its role as the guarantor of international monetary stability, rising competition from export-led industrializing states such as Japan and the newly industrialized countries (NICs), and increased trade subsidies and barriers imposed by the European Economic Community all created a climate of economic uncertainty. A major recession in the early 1980s, brought on partly by another steep rise in the price of oil, further contributed to this uncertainty. Those threatened by job displacement in the industrialized northern states put considerable pressure on governments to slow the pace of trade liberalization and impose protectionist measures to protect vulnerable sectors of the economy. A notable example was the agricultural sector in Western European states. Economic nationalist practices therefore have a powerful domestic constituency in many countries. In difficult economic times, economic nationalist policies become more popular as groups in society look to governments for protection.

Neomercantilists insist that the state is still the primary actor in the global political economy and that MNCs are largely instruments of the states in which they house their headquarters. They also claim that the opening of the world economy to increased trade has led not to a borderless world, as the proponents of globalization proclaim, but to one in which the state continues to act as a protectionist force. Free trade agreements simply reflect the fact that certain states believe that some free trade will benefit them and increase, rather than decrease, the power they wield in the world. As we shall see in Chapter 8, economic nationalism remains an influential perspective in most states, despite ongoing efforts to expand international trade and deepen regional and global free trade agreements. This was especially true in the wake of the economic recession that began in 2008. Anti–free trade movements have maintained or increased their popularity in most countries, supported by individuals and groups concerned about jobs, social programs, culture, and ecology.

LIBERAL APPROACHES TO IPE: CLASSICAL LIBERALISM, KEYNESIANISM, AND INSTITUTIONALISM

The principles of economic liberalism form the foundation of the contemporary global economy, including the international trade system and its related organizations such as the **World Trade Organization (WTO)**. Liberal economics have also determined the shape of the international monetary system. MNCs, as well as smaller firms, conduct their global economic affairs in accordance with liberal market principles. The predominant development strategy directed at LDCs is based on liberal approaches to the generation of wealth and the promotion of economic growth. It is not an exaggeration to suggest that a liberal orthodoxy has dominated the theoretical and policy discourse on global economic affairs.

The foundation of the liberal approach to IPE rests on the work of Adam Smith (1723–90), most specifically in his classic work *An Inquiry into the Nature and Causes of the Wealth of Nations*. Smith's writings were motivated by his opposition to mercantilism, which he argued was not only poor economics, but also a source of "discord and animosity" in international affairs.[13] In contrast, Smith supported the establishment of open markets in which individuals would be free to engage in commerce. The "invisible hand" of unfettered markets could maximize prosperity, and free trade would create "a bond of union and friendship" among nations.[14] From these intellectual beginnings, liberal approaches to IPE emphasize the market and the promotion of individual wealth over protectionism and the accumulation of state power. For liberals, economic actors (whether individuals, firms, or households) will engage in mutually beneficial exchange if given the freedom to do so. While states and their governments will be required to establish laws and enforcement provisions concerning private property and economic transactions, liberals argue that resources are allocated most efficiently through free market activity unburdened by excessive state regulation. Therefore, governments should pursue a hands-off or *laissez-faire* (literally "let do") approach to economic management, permitting individuals, households, and firms the freedom to make their own decisions on economic matters.

Liberals reject the zero-sum-game characterization of realist approaches to IPE, trusting instead that all states can benefit from trade. However, there are significant differences of opinion within the liberal perspective on IPE.[15] We describe these differences in terms of classical liberalism, Keynesianism, and liberal institutionalism.

The Headquarters of the World Trade Organization (WTO) in Geneva, Switzerland. The WTO replaced the General Agreement on Tariffs and Trade (GATT) in 1995, but both were designed to reduce barriers to trade in accordance with liberal economic principles. (AP Photo/Donald Stampfli/CP Archive.)

Classical liberals, like Adam Smith, emphasize *laissez-faire* economic policies and the efficiency of the market in determining the exchange and allocation of money, goods, and resources. Classical liberals are champions of free trade in global politics. In a market-driven international economy, every state will find an economic niche by specializing in the production of goods it can produce most efficiently and trading for those goods it cannot produce efficiently. This **absolute advantage** would mean that every state would gain from free trade with other states. Why waste resources producing goods inefficiently, when you can trade for those goods by selling the goods you do produce efficiently? For example, if Canada can produce wood products more efficiently than India, but India can produce cloth more efficiently than Canada, both countries will benefit from specialization and trade. Each country would no longer be wasting resources on inefficient production. As more and more states engaged in such trade, the collective use of their resources would become more and more efficient, and they would all accumulate greater wealth as a result.

Another classical liberal, David Ricardo (1771–1823) took Smith's logic a step further. Ricardo's work *On the Principles of Political Economy and Taxation* (1817) outlined his theory of **comparative advantage**, which remains the foundation of trade theory to this day.[16] Ricardo's theory of comparative advantage is crucial because it demonstrates why states will and should trade, even if no absolute advantage exists between them. What if state A and state B contemplated a trade relationship, only to find that state A produced *all* goods more efficiently than state B? Would this not mean that neither state would benefit from trade? Ricardo argued that both states could in fact benefit from trade, because state B would still produce some goods comparatively more efficiently than state A. In other words, even though state A produces all goods more efficiently than state B, not all of these goods will be produced with the same margin of efficiency over the goods produced in state B. It is this comparative margin, or difference, that is the basis for a mutually beneficial trade relationship (see Profile 4.2).

Classical liberal economic theory has been challenged in a number of ways. A significant challenge is the unequal distribution of the gains from trade. While liberals typically acknowledge that not all individuals, firms, households, or states will gain equally from free trade, over time these unequal gains can create large asymmetries in wealth and economic development. Another significant challenge to classical liberal economic theory is the widening gap between those who benefit least (the very poor) and those who benefit the most (the very rich). Smith's work was completed before the advent of mobile, transnational capital, which today can usually relocate production processes while seeking the lowest wages, resource prices, and environmental standards. For critics of liberal economic theory, these processes have exacerbated the economic division between the richest and poorest peoples on the planet. Finally, classical liberal economics was never confronted with the large-scale environmental costs associated with free market activity on a global scale. The relationship between environmental degradation and economic growth is now a major point of concern and controversy in IPE.

In contrast to classical liberalism, **Keynesian liberalism** is based on the ideas of John Maynard Keynes (1883–1946). One of the most influential liberal economists of his time, Keynes was critical of both neomercantilism and classical liberal economics.[17] In his view, the classical liberal argument that the pursuit of mutually beneficial exchange in a largely unregulated market would lead to gains for all and society as a whole was flawed. Keynes drew his argument from the experience of the Great Depression, which he believed demonstrated that unregulated market activity would lead to economic instability (such as the 1929 stock market crash) and perpetuate high levels of unemployment (which persisted well into

PROFILE 4.2 Comparative Advantage: An Illustration

To illustrate the theory of comparative advantage, we will use a hypothetical example involving Canada and Mexico (in his *On the Principles of Political Economy, and Taxation,* Ricardo used the example of England and Portugal). We will pick two products (wheat and cloth) and one production input (labour). The table below provides the hypothetical amount of labour (hours of work) required to produce one bushel of wheat and one roll of cloth in Canada and Mexico.

	ROLL OF CLOTH	BUSHEL OF WHEAT
Canada	9 hours	7 hours
Mexico	3 hours	6 hours

Mexico therefore has absolute advantage over Canada in the production of both wheat and cloth, because it requires fewer labour hours to produce both products. However, Canada has a comparatively small labour disadvantage in wheat production, and therefore has a comparative advantage in wheat and Mexico has a comparative advantage in cloth. The two countries can specialize and achieve gains from trade by emphasizing what they produce most efficiently. If Canada were to divert 100 hours of labour from cloth production to wheat production, wheat production would rise by approximately 14 bushels (100 divided by 7), and cloth production would fall by approximately 11 rolls (–100 divided by 9). If Mexico were to divert 50 hours of labour from wheat production to cloth production, cloth production would increase by nearly 17 rolls (50 divided by 3) and wheat production would fall by approximately 8 bushels (–50 divided by 6). So, through greater specialization and trade, Canada and Mexico together produce 6 more rolls of cloth and 6 more bushels of wheat!

	ROLL OF CLOTH	BUSHEL OF WHEAT
Canada	–11	+14
Mexico	+17	–8
Gain	+6	+6

Of course, this is a simplified example. In the complex world of global economics, states have many trading partners, not just one. There are many goods produced, not just two. And there are more inputs into production costs than labour time expended, including social and environmental costs. Nevertheless, this basic concept of comparative advantage forms the foundation of liberal trade theory: in theory, all states benefit from free trade.

the 1930s). This unemployment in turn would lead to a downturn in the economy (because people had less to spend) and a consequent fall in production and investment. In his most important book, *The General Theory of Employment, Interest, and Money* (1936), he challenged the conventional economics of the time, arguing that governments needed to intervene in economic activity to a much greater extent than classical liberals would ever contemplate. Keynes argued that a *laissez-faire* philosophy was harmful during economic downswings and that the state should intervene in the economy, encourage low interest rates, and adopt a fiscal policy that injects money into the economy through increased public expenditure or lower taxes. Keynes's solution to the Depression was for governments to stimulate demand through large public works projects. While this might require running budget deficits in the short term (in effect, governments would borrow money to spend on public works projects) this would benefit society in the long run by increasing employment, and therefore demand, production, and investment. The increased tax revenue generated by a growing economy could then be used to pay off the deficits incurred by government borrowing. In effect, Keynes argued that government intervention in the economy was required to ensure economic

The more, the better? Trade has increased dramatically over the decades, and ports such as Vancouver and Halifax are busier than ever. However, while some economies have benefited from trade, others have not. Gains from trade are unevenly distributed, and environmentalists question the ecological sustainability of economic growth. (CP Photo/Chuck Stoody.)

stability and the larger social good, which could not always be guaranteed by classical liberal economic policy.

Keynes extended his idea to include international economic affairs. He was a critic of the harsh economic prescriptions of neomercantilism. In *The Economic Consequences of the Peace* (1919), Keynes questioned the wisdom of the postwar settlement that imposed heavy reparations on Germany. Although he was generally supportive of free trade, he argued that governments had to be willing to manage such trade, and intervene when necessary to ensure that free trade did not damage domestic employment levels. Keynes thus saw a positive role for restrictions on imports under certain circumstances. International economic activity, he argued, should be managed and planned through multilateral negotiations, in order to ensure international economic stability and the effective coordination of macroeconomic policies. As an economic advisor to the British government, Keynes drafted proposals for the establishment of an International Clearing Union after World War II. In this system, nations with trade deficits would be able to maintain participation in the global economy by drawing on the union, which other states would help fund. The IMF and the **International Bank for Reconstruction and Development (IBRD)** (now known as the **World Bank**) perform a function similar to that of Keynes's proposed union. Although the Keynesian outlook fell into serious disrepute among industrial countries when it was discovered that undisciplined deficit spending by governments led to high levels of public debt, the idea that it is the government's responsibility to create jobs to keep an economy healthy survives, advocated by famous economists such as Canadian-educated John Kenneth Galbraith. Keynes thus established the principles for a more interventionist, managed approach to liberal economics. As Theodore H. Cohn has argued,

> Despite his divergence from liberal orthodoxy, Keynes remained firmly within the liberal-economic tradition, believing in the importance of individual initiative and the inherent efficiency of the market. Greater management, in Keynes's view, would facilitate rather than impede the efficient functioning of world market forces. Thus, Keynes favoured intervention by the government, not to replace capitalism but to rescue and revitalize it. Keynes's views, calling for greater government intervention in the economy, gave rise to the interventionist strand of liberalism.[18]

Finally, **liberal institutionalism** emphasizes the importance of international organizations and regimes in the global economy. We discuss international organizations and regimes in greater detail in Chapter 5, so here we will focus only on the significance of liberal institutionalism in IPE. Regimes are "sets of implicit or explicit principles, norms, rules, and decision-making procedures around which actors' expectations converge."[19] In other words, over time sets of principles, norms, and rules can be established that serve to regulate and guide state behaviour in some issue areas, such as transportation and communication.[20] Liberal institutionalists argue that this desire for coordinating instruments is a logical consequence of cooperation. As states experience gains from cooperation, it is to their mutual benefit to develop mechanisms to govern and regulate their relationship. In IPE, liberal institutionalists point to the creation and rapid growth of regimes established since World War II to regulate economic affairs between states. This wide array of rules determines what kinds of economic activities are allowed or disallowed. Of course, it helps to have these principles, norms, and rules written down, and so it should be no surprise that the world economy is also characterized by a wide array of international agreements, treaties, regulatory agencies, and organizations that serve to manage global economic activity. The relationship between regimes and IGOs is symbiotic. For example, today the WTO and regional trade organizations are part of the global trade regime. These organizations also contribute to the deepening and widening of this regime, as organizations establish new rules and invite new states as members.

For liberal institutionalists, these regimes and organizations matter a great deal, because they serve to entrench liberal economic practices. The greater the cooperation between states, and the more states that participate, the stronger regimes become. States are increasingly bound together in an ever-deepening and ever-widening interdependence, reinforcing the benefits of economic cooperation and the prospects for peace. However, realists and Marxists are less complimentary about the role of regimes. For realists, regimes are merely instruments created and employed by the most powerful states to control international economic activity to their advantage. It is not a coincidence that the United States was the founder and principal maintainer of most of the economic regimes in the world today. On the other hand, Marxists argue that regimes are merely part of the mechanisms of control wielded by economic elites in service of their efforts to exploit others. Like states themselves, regimes and organizations serve the interests of dominant economic classes.

MARXIST APPROACHES TO IPE: DEPENDENCY THEORY, AND WORLD-SYSTEM THEORY

In our discussion of Marxism in Chapter 1, we outlined the core elements of the Marxist approach to global politics. As we have seen, Marxism is grounded by a historical materialist view: economic developments have driven political developments in world history. Marxism is an evolutionary perspective based on transitions from one mode of production to another, holding in common the exploitation of a poor, politically subordinate peasant or working class by a rich, politically dominant landowning or factory-owning class.[21] History is the history of class struggle, as the subordinate class struggles to achieve its liberation from oppression and exploitation. In capitalist systems—the dominant mode of production in modern times—the bourgeoisie (the capitalist class) dominates and exploits the proletariat (the workers). The state is merely an instrument of the bourgeoisie: it is used to maintain their power and privilege, and authorities employed by the state are socialized to adopt conducive values.[22] For Marx, this exploitation cannot end until the capitalist system, the economic foundation of the political order, is overthrown in a revolution of the proletariat that will usher in a classless society free from inequality and therefore free of social conflict.

Karl Marx (1818–83) never developed a comprehensive theory of international politics, but many others have developed Marxist theories of IPE. It was left to activists and theoreticians such as Vladimir Lenin (1870–1924) and Rosa Luxemburg (1870–1919) to build on the work of Marxist and non-Marxist economists (such as John A. Hobson) to develop a theory of imperialism.[23] Marx had predicted that capitalist systems would collapse because of overproduction. As production exceeded demand, employment and wage prospects for the working class would diminish. The proletariat would thus live in growing hardship, and this would eventually spark revolution and the overthrow of the bourgeoisie in the advanced capitalist countries (most notably Germany). However, the revolution did not seem imminent, and Lenin explained this by arguing that the age of European imperialism had delayed the revolution. The colonies of the capitalist states of Europe had brought new sources of cheap labour, raw materials, capital, and new markets to consume products. As a result, the predicted

Still influential. Though few states espouse Marxism as an ideology today, its central proponents continue to inspire political activity around the world. Here, members of the Lebanese Communist Party march through Beirut on May Day, 2008. (AP Photo/Hussein Malla/CP Archive.)

crisis in capitalism had not occurred. However, Lenin argued that once the imperial powers had divided the world between them, their desire for more labour, resources, and markets would drive them into competition and war with each other. In this zero-sum game of competition for imperial possessions, the imperial powers would come into conflict and then engage in war, a war that would precipitate the revolution and overthrow capitalism. Although it was not his own idea, Lenin's theory of imperialism was the foundation for subsequent neo-Marxist work on IPE. The idea that capitalism was extended around the world, and the idea that there was a dominant set of capitalist imperial states that dominated and exploited their colonies, would establish the foundation for dependency theory and world-system theory.

Dependency theory developed in Central and South America in the 1960s, and was almost exclusively concerned with development in relatively impoverished countries (specifically those in Latin America). An important authorial link between Marxism and dependency theory was Paul Baran, who argued that the economic elites in advanced capitalist states used developing states as "source countries" for raw materials and opportunities for corporate profit and investment.[24] Dependency theorists agreed with Baran, pointing to the position of Latin American economies within the economic orbit of the United States, and argued that economic elites in "core" countries such as the

United States kept "periphery" countries such as those in Latin America in a subordinate position of "underdevelopment."[25] This dominance was facilitated by cooperation between Latin American landowners, export merchants, and American economic elites. What dependency theorists called a **comprador** class thus controlled Latin American countries. The interests of these *compradores* were not in the economic development of their country but in the maintenance of their own power and privilege, which was directly linked to the subordinate and exploited status of their country.[26] Although some countries might experience more economic growth than others in this environment, poor countries remained poor by virtue of their subordinate roles in an international capitalist system run by economic elites in core countries, in cooperation with *compradores* in the periphery countries.

Dependency theory was powerfully influenced by the economic and political role of the United States in Latin America before and during the Cold War, which frequently took the form of outright intervention in the affairs of Caribbean and Central and South American countries. For example, the U.S. military occupied the Dominican Republic between 1916 and 1924. Although the occupation came in the wake of successive dictatorships, it also created a political climate favourable to U.S. investment.[27] In another example, the United States engineered the overthrow of the Guatemalan government of Jacobo Arbenz in 1954. Arbenz had been elected in 1950 on a platform of socioeconomic reforms. Fearing (with little justification) that a nationalist, communist regime was taking root, the U.S. Central Intelligence Agency embarked on a campaign of subversion that eventually forced Arbenz to resign and flee the country. The CIA installed Castillo Armas in power, beginning a long period of successive Guatemalan dictators who would be responsible for some of the worst human rights abuses in the Americas. However, the most famous example of U.S. intervention in Latin America involved Chile. In 1970, Salvador Allende Gossens, a self-proclaimed Marxist, was elected president over a candidate favoured by the U.S. government and U.S. businesses in Chile (including Kennecott Copper, Anaconda Copper, International Telephone and Telegraph, and Pepsi-Cola, among others). The Allende government was reviled by the Nixon Administration, both for its rhetoric (which was highly critical of the United States) and for its economic policies (which included the nationalization of some foreign businesses and factories). With the cooperation of U.S. firms, the United States began a campaign to destabilize the Allende government, by cutting off sources of finance and pressuring other countries not to purchase Chilean products. The Chilean economy weakened, and protests began to grow against the government. Finally, in 1973 Allende was overthrown and killed in a military coup led by Augusto Pinochet. The Pinochet regime (which would receive the support of the United States) would go on to become one of the most brutal in South America.[28] Given this record, and the example set by the Cuban revolution, it is not hard to see why dependency theory developed in Latin America, and why it received considerable support in a region that could see for itself what the "core" could do to countries in the "periphery."

World-system theory shares many similarities with dependency theory. The focus of analysis is the world-system, a global economy organized largely according to the logic of capitalism. Much of world-system theory is drawn from the work of Immanuel Wallerstein, who argued that "there is one world system. It is a world-economy and it is by definition capitalist in form."[29] Like dependency theorists, world-system theorists argue that the world is divided between a dominant "core" and an exploited "periphery." As Wallerstein went on to argue, "capitalism involves not only appropriation of the surplus value by an owner from a labourer, but an appropriation of surplus of the whole world-economy by core areas."[30] World-system theorists thus argue that the world economy mimics domestic capitalism on a global scale. Economic elites in the rich industrialized world, using the power of states that they control, dominate and exploit the poor of the world. The instruments of control are the institutions and nonstate actors of the global economy: international organizations and agencies, multinational corporations, and regimes.

World-system theory differs from dependency theory in several respects. First, while dependency theory tends to focus on periphery states, especially those in Latin America, world-system theory examines the entire system, including relations among the core countries. Second, world-system theory allows for some movement by states across the categories of core, periphery, and what world-system theorists call "semi-periphery" countries. These semi-periphery countries are more powerful and economically advanced than periphery countries, and enjoy more autonomy from the core. While semi-periphery countries are still dependent on the core, world-system theorists suggest that countries can on occasion move across these categories, while dependency theorists argued that no periphery countries could escape their subordinate status without revolution. Dependency theory and world-system theory, grounded in the Marxist approach, continue to be relevant perspectives in the contemporary study of IPE. As we shall see, these perspectives play a powerful role informing the views of those critical of liberal theories of progress in developing countries. Many of the antiglobalization perspectives we will explore in Chapter 8 are informed by dependency or world-system interpretations of the global economy.

Finally, many neo-Marxist IPE scholars are influenced by the Gramscian perspective discussed in Chapter 1, and emphasize the significance of the spread of liberal economic beliefs and value systems at the global level. The world political order at any given time in history is determined by the social relations of production, which include not only economic relations but also a set of accompanying beliefs and value systems, reinforced and perpetuated by political, cultural, and social institutions, including formal and informal education systems. In our time, the political order is characterized by capitalism and the accompanying dominance of liberal economic ideas. These ideas have constructed an international hegemonic belief system. Although pockets of active resistance to this liberal orthodoxy exist, the inexorable spread of capitalism is aided by the widespread intellectual acceptance of market values, corresponding legal codes, and the doctrines of economic growth and globalization. The word hegemony is therefore used in a different context here than when employed by realists or liberals. A leading proponent of this view of IPE is the Canadian scholar Robert Cox.[31]

FEMINIST, ECOPOLITICAL, AND CONSTRUCTIVIST APPROACHES TO IPE

From a feminist perspective, the evolution of the global economy has marginalized women and placed them in a condition of economic and social disadvantage and underrepresentation. Discrimination against women is evident across a broad range of economic and social indicators, from land ownership to share of private wealth to equal pay for equal work. Relatively few women are present at the upper levels of the corporate world or the institutions of global economic governance. In contrast, women are disproportionately represented among poor and exploited populations. Feminists also observe that the study of IPE is reflective of patriarchy and the dominance of the male experience in economic matters. Liberal economic theory has emphasized individual self-interest and rational choice, and deemphasized the role of lived experience, differences in power, and other behaviour motivations such as concern for family, community, and social health. These concerns are often more (though not exclusively) the concerns of women and have not been the focus of mainstream economic thought.[32]

Furthermore, economic theory focuses on production and accumulation of money and goods, and the exchange of those goods. Feminists argue that less attention has been paid to reproduction, family, and provisioning, all roles much more associated with women. The result has been the systematic devaluation of home work, child-bearing and -rearing, and serving the family and community, with the consequent devaluation of the status of women in economic and political life. Male and female "jobs" and "work" have thus been viewed differently and rewarded unequally in a male-dominated society. Feminists believe that our notions of what constitutes "production" and the value we associate with "work" have to be changed to achieve gender equality in practice and in economic thought. Feminists also point out that the expansion of global trade has precipitated a deep and often painful social transition in most countries. Issues such as labour and labour mobility, the expansion of the financial and services sector, and the social impact of economic crises are having a very real impact on women and an analysis and response to these issues should include gendered perspectives.

Ecopolitical perspectives in the study of IPE first emerged during the 1960s, when the health and ecological impact of pollution from industry and agriculture became increasingly apparent. Rachel Carson's book *Silent Spring*, published in 1962, detailed the impact of pesticides on the environment and is often credited with starting the modern environmental or "green" movement.[33] The ecopolitical perspective in IPE observes that liberal economic theory does not account for the environmental costs of resource extraction, production, trade, and transportation. In effect, economic growth and development has been decoupled from the ecological costs of economic activity: these costs have been externalized and are not factored in to the final costs of any product or service. In an effort to maximize economic efficiency, businesses and industries actually have a disincentive to protect the environment, because doing so would create costs (for waste treatment, for example) that could make a business or industry uncompetitive. However, untreated waste can have severe impact on the biosphere, local ecology, and human welfare. As a result, on its own the liberal economic system fails to include the importance of ecological endowments that provide the very basis for human, animal, and plant welfare, as well as the existence value of habitat and the world's species. Of course, this criticism can also be applied to other economic systems. During the Cold War, the Soviet Union was steeped in polluting industries and environmentally harmful resource extraction and agricultural practices. The imperatives of industrialization and competition with the West coupled with control of the media and suppression of dissent left little room for the expression of environmental concerns.

The ecopolitical perspective on IPE argues that we must include the environment in our economic calculations, in the costs of doing our business, and in decisions related to what we consume and how we travel. Part of the solution is government regulation and enforcement to ensure that pollution is minimized. However, much of the ecopolitics approach calls for a shift to new models of economic thinking, away from big business and big markets and toward an emphasis on localized and community-based economic activity.[34] Local sourcing for resources and food strengthens community bonds, reduces waste, and minimizes transportation costs. This perspective was best articulated in E. F. Schumacher's famous 1973 book *Small Is Beautiful: Economics as If People Mattered* which called for a new balance between human activity and the environment.[35] The green movement and ecopolitical perspectives on IPE grew in significance with the discovery of the hole in the ozone layer and increased awareness that human activity on the planet was unsustainable. We turn to these issues in Chapter 10, but the global character of environmental issues was beginning to seep into the study of IPE well before climate change emerged as an overarching issue.

Constructivist approaches to IPE focus on the power of concepts and ideas to influence thought and policy. For constructivists, concepts such as the state, the market, and capitalism (among many others) are built on assumptions about a set of patterns and behaviour that are built on contestable foundations. Our ability to think about IPE is clouded by our assumptions of what we think the state, market, and capitalism represent. However, these meanings may differ from person to person or across time and place. Someone living in

Niger or in Belarus is going to have very different views of what the state, the market, and capitalism mean than most people living in Canada or Japan. How can there be eternal truths to comparative advantage, mutually beneficial exchange, or the "invisible hand" of the market if these concepts lack meaning or mean different things to different people? Constructivists also remind us that liberal economic theory and IPE concepts are interwoven into normative assumptions about how markets and capitalism are "good" things to be encouraged and developed, and how economic growth and development are "inevitable" or how there are no alternatives to "globalization." In other words, value systems are inextricably linked with concepts, practices, and historical developments in the study of IPE. The entire discourse of liberal economic theory privileges certain ideas and perspectives over others, creating a dominant perspective that is difficult to challenge. It is this dominant perspective that guides the decision making of key governments and international institutions, a clear illustration of the power of ideas in policy practice. We next briefly discuss one such dominant idea, that of hegemonic stability.

HEGEMONIC STABILITY THEORY AND IPE: IS THE UNITED STATES IN DECLINE?

In Chapter 2, we introduced the theory of hegemonic stability, which holds that a dominant state can exert a stabilizing influence over international affairs, including the management of the world economy. This theory has been one of the most hotly debated and politically significant concepts in the study of global politics since the end of World War II, largely because it has profound implications for the policies (and the very future) of the United States. Although hegemonic stability theory is grounded in realism, there are liberal scholars who support and criticize the theory. In other words, hegemonic stability theory is something of a special case, having won praise and condemnation across theoretical boundaries.

Hegemonic stability theory is grounded in the realist concept of the distribution of power. When one state is so powerful compared to all the others in the system, that state is described as "hegemonic" or a "hegemon." Robert Gilpin characterizes a hegemonic system as one in which "a single powerful state controls or dominates the lesser states in the system."[36] However, the concept of hegemony has been extended beyond the traditional measures of power employed by realists. Wallerstein describes a hegemonic environment as one in which "one power can largely impose its rules and wishes (at the very least by effective veto power) in the economic, political, military, and diplomatic and even cultural arenas."[37] As discussed in the preceding section, Gramscian and constructivist thought extends the idea of hegemony even further to include the dominance of certain ideas and belief systems (such as capitalism and liberal economic theory). Hegemonic states and hegemonic ideas have a symbiotic relationship, each serving to reinforce the dominance of the other. In this way, the status quo is maintained, both in the realm of state power and in the realm of ideas.

In the conventional use of the term, *hegemonic stability theory* holds that the existence of a dominant state, willing and capable of exerting leadership in international economic affairs, is essential for the development and maintenance of a stable international economic order. The hegemon uses its preponderance of power in the system to establish rules, institutions, and regimes, and provides the **public goods** necessary for the maintenance of the system. The implications of hegemonic stability theory are therefore quite stark: when there is no hegemon, or when a hegemon is in decline, the prospects for the creation or maintenance of a stable, open international economic system are poor. As Robert Keohane has argued, "hegemonic structures of power, dominated by a single country, are most conducive to the development of strong international regimes whose rules are relatively precise and well obeyed.... [T]he decline of hegemonic structures of power can be expected to presage a decline in the corresponding international regimes."[38] Some (but not all) liberals regard hegemons as a benevolent presence because the hegemon must be willing to pay a price for its dominant position, and bears a disproportionate share of the burden of maintaining the system.[39] In contrast, realists tend to see the hegemon as more coercive. Neo-Marxists tend to see the hegemon as an exploitative actor, while feminists regard the concept of hegemonic power as emblematic of the focus on very male-centric interpretations of power.

For liberals, hegemons perform two valuable functions that serve to maintain an open and stable international economic order. First, liberals argue that hegemons will provide public goods in order to maintain an open trading system. Public goods (sometimes referred to as collective goods) are goods that, once created, benefit everyone, including those who do not pay to create or maintain the good. Public goods can be used by anyone, and it is difficult or impossible to restrict their use to some while excluding others. Public parks and sidewalks are examples of domestic public goods. For liberals, an open international economy is a public good established and maintained by the current hegemon (the United States) from which all states derive benefit, whether they contribute to its maintenance or not. Second, because public goods can be used by everyone and exclusion is difficult, the natural tendency of all users is to free-ride; that is, to continue to use a public good while contributing nothing to maintain it. Of course, if everyone adopted this approach, the public good (whether a public park, a sidewalk, or the international economic system) could decline into disrepair until it was no longer usable. For liberals, the corrosive impact of free riding on public goods is minimized when a hegemon takes it upon itself to maintain the public good. A hegemon can also reduce free riding by encouraging or threatening other states to bear at least some of the burden of maintaining the good. Therefore, hegemons help to reduce the harmful effects of self-interested free-riding. If there is no hegemon, or a hegemon disappears, free-riding becomes more likely, and the prospects for maintaining public goods become rather poor.

And so, for most liberal economists, the post–World War II United States has carried a disproportionate share of the burden of maintaining the public good of an open, international economic order, from which all other states benefit. Liberals argue that the United States supplies its currency as the central unit of account and reserve in the world economy, and must therefore maintain a money supply that benefits all, not just U.S. interests. The United States must also maintain a relatively open domestic market, even though more cheaply produced goods are free to enter the United States from abroad, thus threatening domestic interests and jobs. In other words, the United States must tolerate balance of trade deficits in order to maintain a global free trade regime. The United States has also had to take the lead coordinating the macroeconomic policies of the world's largest economies, and providing credit as a lender of last resort (via the IMF) when states need to finance deficits or when economic shocks threaten to destabilize the world economy. In short, for liberals a hegemon gives as well as receives in its role, and without U.S. hegemony an open international trading system may never have been built or maintained. However, realists and neo-Marxists have less benevolent views of hegemons. For realists, hegemons maintain their dominant position through the power of reward and threat, and derive a highly disproportionate advantage from this status as compared with any burdens they need to bear. For neo-Marxists, the provision of public goods is merely another instrument of hegemonic control over world capitalism. The hegemon establishes and maintains an open trading system because it is the mechanism through which its elites exert their dominance over structurally disadvantaged countries and the working classes, and transnational economic elites in the periphery collude in this system.

Historically, hegemons rise and decline. The period of British hegemony began to decline in the 1870s and disappeared after World War II. The period of U.S. hegemony began during World War II. Today, the question is whether the United States' hegemonic power is beginning to erode. The question is extremely significant, for two reasons. First, debate over U.S. decline obviously strikes a chord in America, as it calls into question the future of American power, American foreign policy, and America's role in the world; it also has direct implications for Canada, which relies heavily on trade with the United States. Second, the debate over U.S. decline calls into question the future of the international economy, for if the hegemon is in decline, would this not mean the future of the global economic system is in question?

Why do hegemons decline? Periods of hegemony are temporary because of slow but steady changes in the economic fortunes of the most powerful states. Changes in the international distribution of economic power arise from technological innovation and changes in economic efficiency, production costs, and economic competitiveness between states. Eventually, the economic position of a hegemon begins to erode relative to new centres of economic growth and dynamism. Robert Gilpin concludes that "with the inevitable shift in the international distribution of economic and military power from the core to the rising nations … the capacity of the hegemon to maintain the system decreases."[40] In addition, in their effort to maintain the international order, hegemons suffer from what Paul Kennedy has termed "imperial overstretch." Hegemons tend to take on a large number of international commitments, especially military commitments. The investment in these military capabilities draws resources away from economic revitalization and domestic economic development, thus contributing to and even accelerating hegemonic decline. Paul Kennedy's 1987 book titled *The Rise and Fall of the Great Powers* began the enduring debate over U.S. hegemonic decline.[41]

The debate was particularly intense in the 1990s, when the U.S. share of global economic output fell from 50 percent in 1947 to 20 percent.[42] The United States went from being the leading creditor nation to the leading debtor nation, failed to invest in public infrastructure and education, and overstretched itself with large military budgets and extensive overseas military commitments. However, those who disputed the notion that the United States was in decline criticized the declinist thesis. "Revivalists" or "renewalists" argued that the drop in the U.S. share of global output could be explained by the recovery of the war-devastated economies of Europe and Japan after World War II. The U.S. economy was still more than twice as large as any other in the world. As for high levels of U.S. debt, the U.S. economy remained large and robust enough to sustain such a debt burden. U.S. military spending (historically maintained at approximately 3 percent of GDP) was not an unbearable burden (though recent deficit-financed increases related to the "War on Terror" and the Iraq War have reignited this debate). Furthermore, the United States still led the world in cultural influence, innovation, and ideas, and was therefore the world leader in "soft" power.[43] This declinist–revivalist debate continues in the context of the financial and political costs of the Iraq War (see Chapter 6) and the economic damage wrought by the U.S. financial crisis and the related recession (see Chapter 13).

Globalization has brought a new energy to theoretical debates in IPE, and concern over the future of the global economy has never been more widespread. In Chapter 8, we will explore globalization and the theoretical debates that surround it in more detail. But to get there, we need a rough composite of from whence we came. We now turn to a discussion of how the modern world economy developed, and how the principles of liberal economics, in particular, became embedded in the structure and institutions of the contemporary world economy. As we indicated in our overview of civilisations and war and peace in Chapter 2, this is also a necessarily brief discussion and cannot claim to be a complete historical account.

THE EVOLUTION OF THE GLOBAL ECONOMY

Throughout history, groups of people have traded with one another. Trade over wide geographic areas developed around 200 B.C.E. with the rise of the Roman and Han Empires.

Trade flourished within these empires, and luxury goods traded between the empires via the famous Silk Route and by sea routes connecting Indian and Persian ports with those in the Mediterranean. Trade nearly collapsed after the fall of the Roman Empire and the invasion of India and China by "barbarian" peoples. Long-distance trade routes were reopened between 570 and 1000 C.E. With increased trade came the rise of merchant cities such as Bruges, Venice, Baghdad, Samarkand, and Hangchow. A variety of products, ranging from Asian spices to Flemish woollens, were in heavy demand, and merchants began travelling to sell them. As economic activity and wealth grew, demand for exotic luxury items increased. By 1100 C.E., trading centres had been established all over Europe, from Italy to the Baltic, from England as far east as Bohemia. In 1317 the Venetians produced the Flanders galleys, commercial flotillas that made regular passage between the Adriatic and the North seas. In the 1400s, trade flourished in Europe, and financial empires based on international banking rose in importance (for example, the Fuggers of Augsburg and Medicis of Florence).

Extensive long-distance trade did not begin until about 1500. With the adoption of the mariner's compass and improvements in ship design and building, it became possible to sail the open seas, out of sight of land, and still get—roughly—where one wanted to go. The Portuguese were the first to build a sea-based commercial and political empire, but all the major European nations, including the Spanish, Dutch, French, and others, would soon follow. As a result, just as the Westphalian state system was extended through the expansion of the European empires (see Chapter 2), the economic system of Europe was extended around the world in a similar fashion. Through the 1500–1750 time period, the economic principles of mercantilism prevailed, as states sought balance of trade surpluses and the accumulation of gold and silver. Colonialism and mercantilism were thus closely linked, as some overseas colonies provided markets, cheap labour, and resources, and others (especially in Central and South America) provided gold and silver. The economic and trading systems of non-European empires and civilizations initially survived (and even thrived), but increasingly they were reduced to colonial status by the political and economic dominance of the European empires. In this way, the seeds of the current North–South debate were sown.

Asia had long been a source of many highly valued commodities, such as silk and cotton fabrics, rugs, jewellery, porcelains, sugar, and spices (the remarkable rise of Asia-Pacific trade today is not so surprising when we take this historical context into consideration). But the new sea route to the East and the discovery of America in the late 1400s brought a vast increase in trade not only in luxury items but also in bulk commodities such as rice, sugar, and tea. Older commercial activities were transformed by the widening of markets. Spain increasingly drew cereals from Sicily, the Netherlands drew food from Poland, and the French wine districts ate food from northern France. Russia and the Baltic States entered the commercial scene with the growth of shipping and related industries. Trade had become a way of life for many people by the middle of the past millennium.

Arguably, the opening of the Atlantic in the 16th century was the real beginning of a global economy. In this period, the economic dominance of the Mediterranean and the Middle East receded, as western and northern Europe became the new centres of economic activity with trade links to the Americas, Africa, and Asia. The Portuguese and Spanish were the first to profit, and they retained a near-monopoly through most of the 16th century, but their eventual commercial and military decline made room for the British, French, and Dutch empires. However, this economic activity had a dark side. First, the slave trade was one of the largest activities in the world economy. The arrival of European traders in Africa greatly increased the traditional sub-Saharan and Arab slave trades; between 1500 and 1850, white traders forced almost 10 million Africans to the Americas, most of them to the newly opened plantations of the Caribbean, Brazil, and the United States. Second, the colonial powers were adamant about protecting their trade routes and markets. For example, the famous Opium War (1839–42) was caused primarily by British traders, who insisted on trading opium to addicts of the drug in China despite official Chinese protestations. In 1839, opium in British warehouses was destroyed, and in retaliation the British sent warships and troops to attack China's coastal cities (such as Hangchow, Hong Kong, and Canton). Eventually, the victorious British received a $20 million indemnity and temporary colonial possession of Hong Kong, and they opened ports to the opium trade. The Opium War also weakened Imperial China, leaving it vulnerable to demands for treaty ports and trading concessions by Russia, Japan, France, and Germany. Hong Kong was finally returned to Chinese rule at the end of June 1997.

Another great expansion of international trade took place when systems of delivery—ships and trains—acquired new capabilities in the 19th century. As a result of the innovations of the Industrial Revolution, world trade grew threefold between 1870 and 1913, before being curtailed by World War I. Most trade at that time took place between imperial powers and their colonies; the latter would export primary products such as natural resources, and the parent country would export finished products (this pattern of trade persists today in many sectors). Opening up borders to trade was not an easy development, since governments were highly protective of domestic markets and could use the colonies to attain raw materials instead of trade with each other. The defeat of the Corn Laws, which had imposed high tariffs on imports of grain into England, was one of the first major victories for free trade. The Anti–Corn Law League, established in 1838, was composed mostly of industrialists and wage earners, all of whom sought to establish lower corn prices with freer trade. The British landowning aristocracy, however, wanted to protect English agriculture from the onslaught of cheaper, continental products. Pressure from the League and a famine in Ireland ultimately led to the Corn Law's repeal in 1846. Great Britain, by that time an emerging economic state, would become dependent on imports for food and was thus committed to an interdependent global economic system of increased free trade.

However, it was not just the movement of goods that was shaping the emerging global economy. Between 1845 and 1914, some 41 million people migrated to the Americas, especially the United States, from Europe. Others went to Australia and South Africa (see Chapter 11). This migration and the stagnation of industrialized European economies led to the development of the export of capital. British, Dutch, French, Belgian, Swiss, and eventually German investors tried to increase their incomes by buying the stocks of foreign business enterprises and the bonds of foreign businesses and governments. They organized companies of their own to operate in foreign states; and banks began granting loans to each other across the Atlantic. As early as the 1840s, half the annual increase of wealth in Great Britain was going into foreign investments. By 1914 the British had US$20 billion in foreign investments, the French about US$8.7 billion, and the Germans about US$6 billion (these were huge sums of money at the time). The sums went into the Americas, the less affluent regions of Europe, and then after 1890 to Asia and Africa. However, in World War I the British lost about a quarter of their foreign investments, the French about a third, and the Germans everything.

Investment, trade, and monetary policy in the 18th, 19th, and 20th centuries were largely influenced by capitalist principles. Capitalism involves the ownership of means of production and the employment of labourers to produce goods that are then sold on domestic and international markets. As an economic system, capitalism is prone to cycles of boom and depression, the most notable example of the latter being the long depression that set in about 1873 and lasted to about 1893. The growth of capitalism depended partly on the technological changes that ushered in the Industrial Revolution, but in the strict economic sense it was contingent also on a willingness to grant credit and gamble with it. Sometimes this gamble works, in the sense that profits are realized and loans are paid back; other times it does not, and the willingness to loan and gamble recedes. During times of recession, governments began to take a more active role in the economy. Previously, governments had adopted a hands-off or *laissez-faire* approach to their economies, except in the case of tariffs. Governments began taking measures to combat the essential insecurity of private capitalism, adopting additional protective tariffs and social insurance and welfare legislation, and allowing trade unionism to grow in some areas. After 1880, the old orthodoxy of 19th-century unregulated, *laissez-faire* capitalism diminished in an era of interventionist governments.

Investment and trade were both facilitated by the near-universal adoption of the gold standard. England had adopted the gold standard in 1816, when the pound sterling was legally defined as the equivalent of 113 grains of fine gold. This standard led many investors to keep money in London in the form of sterling on deposit. This money, and the military defeat of Napoleon in 1815, established London's reputation as the centre of the world economy and signalled the beginning of Britain's hegemonic status. Western Europe and the United States (the latter was growing into a major economic power, though the American Civil War would forestall this) adopted an exclusively gold standard in the 1830s; a person holding any "civilized" money (pounds, francs, dollars, marks, etc.) could turn it into gold at will, and a person holding gold could turn it into money. Thus citizens from states with different currencies could trade with confidence that the money changing hands could be transformed. Until 1914 exchange rates between the currencies remained very stable, though the gold standard was hard on countries with little gold, and it produced a gradual fall in prices, especially between 1870 and 1900, because (until the gold discoveries in South Africa, Australia, and Alaska in the 1890s) the world's production of gold lagged behind the expanding production of industrial and agricultural goods.

In the 15 years before World War I, world trade increased dramatically. German exports grew more rapidly than British exports at this time, and some historians feel this severe economic competition was one of the primary factors leading to the "war to end all wars." The war would help usher in another economic system, put in place by Lenin's Bolsheviks after the Russian Revolution in 1917 (see Chapter 2). This rejection of capitalism by the Soviet Union produced a wave of fear that other states in Europe or North America might experience a similar revolution. The new Soviet state would pronounce itself owner of all the means of production and, after World War II, would participate in an alternative trade system involving itself and other states based on the socialist economic model.

After World War I, production was at an all-time high, due especially to the mass production of the automobile. However, much of the postwar boom was based on credit and stock market speculation. The Great Depression began as a stock market crisis in New York in October 1929. The crisis was related to speculation; stockbrokers (and many ordinary citizens as well) had purchased large amounts of stock on credit, pushing up stock prices. When prices began to fall, owners of stock had to sell off enough stock to pay back the money they had borrowed, and this snowballed into a huge selloff: between 1929 and 1932, the average value of 50 industrial stocks traded on the New York Stock Exchange dropped from $252 to $61, and 5000 American banks shut down.[44]

As Americans stopped exporting capital and buying foreign goods, world trade decreased. The failure of a leading bank in Vienna in 1931 sent shockwaves across Europe. Massive unemployment was experienced across the globe, and states adopted policies designed to protect themselves. The gold reserve in Britain that had supported the pound sterling declined, and investors converted their pounds into other currencies they felt would be safer. By 1931 Britain had devalued the pound and gone off the gold standard, and other countries soon followed suit. Governments manipulated their currencies to keep up exports (that is, they devalued their currencies, making it cheaper to buy their goods). In response to this global economic crisis, states turned away from multilateral free trade to protectionism, in an effort to insulate their hard-hit industries and labour forces from foreign competition. Tariffs were raised, first by the United States in the famous Smoot–Hawley tariff of 1930 (see below) and then by other countries, which had the effect of almost eliminating trade in some products (such as agricultural products), while quotas were introduced for others. World trade fell from US$35.6 billion in 1929 to US$11.9 billion in 1932. This decline in trade exacerbated the economic crisis and made economic recovery much more difficult and much slower than it could have been. An International Monetary and Economic Conference met in London in 1933, but participants were unable to negotiate a reversal of these restrictions on trade as the world sank deeper into the Depression.

In Germany, Adolf Hitler rose to power on a wave of post-Versailles discontent and tremendous inflation rates. The German economy, in shambles after World War I, did begin to recover as a result of the Dawes Plan. In 1924 an American banker, Charles G. Dawes, proposed a plan under which war reparations would be lowered and bank loans would be extended to Germany to enable it to pay the reduced reparations. Money flowed into Germany from the United States, financing economic recovery and the payment of reparations to Great Britain and France. These reparation payments were in turn used to pay off the debts these countries owed to the United States. The importance of the U.S. economy in this arrangement was

On to Ottawa! Canada did not escape the hardships of the Depression. Thousands of unemployed "rode the rails" in search of jobs. In 1935, many unemployed did so in protest against the conditions in government work camps. Then, as now, there is a direct relationship between economic hardship and political instability. (CP Photo/Toronto Star.)

highlighted in 1929, when the stock market crash stopped the flow of U.S. dollars to Europe. When the Germans could no longer pay their reparations, the British and French could no longer pay their war debts to the United States. To pay these debts, the British and French governments sought to increase their exports to the United States to obtain the needed currency. However, protectionist sentiment (to protect domestic industry) in the United States was high, and the Smoot–Hawley tariff of 1930 raised tariffs against foreign imports to the United States to their highest levels ever. The result was that British and French exports were shut out of the United States. The Smoot–Hawley tariff hampered international trade, blocked collection of war debts, and initiated a chain reaction of protectionism around the world, including the 1932 Ottawa Agreements, which established favourable tariff agreements for the Commonwealth. The Smoot–Hawley tariff also exported the depression to Europe, which, without U.S. dollars, could not finance its debt burdens. The result was economic disaster; businesses closed and unemployment soared. Just as it did in Germany, economic nationalism contributed to political nationalism and the rise of extremist movements, which capitalized on the frustration and resentment over high unemployment and falling living standards. Democratic governments fell in Japan, Austria, and Eastern Europe (with the exception of Czechoslovakia).

The rise of fascism in Spain, Germany, and Italy, and Japanese expansionism in Asia would eventually lead to World War II, but many analysts argue that the effect of the Great Depression and the fall of the multilateral trading system as it had evolved to that point were also partly responsible for the war. During World War II, economic production became war oriented. According to Alvin and Heidi Toffler, the United States manufactured nearly six million rifles and machine guns, more than 300,000 planes, 100,000 tanks and armoured vehicles, 71,000 naval vessels, and 41 billion rounds of ammunition.[45] The United States had built up considerable gold reserves during the 1930s and benefited further from trade with the Allies. As a result, the most powerful military power emerged as the most powerful economic power after the war.

BRETTON WOODS AND THE DEVELOPMENT OF THE WORLD MONETARY SYSTEM

The instability that characterized the interwar period is often attributed to U.S. reluctance to join the League of Nations and provide a leadership role in the world economy. The United States refused to accept the mantle of leadership and fill the void left by the diminishment of the British Empire, which had previously wielded great power within the world economy through the common use of the pound sterling.[46] After World War II the United States emerged as the most powerful economic and military power in the world, especially given the devastation and war-exhaustion of most European and Asian economies. In contrast to the interwar period, the United States was willing to assume the role of a hegemonic power, and to exert leadership in establishing postwar monetary and trade institutions and regimes. In July 1944, even before the end of World War II, representatives of 44 countries met at Bretton Woods, New Hampshire, to construct a stable postwar international economic system. This system came to be called the **Bretton Woods system**, and until 1971 the plans developed at Bretton Woods were to form the foundation of what would be called the **Liberal International Economic Order (LIEO)**, the international economic system of the non-communist world.

The first priority of the Bretton Woods conference was to establish an international financial structure based on fixed currency rates. Floating exchange rates were blamed for the instability and ultimate collapse of the international economy in the interwar period. At Bretton Woods, all countries agreed to fix (or peg) their currencies to the U.S. dollar at a specified rate of exchange and to maintain that rate. The U.S. dollar, in turn, was fixed (or pegged) to gold, at an exchange rate of US$35 an ounce. The United States pledged that it would exchange dollars for gold at any time. As a result, all countries knew the value of their currency in U.S. dollars (and ultimately in gold). They knew this value would not fluctuate unpredictably, because states could borrow from the International Monetary Fund (IMF) (see below) to prevent a weakening of their currency and because any change in exchange rates required international negotiations. As a result, the international monetary system would be predictable and stable. The U.S. dollar became the central unit of account in the international system, used by states to maintain the value of their currency (by using dollars to sell or buy their own currency internationally), to purchase products needed for postwar reconstruction, and to store financial reserves.

The Bretton Woods negotiations also established two institutions to help manage the system and perform central banking functions. The IMF was created to facilitate trade. The IMF had to approve changes in the fixed exchange rate system and possessed a credit fund of US$8.8 billion to lend to countries that were experiencing downward pressure on the value of their currencies. The IBRD, now known as the World Bank, was created to assist war-torn countries in rebuilding their economies by providing short-term financing (see Profile 4.3). Later, both the IMF and the World Bank became prominent lenders to developing countries, a role they still perform today, although not without criticism. In particular, the decision-making systems of both institutions have been accused of being undemocratic and unrepresentative. In the IMF and the World Bank, decisions are made by a vote in the Board of Governors or the Executive Board whose members are nominated (in the former) and elected (in the latter) by member states. The weight of each board member's vote (in effect the weight of each state's vote) is determined by the contribution that state makes to the financial resources of the institution. As a result, the rich developed countries (especially the United States, Japan, Germany, France and Britain) have the greatest influence in the IMF and World Bank and tend to dominate decisions. Together, the IMF and the IBRD are known as the "twin institutions" of the Bretton Woods system. It was clear soon after the war that the Soviet Union, with its commitment to a non-capitalist path, would not participate in the building of the LIEO. It was also clear that all the other states with large economies, most of which required a great deal of reconstruction, were willing to accept American leadership. The United States provided much of the funding for the creation of the United Nations, the IMF, and the IBRD and came to the aid of the Bretton Woods system when it was threatened in 1947.

In 1947, the international problem was a dollar shortage. Quite literally, too few U.S. dollars were circulating in the international system. As discussed above, dollars were in demand for a number of crucial functions, but if enough dollars were not available, what then? More dollars had to be disbursed into the international system if Bretton Woods was to survive. The answer was a massive program of aid to foreign countries so that they would be able to buy the U.S. goods they required for reconstruction. The most famous of these programs was the Marshall Plan, under which 16 Western European countries received more than US$17 billion between 1948 and 1952. The United States also tolerated trade protectionism in Europe and Japan to revive the European and Japanese economies (and thus create more consumers for U.S. products in the future). As a result of the Marshall Plan and trade protectionism abroad, the United States experienced massive balance of payments deficits; that is, more money was flowing out of the country than was coming in. Although this deficit was not a concern in the late 1940s and early 1950s, by the late 1950s it was becoming a problem, and by 1960 the Bretton Woods system was again in trouble.

PROFILE 4.3 The IBRD (the World Bank)

The IBRD (or the World Bank) was established at the Bretton Woods conference in 1944 and is located in Washington, D.C. After the postwar reconstruction of Europe, the Bank began to focus on Southern development. The Bank operates on a weighted voting system, meaning that the more a state contributes, the more say it has in what the Bank does and does not do. Obviously, then, Bank decisions are dominated by the United States, Japan, Germany, and other wealthy states (in 2007, Canada had 2.78 percent of total voting shares). In 1957 the Bank established the International Finance Corporation (IFC) to assist poorer states in obtaining finance from private lenders, and in 1960 the International Development Association (IDA) was established; it makes 35- and 40-year interest-free loans to poorer states (the Bank also includes the Multilateral Investment Guarantee Agency, and the International Centre for Settlement of Investment Disputes). In the 1970s the activities of the Bank accelerated under a campaign to eliminate poverty. However, the Bank's aid was linked to economic and social reforms, many of which harmed the most vulnerable members of society. Critics charge that the Bank has contributed to the perpetuation of poverty by favouring large-scale infrastructure projects that benefit the wealthy and cause environmental damage. The Bank has attempted to reform its policies to account for these negative experiences. Nevertheless, it remains a target of critics who argue that its policies are harmful and counterproductive to development. For example, the Fifty Years is Enough campaign has called for the suspension of all World Bank activities, while the Make Poverty History campaign has called for the restructuring of the Bank to make it more democratic. Today, one of the Bank's core activities is to advance the Millennium Development Goals discussed in Chapter 8. See Department of Finance Canada, *Canada at the IMF and World Bank 2007*, at http://www.fin.gc.ca/bretwood/bretwd07_2e.html.

GATT AND THE DEVELOPMENT OF THE WORLD TRADING SYSTEM

Negotiations on the principles and structure of the postwar trading system began between the United States and Great Britain as early as 1942, with multilateral discussions beginning in 1945. An open trading system was naturally in U.S. interests because it would allow the United States to export products overseas. An open trading system would also allow European and Asian economies to export products to the United States, thus facilitating postwar economic development. There was also an additional interest. Most governments believed the Depression had been prolonged and deepened by protectionism. An open trading system, established by treaty and maintained by the hegemonic United States, would prevent protectionism from stalling economic recovery after World War II. And so, in 1947 the General Agreement on Tariffs and Trade (GATT) was established. GATT was a treaty binding its members to certain rules concerning international commerce. Only 23 countries attended the first GATT conferences in 1947. Originally, the authors of the Bretton Woods system had intended to establish a powerful International Trade Organization (ITO). However, the U.S. Congress objected to an exception for imperial trading systems, which effectively killed the ITO proposal. The GATT system proceeded without the ITO, focusing on a series of trade negotiations. The aim of GATT was to increase trade liberalization. For its part, Canada was an avid supporter of the GATT regime.[47]

GATT was initially designed to promote trade liberalization in two ways. First, because it was an intergovernmental process, GATT provided an important forum for states to negotiate reductions in barriers to trade. GATT was an ongoing process and provided a steadily expanding body of rules and agreements to build upon as more states joined the GATT process (see Profile 4.4). Second, GATT established (and continually developed) sets of norms and rules governing international trade. For the first 30 years of GATT's existence, these norms and rules focused on the reduction of tariffs. Tariffs are essentially taxes imposed by governments on goods originating in another country. In other words, tariffs are taxes on imports. The costs of these taxes are passed on to the domestic consumer in the form of a higher price for the good, making the imported good more expensive and therefore less desirable. Tariffs thus discourage trade. And so GATT emphasized the negotiated reduction of tariffs. The average tariff on a manufactured good among the governments belonging to GATT after World War II was 40 percent. After successive negotiations in GATT, in the early 1970s the average tariff on manufactured goods had fallen to 9 percent.[48] The result was an increase in trade among GATT countries as falling tariffs led to falling prices for imported manufactured goods, which in turn increased demand for imported and exported products.

In order to ensure that the GATT system was fair, GATT rules included the principles of **nondiscrimination** and **reciprocity**. The principle of nondiscrimination specifies that all members of GATT must treat all other members of GATT the same with respect to trade policy. For example, a GATT member could not have a low tariff on a good imported from country A and impose a higher tariff on the same good imported from country B (assuming both state A and state B are members of GATT). The tariff would have to be the same for both countries, and any changes to the tariff would have to be applied equally to all members of GATT who produced that good. In principle, this ensures there is no discrimination in how states treat one another in GATT. This convention is also known as the Most Favoured Nation (MFN) principle. The principle of reciprocity specifies that all members of GATT should make approximately the same value of concessions to each other when making trade policy. For example, if Canada were to reduce its tariffs on rice imported from Japan, Japan should reciprocate by reducing its tariffs on a product it imports from Canada, such as wood products. Moreover, this Japanese reciprocity should lead to approximately the same value of increased trade for Canada in wood products as the Canadian tariff reduction did for Japanese rice. These two principles were crucial for GATT, because they entrenched the idea that all members should benefit from trade, and they should all benefit as equally as possible. In this way, it was hoped that neomercantilist temptations would be minimized.

As GATT evolved and expanded, and world economic activity grew in scope and complexity, member states began to negotiate and implement measures on a variety of other issues related to trade liberalization. One of the first issues to be addressed was **dumping**, the practice of exporting goods to a country and selling them at below the cost of production (in order to seize market share by bankrupting competing producers prior to increasing prices). Dumping was made illegal under GATT, although accusations of dumping remain commonplace in the global economy. By the 1980s, **nontariff barriers** to trade were under discussion. There was growing concern that countries were using health and safety regulations, labelling laws, and

---

PROFILE 4.4 **Multilateral Negotiations Under GATT and Number of Participants**

1. Geneva, 1947: 23 states
2. Annency (France), 1949: 13 states
3. Torquay (Britain), 1950–51: 38 states
4. Geneva, 1955–56: 26 states
5. Dillon Round, 1960–61: 26 states
6. Kennedy Round, 1964–67: 62 states
7. Tokyo Round, 1973–79: 102 states
8. Uruguay Round, 1986–94: 123 states

government contracting rules as barriers to trade (that is, to exclude foreign products from their market to favour domestic producers). This of course led to debates on whether such regulations were unfair trade practices or justifiable efforts by governments to regulate their economies and societies. Under the Tokyo and Uruguay Rounds of GATT, some progress was made on the issue of nontariff barriers, but, as we shall see, this debate continues to rage today. The Uruguay Round also began to create rules governing intellectual property rights. Intellectual property involves creations of the imagination, including artistic works, literature, symbols and logos, among many others. The holder of the patent or copyright for such creations has the exclusive right to profit from a piece of music, computer software, image, or brand name. Since the 1980s, an international problem has emerged surrounding the issue of copyright infringement and piracy. Companies in some parts of the world turn out counterfeit, unlicensed versions of these creations at low cost for their own profit, costing the patent holder thousands, millions, or billions of dollars in lost revenue and reducing the incentives to produce creations of imagination in the first place. As we shall see in Chapter 8, the negotiation of **Trade-Related Intellectual Property Rights (TRIPs)**, which require member states to create and enforce copyright rules, has been a controversial issue in IPE. Some critics charge that TRIPs agreements protect the profits of large firms, and high licensing or user fees prevent developing countries from using technology and ideas that might improve their social condition.

The Uruguay Round also created a **General Agreement on Trade in Services (GATS)** to govern the growing international trade in the service sector. Services are economic activities such as banking, insurance, tourism, and transportation, to name a few. The expansion of the service sector in the 1980s was addressed in GATT because service sector companies were finding it very difficult to operate in other countries. The GATS agreement began the process of liberalizing trade in services, an effort that continues today, though not without controversy. GATT was also forced to confront a growing problem in the world economy: the divide between rich countries and poor countries. Decolonization brought a large number of new (and generally poor) states into the international system, and large numbers of these states joined GATT. The poor states of the developing world called for greater access to the markets of rich states, through the lowering of tariffs on products exported by developing countries. Greater access to rich world markets would enable poor countries to generate increased revenues through increased exports. For the most part, rich states were reluctant to do this because of the threat the (generally cheaper) goods of the developing world posed to domestic industries and agriculture. While a **Generalized System of Preferences** was established in GATT in the 1960s (allowing industrialized states to lower tariffs on imports from developing countries to levels below the tariffs imposed on the same goods from developed countries), this system never succeeded in addressing the North–South divide in the global economy. As we shall see in Chapter 8, this issue has only intensified in contemporary debates over globalization.

Agreements in GATT were not reached without considerable debate at the intergovernmental level, and of course most governments faced domestic political opposition to many GATT measures. GATT agreements reached at the end of each round always reflected what was possible through negotiation. States sought to protect their economic and social interests in the GATT negotiations, and realists would remind us that GATT agreements reflected these interests. States negotiated exemptions for certain sectors of economic and social activity. For example, many countries (including Western European states, the United States, and Canada) protected their agricultural sector from high levels of trade liberalization in the early rounds of GATT, enabling them to maintain subsidies and high tariffs in this politically sensitive sector. Canada and other countries (especially France) fought to protect their cultural sector against the perceived threat of U.S. cultural influences. Of course, states also found themselves in trade disputes with other GATT members. Trade disputes arise when one or more states feel that other GATT states are engaging in economic or public policy that is against the letter or the spirit of GATT rules. Trade disputes became a central feature of global politics. Major disputes, such as those between the United States and Japan over automobile imports, and the United States and the EEC over agricultural trade, received considerable media and public attention.

Though the successive rounds of GATT succeeded in reducing tariffs and facilitating increased levels of world trade, the 1970s and 1980s saw a rise in protectionism. The final concluded round of GATT negotiations (the eighth) may have been the most difficult. The Uruguay Round began in 1986 and involved 107 countries (including the individual members of the EEC). Only the Soviet Union and China sat out the negotiations. On April 15, 1994, at Marrakesh, Morocco, the final result of these lengthy negotiations (some refer to GATT as the "General Agreement to Talk and Talk") was released to the public. Under this new world trade agreement, 123 countries (the membership of GATT by 1994) agreed on a set of rules that would reduce tariffs by approximately one-third. Since 1994, more states have signed the agreement, and the countries that are party to the Uruguay Round agreement account for 90 percent of world trade. Finally, the agreement also established the World Trade Organization (WTO). We will explore the WTO further in Chapter 8.

THE DECLINE AND FALL OF THE BRETTON WOODS SYSTEM

By 1960, the problems facing the Bretton Woods system were in many ways different from the ones it faced in 1947. The persistent balance of payments deficits experienced by the United States meant that more and more dollars were in circulation in the international system. The deficits, caused by U.S. military activities around the world, military and economic aid, and private investment in foreign countries, were increasingly out of control. The dollar shortage had turned into the dollar glut. In 1960, for the first time, more dollars were in circulation than there was gold in U.S. reserves. This imbalance meant that the United States would not be able to exchange gold for dollars at $35 an ounce. Not surprisingly, many began to question the strength of the U.S. dollar as a reserve currency and feared that it would be devalued. As a result, many holders of U.S. dollars began to convert their dollars into gold, creating the first dollar crisis.

Other developments also threatened the position of the dollar. The economies of Western Europe and Japan had recovered from the war, and the need for U.S. dollars and U.S. products lessened. The IMF was moving away from reliance on the U.S. dollar toward Special Drawing Rights (SDRs), a basket of major currencies that could be drawn on by countries in search of financing. (Because SDRs were a blend of currencies, they were seen as more stable than gold or U.S. dollars.) The expenditures of the Vietnam War and President Lyndon Johnson's War on Poverty had also eroded the competitiveness of the U.S. economy. And finally, in 1971, the United States experienced a balance of trade deficit (with more goods imported into the country than were exported) for the first time. This deficit threatened jobs at home and increased international tensions, as the U.S. government blamed Western Europe and Japan for maintaining undervalued currencies (currency values that did not reflect the true cost of goods and services in those countries). This undervaluing in turn made foreign products more attractive for consumers in the United States, which contributed to the U.S. balance of trade deficit.

On August 15, 1971, the Nixon administration responded to the eroding position of the U.S. economy by announcing that it would no longer exchange dollars for gold. A tariff was placed on goods entering the United States, and the U.S. dollar was devalued to increase exports.[49] For all intents and purposes, the Bretton Woods system had collapsed. This collapse had two general consequences. First, the international monetary system was transformed. With the collapse of the fixed exchange rate system, the value of currencies now floated freely in international financial markets. The value of a currency was now based on perceptions of the strength and health of a state's economy; market forces, rather than government intervention, determined a currency's value. The financial predictability of Bretton Woods vanished, replaced with the volatile financial markets we are familiar with today (see Profile 4.5). Second, it was apparent by 1971 that the United States could no longer unilaterally regulate the global economic system. Economic power had become more dispersed in the international system, and although the United States was still by far the world's largest economy, it was no longer capable of exerting leadership unilaterally, and other countries were no longer willing to unconditionally accept that leadership. The management of the international economy began to shift from a hegemonic management system to an increasingly multilateral management system. Of course, this shift to a new international monetary system had implications for other countries, including Canada (see Profile 4.6).

THE POLITICS OF OIL

The global economy faced another challenge in the wake of the collapse of Bretton Woods: the formation of OPEC in 1960 by four Middle Eastern states and Venezuela initially to fight proposed oil price cuts by oil companies and later to pressure transnational oil corporations to give host-country governments a greater share of the immense profits. By the early 1970s OPEC was winning significant concessions and had raised the price of oil. It is important to keep in mind that oil has been the predominant fuel of industrialization since the latter half of the 20th century, especially in the United States, Western Europe, and Japan. The pursuit of oil, its role in the global economy, and the geopolitical and environmental implications of humanity's extraordinary dependence on this substance has inspired a great body of literature.[50] OPEC is a **cartel**, a producer's organization that seeks to raise the price of a good by reducing its supply through controls on production. In 1973, in reaction to U.S. support for Israel in the 1973 Arab–Israeli War, OPEC countries initiated a cutback in oil production and imposed an oil embargo against the United States. World oil prices rose dramatically, from $2.50 a barrel in 1973 to $11.65 in 1974 (a barrel is a standard measure for petroleum, equivalent to 42 U.S. gallons or 159 litres). The oil shock created havoc in the West and particularly in the United States, the world's leading importer of oil. World recession followed, as countries had to spend more for energy. Dollars also flowed to OPEC countries in such huge amounts ($70 billion in 1974 alone) that the supply of dollars in the international system depressed the value of the dollar still further.

Some equilibrium was achieved when oil prices began to decline in the late 1970s due to a fall in demand through conservation efforts, reduced consumption, the discovery of new deposits elsewhere, and a shift to alternative sources of energy. However, another oil shock followed after the Iranian revolution in 1979, as world prices of oil shot up to $50 a barrel. Global recession once again followed, although, again, conservation measures and the exploitation of new sources of oil eventually reduced pressure on world oil prices. However, to this day many of the world's leading industrial economies (especially those in Europe and Asia) are heavily reliant on Middle Eastern oil. In fact, many would argue that the war in the Persian Gulf in 1991 and the Iraq War in 2003 were related directly to the strategic importance of oil. Oil is also a key factor in the politics of export-dependent states such as Nigeria and Venezuela; some analysts refer to states with large oil reserves and military governments

PROFILE 4.5 Money and Floating Exchange Rates

Toronto Stock Exchange. Photo by Gordon Powley taken c. June 17, 1952 (© Toronto Star Syndicate 2003. All rights reserved. CP Photo.)

Money performs several different functions in the international economy. Currencies must be accepted and recognized so that actors possessing currency can use it to purchase goods and services from other actors. Money serves as a store of value, and money must be a standard of deferred payment so that actors will be willing to lend money knowing that the money will still have purchasing power when the loan is repaid. This belief is important because the value of money can erode through inflation. Inflation occurs when the supply of money exceeds the value of goods and services produced in an economy. As a currency becomes inflated, it loses purchasing power and becomes a poor store of value and less acceptable as an exchange for the payment of debts. As a result, governments around the world try to keep inflation as low as possible.

Changes in currency exchange rates occur when international evaluations of a country's economy and its ability to maintain the value of its money change due to political or economic events or trends. If a country has a healthy and growing economy, its currency will rise relative to other currencies (one unit of the currency will buy more of another currency) because it becomes more desirable as a store of value or a medium of exchange. If, however, a country's economy is performing poorly, its currency will fall relative to other currencies (one unit of

the currency will buy less of another currency) because it is less desirable as a store of value or a medium of exchange. Of course, since all currencies are floating relative to each other, the exchange rates between them are dependent on the relative performance of their economies. Who makes these international evaluations of the performance of state economies? International organizations, governments, banks and financial institutions (such as investment houses), corporations, and individuals all contribute to the general appraisal of a state's economy (although certain institutions play a greater role than others). Much of the activity in international financial markets is based on currency speculation, an effort to make money by buying it and selling it at a profit. In essence, speculators gamble (based on economic and political indicators) that the value of a currency will increase in the future: they will buy the currency, store it, and sell it when the value of the currency is higher (thus making a profit).

As a result, the capacity of a state government to influence the value of its own currency is limited, because the value of the currency is based on what others think of the state's economy. However, governments will try to act in support of their currencies, because the value of a currency (and especially its stability relative to other currencies) is extremely important for

(continued)

PROFILE 4.5 Money and Floating Exchange Rates (*continued*)

exporters and importers of goods and services, since they must purchase or sell their goods and services across state borders in accordance with current exchange rates. Governments will therefore try to follow responsible fiscal policies so as not to damage the value of their currency. Governments intervene by buying or selling their own currency in the international system, thereby increasing or decreasing the value of the currency by affecting the

international demand for it. One of the great challenges of the post–Bretton Woods system was adjusting to the fact that the value of currencies could fluctuate quite dramatically and that this fluctuation was due to forces largely out of state control. Today, even small changes in the value of currencies are important knowledge, whether you are planning a holiday or managing a government's financial reserves.

as "petro-tyrannies."[51] It can also be argued that the sudden influx of petrodollars to Western banks encouraged the latter to make hazardous loans to Southern state governments, stimulating the developing countries' debt crisis. As we shall see in later sections of this textbook, the shock of high oil prices in 2008, combined with newfound awareness of climate change issues, may be the beginning of a profound revolution in human affairs as we adjust to a

PROFILE 4.6 Canada and Floating Exchange Rates

The value of the Canadian dollar, like that of most other currencies, is largely determined by financial markets. Currency traders, buyers, speculators, banks, and foreign governments evaluate the attractiveness of the Canadian dollar on the basis of the health of the Canadian economy, the economic policies of Canadian federal and provincial governments, and political developments in Canada. If the Canadian economy shows disappointing trends (such as lower growth), the Canadian dollar is less attractive to foreign-currency holders and the value of the Canadian currency will decline. Similarly, if the Canadian government follows economic policies viewed as fiscally irresponsible (such as increased budget deficits), the value of the Canadian dollar will decline. Political developments may also cause the value of the Canadian dollar to fluctuate. For example, in the 1997 federal elections in Canada, early returns indicated a possible minority government for the Liberal Party. A minority government may have meant instability in Canada's political scene, and the value of the Canadian dollar dropped as speculators, banks, and governments found the Canadian dollar less attractive. As the election results showed a slim Liberal

majority government, the dollar rebounded somewhat on international markets. Canada, like most countries, is faced with two dilemmas in this market-oriented monetary environment. Canadian governments must make economic policy with an eye on the possible reaction of international financial markets, which constrains the government's ability to make decisions on the basis of domestic needs. The Canadian government must also decide when to intervene to prop up the dollar by buying Canadian dollars on international markets (creating a demand for Canadian dollars, which increases the value of the currency). Doing this, of course, costs money. Because Canada is a major exporter and importer, currency fluctuations are of tremendous importance to the Canadian economy. In late 2003 and early 2004, the increasing value of the Canadian dollar relative to the U.S. dollar caused consternation among Canadian exporters, as the higher Canadian dollar made Canadian exports more expensive to consumers (especially consumers in the United States). On the other hand, many imported products dropped in price, to the pleasure of many Canadian consumers! By 2009 the Canadian dollar had again settled to a value below that of its American counterpart.

post-oil global economy. However, we are some way off from this achievement and the historical importance of this special commodity cannot be overemphasized.

THE GROUP OF SEVEN (AND THEN THERE WERE EIGHT)

Since 1975, a very exclusive forum has met to discuss and reach agreement on economic issues. The Group of Seven (G-7) countries are Canada, France, Germany, Great Britain, Italy, Japan, and the United States. Initially known as the Group of Five (G-5) before the admission of Canada and Italy in 1976, the G-7 is not an international organization. Rather, it is a forum for discussion and coordination on a wide range of political and economic issues. In short, the G-7 has a deliberative function (members meet to create understanding and awareness), a directive function (summits establish agendas and priorities), and a decisional function (members reach joint agreements on programs, targets, and timetables). Summits of the leaders of the G-7 countries are held on a yearly basis. In the early years of the G-5/G-7, the primary role of the forum was to coordinate the management of exchange rates and domestic interest rates. This role is significant because it signalled the inability of the United States to manage the global economic system on its own, and it committed the largest economies of the free world to cooperation on economic policy to attempt to manage the international economy. In addition, the early meetings marked the return of Japan to global prominence.

The G-7 summit in 1994 was held in Naples, where leaders agreed to revitalize international economic institutions and integrate the former communist countries into the global economic system more rapidly. This summit was also notable for the fact that Russian President Boris Yeltsin was invited. Although Russia was not invited to become a full economic member of the forum, it has attended the G-7 summits every year since Naples (leading some to refer to the G-7 as the G-8 or simply the Eight; the President of the EU also participates). In 1995 the G-8 summit was held in Halifax, where leaders discussed the collapse of the Mexican peso and the progress achieved in creating new financial institutions. In recent years, G-8 summits in St. Petersburg, Russia (2006), Heiligendamm, Germany (2007), Toyako, Japan (2008), and La Maddalena, Italy (2009) have addressed a wide range of political issues, including terrorism and security challenges, the environment, food and oil prices, and development. This raises questions about whether the G-8 is becoming something akin to an elitist concert of powers (similar questions have been raised about the high-level meetings of economic elites in Davos, Switzerland each year).

Membership in the G-8 has also become an issue. As a forum for the world's largest democratic market economies, the G-8 membership is rather anachronistic. If economic size were the sole measure of membership, for example, Canada would no longer be a member of the group; China, India and Brazil certainly would. Canada's continued membership in the G-8 is a reflection of Canada's international diplomatic profile, its tradition of involvement in international economic and political issues, and the unwillingness of other G-8 countries to discuss the politically sensitive issue of membership criteria. In part, this led to the creation of the G20 forum in 1999, a meeting of finance ministers and central bank governors from the 20 largest economies in the world (including the European Union). The G20 devotes most of its attention to financial and development policy coordination among member states. It met at the Heads of Government level for the first time in November 2008, possibly indicating that its role may be enhanced and become more significant in the future. In another relatively exclusive forum, the **Trilateral Commission**, economic experts from North America, Europe, and Japan meet to discuss future relations. The 29 states in the **Organisation for Economic Co-operation and Development (OECD)** carry out research and consultations on promoting free trade and economic efficiency. OECD countries produce two-thirds of the world's goods and services. The organization is often criticized as a rich countries' club, though Mexico and South Korea have both won admission.

As we have seen, the global economy has evolved considerably since the end of World War II, through a combination of long-term trends (such as economic growth, trade, technological innovations, and the decline of U.S. dominance, or hegemony, in the system) and short-term shocks (such as the collapse of Bretton Woods, the oil shocks, and the fall of the Soviet Union). In general, the politics of the global economy have evolved from a largely unilateral or hegemonic management of the system to a multilateral management effort. The global economy we live in today is the product of a conscious effort to create an open trading system at the end of World War II based on liberal economic principles, and of the subsequent political and economic events that shaped the 20th century.

CONCLUSIONS

As the Cold War ended, the global economy was as complex as ever. A clear dividing line remained between rich and poor, largely in North–South terms. However, it was becoming quite apparent that the Soviet Union and the Eastern European states were in economic disarray. They had to be integrated into the world economy somehow, and they embarked on a program of privatization that, initially at least, caused a great deal of hardship. China was charting a new course toward greater privatization and was experiencing rapid economic growth based on cheap labour and increased exports. Other Asian countries were also continuing down the export-led development path with record growth, although the Asian financial crisis of 1997 (see Chapter 8) would slow growth down for a few years. Canada had entered into NAFTA with the U.S. and Mexico, and Europe was forging ahead with its problematic economic and political integration. Many states in Sub-Saharan Africa and Latin America were mired in development dilemmas related to debt and democracy. The environmental problems that had resulted from years of global industrialization and population growth became topics of great concern as the world prepared for the United Nations Conference on Environment and Development, held in Rio de Janeiro, Brazil, in 1992. MNCs were growing in number and in size, which raised questions about the impact such firms were having on trade and development.

Poverty and wealth, arguably the two central themes of economic history, continue to coexist. So, too, do the central perspectives on IPE we have outlined. In this chapter, we have emphasized several divergent perspectives: neomercantilism, liberalism, neo-Marxism, feminism, global ecopolitics, constructivism, and hegemonic stability theory. We have provided a brief outline of the recent evolution of trade and finance in the international economy and the principles on which this system is based. In Chapter 8, we will look at the modern world economy and discuss some of the prevalent concerns facing those who study IPE today. We turn now to an examination of what many analysts feel are the principal potential facilitators of both peace and economic progress on a global scale: international institutions.

Endnotes

1. M. Waters, *Globalization* (London: Routledge, 1995), 66–67; L. Lapham, "Notebook: Estate Sale," *Harper's Magazine*, May 2008, 9–12, 11; J. Frieden, *Global Capitalism: Its Fall and Rise in the Twentieth Century* (New York: W. W. Norton and Company, 2006), xvi.

2. T. Friedman, *The World Is Flat: A Brief History of the Twenty-First Century* (New York: Farrar, Straus and Giroux, 2005).

3. P. Collier, *The Bottom Billion: Why the Poorest Countries are Failing and What Can be Done About It* (Oxford: Oxford University Press, 2007).

4. R. Isaak, *Managing World Economic Change: International Political Economy*, 3rd ed. (Upper Saddle River, NJ: Prentice-Hall, 2000), 2.

5. T. Cohn, *Global Political Economy: Theory and Practice*, 2nd ed. (Toronto: Longman, 2003), 6.

6. K. Polanyi, *The Great Transformation: The Political and Economic Origins of Our Time* (New York: Beacon Press, 1944).

7. T. Oatley, *International Political Economy: Interests and Institutions in the Global Economy* (New York: Pearson Education, 2004), 3.

8. See, for example, P. Krugman, and M. Obstfeld, *International Economics: Theory and Policy* (New York: HarperCollins, 1991); and J. D. Richardson, *Understanding International Economics: Theory and Practice* (Boston: Little, Brown and Company, 1980). For a study of the interaction between politics and economics, see J. Grieco and J. Ikenberry, *State Power and World Markets: The International Political Economy* (New York: W. W. Norton, 2003).

9. C. E. Lindblom, *Politics and Markets: The World's Political Economic Systems* (New York: Basic Books, 1977).

10. R. Gilpin, *The Political Economy of International Relations* (Princeton: Princeton University Press, 1987).

11. See R. S. Walters and R. H. Blake, *The Politics of Global Economic Relations*, 4th ed. (Englewood Cliffs, NJ: Prentice-Hall, 1992).

12. For a classic text, see R. Rosecrance, *The Rise of the Trading State: Commerce and Conquest in the Modern World* (New York: Basic Books, 1986).

13. A. Smith, *An Inquiry into the Nature and Causes of the Wealth of Nations*, vol. 1, bk. 4 (London: Dent and Sons, 1910), 436.

14. Ibid., 436.

15. Cohn suggests there are three variants of liberalism: orthodox, interventionist, and institutional. Cohn, 93; Michael Doyle writes of liberal institutionalism, commercial pacifism, and liberal internationalism in his *Ways of War and Peace: Realism, Liberalism, and Socialism* (New York: W. W. Norton, 1997).

16. For a discussion of international trade theory and its evolution, see D. Irwin, *Against the Tide: An Intellectual History of Free Trade* (Princeton: Princeton University Press, 1996).

17. For a discussion of the impact of Keynes's ideas, see P. Hall, ed., *The Political Power of Economic Ideas: Keynesianism Across Nations* (Princeton: Princeton University Press, 1989).

18. Cohn, 98.

19. S. Krasner, "Structural Causes and Regime Consequences: Regimes as Intervening Variables," in same, ed., *International Regimes* (Ithaca, NY: Cornell University Press, 1983), 2. See also M. Zacher, "Toward a Theory of International Regimes," *Journal of International Affairs* 44, no. 1 (1990), 139–58; and O. Young, "The Politics of International Regime Formation: Managing Natural Resources and the Environment," *International Organization* 43, no. 3 (1989), 349–75.

20. See, for example, M. Zacher with B. Sutton, *Governing Global Networks: International Regimes for Transportation and Communication* (Cambridge, UK: Cambridge University Press, 1996); P. Kien-hong Yu, *International Governance, Regimes, and Globalization: an East Asian Perspective* (New York: BrownWalker, 2008).

21. K. Marx and F. Engels, *The Communist Manifesto* (New York: International Publishers, 1948). Much more important, from a theoretical viewpoint, was Marx's landmark study, *Das Capital*, and his earlier, more philosophical work.

22. R. Miliband, *The State in Capitalist Society* (New York: Basic Books, 1969).

23. See V. I. Lenin, *Imperialism: The Highest Stage of Capitalism*, rev. trans. (New York: International Publishers, 1939), and R. Luxemburg, *The Accumulation of Capital* (London: Routledge, 2003).

24. See P. Baran, *The Political Economy of Growth* (New York: Monthly Review Press, 1962), 12. On the political history of what is often referred to as the "Third World," see L. S. Stavrianos, *Global Rift: The Third World Comes of Age* (New York: William Morrow, 1981).

25. See, for example, A. G. Frank, *Latin America, Underdevelopment or Revolution: Essays on the Development of Underdevelopment and the Immediate Enemy* (New York: Monthly Review Press, 1970). For an excellent review of dependency theory, see M. Blomstrom and B. Hettne, *Development Theory in Transition, The Dependency Debate and Beyond: Third World Responses* (London: Zed Books, 1984); and P. Evans's classic *Dependent Development: The Alliance of Multinational, State, and Local Capital in Brazil* (Princeton: Princeton University Press, 1979). For an African perspective, see S. Amin, *Accumulation on a World Scale: A Critique of the Theory of Development*, vols. 1 and 2 (New York: Monthly Review Press, 1974).

26. See F. Cardoso and E. Faletto, *Dependency and Development in Latin America*, trans M. Urquid (Berkeley: University of California Press, 1979).

27. See P. Gleijeses, *The Dominican Crisis: The 1965 Constitutional Revolt and American Intervention*, trans. L. Lipson (Baltimore, MD: Johns Hopkins University Press, 1978).

28. See R. Sandford, *The Murder of Allende and the End of the Chilean Way to Socialism*, trans. A. Conrad (New York: Harper and Row, 1976). For more on U.S. foreign policy in Latin America, see R. Pastor, *Exiting the Whirlpool: US Foreign Policy Toward Latin America and the Caribbean* (Boulder, CO: Westview Press, 2001).

29. I. Wallerstein, "The Rise and Future Demise of the World Capitalist System: Concepts for Comparative Analysis," in same, *The Capitalist World-Economy* (New York: Cambridge University Press, 1979), 35. See also F. Braudel, *Civilization and Capitalism: 15th–18th Century*, 3 vols. (New York: Harper and Row, 1981, 1982, 1984).

30. Ibid., 18–19.

31. R. Cox, *Production, Power, and World Order: Social Forces in the Making of History* (New York: Columbia University Press, 1987).

32. See G. Waylen, "Gender, Feminism, and Political Economy," *New Political Economy* 2, no. 2 (July 1997), 205–220, and J. A. Nelson, "Feminism and Economics," *The Journal of Economic Perspectives* 9, no. 2 (Spring 1995), 131–148.

33. R. Carson, *Silent Spring* (Boston: Houghton Mifflin, 1962).

34. See Eric Helleiner, "International Political Economy and the Greens," *International Political Economy* 1, no. 1 (March 1996), 59–78.

35. E. F. Schumacher, *Small Is Beautiful: Economics as If People Mattered* (New York: Harper Perennial, 1973).

36. R. Gilpin, *War and Change in World Politics* (Cambridge, UK: Cambridge University Press, 1981), 29.

37. I. Wallerstein, "The Three Instances of Hegemony in the History of the Capitalist World Economy," in same, *The Politics of the World-Economy: The States, the Movements, and the Civilizations* (Cambridge, UK: Cambridge University Press, 1984), 38.

38. R. Keohane, "The Theory of Hegemonic Stability and Changes in International Economic Regimes, 1967–1977," in O. Holsti, R. Siverson, and A. George, eds., *Change in the International System* (Boulder, CO: Westview Press, 1980), 132.

39. See C. Kindleberger, *The World in Depression, 1929–1939* (Berkeley: University of California Press, 1973).

40. Gilpin, *The Political Economy of International Relations*, 78.

41. P. Kennedy, *The Rise and Fall of the Great Powers* (New York: Random House, 1987).

42. D. White, "Mutable Destiny: The End of the American Century?," *Harvard International Review* 20 (Winter 1998), 42–47.

43. For examples of revivalist writings, see J. Nye Jr., *Bound to Lead: The Changing Nature of American Power* (New York: Basic Books, 1990); and S. Strange, "The Persistent Myth of Lost Hegemony," *International Organization* 41, no. 4 (Autumn 1987), 551–74.

44. On the causes and consequences of Black October 1929, see J. K. Galbraith, *The Great Crash: 1929* (1954; Boston: Houghton Mifflin, 1988).

45. A. Toffler and H. Toffler, *War and Anti-War: Survival at the Dawn of the 21st Century* (Boston: Little, Brown and Company, 1993), 40. See also N. Polmar and T. Allen, *World War II: America at War, 1941–1945* (New York: Random House, 1991).

46. Kindleberger, op. cit.

47. See F. Stone, *Canada, the GATT and the International System* (Montreal: Institute for Research on Public Policy, 1984).

48. Oatley, 20.

49. See F. Block, *The Origins of International Economic Disorder* (Berkeley: University of California Press, 1977). This tariff increase especially angered Ottawa, since Canada and the United States had such a close trading relationship by that time.

50. See for example A. A. Kubursi and S. Mansur, "The Political Economy of Middle Eastern Oil," in R. Stubbs and G. Underhill, eds., *Political Economy and the Changing Global Order* (Toronto: McClelland and Stewart, 1994), 313–27, 324. See also D. Yergin, *The Prize: The Epic Quest for Oil, Money and Power* (New York: Simon and Schuster, 1991).

51. See J. Bacher, *Petrotyranny* (New York: Science for Peace, 2000).

Suggested Websites

G-8 Information Centre
http://www.g7.utoronto.ca

Global Exchange
http://www.globalexchange.org/index.html

History of Economics Internet references
http://home.tvd.be/cr27486/hope.html

International Monetary Fund
http://www.imf.org

International Trade Canada (ITC)
http://www.itcan-cican.gc.ca/menu-en.asp

OPEC: Organization of the Petroleum Exporting Countries
http://www.opec.org

Organisation for Economic Co-operation and Development
http://www.oecd.org/home

Routledge Journal: Review of IPE
http://www.tandf.co.uk/journals/titles/09692290.asp

University of Puget Sound International Political Economy Program
http://www.ups.edu/ipe/home2.htm

WebEc
http://www.helsinki.fi/WebEc/webecf.html

World Bank Group
http://www.worldbank.org

World Trade Organization
http://www.wto.org

WWW Virtual Library: Resources on International Economics and Business
http://www.etown.edu/vl/intlbus.html

International Institutions and Law

We the Peoples of the United Nations, determined to save succeeding generations from the scourge of war ... and to reaffirm faith in fundamental human rights, in the dignity and worth of the human person, in the equal rights of men and women and of nations large and small, and to establish conditions under which justice and respect for the obligations arising from treaties and other sources of international law can be maintained, and to promote social progress and better standards of life in larger freedom ... HAVE RESOLVED TO COMBINE OUR EFFORTS TO ACCOMPLISH THESE AIMS.

—Preamble, The Charter of the United Nations, 1945

The globalization of law is an integral aspect of the globalization of capitalism. The law globalizes rules that facilitate transnational patterns of capital accumulation, attenuating certain regulatory capacities of states, while advancing others.

—A. Claire Cutler[1]

INTRODUCTION

There are many ways of looking at international organizations (IOs) and international law (IL), and some truth to all of them. IOs and IL can be seen as the conceptual and regulatory core of the international society of states, as the instrumental arm of what is popularly termed **global governance**. Liberal institutionalists tend to view IOs and international regimes as institutional solutions to market failure problems, reducing uncertainty and promoting further cooperation. Realists are rather less enthusiastic about the purpose and prospects of international institutions and law, which they view primarily as vessels or forums for the pursuit of national interests. They ascribe little autonomy to IOs, and little causal significance to IL, but certainly recognize the potential of IOs to intervene in conflict situations, and to present both obstacles and opportunities to rational decision makers. Neo-Marxists and Gramscians would argue that important elements of what Marx would call the "superstructure" of the capitalist system—the institutions and ideologies enforcing and justifying the socioeconomic order—can be found at the IO and IL level. Historically, law has protected property, including of course the territorial right to sovereignty held by states (or by those elites who determine the national interest for states). At the same time, however, many constructivists and feminists see the UN and IL as possible conduits for serious reforms toward a more equitable world order, instruments for enhancing the observation of human rights standards, and the global redistribution of wealth. Constructivists argue that by participating in IOs such as the EU or African Union (AU), states slowly change their own self-identities, and thus their estimation of self-interest in the process.

Taken together, the study of IOs, IL, and other forms of multilateral cooperation is increasingly referred to as global governance. Of course, this term does not refer to an extant, or even the future existence, of a world government, but to efforts to manage common action problems with decentralized yet coordinated political authority and regulation. However, the subfield of international organization still revolves largely around what Plano and Olton term a "formal arrangement transcending national boundaries that provides for the establishment of institutional machinery to facilitate cooperation among members in security, economic, social or related fields."[2] Generally, two types of IOs exist: **intergovernmental organizations (IGOs)** and nongovernmental organizations (NGOs). All IGOs share a number of characteristics. First, they comprise states and only states (although in some cases nonstate actors may be represented, or have "observer status"). Second, IGOs are created by treaties between states and, therefore, have legal standing under IL; they have, for example, the right to immunity from jurisdiction of state courts for acts and activities performed by the organization. Third, they hold regular meetings attended by delegates from member states. Those delegates represent the policies and interests of their respective countries. Fourth, IGOs have permanent headquarters and an executive secretariat that runs the day-to-day activities of the organization. Finally, IGOs have permanent administrative employees who work for the organization and do not represent their governments; rather, they are international bureaucrats. Although these employees do not renounce their citizenships, they serve the organization, not their respective states. Such organizations have proliferated in number, especially in the 20th century. In 1909, there were 37 IGOs; in 1960, there were 154; in 1987, there were 381; and there are currently more than 400. As we will see, these organizations perform a wide variety of functions in the international system, and states have increasingly interacted and cooperated with each other through the mechanisms provided by IGOs. In addition, such institutions are vital to less powerful states, such as Canada, that have many connections to the international diplomatic scene but a limited capacity to influence international events on their own. Many Canadians, such as Lester Pearson, Yves Fortier, Stephen Lewis, Elizabeth Dowdeswell, Douglas Roche, Louise Arbour, Maurice Strong, and Louise Fréchette, have played high-profile roles at the United Nations.

It is important to recognize the wide scope of activities in which international organizations engage. The UN, for example, is involved in issue-areas as diverse as international and civil war, technology, gender relations, humanitarian assistance and disaster relief, literacy, pollution abatement, decolonization, human rights and IL, disarmament, important treaties such as the nuclear **Non-Proliferation Treaty**, and significant conferences such as the June 2008 Global Food Security Summit in Rome. The various specialized agencies and programs of the UN include the International Research and Training Institute for the Advancement of Women,

A challenging occupation. United Nations General Secretary Ban Ki-moon addresses the UN General Assembly, September 2008. (AP Photo/Julie Jacobson/CP Photo.)

the UN Population Fund, the UN Office for the Coordination of Humanitarian Affairs, the International Civil Aviation Organization, the World Intellectual Property Organization, all of the UN-mandated peacekeeping operations in effect around the globe, UNAIDS, and many others. As well, we have seen the rise of a particular single actor, the **Secretary-General**, from the preconceived role of an international bureaucrat to that of a globetrotting mediator.

Several types of IGOs exist. The UN is a *multipurpose, universal-membership* organization. It serves many functions and can be joined by all states in the international system, providing the Security Council's permanent members and two-thirds of the General Assembly agree.[3] Importantly, the UN universe includes more than 30 major agencies and programs such as the International Labour Organization (ILO), the **Food and Agriculture Organization of the UN (FAO)**, the **UN Educational, Scientific and Cultural Organization (UNESCO)**, the International Maritime Organization (IMO), the **UN Conference on Trade and Development (UNCTAD)**, and the **UN Development Programme (UNDP)**, in addition to those mentioned earlier. Multipurpose, universal-membership organizations may be contrasted with *regional* and *functional* organizations, which manage issues at a regional level or are designed for a specific purpose. In fact, most IGOs fall into the latter category. The most famous regional IGO is the European Union, which was known as the European Community (EC) before 1994; indeed, the EU has coordinated policies to such a degree that it is often called a *supranational* institution. Other multipurpose regional organizations include the Organization of American States (OAS), the African Union, the Association of Southeast Asian Nations (ASEAN), and the **Arab League**. Single-purpose, or functional, regional organizations include the **Asian Development Bank**, the North Atlantic Treaty Organization (NATO), the **Northwest Atlantic Fisheries Organization (NAFO)**, and the Organization of the Petroleum Exporting Countries (OPEC). Lest we think only the UN has potential global membership, we should keep in mind the existence of open-membership organizations that have single functions, such as the various UN agencies[4] mentioned above, the International Organization for Migration (IOM), and the International Whaling Commission (IWC). Not all states have joined these organizations, but they may if they desire.

INTERNATIONAL ORGANIZATIONS AND REGIMES IN HISTORY

People watching the Olympic Games may be surprised to learn that the Games, which originally organized peaceful competition among Greek city-states, were once an early ancestor of the modern IO.[5] But when we speak of modern, formal IOs, such as the League of Nations (1919–46) and the current UN system (1945–present), we are discussing relatively recent developments.

Both the League and the UN were established for two primary reasons. The first is practicality. Once the nation-state system was established and contacts between states expanded, it became clear that governments would have to maintain linkages that facilitated communication and coordination. As economic interdependence between states grew, it became necessary to establish new lines of communication and to reduce the probability of unexpected events. Trade relations are very dependent on order, the ability to expect payment for goods, fair treatment in foreign markets, freedom from piracy, and other factors. Secondly, IOs can serve a much broader purpose, such as the establishment or maintenance of world order and peace—this is the official mandate of the UN itself, which was established following the most destructive war in global history. However, we should stress how these rationales complement each other. Simply put, most functional organizations are based on some set of guiding principles (or ideals), but their creation is also necessitated by the practical circumstances surrounding them. For example, two early IOs still in operation today are the **International**

Telecommunication Union (1865) and the **Universal Postal Union** (1874), both created for rather specific purposes (telegraphs and postage between nations).[6] Another early IO with a clear functional purpose was the **International Office of Weights and Measures**, established in 1875. Yet behind this functional cooperation was a belief, held by participating government and industry representatives, that telegrams, mail, and common measurement standards were good for business, if not for world peace itself. Liberal values on international political economy, as discussed in the previous chapter, surface again here: increased trade and communication is assumed by many to be the best path toward a peaceful international system, and IOs provide the regulatory standards and predictability that trade and communication systems require.

We can see, then, that it is tempting to conclude that IOs are similar in their wide range of functions to domestic governments, though they do not often disrupt the cardinal principle of state sovereignty. IL, on which we focus later in this chapter, evolved alongside the IO, though it has a much more complex history predating the contemporary era. International treaty law is especially important, since it often establishes the legality of IOs themselves.

THE LEAGUE OF NATIONS

As discussed in Chapter 2, the **League of Nations** was created at the end of World War I, inspired by idealism and the associated hope for a world free from war. Two basic principles underlay the League's system of peace maintenance. First, members agreed to respect and preserve the territorial integrity and political independence of other states. Second, any war or threat of war was considered a matter of concern to the entire League. While the major emphasis of the League's Covenant was on maintaining international peace and stability, some recognition was also given to promoting economic and social cooperation. The Covenant did not provide any special machinery for overseeing these efforts, though a commitment was included for the establishment of one or more organizations to secure "fair and humane conditions of labor for men, women and children" (Article 23), and an autonomous International Labor Office (ILO) was established as part of the Treaty of Versailles (the ILO is still in existence as the International Labour Organization).

League organization centred around three major organs: the Assembly, to which all member-states belonged; the Council, to which a select few belonged; and the Secretariat. The League also established a Permanent Court of International Justice in 1921 to resolve disputes between members of the international community. From the outset the Permanent Court's role was not considered of primary importance, mirroring the present International Court of Justice in the UN system, which retains some symbolic significance but is not a decisive factor in world affairs. The League Assembly and the Council were the two main deliberative organs of the League. In both organs, each state possessed one vote. The Assembly was primarily responsible for discussing important issues confronting either individual members of the League or the international community as a whole. The Council was primarily responsible for discussing the maintenance of peace. Originally, the Council was to be composed of five permanent and four elected members. However, despite the fact that U.S. President Woodrow Wilson was the primary champion of the League, the United States never joined the organization (the U.S. Senate did not ratify the Treaty of Versailles, preferring its old isolationist foreign policy). As a result, Great Britain, Italy, Japan, and France were the original permanent members. Germany was given Permanent Council status on its admission to the League in 1926, and the Soviet Union was given the same status in 1934. Germany and Japan would eventually withdraw from the League, and the Soviet Union was expelled in 1939 for its invasion of Finland.

Despite the failure of the League to prevent war, the operations of the Secretariat, which was charged with administrative duties, were widely regarded as a success. As Egon Ranshofen-Wertheimer has observed, "The League has shown that it is possible to establish an integrated body of international officials, loyal to the international agency and ready to discharge faithfully the international obligations incumbent upon them. It was not for lack of executive efficiency that the League system failed."[7] Beyond this administrative precedent, the League of Nations established or incorporated bureaus and committees dealing with disease, communications, traffic in arms, slavery, drugs, labour, women, and children. In 1925, it played an important role in bringing about the peaceful resolution of the Greek–Bulgarian border dispute. By 1921, 48 members had joined the League and by mid-1929, 46 states had ratified the 1928 Kellogg–Briand Pact, in theory committing signatories to the peaceful settlement of disputes. The League considered 66 disputes and conflicts between 1920 and 1939, and in 35 of them, it was able to contribute to a peaceful resolution. The League was linked to several semiautonomous organizations, such as the Economic and Financial Organization, the Health Organization, the Organizations for Communications and Transit, the High Commissioner for Refugees, and the Intergovernmental Committees on the Drug Traffic, Traffic in Women, the Protection of Children, and Intellectual Co-operation. Nevertheless, despite the Wilsonian idealism that surrounded the formation of the League, its "primary purpose, like that of the Concert of Europe, was to assist in the management of a multipolar balance of power, not to replace it with a universal system."[8]

Unfortunately, the League's ability to alleviate serious disputes was limited. As discussed in Chapter 2, when the Japanese launched a series of attacks against Manchuria in 1931, some Council members, including Great Britain and France, were unwilling to apply economic and military sanctions, which seriously undermined the League's ability and willingness to discourage members of the international community from resorting to arms to achieve their objectives. Another serious blow to the League's credibility came in 1935, when the League was unable to deter Italy's invasion of Ethiopia, although the economic sanctions imposed on Italy were the first on behalf of the international community, setting an important precedent for the use of economic sanctions by the UN.

Several reasons have been advanced for the League's demise. Some attribute it to the absence of the United States and, during shorter periods, to the absence of the Soviet Union and Germany (this lack of leadership helped give rise to theories about hegemonic stability discussed in previous chapters). Its collapse can be linked to the inherent deficiencies of its Covenant, including Article 5, requiring unanimity on all major Assembly and Council decisions. Yet, in the critical tests, such as Japan and Ethiopia, it appeared to be the lack of political will among the members of the League, rather than the available machinery, that was primarily responsible for the League's failings. Finally, the aggressive foreign policies of the Axis powers made a successful League impossible. The League of Nations, reduced to insignificance by the cataclysm of World War II, was officially disbanded in April 1946. The demise of the League is often cited by realists as evidence of the inherent limitations of international institutions and international law in an anarchic world.

THE UNITED NATIONS ORGANIZATION

Plans to create the UN began during World War II. The term "United Nations" originated in the Washington Declaration of 1942 in which 26 Allied countries pledged to fight Germany, Japan, and Italy; before that, the Declaration of Principles (the **Atlantic Charter**) expressed similar concerns. By October 1943, the governments of the United States, Great Britain, the Soviet Union, and China were prepared to issue a clear statement of their intention to establish a general IO. That year, further steps were taken to create several agencies that would eventually fall under the auspices of the UN or that would come to be closely associated with it. The Food and Agriculture Organization (FAO) would be established in 1945, and, as a result of the Bretton Woods conference in 1944, the IMF and the IBRD were created. At the Dumbarton Oaks Conference of August 21, 1944, representatives from the United States, Great Britain, and the U.S.S.R. (China participated in the second phase of negotiations) began to map out a blueprint for a new world body. At the famous Yalta Conference of February 1945, progress was made on filling several of the technical gaps that remained open at the Dumbarton Oaks Conference. Two more important conferences took place before the organization was officially born. In February and March 1945, representatives from the United States and its Latin American allies met in Mexico City to discuss their plans for a general IO. At the same time, a committee of jurists representing virtually all the states that would attend the San Francisco conference met in Washington to discuss the creation of an International Court of Justice (ICJ), which would replace the Permanent Court of International Justice established under the League of Nations.

Inis Claude states that it was important to begin discussing plans for the creation of the United Nations before the end of war for two main reasons. First, as former U.S. Secretary of State Cordell Hull pointed out, if negotiations for an IO had been left to the end of the war, it would have been much more difficult to reach a consensus on how to create the organization, since politicians would be too preoccupied with political, economic, and social issues at home. Second, it was extremely important to avoid creating an unnecessarily close relationship between the UN and the peace settlement. In other words, the founders of the UN did not want it to appear as if the rights and obligations contained in the UN Charter were being imposed on states as part of the peace settlement, which appeared to be the case with the League. Rather, the UN was to be created expressly for "all peace loving nations," which opened up the possibility of accepting postwar Germany and Japan to join in the hope of bringing about lasting peace.[9]

In addition, it is important not to dismiss the psychological and political factors motivating diplomats from countries such as Canada to support the creation of the UN. Canadians, for example, believed that—in contradistinction to the League of Nations experience—the United States had to be engaged in postwar affairs, and saw the UN as a means to ensure this. Yet a close reading of the UN Charter indicates that although this document is approximately four times longer than the League's Covenant, it nonetheless contains many of the same features. Not unlike the Covenant, the Charter refers to the principal organs of the UN and the functions each should perform. Moreover, it clearly sets out the primary purpose of the UN, the maintenance of international peace and security, and how this commitment can be fulfilled. Furthermore, like the Covenant, the Charter emphasizes the inherent responsibility of all member states to deter aggression.

Canadian delegation to the United Nations conference in London, January 1946. Vincent Massey, Canadian High Commissioner to the United Kingdom (left), stands next to Minister of Justice Louis St. Laurent, Secretary of State Paul Martin Sr., and Associate Under-Secretary of State for External Affairs Hume Wrong. (CP Picture Archive.)

The climactic event in the long and arduous process of building a new IO took place in San Francisco in the spring of 1945.

Representatives from 50 nations deliberated for two months before they could agree on the final version of the UN Charter. On June 26, 1945, the Charter was signed, but it was not until January 10, 1946, that the first session of the General Assembly was held in London. Eventually, UN headquarters would be moved to its permanent home in New York City, a building now easily recognized around the world (see Profile 5.1). Although initial hopes for the organization were high (especially in Canada), the superpower confrontation effectively paralyzed the UN's capacity to mount collective security efforts. This incapacity did not mean that the UN was inactive. On the contrary, the UN performed many other crucial functions, most prominently in the process of decolonization, peacekeeping, and aid and development.

The UN has six principal organs (see Figure 5.1). At its heart is the **General Assembly** (GA), a forum in which all states can send representatives to sit in session, present opinions, and vote on resolutions, which need a two-thirds majority to pass (see Profile 5.2). It is true that GA resolutions cannot force other UN members to act; however, since those resolutions are considered by many to carry the weight of world opinion, they remain significant. The GA also makes key decisions regarding who gets to join the organization, what the Economic and Social Council (ECOSOC) does, and the spending powers of the organization. The GA has exclusive authority over the budget of the UN and elections to the Security Council and ECOSOC, but needs a recommendation from the Security Council to take action on the appointment of the secretary-general, UN membership, and amendments to the Charter. The Assembly and Security Council are jointly responsible for electing the judges of the International Court of Justice (ICJ).

The **Security Council** includes five permanent members, including the People's Republic of China, France, the Russian Federation, the United Kingdom, and the United States. Each of these states has a veto over any substantive matter that comes before the Council. There are

---

PROFILE 5.1 **Locating the United Nations**

What if you had built a world organization on which a new global order was to be based but didn't know where to put it? Locating the UN was, in fact, one of the first problems faced by the organization. This issue was obviously important since it was initially believed that a truly global organization could hardly be located anywhere closely affiliated with a major power, such as in Washington or Moscow, and it would be unsafe to locate it in an unstable state where political authority itself was contested, such as in China or soon-to-be-independent India. In all probability, the idea of locating the UN in a Southern state was never taken seriously; the first Southern Hemisphere location of a UN agency was in Nairobi, Kenya, and this was the headquarters of the UN Environment Programme established in the early 1970s. Germany, Japan, and Italy were (of course) out of the question as hosts of the new UN, as was any truly neutral place, such as the inaccessible Antarctic. The Swiss, hosts to the League of Nations and the first temporary location of the General Assembly of the UN, were reluctant to assume the responsibility of long-term UN involvement; they refused to host a UN capable of making decisions related to the use of force, which is of course precisely what Chapter 7 of the UN Charter authorizes the Security Council to do. (Switzerland joined the UN in 2002.) Europe was in a state of financial chaos and most of its capital cities were literally in physical ruin. The only country in a position of relative economic strength was the United States, and it was the American philanthropist John Davison Rockefeller Jr. who supplied the initial capital to build the UN in New York City. However, most specialized agencies and Conventions have Secretariats in other world cities, such as Geneva, Vienna, Rome, Paris, Nairobi, and Montreal.

Figure 5.1 The United Nations System

THE UNITED NATIONS SYSTEM

International Court of Justice	General Assembly (GA)	Economic and Social Council (ECOSOC)	Security Council	Secretariat	Trusteeship Council

- Main and other sessional committees
- Standing committees and ad hoc bodies
- Other subsidiary organs and related bodies

▲ **UNRWA**
United Nations Relief and Works Agency for Palestine Refugees in the Near East

■ **IAEA**
International Atomic Energy Agency

▲ **INSTRAW**
International Research and Training Institute for the Advancement of Women

▲ **UNCHS**
United Nations Centre for Human Settlements (Habitat)

▲ **UNCTAD**
United Nations Conference on Trade and Development

▲ **UNDCP**
United Nations International Drug Control Program

▲ **UNDP**
United Nations Development Programme

▲ **UNEP**
United Nations Environment Program

▲ **UNFPA**
United Nations Population Fund

▲ **UNHCR**
Office of the United Nations High Commissioner for Refugees

▲ **UNICEF**
United Nations Children's Fund

▲ **UNIFEM**
United Nations Development Fund for Women

▲ **UNITAR**
United Nations Institute for Training and Research

▲ **UNU**
United Nations University

▲ **WFC**
World Food Council

▲ **WFP**
World Food Program

▲ **ITC**
International Trade Centre UNCTAD/GATT

- **FUNCTIONAL COMMISSIONS**
  - Commission for Social Development
  - Commission on Crime Prevention and Criminal Justice
  - Commission on Human Rights
  - Commission on Narcotic Drugs
  - Commission on Science and Technology for Development
  - Commission on Sustainable Development
  - Commission on the Status of Women
  - Population Commission
  - Statistical Commission

- **REGIONAL COMMISSIONS**
  - Economic Commission for Africa (ECA)
  - Economic Commission for Europe (ECE)
  - Economic Commission for Latin America and the Caribbean (ECIAC)
  - Economic and Social Commission for Asia and the Pacific (ESCAP)
  - Economic and Social Commission for Western Asia (ESCWA)

- **SESSIONAL AND STANDING COMMITTEES**

- **EXPERT, AD HOC AND RELATED BODIES**

■ **ILO**
International Labour Organization

■ **FAO**
Food and Agriculture Organization of the United Nations

■ **UNESCO**
United Nations Educational, Scientific and Cultural Organization

■ **WHO**
World Health Organization

World Bank Group
■ **IBRD**
International Bank for Reconstruction and Development (World Bank)
■ **IDA**
International Development Association
■ **IFC**
International Finance Corporation
■ **MIGA**
Multilateral Investment Guarantee Agency

■ **IMF**
International Monetary Fund

■ **ICAO**
International Civil Aviation Organization

■ **UPU**
Universal Postal Union

■ **ITU**
International Telecommunication Union

■ **WMO**
World Meteorological Organization

■ **IMO**
International Maritime Organization

■ **WIPO**
World Intellectual Property Organization

■ **IFAD**
International Fund for Agricultural Development

■ **UNIDO**
United Nations Industrial Development Organization

■ **GATT**
General Agreements on Tariffs and Trade

- Military Staff Committee
- Standing committees and ad hoc bodies
- Peacekeeping operations

▲ United Nations programs and organs (representative list only)
■ Specialized agencies and other autonomous organizations within the system
• Other commissions, committees, and ad hoc and related bodies

SOURCE: *THE CANADIAN REFERENCE GUIDE TO THE UNITED NATIONS,* FOREIGN AFFAIRS CANADA, 2000. REPRODUCED WITH THE PERMISSION OF THE MINISTER OF PUBLIC WORKS AND GOVERNMENT SERVICES CANADA, 2009.

Member States of the United Nations as of July 2009

MEMBER (DATE OF ADMISSION)

Afghanistan (November 19, 1946)

Albania (December 14, 1955)

Algeria (October 8, 1962)

Andorra (July 28, 1993)

Angola (December 1, 1976)

Antigua and Barbuda (November 11, 1981)

Argentina (October 24, 1945)

Armenia (March 2, 1992)

Australia (November 1, 1945)

Austria (December 14, 1955)

Azerbaijan (March 9, 1992)

Bahamas (September 18, 1973)

Bahrain (September 21, 1971)

Bangladesh (September 17, 1974)

Barbados (December 9, 1966)

Belarus (October 24, 1945)

Belgium (December 27, 1945)

Belize (September 25, 1981)

Benin (September 20, 1960)

Bhutan (September 21, 1971)

Bolivia (November 14, 1945)

Bosnia and Herzegovina (May 22, 1992)

Botswana (October 17, 1966)

Brazil (October 24, 1945)

Brunei Darussalam (September 21, 1984)

Bulgaria (December 14, 1955)

Burkina Faso (September 20, 1960)

Burundi (September 18, 1962)

Cambodia (December 14, 1955)

Cameroon (September 20, 1960)

Canada (November 9, 1945)

Cape Verde (September 16, 1975)

Central African Republic (September 20, 1960)

Chad (September 20, 1960)

Chile (October 24, 1945)

China (October 24, 1945)

Colombia (November 5, 1945)

Comoros (November 12, 1975)

Congo (September 20, 1960)

Costa Rica (November 2, 1945)

Côte d'Ivoire (September 20, 1960)

Croatia (May 22 1992)

Cuba (October 24, 1945)

Cyprus (September 20, 1960)

Czech Republic (January 19, 1993)

Democratic People's Republic of Korea (September 17, 1991)

Democratic Republic of the Congo (September 20, 1960)

Denmark (October 24, 1945)

Djibouti (September 20, 1977)

Dominica (December 18, 1978)

Dominican Republic (October 24, 1945)

Ecuador (December 21, 1945)

Egypt (October 24, 1945)

El Salvador (October 24, 1945)

Equatorial Guinea (November 12, 1968)

Eritrea (May 28 1993)

Estonia (September 17, 1991)

Ethiopia (November 13, 1945)

Fiji (October 13, 1970)

Finland (December 14, 1955)

France (October 24, 1945)

Gabon (September 20, 1960)

Gambia (September 21, 1965)

Georgia (July 31, 1992)

Germany (September 18, 1973)

Ghana (March 8, 1957)

Greece (October 25, 1945)

Grenada (September 17, 1974)

Guatemala (November 21, 1945)

Guinea (December 12, 1958)

Guinea-Bissau (September 17, 1974)

Guyana (September 20, 1966)

Haiti (October 24, 1945)

Honduras (December 17, 1945)

Hungary (December 14, 1955)

Iceland (November 19, 1946)

India (October 30, 1945)

Indonesia (September 28, 1950)

Iraq (December 21, 1945)

Ireland (December 14, 1955)

Islamic Republic of Iran (October 24, 1945)

Israel (May 11, 1949)

Italy (December 14, 1955)

Jamaica (September 18, 1962)

Japan (December 18, 1956)

Jordan (December 14, 1955)

Kazakhstan (March 2, 1992)

Kenya (December 16, 1963)

Kiribati (September 14, 1999)

Kuwait (May 14, 1963)

Kyrgyzstan (March 2, 1992)

Lao People's Democratic Republic (December 14, 1955)

Latvia (September 17, 1991)

Lebanon (October 24, 1945)

Lesotho (October 17, 1966)

Liberia (November 2, 1945)

(continued)

PROFILE 5.2 Member States of the United Nations as of July 2009 (*continued*)

Libyan Arab Jamahiriya (December 14, 1955)

Liechtenstein (September 18, 1990)

Lithuania (September 17, 1991)

Luxembourg (October 24, 1945)

Madagascar (September 20, 1960)

Malawi (December 1, 1964)

Malaysia (September 17, 1957)

Maldives (September 21, 1965)

Mali (September 28, 1960)

Malta (December 1, 1964)

Marshall Islands (September 17, 1991)

Mauritania (October 7, 1961)

Mauritius (April 24, 1968)

Mexico (November 7, 1945)

Micronesia (States Federated of) (September 17, 1991)

Monaco (May 28, 1993)

Mongolia (October 27, 1961)

Montenegro (June 28, 2006)

Morocco (November 12, 1956)

Mozambique (September 16, 1975)

Myanmar (April 19, 1948)

Namibia (April 23, 1990)

Nauru (September 14, 1999)

Nepal (December 14, 1955)

Netherlands (December 10, 1945)

New Zealand (October 24, 1945)

Nicaragua (October 24, 1945)

Niger (September 20, 1960)

Nigeria (October 7, 1960)

Norway (November 27, 1945)

Oman (October 7, 1971)

Pakistan (September 30, 1947)

Palau (December 15, 1994)

Panama (November 13, 1945)

Papua New Guinea (October 10, 1975)

Peru (October 31, 1945)

Philippines (October 24, 1945)

Poland (October 24, 1945)

Portugal (December 14, 1955)

Qatar (September 21, 1971)

Republic of Korea (September 17, 1991)

Republic of Moldova (March 2, 1992)

Romania (December 14, 1955)

Russian Federation (October 24, 1945)

Rwanda (September 18, 1962)

Saint Kitts and Nevis (September 23, 1983)

Saint Lucia (September 18, 1979)

Saint Vincent and the Grenadines (September 16, 1980)

Samoa (December 15, 1976)

San Marino (March 2, 1992)

Sao Tome and Principe (September 16, 1975)

Saudi Arabia (October 24, 1945)

Senegal (September 28, 1960)

Serbia (November 1, 2000)

Seychelles (September 21, 1976)

Sierra Leone (September 27, 1961)

Singapore (September 21, 1965)

Slovakia (January 19, 1993)

Slovenia (May 22, 1992)

Solomon Islands (September 19, 1978)

Somalia (September 20, 1960)

South Africa (November 7, 1945)

Spain (December 14, 1955)

Sri Lanka (December 14, 1955)

Sudan (November 12, 1956)

Suriname (December 4, 1975)

Swaziland (September 24, 1968)

Sweden (November 19, 1946)

Syrian Arab Republic (October 24, 1945)

Tajikistan (March 2, 1992)

Thailand (December 16, 1946)

The former Yugoslav Republic of Macedonia (April 8, 1993)

Timor-Leste (September 27, 2002)

Togo (September 20, 1960)

Tonga (September 14, 1999)

Trinidad and Tobago (September 18, 1962)

Tunisia (November 12, 1956)

Turkey (October 24, 1945)

Turkmenistan (March 2, 1992)

Tuvalu (September 5, 2000)

Uganda (October 25, 1962)

Ukraine (October 24, 1945)

United Arab Emirates (December 9, 1971)

United Kingdom of Great Britain and Northern Ireland (October 24, 1945)

United Republic of Tanzania (December 14, 1961)

United States of America (October 24, 1945)

Uruguay (December 18, 1945)

Uzbekistan (March 2, 1992)

Vanuatu (September 15, 1981)

Venezuela (November 15, 1945)

Viet Nam (September 20, 1977)

Yemen (September 30, 1947)

Zambia (December 1, 1964)

Zimbabwe (August 25, 1980)

also ten nonpermanent members (originally there were six), elected by the General Assembly in accordance with an agreed-upon geographical formula for two-year terms. A substantive matter (as opposed to a procedural one) requires nine positive votes and the absence of a veto to pass in the Council. The Council meets whenever the Secretary-General decides a matter has come up that demands its attention. Simultaneous translation allows it to operate in six official languages: Arabic, Chinese, English, French, Spanish, and Russian. Sydney Bailey and Sam Davis write that one diplomat, Victor Andres Belaunde of Peru, "used to choose a language to suit his mood: French when he wanted to be precise, English when he wanted to understate, Spanish when he wanted to exaggerate."[10] The Security Council is still the primary organ dealing with questions of international peace and security, and in particular collective security, a concept embraced originally by the UN's founders despite its apparent failure during the interwar period (see Profile 5.3). Canada has been elected six times to a nonpermanent seat on the Council: 1948–49, 1958–59, 1967–68, 1977–78, 1989–90, and 1999–2000, and is expecting reelection in the autumn of 2010.

The **Economic and Social Council (ECOSOC)** comprises 54 members elected by the General Assembly for a term of three years. ECOSOC has established several regional and functional commissions and other bodies, considers general policy questions regarding economic and social development, and makes recommendations. The **Trusteeship Council** was set up to help manage trust territories after World War II but is no longer an active body. The **Secretariat** is the administrative arm of the organization, comprising the Secretary-General and staff appointed by that person. Staff members are supposed to act as truly international civil servants, discarding any national obligations they may have toward their home state. The Secretariat has been trusted with increasingly important matters since the formation of the UN, and the Secretary-General has participated in, or has had representatives participate in, many diplomatic missions through the "good offices" function. The sixth principal organ of the UN, the **International Court of Justice (ICJ)**, is discussed in our examination of IL later in the chapter.

The demands placed on the UN are quite extraordinary. In addition to its diplomatic and moral role in global politics, the UN now has over 100,000 employees worldwide. The

---

PROFILE 5.3 Collective Security and the UN

Collective security is a system of international order in which all states respect recognized territorial boundaries and in which aggression by any state is met by a collective response. In other words, an attack on one will be considered an attack on all and dealt with accordingly. This ideal differs from collective defence systems, which are traditional alliances aimed at potential aggressors outside the membership of the system. Collective security is an ideal system that has yet to be fully realized by the international community. The League of Nations was a collective security organization, as is the United Nations. The UN rarely exercised its collective security provisions during the Cold War, due to the use (or threatened use) of the veto. It came close to doing so in the Korean War, but the Soviet Union was absent from the Security Council vote on Korea. Some argue that the response to Iraq's invasion of Kuwait in 1990–91 was an instance of collective security in action; others insist it was merely an example of American-orchestrated power. NATO chose to avoid the Security Council altogether when it launched its air war over Serbia in 1999, aware that the Russians and Chinese would most likely veto military action; and the United States did not seek final Security Council authorization before it and the United Kingdom launched the invasion of Iraq in 2003.

UN deployed over 88,000 uniformed peacekeepers in mid-2008. The Office of the High Commissioner for Human Rights (a post held by a Canadian, Louise Arbour, until June 2008) has 11 country offices and seven regional offices. The UN Development Program has a presence in 166 countries. Each year, humanitarian programs operated through the UN deliver emergency supplies to over 30 million people, and the World Food Program delivers emergency food aid to over 70 million people. However, despite the UN's profile in the world, and despite the wide variety of political, economic, and social functions it performs, the organization operates in a state of permanent financial crisis. The annual regular budget of the UN is approximately US$1.925 billion per year, although adding the separate peacekeeping budget, the expenditures of all funds and programs, and the budgets of the specialized agencies the entire UN system spends approximately US$15 billion a year (excluding the IMF and the World Bank). Compared to the spending of other institutions the UN budget is remarkably modest. For example, the City of New York spent over US$43 billion in 2007.[11]

The money in the UN regular budget is paid to the UN in the form of dues from member states (peacekeeping costs are assessed separately). The UN is often in financial crisis because many members fail to pay their dues. During the 1990s, the biggest debtor was the United States, although it has paid up much of its debt—after prolonged negotiations. The United States argued that the mechanism used to determine dues was unfair. Member states are expected to contribute a certain percentage of the UN budget based on the size of their gross national product (GNP). As a result, because the United States had typically generated about a third to a quarter of world GNP, it was expected to pay much more than other states. However, with the increased growth in the economies of Europe and Japan over the past two decades, the United States argued that it was paying more than its share, and demanded that its contribution be capped at 22 percent. This was agreed to in 1999, and the U.S. began paying back some (though not all) of its dues. Many other countries are also in arrears to the UN. As of 2008, the UN was owed US$1.6 billion in unpaid dues to the regular budget (the U.S. still owed US$846 million, or 52 percent of the total). In addition, over the past few decades the United States has on occasion unilaterally withdrawn funding for various agencies, such as the United Nations Population Fund, which promotes family planning and contraception. Given the enormous responsibilities and tasks the UN is assigned by its member states, it is a source of great shame and frustration for UN advocates around the world that inadequate funding continues to plague the organization.

The UN has also been criticized for being unrepresentative, with the composition of the Security Council reflecting the old distribution of power and excluding important countries (especially Japan, Germany, Brazil, and India), and for being overly bureaucratic. In recent decades there has been much discussion of UN reform. Some substantive developments include the creation in 2005 of a Peacebuilding Commission and a Peacebuilding Fund to increase the ability of the UN to engage in post-conflict reconstruction. In 2006, the UN Security Council passed resolution 1674 on the Protection of Civilians in Armed Conflict, for the first time affirming the "Responsibility to Protect" doctrine (see Chapter Seven).[12] A Human Rights Council was created in 2006 (replacing the Human Rights Commission) in order to strengthen the UN's role in monitoring and promoting human rights. A Department of Field Support was created in 2007 to enhance the ability of the UN system to provide logistics assistance to peacekeeping and other UN missions. Many other reforms were made to UN structures, procedures, and programs. However, the solution to the major issue of reforming the UN Security Council has proven elusive.

Ultimately, the UN can be only as effective as its members want it to be. National interests, concerns over protecting sovereignty, and economic and political disputes between states continue to plague the United Nations. Indeed, many political leaders (often from lower-income states) want to avoid a stronger UN; they are concerned that the UN might become an instrument used by rich states to dominate or intimidate others. A vocal domestic anti-UN political current has also marked the American approach to the UN, and this was especially evident during the recent Bush administration. However, contrary to the blatantly erroneous allegations of some individuals and groups, the UN is nowhere close to becoming a world government with any substantive supranational authority, though myths of "UN hegemony" (and even a UN army) persist.

For the most part, smaller states such as Canada tend to be supportive of the UN, showing generally consistent dedication to paying their dues and contributing to peacekeeping missions.[13] Many countries view the UN as the cornerstone of an international legal system, and Security Council authorization is often seen as the most important form of legitimation for collective security–related military operations. However, a large rift has grown between theory and practice, since neither NATO's attack on Serbia in 1999 nor the "coalition" invasion of Iraq in 2003 were given explicit Security Council approval (vetoes from Russia over Serbia and from France over Iraq were almost certain). Nonetheless, the UN and its agencies perform so many valuable functions that if it did not exist, it would likely have to be created. In the end the UN does what its members allow it to do, and the political will and resource capacity of its members sets its limitations.

NON-UN IGOS

The UN, of course, is not the only IGO in the international system. Arguably, the most advanced supranational institution is the European Union: it can be seen as an ongoing experiment in political integration, challenging many aspects of the sovereign statehood that characterized the European system for so long. The EU is a much more demanding institution than the UN, since it has more regulatory and legal powers within member states. But there are other IGOs of great significance as well. While space does not permit an exhaustive survey, here is an overview of some other prominent IGOs that have special relevance for Canada and other middle powers.

- *The North Atlantic Treaty Organization.* NATO (also informally called the Atlantic Alliance) was established in 1949 to deter a Soviet invasion of Western Europe and to solidify American leadership (Canada was a founding member.) After the Cold War, NATO adopted a New Strategic Concept, which reduced its standing military forces and created a force structure oriented toward crisis response. NATO has established close relationships with other European institutions and was actively involved in peacekeeping operations in the former Yugoslavia in the 1990s. In a controversial action, NATO embarked on a bombing campaign against Serbia in 1999 in response to human rights abuses in the Serbian province of Kosovo. In 2003, NATO took over responsibility for the International Security Assistance Force (ISAF) in Afghanistan, a mission that has caused controversy among and within member states. NATO has grown since the end of the Cold War: Poland, Hungary, and the Czech Republic joined in 1999 and seven more countries—Bulgaria, Estonia, Latvia, Lithuania, Romania, Slovakia, and Slovenia—joined in 2004. In 2009, Albania and Croatia joined the Alliance, bringing NATO membership to 28 states. NATO's headquarters are in Brussels, Belgium.
- *The Commonwealth.* The origins of the Commonwealth lie in the British Empire. World War I, the adoption of the famous Balfour Declaration at the 1926 Imperial Conference, and the institution's formal creation in 1931 under the Statute of

Westminster were the defining events in the formation of the Commonwealth and the independence of its early members (which included Canada and Newfoundland). The Commonwealth expanded during the decolonization era, though South Africa was expelled, and in 1965 a Secretariat was established. A major issue facing the Commonwealth during the Cold War was the apartheid regime in South Africa; its eventual collapse led to the readmission of South Africa in 1994. Today, human rights, democracy, and development are the major concerns of the Commonwealth (see Profile 5.4), with Nigeria and Zimbabwe both presenting major problems and Commonwealth suspensions (Zimbabwe withdrew in late 2003, and Fiji remains suspended as of 2009). Another important cultural and diplomatic organization, with ties to Canada's French colonial past, is La Francophonie.

- *The Organization of American States.* According to its own literature, the OAS is the oldest regional intergovernmental organization in the world, with its origins in the 1826 Congress of Panama. The Charter of the present OAS was signed in 1948 and entered into force in 1951. The OAS has a troubled history, both because of the political instability of Central and South America and because of the disturbing tendency of the United States to engage in unilateral action (including invasions and interventions) in the region. As a result, the OAS has been frequently maligned as ineffective and dominated by Washington. Today, the principal activities of the OAS are focused on democratic values, trade, and economic development. The OAS has also

---

PROFILE 5.4 **Membership in the Commonwealth**

The 53 Commonwealth states have an estimated 1.7 billion citizens. Members are listed below:

Antigua & Barbuda	Kiribati	Singapore
Australia	Lesotho	Solomon Islands
Bangladesh	Malawi	South Africa
Barbados	Malaysia	Sri Lanka
Belize	Maldives	St Kitts & Nevis
Botswana	Malta	St Lucia
Brunei Darussalam	Mauritius	St Vincent & the Grenadines
Cameroon	Mozambique	Swaziland
Canada	Namibia	Tanzania (United Republic of)
Cyprus	Nauru (in arrears as of January 2009)	The Bahamas
Dominica		The Gambia
Fiji Islands (suspended 2006)	New Zealand	Tonga
Ghana	Nigeria	Trinidad & Tobago
Grenada	Pakistan	Tuvalu
Guyana	Papua New Guinea	Uganda
India	Samoa	United Kingdom
Jamaica	Seychelles	Vanuatu
Kenya	Sierra Leone	Zambia

played a minor role in political oversight and mediation, frequently deploying election observers and negotiating teams. The OAS had 35 members in 2009 (Canada joined in 1990) and is headquartered in Washington, D.C.

- *The African Union.* In 2002, the 53-member AU was established from the foundations of the Organization of African Unity (OAU), which had failed to respond to the crises in Rwanda, the Congo, and Somalia. The AU vision is to strengthen cooperation on African security affairs, development, and corruption. Notably, it explicitly recognizes the right to humanitarian intervention. The AU has deployed badly prepared peace-keeping missions in Burundi and Darfur in 2003 (the latter in cooperation with the UN as of 2008), and Somalia in 2007. An AU force restored stability to the Comoros in 2008. It oversees the New Partnership for Africa's Development (NEPAD) which establishes partnerships with industrialized countries to increase the economic development of Africa. However, the AU is beset with problems familiar to many international organizations. It relies on consensus of its members in order to act, and this has weakened the organization's ability to respond to human rights problems in Africa such as the governance of Zimbabwe, and the organization is seriously underfunded (in 2006 only 12 countries paid their membership dues).

NONGOVERNMENTAL ORGANIZATIONS

In Chapter 4, we mentioned the growing importance of international nongovernmental organizations (NGOs) in world affairs. An important distinction must be made between multinational corporations (MNCs) and NGOs. MNCs are profit-generating businesses with operations in more than one country. NGOs are not for profit organizations of individuals dedicated to a particular cause and/or representing particular social movements. We discussed the importance of MNCs and international financial institutions (IFIs) in the previous chapter, and thus will focus largely on NGOs here, but should note that private-sector actors are obviously heavily involved in global governance efforts today. Indeed, James Rosenau has written of the "bifurcation of global structures into the old state-centric world and the relatively ascendant multicentric world, composed of sovereignty-free actors including MNCs, ethnic minorities, subnational governments and bureaucracies, professional societies, and transnational organizations."[14] Most visibly, the rising influence of groups such as Amnesty International, CARE, Médecins sans Frontières, and the International Committee of the Red Cross/Red Crescent is viewed by many as a positive development in human rights and humanitarian issues. Labour unions are increasingly internationalized as well, and are major voices in global activism on working conditions and the rights of labourers among many other issues. While NGOs may not have the military power or diplomatic resources of states, they do possess an inherent ability to change shape, to submerge and resurface, and to make decisions rapidly, all important tools of survival. Meanwhile, the IOs that form the core of state-centric diplomacy, in particular the immense UN system, can act as channels or conduits between the state and the NGO community.

While NGOs may not have access to the same resources as states, they are increasingly important and visible actors in the global system. In 1972 about 2,100 NGOs existed; in 1982 more than 4,200 had been established, and by 1993 more than 4,800 had been registered with the Union of International Associations in Brussels. Remarkably, current estimates run as high as 40,000 international NGOs. Most are private organizations, founded by individuals or groups and funded from donations, grants, IGO budgets, or governments. These individuals or groups do not formally represent their states or governments, although they continue to be citizens of states, and many do collaborate extensively with governments. It is impossible to list the wide variety of NGO activities here, but a partial list would include the following:

- *Humanitarian NGOs.* These NGOs undertake aid efforts to assist in the alleviation of human suffering. The **International Committee of the Red Cross** (ICRC; "Red Crescent" in Muslim societies) provides medical assistance to victims of war and armed conflict. CARE International provides developmental and emergency care to poor peoples and victims of natural disasters and conflicts. Save the Children focuses on alleviating child poverty.

- *Human rights NGOs.* Human rights NGOs monitor and investigate human rights abuses worldwide and put pressure on governments to improve their human rights records or take action against other governments with poor human rights records. The most prominent example is Amnesty International.

- *Corporate lobby groups.* Corporations typically pool their money and expertise to create lobby groups with international reach. Examples include the Trilateral Commission, the European Roundtable of Industrialists, the Canadian Business Council on National Issues, the Davos World Economic Forum, and the International Chamber of Commerce.

- *Scientific and technical organizations.* Scientific and technical NGOs work to increase scientific cooperation, achieve standardization, and promote research and development. Examples include the Council of Scientific Unions, the International Peace Research Institute, and the European Space Agency.

- *Sports bodies.* Sporting organizations manage international sporting events and frequently find themselves involved in world politics, as sport is often employed for political purposes (such as the former ban on South African athletes, or boycotts and protests related to the Olympic Games). The International Olympic Committee (IOC) is the most prominent sports-related NGO.

- *Professional associations.* Professional associations exist to promote the interests of their members and interaction among them. Examples include the International Federation of Airline Pilots and the International Studies Association (a favourite of many IR scholars!).

- *Environmental groups.* Environmental NGOs promote awareness on environmental issues and often mount protests and publicity campaigns to this end. Three well-known environmental NGOs are Greenpeace, the International Fund for Animal Welfare, and Friends of the Earth.

- *Women's issues NGOs.* These NGOs exist to promote the political and economic advancement of women. Examples include the parallel Women's Forum of the ECOSOC Commission on the Status of Women, and the Associated Country Women of the World.

- *Philanthropic organizations.* A large number of trusts and foundations provide grants and sponsor projects on a variety of international issues. Although not strictly international NGOs because they are chartered under the domestic law of one state, organizations such as the Ford Foundation and Rockefeller Foundation have supported the NGO community and continue to do so.

- *Religious organizations.* A large number of religious NGOs exist, including the Roman Catholic Church and the World Jewish Congress. Multifaith NGOs include the International Association for Religious Freedom and the World Congress of Faiths.

They promote religious activities and are often directly involved in transnational political campaigns related to lifestyle and other moral choices.

NGOs perform many functions in global politics: they facilitate communication between interested individuals; act as pressure groups to change government policies; offer information-gathering resources, often when no other reliable source exists; distribute aid and knowledge; and play an important role in the formulation of state or IGO policy in cooperation with governments. Indeed, there is a growing tendency toward institutionalized interaction between official multilateral organizations and NGOs with more specific agendas. Such hybrids include the Arctic Council, which is composed of eight Arctic states—Canada, Denmark (for Greenland), Finland, Iceland, Norway, the Russian Federation, Sweden, and the United States—as well as six initial permanent participant groups—the Inuit Circumpolar Conference; the Saami Council; and the Russian Association of Indigenous Peoples of the North; the Aleut International Association; the Arctic Athabascan Council; and the Gwich'in Council International. It is not insignificant that these groups have been guaranteed a permanent status on the Council, even if they will have less influence than the formal governments involved. The Council is supposed to be a "high-level permanent intergovernmental forum to provide for co-operation, co-ordination and interaction among the Arctic states, the Arctic indigenous communities and other Arctic inhabitants on common Arctic issues [including] economic and social development, improved health conditions and cultural well-being."[15] In another somewhat ironic example, even legislators have an NGO, called Parliamentarians for Global Action. Here we see the ultimate meshing of the public sector and the nonprofit NGO.

At the UN, NGOs have consultative status in many agencies. As A. LeRoy Bennett writes,

> The most sought-after consultative status is granted by the Economic and Social Council. The breadth of ECOSOC's mandate explains the large number of NGOs that have been granted consultative status, including more than 800 organizations divided into three categories according to the extent of their involvement in ECOSOC's program.... The relationships between United Nations agencies and hundreds of NGOs demonstrates the impossibility of effectively separating public from private organizations.[16]

Bailey and Daws argue that NGOs play an important role within ECOSOC, "so long as they do not try to usurp the functions of governments."[17] Meanwhile, David Keen, who is concerned with refugees' rights, argues that while NGOs can contribute immensely to such UN-related activities as humanitarian relief, "this trend nevertheless carries risks. It represents a shift in welfare responsibilities away from government-funded bodies in the UN towards organizations largely funded from private contributions.... Linking the welfare of millions with private charity—which is unpredictable and makes planning difficult—seems a poor alternative to establishing an international system in which refugees' rights to welfare are guaranteed by regularized public contributions and clear legal obligations."[18]

Some analysts even suggest that transnational environmental activist groups, such as the World Wildlife Fund, Friends of the Earth, Greenpeace, Conservation International, and Earth Island Institute are formative agents in the development of a new **global civil society**, both as part of and in opposition to the evolution of global governance.[19] A wide variety of

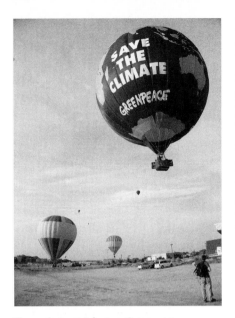

The environmental group Greenpeace launches its new Stop Global Warming, Save the Climate hot-air balloon in Albuquerque, New Mexico, 2008. NGOs like Greenpeace are increasingly active on a wide range of international issues. (AP Photo/Susan Montoya Bryan/CP Images.)

NGOs cluster around certain issue-areas and coordinate their activities. For example, the annual meeting of the International Whaling Commission habitually attracts representatives from more than 90 NGOs. Similarly, in the political arena, groups such as Amnesty International and Human Rights Watch play a key role in monitoring and exposing violations of human rights by governments. A number of NGOs dedicated to human rights issues cooperate under a loose framework known as the social justice movement. Others, such as CARE International, play a constructive role in both long-term and emergency development and relief efforts. And NGOs, domestic and international, have always been the active force behind what has been broadly labelled the **peace movement** in both international and domestic contexts.[20] However, the tendency to equate NGO activity with the broader political concept of civil society may be criticized as an oversimplification, and we would then have to include organizations such as the National Rifle Association and even pro-racist groups with internationally organized memberships.

Throughout the remainder of this text we will refer often to various NGOs that have been involved in global politics. Whether we are on the verge of a new global civil society is highly debatable, but we are undeniably living in an era in which nonstate actors have increased their ability to influence the work of governments and IOs alike. All of these organizations operate in what English school realists call an *anarchical society*, a complicated environment dominated by sovereign states that are loosely bound together with institutions, nonstate actors, and a growing set of norms and rules that constitute a social system. We turn next to those formal rules which form the basis of international law.

INTERNATIONAL LAW

Many would argue that IL has its origins in the Roman Empire, when Roman judges settled disputes between persons of different regions with conflicting local customs. Roman law held that no custom was necessarily right, that a higher universal law existed that was inherently fair and would apply to all. This **natural law**, or law of nature, would arise from human reason and nature itself, and it would derive its force from being enacted by a proper authority. This authority, attributed (not surprisingly) to the emperor, was called *majestas*, or sovereign power. Thus the central question of IL remains the achievement of global standards that can be applied within the context of respect for the individualism of different localities and geographic areas of the world (see Profile 5.5). In addition, the international legal system, like the Westphalian state system and the international economic system, resulted from the expansion of the European empires. As a result, Western values and legal concepts dominate IL and are often the source of considerable friction between Western countries and the Islamic and Asian world.

IL is often dismissed as a weak force in world politics because it is based on voluntarism, or states' willingness to commit themselves to its realization, rather than on any physical body capable of enforcing it. Though no legal authority exists that can enforce IL in the same way domestic courts can enforce national laws, as A. LeRoy Bennett writes, an

PROFILE 5.5 Hugo Grotius (1583–1645)

Grotius was a Dutch jurist and diplomat (in Swedish service). His most famous work, *De jure belli ac pacis* (*On the Law of War and Peace*), is regarded as one of the intellectual foundations of IL. Grotian thought offers an alternative perspective on international relations from that of Machiavelli or his English contemporary, Thomas Hobbes. This perspective, referred to as the *Grotian tradition*, seeks to establish order and escape anarchy in the international system through the creation of IL. For Grotius, the origins of IL rested in natural law principles and in treaties and covenants established between states. In addition, Grotian thought recognizes the existence of values and norms that influence the behaviour of states and help to maintain order among them. Grotius believed that IL should be binding on states even in the absence of a central authority to enforce them. In this sense, Grotius was advocating the building of a world as it ought to be, rather than describing the world as it existed.

Four key Grotian ideas have had an enduring legacy in international relations:

1. States should refrain from interference in the internal affairs of others, by not seeking to impose their ideologies (in Grotius's time, Catholicism and Protestantism) on others.

2. A law of nature exists that is higher than human affairs but can be known through reason.

3. Acceptance of the principles of this natural law is the only escape from anarchy.

4. An assembly of nations ought to be created to enforce such laws.

Grotius is recognized as one of the key founders of the constitutive concepts behind IL and IOs. In international relations theory, the Grotian perspective is similar to that of the English School/liberal realists discussed in Chapter 1.

SEE L. VAN SOMEREN, *UMPIRE TO THE NATIONS: HUGO GROTIUS* (LONDON: DENNIS DOBSON, 1965); AND S. TARZI, "THE ROLE OF NORMS AND REGIMES IN WORLD AFFAIRS: A GROTIAN PERSPECTIVE," *INTERNATIONAL RELATIONS* 14, NO. 3 (1998), 71–84.

assessment "of the deficiencies of IL may lead erroneously to the conclusion that no legal principles operate across national boundaries, but an inadequate system does not signify the absence of any system."[21] Most scholars of IL accept its inherent weakness as the price of protecting state sovereignty, but do not dismiss its potential as a unifying and even pacifying force.

Formal public international law encompasses the affairs of states, while private international law largely concerns the transactions of companies doing business in the international arena. The latter is the more lucrative for aspiring lawyers, while the former, arguably, has more important implications for global politics. We should further distinguish between the progressive development of IL and the codification of IL. The first aims at developing new law (*lex ferenda*), while codification aims essentially at clarifying existing law (*lex lata*). In practice, a bit of both occurs. Finally, many analysts distinguish between hard law, codified by treaties and enforced by some sort of punishment mechanism, and soft law, which consists mainly of declaratory statements emerging from the GA and elsewhere.

IL is derived from many sources, including treaties, customs, and legal scholarship. Of these, treaties are the most important, since they are largely seen to bind states to agreements. Tens of thousands of bilateral and multilateral agreements exist today, a sign of the spread of diplomatic activity as well as faith in IL. Treaties are assumed to be binding on successor governments, no matter how those governments come into power. Many treaties, however, have escape clauses that permit states to withdraw their obligations without penalty, and other clauses that allow disputants to use the International Court of Justice (often referred to as the World Court) to settle arguments over their interpretation.

Arguably, the most important treaty is the Charter of the United Nations, which enshrines the primacy of the principle of state sovereignty, the most important principle in contemporary IL. The UN Charter attempts to strike a balance between the principle of state sovereignty and the need for collective responses to international issues. For example, although states that sign the UN Charter do commit themselves to collective security and in theory surrender some of their sovereign authority to make foreign policy decisions to the greater body called the United Nations, it is the Security Council, comprising a mere 15 members (five of which, we will recall, have disproportionate power as permanent members), that ultimately decides when collective security has been breached and when the UN can take action. In addition, in practice many states have not contributed to collective security or peacekeeping efforts by the UN. Participation is largely voluntary, and no system exists to force or compel states to contribute to UN operations. Another example of the protection of sovereignty in the Charter is the contrast between supranational jurisdiction and two conflicting perspectives on the legitimate prosecution of crimes. The territorial principle suggests that courts in the country where the crime is committed should have first crack at prosecution. The nationality principle implies that states can assert their jurisdiction over the conduct of nationals anywhere, including outside their home state.

IL is also derived from customary law, which stresses the validity of repeated modes of interaction over time. In what is known as the positivist view, customs that occur over time can be said to constitute some form of law, while natural law or divine law (said to have come from the heavens) is rejected. Customary law has an important psychological element in the sense that it requires "a conviction felt by states that a certain form of conduct is permitted by international law."[22] For example, in the so-called Fisheries Case in the International Court of Justice (*United Kingdom vs. Norway, 1949–51*), the United Kingdom complained that Norway had reserved an exclusive fishing zone for its nationals within a four-mile zone (about 6.5 kilometres) that had been drawn according to several fixed points along the coastline instead of using the configuration of the actual coastline itself. The Court found that Norway had been using this method for decades without any objections by other states and that, therefore, it was permissible under customary IL. The ICJ can also refer to legal scholarship, the judgments of international arbitrational bodies such as itself, as well as the writings of highly respected experts in the field, when arriving at decisions.

If no global police force exists to enforce IL, are there mechanisms at least to encourage compliance? The short answer is yes. States that reject or deliberately disobey IL can be subject to **reprisals** (actions that would have been illegal under IL may be legal if taken in response to the illegal actions of another state). The most extreme example of this action is the outright declaration of war on a state, as was seen when Iraq violated the sovereignty of Kuwait, and the Security Council voted in November 1990 to authorize the use of force against Iraq. (Cuba and Yemen voted against the relevant resolution, and China abstained.) Bilateral or multilateral sanctions can also be applied.[23] In the bilateral case a state will suspend or reduce its customary trade relationship with another state, and in the multilateral case a number of states will join to impose sanctions on a target state. As we will see in Chapter 7, the efficacy of sanctions is a hot topic of policy debate. For example, some say sanctions helped change apartheid South Africa, while others (such as former British Prime Minister Margaret Thatcher) argue that South Africa changed despite them. On the other hand, multilateral sanctions will usually have a greater impact on the offending state than will bilateral sanctions. A sanctioned state can, over time, assume the status of a pariah in the world community.

Nigeria, Burma, Iraq, Iran, Serbia, Sudan, Zimbabwe, and Libya are examples of states that at one time or another have achieved this dubious distinction (Libya rehabilitated itself by renouncing weapons of mass destruction in 2004). However, when more powerful states violate IL much less is done by the world community. Russia's activities in Chechnya, China's actions in Tibet, and the American/British invasion of Iraq are all, arguably, violent examples of breaches of global norms without direct legal responses.

Certain conventions related to international diplomacy also have international legal status. Embassies in foreign states are considered part of the embassy state's territory. As a result, the laws of the embassy state apply there, not the local laws of the land. When Iranian students seized and occupied the American embassy in Iran in 1979 following the Islamic revolution there, it was widely considered a breach of IL. Since host governments are expected to use force to protect the sanctity of embassies, the Iranian government was condemned as an accomplice. Another important convention is the extension of diplomatic immunity to foreign diplomatic staff (though there are some constraints on their right to travel). Because this means the law of the local state does not apply to foreign diplomats, the worst a state can do to a diplomat suspected of engaging in criminal acts is expel that person from the country. This treatment opens up room for espionage activities and can elicit a rather indignant response among the local population.

There are other bodies of IL as well. International criminal law has been defined as a "complex set of norms and conflict-resolving mechanisms adhered to by sovereigns within a particular jurisdictional unit, through agreement or the use of sanctions."[24] As such, it encompasses slavery, terrorism, hijacking, drug trafficking, genocide, piracy, acts against the peace, acts of aggression, and war crimes. International humanitarian law, on the other hand, refers to laws designed specifically to limit the harm to noncombatants during wartime. A great deal of jurisdictional overlap exists between this body of IL and domestic law in most states. This jurisdictional overlap sometimes creates tensions between those advocating prosecution under domestic law and those advocating prosecution under IL. A major development in the realm of international criminal and humanitarian law occurred in 1997 when the Treaty of Rome established the **International Criminal Court (ICC)**. The ICC has the unique ability to prosecute individuals charged with crimes against humanity, and began hearing cases in 2008 (we examine the ICC in more detail in Chapter 9).

Another distinction should be made between international public law (which we have discussed so far) and international private law, which refers to legal contracts between individuals and, more often, firms engaged in trade and investment. The vast majority of international lawyers are in fact employed by MNCs, though they must understand international public law in order to represent their clients. Sometimes, the concerns of private and public IL converge in a single case. For several years, three judges from the United States, three from Iran, and three from other countries met to negotiate the issue of financial compensation following the Iranian revolution in 1979. The Iran–United States Claims Tribunal convened in an unmarked building on the outskirts of The Hague. As Abner Katzman writes, "despite the backdrop of political bitterness, the daily hearings in the marble and wood-paneled chambers have resolved almost 4000 cases arising from expropriations, the freezing of assets, and broken contracts. That has meant about $2.1 billion (U.S.) for American claimants and about $9 billion to Iranians, with a billion more in interest." The tribunal also facilitated the settlement of a $61.8 million payment the Americans made to Iran after the cruiser USS *Vincennes* shot down an Iran Air A-300 Airbus over the Persian Gulf on July 3, 1988. The Airbus case had been before the ICJ for years before both sides agreed that it would be easier to deal with through the tribunal.[25]

However, this case is by no means typical, since political divisions will often undermine attempts to achieve consensus and healthy compliance levels with IL. The prevalent cynicism about the efficacy of IL is understandable. However, that a body of legal thought and historic precedents pertaining to international relations exists at all is impressive. In a speech to the General Assembly of the UN in New York, the former president of the ICJ, Judge Nagendra Singh, argues we should not be

> mesmerized by the simplistic notion of politics and law as antipoles. On the contrary, the law made by treaties is a law made by political decisions; the law codified in conventions is a law confirming the *opinio juris* of political entities; while the law of custom registers the regularity of State conduct. But in all three the keynotes are balance and reconciliation, tolerance and mutual regard: in a nutshell, the evidence that politics can, and must, transcend the partisan, the provisional, and the parochial.[26]

Others, such as Theodore Couloumbis and James Wolfe, are less sanguine:

> Without worldwide consensus on vital international issues, without central global authorities, without a legislature, without effective courts, given the existence of large autonomous subjects with powerful military establishments, given further the permanent companion of human history called war … in these circumstances, all that international law can hope to accomplish is to limit violence [and] to substitute for it at times.[27]

The UN has developed a complex network of international legal specialists and governmental representation over the years. Two important bodies are the International Law Commission, which is an independent body of 34 legal experts who meet once a year in Geneva to work on the codification of existing laws, and the Sixth Committee of the General Assembly, the Legal Committee. The Legal Committee is filled with governmental representatives who report to the GA on current developments in IL and also draft conventions. Although many other parts to the giant puzzle of contemporary IL exist, the most prominent institution is the International Court of Justice, also known as the World Court.

THE INTERNATIONAL COURT OF JUSTICE

Established in 1946, the ICJ is the principal judicial organ of the UN and meets at The Hague in the Netherlands. Its 15 judges are elected by separate votes (simple majorities required) in the Security Council and the General Assembly, and they are intended to reflect the world's leading civilizations and judicial systems. The judges serve nine-year terms. Decisions are taken in private by a majority vote, the quorum being nine. Cases are brought before the ICJ voluntarily when both states seek a ruling, but the Court also provides **advisory opinions** at the request of the General Assembly, individual states, or any of the specialized agencies. All members of the UN belong to the Court, although many have opted out of accepting its compulsory jurisdiction (the ability to call states before it at will and enforce decisions). Article 36 of the ICJ Statute says that states may agree in advance to adhere to compulsory jurisdiction. In 1946 the United States made a reservation (known as the Connally Amendment) that asserts the right to exclude disputes believed to fall under domestic jurisdiction, and most states have adopted similar reservations. Thus the ICJ is nothing like a domestic court of law.

Most states have signed the treaty establishing the Court, but only about one-third have signed the Optional Clause, which would give the Court unconditional jurisdiction in certain cases.[28] The United States withdrew from the Optional Clause when it refused to allow the Court's 1986 decision regarding the mining of Nicaraguan harbours to affect its foreign policy. Israel has withdrawn its acceptance of the Optional Clause as well. Canada put forth a reservation over the issue of extending Canadian sovereign jurisdiction in Arctic waters in the early 1970s.[29] However, literally hundreds of bilateral and multilateral treaties contain clauses agreeing that the parties will submit any disputes over the terms of the treaty to the ICJ. And the Court has jurisdiction over a number of specialized human rights conventions, including the Convention on Genocide; the Supplementary Convention on the Abolition of Slavery, the Slave Trade and Institutions and Practices Similar to Slavery; the Convention on the Political Rights of Women; the Convention Relating to the Status of Refugees; and the Convention on the Reduction of Statelessness. The ICJ also works in conjunction with other legal bodies. For example, the European Convention for the Protection of Human Rights and Freedoms (1950) allows individuals to petition the European Commission on Human Rights, which may ask the European Court of Human Rights to enforce the relevant UN convention.

In some cases, states employ the ICJ as a mediator. For example, in 1992, El Salvador and Honduras used the Court to settle territorial disputes along six stretches of border, three islands, and territorial waters. The disputes had been one of the causes of a war in 1969. The commonly accepted five-judge panel was headed by a Brazilian, and included judges from El Salvador, Honduras, Britain, and Japan. The Court drew borders in the ruling that gave about two-thirds of the total land to Honduras and split the territorial waters among both countries and Nicaragua, and all the relevant governments pledged to abide by the decision. Thus, a potentially violent conflict was avoided by the use of the ICJ. Canada and the United States have similarly used the Court to determine fishing rights off the East Coast.

The Court has also gone beyond its role as mediator and passed commentary. In 1996 it found that the use or threat to use nuclear weapons is "generally illegal under international law." The Court added that it was impossible to say whether the weapons would be illegal to use in self-defence, however. This hardly challenges the theory of deterrence, which, as we saw in Chapter 3, is based on the idea that nuclear weapons would be used only in self-defence anyway. This opinion was also a nonbinding one sought by the General Assembly, and the presiding judge, Mohammed Bedjaoui of Algeria, had to break a 7–7 tie on crucial paragraphs of the ruling. Yet, despite all this ambiguity, many have interpreted the Court's ruling as a strong push toward the negotiation of a Comprehensive Test Ban Treaty, which was signed in 1996. Canada's former disarmament ambassador, Douglas Roche, believes the Court was telling the nuclear five "to get on with it."[30] However, it is rather contestable whether an ICJ ruling on such a matter will have any significant influence when it comes to a topic state leaders tend to hold so dear to national

The World Court at work. The ICJ convenes on September 8, 2008 to hear charges of harassment and persecution brought by the government of Georgia against the government of Russia. The charges opened up a legal front in the armed conflict between Georgia and Russia over the territories of South Ossetia and Abkhazia in 2008. (AP Photo/Evert-Jan Daniels/CP Archive.)

security. For example, the 2004 ruling condemning the construction of a "security fence" by Israel in the Occupied Territories has been ignored. Canada abstained from the GA vote calling for the trial, claiming it was asking the Court to render a political, and not a legal, decision. However, the distinction between these two modes of decision remains unclear.

THEORY AND INTERNATIONAL ORGANIZATIONS

Three interpretations of the role and influence of IOs stand out in the literature. The central question pursued here is how much influence and autonomy IOs have in global politics. We have seen already that both IGOs and NGOs have increased in size and scope. But has this change resulted in a commensurate increase in their abilities to affect human or state behaviour? Are IGOs actually capable of making independent decisions, free from the constraints of members' objections? Are they places where the interests and expectations of various actors merely converge, or have they assumed a causal role in global politics themselves? Do NGOs influence global politics in decisive ways? Do they constitute the emergence of a global civil society that transcends the state, or are they primarily reflective of existing patterns of power and privilege in the world?

First, MNCs and NGOs have some automatic freedom from governments since they are not official representatives of states and exist to pursue their own objective, be it profit, charity, or value promotion. However, powerful though they may be, they are still subject to the national laws that exist where they operate, as well as the constraints imposed by the international system. But what about intergovernmental organizations themselves? The three main perspectives regarding the role of IGOs are simplified immediately below. Keep in mind that one can view the question of the effect of IL in much the same manner.

- IGOs are seen as mere instruments of foreign policy: they are little more than political arenas in which members (states) pursue their self-interest.

- IGOs are seen as "intervening variables"; that is, IGOs and international regimes intervene between causes and outcomes in world politics. As a result, they have some limited influence in global politics.

- IGOs can be seen as autonomous and influential actors, able to command their own resources and significantly alter the international system.[31]

As mentioned in the introduction to this chapter, both realists and Marxists tend to reject the notion of IO autonomy. For realists, IGOs merely reflect the character of power politics and the dynamics of cooperation as a form of self-help in an anarchic world. Like alliances, IGOs will form or dissolve when states decide to create them or eliminate them. When IGOs act in global politics, these actions reflect the extent to which states are willing to cooperate. Realists argue that this is why IGOs frequently fail to act in response to global events or only act in limited ways. No international institution can act without the agreement of its member states and most decisions are the result of consensus or the lowest common denominator among the membership (see the discussion of decision making in Chapter 3). For realists, NGOs lack true power and rely on lobbying state publics and governments to obtain their goals. Ultimately, NGOs rely heavily on states to adopt their beliefs, implement their policy prescriptions, and fund their programs in order to make change in global politics. For neo-Marxists, IGOs and NGOs merely reflect the character of global capitalism and the interests of the rich elites and the rich states. Both are part of the global power structure characterized by dominance and exploitation. Like the state itself, IGOs and NGOs are tools of the rich classes and rich states used to enforce their will and maintain their power. Gramscian approaches argue that NGOs and IGOs also act as conduits for the dissemination of liberal value systems that are part of the power structure of global capitalism.

In contrast, liberals tend to see the most potential for IOs, so much so that the literature refers to liberal institutionalism as a genuine perspective (see Chapter 1). The core belief held by liberal institutionalists is that international regimes and institutions can facilitate agreements among states. IOs operate as modifiers of state behaviour or, as Stephen Krasner and others put it, as "intervening variables." Although diplomacy is still the prerogative of states, the IOs to which they belong (and, in the broader sense, the regimes) at least partially shape their behaviour. Some would suggest that IOs are perhaps even supplanting the state in importance as global governance progresses. In other words, IOs are gaining autonomy from the governments that send representatives to them and have an independent voice in world affairs. Within the liberal perspective we may identify at least two prevalent strains of theory: **functionalism** and **regime theory**.

FUNCTIONALISM

Integration theorists have written of the gradual establishment of supranational governments, be they along federal or confederal lines. Functionalism, with roots in the writings of David Mitrany, emerged as a branch of such thinking following World War II.[32] Functionalists envisioned global political integration as a process arising out of technical cooperation among nation-states. Meanwhile, neo-functionalists stressed the role of mutual self-interest in the construction of regional institutions whose success would "spill over into other areas of interaction."[33] Functionalists believed that positive experiences with cooperation between peoples and governments would encourage further cooperation and increased institutional and political integration; in this sense they were to some extent constructivist in orientation. In the development of larger political communities, form should follow function. IOs should be constructed according to the specific needs they can satisfy for the citizens of states, and eventually those citizens will come to realize that their loyalty to the nation-state is itself misplaced. The European Union has been the traditional source of empirical inspiration for functionalism and neo-functionalism (see Profile 5.6). Regional economic arrangements are heralded as embryonic political communities, since a "regional market's institutional machinery, its harmonization of economic policies, and the spillover effect of its successes may help create an awareness within the region of the advantages of the integrative process."[34]

For functionalism to make sense, it has to be manifested at the institution-building level: the granting of authority to supranational entities in which a scientific or technocratic consensus determines policy. Although examples of this authority occur in limited areas, it is impossible to talk seriously of apolitical international relations. First, policies will reflect the operative ideologies of the decision makers, regardless of how objective their research and suggestions might be. Second, the sacrifice of state sovereignty such institutions demand can be viewed as a short-term commitment, rather than the kind of permanent obligation required to transform global politics. Third, aware of the possibility that political interests will usually interfere with scientific or technocratic calculations, political scientists have been rather skeptical about the idea of functionalist bodies capable of freeing themselves from the political demands of individual members. Neo-functionalists argue that, in some cases, self-interest will be best pursued by such cooperation, which will then spill over into other areas. However, the evidence in terms of a neo-functionalist trend in the continuing evolution of the European Union (often considered the most fertile proving ground for neo-functionalism) seems rather bleak.[35]

PROFILE 5.6 The European Union

The EU is widely regarded as the most advanced case of contemporary political integration among states. It began with three largely functional "communities" established by post–World War II Western European states: the European Coal and Steel Community (1952), the European Economic Community (1957), and the European Atomic Agency (EURATOM) (1957). In 1967 these three institutions merged and became the European Community. Increased integration at the economic and political level prompted the establishment of the European Union in 1993. The original membership included France, Germany, Italy, Belgium, the Netherlands, and Luxembourg. The United Kingdom, Denmark, and Eire (Ireland) joined in 1973; Greece in 1981; Spain and Portugal in 1986; Austria, Finland, and Sweden in 1995. In May 2004, a group of 10 states joined the EU: Estonia, Latvia, Lithuania, Poland, the Czech Republic, Hungary, Slovakia, Slovenia, Malta, and Cyprus. In 2007, Bulgaria and Romania joined as well. Even Turkey might join in the future, although consideration of Turkey raises interesting questions about what exactly it means to be "European." Collectively, the 27 countries of the EU have 500 million citizens and account for almost a third of world economic output. The EU has developed many common policies. It is a single market, providing for the free movement of people, goods and finance within its borders. It maintains common trade, agricultural, and fisheries policies. And it maintains a regional development policy to assist economically weaker areas in the Union. The EU is the most highly institutionalized international organization in the world: the European Commission is composed of member states and is the executive branch of the EU; the Council of the EU and a European Parliament compose the legislative branch; the European Court of Justice manages legal affairs; and the European Central Bank manages monetary policy. The EU is increasingly an actor on the world stage. Member states will often forge common positions on issues, and then represent themselves as a single, united block in international negotiations. For example, the EU has forged common positions on climate change, global trade rules, and genetically modified organisms.

The EU can be seen as a bold experiment in political integration, involving the forging of a new identity that supersedes the identities of its collective units. However, the EU has always encountered resistance to its integration plans. Governments have often proved reluctant to agree to certain proposals or policies, attempting to block them outright or refusing to adopt them. And many people in Europe are sceptical of too much economic integration and are even more sceptical of too much political integration. This has resulted in widespread suspicion and even hostility to the EU, often expressed by nationalist elements, who feel that Brussels has acquired too much influence over sovereign state affairs. Indeed, EU regulations cover everything from recycled beer cans to the enforcement of the European Convention on Human Rights. Although the EU principle of *subsidiarity* suggests that the European Council should intervene only when lower jurisdictions cannot deal adequately with issues, this has not been sufficient to satisfy anti-EU sentiments. The adoption of the euro as a single currency (see Chapter 8) further unifies and divides Europeans, as does the enlargement of the EU itself. Many argue that the entry of Eastern European states has harmed the EU's economy, as millions of labourers flood westward looking for work. As a result, deepening and strengthening European integration has proved to be a difficult task in recent years. In 2005, French and Dutch voters rejected a new EU constitution that would have strengthened EU institutions and foreign policy machinery. And in June 2008 Irish voters rejected another constitution proposal, plunging the future of European integration into uncertainty. For more on the EU, see the *Journal of European Integration*, an academic journal dedicated to the study of European cooperation and institution-building.

One observation that flows from the functionalist literature has a special resonance for global politics today: the notion that the modern state is poorly equipped to deal with the daily needs of contemporary citizens. In a certain sense, little doubt exists that a growing number of states, due to ecological and other problems, are incapable of effective governance. Lynton Caldwell writes of the potential spread of what he terms "socioecological insolvency," wherein "a state has exhausted its material means of self-support and no longer provides to its people the elementary services of government."[36] Furthermore, functionalism stresses the possible emergence of some form of global technocratic social democracy and predicts the formation of groups of international scientists acting in concert to influence policy. These groups are commonly referred to as "epistemic communities."[37] However, none of these developments necessarily means the end of the sovereign state system or the end to conflicts between states.

REGIME THEORY

It is more common today for students of IOs to discuss institutionalism rather than integration, accepting the inconvenient fact that the nation-state just will not go away. Oran Young's differentiation between institutions ("social practices consisting of easily recognised roles coupled with clusters of rules or conventions governing relations among the occupants of those roles") and organizations ("material, extant entities that possess legal sovereignty and physical artifacts, such as office buildings") is helpful.[38] The first category is currently manifested in academic inquiry by what has been popularly labelled *regime theory*, stemming from the liberal preoccupation with the concept of interdependence in world politics. To cope with this interdependence, states form regimes, defined succinctly by Stephen Krasner as sets of norms, principles, rules, and decision-making procedures around which actors' expectations converge. Regimes do not change the fundamental structures of political power, but they may influence the ultimate outcome of behaviour emanating from the international system.[39] Of course, one may be more or less enthusiastic about just how "intervening" these variables are. This intervention does not always seem to matter in its current usage; the term *regime* has acquired fantastic flexibility. A loose definition of what exactly constitutes a regime or institution—a tight definition would be unnecessarily constraining—leads to the conclusion that most areas of international collaboration are regimes whether or not some hegemonic leader provides the "public good" of leadership. What were once functionalist projects, for example, have become regimes.[40]

Regime analysis may seem a shallow, even cosmetic, perspective by those obsessed with grand theories that attempt to explain everything. Others argue that any study of regimes must reflect the social constructions or normative contexts that influence these interactive activities. The identification of the latter can be only an imprecise enterprise, perhaps largely determined by the intellectual perspective of the observer. This contribution belongs to the constructivists mentioned in Chapter 1, who suggest that agents and structures co-evolve as participants acquire intersubjective understandings of each other and themselves. Prolonged exposure to certain institutions will affect the perceptions of policymakers and thus their policies, for better or for worse. Feminists also tend to be supportive of regime building, which can promote greater awareness and understanding of gender issues in global politics, as well as establishing international laws and norms to address the political and economic marginalization of women and issues ranging from international humanitarian law to the sex trade.

International institutions do help us define acceptable behaviour, though this is not an inherently progressive function. This process of definition may involve delegitimation: redefining certain types of behaviour as illegitimate and attempting to proscribe them. In these cases we see the development of global prohibition regimes: they are guided by norms that "strictly circumscribe the conditions under which states can participate in and authorize these activities and proscribe all involvement by nonstate actors."[41] Slavery is often used as an example of an international activity that came to be viewed as inhumane by key actors in the global system, which led to a global prohibition regime outlawing the world slave trade (although that trade persists in many forms today). At the same time, regulatory regimes have a corresponding positive function, to legitimize behaviour that is taking place. This legitimization could include, for example, behaviour that is arguably hazardous to environmental health, such as the spread of nuclear power, which is one of the stated goals of the **International Atomic Energy Agency**. The tendency to equate regime formation with a progressive evolution in world affairs overlooks the dual nature of institutions and organizations that have both promotional and regulatory roles. Finally, mainstream regime theory is often criticized for overlooking the contemporary role of nongovernmental actors, despite the fact that the rise of such actors helped promote thinking about interdependence.

CONCLUSIONS

This chapter has argued that IOs are highly relevant in global politics. We offered a brief historical look at international institutions in history, including the development of the League of Nations and the United Nations. Next, we discussed IL and some of its key terminology before turning to the International Court of Justice. Though IL has limited direct utility and relies on consent rather than any strong coercive powers, it contributes to the popularization of important issues, such as the validity of nuclear weapons, and can promote human rights and compliance with regime agreements designed to preserve the environment. However, certain states will consider themselves above the law, and this belief leads to a crisis of legitimacy for institutions such as the ICJ. As the noted scholar Martin Wight once commented, IL has a tendency to "crawl in the mud of legal positivism."[42] Yet IL remains a core component of efforts to build a more tightly knit global society—for better or for worse.

We finished the chapter by discussing theoretical perspectives pertaining to the role of IOs and IL. Realists and neo-Marxist theorists feel that IOs and IL serve the interests of the more powerful states or classes. Liberal institutionalists, constructivists, and feminists hold a more positive view of institutions and organizations, regarding them as important actors that can be used to lower levels of conflict and promote greater understanding and well-being. Students might reflect on this question of the influence and autonomy of IOs when reading the remainder of this book, since IOs (and IL) factor into all of the issue-areas we examine. One of the more fundamental questions concerns whether we can speak appreciably about a new era of global governance today, or whether unilateralism in foreign policy, ongoing points of divergence among rich and poor states, the privatization of security forces, and other factors make the very notion of global governance problematic, at least at this time. This question is a dominant one for experts examining contemporary global politics, and we turn to these issues in the next section of this book.

Endnotes

1. A. Claire Cutler, "Historical Materialism, Globalization, and Law," in M. Rupert and H. Smith, eds., *Historical Materialism and Globalization* (London: Routledge, 2002), 230–56, 231.

2. J. Plano and R. Olton, *The International Relations Dictionary*, 4th ed. (Santa Barbara: ABC-CLIO, 1988), 416. This dictionary has become standard in the international relations field. See also the journal *International Organisation* and (for a constructivist take) M. Barnett and M. Finnemore, *Rules for the World: International Organizations in Global Politics* (Ithaca: Cornell University Press, 2004). On global governance see J. Rosenau and E.-O. Czempiel, eds. *Governance Without Government: Order and Change in*

World Politics (Cambridge: Cambridge University Press, 1992); the flagship journal of the Academic Union for the Study of the UN System, *Global Governance: A Review of Mulitlateralism*; and J. Muldoon, *The Architecture of Global Governance: An Introduction to the Study of International Organizations* (Cambridge, MA: Westview, 2004). The standard realist response has become J. Grieco, "Anarchy and the Limits of Cooperation: A Realist Critique of the Newest Liberal Institutionalism," *International Organization* 42 (Summer 1988), 485–507.

3. States can also be expelled, though this is rare. It is still a matter of some contention regarding which states belong to the UN, since China has resolutely disallowed the Republic of Taiwan from joining, claiming it is still part of mainland China. Despite hosting many of its key institutions, Switzerland refused to join the UN for many years, protecting its policy of neutrality (since collective security would commit it to taking sides in a UN-approved war). However, after a national referendum on the subject, Switzerland finally officially joined in 2002. Yet another controversy is related to the unilateral declaration of independence by Kosovo, which now seeks its own seat in the General Assembly.

4. This difference may lead to understandable confusion for the nonspecialist. The agencies of the UN (WHO, UNESCO, etc.) are in and of themselves IOs, with working constitutions and general and executive assemblies. However, they are generally considered part of a larger organizational entity, the UN Organization. On the UN system see P. Baehr and L. Gordenker, *The United Nations: Reality and Ideal*, 4th edition (New York: Palgrave Macmillan, 2006).

5. The games were held from 776 B.C.E. to 393 C.E., every four years at Olympia, in honour of Zeus; they resumed in their present format in 1896. At present, the International Olympic Committee is a universal-membership, single-purpose IO, with headquarters in Lausanne, France. Recent corruption scandals have plagued the IOC.

6. The ITU was originally created as the International Telegraph Union; the title was changed in 1934. The ITU became a UN specialized agency in 1947. Headquarters are in Geneva. See G. Codding and A. Rutkowski, *The International Telecommunication Union in a Changing World* (Dedham, MA: Artech House, 1982). The UPU was established when the first International Postal Convention was signed, creating the General Union of Posts; its name was changed to the UPU four years later. Stamp collectors will recognize the importance of the Convention, which gave every member-state full use of postal services throughout the world. Headquarters are in Bern, Switzerland, where the International Copyright Union is also stationed. See G. Codding, *The Universal Postal Union* (New York: New York University Press, 1964).

7. *The International Secretariat* (Washington, DC: Carnegie Endowment for International Peace, 1945), 428. For a first-hand account of the role of secretariats, see J. Mathiason, *Invisible Governance: International Secretariats in Global Politics* (New York: Kumarian, 2007).

8. B. Hughes, *Continuity and Change in World Politics: The Clash of Perspectives*, 2nd ed. (Englewood Cliffs, NJ: Prentice-Hall, 1994), 73.

9. Claude's classic text is *Swords into Ploughshares*, 4th ed. (New York: Random House, 1971). See also L. Goodrich, L. "From League of Nations to United Nations," *International Organization*, February 1947, 3–21; and for a recent account, P. Kennedy, *The Parliament of Man: the Past, Present and Future of the United Nations* (New York: Random House, 2006).

10. *The United Nations: A Concise Political Guide*, 3rd ed. (London: Macmillan, 1995).

11. Office of Management and Budget, *The City of New York Executive Budget Fiscal Year 2009, Budget Summary*, http://www.nyc.gov/html/omb/pdf/sum5_08.pdf (accessed May 29, 2008).

12. United Nations Security Council Resolution 1674, S/RES/1674 (April 28, 2006).

13. See F. H. Suward and E. McInnis, "Forming the UN, 1945," in D. Munton and J. Kirton, eds., *Canadian Foreign Policy: Selected Cases* (Scarborough, ON: Prentice-Hall, 1992), 4–18, for more on the initial Canadian position.

14. For a concise summary, see J. Rosenau's article "Normative Challenges in a Turbulent World," *Ethics and International Affairs* 6 (1992), 1–20. A (much) lengthier exposition is found in his *Turbulence in World Politics: A Theory of Change and Continuity* (Princeton: Princeton University Press, 1990). On the private sector, see D. Fuchs, *Business Power in Global Governance* (Boulder, CO: Lynne Rienner, 2007); on the role of various actors in modern conflict zones, see M. Duffield, *Global Governance and the New Wars: The Merging of Development and Security* (London: Zed, 2001).

15. Canada, Department of Foreign Affairs and International Trade, press release, September 19, 1996.

16. A. LeRoy Bennett, *International Organizations: Principles and Issues*, 6th ed. (Englewood Cliffs, NJ: Prentice Hall, 1995), 272.

17. S. Bailey and S. Daws, *The United Nations: A Concise Political Guide*, 3rd ed. (Lanham, MD: Barnes and Noble, 1995).

18. D. Keen, *Refugees: Rationing the Right to Life* (London: Zed, 1992), 40.

19. P. Wapner, "Politics Beyond the State: Environmental Activism and World Civic Politics," *World Politics* 47 (1995), 311–40; J. Fisher, *The Road from Rio: Sustainable Development and the Nongovernmental Movement in the Third World* (Westport, CT: Praeger, 1993); J. McCormick, *Reclaiming Paradise: The Global Environmental Movement* (Bloomington: Indiana University Press, 1989); and P. Willetts, ed., *"The Conscience of the World": The Influence of Non-Governmental Organizations in the UN System* (Washington, DC: Brookings, 1996); on the role of IL, see R. Falk, R. *Law in a Merging Global Village: A Post-Westphalian Perspective* (Ardsley, NY: Transnational Publishers, 1998). See also the review essay by R. Reitan, "A Global Civil Society in a World Polity, or Angels and Nomads Against Empire?," *Global Governance* 13 (2007), 445–460.

20. R. Angell, *Peace on the March: Transnational Participation* (New York: Van Nostrand Reinhold, 1969); for a Canadian history, see T. Socknat, *Witness Against War: Pacifism in Canada 1900–1945* (Toronto: University of Toronto Press, 1987).

21. LeRoy Bennett, op. cit., 180.

22. M. Akehurst, *A Modern Introduction to International Law*, 3rd ed. (London: George Allen and Unwin, 1977), 35. See also A. Cassese, *International Law* (Oxford: Oxford University Press, 2001); G. von Glahn, *Law Among Nations: An Introduction to Public International Law* (New York: Macmillan, 1965); and M. Byers, ed., *The Role of Law in International Politics: Essays in International Relations and International Law* (Oxford: Oxford University Press, 2000).

23. On sanctions, see especially M. Doxey, *Economic Sanctions and International Enforcement*, 2nd ed. (New York: Oxford University Press, 1980).

24. C. Bassiouni and V. P. Nanda, eds., *A Treatise on International Criminal Law: Crime and Punishment*. vol. 1 (Springfield, IL: Charles Thomas, 1973), 5.

25. A. Katzman, "U.S., Iran Claims Settled Quietly," *The Globe and Mail*, March 20, 1996.

26. Reprinted in *The International Court of Justice*, 3rd ed. (The Hague: ICJ, 1986), 144.

27. T. Couloumbis and J. Wolfe, *Power and Justice: Introduction to International Relations*, 3rd ed. (Englewood Cliffs, NJ: Prentice-Hall, 1986), 259.

28. This is Article 36 of the Statute of the ICJ, which provides in Section 2 that any party can recognize as compulsory the jurisdiction of the Court in legal disputes concerning the interpretation of a treaty; any question of international law; the existence of any fact that, if established, would constitute a breach of an international obligation; and the nature or extent of the reparation to be made for the breach of an international obligation. By July 1993, only 56 states had filed declarations of acceptance of the Optional Clause.

29. See K. Kirton and D. Munton, "Protecting the Canadian Arctic: The Manhattan Voyages, 1969–1970," in K. Kirton and D. Munton, eds., *Canadian Foreign Policy: Selected Cases* (Scarborough: Prentice-Hall, 1992), 205–26, 220.

30. *The Globe and Mail*, July 9, 1996, A8. For a broad discussion of this important theme, see N. Singh and E. McWhinney, *Nuclear Weapons and Contemporary International Law*, 2nd ed. (Dordrecht, Netherlands: Martinus Nijhoff, 1989).

31. For another summary, see C. Pentland, "International Organizations," in J. Rosenau, K. W. Thompson, and G. Boyd, eds., *World Politics* (New York: The Free Press, 1976), 624–39.

32. Mitrany's classic text is *A Working Peace System: An Argument for the Functional Development of International Organisation* (London: RIIA, 1943).

33. Most famously, see E. Haas, *Beyond the Nation-State* (Stanford: Stanford University Press, 1964); and A. Groom and P. Taylor, eds., *Functionalism: Theory and Practice in International Relations* (London: University of London, 1975).

34. R. Riggs and J. Plano, *The United Nations: International Organizations and World Politics* (Chicago: Dorsey, 1988), 290.

35. See, in particular, M. Huelshoff and T. Pfeiffer, "Environmental Policy in the EC: Neo-Functionalist Sovereignty Transfer or Neo-Realist Gate-Keeping?," *International Journal* 47, no. 1 (1992), 136–58. See also B. Rosamond, *Theories of European Integration* (New York: St. Martin's Press, 2000).

36. L. Caldwell, *International Environmental Policy: Emergence and Dimensions*, 2nd ed. (Durham: Duke University Press, 1990), 328. We expand on this theme in Chapter 11.

37. See P. Haas, "Introduction: Epistemic Communities and International Policy Coordination," *International Organization* 46, no. 1 (1992), 1–35.

38. O. Young, *International Cooperation: Building Regimes for Natural Resources and the Environment* (Ithaca, NY: Cornell University Press, 1989), 32. For example, the University of British Columbia is an organization, and the Canadian postsecondary school system is an institution; the International Atomic Energy Agency is an organization, and the nonproliferation regime is an institution; the Las Vegas Wedding Chapel is an organization, and marriage is an institution.

39. For standard texts, see S. Krasner, "Structural Causes and Regime Consequences: Regimes as Intervening Variables," in S. Krasner, ed., *International Regimes* (Ithaca, NY: Cornell University Press, 1983), 1–22; R. Keohane, *After Hegemony: Cooperation and Discord in the World Political Economy* (Princeton: Princeton University Press, 1984); M. Zacher, "Toward a Theory of International Regimes," *Journal of International Affairs* 44, no. 1 (1990), 139–58; and O. Young, "The Politics of International Regime Formation: Managing Natural Resources and the Environment," *International Organization* 43, no. 3 (1989), 349–75.

40. For example, see P. Sands, "EC Environmental Law: The Evolution of a Regional Regime of International Environmental Protection," *Yale Law Journal* 100, no. 8 (1991), 2511–23.

41. E. Nadelmann, "Global Prohibition Regimes: The Evolution of Norms in International Society," *International Organization* 44, 4 (1990), 481–526.

42. M. Wight, "Why Is There No International Theory?," in H. Butterfield and M. Wight, eds., *Diplomatic Investigations* (Cambridge, MA: Harvard University Press, 1968), 29.

Suggested Websites

Amnesty International
http://www.amnesty.org

European Union Newsweb
http://www.eurunion.org/states/home.htm

The Fletcher School of Law and Diplomacy
http://fletcher.tufts.edu

The Global Policy Forum
http://www.globalpolicy.org

International Court of Justice
http://www.icj-cij.org

International Monetary Fund
http://www.imf.org

Union of International Associations
http://www.uia.org

United Nations (the best place to begin any search for IOs)
http://www.un.org

WashLaw Web
http://www.washlaw.edu

World Bank Group
http://www.worldbank.org

PART TWO

Currents

This section explores the central issues and debates that characterize contemporary global politics. In the preceding section we presented an overview of the historical and intellectual roots that have contributed to the evolution of the international system and our understanding of it. We now turn to an examination of current international security issues, contemporary conflict management efforts, the globalization of the world economy, the problem of inequality, and human rights. As we will see, the dual process of convergence/divergence continues to define the political landscape and challenge our ability to make safe assumptions about the future, and all of the theoretical perspectives introduced in Chapter 1 retain their relevance. We have tried to provide as complete an overview of current world affairs as possible but make no claim to have captured them all in the brief space of four chapters.

International Security After the Cold War

The supreme importance of the military instrument lies in the fact that the ultimate ratio of power in international relations is war.

—*Edward Hallett Carr (1942)*[1]

More than six years after the start of the "war on terror," America and its allies are less safe, their enemies stronger and more numerous, and the war's key geographic battleground, the greater Middle East, dangerously unstable.

—*Philip H. Gordon (2008)*[2]

INTRODUCTION: THE CHANGING NATURE OF INTERNATIONAL SECURITY

What is *security*? What does it mean to be secure? Dictionary definitions suggest that security is freedom from threats or dangers, but who or what is being threatened or endangered? And who or what is doing the threatening and endangering? Traditionally, international security has focused on the security of states, and as a result security is most frequently conceptualized as the security of a state from external threats to its territorial integrity, political independence, and general way of life. For realists, the most important challenge has been the military threat posed by other states, although revolutionary movements, secessionist movements, and terrorist groups have also been long regarded as threats to state security. However, this rather restrictive view of security has been challenged in recent decades, both by theoretical schools that do not accept a state-centric interpretation of global politics, and by changes in the structure of the international system itself.[3]

As a result, the subject matter of security studies now includes a range of threats that are not state-centric or military in nature. For example, environmental degradation, cultural influences, modernization, economic integration, and the migration of peoples may be interpreted as threats to the well-being or even the survival of societies. Furthermore, the study of security is increasingly focused on actors and forces other than the state: certain ideologies, individuals, groups, or socioeconomic conditions existing within or across state boundaries may represent a threat to human communities. Of course, states are still highly relevant actors: as Peter Andreas argues, "clandestine transnational actors" are shifting conceptions of borders and security away from military defence and toward policing, and therefore "territoriality is persisting—but with a shift in emphasis."[4] Furthermore, states still go to war, and threaten the security of individuals or groups through a variety of repressive measures including the use of military or police force, discriminatory legislation, or economic policies. Nevertheless, in moving the reference point of security away from a focus purely on the state and military power, liberal, neo-Marxist, and feminist scholars have all contributed to an expansion of the concept of security long dominated by realist interpretations of international politics. Constructivists have also made a significant contribution to security studies in the form of securitization theory, emphasizing that security is not an objective term but is constructed through social processes. Certain issues are "securitized" through speech, the media, and other forms of social dialogue, becoming security issues because they are represented as such in a society, thus influencing how people subsequently approach these issues.[5]

The end of the Cold War had a profound effect on the study of international security. The focus on the superpower rivalry vanished, and a wide range of other security concerns moved to centre stage. Many of these concerns were not new, but the end of the Cold War served to bring them to the forefront of the international security agenda. Profile 6.1 illustrates how the security agenda has shifted since the end of the Cold War. Today, several issues occupy the attention of most international security scholars and analysts:

- *The origins and causes of conflict in the international system.* This work now includes a growing literature on the origins of civil wars and ethnic conflicts, as well as research into the link between poverty and war, environmental degradation and war, and economic incentives for war.

- *National security.* Interstate security concerns have not vanished, and state governments continue to grapple with a broad range of security threats to their territorial integrity, the independence of their political institutions, and their way of life. Other interests may include defending strategic territory and allies, combating international criminal organizations, and securing access to vital resources such as oil or natural gas (often referred to as "energy security").

- *Group security.* The focus of this growing area of study is ethnic, religious, clan, or factional groups. The issues of group security revolve around minority rights, economic and political grievances, **self-determination**, and in some cases separatism. In most violent conflicts today, some or all of the actors involved are groups.

- *Nuclear weapons safety and nuclear weapons proliferation.* While issues such as the safety and security of nuclear arsenals in the United States and Russia continue to receive some attention, the bulk of the focus on nuclear weapons is now directed to the possibility of a nuclear war between India and Pakistan, the spread of nuclear weapons technology to countries such as North Korea and Iran, and the remote though much-feared prospect of a terrorist attack using nuclear weapons.

- *Chemical and biological weapons proliferation.* The spread of chemical and biological weapons and their possible use by states and/or terrorist groups is now one of the most prominent security concerns in global politics.

- *The spread of conventional weapons.* While a great deal of attention is placed on nuclear, chemical, and biological weapons (sometimes collectively referred to as "weapons of mass destruction" or WMD), the fact remains that conventional arms buildups are a major concern in many regions. Most organized political violence is conducted with so-called conventional weapons, mostly small arms and light weapons such as assault rifles or rocket-propelled grenades.

PROFILE 6.1	**The International Security Agenda: Cold War and Post–Cold War**		
COLD WAR		**CONTEMPORARY**	
East–West	Preoccupation with super-power confrontation as the source of the next world war	North–South	Growing awareness of global disparities and poverty as a source of conflict
Interstate	Study of wars between states	Intrastate	Study of wars within states: ethnic, religious, and factional conflicts between substate actors
Nuclear strategy	Focus on deterrence and nuclear weapons programs	Nuclear, biological, and chemical weapons proliferation	Concern with the spread of nuclear weapons to substate groups; continued concern over rogue nuclear states
Alliances	Study of alliance formation, East and West blocs	Zones of peace and instability	Study of actors and structures (especially institutions) in peaceful regions as compared with warring regions
Military	Focus on military security and military as foreign policy instrument	Economic, social, and environmental	Examination of security implications of economic conflict, resource scarcity, environmental degradation, and organized crime
High-intensity conflict (HIC)	Focus on large-scale wars between powerful states and development of sophisticated weapons	Low-intensity conflict (LIC) and counterterrorism	Focus on insurgency wars and terrorist groups
War in Europe	Concern with NATO/Warsaw Pact HIC in Europe	Regional conflicts	Concern with outbreak and spread of war and instability in the world's regions
Superpower arms control	Effort to control super-power arms race especially with agreements on nuclear weapons	Global arms control	Effort to control spread of weapons around the world

- *Terrorism.* While terrorism has been an international security issue for decades, since the September 11 attacks on the United States it has become the most important security priority of the U.S. and Canadian and many other governments around the world.

- *Global criminal activity.* The focus on the role played by nonstate actors also encourages more concerted efforts to examine the spread of international organized crime, which is currently accountable for a large chunk of global economic activity, threatening both the legitimacy of states and the well-being of human communities.

- *Human security.* The focus of human security is on the individual as the object of security. The objective is the freedom of individuals from violent or nonviolent threats to their rights, safety, and lives. The human security agenda has developed considerably in recent years, led by countries such as Canada that have pursued a wide range of policies and programs including the Ottawa Treaty to ban land mines, the International Criminal Court, and international agreements on war-affected children and child labour, to name a few. We will explore human security in more depth in subsequent chapters.

- *Regional security studies.* Much more attention is now devoted to regional security dynamics, especially in West Africa and sub-Saharan Africa, the Middle East, the Persian Gulf, South Asia, Central Asia, and Southeast Asia, as well as Latin America. Regional security issues often include armed conflict, weapons proliferation, criminal activity, and piracy.

- *Environmental security.* The focus of environmental security is on threats to ecological health, the maintenance or improvement of ecological health, the impact of ecological degradation on individuals and human communities (from states to villages), acts of ecocide, and the reciprocal effect of environmental scarcity and armed conflict. This concept of security is an important element of the global ecopolitics approach we discuss in Chapter 10.

This chapter first explores the problems of interstate and intrastate war, a traditional concern of security studies that remains relevant today. We will then address some of the security challenges that have grown in prominence with an increasingly interdependent world: the proliferation of weapons; terrorism; and the growth of international organized crime.

WAR IN CONTEMPORARY GLOBAL POLITICS

War or armed conflict is a period of armed hostilities within or between states or other collectives (such as ethnic groups or political factions). The historian John Keegan has devised what may be the most concise definition of war: collective killing for a collective purpose.[6] In his famous work *On War*, Karl von Clausewitz characterizes war as a "continuation of politics by other means" and therefore focuses on armed conflict as a political act. However, a debate exists over the relative importance of politics, economics, and culture in the origin and fighting of wars.[7] In war, killing and physical destruction are both expected and condoned, although the participants are expected to follow the boundaries and constraints established by existing laws or norms. Armed conflict has caused immeasurable suffering and destruction in human history: one estimate suggests that between 1500 and 1989 there were approximately 589 wars in the international system, which caused approximately 141,901,000 deaths.[8]

Several trends can be identified in the nature of contemporary armed conflict. Between 1945 and 2006, there were 232 armed conflicts in the world.[9] During this period there were no wars between great powers, although they were certainly involved in wars (such as Korea, Vietnam, the Falklands, and the Gulf War). Instead, most of these wars have taken place between or within smaller countries in the Middle East, Africa, and Asia. Another trend is the increased frequency of wars within states, known as *intrastate conflicts* (see Figure 6.1). Of the 122 armed conflicts waged between 1989 and 2006, 89 were intrastate conflicts and 33 were interstate (wars between states).[10] Between 1998 and 2007 we witnessed only a few interstate wars: Eritrea and Ethiopia; India and Pakistan; the NATO air war against Serbia; the initial phases of the Iraq War and the war in Afghanistan; and the Israeli invasion of Lebanon. In August 2008 Russia and Georgia clashed over South Ossetia, although this brief but intense conflict was grounded in a larger dispute over South Ossetian independence from Georgia. Overall, the frequency of armed conflict is in decline: in 2006, there were 32 armed conflicts in the world, down from 52 in 1991–1992.[11] Finally, while war-related casualties are also on the decline, increasingly the victims of armed conflict are civilians. In World War I, 15 percent of the fatalities were civilians. In World II, this percentage rose to 65 (including Holocaust victims). In wars since 1945, more than 90 percent of casualties have been civilians.[12]

Figure 6.1 Number of Armed Conflicts by Type, 1946–2007

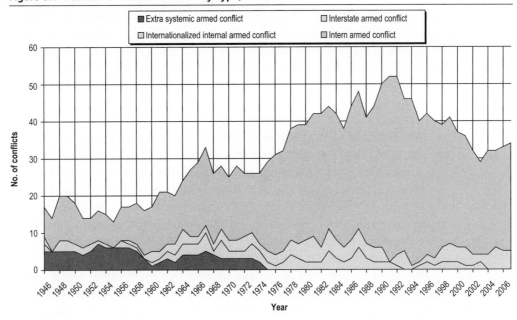

SOURCE: UPPSALA CONFLICT DATA PROGRAM (DATE OF RETRIEVAL: 2008/12/18) UCDP DATABASE: WWW.UCDP.UU.SE/DATABASE, UPPSALA UNIVERSITY ©2008.

In the years immediately following the end of the Cold War, there was an encouraging decline in global military spending. Most of this decline came from the dramatic fall in military expenditures in Eastern Europe and the former Soviet Union.[13] However, since 1998 world military spending has steadily increased. In 2007, world military expenditures totalled over US$1.3 trillion, amounting to 2.5 percent of world gross domestic product (GDP) and representing US$202 per person on the planet. Most of the increase in world military spending is due to the surge in U.S. expenditures following the September 11, 2001 attacks and the wars in Afghanistan and Iraq. Between 2001 and 2007 US military spending increased by 59 percent. The United States accounted for 45 percent of world military expenditures in 2007. The top five countries (the United States, Japan, the United Kingdom, France, and China) account for approximately 65 percent of world military spending.[14]

THEORIZING ABOUT THE ORIGINS OF WAR

Not surprisingly, many efforts have been made to understand the phenomenon of war and explain its causes. The difficulty with this enterprise is our inability to confidently generalize from one war to the next. After all, every war has unique and multifaceted causes. As

Intrastate conflict in the Congo. A young displaced child speaks with government soldiers in the war-torn Eastern Congo, November 2008. (AP Photo/Jerome Delay/ CP Archive.)

Quincy Wright has observed: "A war, in reality, results from a total situation involving ultimately almost everything that has happened to the human race up to the time the war begins."[15] We can, however, build narrower categories of possible explanations of war by exploring the three levels of analysis introduced in Chapter 1: causes of war at the individual level, the state or group level, and the systemic level. Using the individual level of analysis, we would find the cause of war in ourselves, in our nature as a species. But where does this nature come from? Early psychologists suggested that humans are inherently aggressive and war is therefore inevitable. In a letter to Albert Einstein, Sigmund Freud suggested that humans possess a death instinct, a desire to destroy and kill.[16] Konrad Lorenz, an anthropologist, referred to humans as killer apes, one of very few species that kills its own kind.[17] On the other hand, behavioural sociologists suggest that aggressive and violent behaviour is not innate but learned. Human society developed in such a way as to reward aggressive individuals and social organizations, and these traits were in turn passed on to future generations. Some feminists have argued that aggression is related to gender, with most males being more aggressive than females (whether through biology or social conditioning). Still other theories suggest that the origins of war lie in individual personalities or in misperception.[18]

The state or group level of analysis suggests that the cause of war is to be found in the social and political characteristics of states or groups. Put simply, some states or groups are more prone to war than others. Cultural determinists such as anthropologist Margaret Mead argue that war is an invention and that some cultures never experienced war, such as some of the indigenous peoples of the South Pacific.[19] However, most societies and civilizations have experienced war. An enduring debate exists over what kinds of states or groups are inherently more warlike, and not surprisingly the prevailing consensus has changed over time. Today, it is generally held that states or groups with authoritarian internal structures are more warlike because the leaders of such states are isolated from the will of their peoples and lack any checks or controls on their exercise of power. In contrast, democratic states are regarded as inherently peaceful, an assumption we will examine further in the next chapter. However, in the past monarchies were regarded as stable and responsible forms of government while republics were seen as impetuous, aggressive, and dangerous. During the Cold War, capitalist states regarded themselves as inherently peaceful and so-called "communist" states as inherently aggressive, while the so-called communist states regarded capitalist states as warlike, seeking markets abroad through imperialism. Great powers have been seen as aggressive actors while small states have been seen as less war-prone (echoes of this sentiment can be found in some Canadian attitudes toward the United States). In other words, the conception of what is a war-prone state or group has changed over time and according to political or ideological perspectives.

Finally, the system level of analysis finds the origins of war in the nature of international politics itself. As discussed in Chapter 1, this view is widely held by structural realists. The principal source of war is anarchy (the absence of central authority) and the distribution of power (the number of poles in the system). Individual aggressiveness and the internal character of states and groups are less important as explanatory factors. Wars arise not necessarily from belligerence, but because, as Kenneth Waltz argues, "There is nothing to prevent them."[20] The insecurity of an anarchic environment will lead to the security dilemma, arms races, and competing alliances (see Chapter 2). One of the more popular systemic-level explanations of war has been the concept of hegemonic war. Some realist scholars have suggested that history oscillates between **long cycles** of war and peace between great powers, with a general war breaking out approximately every 100 years.[21] Long-cycle theory is based on the rise and decline of hegemonic powers. At their height, they maintain systemic stability by establishing order, usually in the form of rules governing trade and security. However, as these hegemonic powers decline due to overextension, costs of empire, and the rise of challengers to their position, the preeminence of the hegemon is delegitimized, and war breaks out between the declining hegemon and its challengers. At the conclusion of the war, a new hegemon emerges and the cycle begins anew. In this view, the outbreak of war is linked to the fortunes of hegemonic powers. Smaller wars, such as the Vietnam conflict in the 1960s and 1970s, are seen as proxy wars among competing hegemons. Using the individual, state or group, and system levels of analysis can therefore provide insights into the origins of any war.

War has been a central subject of debate between the principal theoretical frameworks employed in the study of global politics. While realists argue that war is inevitable due to the lack of trust and the primacy of self-interest in an anarchic international system, liberals see war as a reflection of weak global governance mechanisms and the existence of authoritarian governments. For liberals, war is not inevitable: it can be prevented through the development of effective international institutions and law, and the spread of economic interdependence and democracy. In contrast, neo-Marxists regard war as an extension of the interests of rich elites, who use the power of the states they control (including military power) to protect and promote their own interests. War is therefore an extension of imperialism. Constructivists assert that wars are caused by socially constructed belief systems such as historical grievances, political or religious ideologies, nationalism, and racism. Wars can be avoided by challenging and exposing these constructions through education and improved understanding of the "other" in order to undermine the stereotypes born of ignorance and prejudiced social discourse. Feminists point out that war is a product of male perspectives on power and security, perspectives that are further illustrated by the long history of abuse committed by armies against women. The answer to war is to challenge male approaches to power by emphasizing the importance of cooperation and the security of individuals and communities. Arguments based on these perspectives are in evidence whenever war is publicly discussed, illustrating the ongoing relevance and importance of theoretical debates in global politics.

INTERSTATE WARFARE: FROM THE GULF WAR TO THE IRAQ WAR

The 1990–91 Gulf War and the 2003 Iraq War demonstrated the ongoing significance of interstate war in global politics. On August 28, 1990, Iraq invaded and occupied neighbouring Kuwait. Iraq's dire economic situation after an eight-year war with Iran prompted Iraqi leader Saddam Hussein to seize Kuwait for both immediate economic gain and long-term control over a significant portion of Middle East oil reserves. Almost every country in the world condemned the Iraqi invasion of Kuwait, and at the UN a series of resolutions called for Iraqi withdrawal, imposed severe economic sanctions against Iraq, and eventually authorized the use of force against Iraq. An American-led military coalition assembled by U.S. President George Bush (Sr.) began to deploy military capabilities to the Gulf. Great Britain, France, Saudi Arabia, Syria, Egypt, Canada, and many other countries joined the coalition (which received its mandate from the UN Security Council). By the time war broke out, the coalition had amassed 750,000 personnel in the Gulf, three-quarters of them American. Public opinion in most coalition countries was not solidly behind the war and antiwar demonstrations took place in many countries.

In response, the Iraqi government deployed more than 400,000 troops to defend its gains in Kuwait. However, in terms of troop and equipment quality, the Iraqi army was no match for the modern armies fielded by the U.S.-led coalition. In the end, Saddam Hussein was unwilling to meet coalition demands that he withdraw unconditionally from Kuwait, and economic sanctions were judged (prematurely in the minds of many critics) as too slow by an impatient Bush administration in Washington. The military campaign began on January 17,

1991, with a 40-day air campaign against Iraq and Iraqi forces in Kuwait. Iraq responded by launching missile attacks against Saudi Arabia and Israel, which failed to cause serious damage or bring Israel into the war. The war ended with a 100-hour ground offensive into Iraq and Kuwait, which succeeded in routing Iraqi forces. A ceasefire was called on February 27, 1991.

After the war, Iraq was expected to abide by all UN Security Council resolutions, including the renunciation of claims to Kuwait, the payment of reparations, and the destruction of its weapons of mass destruction program. The costs of the war were high. In monetary terms, the war cost more than US$150 billion, mostly paid for by Saudi Arabia, Kuwait, Germany, and Japan. The coalition suffered approximately 240 casualties, while estimates of Iraqi military casualties range between 20,000 and 85,000. Estimates of Iraqi civilian deaths range between 2,300 and 100,000. The war also caused the displacement of four to five million people, mostly migrant workers living in Iraq, Kuwait, and Saudi Arabia.[22] During the war, Kurds in the north of Iraq and Shiite Muslims in the south both rebelled against Saddam Hussein's rule with U.S. support. These uprisings were brutally suppressed by Saddam Hussein with the full knowledge of coalition forces until large parts of northern and southern Iraq were declared to be safe havens, protected by coalition airpower. The environmental impact of the war was also enormous. Iraq intentionally released vast quantities of crude oil into the Gulf in an effort to foul Saudi Arabian coastal areas, destroying fish and wildlife habitat. During their retreat from Kuwait, Iraqi forces blew up hundreds of Kuwaiti oil wells, which sent black smoke into the atmosphere over a wide area.

The Gulf War was successful in that it achieved its stated objective: the removal of the Iraqi military from Kuwait and the restoration of the Kuwaiti government. However, the war also left a number of unresolved issues. First, Saddam Hussein remained the leader of Iraq. Second, UN weapons inspectors entered Iraq to begin destroying Iraq's WMD programs. However, these inspectors encountered a systematic effort by Iraq to hide these programs. Third, coalition airpower remained in place over northern and southern Iraq, enforcing the no-fly zones over these safe havens. Periodically, air strikes were launched to punish Iraqi forces for threatening the no-fly zones and to compel Iraq to cooperate fully with UN weapons inspectors. This continued military presence of coalition airpower over Iraq and the presence of the United States and other Western countries in Saudi Arabia (the location of the holy sites of Mecca and Medina) during the war contributed to an increasing anti-American sentiment in the region. Fourth, UN sanctions remained in force against Iraq, aimed at pressuring Saddam Hussein to completely destroy his WMD program. These sanctions became increasingly controversial, as they crippled Iraq's economy and caused hardship to Iraqi civilians, who faced shortages of basic goods and medical and safety equipment (we examine the issue of sanctions in Chapter 7). The Iraqi population suffered from increased rates of disease, malnutrition, poverty, and infant mortality. In response, a growing protest movement argued that the sanctions should be lifted or modified to alleviate human suffering in Iraq. These issues would keep Iraq high on the list of international crisis points through the 1990s and the years of the Clinton administration.

After the terrorist attacks of September 11, 2001, terrorism became the primary security threat to the United States. Terrorism, and the states that supported it, became the focus of a "war on terror" launched by the new administration of George W. Bush, the son of former U.S. President George Bush (Sr.). Initially supported by widespread public and government opinion, and backed by UN Security Council resolutions, the United States identified Al-Qaeda and its leader, Osama Bin Laden, as the group responsible for the attacks. A United States–led coalition, which included Canada, launched a war to overthrow the Taliban government in Afghanistan (we examine terrorism and September 11 later in this chapter). However, the "War on Terror" would not stop in Afghanistan. On January 29, 2002, in his State of the Union address, President Bush referred to North Korea, Iran, and Iraq as an "axis of evil" that threatened the United States and world peace. For many senior officials in the new Bush administration, Saddam Hussein was an unresolved piece of business and the most important security threat facing the United States.[23] Despite the lack of evidence suggesting a substantive link between Al-Qaeda and Saddam Hussein, the Iraq agenda and the "War on Terror" began to converge in Washington. The Bush administration began an effort to build international support against Iraq. The United States received considerable diplomatic support from the United Kingdom, and British Prime Minister Tony Blair would be a forceful spokesman for the case against Iraq and the decision to go to war.

However, there was considerable opposition to U.S. efforts, and support was not as forthcoming as it had been in the 1990–91 Gulf War. Many governments simply did not agree that Iraq was an immediate threat to American or world security and did not see any connection between the September 11 attacks and Saddam Hussein. There was widespread suspicion of American motives, particularly in the Middle East, where American policy was seen as an expression of a U.S. desire to remove Saddam Hussein and control Iraqi oil. Moreover, the prospect of American-led military action against Iraq was deeply unpopular in almost all countries. As the threat of war grew so did antiwar protests, which culminated in a global "Day of Action" on February 15, 2003, a worldwide protest of millions of people coordinated over the Internet. There was also a growing concern over the policies of the Bush administration and the direction the war on terror was taking. At a speech at West Point Military Academy in June 2002, President Bush stated that U.S. security would require Americans "to be ready for preemptive action when necessary."[24] The United States released a new national security strategy document in September 2002, which stated that "while the United States will constantly strive to enlist the support of the international community, we will not hesitate to act alone, if necessary, to exercise our right of self-defense by acting preemptively against such terrorists, to prevent them from doing harm against our people and our country."[25] These proclamations increased suspicion that the United States was moving toward a unilateral, preemptive approach to its security priorities in general and Iraq in particular.

Prior to the outbreak of war, there was a period of frantic and often acrimonious diplomacy. The Bush administration, unwavering in its conviction that Iraq represented a threat to America and world peace, sought to persuade the UN Security Council to adopt a harder line against Iraq. The United States sought to obtain a Security Council resolution authorizing force against Iraq because of the legitimacy that resolution would provide to any war, and because domestic and international opinion was much more supportive of a war that had UN approval. The U.S. proposed a draft resolution with a strict deadline and an authorization to use force if Iraq did not comply fully with its weapons inspection obligations. France was opposed to such a resolution, and instead proposed a call for the return of inspectors to Iraq, but with no firm

Making the case against war. A peace march moves through London's Piccadilly toward Hyde Park on February 15, 2003, as part of the global "Day of Action" in protest against the eventual invasion of Iraq. (AP Photo/Kirsty Wigglesworth/CP Archive.)

deadline and no commitment to use force. The UN Security Council passed Resolution 1441, an awkward compromise between the French and U.S. positions, and weapons inspectors did return to Iraq in November. However, by January 2003 the head of the UN inspection commission, Hans Blix, estimated that their work would take another year to complete.[26] Seeking to speed up the process and obtain UN authorization to use force, in February the United States, Spain, and the United Kingdom drafted a resolution explicitly authorizing force against Iraq. The U.S. Secretary of State Colin Powell made a lengthy presentation to the Security Council on February 5, 2003, in which he outlined the suspected Iraqi WMD programs, Iraq's circumventions of UN sanctions, connections to Al-Qaeda, and human rights violations by the Iraqi government.[27] France, Russia, and China (along with Germany, a nonpermanent Council member), were opposed to the draft resolution, believing that Iraq should be given more time to comply with UN resolutions. France even threatened to use its veto to stop any resolution authorizing force against Iraq. When it became clear that a resolution authorizing force against Iraq would not be passed by the Security Council, it was withdrawn. The diplomatic effort at the UN was over. On March 17, 2003, U.S. President George Bush gave Saddam Hussein 48 hours to leave Iraq.

The military campaign against Iraq began on March 19, 2003. Unlike the Gulf War in 1990–91, there were significantly fewer states willing to assist the United States militarily or financially. Of the 30 countries that openly supported the effort diplomatically, only the United States, Britain, and Australia contributed military forces, while some countries in the Gulf allowed their airspace or territory to be used by coalition forces. Turkey, a traditional ally of the United States, refused to permit coalition forces to use Turkish land bases for the attacks on Iraq. Canada, another traditional ally of the United States, also refused to participate in the war in the absence of a UN Security Council resolution. No Middle Eastern or Muslim countries contributed military forces. Nevertheless, the military campaign was swift and

Making the case for war. The scene in the United Nations Security Council on February 5, 2003, as U.S. Secretary of State Colin Powell (seated at round table, first from left) presents evidence of Iraq's weapons of mass destruction program. He would later regret this moment. (Action Press/UN Photo/CP Archive.)

successful. With air supremacy gained almost immediately, U.S. and British forces moved into Iraq from Kuwait on March 20. In the north, U.S. Special Forces, airborne troops, and Kurdish fighters advanced on regime strongholds north of Baghdad. Despite some resistance and bad sandstorms, U.S. forces advancing from the south reached Baghdad by April 3. By April 9, the regime in Baghdad had ceased to function, Saddam Hussein had fled, and U.S. troops controlled the city. On May 1, beneath an enormous banner reading "Mission Accomplished" hanging from the control tower of the U.S. aircraft carrier *Abraham Lincoln*, President Bush declared that major combat operations were over. Saddam Hussein was captured in a small, underground hideaway on December 13.

Since the invasion of Iraq, the country has been characterized by political instability and ongoing violence. The institutions and capacities of the Iraqi state essentially collapsed after the invasion, leaving a governance and security vacuum. The situation was exacerbated by poor preparation and decision making by the Bush administration and U.S. civilian and military leaders responsible for governing Iraq.[28] Violence initially took the form of crime and looting, but soon an al-Qaeda-led and -inspired insurgency emerged, followed by sectarian violence between Iraq's main religious communal groups, the Kurds, Shias, and Sunnis. To make matters worse, tribal factions also fought each other, resulting in a complex pattern of violence that included criminality, kidnappings, assassinations, attacks on United States and coalition forces, sectarian terrorism, and political feuds. From 2005 through 2009 U.S. and coalition forces in Iraq (complemented by a slowly reconstituted Iraqi military) struggled to maintain order and security. All-out civil war was a distinct possibility, as violence increased and the Iraqi government was deeply divided along sectarian lines and proved largely incapable of governing.

The long-term prospects for peace in Iraq remain bleak, because the formation of a government capable of forging national unity continues to be elusive—or, as some observers have suggested, impossible.[29] The U.S. government's 2007 National Intelligence Estimate for Iraq warned that a significant deterioration in the security situation might lead to state collapse with three possible outcomes: partition into Kurdish, Shia, and Sunni territories; the emergence of a Shia "strongman"; or the anarchic fragmentation of Iraqi society.[30]

The Iraq War leaves any student or analyst of global politics with many questions and unknowns. However, we can with confidence raise the following questions, issues, and criticisms:

- What were the human and monetary costs of the war? At its peak, the U.S.–led coalition deployed over 500,000 personnel, over 90 percent of these being American. When President Bush declared the war over on May 1, 2003, the coalition had suffered 172 fatalities. However, as of June 2009 over 4,200 U.S. military personnel had been killed in Iraq, and over 30,000 wounded (the United Kingdom had suffered 174 deaths, and other coalition countries a total of 133).[31] Estimates of Iraqi military and civilian casualties vary: one conservative estimate based on confirmed press reports of civilian deaths provides a range of between 82,625 and 92,149 Iraqi civilian deaths from violence between 2003 and February 2008.[32] However, another report based on household surveys estimated that approximately 1,033,000 Iraqi civilians were killed between 2003 and August 2007.[33] Large numbers of Iraqi citizens have become refugees or **internally displaced persons (IDPs)**. The **United Nations High Commissioner for Refugees (UNHCR)** estimates that some two million Iraqis have fled the country.[34] A report released in March 2008 estimated that over 2.7 million Iraqis have been internally displaced.[35] Meanwhile, the monetary costs of the Iraq war to the U.S. treasury are staggering. The U.S. Congressional Budget Office released a report in October 2007 estimating that the Department of Defense had spent US$413 billion in Iraq between 2003 and 2007. The report estimated that the combined costs of the Iraq war, the war in Afghanistan, and the war on terror would cost the U.S. government between US$1.2 trillion and US$1.7 trillion between 2001 and 2017.[36] However, a 2006 study by Linda Bilmes and Nobel Prize winner Joseph Stiglitz estimated that the total costs of the war in Iraq alone would exceed US$2 trillion. Two years later, the same authors revised their findings, estimating that the Iraq War will cost America US$3 trillion.[37] It is worth remembering that cost estimates issued by the Bush administration prior to the war ranged between US$50 billion to US$200 billion.

- What was the Bush administration's motive for going to war? It seems likely there were a number of factors. The perceived threat of weapons of mass destruction unified the administration, even if this perception was based on the flimsiest of evidence. Certainly, Iraq and Saddam Hussein was unfinished business for a number of leading figures in the administration that were in government during the 1990–91 Gulf War. In fact, some critics have charged that the administration was so focused on Iraq that it ignored the threat posed by Al-Qaeda prior to September 11.[38] Still others saw a war as an opportunity to reorder the Middle East, by affecting regime change in Baghdad and installing a "democracy" in the region.[39] Much was made of the U.S. desire to control Iraqi oil (the "No War for Oil" slogan was a popular feature of the antiwar protests) and of the Bush administration's connections with the oil industry.[40] Certainly, controlling Iraq would make the politics of the international oil market much more favourable to the United States. However, although oil was a motive, it was likely not the only one: if it had been, America might have reasonably decided to cut a deal with Saddam Hussein. After all, earlier U.S. governments had done so, and had made similar arrangements with other authoritarian regimes. All these motives seem to have combined to take Bush and his senior advisors, including Secretary of Defense Donald Rumsfeld, National Security Advisor Condoleezza Rice, Vice-President Richard Cheney, and a much more reluctant Secretary of State Colin Powell, toward war.[41]

- Was the Iraq War a "war of necessity"? In making the case for war, the Bush administration maintained that the war was necessary. However, as more information comes to light this is an increasingly improbable argument. The evident enthusiasm for the military option within the administration rode roughshod over any alternatives, and belies the notion that war was undertaken as a last resort. The extent to which the primary case for war (Iraq's possession of weapons of mass destruction and complicity in the September 11 attacks) was fabricated undermines the argument that war was the only reasonable choice. Alternatively, a policy of "vigilant containment" may have been more appropriate.[42] Above all else, Saddam Hussein was interested in maintaining his own power, and therefore it was unlikely he would support or initiate an attack against the United States with weapons of mass destruction that would invite his own destruction in return. Another option was to remove Saddam Hussein through covert action, although there is some evidence to suggest such an effort may have been in place since 1991, to no avail. The Iraq War also diverted enormous resources and extensive diplomatic energy away from more immediate terrorist threats and the ongoing effort to rebuild Afghanistan. Certainly, the failure to obtain UN Security Council authorization was a major blow to the legitimacy of the war. For all of these reasons, the Iraq War may have been, as one of its critics suggested, "the wrong war, in the wrong place, at the wrong time, against the wrong enemy."[43]

- What happened to the weapons of mass destruction? The primary stated rationale for the war on Iraq was the danger posed by Iraqi WMDs. Bush administration officials had repeatedly stated that there was "no doubt" that Iraq possessed chemical weapons, and was close to acquiring biological and nuclear weapons. Therefore, Iraq was an "immediate threat" to United States and global security. The case presented to the UN Security Council and the world was almost exclusively devoted to the WMD issue. And yet, after the war was over, inspectors found no evidence that Iraq possessed weapons of mass destruction. There was, of course, evidence of past weapons development and possession, but these were well known. This has led to charges that President George Bush and Prime Minister Tony Blair had engaged in a deliberate deception. In one striking example, the Bush administration continued to use a story about Iraq's efforts to acquire uranium from Niger even when the story had been proven false by American investigators. Attention has also been focused on the U.S. National Intelligence Estimate on Iraq that proved to be systematically inaccurate for a number of reasons. First, the starting assumption was that Iraq would never give up its weapons of mass destruction. However, by the mid-1990s it appears that Saddam Hussein had decided to scale down his WMD program to avoid detection. This change in policy was apparently missed by intelligence agencies. Second, when UN inspectors left Iraq in 1998 the primary source of intelligence gathering and verification dried up, leaving intelligence officials relying on suspect information that could not be independently confirmed. Lacking good data, they began to rely on their assumptions concerning Iraqi intentions. Third, in an exhibition of "groupthink" behaviour the Bush administration was clearly receptive to information that confirmed its beliefs about Saddam Hussein, and doubted or rejected contrary intelligence information. Efforts appear to have been made to manipulate intelligence by selecting certain pieces of information for reports to senior officials while excluding others. Fourth, the Bush administration has been accused of distorting intelligence reports to enhance the public case for war. Administration officials would cite "worst-case" estimates from intelligence reports, but not the estimates considered most likely by the intelligence community. This is an especially damaging accusation for, if true, it represents a deliberate effort to mislead not only the American public, but also world governments and world opinion.[44]

- Why was the United States so poorly prepared to stabilize and rebuild postwar Iraq? The U.S. and its coalition partners encountered enormous problems dealing with stability in postwar Iraq. There was no clear transition government ready to put in place, there were an insufficient number of troops available to maintain order and prevent theft and looting, there were insufficient resources available to repair infrastructure, institutions and government agencies had ceased to function, and few good communications channels had been opened with the local population. Critics charged that the Bush administration was unprepared for the magnitude of the rebuilding project and the challenges of governance. However, the criticisms were wide of the mark. In fact, a great deal of planning for the challenges of rebuilding Iraq had been done in the U.S. government. As early as late 2001, what would become the Future of Iraq Project was already under way in the State Department, preparing for a possible postwar Iraq scenario. In the year prior to the war, experts inside and outside government had warned Congressional committees that the challenges of postwar Iraq would be greater than the challenges of defeating the Saddam Hussein regime. The United States Agency for International Development formed an Iraq Working Group that accumulated the experience of U.S. nongovernmental organizations in postwar environments. The U.S. Army conducted studies on the numbers of soldiers necessary to invade Iraq and maintain order afterward. The problem was not that these studies had never been carried out, or that the studies had failed to anticipate the postwar challenges correctly. The problem was that senior officials in the Bush administration routinely and systematically ignored or dismissed these studies and reports. Supremely confident in their approach, administration officials—through a combination of arrogance, ignorance, and carelessness—chose to treat warnings about the challenges of postwar Iraq as antiwar sentiment.[45] Subsequently, the U.S. lost immeasurable credibility both inside and outside Iraq, and the Iraqi people endured a great deal of unnecessary suffering.[46]

• The image of the United States in the world. Perhaps the greatest criticism that can be brought to bear on the decision to launch the Iraq War is the damage it has done to the legitimacy, prestige, and image of the United States. In the wake of September 11, the U.S. received the sympathy and support of most governments and most peoples around the world. Unprecedented advances in cooperation on counterterrorism and intelligence gathering followed. The war in Afghanistan, though not without controversy, was supported by the vast majority of the world's governments. And yet, in less than two years, the United States had effectively squandered that sympathy and political support.[47] The credibility of the U.S. has been damaged worldwide by a combination of the lack of a UN Security Council authorization for the war, the failure to find any weapons of mass destruction, poor political and military planning for a postwar Iraq, revelations of the torture of Iraqi prisoners held by U.S. forces in prisons such as Abu Ghraib, civilian casualties, and the careless use of deadly force by some private security contractors operating in Iraq. The war has had a very negative impact on popular opinion of the United States in most countries, especially in the Middle East.[48] The consequences of this are significant in security terms. According to the U.S. government's own 2006 National Intelligence Estimate, the Iraq War has exacerbated anti-U.S. sentiment in the Islamic world, increased sympathies with

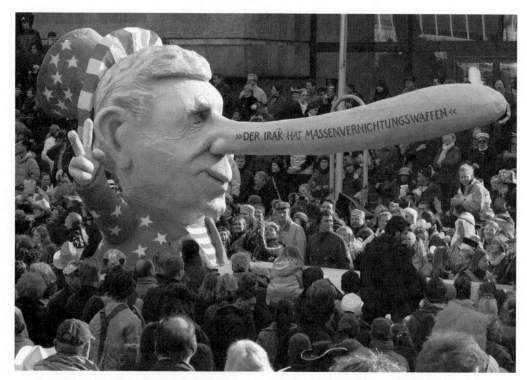

Loss of credibility. U.S. President George Bush is depicted with a Pinocchio nose on a float in the annual carnival parade in Düsseldorf, Germany, in February 2004. The writing on the nose reads: "Iraq possesses weapons of mass destruction." (CP Photo/Frank Augstein/CP Archive.)

extremist movements, and facilitated terrorist recruitment.[49] The Iraq war is also increasingly unpopular in the United States; in a poll conducted in November of 2007, 62 percent of Americans believed the Iraq War was a mistake.[50]

The future of Iraq is uncertain. While the end of the Saddam Hussein regime should not be lamented, the future of Iraq may be characterized by ongoing violence and social upheaval, the division of the country into Kurdish, Shiite, and Sunni blocs, or the emergence of another authoritarian ruler. There are some signs of improvement in daily life in Iraq: violent incidents declined through 2007 and 2008; some parts of the country (most notably in the north) are relatively stable; government services are being restored; and the economy has shown some signs of growth. Nevertheless, if a path to effective government and sectarian peace cannot be found, the prospects for the future will be increasingly grim. Of course, one must dare to hope that the future of Iraq will be a better one, where a democratic system and economic development can offer a better choice than extremism and violence. The challenges are formidable, and depend on the willingness of Iraq's political leadership to overcome their differences and the willingness of countries (especially the United States) to commit the resources necessary for the length of time necessary to consolidate peace and stability.[51] In February 2009 U.S. President Obama announced that the U.S. combat mission in Iraq would come to an end in August 2010, with perhaps as many as 50,000 U.S. troops remaining in the country in a "training and support" role until 2011. In a global context, perhaps the Obama administration will be able to repair the damage the Iraq War has inflicted on the image and legitimacy of the United States, and rebuild relations with both its allies and more mistrustful countries. This will require a more concerted effort by the U.S. government to engage in multilateral forums and compromise for the sake of achieving a broader consensus on postwar Iraq.

The Gulf War of 1990–91 and the Iraq War of 2003 remind us that interstate wars may still occur in an era of intrastate conflict and transnational security concerns. However, we must avoid thinking of interstate war in terms of only these two conflicts. Examples abound of high levels of tension and rivalry between states in the contemporary international system that could lead to future wars:

- Greece and Turkey both claim control over islands in the Aegean Sea and have clashed over the control of Cyprus, an island divided between Greek Cypriots and Turkish Cypriots.
- India and Pakistan have fought three wars since the end of World War II and continue to clash over territorial and religious issues. In 1998, both countries tested nuclear weapons, raising the prospect of a nuclear war in South Asia.
- China, Vietnam, Malaysia, Brunei, and the Philippines are the principals in a dispute over the Spratly Islands, a chain of small volcanic outcroppings in the South China Sea. Small violent clashes have occurred over the possession of these islands and the right to exploit fishing and mineral resources and conduct oil exploration in the territorial limit around them.
- China and Taiwan have an unresolved conflict over the status of Taiwan, with Taiwan claiming (though not declaring) independence while China insists Taiwan is a part of China.
- Israel and Syria have fought each other in the Arab–Israeli wars, and continue to dispute possession of the Golan Heights. Their interests and allies also clash in Lebanon.
- North Korea and South Korea have not fought each other since 1953, but a very high level of tension remains on the Korean peninsula, especially after two North Korean nuclear tests in 2006 and 2009.

- Peru and Ecuador have clashed over their disputed border since the last major war between these two countries in 1941. The latest border skirmishes took place in 1995.

- Ethiopia and Eritrea fought a war over territory and economic issues between 1998 and 2000. The war ended in December 2000, and a UN peacekeeping force was deployed to the border between the two states. However, the underlying territorial and economic issues have not been resolved, and there are concerns that another war could break out in the future.

- Cameroon and Nigeria nearly went to war in 1981 over two long-standing territorial disputes over the Bakassi peninsula and the border around Lake Chad. Tensions have increased in recent years, exacerbated by disputes over offshore oil resources in the Gulf of Guinea.

- Venezuela, Ecuador, and Colombia became embroiled in a crisis in 2008 when Colombian troops crossed the border into Ecuador to combat insurgents. All three countries sent military forces to their borders and the crisis was only defused through diplomatic efforts at the Organisation of American States.

- Russia and Georgia fought a war in August 2008 over two separatist regions of Georgia, Abkhazia and South Ossetia. The status of these territories, which Georgia claims as part of its sovereign territory and Russia recognizes as independent states, continues to be a source of tension between the two governments.

Warfare between these states remains a very real possibility, and of course other interstate wars could break out almost anywhere with virtually no warning. Realists remind us that many states continue to regard their neighbours with suspicion, have unresolved territorial or political disputes, and have a history of conflict.

INTRASTATE CONFLICT

As indicated earlier in this chapter, one of the most noticeable trends in international security is the extent to which traditional conflicts between states—interstate conflicts—have been less frequent, while conflicts within states—intrastate conflicts—have increased in frequency. In fact, the vast majority of recent conflicts have occurred at the substate level. These conflicts are often generically referred to as **ethnic conflicts**, but not all intrastate conflicts are ethnic conflicts. In many cases, they may be conflicts between religious communities, clans, or political factions, and some would argue that class relations are central factors in most of them. As a result, in this chapter we use the term **communal conflicts** to describe wars that take place between communal groups of all types at the substate level.[52]

Communal groups come in many forms, but they all share one important quality: a sense of common identity. Ted Robert Gurr calls this shared sense of identity a "psychological community" that is enduring and differentiates the group from others.[53] This sense of identity gives the group the internal solidarity and the capacity for collective action. Without this quality (if group identification is weak) there is seldom the potential for organized collective action by the group. Communal identities can be based on one or more of the following characteristics:

- Ethnicity (race, custom)

- Historical experience or myth

- Religious beliefs

- Region of residence
- Familial ties (clan systems)

It is important to note that communal group identity is not a menu or checklist of items that identify a group. Communal identity is bestowed on individuals by virtue of birth, but it is not a fixed or permanent characteristic of all individuals within a group. Communal identity may be more or less active in some individuals at any given time, depending on the issues at stake. Communal identity also has a voluntary element, in the sense that individuals within a group have a certain element of choice over how much they want to identify themselves by communal group loyalty. Some of these communal characteristics are more subject to individual choice than others. Obviously, physical characteristics are not a matter of choice. However, observing religious beliefs or social customs is more subject to individual choice, though it is irresponsible to generalize across cultures in this respect.

Communal groups are fluid entities, and their self-identities may vary over time. Some communal groups may be assimilated into larger ones; and the unity of some groups may be influenced by their position within a larger society. On the one hand, if a group comes under external pressure (by, for example, a threat to its religious beliefs or social customs), its sense of identity and capacity for communal action may increase. On the other hand, if the group has its basic desires accommodated within a larger social structure, the identity and capacity for action may decline. Communal identity can also be affected over time by other social constructions. Myth and legend, passed down from generation to generation, can keep beliefs, values, and shared history alive. Communal identity can also be reinforced and even constructed through schooling and social life. Nation-states often aspire to communal status: the modern state spends time and money on fostering solidarity at the national level. In some cases, such as the former Yugoslavia or the former Czechoslovakia, the effort fails completely because substate communal loyalties persevere and triumph over state nationalism.

EXPLAINING COMMUNAL CONFLICT

Why do communal conflicts erupt? It is tempting to point to a particular causal factor and declare that it is the cause, and the only cause, of that conflict. In some cases, this declaration may be accurate. However, in most cases, multiple causal factors are behind the outbreak of a communal conflict, and while some may be more readily apparent than others, no one factor is solely to blame. Communal conflicts may originate in one or more of the following situations.

1. *Grievances.* One communal group within a society may have a grievance against other groups or against the state itself. These grievances may take several forms, including:
   - *Economic grievances.* Communal conflicts can be conflicts over entitlements and resources and the right or power to control them. In this sense, communal conflicts are struggles against entrenched economic discrimination. Often, one communal group will control these resources and the means of distributing them, and this control will lead to conflict between the advantaged and the disadvantaged groups.
   - *Political grievances.* Communal conflicts may be conflicts over political rights and freedoms. In this sense, these conflicts are struggles against political discrimination, which may take the form of efforts to gain the right to vote, practise a religion, travel, organize, or secure protection from human rights abuses. In addition, the conflict may be a struggle for representation in the institutions of the state, government, the army, the police, or the bureaucracy.

2. *Autonomy and independence.* In other cases, conflict may develop out of the desire of a communal group for greater political and cultural autonomy or independence. It is perhaps ironic that many intrastate conflicts are motivated at least in part by the desire of one or more communal groups to establish a state. Most communal groups regard a certain defined territory (which they may or may not occupy) as part of their ethnic endowment or as their natural homeland. Conflict may develop between rival communal groups that claim the same stretches of territory.

3. *Social change.* In other cases, conflict may erupt when a communal group feels threatened by change, such as modernization. This change may take the form of the threat posed by industrialization or commercialization or by government policies that threaten their political, economic, territorial, or cultural position in society. In such cases, communal groups will mobilize in defence of their way of life.

4. *Primordialism.* Another explanation is that communal conflicts develop out of the hatreds that various particular communal groups feel for one another. These hatreds usually have a long historical record, and the communal groups involved have long memories of past injustices perpetrated generations ago. This explanation suggests that communal conflicts start at the grassroots level between peoples.

5. *Incitement by leaders.* Another explanation suggests that communal conflicts originate with self-aggrandizing leaders who incite nationalist, ethnic, or religious bigotry for their own political ends. Such leaders may attempt to mobilize public support for their goals of territorial expansion or ethnic purification by vilifying other communal groups. Nationalist leaders may create scapegoats for economic and social hardships at home, or incite conflict between groups to justify oppressive state control. This "instrumental" explanation suggests that communal conflicts begin at the *elite* level, not at the grassroots level.

6. *State nationalism versus ethnonationalism.* Conflicts can originate in a clash between the state and ethnic groups. The nation-state is built on an internal tension between the sovereignty of the state based on territorial demarcation and the imposition of this sovereignty on the ethnic, cultural, and religious divisions of the world. In an effort to achieve domestic social unity, political leaders may seek to emphasize a sense of common identity based on loyalty to the state. However, this effort may threaten communal group identity and loyalty, sparking conflict.

7. *The loss of the political centre.* The structural explanation for communal conflict suggests that when governments are too weak to maintain order and protect the security of individual groups within the country, communal groups are plunged into a condition of anarchy. This may occur when empires or states collapse. When this happens, the human geography of their territory resembles a patchwork of peoples with enclaves of one group often surrounded by others. In such situations, a security dilemma can develop among peoples as it has developed among states. Other groups are seen as potential threats, and attempts to protect group security become interpreted as hostile acts by neighbours, starting (or renewing) a cycle of mistrust or hostility.

8. *Symbolic politics.* The symbolic politics approach suggests that symbols and myths are the key to understanding ethnic conflicts. Symbolic politics is "any sort of political activity focused on arousing emotions rather than addressing interests."[54] Ethnic conflicts begin when symbolic politics involving hostile myths and ethnic fears are mobilized within ethnic groups in the absence of a political centre willing and capable of stopping this mobilization. When this happens, people make decisions increasingly

on the basis of emotional attachments to ideas and values, preconceptions of enemies and heroes, and interpretations of right and wrong. This can lead communal groups toward confrontation and war.

THE NATURE OF COMMUNAL WAR

Intrastate wars have a very different profile than the wars of the past. As Kalevi Holsti has observed, "There are no declarations of war, there are no seasons for campaigning, and few end with peace treaties. Decisive battles are few. Attrition, terror, psychology, and actions against civilians highlight 'combat.' Rather than highly organized armed forces based on a strict command hierarchy, wars are fought by loosely knit groups of regulars, irregulars, cells, and not infrequently by locally based warlords under little or no central authority."[55] In particular, the violence and brutality of contemporary communal conflicts has shocked and appalled most observers, and this sentiment is in no small part responsible for the many international efforts to terminate or manage these conflicts. However, wars have always been brutal, even so-called good or just wars. In World War II, for example, entire cities were laid waste in an effort to destroy manufacturing facilities and to weaken the morale of the civilian population. Massacres and rapes were not uncommon. What is it about communal conflicts that strike such a chord of repulsion? Is it the way these wars have been presented to viewers on television? Is it because the relatively small number of casualties involved enables us to sympathize with the victims on an individual level in a way that we cannot with the abstraction of high casualties? Or is there a qualitative difference between these wars and interstate conflicts?

One significant difference may be the extent to which civilians are intentional targets in communal conflicts. Civilians are the centre of group power, the source of soldiers, food, and support, and so they are attacked to weaken the military potential of the communal group. Furthermore, in communal conflicts territory is considered conquered only when all or most members of the other ethnic group have been removed and people of the victor's ethnic group have been brought in to replace them. Therefore, forcing populations to leave is a cornerstone of military campaigns in communal conflicts. The term **ethnic cleansing** has been coined to refer to this practice. Ethnic cleansing is the forced removal of peoples from their area of residence (see Chapter 9). The instruments of ethnic cleansing include forced deportation, mass murder, the destruction of homes and property, and the spread of fear and terror. Mass rape has also been used as a weapon in such conflicts, most notably in the former Yugoslavia, Rwanda, Sudan, and the Congo. Beyond the obvious pain and trauma to individuals, rape spreads fear among the female population, compelling the women of a communal group to flee. In recognition of the significance of rape in armed conflict, in June 2008 the UN Security Council classified rape as a tactic of war and a threat to international security. Rape is also recognized by the International Criminal Court's 1998 Rome Statute as a potential war crime. For all these reasons, the violence of communal conflicts is regarded as especially brutal, even by the standards of behaviour found in the history of warfare.

Finally, ethnic conflicts often have a powerful economic component that is sometimes overlooked. While the tendency of the observer is to focus on political, territorial, and religious aspects of the conflict, these may in fact be secondary to the economic gains the continuation of a war can bring to certain groups or individuals. Mats Berdal and David M. Malone suggest that civil wars of all kinds, including ethnic wars, have been "driven not by a Clausewitzian logic of forwarding a set of political aims, but rather by powerful economic motives and agendas."[56] For example, a rebel leader in Liberia was estimated to have made more than US$400 million a year from the war between 1992 and 1996. In Angola, the rebel group controlled 70 percent of the country's diamond production, creating an international reaction against "conflict diamonds" that were financing an ongoing war. In Cambodia, senior commanders in the rebel groups and the government's army alike were often more interested in reaping the profits of illegal logging and trading in gems than in the politics of the war.[57] As David Keen has suggested,

> Conflict can create war economies, often in the regions controlled by rebels or warlords and linked to international trading networks; members of armed gangs can benefit from looting; and regimes can use violence to deflect opposition, reward supporters or maintain their access to resources. Under these circumstances, ending civil wars becomes difficult. Winning may not be desirable: the point of war may be precisely the legitimacy which it confers on actions that in peacetime would be punishable as crimes.[58]

This connection between ethnic conflict, civil wars, and economic gain must of course be addressed in any conflict management efforts designed to end such wars.

The case studies below provide vivid illustrations of the dynamics of communal conflict. What is evident is that many similarities exist between intrastate conflicts, but that understanding the origins and dynamics of each conflict requires careful consideration of the circumstances unique to each war.

- *The collapse of Yugoslavia.* Yugoslavia was a federal state composed of eight republics and provinces, presided over by the dictator Josef Tito. Yugoslavia was a multiethnic state, composed of Serbian, Croatian, Muslim (Bosniac), Slovenian, Albanian, and a variety of other communal groups. When Tito died in 1980, the federal structure and the federal army became increasingly dominated by Serbia, alienating the republics of Slovenia and Croatia, which sought to leave the federation and declare independence. Violence broke out in 1990 and Slovenia and Croatia declared independence in June 1991. The Serbian-dominated federal army was instructed by Serbian President Slobodan Milošević to use force to keep Slovenia and Croatia in the federation, but this effort failed. In April 1992, war spread to Bosnia, where the Bosnian Muslim government, having declared independence, wanted to preserve a multiethnic state. However, nationalist movements in the Serbian and Croatian regions of Bosnia sought independence and eventual amalgamation with Serbia and Croatia respectively. Months of heavy fighting followed, characterized by ethnic cleansing and massacres, artillery bombardment of cities, and battles for control of ethnic enclaves. The initial success of the Bosnian Serbs, supported by the Milosevic government in Belgrade, was reversed by a combination of a Muslim–Croat alliance, the withdrawal of Serbian support (the result of UN sanctions), and the intervention of NATO in support of the UN. At the end of 1995, after more than three years of war, a peace was brokered in Bosnia, leading to the Dayton Agreement and the deployment of 60,000 heavily armed NATO troops authorized to use force to maintain the peace. While communal tensions remain high in Kosovo (see Chapter 7) an uneasy peace now exists in what is essentially an ethnically divided Bosnia. Slovenia and Croatia are now member states of NATO.
- *Somalia.* Somalia emerged as an independent state out of colonial Africa in July 1960. However, it was a state deeply divided along clan lines. In 1969, Major-General Mohammed Siad Barre seized power and attempted to establish a socialist state. Barre

was ousted in 1991 by a coalition of opposition clans. This coalition soon collapsed and months of war followed, destroying what was left of the infrastructure of Somalia. A humanitarian disaster of enormous proportions gained the attention of the UN and the international community, which responded in an effort to bring humanitarian relief and peace to Somalia. Yet while the humanitarian relief effort was largely successful, the peace efforts were not. Clan conflict continued in Somalia, with UN peacekeepers and American-led coalition forces engaging in armed clashes with local clan militias. The international presence was withdrawn in March 1995, and violence between the rival clan factions has continued. The country remains deeply divided between rival political movements based on clan divisions, and is often described as a "failed state" with no effective central government and poor prospects for long-term peace and development. Somalia is a continuing source of regional instability: the outbreak of armed conflict in 2006 between an alliance of warlords and Islamic militias led to Ethiopian intervention in the war. The chaotic environment in Somalia has also made the country a haven for drug and arms trafficking, terrorists, and pirates who seize merchant ships and their crews off the coast of Somalia for their cargoes and for ransom.

- *Chechnya/Russia.* A centuries-old history of conquest, repression, and deportation has left a legacy of bitter relations between Moscow and Chechnya, the most homogeneous Muslim republic in the Russian Federation. When the Soviet Union collapsed in 1991, Chechen leaders claimed the right of self-determination and independence for Chechnya, while the Russian government maintained that Chechnya was part of Russia. In 1993, the Russian government under Boris Yeltsin decided to use military force to crush Chechen independence. The first round of violence lasted two years, resulting in 100,000 casualties and nearly 400,000 refugees. Most of the major cities and towns of Chechnya were devastated by indiscriminate artillery and air bombardment, including the capital, Grozny. The war was very unpopular in Russia, and a ceasefire in August 1996 saw the withdrawal of Russian troops from Chechnya and an agreement to defer the status of Chechnya for five years. In August 1999 war returned to Chechnya as the Russian government under President Vladimir Putin sought to crush the Chechen independence movement. The so-called Second Chechen War received more popular support in Russia after a series of bombings in Moscow was attributed to Chechens, although rumours persist that the blasts were set by Russian authorities to gain popular support for a war in Chechnya. Through the indiscriminate use of firepower and the deployment of 90,000 troops, Russia gained control over most of Chechnya. Years later, Chechnya still faces the legacy of both wars: a destroyed civilian infrastructure; a countryside ridden with land mines; and a population harbouring a fierce hatred of Moscow and the pro-Russian government that now rules the region.

- *Israel and the Palestinian people.* This decades-old conflict between the Jewish and Palestinian peoples has defied efforts to build a permanent peace. In September 1993, a peace process culminated in the signing of an agreement between Israel and the Palestine Liberation Organization (PLO). However, the peace process began to unravel after the assassination of Israeli Prime Minister Yitzhak Rabin in November 1995. Another attempt to forge peace under the "Road Map" plan devised by the Bush administration in 2002 has also failed (we will examine these conflict management efforts in Chapter 7). Little progress has been made on outstanding issues such as the future of Jerusalem, the return of refugees, Israeli settlements, and division of territory and land. A number of Palestinian terrorist groups have employed suicide bombers against civilian and military targets in Israel. The Israeli government has responded with a hard-line policy of doubtful legality including air strikes, military incursions into Palestinian self-rule areas, economic coercion, and restrictions on Palestinian freedom of movement. These policies have in turn inflamed Palestinian sentiment toward Israel. In 2002, Israel began construction of a "security fence," which has become another source of tension between Israel and Palestinians. Unilateral Israeli withdrawal from the Gaza Strip in 2005 and the subsequent seizure of the territory by the Islamist movement Hamas in 2007 has led to further armed conflict, including rocket fire by Hamas militias in Gaza against Israeli towns and Israeli attacks against Hamas targets, punctuated by a major armed incursion into Gaza by the Israeli Army in 2008–2009.

- *The Kurds.* The Kurdish people are an ethnic group living in a large territory currently controlled by Turkey, Iraq, Iran, and Syria. Kurdish efforts to establish their own state (Kurdistan) have led to periodic violence and terrorism by Kurdish separatist groups and brutal suppressions of Kurds by the governments of Turkey and Iraq. The Kurds in northern Iraq have had considerable autonomy over their own affairs since the 1990–91 Gulf War and the 2003 Iraq War. The future of the Kurds living in post-Saddam Iraq is unclear. Nationalist sentiment already runs high, and if the government of Iraq fails to satisfy Kurdish desires for regional autonomy and input into central government positions, renewed calls for separatism and independence are likely, and the possibility of violence will increase.

- *The Sudan.* The intrastate war in Sudan has waged since 1956, apart from a nine-year break in the 1970s. The war has pitted an Arab Muslim government in the north against African Christian and animist militias in the south and west. The conflict has been waged over territory, religious practices, separatist claims, and oil. In 2002, peace talks began between the government and rebel groups, and significant progress was made by 2003 when the two sides had agreed on regional autonomy for the south, the sharing of oil revenues, and religious practices. A peace agreement was finally signed on May 26, 2004. However, it became clear that yet another humanitarian disaster was looming in the Darfur region of western Sudan. A bloody armed conflict broke out in 2003 in Darfur, when two political movements composed of local African tribal groups rebelled against the government. In an effort to defeat the rebellion, the Sudanese government armed and supported an Arab "Janjaweed" militia, which conducted an ethnic cleansing campaign against the African population of Darfur. According to most estimates, approximately 300,000 people in Darfur have been killed, and over two million have been displaced.[59]

The cases we have examined here represent only a small percentage of the number of ongoing intrastate, communal conflicts in global politics. Every year, new conflicts emerge and many descend into violence. As a result, one of the core questions facing international conflict management is how such conflicts can be avoided and stopped. We will explore this question in Chapter 7. Of course, even a casual observer of the world's interstate and intrastate conflicts cannot help but notice the availability of weapons. We turn now to a discussion of the weapons proliferation problem in global politics.

THE PROLIFERATION OF WEAPONS

The proliferation, or spread, of weapons around the world is a major international security issue. While most attention is directed toward the spread of weapons of mass destruction (nuclear, biological, and chemical weapons), the spread of conventional weapons is also a matter of grave concern. Conventional weapons include a wide variety of weapons systems such as aircraft, naval vessels, missiles, and armoured vehicles, as well as individual small arms and light weapons such as assault rifles, rocket-propelled grenades, and land mines. The proliferation of weapons is regarded with anxiety because regional arms races can exacerbate existing tensions or raise levels of distrust and hostility. In addition, should war break out the combatants will be equipped with more modern weapons technology capable of high levels of destruction. Concern also exists that substate groups such as terrorist organizations are acquiring increasingly sophisticated weapons systems, including chemical and biological weapons. As a result, the control of the spread of weapons systems and weapons technology is regarded as an important contribution to both preventing war and reducing the level of violence in the international system.

THE PROLIFERATION OF NUCLEAR WEAPONS

One of the greatest concerns today is the prospect of the spread of nuclear weapons capabilities to more states and perhaps to substate actors. Today, eight countries possess nuclear weapons, with one of them (Israel) an undeclared nuclear power (Israel has never formally acknowledged the possession of nuclear weapons). Four other countries had acquired nuclear weapons but subsequently relinquished them (see Profile 6.2). Many other countries had active nuclear weapons programs at one time. Today, the two most prominent proliferation concerns are with the states of North Korea and Iran. Some scholars—in particular, some structural realists—have argued that nuclear weapons can have a steadying effect on regional stability.[60] As Kenneth Waltz argues, "the presence of nuclear weapons makes states exceedingly cautious. Why fight if you can't win much and might lose everything?"[61] However, the prevailing view is that the spread of nuclear weapons is inherently dangerous.[62] If more decision makers have the option of using nuclear weapons, then nuclear weapons are more likely to be used. The prospects for accidental or unauthorized nuclear release will increase, especially as many new nuclear-weapons states may not invest the same effort or resources into the development of effective command and control systems. In addition, small nuclear arsenals may be more vulnerable to preemptive strikes, thus increasing the incentives to use nuclear weapons first in crisis or war. Finally, the monetary and environmental costs of nuclear arms races are tremendous, as the Russians and Americans are well aware.

Several rationales may motivate state leaders to develop a nuclear weapons capability. First, they may want to acquire nuclear weapons for security reasons, perceiving a threat from another country and seeking the bomb to act as a deterrent or as a weapon of last resort. Certainly, these reasons were important considerations in the respective decisions by the Soviet Union and by Pakistan to develop a nuclear capability. Second, state leaders may seek the prestige such a capability would bring to a country: nuclear weapons are equated with modernization and development. This idea was a factor in the Chinese and Indian nuclear weapons programs. Others might be seeking security, autonomy, and independence—the ability to be self-reliant when it comes to nuclear weapons. These factors were important in the motivation behind the development of France's *Force de Frappe*. Alternatively, some countries might develop (or attempt to develop) nuclear weapons because of isolation (South Africa) or ambition (Iraq). As we saw in Chapter 3, another possible explanation is the influence of domestic politics: nuclear weapons may be acquired to advance the interests of domestic groups, industries, and bureaucracies.[63]

What is required to become a nuclear-weapons state? For any country seeking to develop nuclear weapons, several steps must be taken. First, the political will to develop the weapons must exist. Canada, for example, could build nuclear weapons tomorrow, but successive

PROFILE 6.2 — Nuclear-Weapons States: Past, Present, and Future

NUCLEAR-WEAPONS STATES	FORMER NUCLEAR-WEAPONS STATES	STATES WITH PAST NUCLEAR-WEAPONS PROGRAMS	FUTURE NUCLEAR-WEAPONS STATES?
United States (1945)	South Africa[c]	Iraq[e]	Iran
Russia (1949)	Ukraine[d]	Libya[f]	Syria
United Kingdom (1952)	Belarus[d]	Argentina	
France (1960)	Kazakhstan[d]	Brazil	
China (1964)		South Korea	
Israel (1969)[a]		Taiwan	
India (1974)			
Pakistan (1998)			
North Korea (2006)[b]			

[a] Undeclared nuclear-weapons state. The precise year of acquisition is unknown, and it is not known if Israel has conducted a test.
[b] In April 2003, North Korea informed U.S. officials it possessed a nuclear bomb. North Korea conducted one nuclear test in 2006, and another in 2009.
[c] South Africa developed nuclear weapons in the 1970s but unilaterally dismantled the weapons and the program in 1991.
[d] Ukraine, Belarus, and Kazakhstan all inherited the nuclear weapons on their soil after the collapse of the Soviet Union, but all three relinquished possession of those weapons.
[e] A significant nuclear weapons program was disrupted by the 1990–91 Gulf War. Ceasefire terms required Iraq to eliminate all nuclear-related facilities and materials. No nuclear weapons were found at the conclusion of 2003 Iraq War.
[f] Renounced its secret nuclear weapons program in 2003.

Canadian governments have decided not to do so. Second, a country must acquire the knowledge base required to build nuclear weapons. A country must develop its own nuclear scientists and technicians or purchase the services of foreign scientists and technicians. Third, a country must build the nuclear, industrial, and manufacturing infrastructure required to build a bomb. This infrastructure may involve the construction of a nuclear reactor, uranium enrichment facilities, and laboratories and manufacturing plants. All this infrastructure takes time to build, is costly, and may be detected if the program is a clandestine one. Fourth, the country must acquire fissile material—highly enriched uranium or plutonium—for the bomb. This acquisition is often the most difficult challenge for would-be nuclear states, for this material is rare and must be purchased from abroad or mined and enriched at home. Finally, a bomb design must be adopted and a decision made to assemble and deploy the weapons. A test may be necessary, although computer models have improved to the point where a country can have a high expectation that its bomb will work even if it is not tested. We will explore international efforts to prevent the proliferation of nuclear weapons in the next chapter, but the greatest obstacles to the spread of nuclear weapons remain the technical difficulty, costs, and long time frame associated with a nuclear weapons program.

A small number of states continue their attempts to develop nuclear weapons, and have resorted to building clandestine nuclear facilities with the help of international smuggling networks. The most famous of these networks was headed by Dr. Abdul Khan, the chief of Pakistan's nuclear weapons programs since the 1970s. The "Khan network" operated out of Pakistan, using companies in Japan, Germany, Turkey, South Africa, Dubai, Switzerland, South Korea, Thailand, China, and the Netherlands as intermediaries. The Khan network provided assistance to Iran, Libya, and North Korea in the form of uranium separation and enrichment equipment components. The network was exposed in 2004, but Dr. Khan, a national hero in Pakistan for his role in developing Pakistan's nuclear arsenal, was pardoned. In the past few years, two of the countries assisted by Khan's network—North Korea and Iran—have been the focus of proliferation fears.

North Korea began its nuclear weapons program in 1964. Under increasing international suspicion, North Korea was suspected of having produced plutonium for a nuclear bomb by the early 1990s. The international response was to call for inspections of North Korea's nuclear facilities, which North Korea refused to permit. In 1994 negotiations between the United States and North Korea led to a Framework Agreement in which the North Korean government agreed to stop its nuclear weapons program and give international inspectors leave to enter, in return for assistance in building replacement reactors for civilian use and regular supplies of fuel oil. In October 2002 North Korean officials admitted to having a program to enrich uranium for use in nuclear weapons, a violation of the 1994 agreement. In April 2003, a North Korean official informed U.S. representatives that North Korea had at least one nuclear weapon.[64] The already tense situation became a crisis when North Korea conducted a nuclear test on October 9, 2006. The motive behind the test is unclear: perhaps the Kim Jong-Il government felt a test would allow the impoverished and isolated North Korea to negotiate from a position of strength; perhaps the test was a domestic political statement reinforcing Kim Jong-Il's power; or perhaps North Korea's government feared a preemptive attack on their nuclear facilities. Whatever the motive, the test certainly gained the world's attention. The initial reaction to the test was international condemnation (even from China, North Korea's only ally) and the imposition of additional sanctions on the country.

The U.S. government had traditionally taken a hard line on North Korean nuclear proliferation, but in the wake of the North Korean test it changed course and began direct negotiations with the Kim Jong-Il government. This shift in policy led to the resumption of the so-called Six Party Talks (China, North Korea, South Korea, Japan, Russia, and the U.S.) which had been the primary diplomatic conflict management mechanism used to negotiate with North Korea since 2003. On February 13, 2007 an agreement on a "Denuclearization Action Plan" was reached in which North Korea agreed to shut down its nuclear weapons facilities and accept International Atomic Energy Agency (IAEA) inspectors. In return, the United States and other Six Party Talks members agreed to provide economic, energy, and humanitarian assistance to North Korea, and Japan and the U.S. agreed to move toward the normalization of political relations with the Kim Jong-Il government. The United States also agreed to lift its restrictions on trade with North Korea and remove the country from its list of state sponsors of terrorism. It is unclear whether this agreement will be fully implemented. Previous agreements in 1994 and 2005 unravelled due to mutual distrust and internal North Korean politics.[65] The Denuclearization Action Plan nearly unravelled in 2008 over the issue of North Korea's removal from the U.S. state sponsors of terrorism list. After negotiations, North Korea was removed from the list in October 2008. Critics argued that the agreement rewarded North Korea for acquiring nuclear weapons, and did not address the issue of North Korea's existing nuclear weapons. Nevertheless, it represented a major diplomatic breakthrough on a nuclear proliferation crisis that has endured since the 1990s. However, North Korea's subsequent nuclear test in the spring of 2009 raised tensions and threw the future of the Denuclearization Action Plan into doubt.

Tensions over Iran's nuclear program have risen dramatically over the past few years. Unlike North Korea, Iran has neither declared that it has nuclear weapons nor carried out a test. Iran is considered a proliferation concern because it does possess a nuclear energy program but refuses to stop uranium enrichment (a key step in acquiring the fissile material for a nuclear bomb) and refuses to allow unrestricted inspection of its nuclear facilities. The United States and many other countries fear that Iran's nuclear energy program is being used to develop a bomb. The UN Security Council has repeatedly called on Iran to suspend its enrichment activities and cooperate fully with the IAEA. The controversial President of Iran, Mahmoud Ahmadinejad, has rejected these resolutions, arguing that Iran's enrichment program is entirely peaceful. However, the Iranian government has been less than cooperative on the issue. In 2003 Iran had signed an Additional Protocol arrangement with the IAEA, which resulted in some of its enrichment equipment being sealed in special storage sites under IAEA supervision. Iran also agreed to additional regular IAEA inspections of its nuclear facilities to verify their strictly civilian use. In 2006 Iran withdrew from this agreement, broke the seal on the storage sites, and resumed enrichment activity. In December 2006 the UN imposed sanctions on Iran, seeking to pressure the Iranian government to comply with UN Security Council resolutions.

As the crisis intensified, there was growing concern that Israel or the United States might carry out a preemptive military strike on Iranian nuclear facilities despite serious practical challenges and political risks.[66] Additional sanctions were placed on Iran in March 2007, but with little effect. International diplomacy toward Iran is complicated by divisions between the United States, Europe, China and Russia on how to deal with the Iranian nuclear crisis. The U.S. has been the most insistent on diplomatic pressure and sanctions as part of its larger efforts to isolate Iran. European governments have emphasized dialogue and negotiation, while Russia and China have viewed the U.S. position as too aggressive and have been more reluctant to exert pressure on Iran (although Russia imposed additional sanctions on Iran in May 2008). President Ahmadinejad has used the nuclear issue as a means of rallying domestic support and positioning himself as a defender of Iranian national pride and technological prowess.[67] As a result, an uneasy stalemate has developed, with the international community divided on how to proceed and Iran "playing it by ear."[68] The ability of the U.S. government to pressure Iran has been limited due to the imbroglio in Iraq and the release of the U.S. government's 2007 National Intelligence Estimate (NIE) which concluded with "high confidence" that Iran had halted its nuclear weapons program in 2003.[69] Nevertheless, the NIE also concluded that Iran's enrichment activities might lead to the development of a bomb "if a decision is made to do so" perhaps by 2010 to 2015. A nuclear-armed Iran would be considered a major security threat in a region already beset with conflict management challenges and another nuclear power—Israel.

Of course, states are not the only actors who may be interested in acquiring nuclear weapons. Concern is increasing that nuclear weapons may fall into the hands of substate groups, especially terrorist organizations. This fear has been magnified by concern over the security of weapons grade materials, technology, and warheads from the former Soviet Union and Russia.[70] While the concern is considerable, the likelihood of a terrorist organization acquiring a nuclear device or the capability to produce one is often overstated.[71] Terrorist organizations may not be able to achieve their goals with a weapon so destructive, and its use (or the threat of its use) might be counterproductive. Developing nuclear weapons is costly and, as noted above, requires a large physical infrastructure. Stealing a weapon is also a difficult proposition, but even if a warhead could be obtained the terrorists would still have to find someone with the knowledge to detonate the bomb, which is a rare talent. Nevertheless, the threat of nuclear terrorism cannot be ignored, because the use of even trace amounts of plutonium in a "radiological" or "dirty" bomb is a grave possibility with enormous implications.

A NUCLEAR SOUTH ASIA

One of the most significant developments in nuclear weapons proliferation occurred in May 1998. From May 11 to 13, India conducted five nuclear tests, and Pakistan followed suit with six tests between May 28 and 30. While India had tested a nuclear device in 1974 and Pakistan was thought to have nuclear weapons by 1992, these tests heightened tensions in South Asia and increased awareness of the dangers of nuclear proliferation. International condemnation was swift, as countries such as the United States, Japan, Australia, and Canada imposed sanctions on India and Pakistan. The sanctions hurt both economies (especially Pakistan's), but neither country showed any indication of renouncing its nuclear weapons program. Although both countries were accused of violating international norms on nuclear testing and damaging the nonproliferation regime, Indian and Pakistani officials argued that such accusations were hypocritical. After all, they argued, most of their accusers possessed nuclear weapons or benefited from the security provided by them. Did not India and Pakistan have the same right as sovereign states to respond to their own security requirements?

As we indicated in Chapter 3, the relevance of nuclear deterrence did not end with the Cold War. Nuclear deterrence is alive and well in South Asia, with concerns that two countries that have fought three wars might fight a fourth war with nuclear weapons. These concerns were exacerbated by the development of ballistic missiles by both countries. However, the nuclear tests have imposed the same threat of mutual annihilation on India and Pakistan that existed between the superpowers during the Cold War. Indeed, on February 20, 2000, the leaders of India and Pakistan inaugurated the first bus service between the two countries in 50 years, using the occasion to reinforce their desire for peace and to avoid a nuclear war. It seemed that the nuclear weapons might compel the two states toward a closer political relationship, much in the same way the United States and the U.S.S.R. established a closer (though still antagonistic) relationship as the Cold War progressed. In the summer of 2000, a border skirmish in Kashmir between Pakistani-backed separatists and the Indian military increased tensions between the two countries. In late November 2008, terrorist attacks in Mumbai, India were linked to Pakistan, creating a crisis between the two countries. These incidents illustrate that the possession of nuclear weapons will not necessarily prevent conflict between India and Pakistan.

In Chapter 3 we discussed some varying explanations for why India and Pakistan tested nuclear weapons in 1998. Several factors played a role in India, including the enthusiasm of nuclear scientists, the Indian government's desire to increase domestic support, the threat from Pakistan and China, and the desire to be seen as a great power. Pakistan's government was under enormous pressure to respond to the Indian tests and not appear weak. Growing conventional military inferiority meant nuclear weapons promised security from India. And the Pakistani military, a strong force in Pakistani politics, was largely in favour of the tests. Public opinion in both countries was solidly behind the tests, with large crowds celebrating in an atmosphere of national fervour. Yet there were dissenters: in 1998, thousands of protestors marched in India and Pakistan to oppose the tests. It is possible that these groups will be the beginning of growing regional antinuclear movements similar to those that existed in the West during the Cold War. As one Indian commentator lamented, "A country that has nearly half its population living in absolute poverty, that has an illiterate population more than 2.5 times that of Sub-Saharan Africa, that has more than half its children over the age of four living in malnourishment can never be a superpower."[72] To outsiders, foreign governments, and opponents of nuclear weapons, the tests were sadly inappropriate for two countries mired in poverty and struck a serious blow to efforts to reduce the stockpile of nuclear armaments. Furthermore, increased violence and instability in Pakistan have raised concerns about the safety and security of the country's nuclear weapons. If Pakistan were to become a failed state, what would happen to its nuclear arsenal?

THE PROLIFERATION OF CHEMICAL AND BIOLOGICAL WEAPONS

Although the proliferation of nuclear weapons has attracted much of the attention of scholars, government officials, and the public, the proliferation of chemical and biological weapons may be a more urgent and pressing concern. Chemical and biological warfare involves the dissemination of chemicals or living organisms over military or civilian targets. The primary vector—that is, the medium through which the chemical or biological warfare agent reaches a human being—is the atmosphere, although these weapons can be transmitted to humans through water and surface contact as well. Chemical agents include mustard gas, phosgene, cyanide, and the nerve agents sarin, soman, and tabun, among many others. Biological weapons are living organisms that multiply within the host, eventually killing it. Biological agents include plague, dysentery, typhus, anthrax, smallpox, yellow fever, and botulism. Research and development have produced newer and deadlier chemicals, and biotechnology has led to the development of various engineered bacteria and viruses.

Chemical weapons were used extensively in World War I. The Japanese Imperial Army used chemical and biological weapons in China during World War II. Chemical weapons were used by the United States in Vietnam, in the form of napalm, defoliants, and tear gas. There were persistent allegations of chemical weapons use by the Soviet Union in Afghanistan. During the Iran–Iraq War (1980–88), Iraq used chemical weapons at the front against Iranian troops and also used chemical weapons against a Kurdish rebellion in northern Iraq. In 1995, nerve gas was used in a terrorist attack in the Tokyo subway system. Chemical weapons have limited utility against well-trained and well-equipped military personnel. Against such forces, they are largely of nuisance value, forcing soldiers to wear hot, cumbersome, and restrictive protective clothing. Biological weapons have a limited battlefield utility, as they take time to incapacitate or kill. However, both chemical and biological weapons can be devastating against unprotected military personnel or civilians, which is why they are classified as weapons of mass destruction.

Why would political or military leaders want to acquire chemical or biological weapons? Some countries may acquire such weapons for use on the battlefield, particularly if their prospective opponent is not well equipped with protective clothing. The use of gas by Iraq during the Iran–Iraq War demonstrated the utility and effectiveness of such weapons against unprepared opponents. Other countries may acquire these weapons for deterrent purposes, reasoning that if they possess such weapons, other countries will be reluctant to attack them. Compared with the costs associated with nuclear weapons, chemical and biological weapons are relatively inexpensive to develop and produce. As a result, chemical and biological weapons have been called "the poor state's nuclear weapon." Furthermore, the technology used to produce such weapons is readily available because it is very similar to that used in the fertilizer or chemical industry. The materials required are also not difficult to obtain as the precursors, or component chemicals, for most chemical weapons are common industrial compounds that can be purchased openly on the international market. Research facilities need not be large or expensive: one U.S. study managed to build a small biological weapons facility for US$1.6 million.[73] In short, countries unwilling to invest the time and expense of developing nuclear weapons may find chemical or biological weapons an effective and economical alternative (see Profile 6.3).

THE PROLIFERATION OF CONVENTIONAL WEAPONS

Although weapons of mass destruction get more publicity, conventional weapons have been responsible for the overwhelming majority of deaths and casualties in the world's wars since 1945. For the most part, these casualties are caused by small arms and light weapons, such as military rifles, grenades, rocket launchers, and land mines. The problem of conventional weapons proliferation has two dimensions: the legal international arms trade and the covert or illicit arms trade. The bulk of conventional weapons that change hands in the international

PROFILE 6.3 States with Chemical and Biological Weapons

	CHEMICAL WEAPONS	BIOLOGICAL WEAPONS
KNOWN	Iran, Libya, North Korea, Syria	
PROBABLE	China, Egypt, Ethiopia, Israel, Myanmar, Pakistan, Taiwan	China, Cuba, Egypt, Iran, Libya, North Korea, Russia, Syria
POSSIBLE	Algeria, Cuba, Sudan, Vietnam	Algeria, India, Israel, Pakistan, Sudan, Taiwan
FORMER	Canada, France, Germany, India, Italy, Japan, South Africa, United Kingdom, United States, Yugoslavia (Federal Republic of)	France, Germany, Iraq, Japan, South Africa, United Kingdom, United States

SOURCE: "CHEMICAL AND BIOLOGICAL WEAPONS: POSSESSION AND PROGRAMS PAST AND PRESENT," CENTER FOR NONPROLIFERATION STUDIES, MONTEREY INSTITUTE OF INTERNATIONAL STUDIES, HTTP://CNS.MIIS.EDU/RESEARCH/CBW/POSSESS.HTM (ACCESSED JUNE 28, 2004).

system do so through the perfectly legal international arms trade, consisting of arms deliveries between governments and between corporate manufacturers and governments. In 2006 the value of the world arms trade was approximately US$45.6 billion.[74] Five countries—the United States, Russia, Germany, France, and the United Kingdom—accounted for 80 percent of the supply of arms between 2003 and 2007 (see Profile 6.4).[75] In this period, Asia imported 37 percent of all arms transfers, while Europe accounted for 23 percent and the Middle East 22 percent. In monetary terms, the United States led all arms exporting countries with US$34.5 billion in sales between 2003 and 2007, while China was the leading importer with US$13.5 billion in purchases (see Figures 6.2 and 6.3).

Another point of concern is the quality of many weapons now being purchased: many countries are purchasing weapons that represent significant improvements over their past inventories. Particular concern exists over the spread of ballistic missile capabilities, which could be used

PROFILE 6.4 The Five Largest Suppliers of Major Conventional Weapons and Their Main Recipients, 2003–2007

SUPPLIER	SHARE OF GLOBAL ARMS TRANSFERS, %	NUMBER OF RECIPIENT COUNTRIES	MAIN RECIPIENTS (SHARE OF SUPPLIERS' TRANSFERS, %
United States	31	71	South Korea (12), Israel (12), UAE (9), Greece (8)
Russia	25	45	China (45), India (22), Venezuela (5), Algeria (4)
Germany	10	49	Turkey (15), Greece (14), South Africa (12), Australia (9)
France	9	43	UAE (41), Greece (12), Saudi Arabia (9), Singapore (7)
United Kingdom	4	38	United States (17), Romania (9), Chile (9), India (8)

SOURCE: STOCKHOLM INTERNATIONAL PEACE RESEARCH INSTITUTE, *SIPRI YEARBOOK, 2008* (OXFORD: OXFORD UNIVERSITY PRESS, 2008), 294.

Figure 6.2 Leading Suppliers of Major Conventional Weapons by Value, 2003–2007

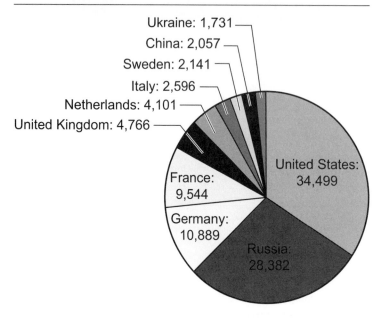

Ukraine: 1,731
China: 2,057
Sweden: 2,141
Italy: 2,596
Netherlands: 4,101
United Kingdom: 4,766
France: 9,544
Germany: 10,889
Russia: 28,382
United States: 34,499

Total value: US$ millions 111,528

SOURCE: DATA FROM STOCKHOLM INTERNATIONAL PEACE RESEARCH INSTITUTE, *SIPRI YEARBOOK, 2007* (OXFORD: OXFORD UNIVERSITY PRESS, 2007), 422.

Figure 6.3 Leading Recipients of Major Conventional Weapons by Value, 2003–2007

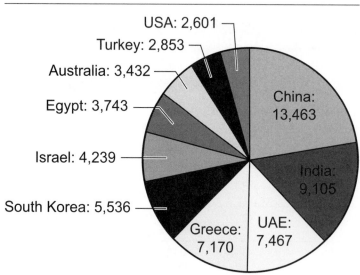

USA: 2,601
Turkey: 2,853
Australia: 3,432
Egypt: 3,743
Israel: 4,239
South Korea: 5,536
Greece: 7,170
UAE: 7,467
India: 9,105
China: 13,463

Total value: US$ millions 111,528

SOURCE: DATA FROM STOCKHOLM INTERNATIONAL PEACE RESEARCH INSTITUTE, *SIPRI YEARBOOK, 2007* (OXFORD: OXFORD UNIVERSITY PRESS, 2007), 418.

to deliver nuclear, chemical, or biological weapons in various regional settings. In addition, many countries are acquiring sea-skimming anti-ship missiles, modern tanks, new fighter aircraft, submarines, and precision-guided munitions. Competition has also led most arms companies to offer generous offset packages to prospective buyers, which take a variety of forms. The importing country might be permitted to manufacture certain components of the weapon domestically under licence (and perhaps in time the entire weapon). Some offset packages permit the permanent transfer of technology to the recipient country. Governments may assist their own arms industries by lifting export restrictions on certain armaments. In other cases, governments may offer financing or credit to prospective buyers to secure the contract for their own arms industry.

The arms industry itself is also in the process of transformation. Just as global economic interdependence has facilitated the internationalization of civilian business, finance, and manufacturing, it has also facilitated the internationalization of the arms industry. Weapons systems can now use components and technology from a variety of different countries and corporations. Transfer of weapons technology between corporate subsidiaries is increasingly common.[76] Why do governments help domestic weapons manufacturers sell their product abroad? In some cases, hard currency is the main motivation, especially if that country is in dire need of cash. For some countries (such as Russia), military hardware is a significant export and hard-currency earner in the country's economy. Jobs are another incentive to secure arms deals abroad. Producing states will encourage arms exports to maintain production activity and the employment that activity brings. Producing states may also want to maintain their manufacturing capability (sometimes called the *defence industrial base*) and keep their production lines open for future sales. As long as the production line is busy, the skilled workforce, design teams, and manufacturing facilities will remain intact. If the production line has to close down, these assets may be lost. Finally, producers may want to encourage sales abroad to lower the unit cost of the weapon. If a weapons system has a long production run and large numbers are produced, the costs of that weapon on a per-unit basis will be lower than if the weapons system was manufactured in lower quantities. The larger the production run, the lower the costs of each individual weapons system, making the weapons system more affordable, both for foreign buyers and for domestic purchasers.

In comparison to the legal arms trade, the covert arms trade is harder to track. The value of the covert trade in armaments (or *gunrunning*, as it is sometimes called) is estimated at between US$2 billion and US$10 billion per year.[77] International arms dealers (often referred to as *brokers*) purchase weapons and stockpile them for sale on the black market, or broker sales between sellers and buyers. The weapons may have been purchased legitimately, stolen from military stocks, diverted from their original destinations, or purchased in war-torn regions from individuals or groups that have a large surplus of weapons available for sale to any bidder. In some cases, weapons available for illegal sales may be sold by companies that failed to observe embargoes or export rules, sometimes with the tacit approval of governments. The weapons are then transported through transshipment points to their buyers.

The challenge of responding to the illegal trade in weapons is illustrated by the case of Victor Bout, the notorious "Merchant of Death." For two decades, Bout supplied weapons to many of the world's conflicts, often in violation of UN arms embargoes. Bout also supplied weapons to dictators and terrorist groups. Wanted since 2002, Bout evaded capture for years by exploiting the gaps between national and international laws and weak enforcement capacities. In March 2008 authorities in Thailand arrested Bout, but inevitably others will rise to take his place.[78]

INTERNATIONAL TERRORISM

Few international events have the emotional impact that incidents of terrorism generate. In many cases, incidents are often broadcast live around the world by the global media. The surprise that attends most acts of terrorism contributes to this international impact; without warning, a plane is hijacked, a bomb explodes, or individuals are kidnapped or taken hostage. And yet, many more cases go unnoticed or unreported. Terrorism directly or indirectly affects the policies of all actors in global politics, and terrorist activity often stretches across borders and regions. In this sense, it is a transnational security concern. Huge sums are spent every year on counterterrorism and security measures at airports, government buildings, business facilities, and public places. The terrorist attacks committed against the United States on September 11, 2001 brought all of the debates about terrorism and counterterrorism into sharp relief and raised the profile of international terrorism to a level never witnessed before. The United States and many other countries now regard international terrorism as the most important security threat they face. People living in Canada have been fortunate as Canada has been relatively unscathed by terrorist attacks. Although 25 Canadians died in the September 11 attacks, and there can be no doubt that international terrorists use Canada as a travel conduit, a location for fundraising, and a place where a small minority of sympathetic individuals might be found, incidents of international terrorism in Canada have been rare.

Terrorism is far from a recent phenomenon. Terrorist incidents, or the causes that motivate them, often have deep historical roots. Traditionally, terrorism has been the weapon of the weak, employed as a political instrument by individuals or groups seeking to reject authority, generate social change, promote revolution, or spread fear. Historical examples of the use of terrorism include the Zealots, a Jewish sect that appeared in B.C.E. 6 and used assassinations in an effort to force the Roman Empire out of Palestine. In the Middle East between 1090 and 1275 C.E., Muslims known as *hashashin* (from which the word "assassin" originates) carried out many political and religious killings on behalf of their political and spiritual leaders. In 1605, a group of English Catholics conspired to blow up James I of England, in the failed "gunpowder plot." At the end of the 19th century, political assassinations by anarchists claimed U.S. President William McKinley, French President Sadi Carnot, the Empress Elizabeth of Austria, and Spanish Prime Minister Antonio Canovas. World War I began with an act of terrorism—the assassination of Austrian Archduke Franz Ferdinand—by a Serbian terrorist organization called the Black Hand. In an eerie precursor to contemporary car bombings, in 1920 a horse-drawn cart exploded on Wall Street in New York City, killing 40 and injuring 300 in an attack that remains unsolved. In 1946, the Jewish Irgun Tsvai-Leumi bombed the King David Hotel, the headquarters of the British Secretariat in Palestine, killing 91 people. At the 1972 Olympics in Munich, the Palestinian group Black September killed 11 Israeli athletes. Also in 1972, "Bloody Friday" claimed nine lives and injured 130 as 22 bombs planted by the Irish Republican Army exploded in and around Belfast. In 1980, government-backed death squads in El Salvador killed a Catholic priest and four U.S. nuns. In 1985, a bomb placed on board Air India Flight 182 by Sikh extremists at Vancouver International Airport killed 329 people. North Korean agents planted a bomb on Korean Airlines Flight 858 in 1987, killing all 115 on board. In 1993, a car bomb exploded in the underground parking lot of the World Trade Center Towers in New York, killing six. In 1995, a Japanese cult named Aum Shinrikyo released sarin nerve gas in the Tokyo subway system, killing 12 and injuring 5,000. In the same year, 168 people were killed when Timothy McVeigh and his associates detonated a truck bomb outside the federal building in Oklahoma City. In 1999, Ahmed Rassam, an Algerian national, was arrested crossing the Canada–United States border with explosive materials for a bomb intended to attack Los Angeles International Airport. These incidents are but a small fraction of the terrorist acts perpetrated over the years, and illustrate how terrorism as a historical phenomenon cuts across countries, regions, and cultures.

There is no universally accepted definition of terrorism in international law. Definitions of terrorism are notoriously difficult to construct, in part because terrorism is a politically charged word, and is often used inappropriately for political purposes. The familiar adage "one person's terrorist is another's freedom fighter" illustrates the relative nature of the term. Many different types of terrorism occur, and it is difficult to establish a single definition that accounts for all of them. Walter Laqueur defines terrorism as "the substate application of violence or threatened violence intended to sow panic in a society, to weaken or even overthrow the incumbents, and to bring about political change."[79] Cindy Combs defines terrorism as "a synthesis of war and theatre, a dramatization of the most proscribed kind of violence—that which is perpetrated on innocent victims—played before an audience in the hope of creating a mood of fear, for political purposes."[80] Paul Wilkinson's definition is more comprehensive:

> Terrorism is the systematic use of coercive intimidation, usually to serve political ends. It is used to create and exploit a climate of fear among a wider target group than the immediate victims of the violence, often to publicize a cause, as well as to coerce a target into acceding to terrorist aims. Terrorism may be used on its own or as part of a wider conventional war. It can be employed by desperate and weak minorities, by states as a tool of domestic and foreign policy, or by belligerents as an

accompaniment or additional weapon in all types and stages of warfare. A common feature is that innocent civilians, sometimes foreigners who know nothing of the terrorist's political quarrel, are killed or injured.[81]

Many definitions of contemporary terrorism also reflect the "stateless" quality of some terrorist acts. As Suman Gupta argues, for many terrorist acts "the motives and/or agencies and/or effects cross the boundaries of nation-states, and are not necessarily conducted (certainly seldom directly) at the behest of any nation-state."[82]

Paul Wilkinson's definition reminds us that individuals and groups are not the only perpetrators of terrorism. Although the image of the small terrorist cell operating in a clandestine fashion in the city or countryside is the most popular conception of terrorism, much of the terrorism in the world is planned and executed by states against their own citizens. **State terrorism** is employed by states within their own borders to suppress dissent and silence opposition. Such campaigns frequently involve massive human rights violations, an issue we shall return to in later chapters. State terrorism also has deep historical roots. The Roman emperor Nero killed large numbers of suspected political opponents, including members of his own family. In the French Revolution, state terrorism was employed as a tool of the French Republic to get rid of its enemies. During the years of racial segregation, or apartheid, in South Africa, government hit squads killed political opponents of the regime to spread fear and to intimidate others. In the late 1970s, the Khmer Rouge in Cambodia systematically murdered approximately 1.5 to 2 million people in an effort to fulfill a bizarre ideological purification of the country. The military government of Argentina was responsible for the deaths of almost 10,000 people in 1976–77 alone. In the 1980s, the government of Guatemala used death squads to conduct assassinations and kidnappings of political opponents. Accusations of state terrorism have been directed against Israel for its actions against Palestinians. Such state terrorism differs from **state-sponsored terrorism**, which is the support of international terrorist individuals or groups by a government. Libya once provided sanctuary and assistance to the Abu Nidal Organization, and Iran has supported the operations of Hamas and Hizbollah, among others. Many accusations of state-sponsored terrorism have been directed against the United States: the arming and training of the Contras in Nicaragua in their effort to overthrow the Sandinista government is but one example.

THE ORIGINS AND CAUSES OF TERRORISM

State terrorism is designed to eliminate political opposition, and the killers and torturers who engage in it are paid for their work, which can even become routine for them. But what causes the nonstate terrorist to commit acts of violence against innocent people? In most cases, terrorist acts will be committed for a number of motives. If appropriate and effective counterterrorist strategies are to be developed, an understanding of these motives is essential. Studies of terrorism and terrorists suggest that terrorism can be explained by the following factors:

Individual and Group Psychology

Some researchers suggest that the root cause of terrorism is the psychological makeup of the individuals who participate in terrorist activities. In particular, personal motivations such as the desire for glory, romantic visions of sacrifice and struggle for a cause, feelings of obligation or duty to family or community, the sense of identity and community found in terrorist cells, or a desire for revenge are powerful explanations for terrorist actions. Some psychologists and psychiatrists suggest that personality disorders or even mental illness may explain terrorist activity.

Ideological Fanaticism

Terrorism can originate from the commitment of individuals and groups to a particular political idea and their efforts to promote this political idea through violence. Ideologies such as Marxism-Leninism, fascism, and extreme racism offer a framework for interpreting social injustice and inequality and identifying those responsible, and provide a program of action to build a better society. Terrorists are thus committed to the idea of social change through violence.

Religious Fanaticism

Terrorist acts may originate in religious extremism, drawn from literal interpretations of religious beliefs. Often, religious fanaticism employs a belief system that is in fact a perversion of the principles of that religion. Terrorist acts are carried out by individuals or groups seeking to advance their religious views, secure religious rights or freedoms, or wage a holy war against their religious enemies.

Grievance and Cycles of Violence

Terrorist acts may originate with the grievances of a particular group. This group may be the target of discrimination and repression, which may include economic, political, or religious persecution. In some instances, this persecution may be violent. Although the relationship between poverty and terrorism is uncertain, the combination of economic and political grievances can create angry and resentful individuals, who can then be recruited and indoctrinated to carry out acts of violence against the perceived enemy.

Nationalism and Separatism

Terrorism may also originate from the desire of individuals within a larger community for greater political autonomy or even full independence. While this desire often originates with a history of grievances, the specific aim of the terrorist activity is to advance the political independence of a group.

Activist Fanaticism

Terrorist activity may also originate from a very specific issue or controversy that provokes certain individuals or groups to violence. The aim of such violence is to prevent certain political or social activity or to force their belief systems on others. Such issues include abortion, animal rights, racial superiority, and environmental protection.

Despite the shock and horror terrorism evokes, it is seldom successful in achieving its stated objectives. While terrorist activity is designed to promote a cause, it can often have the opposite effect. It can alienate other supporters of the cause who do not believe that violence is the appropriate instrument for advancing their interests or beliefs. it can also discredit moderates, who become associated with the violence even though they have no connection to it. While a harsh backlash against terrorists by a central authority can drive more people to the terrorists' cause, these measures can also lead to persecution and repression of the people or group the terrorist organization is supposedly fighting for.

SEPTEMBER 11, 2001

On the morning of September 11, 2001, nineteen terrorists used box cutters and verbal threats to hijack four civilian airliners in the United States. They overpowered the crews and commandeered the planes. Two of the aircraft were deliberately crashed into the two towers of the World Trade Center in New York, which subsequently collapsed due to the structural

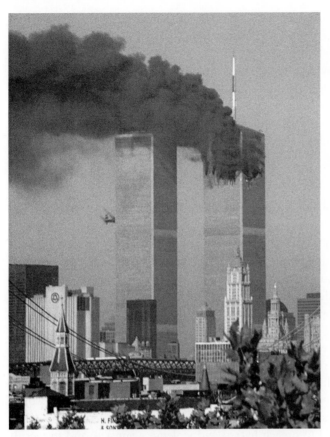

9:03 a.m., September 11, 2001. United Airlines Flight 175 strikes the south tower of the World Trade Center in New York, just 18 minutes after American Airlines Flight 11 hit the north tower. Both towers subsequently collapsed. (AP Photo/Moshe Bursuker/CP Archive.)

damage and fire caused by the collisions. The third hijacked plane was crashed into the Pentagon, the headquarters of the American military establishment. The fourth plane, whose target was believed to have been either the Capitol Building or the White House, crashed into a field in Pennsylvania when the passengers tried to overpower the hijackers. Over 3,000 people were killed that morning. For most, it was a day of profound shock and dismay, as well as fear and uncertainty of what might happen next. All civilian airline traffic in the United States was grounded, and most flights inbound from other parts of the world were diverted to Canada. The Canada–United States border was closed, bringing cross-border travel and commerce to a halt. In the following days, as transportation systems in North America resumed operation and cleanup efforts started to remove rubble and human remains, expressions of sympathy and support were extended to the United States from around the world.

Though many reasonable questions remain about the origin and execution of the September 11 attacks, they are generally assumed to be the result of years of planning and preparation by Al-Qaeda, a terrorist group lead by Osama Bin Laden. As early as two days after the attacks, official suspicion fell on Al-Qaeda, as the organization had been responsible for the bombing of the World Trade Center in 1993, the bombings of U.S. embassies in Africa in 1998, and an attack on a U.S. warship in 2000. The Clinton administration had identified Al-Qaeda as America's top security threat, and had attempted to disrupt its operations and capture Osama Bin Laden. Al-Qaeda was a formidable network of loosely associated terrorist cells, controlled by a leadership group under Bin Laden. With operations in over 50 countries, Al-Qaeda engaged in the planning and execution of terrorist attacks, fundraising efforts, and training thousands of terrorist fighters (primarily in bases in Afghanistan). On September 17, Osama Bin Laden was formally accused as the perpetrator of the attacks. On September 20, President George W. Bush launched a "war on terror," declaring: "Our war on terror begins with Al-Qaeda, but it does not end there. It will not end until every terrorist group of global reach has been found, stopped and defeated."[83]

The motive for the September 11 attacks has been the subject of considerable debate and controversy. The increasing resentment directed against the United States in large parts of the world in general and the Islamic world in particular was well understood by observers of global politics (though not the American population at large). Anti-American sentiment was built on a wide array of grievances that include U.S. support for Israel (and therefore complicity in the repression of the Palestinian people), U.S. assistance to repressive regimes in the Islamic world, the growing cultural influences of the United States, and a reaction against Western modernization and globalization, which is led in large part by Washington. The world perspective of Osama Bin Laden and the Al-Qaeda ideology used an extreme interpretation of these grievances, and combined them with a particular brand of Islamic fundamentalism, to recruit and train young volunteers for a perverse form of *jihad* or holy war against America and the West. However, there may also have been a broader political purpose behind the attacks. Al-Qaeda had long regarded most Middle Eastern governments as enemies of Islam. The September 11 attacks may have been intended to precipitate an American reaction that would lead to a general uprising and revolution across the Arab world. Critics of U.S. foreign policy also pointed out that Bin Laden (virtually unknown at this time) and other extremists had received U.S. assistance during the Cold War in their fight against the Soviet occupation of Afghanistan.[84]

Of course, any suggestion that American foreign policy may have been even partially responsible for the September 11 attacks was rejected by Washington, which quickly cast the attacks as an act of unjustified aggression by extremists. In one sense, this sentiment is understandable, as none of the 3,000 people who were killed in the attacks had any hand in the real or imagined grievances of the attackers (of course, it is hard to imagine any political leader acknowledging that a terrorist attack might have been understandable). Moreover, one cannot blame U.S. foreign policy in isolation from other factors, including the hate- and ambition-inspired motives of terrorist leaders and the propaganda and invective they employ to guide others to kill in the name of faith or politics. It is difficult to imagine any political initiatives that could satisfy Al-Qaeda, whose spokesman, Suleiman Abu Ghaith, stated that there could be no truce until four million Americans had been killed.[85] However, in another sense this rejection of responsibility by the American government is a counterproductive sentiment, for it absolves the United States of any critical reflection on its role in the world. The U.S. cannot detach itself or its policy decisions from the political and economic grievances that even now are being used to preach hatred and violence against it, and to recruit future generations of poor, desperate, ignorant, angry, and easily misled youth to be the next generation of terrorists.

THE WAR IN AFGHANISTAN

Once Al-Qaeda was identified as the perpetrator, the United States began to move against the group's primary base of operations in Afghanistan. The country was ruled by the Taliban, a predominantly ethnic Pashtun group that had seized power over most of Afghanistan in 1997 (with the exception of anti-Taliban regions in the north). Composed largely of students of religious schools preaching an extremist form of Islam, the Taliban government was already isolated from the international community for its harsh imposition of Islamic law and its treatment of women. The United States accused the Taliban government of harbouring Al-Qaeda terrorists and Osama Bin Laden and demanded they be handed over to American authorities. The Taliban government refused, and the diplomatic efforts of Pakistan and Saudi Arabia to change the Taliban government's position were unsuccessful. The Bush administration began a war against Afghanistan on October 7, 2001 with the stated objectives of destroying Al-Qaeda, capturing Osama Bin Laden, and overthrowing the Taliban government. The war in Afghanistan received considerable international support. Thirty-three countries offered military forces, and many others offered political support. There was controversy over the legalities of military action against Afghanistan. Critics charged that the operation did not have the explicit authorization of the UN Security Council and was therefore illegal. Others argued that because the United States was responding to the September 11 attacks, military action against Afghanistan was legal under the right of self defence. While legal experts deliberated, the military campaign moved swiftly. Through a combination of Special Forces personnel on the ground cooperating with anti-Taliban forces in the north, and the extensive use of airpower, the U.S.–led coalition successfully overthrew the Taliban government in November. Many senior Taliban and Al-Qaeda figures were captured or killed, but Osama Bin Laden himself eluded capture or death.

Political events also moved swiftly. Under the Bonn Agreement of December 2001 an Afghan Interim Authority was established, beginning a process designed to establish a new government in Afghanistan. In January 2002 a UN International Security and Assistance Force (ISAF) deployed to Kabul to assist in providing security in the area around the capital, while U.S.-led coalition forces under Operation Enduring Freedom fought surviving Taliban and Al-Qaeda forces in the west and south of Afghanistan. In 2003 the North Atlantic Treaty Organization (NATO) assumed control over ISAF (a transition authorized by the UN Security Council). Although Taliban and Al-Qaeda resistance continued, there was some optimism as the Bonn process led to the adoption of a new constitution and the election of Hamid Karzai as President in 2004. A National Assembly and Provincial Councils were elected in 2005. NATO expanded ISAF operations across the country between 2003 and 2006, establishing Provincial Reconstruction Teams (PRTs) under the control of NATO member states in most Afghan provinces. The PRTs were designed to provide security assets and development resources that together would defeat the Taliban insurgency and assist with the economic reconstruction and development of the country. However, the optimism proved to be short-lived. In recent years the conflict in Afghanistan has been characterized by a resurgent Taliban, an increase in narcotics production, and the weakness of the central government in Kabul.

The security situation in Afghanistan has deteriorated steadily since 2001.[86] The number of violent incidents in the country increased dramatically through 2006 to mid-2009, spreading geographically to include previously safe parts of the country. A resilient insurgency has shifted tactics from larger-scale operations to suicide bombings, the use of improvised explosive devices (IEDs), and smaller-scale "hit and run" attacks. While these tactics are incapable of holding territory against NATO forces, they are difficult to counter and have increased the sense of insecurity in the country, especially in the southern and eastern provinces. The conflict in Afghanistan is best described as an insurgency war, with ISAF troops and Afghan government forces trying to defeat a resurgent Taliban and maintain or establish a safe and secure environment for reconstruction and development efforts, efforts regarded as essential to gaining victory over the insurgency by winning the "hearts and minds" of the Afghan people.

However, attempts to improve the security situation have met with a number of challenges. The mountainous terrain of Afghanistan is ideal for insurgency warfare. The complex social structures of the country rooted in ethnolinguistic and tribal relations have complicated political reconciliation and federal and provincial governance. The historical antipathy of the Afghan people to foreign involvement in their country (drawn from experiences with the British Empire and the Soviet Union) has been an obstacle to trust and cooperation between ISAF and the Afghan government and people.[87] Civilian casualties caused by NATO air strikes have provoked much additional resentment. Despite having 47,000 troops in the country as of mid-2008, ISAF lacked sufficient resources to effectively control the countryside. Some NATO governments have proved reluctant to commit their militaries to the more dangerous, combat-intensive mission in the southern part of the country, largely due to public opposition. This has lead to tension within the Alliance. In fact, Canada threatened to withdraw from Afghanistan unless other NATO countries contributed more to the operations in Kandahar Province, where the Canadian PRT is located (see Profile 6.5). Amid concerns that the war in Afghanistan was being lost, in early 2009 the Obama administration decided to send an additional 17,000 U.S. troops to Afghanistan, with plans to send more in the near future.

PROFILE 6.5 Canada in Afghanistan

In the wake of the September 11, 2001 attacks, Canada added its voice to the international condemnation of Afghanistan and supported U.S. diplomatic efforts to pressure the Taliban government into surrendering Bin Laden and the al-Qaeda leadership. When the U.S.-led military campaign began in October 2001, Canada deployed a naval task force to the Persian Gulf in support of coalition operations in the region. In February 2002 a battle group of 800 personnel were deployed to Kandahar Province in Afghanistan to assist U.S. and coalition forces in the U.S.-led Operation Enduring Freedom against the Taliban and al-Qaeda fighters. There was some opposition to Canada's participation in the war in Afghanistan: some felt Canada was abandoning its peacekeeping tradition and following Washington too closely. However, for the most part there was widespread support for Canada's contribution as a justifiable response to terrorism and an expression of Canada's commitment to the United States. The Canadian battle group was withdrawn from Afghanistan in July 2002. In February 2003 the Canadian government announced it would send Canadian troops back to Afghanistan. The decision was widely viewed as a tactic to avoid the deployment of Canadian ground forces in the Iraq War. From August 2003 to December 2005, Canada's military commitment was based in Kabul, as part of the NATO-led, UN-mandated International Security Assistance Force (ISAF)

which was to provide the security required for the rebuilding of Afghanistan (Canada would command ISAF for much of 2004). In August 2005, Canada assumed responsibility for the Kandahar Provincial Reconstruction Team (PRT), and Canadian forces were redeployed from Kabul to the volatile southern province. The Canadian effort in Kandahar has been multi-dimensional: in addition to providing security, the PRT is responsible for assisting Afghan reconstruction and development. The mission in Afghanistan has been a high-profile component of Canadian foreign policy: Afghanistan has been the largest overseas deployment of Canadian troops and the largest recipient of Canadian development assistance funding since 2005. Afghanistan has become a major political issue in Canada. Supporters of the mission argue that Canada has an interest in the stability of the country and should honour its commitments to its NATO allies. Critics argue the conflict is too closely connected to the U.S. "war on terror," and has been beset with poor planning, inadequate resources, and insufficient efforts to rebuild the country. The cost has been high: as of 2009, 120 Canadian soldiers had been killed in Afghanistan since February 2002. Canada intends to withdraw its military commitment from Afghanistan in 2011.

FOR AN ACCOUNT OF THE POLITICS OF CANADA'S ENGAGEMENT IN AFGHANISTAN, SEE J. G. STEIN AND E. LANG, *THE UNEXPECTED WAR: CANADA IN KANDAHAR* (TORONTO: VIKING CANADA, 2007).

Several NATO countries also pledged to increase their military and development assistance contributions to the country. However, the Taliban have relatively safe sanctuary in western areas of neighbouring Pakistan, which they have used as a base of operations and a recruitment ground for new fighters. In response, U.S. air strikes and Pakistan military campaigns against the Taliban in western Pakistan accelerated in 2008 and 2009. It is becoming increasingly clear that the war in Afghanistan has widened into a regional conflict that threatens the political stability of Pakistan itself.

One of the most serious challenges facing Afghanistan and the international effort in that country is the narcotics trade. Poppy growth and cultivation has increased steadily since 2001. Afghanistan is responsible for over 90 percent of the world's production of opium, and the annual crop accounted for about one-third of the country's gross domestic product (GDP) in 2007.[88] The problem is that poppy cultivation is the best economic option for many Afghan farmers: foodstuffs or other produce cannot match opium in value. The Taliban and local warlords (including some that are nominal allies of the ISAF presence) use the

A Canadian soldier on patrol in Arghandab, Kandahar province. In 2008, there were approximately 2,500 Canadian soldiers serving in the International Security Assistance Force (ISAF) in Afghanistan. (AP Photo/Alluaddin Khan/CP Archive.)

revenues from poppy production to finance their activities, creating a direct relationship between poppy cultivation and the insurgency. This has led to concern that Afghanistan is becoming a "narco-mafia state," with the economy of some areas of the country dominated by poppy cultivation and drug-related corruption reaching the highest levels of government.[89] Proposed responses have ranged from eradication (which risks alienating local populations, harming local ecology, and plunging dependent farmers into poverty) to legal purchase of opium for medical codeine and morphine (which would not yield the same return as opium for the drug trade). It is likely that only a combination of responses will be successful. Reducing the area under poppy cultivation is essential, but only in the context of some income-replacement or alternative crop program. Restoration of agricultural infrastructure has a high priority, but requires security against insurgent attack. And reducing demand in the primary market for Afghanistan's opium—Europe—would also help.

The prospect for stability and economic development in Afghanistan ultimately depends on effective governance. Initial optimism about the prospects for the Karzai government has changed to skepticism, largely due to the lack of capacity of the government, its poor or even nonexistent control over large parts of the country, and persistent problems with corruption. Positive developments are in evidence: GDP grew by 8 percent in 2006, enrolment in school increased dramatically between 2001 and 2008, and cultural life (virtually nonexistent under the Taliban) experienced something of a renewal.[90] However, this must be appreciated against the backdrop of a federal government that lacks capacity, has difficulty delivering services beyond certain parts of the country, struggles to maintain its authority in the face of regional and provincial opposition, and is beset by corruption. There is widespread agreement that strengthening the institutions of the Afghan government, as well as the Afghan National Army (ANA) and the Afghan National Police (ANP), are essential if ISAF is to be able to withdraw from a country that is relatively stable and secure. Thus far, international economic assistance devoted to Afghanistan has not met the demand, raising the possibility that ISAF contributors will tire of the mission and withdraw their military and financial support even if the Afghan government is not ready to assume the burdens of security and governance.

INTERNATIONAL TERRORISM AFTER SEPTEMBER 11

Terrorism continues to be one of the major security issues in global politics. Terrorism is a focus of the security strategy of many states and a domestic security concern for governments worldwide. In the past few years, the discourse on terrorism in most industrialized countries has focused on what has been called "Islamist terrorism," a reference to terrorist groups and acts inspired by extremist or fundamentalist interpretations of Islam. In particular, attention has focused on al-Qaeda, the organization held responsible for the September 11, 2001 attacks. On the one hand, this emphasis on Islamist terrorism and al-Qaeda is understandable, given the focus on Iraq, Afghanistan, Pakistan, and other Islamic countries in the U.S. war on terror. Numerous terrorist groups are guided by extremist Islamic ideology and operate in countries from Morocco to Indonesia. Furthermore, al-Qaeda has proved to be a resilient and dangerous entity, inspiring and conducting acts of violence in many parts of the world. On the other hand, the emphasis on Islamic-inspired terrorism has led to an unfortunate and inaccurate association of Islam with terrorism, a dangerous trend toward the assumption that the "clash of civilizations" thesis (discussed in Chapter 13) is now a reality, and a relative neglect of other forms of terrorism (especially state and state-sponsored terrorism) in other parts of the world. Critics of the war on terror and other national counterterrorism campaigns have argued that the focus on "Islamic terrorism" has led to prejudice and racial profiling against Muslims and people of Arab descent, while the means used to combat terrorism are increasingly threatening the civil liberties essential to a free and democratic society.

In the past few years, al-Qaeda has continued to be the primary focus of global antiterrorism efforts, largely because these efforts are led (or greatly influenced) by American policy. It is sobering to consider that after years of effort to eradicate al-Qaeda it has survived and remains capable of carrying out terrorist attacks (even the leader of al-Qaeda, Osama Bin Laden, remains at large). This is due in large part to the evolution of al-Qaeda from a relatively coherent and structured organization based in Afghanistan to a decentralized network inspired by al-Qaeda ideology and tactics. Terrorist attacks are no longer planned or executed by a central leadership, but instead are carried out by local or "home-grown" individuals or "franchise" groups sympathetic to al-Qaeda's visions and goals.[91] Using the Internet, al-Qaeda has remade itself into a global conduit for two basic messages: a simple narrative of Muslim oppression at the hands of unbelievers; and a call for violent "resistance" through *jihad*. The narrative of the oppression of Muslims is characterized by references to Western occupation of Muslim lands (particularly Iraq and Afghanistan), anti-Israeli and anti-Jewish sentiments, a deep hatred of America, and calls for the overthrow of existing secular governments in the Islamic world such as Saudi Arabia, Egypt, and Pakistan.

The call for violent resistance is characterized by online "terrorism manuals" that provide instructions for the manufacture of explosives and bombs and information on the planning and execution of terrorist attacks. While *jihad* is generally understood by most Islamic scholars and imams as a personal struggle for spiritual purity, *jihad* in the al-Qaeda formulation is literally a call to violent action to overthrow the oppressors of the Islamic world. This potent combination of a narrative of grievance and a call to violence by an evasive Web-based ideology with little or no centralized command or leadership has proven a difficult challenge for governments throughout the world.[92] As Audrey Kurth Cronin argues: "Al-Qaeda's most potent sources of strength are its powerful image and carefully crafted narrative, assets constructed through a widespread, well-developed, and sophisticated effort to build popular support for the cause.... Al-Qaeda is at heart a brilliant propaganda and image machine whose primary purpose has been to convince Muslims that they can defeat the West and in this way solve their problems."[93] In Europe, Canada, and the United States, there is growing concern that Al-Qaeda's message is finding a sympathetic audience among some alienated and disaffected Muslim youth, sparking national debates on the assimilation and integration of Muslims into society and the role of racism and religious bigotry in social attitudes toward Muslim immigrant communities.

Counterterrorism efforts have had only limited success against Al-Qaeda. U.S. counterterrorism strategy has emphasized the use of military power projection and the physical security of American territory. While some successes have been achieved, such as the killing or capture of many senior al-Qaeda leaders, the U.S. war on terror has been heavily criticized; it has been widely interpreted in the Muslim world as a war on Islam, with the invasions of Iraq (and to a lesser extent Afghanistan) seen as the primary evidence of a Western "crusade" that has provoked increased anti-U.S. and anti-Western sentiment. The emphasis on military power in U.S. counterterrorism policy has been criticized as misplaced and counterproductive, marginalizing the importance of intelligence, policing, and political and social policy as responses to terrorism. The war on terror has sparked global protest over U.S. violations of human rights and international law. Examples include: the maintenance of a detention centre at the U.S. military base in Guantanamo Bay where detained terrorist suspects were held without protection under the Geneva Conventions or U.S. domestic law; the practice of "extraordinary rendition" (the transport of terrorist suspects to third countries for interrogation and torture) by the Central Intelligence Agency outside of legal procedures; and the use of "enhanced interrogation" techniques that include sleep deprivation and "waterboarding" (a torture technique that simulates drowning). Finally, U.S. counterterrorism policy has raised serious civil liberties concerns, particularly with respect to the privacy of financial data, voice and e-mail communications, search and seizure, and airline passenger information. Taken together, these criticisms reflect a deep ambivalence about the effectiveness of the U.S. war on terror and a growing opposition to the policies and techniques employed by America, which have undermined international support for U.S. policies on a wide range of counterterrorism and human rights issues. Significantly, establishing a timetable for closing Guantanamo Bay and banning "waterboarding" were among the first acts of the Obama administration (although as of early 2009 rendition was still permitted).

As noted earlier, the attention placed on Al-Qaeda and on "Islamic-inspired" terrorism has obscured the fact that terrorism is a much wider phenomenon and is inspired by a wide variety of causes and carried out by a wide variety of groups. Any number of causes can drive individuals or groups to carry out terrorist acts. For example, in recent years terrorist attacks have been carried out by Tamil Tiger separatists in Sri Lanka, *Fuerzas Armadas Revolucionarias de Colombia* (FARC) rebels in Colombia, the *Ejercito Popular Revolucionario* (EPR) in Mexico, and Basque *Euskadi Ta Askatasuna* (ETA) separatists in Spain. Furthermore, governments have carried out acts that can be described as state terrorism, whether it is the suppression of protests in Burma or the policies of the Sudanese government in Darfur. Whatever the origin or motive, terrorism is likely to remain a feature of global politics in the future. While the technology required to carry out bombings or other forms of terrorist attacks remains relatively simple, the use of Internet communication and Web-based information dissemination has become a prominent feature of contemporary terrorism.[94] Concerns remain that terrorists might acquire and use chemical and biological weapons (see Profile 6.6) or perhaps even radiological and nuclear weapons.[95] However, it is more likely that the current trend toward globally inspired but locally derived terrorist activity using bombs and suicide bombers will continue to be the dominant form of terrorism in the future.

Another characteristic of contemporary international terrorism is the growing link between different terrorist individuals and groups. International terrorist networks exist, although estimates of their extent vary. Such networks facilitate the sharing of memberships, training facilities, weapons, information, and finance, and reduce reliance on client states for sponsorship. Some analysts have argued that globalization is enhancing the terrorist threat: Audrey Kurth Cronin contends that "the current wave of international terrorism, characterized by unpredictable and unprecedented threats from nonstate actors, not only is a reaction to globalization but is facilitated by it."[96] However, others claim that globalization also provides opportunities to combat terrorism. As Kendall Hoyt and Stephen G. Brooks argue, "many of the most effective tools for dealing with the terrorist threat are themselves partly

PROFILE 6.6 The Tokyo Subway Attack

In March 1995, 12 people were killed and more than 5,000 injured by a sarin nerve gas attack on several Tokyo subway lines. The attack was carried out by members of a religious cult known as Aum Shinrikyo (Supreme Truth), a well-financed organization with more than 10,000 members in Japan and some 100,000 abroad. Asahara Shoko founded the cult in 1994, and his teachings spoke of an imminent Armageddon for modern society, which he believed was corrupt. Although many more casualties have been caused by terrorist bombings and shootings around the world, the Aum Shinrikyo acts are especially disturbing. For the first time, chemical weapons have been used on a large scale in an urban terrorist act. The cult maintained front companies and laboratories that employed highly skilled technicians and graduate microbiologists to develop and produce the gas used in the subway attack. In addition, the cult was a religious organization, not a political one, and was interested in promoting a theological outcome, not one designed to advance a political agenda or extract concessions from the Japanese government. As such, its actions cannot be responsive to political change designed to eliminate the root causes of terrorism. Asahara Shoko was found guilty of murder in 2004 and was sentenced to death. His appeal was denied in 2006 and he is awaiting execution.

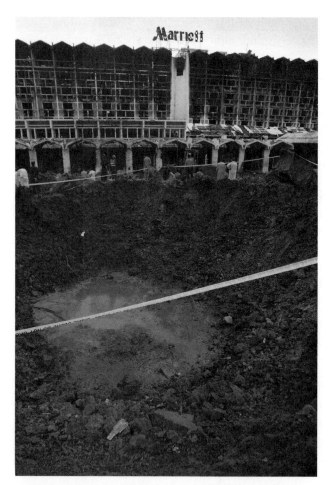

The aftermath of a terrorist attack. A view of the crater caused by the massive truck bombing of the Marriott Hotel in Islamabad, Pakistan, on September 20, 2008. The explosion killed 40 people and injured more than 250. (AP Photo/Anjum Naveed/CP Archive.)

the product of globalization."[97] Another trend is the emergence of many terrorist groups that have somewhat different motivations than traditional terrorist groups. Most terrorism is motivated by a set of goals that can be quantified in terms of land, political power, or independence. However, the objectives of what Walter Laqueur has called "postmodern terrorism" are inspired by religious or cult beliefs or by racial hatred. These motives are not so amenable to conflict management efforts or negotiated settlements, and so there is considerable concern that such groups cannot be addressed by responding to root causes or by offering concessions. Perhaps most disturbing of all is the fact that these groups seem to have turned away from hijackings and the targeting of specific individuals and toward more indiscriminate killing.[98]

September 11 has led counterterrorism experts into a dangerous game of speculation as to what type of attacks terrorist groups may undertake in the future. Since September 11, terrorists have attacked nightclubs and street markets, civilian aircraft, embassy buildings, and train stations, to name a few. They might attack nuclear power plants or chemical industries with potentially devastating effects. Port facilities might be attacked using bombs planted on commercial ships or small civilian craft. National transportation infrastructure such as bridges, pipelines, power cables, dams, subways, and railways are all considered vulnerable. Portable surface-to-air missiles might be used against civilian airliners. More ominously, terrorists with chemical or biological weapons might attack water supplies, public places, or urban areas using "crop duster" aircraft intended to spray agricultural pesticides. The anthrax attacks in the United States after September 11 used the postal service to deliver anthrax spores to a range of individuals in letter-sized envelopes. It is also possible that terrorists will turn to "weapons of mass disruption" in the future, choosing to attack computer and telecommunications networks in what are sometimes called "cyber-attacks."[99] Furthermore, terrorists do not have to actually plant a bomb or conduct an attack; often the mere threat that a bomb exists or an attack is imminent can cause mass fear and disruption of transportation systems. In other words, wherever we look we are likely to see opportunities for terrorists. While such an exercise can be prudent if it leads to sound security improvements, it can also lead to an exaggerated sense of vulnerability and fear, and the expenditure of large amounts of resources to defend against an attack that may never come.

COMBATING TERRORISM: APPROACHES AND METHODS

Can international terrorism be stopped? Can a war on terrorism be won? Asking this question demands some humility, for terrorism has been an enduring feature of the history of human violence. However, terrorist groups can be defeated with a combination of sound policies. First, few if any counterterrorism efforts can be successful without some effort to address root causes and motives. To the extent that terrorism is rooted in grievances, injustices, and a desire for autonomy or independence, efforts to address such grievances or desires might reduce or eliminate terrorist activity. Of course, particularly radical or extremist individuals or groups might not be satisfied with any level of accommodation short of their objectives, and would continue to engage in acts of violence. However, these individuals and groups would be increasingly isolated from their broader community, and easier to combat with law enforcement efforts. Of course, this approach presumes that governments or societies are willing to address root causes. In many cases, governments and publics are committed to preserving the status quo, and are highly resistant to making the economic, political, or social changes required. Furthermore, in many regions of the world, poverty, despair, hatred, and other social ills are so pervasive that eliminating the terrorism that develops from such conditions would require revolutionary changes, which may be beyond the resources as well as the political will of governments. The motives of terrorists must also be understood if responses are to be effective: if terrorists are motivated by political aims, certain responses may be effective, but if terrorists are motivated by affective or emotional ties to each other and the group, different responses may be in order.[100]

Second, governments can employ military and/or police force against terrorist organizations or the states that sponsor their activities. Such counterterrorist operations might include the use of highly trained teams of police or military personnel in large-scale search operations or the bombing of terrorist training grounds and facilities from the air. However, the usefulness of the military against terrorist organizations is limited. Terrorist organizations are hard to track and target because they are often small, and compartmentalized into highly secretive cells. Military operations against terrorists also face tactical and political obstacles. Terrorist facilities are often located in sponsoring states, and any attack against them would have to take into account the military capability of the host state as well as the political repercussions of attacking its territory. Often, military force is a very blunt instrument and attacking terrorists or their facilities can lead to the deaths of innocent individuals. As a result, the use of military force can create new grievances and new martyrs for the terrorist cause. Furthermore, constructivists would remind us that using the language of war can influence our thinking about counterterrorism. For example, by declaring a "war on terror" the Bush administration did manage to capture a mood of sadness and anger that prevailed in the United States immediately after September 11. However, by using this language the administration also (intentionally or unintentionally) militarized the campaign against terrorism. The language of war focused discussion on military responses, while reducing the importance of non-military responses and the need to address the root causes of terrorism.

Third, efforts can be made to reduce the vulnerability of a country and its people to terrorist attacks. Physical security around prominent government buildings, transportation infrastructure such as airports, and public places and events can make it more difficult for terrorists to attack such targets. The security of computer networks can be improved. The increased use of police and surveillance of public places can also increase security. Immigration and refugee applicants can be screened more thoroughly, and visitors to a country can be subjected to a higher level of search and investigation. However, these measures all carry the risk of infringing on people's rights, the selective application of security measures to certain minority groups, and the creation of obstacles to the free movement of goods and services. There is also a practical limitation on efforts to increase the physical security of a society: the scale of cross-border traffic and trade is simply immense, and security measures are at odds with the economic advantages of the free flow of goods and services. For example, after September 11 the United States faces the challenge of improving its national security against future terrorist attacks. However, the U.S. has 301 ports of entry and 420 commercial airports. Inside the United States are 103 nuclear power plants, 2,800 other power plants, and 600,000 bridges. Over 14 million shipping containers enter the United States every year, and only 2 percent of these are inspected. Every day, 1.3 million people, 340,000 vehicles, and 58,000 cargo shipments enter the country.[101]

Fourth, governments can seek to strengthen international cooperation on counterterrorism. In order to meet the threat posed by international terrorist networks, states must design comprehensive and integrated strategy incorporating economic, political, legal, diplomatic, cultural, and military responses. Intelligence agencies must cooperate to share information and coordinate law enforcement efforts. Intelligence agencies and financial institutions must also cooperate to combat terrorist financing. States can establish bilateral agreements on extradition of terrorists for trial. For example, the political offence exception rule in extradition law allows defendants accused of terrorist acts to claim that they were engaged in political acts of conscience so that they are not subject to extradition. Bilateral agreements, such as the United States–United Kingdom extradition treaty can remove this exception from certain acts of terrorism, such as skyjacking. A number of international multilateral treaties on terrorism also exist, though many states have yet to sign them (see Profile 6.7). However, in democratic societies, strengthening domestic law to combat terrorism is a serious matter, raising the danger of excessive restriction of freedoms and a slide into authoritarianism in the name of combating subversion.

A last point to be made about terrorism is the complex role of the media in covering terrorist events. Publicity is a major objective behind terrorist activities. Acts of terrorism bring attention not only to the attack itself but also to the individuals and groups who carried out the act, the cause or aim they purport to achieve, and the grievances or injustices they are struggling against. Terrorism attracts the attention of the media, the public, and government officials and elected leaders. The role of the media in covering terrorist incidents is controversial. Some argue that media coverage of terrorist incidents encourages terrorism (by providing terrorists with the publicity they seek) and that such coverage lacks sophistication and a high level of informed comment. Others argue that a free media is an essential component of a free

PROFILE 6.7 International Agreements on Terrorism

There are 12 major multilateral conventions on terrorism. In addition, there are many other instruments, treaties, and agreements between states on counterterrorism.

1963   Convention on Offences and Certain Other Acts Committed on Board Aircraft (Tokyo Convention)

1970   The Hague Convention for the Suppression of Unlawful Seizure of Aircraft (Hague Convention)

1971   Convention for the Suppression of Unlawful Acts Against the Safety of Civil Aviation (Montreal Convention)

1973   Convention on the Prevention and Punishment of Crimes Against Internationally Protected Persons, Including Diplomatic Agents

1979   International Convention on the Taking of Hostages (Hostages Convention)

1980   Convention on the Physical Protection of Nuclear Material (Nuclear Materials Convention)

1988   Convention for the Suppression of Unlawful Acts Against the Safety of Maritime Navigation

1988   Convention for the Suppression of Unlawful Acts of Violence at Airports Serving International Civil Aviation

1988   Protocol for the Suppression of Unlawful Acts Against the Safety of Fixed Platforms Located on the Continental Shelf

1991   Convention on the Marking of Plastic Explosives for the Purpose of Detection

1997   International Convention on the Suppression of Terrorist Bombings

1999   International Convention for the Suppression of the Financing of Terrorism

society and that media reporting on terrorism, as long as it remains within appropriate ethical and legal boundaries, should not be constrained.

INTERNATIONAL ORGANIZED CRIME

Traditionally, organized crime has been regarded as a domestic political problem for societies and governments. While this is still largely the case, criminal activity has become increasingly internationalized, and international organized crime is now considered a serious global security issue and a threat to the social, economic and political stability of societies worldwide. International organized crime manifests itself in many forms, including trafficking in human beings, drugs, endangered species, toxic waste, and weapons, as well as money laundering, prostitution, kidnapping for ransom, and piracy. The increased attention placed on transnational organized crime is reflected in international agreements. At the 1995 G-7 summit in Halifax, the participating states declared that organized crime represented a growing threat to the security of the G-7 countries.[102] In December 2000, the United Nations Convention Against Transnational Organized Crime was established, obligating member states to cooperate on extradition, mutual legal assistance, and joint investigations. Member states are also obligated to establish domestic laws against participation in international criminal groups, money-laundering activities, corruption, and obstruction of justice. Two optional protocols to the convention cover trafficking in humans and the exploitation of women and children for sexual activities or sweatshop labour. In October 2003, the United Nations Convention Against Corruption was established, aimed at eliminating the growing threat presented by criminal activity to election and political party financing, judicial neutrality, and fair government contracting. Transnational crime has been identified as an international security issue for the following reasons:

- International criminal activity has escalated in terms of monetary scale and international scope. The retail value of the global drug trade alone was estimated at US$320 billion in 2005. The value of global human trafficking is approximately US$32 billion.[103]

- Organized crime has expanded into international banking, investment, finance, and business activity. Money laundering (the conversion of illicitly gained property or money into legal property and currency) is a major international enterprise, estimated at 2 to 5 percent of the global economy.[104] Using 2006 world GDP figures this would place the value of laundered money at approximately US$1.18–2.95 trillion annually. Before it was exposed, the infamous Bank of Credit and Commerce International (BCCI) served as a money-laundering and criminal finance system for organized crime. For most of its 1.4 million depositors, the BCCI was a bank like any other. Furthermore, international criminal organizations are not the only actors that conduct illegal financial activities. Banks and government officials often commit financial fraud and conduct illegal transactions.[105]

- Criminal organizations have become threats to governments. In Italy, the Mafia has used assassinations and bombings to intimidate the Italian government and Italian law enforcement authorities. In Colombia, drug cartels have killed judges and politicians. In Mexico, thousands of people have been killed in drug-trafficking-related violence since 2006, and threats and attacks against government officials have become commonplace.

- Criminal organizations can erode the social fabric of a country, undermining political authority and corrupting the economic and political leadership of states and their governments. In some cases, however, this is because criminal organizations actually improve the standard of living of rural workers or inner-city youths, whereas governments neglect them.

- In some countries, organized crime represents a threat to the conventional economy and the ability of the government to manage it. In Russia, organized crime accounts for a major portion of economic activity that is beyond government regulation and taxation. Organized crime figures are believed to exert a considerable influence over the energy sector in Russia.

- Worrisome indications exist that organized crime may be involved in the international sale of materials required for the production of weapons of mass destruction, in particular nuclear materials, which have appeared in small quantities for sale in Europe.

- The distinction between organized crime and terrorist and revolutionary movements is blurring as terrorist and revolutionary organizations obtain funding from the sale of drugs and as governments funnel money from illegal arms sales to revolutionary militias. International criminal organizations are allegedly facilitating illicit transfers of weapons and financing to terrorist and insurgency groups.[106]

Organized crime exists in virtually all societies in all regions of the world, but the United States, Canada, Mexico, Colombia, Italy, Russia, China, and Japan harbour particularly powerful criminal organizations. Many of these organizations have been increasing their cooperation with one another across state and regional boundaries. In North America and Italy, the Mafia, or Cosa Nostra—with operations in 40 other countries—dominates organized crime. Its activities include drug trafficking, union control and corruption, loan sharking, illegal gambling, prostitution, and financial fraud. Mexican crime organizations smuggle drugs on behalf of the South American drug cartels and smuggle illegal immigrants (with the assistance of the Chinese Triads) into the United States. In Russia, the Russian *mafiya* has expanded rapidly, making inroads into North America and Europe. Its activities include slavery, theft, extortion, murder, money laundering, and poppy production (for the world heroin market). In Asia, the Six Great Triads (based largely in Hong Kong and Taiwan) form the largest and oldest criminal network in the world. They are involved in drug trafficking, arms trafficking, illegal immigration, gambling, prostitution, fraud, and product piracy. The Japanese *boryokudan*, or *yakuza* (the name used in the West for Japanese organized crime syndicates), also operate throughout Asia.

The expansion of crime into an international activity and the growing communication and cooperation among organized crime syndicates has been facilitated by the growth of global interdependence. Other contributing factors include the collapse of communism in the Soviet Union and the growth of capitalism in China, which have removed social barriers to criminal activity in those countries. The establishment of free trade areas and customs unions (especially in North America and Europe) has facilitated the flow of criminal goods and services across borders. The weakening of state authority in many countries has eroded the capacity of police and judicial systems to combat organized crime. Some governments are quite literally supportive of, and supported by, organized crime. Criminal organizations often form alliances and agreements, designed for mutual benefit. Of course, these arrangements between criminal organizations are often fleeting and are based purely on self-interest; few other incentives hold such alliances together. In addition, the world of international organized crime is also one of conflict, as criminal organizations often seek to eliminate their competitors by whatever means necessary.

As the operations of criminal organizations have become increasingly international, the effort to combat international crime has involved greater cooperation and coordination of effort between countries. The United States, for example, has developed a very high level of cooperation with many South American countries to assist in the effort against the drug cartels. This cooperation involves agreements on punishments and extradition, law enforcement coordination, intelligence sharing, and military cooperation. As international crime is likely only to increase, measures such as these may become increasingly common as governments seek to join forces to combat criminal organizations that possess resources greater than those of many states. Meanwhile, unless the demand for drugs in the United States is reduced, there is little hope that the drug trade can be defeated, even as the U.S. continues to wage a largely futile war on drugs in the Caribbean and South America. In 2000, the United States committed US$1.3 billion to "Plan Colombia," an effort to eradicate that country's coca production. This plan was expanded under the Bush administration in 2001 and again in 2004, to include a controversial increase in military aid, larger numbers of U.S. military advisors and private security contractors, and aerial fumigation of crops. Critics charge that this military aid is undermining Colombian democracy, ignoring the social plight of Colombia's poor, and supporting paramilitary groups that have been accused of human rights violations. Mexico has also been embroiled in a drug war since 2006, but despite high levels of cooperation between the United States, Canada, and Mexico and the deployment of tens of thousands of Mexican army troops, drug trafficking and its attendant violence showed no signs of abating in early 2009.

CONCLUSIONS

In this chapter, we have explored some of the major issues facing international security in contemporary global politics. One positive is that the likelihood of a great-power war remains low. However, in much of the rest of the world, there has been no respite from regional wars or the threat of the outbreak of such wars. Indeed, it is possible to speak of the world in terms of zones of peace and zones of instability. Zones of peace, such as North America and Western Europe, enjoy relative peace and freedom from the threat of war, a high level of prosperity, and high levels of economic and political cooperation. Within zones of instability, wars rage, threatening daily life, and economic and political cooperation is limited or fragile. Will more regions become increasingly stable and free of conflict, or will instability and violence spread? We have also looked at weapons proliferation, intrastate conflict, international terrorism, and transnational organized crime. These are just some of the issues that are currently shaping the current international security field, and we will encounter others in subsequent chapters. We now turn our attention to the efforts made to prevent, control, or manage warfare and international security challenges, efforts collectively known as *conflict management*.

Endnotes

1. E. H. Carr, *The Twenty Years' Crisis 1919–1939: An Introduction to the Study of International Relations* (London: Macmillan, 1942), 139.
2. P. H. Gordon, "Winning the Right War," *Survival* 39, no. 4 (Winter 2007–2008), 17.
3. See, for example, K. Krause and M. C. Williams, "Broadening the Agenda of Security Studies? Politics and Methods," *Mershon International Studies Review* 40 (1996), 229–54; S. Smith, "The Increasing Insecurity of Security Studies," *Contemporary Security Policy* 20 (1999), 72–101; P. Stoett, *Human and Global Security: An Exploration of Terms* (Toronto: University of Toronto Press, 2000); and Carl Bildt, "Address to the IISS 50th Anniversary Dinner," in *Perspectives on International Security.* Adelphi Paper 48, nos. 400–401 (October 2008) (New York: Routledge, 2008), 29–34.
4. P. Andreas, "Redrawing the Line: Borders and Security in the 21st Century," *International Security* 28 (Fall 2003), 78. See also C. Coker, *Globalisation and Insecurity in the Twenty-First Century: NATO and the Management of Risk,* Adelphi Paper 345 (Oxford: Oxford University Press, 2002); and B. Buzan, O. Waever, and J. de Wilde, *Security: A New Framework for Analysis* (Boulder, CO: Lynne Rienner, 1998).
5. See M. C. Williams, "Words, Images, Enemies: Securitization and International Politics," *International Studies Quarterly* 47 (December 2003), 511–31; and T. Farrell, "Constructivist Security Studies: Portrait of a Research Program," *International Studies Review* 4 (Spring 2002), 49–72; and the groundbreaking book by D. Campbell, *Writing Security: United States Foreign Policy and the Politics of Identity* (Minneapolis: University of Minneapolis Press, 1992).
6. J. Keegan, *A History of Warfare* (New York: Alfred A. Knopf, 1993).
7. See for example, J. Keegan, *A History of Warfare* (New York: Alfred A. Knopf, 1993); and J. A. Lynn, *Battle: A History of Combat and Culture* (Boulder, CO: Westview Press, 2003).
8. See R. L. Sivard, *World Military and Social Expenditures 1991* (Washington, DC: World Priorities, 1991), 20.
9. L. Harbon and P. Wallensteen, "Armed Conflict, 1989–2006," *Journal of Peace Research* 44, no. 3 (September 2007), 623. The data from this study is drawn from the Uppsala University Conflict Data Program and the international Peace Research Institute, Oslo (PRIO), which defines an armed conflict as a conflict with 25 or more battle-related deaths per year. Other data sets record major armed conflicts of 1,000 battle-related deaths per year. Using this measure, there were 17 major armed conflicts active in the world in 2006, down from 28 in 1998. See Stockholm International Peace Research Institute, *SIPRI Yearbook, 2007* (Oxford: Oxford University Press, 2007), 79.
10. Harbon and Wallensteen, 623.
11. Ibid., 623.
12. See G. Strada, "The Horror of Landmines," *Scientific American,* May 1996, 40.
13. Stockholm International Peace Research Institute, *SIPRI Yearbook, 2003* (Oxford: Oxford University Press, 2003), 109.
14. "Military Expenditure Summary," *SIPRI Yearbook, 2008,* http://yearbook2008.sipri.org/05/ (accessed February 6, 2009).
15. Q. Wright, *A Study of War,* vol. 1 (Chicago: University of Chicago Press, 1942), 17.
16. S. Freud, *Civilization, Society, and Religion,* ed. A. Dickson, trans. J. Strachey (New York: Penguin Books, 1985), 357.

17. K. Lorenz, *On Aggression* (New York: Harcourt Brace, 1966). See also P. Shaw and Y. Wong, "Ethnic Mobilization and the Seeds of Warfare: An Evolutionary Perspective," *International Studies Quarterly* 31, no. 1 (1987), 5–32.

18. See J. G. Stoessinger, *Why Nations Go to War*, 10th ed. (Belmont, CA: Wadsworth Publishing, 2007), and R. Jervis, *Perception and Misperception in International Politics* (Princeton: Princeton University Press, 1976), 154; and M. G. Hermann, "Explaining Foreign Policy Behaviour Using the Personal Characteristics of Political Leaders," *International Studies Quarterly* 24 (March 1980), 8.

19. See the discussion in J. Keegan, *A History of Warfare*, 86–89.

20. K. Waltz, *Man, the State, and War* (New York: Columbia University Press, 1959), 232.

21. See G. Modelski, *Exploring Long Cycles* (Boulder, CO: Lynne Rienner, 1987); and W. Thompson, *On Global War: Historical-Structural Approaches to World Politics* (Columbia, SC: University of South Carolina Press, 1988).

22. See L. Freedman and E. Karsh, *The Gulf Conflict 1990–1991: Diplomacy and War in the New World Order* (Princeton: Princeton University Press, 1993), 408–09. See also A. H. Cordesman and A. Wagner, *The Gulf War* (Boulder, CO: Westview Press, 1996).

23. For an interesting prewar assessment of U.S. interests and objectives, see P. H. Gordon, M. Indyk, and M. E. O'Hanlon, "Getting Serious About Iraq," *Survival* 44 (Autumn 2002), 9–22. For another prewar assessment, see C. Kaysen et al., *War with Iraq: Costs, Consequences, and Alternatives* (Cambridge, MA: American Academy of Arts and Sciences, 2002). For further background material on the Iraq war, see M. L. Sifry and C. Cerf, eds., *The Iraq War Reader: History, Documents, Opinions* (New York, Touchstone Books, 2003); and A. H. Cordesman, *The Iraq War* (Westport: Praeger, 2003).

24. Remarks by the President at 2002 Graduation Exercise of the United States Military Academy, West Point, New York, June 1, 2002.

25. "The National Security Strategy of the United States of America," September 2002, 6, 14, http://www.informationclearinghouse.info/article2320.htm (accessed June 7, 2009).

26. See G. Forden, "Intention to Deceive: Iraqi Misdirection of UN Inspectors," *Jane's Intelligence Review* 16 (March 2004), 30–39.

27. Remarks to the United Nations Security Council by Secretary of State Colin L. Powell, New York City, February 5, 2003.

28. For an excellent overview see T. E. Ricks, *Fiasco: The American Military Adventure in Iraq* (New York: Penguin Books, 2007).

29. For example, see P. W. Galbraith, "After Iraq: Picking up the Pieces," *Current History* 106, no. 705 (December 2007), 403–408.

30. "Unclassified Key Judgments of the National Intelligence Estimate," *Prospects for Iraq's Stability: A Challenging Road Ahead* (Washington, DC: Office of the Director of National Intelligence, 2007), 8–9.

31. Data from "Iraq Figures Since 2003," *The Associated Press*, February 4, 2008, and GlobalSecurity.org, www.globalsecurity.org/military/ops/iraq_casualties.html.

32. "Iraq Body Count," http://www.iraqbodycount.org/database/? (accessed June 7, 2009).

33. See Opinion Business Research, "New Analysis 'Confirms' 1 Million+ Iraqi Casualties," press release, January 28, 2008, http://www.opinion.co.uk/Newsroom_details.aspx?NewsId=88 (accessed April 3, 2008).

34. United Nations High Commissioner for Refugees, "The Situation in Iraq," http://www.unhcr.org/iraq.html (accessed April 4, 2008).

35. "Internally Displaced Persons in Iraq Update—24 March 2008," *IDP Working Group*, http://www.humansecuritygateway.info/documents/UNHCR_Iraq_IDPWG.pdf (accessed April 3, 2008).

36. See "Estimated Costs of U.S. Operations in Iraq and Afghanistan and of Other Activities Related to the War on Terrorism," CBO testimony before the Committee on the Budget, U.S. House of Representatives (accessed October 24, 2007).

37. L. Bilmes and J. E. Stiglitz, *The Economic Costs of the Iraq War: An Appraisal Three Years After the Beginning of the Conflict*, Working Paper No. 12054 (Cambridge, MA: National Bureau of Economic Research, February 2006), and J. E. Stiglitz and Linda J. Bilmes, *The Three Trillion Dollar War: The True Cost of the Iraq Conflict* (New York: W. W. Norton, 2008).

38. See R. A. Clarke, *Against All Enemies: Inside America's War on Terror—What Really Happened* (New York: The Free Press, 2004).

39. A. R. Norton, "Making War, Making Peace: The Middle East Entangles America," *Current History* 103 (January 2004), 3–7.

40. See L. McQuaig, *It's the Crude, Dude: War, Big Oil, and the Fight for the Planet* (Toronto: Doubleday, 2004).

41. For different accounts of the decision making within the Bush administration, see D. J. Feith, *War and Decision: Inside the Pentagon at the Dawn of the War on Terrorism* (New York: Harper Collins, 2008) and M. Isikoff and D. Corn, *Hubris: The Inside Story of Spin, Scandal, and the Selling of the Iraq War* (New York: Random House, 2006).

42. On the case for vigilant containment, see J. J. Mearsheimer and S. M. Walt, "An Unnecessary War," *Foreign Policy* 134 (January/February 2003), 50–59.

43. Former U.K. Defence Minister Peter Kilfoyle, quoted in N. Watt and M. White, "Wrong War, Wrong Time, Wrong Enemy, Warns Labour Rebel," *The Guardian*, March 19, 2003.

44. Kenneth M. Pollack, "Spies, Lies, and Weapons: What Went Wrong," *The Atlantic Monthly*, January/February 2004, 78–92.

45. James Fallows, "Blind into Baghdad," *The Atlantic Monthly*, January/February 2004, 52–74.

46. Norton, 4.

47. For a collection of observations, see "A Special Survey: U.S. Foreign Policy, Seen from the Other Side," *Bulletin of the Atomic Scientists* 60 (March/April 2004), 18–34.

48. See, for example, *A Year After Iraq War: Mistrust of America in Europe Ever Higher, Muslim Anger Persists* (Washington, DC: The Pew Research Center for the People and the Press, 2004), and PEW Global Attitudes Project, "Conflicting Views in a Divided World 2006" (Washington, DC: The Pew Research Center, 2006).

49. "Declassified Key Judgments of the National Intelligence Estimate," *Trends in Global Terrorism: Implications for the United States* (Washington, DC: Office of the Director of National Intelligence, 2006), 2.

50. "American Majority Sees Iraq War as a Mistake," *Angus Reid Global Monitor: Polls and Research*, http://www.angus-reid.com/polls/view/american_majority_sees_iraq_war_as_a_mistake (accessed April 3, 2008).

51. See J. S. Yaphe, "Iraq: Are We There Yet?," *Current History* 107 (December 2008), 403–409; D. Byman, "Constructing a Democratic Iraq: Challenges and Opportunities," *International Security* 28 (Summer 2003), 47–78; and A. Sorensen, "Iraq's Reluctant Nation Builders," *Current History* 102 (December 2003), 407–10. For a broad discussion of postwar issues, see "From Victory to Success: Afterwar Policy in Iraq," *Foreign Policy* 137 (July/August 2003), 50–72.

52. This term is employed by Ted Robert Gurr, *Minorities at Risk: A Global View of Ethnopolitical Conflicts* (Washington, DC: United States Institute of Peace, 1993).

53. Gurr, *Minorities at Risk*, 3.

54. See S. J. Kaufman, *Modern Hatreds: The Symbolic Politics of Ethnic War* (Ithaca, NY: Cornell University Press, 2001).

55. See K. J. Holsti, *The State, War, and the State of War* (Cambridge, UK: Cambridge University Press, 1996), 20.

56. M. Berdal and D. M. Malone, "Introduction," in M. Berdal and D. M. Malone, eds., *Greed and Grievance: Economic Agendas in Civil Wars* (Boulder, CO: Lynne Rienner, 2001), 4.

57. Berdal and Malone, 5.

58. D. Keen, *The Economic Functions of Violence in Civil Wars*, Adelphi Paper 320 (Oxford: Oxford University Press, 1998), 11–12.

59. See International Institute for Strategic Studies, *Strategic Survey 2008* (New York: Routledge, 2008), 250.

60. See B. Bueno de Mesquita and W.H. Riker, "An Assessment of the Merits of Selective Proliferation," *Journal of Conflict Resolution* 26 (June 1982), 283–306; J. Mearsheimer, "The Case for a Ukrainian Nuclear Deterrent," *Foreign Affairs* 72 (Summer 1993), 50–66; and K. Waltz, "Nuclear Myths and Political Realities," *American Political Science Review* 84 (September 1990), 731–45.

61. K. Waltz, *The Spread of Nuclear Weapons: More May Be Better*, Adelphi Paper 171 (London: International Institute for Strategic Studies, Autumn 1981), 5.

62. See L. Dunn, *Containing Nuclear Proliferation*, Adelphi Paper 263 (London: Oxford University Press, 1991); K. Kaiser, "Non-Proliferation and Nuclear Deterrence," *Survival* 31 (March/April 1989), 123–36; and S. Miller, "The Case Against a Ukrainian Nuclear Deterrent," *Foreign Affairs* 72 (Summer 1993), 67–80. See also N. Tannenwald, *The Nuclear Taboo: The United States and the Non-Use of Nuclear Weapons Since 1945* (Cambridge: Cambridge University Press, 2008).

63. For three models of weapons proliferation incentives, see S. Sagan, "Why Do States Build Nuclear Weapons? Three Models in Search of a Bomb," *International Security* 21 (Winter 1996/97), 54–86. See also E. Solingen, *Nuclear Logics: Contrasting Paths in East Asia and the Middle East* (Princeton: Princeton University Press, 2007).

64. See P. Kerr, "North Korea Crisis Chronology," *Arms Control Today* 33 (June 2003).

65. J. A. Foley, "Fail-Safe: North Korea's Stability Paradox," *Jane's Intelligence Review* 19, no. 10 (October 2007), 30–37.

66. T. Ripley, "Mission Improbable: Could Israel Attack Iran?," *Jane's Intelligence Review* 19, no. 11 (November 2007), 26–31.

67. See A. M. Ansari, *Iran Under Ahmadinejad: The Politics of Confrontation*, Adelphi Paper 393 (London: Routledge and the International Institute for Strategic Studies, 2007), 50.

68. S. Chubin, *Iran's Nuclear Ambitions* (Washington, DC: Carnegie Endowment for International Peace, 2006), 13.

69. National Intelligence Council, "National Intelligence Estimate—Iran: Nuclear Intentions and Capabilities" (November 2007), GlobalSecurity.org, http://www.globalsecurity.org/intell/library/reports/2007/nie_iran-nuclear_20071203.htm (accessed June 7, 2009).

70. See R. Molander and P. Wilson, "On Dealing with the Prospect of Nuclear Chaos," *The Washington Quarterly* 17 (1994), 32; and Jon B. Wolfstahl and Tom Z. Collina, "Nuclear Terrorism and Warhead Control in Russia," *Survival* 44 (Summer 2002), 71–84.

71. R. M. Frost, *Nuclear Terrorism After 9/11*, Adelphi Paper 378 (London: Routledge and the International Institute for Strategic Studies, 2005).

72. T. Singh, "Get Back to Basics," *India Today*, June 8, 1998.

73. See J. Miller, S. Engleberg, and W. Broad, *Germs: Biological Weapons and America's Secret War* (New York: Simon and Schuster, 2001), 297–98.

74. Stockholm International Peace Research Institute, *SIPRI Yearbook, 2008* (Oxford: Oxford University Press, 2008), 295.

75. Stockholm International Peace Research Institute, 293.

76. N. Cooper, "What's the Point of Arms Transfer Controls?," *Contemporary Security Policy* 27, no. 1 (2006), 123.

77. "The Covert Arms Trade," *The Economist*, February 12, 1994, 21. For more information on small arms and light weapons see *Small Arms Survey 2008: Risk and Resilience* (Cambridge: Cambridge University Press, 2008).

78. See R. Stohl and D. Tuttle, "Merchant of Death Arrested in Thailand," Center for Defence Information (March 10, 2008), http://www.cdi.org/program/document.cfm?DocumentID=4231&StartRow=1&ListRows=10&appendURL=&Orderby=D.DateLastUpdated&ProgramID=73&from_page=index.cfm (accessed June 20, 2008).

79. W. Laqueur, "Postmodern Terrorism," *Foreign Affairs* 75 (September/October 1996), 24–36.

80. C. Combs, *Terrorism in the Twenty-First Century* (Upper Saddle River, NJ: Prentice Hall, 1997), 8.

81. P. Wilkinson, "A European Viewpoint on Terrorism," in J. S. Nye Jr., Y. Satoh, and P. Wilkinson, *Addressing the New International Terrorism: Prevention, Intervention, and Multilateral Cooperation*, Report to the Trilateral Commission (Washington, DC: The Trilateral Commission, 2003), 21.

82. S. Gupta, *The Replication of Violence: Thoughts on International Terrorism After September 11th 2001* (London: Pluto Press, 2002), 1.

83. U.S. President George W. Bush, "Address to a Joint Session of Congress and the American People" (Washington, DC: Office of the Press Secretary, September 20, 2001).

84. See S. Coll, *Ghost Wars: The Secret History of the CIA, Afghanistan, and Bin Laden: From the Soviet Invasion to September 10, 2001* (New York: Penguin Books, 2005). See also R. Gutman, *How We Missed the Story: Osama Bin Laden, the Taliban, and the Hijacking of Afghanistan* (Washington, DC: United States Institute of Peace Press, 2008).

85. Quoted in International Institute for Strategic Studies, *The Military Balance, 2003–2004* (London: Oxford University Press, 2003), 356, and Graham Allison, *Nuclear Terrorism: The Ultimate Preventable Catastrophe* (Cambridge: Times Books, 2004), 12.

86. For a review of the security challenges facing Afghanistan, see C. Hodes and M. Sedra, *The Search for Security in Post-Taliban Afghanistan*, Adelphi Paper 391 (London: Routledge and the International Institute for Strategic Studies, 2007), and Adam Roberts, "Doctrine and Reality in Afghanistan," *Survival* 51, no. 1 (February/March 2009), 29–60.

87. For a historical account of Afghanistan's struggles with governance and foreign occupation, see M. Ewans, *Afghanistan: A Short History of Its People and Politics* (Hew York: Harper Collins, 2002).

88. See "Policing a Whirlwind," *The Economist* 385 (December 2007), 33.

89. See C. Hodes and M. Sedra, 8, and J. Wright, "Blood Flowers: Afghanistan's Opium Industry Remains Robust," *Jane's Intelligence Review* 21, no. 1 (January 2009), 38–43.

90. The International Institute for Strategic Studies, "Afghanistan: Spreading Insurgency," *Strategic Survey 2007* (New York: Routledge, 2007), 370.

91. B. Riedel, "The Return of the Knights: Al-Qaeda and the Fruits of Middle East Disorder," *Survival* 49, no. 3 (Autumn 2007), 107–120.

92. N. Labi, "Jihad 2.0," *The Atlantic Monthly* 297, no. 6 (July/August 2006), 102–108. See also M. Sageman, *Leaderless Jihad: Terror Networks in the Twenty-First Century* (Philadelphia: University of Pennsylvania Press, 2008).

93. A. K. Cronin, *Ending Terrorism: Lessons for Defeating al-Qaeda,* Adelphi Paper 394 (London: Routledge and the International Institute for Strategic Studies, 2008), 53. See also B. Singh, *The Talibanization of Southeast Asia: Losing the War on Terror to Islamist Extremists* (Westport, CT: Praeger Security International, 2007).

94. See G. Weimann, *Terror on the Internet: The New Arena, The New Challenges* (Washington, DC: The United States Institute of Peace Press, 2006).

95. On chemical and biological weapons terrorism, see A. Stenersen, "Chem-Bio Cyber Class: Assessing Jihadist Chemical and Biological Manuals," *Jane's Intelligence Review* 19, no. 9 (September 2007), 8–13. On nuclear terrorism, see R. M. Frost, *Nuclear Terrorism After 9/11,* Adelphi Paper 378 (London: Routledge and the International Institute for Strategic Studies, 2005), and J. M. Acton et al., "Beyond the Dirty Bomb: Re-thinking Radiological Terror," *Survival* 49, no. 3 (Autumn 2007), 151–168.

96. A. K. Cronin, "Behind the Curve: Globalization and International Terrorism," *International Security* 27 (Winter 2002/2003), 30.

97. K. Hoyt and S. G. Brooks, "A Double-Edged Word: Globalization and Biosecurity," *International Security* 28 (Winter 2003/2004), 124.

98. Laqueur, 25.

99. S. J. Lukasik, S. E. Goodman, and D. W. Longhurst, *Protecting Critical Infrastructures Against Cyber-Attack,* Adelphi Paper 359 (Oxford: Oxford University Press, 2003).

100. M. Abrahms, "What Terrorists Really Want: Terrorist Motives and Counterterrorism Strategy," *International Security* 32, no. 4 (Spring 2008), 78–105. See also B. L. Nacos, *Terrorism and Counterterrorism: Understanding Threats and Responses in the Post-9/11 World* (New York: Penguin, 2006).

101. *Jane's Sentinel Security Assessment: North America, 2002* (Coulsdon, Surrey: Jane's Information Group Limited, 2002), 149.

102. Robert Chote and Peter Norman, "Leaders Zero In on Crime and Nuclear Safety," *Financial Times,* June 19, 1995, 5.

103. *World Drug Report 2007* (New York: United Nations Office on Drugs and Crime, 2007, 170.

104. See P. A. Schott, *Reference Guide to Anti-Money Laundering and Combating the Financing of Terrorism,* 2nd ed. (Washington, DC: The International Bank for Reconstruction and Development and the International Monetary Fund, 2006), I-6.

105. See A. A. Block and C. A. Weaver, *All Is Clouded by Desire: Global Banking, Money Laundering, and International Organized Crime* (Westport, CT: Greenwood Publishing, 2004).

106. See *Overview of the Law Enforcement Strategy Used to Combat International Organized Crime* (Washington, DC: U.S. Department of Justice, April 2008), 3.

Suggested Websites

Center for Defense Information
http://www.cdi.org

DefenseLINK: United States Department of Defense
http://www.defenselink.mil

Federation of American Scientists
http://www.fas.org

International Crisis Group
http://www.crisisweb.org/home/index.cfm

International Peace Academy
http://www.ipacademy.org

International Relations and Security Network
http://www.isn.ethz.ch

Stockholm International Peace Research Institute
http://www.sipri.se

United Nations
http://www.un.org

Conflict Management in Global Politics

Since the end of the Cold War the UN has led an upsurge of international activism that has played a critical role in reducing the number of violent conflicts.

—*Human Security Report*[1]

For most of history, war has been a more or less functional institution, providing benefits for those societies that were good at it, although the cost in money, in lives, and in suffering was always significant. Only in the past century have large numbers of people begun to question the basic assumption of civilized societies that war is inevitable and often useful....

—*Gwynne Dyer*[2]

RESPONDING TO THE INTERNATIONAL SECURITY AGENDA

In Chapter 6, we examined some of the key issues and challenges facing the contemporary international system from a security studies perspective. In this chapter we discuss the range of instruments available to prevent, manage, and resolve conflict in global politics: diplomacy; arms control and disarmament; the concept of human security; the use of international organizations (IOs) and law; peacekeeping and humanitarian intervention; sanctions; and democratization. Our aim in this chapter is to evaluate what might be called the international conflict management tool kit. What instruments have been developed to eliminate, prevent, control, or reduce security threats and challenges in global politics? To what extent have these instruments been useful or found wanting? It is easy to become skeptical and even pessimistic about the prospects for conflict management efforts, especially when international news coverage is dominated by warfare, terrorism, and crisis. This can blind us to the reality that most conflict in global politics is managed or even resolved without resort to violence. Hopefully, we can strengthen these conflict management tools and promote an increased willingness to apply them to the more serious and intractable armed conflicts and security problems in global politics.

The theoretical frameworks discussed in Chapter 1 provide many insights into the nature of conflict management in global politics. Realism is not overly optimistic about the prospects for managing or reducing conflict. Realists acknowledge that states will establish alliances and treaties, international institutions, and laws in an attempt to avoid conflict, but this cooperation is merely a form of self-help and will not endure when states feel it is no longer in their best interests to cooperate. For realists, war can be deterred through military power (at least for a period of time) but in general conflict management efforts are prone to defections and breakdowns due to the distrust and hostility endemic in an anarchic international system. Liberals are much more optimistic about the prospects for successful conflict management. For liberals, it is possible to make progress toward a more peaceful and stable world by addressing the root causes of war and other security challenges: distrust, insecurity, and authoritarian governments. Liberals generally believe that economic interdependence, international institutions, law, and the spread of democracy will reduce and even eliminate these root causes and promote international peace and security.

Critical theorists take a different approach to conflict management. Neo-Marxists argue that most conflict management efforts fail to address the deep economic and political inequities that are the cause of global conflict. War and other security challenges will never be resolved until the capitalist system, and the exploitation of the poor by the rich, is replaced by communism and its promise of an equitable socioeconomic system. Constructivists are optimistic that sound conflict management approaches can promote understanding and the development of norms and rules in global politics. This requires an understanding of the deeply embedded belief systems that cause insecurity and conflict, and the need for efforts to overcome these belief systems through education, dialogue, and the promotion of common interests and values. Establishing global norms and rules on the basis of shared belief systems and goals will begin the construction of a new international system less rooted in prejudice, intolerance, and other belief systems that contribute to insecurity and conflict. Feminists see most conflict management approaches as a reflection of male dominance in global politics. These efforts are characterized by male conceptions of conflict, peace, and security and deemphasize or devalue the importance of women, community, and social health. Feminists suggest that more women should become engaged in conflict management at all levels, and more emphasis should be placed on human security and more community-oriented paths to peace and security. The ecopolitical viewpoint suggests that our treatment of local ecosystems and the global environment must change if social and political harmony are to be achieved.

All these perspectives shed light on our conflict management tool kit, and you should bear them in mind as you read this chapter. We begin our examination of conflict management instruments with the nature and practice of diplomacy.

THE NATURE OF DIPLOMACY

Diplomacy has survived the many changes in international relations and societies from the ancient world to today.[3] Definitions of diplomacy traditionally have been confined to statecraft and the activities of professional diplomats. In this sense, diplomacy can be defined simply as the purposeful communication between states. However, the definition of diplomacy is widening to include diplomatic activities conducted by groups, and individuals who may not be in formal positions of political power. In more traditional approaches to diplomacy, the concepts of representation and communication are fundamental components of diplomatic activity. Representatives of states are acting on behalf of the government of that state, and are almost always acting under the instructions of their government. In fact, one study has suggested that diplomats adopt the identity of their state as part of their own personal identities.[4]

The protocols and formalities of diplomatic practice allow states to interact with one another (and with nonstate actors) using established and mutually acceptable procedures.

Public and private diplomatic affairs are highly formalized events, characterized by painstaking attention to tradition and protocol. For example, when a **head of state** makes a formal visit to a foreign country, an elaborate reception protocol demands a formal reception at the airport, a red carpet, a greeting line of dignitaries, an honour guard (dutifully inspected), a band (playing the national anthem of the visitor), an escorted motorcade to a hotel or the seat of government, and at least one formal state dinner. While the receptions for visitors or diplomats of lesser rank are not as elaborate, they are no less established as conventions. Though many of the trappings of past diplomatic practice have been discarded many of the key traditions, such as diplomatic immunity, endure. As we discussed in Chapter 5, states that have embassies in foreign countries can legitimately lay claim to that space as part of their own territory. This principle of **extraterritoriality** is a cornerstone of diplomatic tradition. According to Garret Mattingly, it evolved in the early days of the Westphalian state system, when states "found they could only communicate with one another by tolerating within themselves little islands of alien sovereignty."[5] Diplomatic protocols help avoid individuals, groups, and states from clashing on issues of symbolism and prestige and maintains the image that diplomats, officials, and leaders of equivalent rank are treated as equals. Formality and protocol also reduce the chance that personality conflicts might interfere with communication between governments. Nevertheless, personalities are often a crucial influence on affairs of state. Canadians, for example, have an interest in the personal relationship between their prime minister and the president of the United States, with some expressing anxiety when the two leaders do not get along, and others upset when they seem to get along too well.

However, diplomacy has undergone some significant changes, particularly in the latter half of the 20th century. Decolonization and increased global interdependence have forced diplomatic services to adjust to larger numbers of states and a much wider variety of language and cultures. The increasing number of states in the world has increased the relevance of multilateral diplomacy and conference diplomacy, because the process of diplomatic exchange simply becomes more efficient if all of the states involved are represented around a single table (although this does not mean the chances of an agreement are any greater). Furthermore, the growing complexity of the diplomatic agenda requires more and more specific technical knowledge on matters as varied as satellites to coral reef management. As a result, communication and dialogue between government agencies other than foreign ministries (sometimes called "paradiplomacy") has become ever more common.[6] The character of diplomatic life has also changed. Developments in global communications have made contact between governments and their representatives abroad virtually instantaneous. Gone are the days when diplomatic pouches would outline broad policy and give a diplomat considerable leeway to make decisions. Another change in the character of diplomacy is the expanding role of nonstate actors such as humanitarian and aid organizations, multinational corporations, private military companies, and communal groups in the conduct of international affairs. Governments now interact with such nonstate actors to an unprecedented degree, and often make use of them in their own diplomatic planning and foreign policy initiatives. Frequently, diplomatic activity is conducted through informal social contacts between individuals and groups in two or more countries. This is sometimes called *track-two diplomacy*, which has proven its value as a means of communication between governments that do not have formal diplomatic ties or have a very poor political relationship.

As indicated in Chapter 3, foreign policy remains a relatively closed area of government activity. Nevertheless, increased access to information has made diplomacy a much more public affair. Public opinion may compel leaders to act in ways that are contrary to the advice of the diplomatic service. In one sense public opinion may cause the diplomacy of a state or group to be more reflective of the body of the people. However, it may also lead to rash or dangerous diplomacy designed primarily to capture public loyalty or votes. Finally, another change in diplomacy is the increasing importance attached to summit diplomacy, the formal meeting of heads of state and government. Summit diplomacy has both its advocates and its detractors. Summits can enable leaders to establish a personal rapport and remove the frustrating constraints of the slow and bureaucratic diplomatic process. The **Camp David** accords, the product of a summit between Egyptian President Anwar el-Sadat and Israeli Prime Minister Menachem Begin at U.S. President Jimmy Carter's official Maryland retreat in 1978, were a success because of the face-to-face meetings between the two leaders. However, summitry can lead to ill-advised decisions made by leaders without adequate consultation with experts or time for reflection. At the Yalta Conference in 1945 (discussed in Chapter 2) between Winston Churchill, Franklin Roosevelt, and Josef Stalin, Roosevelt acquiesced to an agreement that would divide Europe into spheres of influence and pave the way for Soviet domination of Eastern Europe (although there is debate about how much of a choice Roosevelt had). Summits have also been criticized as being little more than photo opportunities and high-security cocktail parties, involving only the signing of agreements worked out in advance by diplomats. Summits can also attract large protest gatherings, as demonstrated during the 2007 G-8 Summit in Heiligendamm, Germany. These protests against the pace of globalization, the lack of development aid, and the failure to address human rights concerns are indicative of the gap between formal state-level diplomacy and the wishes, priorities, and policy prescriptions of a growing international civil society movement of activists and NGOs dedicated to these issues. However, conflict management almost always involves states and the formal instruments of negotiation and diplomacy.

DIPLOMATIC TECHNIQUES AND CONFLICT MANAGEMENT

While diplomacy is an everyday feature of global politics, it is also the foundation of efforts to prevent, contain, and manage international conflict. Of course, diplomacy may also be quite bellicose and militaristic, and even diplomatic efforts intended to avoid war can use threats and intimidation to achieve state objectives.[7] Throughout history, states and groups have employed a variety of diplomatic techniques to secure their goals. These techniques can essentially be reduced to the use of threats and promises. The effectiveness of diplomatic techniques as conflict management instruments depends heavily on one variable: whether a set of proposals can be developed that each party prefers over reaching no agreement at all or over using violence to settle their dispute. In the absence of a set of outcomes acceptable to all sides, diplomacy will fail as a means of preventing, controlling, or managing conflict. Conflict management diplomacy is about facilitating and encouraging the development of such outcomes.[8] One of the ironies of diplomacy as a conflict management tool is that in periods of war or crisis, at precisely the time when effective diplomatic communication is most valuable, such communication is least frequent. Often, countries in a dispute will break off diplomatic relations, necessitating an eventual reopening of communication or the involvement of a third party. Several diplomatic techniques have been employed to facilitate conflict management efforts.

SIGNALLING

States and groups use signals to communicate intent, commitment, and displeasure. Signals may be very overt, coming in the form of speeches, written statements or proclamations, or direct diplomatic contact with individual representatives of other states or groups. Statements expressing the Canadian government's concern about human rights in China or Burma, or its displeasure at Russian warplanes entering Canadian airspace in February 2009, are examples of direct government-to-government signalling. At other times, signals may be less overt, and may come in the form of deliberate symbolic actions such as official or unofficial visits, the recall of ambassadors, or displays of military power. The problem with all signals is that they can be misunderstood or misinterpreted and sometimes missed altogether. And some signals can be very circumspect; in a particularly famous example, China invited the U.S. table tennis team to visit China during an international table tennis tournament in Japan in 1971. After some deliberation, it was decided (correctly) that this was an overture by the Chinese leadership to improve relations between China and the United States. Thus, the term *Ping-Pong diplomacy* was coined.

BARGAINING AND NEGOTIATION

Another technique is the use of bargaining, an attempt to reach an agreement on issues of symbolic or substantive value to all parties. Bargaining and negotiation (bargaining in a formal setting) establishes how such symbolic and substantive desires and aims will be exchanged and divided among the parties. Not all agreements will be equally beneficial to all sides. This imbalance occurs because parties to a dispute bring different means of leverage to the bargaining or negotiation process. As realists would quickly remind us, leverage originates mainly with power capabilities, and these can be employed by offering rewards; issuing threats; or appealing to sentiments of friendship, allegiance, or shared ideology or religion. When one or some parties have leverage over the others, unequal arrangements are frequently (though not always) the result.[9] Over time, several tactics for successful negotiation have emerged:

- Discourage zero-sum (win–lose) views of the issues.
- Establish a fair compromise to ensure a lasting settlement.
- Avoid ultimatums and posturing; encourage dialogue and debate.
- Avoid humiliating one's opponents.
- Blend rewards and threats.
- Avoid personal *ad hominem* attacks on the other party.
- Look for bridges, solutions acceptable to both sides but different from the positions taken at the beginning of negotiations.
- Look for nonspecific compensation, in which one side gets what it wants but gives up something that was not part of the original dispute or discussion.
- Divide the issue into separate and more manageable subjects for agreement.

THIRD-PARTY MEDIATION

Third parties, whether individuals, groups, organizations, or states, can be invited by the parties to assist the process of reaching a settlement. Mediation is a more common form of diplomatic conflict management than bilateral negotiations between parties.[10] Third parties can offer a number of services, which include:

- providing **good offices** (acting as a conduit for communication), a role often performed by the UN Secretary-General;
- providing a neutral site for negotiations (a role often performed by Switzerland, and specifically the city of Geneva);

- clarifying facts and evidence (which may involve providing figures or conducting fact-finding missions);

- acting as a mediator by becoming active in negotiations, making suggestions that might be agreeable to all sides, and breaking deadlocks when they occur;

- acting as an arbitrator (making a judgment on the dispute and establishing a fair settlement) with the consent of the parties; and

- acting as an adjudicator (making a judgment with reference to international law).

Naturally, any international actor entrusted with such roles must be acceptable to all sides, be perceived as neutral with little or no agenda of its own, and be capable of performing such tasks. In the end, the parties to the conflict retain the power to decide on outcomes: despite the best efforts of a mediator, the parties to a conflict may choose to abandon mediated talks or to reject some or all of the terms of any agreement that is reached. This is also true of international law in general, as is discussed in Chapter 5.

DIPLOMACY AND CONFLICT MANAGEMENT IN GLOBAL POLITICS

The record of diplomatic efforts to prevent, control, or manage conflicts is mixed. Certainly there have been spectacular failures, most notably in the weeks before the outbreak of World War I. Of course, when wars do break out, any diplomatic efforts to prevent them are by definition failures. However, there have been successful cases of diplomatic conflict management. For example, in 1987, Costa Rican President Oscar Arias designed a peace accord for Central America involving Costa Rica, El Salvador, Nicaragua, Honduras, and Guatemala. All parties agreed to eliminate restrictions on dissent, offer political amnesty to rebel movements, hold national elections, negotiate ceasefires between governments and rebel groups, deny the use of their territory to rebel groups from other countries, and cut off superpower aid to rebel groups. It was a remarkable achievement, and although never fully implemented, the Arias Plan won Oscar Arias the 1987 Nobel Peace Prize. In another example, India and Pakistan were poised on the brink of war in 2002, with the threat of nuclear hostilities hovering over the crisis. However, because of diplomatic intervention from abroad, exchanges between the two countries led to the defusing of the crisis, though not to a resolution of the underlying issues between the two states. Two of the most high-profile diplomatic conflict management efforts in recent years have been the Middle East peace process and the Northern Ireland peace process. Thus far, these two efforts have yielded different outcomes, illustrating both the limits and possibilities of diplomacy as a conflict management instrument.

DIPLOMACY AND CONFLICT MANAGEMENT IN THE MIDDLE EAST

Since the late 1940s, the key component of the Middle East peace process has been the Israeli–Palestinian conflict. Other actors such as Syria and Egypt and various armed groups in Lebanon are also part of the conflict management equation, but a lasting peace in the Middle East is heavily dependent on an Israeli–Palestinian accommodation. Though there are many complex issues involved, at the root of the conflict is : both Israelis and Palestinians claim the same territory, and so conflict management efforts have concentrated on issues such as control of land, Palestinian independence and statehood, control of Jerusalem (which both sides regard as their indivisible capital as well as a holy centre), the return of Palestinian refugees to their homes in Israel, Israeli settlements on the West Bank, economic opportunity for Palestinians, and access to water resources. For decades, this conflict resisted all international efforts to achieve a diplomatic resolution between the Palestine Liberation Organization (PLO) and the government of Israel. The conflict has been characterized by acts of terrorism, assassinations, military action, civil disturbance (such as the Palestinian youth uprising, or *Intifada*), and economic coercion.

A diplomatic breakthrough occurred in September 1993. Israeli and PLO officials had been meeting in secret in Oslo, Norway. With the third-party mediation of the Norwegian government, negotiators reached agreement on a Declaration of Principles signed in Washington by Israeli Prime Minister Yitzak Rabin (who was assassinated in 1995) and PLO Chairman Yasser Arafat on September 13, 1993. In this declaration, Israel recognized the PLO as the legitimate representative of the Palestinian people, and the PLO recognized Israel's right to exist and renounced terrorism. The declaration also included the goals of future negotiations, the most important of which was Israeli withdrawal from the Gaza Strip and the West Bank, and self-rule for Palestinians in those territories under a new Palestinian Authority. However, the hope that this agreement might pave the way to peace was dashed. While some parts of the agreement were partially implemented, disputes over outstanding issues such as sovereignty over Jerusalem and the border between Israel and a future Palestinian state began to erode support for the agreement on both sides. The continued development of Israeli settlements in the West Bank caused consternation among Palestinians, and renewed terrorist attacks by Palestinian groups caused outrage in Israel. Israel criticized the Palestinian Authority for not doing enough to stop the attacks and suspended implementation of the agreement. In July 2000 Israeli Prime Minister Ehud Barak and Yasser Arafat held a summit mediated by U.S. President Bill Clinton, but this meeting failed to resolve the key issues.[11]

As frustration with the peace process grew, the economic hardships facing Palestinians were mounting, Israeli settlements were still being built, and terrorist attacks were still being committed. Both sides were preparing for a renewal of violence. Some Palestinian leaders

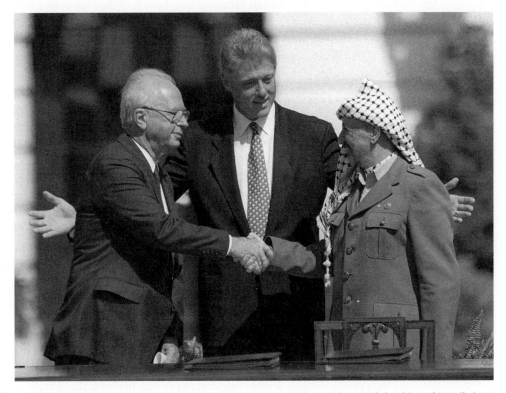

A moment of hope. The signing of the 1993 peace accords by Israeli Prime Minister Yitzhak Rabin and PLO Chairman Yasser Arafat with U.S. President Bill Clinton in the background. This agreement was achieved with the mediation assistance of Norway and the United States. (AP Photo/Ron Edmonds, File/CP Archive.)

began to call for an uprising to compel Israel to agree to a separate Palestinian state, while the Israel Defense Forces (IDF) prepared to crush any Palestinian uprising. All that was needed was a spark, and that spark came when the Likud party leader Ariel Sharon (a man many Palestinians accused of being a war criminal), visited the Temple Mount/Haram al-Sharif, a site considered holy to both Muslims and Jews, in the fall of 2000. Palestinians were outraged that Sharon would visit a site considered holy to Muslims, while many conservative Israelis were outraged at the idea that Sharon should not be able to visit a site holy to Jews. In the wake of the visit, neither side showed any restraint: the El-Aqsa Intifada was launched in September 2000, and the IDF responded with a massive campaign to suppress the Palestinian uprising.[12] Suicide bombings by Palestinian militant groups increased, while the Israeli army conducted frequent raids into Palestinian areas, killing terrorist suspects and civilians, destroying buildings and homes, and arresting suspected militants. By the end of that year, 300 Palestinians and 38 Israelis had been killed.

The ongoing violence once again led to international efforts to find a resolution to the conflict. The new U.S. President, George W. Bush, called for an end to the construction of Israeli settlements in the West Bank, a cessation of Palestinian attacks, and the creation of a Palestinian state. However, active U.S. economic and military support for Israel, efforts to undercut the leadership of Yasser Arafat, and muted criticisms of Israeli military action against Palestinians continued to frustrate the Palestinian leadership and most of the Arab world, and undermined the ability of the United States to break the negotiation deadlock.[13] In February 2002 Saudi Arabia proposed a "grand bargain" that called for Israeli withdrawal to pre-1967 boundaries in exchange for full normalization of relations with all Arab states. The U.S. signalled its support for the proposal, but Israel was less enthusiastic as the proposal called for a Palestinian capital in East Jerusalem and openly supported the El-Aqsa Intifada. Any momentum the Saudi Arabian proposal may have had died away in a renewal of suicide bombings and Israeli reprisals.[14] The violence continued through 2002 and 2003, as suicide bombings and Israeli military actions in the West Bank and the Gaza Strip escalated.

In early 2002, Israel began construction of a "security fence" designed to close off the border between Israel and the West Bank, with five crossing points for Palestinian workers and tourists. The wall, which the Israeli government maintains is a necessary barrier to prevent the movement of terrorists into Israel, not only cuts through communities and separates many Palestinians from their work in Israel, but also cuts into the West Bank and therefore is seen by Palestinians as an effort by Israel to annex land.[15] The deterioration of the situation prompted another round of international efforts to achieve a settlement. In April 2003, yet another peace plan was unveiled. Known as the "Road Map," this plan was designed and endorsed by the United States, Russia, the EU, and the UN. It called for a comprehensive settlement of the Israeli–Palestinian dispute by 2005. In the agreement, a ceasefire would be established; the Palestinian Authority would carry out reforms; Israel would dismantle illegal settlements set up since 2001; a Palestinian state would be created; and negotiations would be conducted on final borders, the status of Jerusalem, and the right of return for Palestinian refugees. However, the "road map to nowhere" achieved little.[16] Dozens of terrorist attacks had to be thwarted during the supposed ceasefire, and Israel dismantled only a few of the illegal settlements and continued building the "security fence," which was still under construction in 2009.

Since 2004, dramatic developments in Palestinian politics have altered the conflict management environment. In November 2004 Yasser Arafat, the leader of the Palestinian Authority and for decades the most visible international symbol of the Palestinian cause, died. This set the stage for a power struggle within Palestinian politics, between the "Fatah" movement once led by Arafat and the rival Islamic-based "Hamas" movement. Presidential elections in 2005 brought Mahmoud Abbas to the Palestinian Authority presidency. Abbas (also called Abu

The "security fence" under construction. This section of the Israeli security fence was being built on the outskirts of Jerusalem, through the village of Abu Dis, January 2004. (AP Photo/Enric Marti/CP Archive.)

Mazen) was considered a moderate Fatah leader and his election created hope for progress in peace talks. However, in parliamentary elections held in January 2006 it was Hamas, not Fatah, that gained a majority in the Palestinian parliament and Hamas' Ismail Haniya became prime minister. The election of the militant and openly anti-Israeli Hamas (the movement refuses to accept Israel's right to exist) stunned many international observers, but in retrospect the results were a reflection of Hamas' efforts to build goodwill in the Palestinian population, widespread frustration with the corruption of Fatah, and divisions within the Fatah movement that divided their voters between too many candidates.[17] The international reaction to the election of Hamas was swift: the United States rejected the election results and halted most of its aid to the Palestinians; Israel cut its ties to the Palestinian Authority; and Europe (traditionally more supportive of the Palestinian cause) withdrew much of its support as well.

The election of Hamas also created conflict among the Palestinian people. The Palestinian Authority was now deadlocked between a Fatah President (Abbas) and a Hamas Prime Minister (Haniya) who disagreed fundamentally on a wide range of issues. Tensions between Fatah and Hamas grew and violence between their respective supporters broke out in 2006, escalating to include daily assassinations and gun battles by the end of the year. Bolstered by U.S. and Israeli support, President Abbas began a buildup of Fatah's security forces to wrestle control of the Palestinian Authority from Hamas. However, in June 2007 Hamas militias struck first, overwhelming Fatah supporters in the Gaza Strip, which since an Israeli withdrawal in August 2005 had been controlled by the Palestinian Authority. In response, President Abbas dissolved the unity government, rounded up Hamas supporters, and appointed an emergency cabinet controlled by Fatah with no Hamas representation. As a result, the Palestinian government and people were now divided between the Fatah-controlled West Bank and the Hamas-controlled Gaza Strip.

The Hamas coup in Gaza took international observers and governments by surprise. This development has seriously complicated conflict management efforts in the region, because there are now two very different movements claiming to speak for the Palestinian people and two separate Palestinian territories under different political and administrative control. The governments of the United States, Europe, and Israel are pursuing a "West Bank first" strategy of supporting Fatah, but this seems to be more of a reactive policy rather than a coherent conflict management approach to the conflict.[18] This strategy has resulted in diplomatic support for President Abbas. In contrast, the Hamas-controlled Gaza Strip has been isolated politically and economically and is surrounded by fences and barriers and virtually cut off from the world by an Israeli land, air, and sea cordon. However, Hamas has demonstrated that it cannot be ignored. Hundreds of crude rockets (often referred to as *Qassam* rockets) have been launched from Gaza into nearby Israeli towns inflicting civilian casualties. The response of the Israeli military (air strikes and incursions) resulted in hundreds of civilian casualties in Gaza during an intense military operation in December/January 2008–2009. The campaign left much of Gaza in physical ruins, and served to exacerbate an ongoing humanitarian crisis reflecting Gaza's isolated position. Unemployment exceeds 70 percent, and 42 percent of Gazan households live in extreme poverty. Due to the ongoing Israeli blockade of Gaza, food is often in short supply, and electricity and water services are often interrupted. Basic health services are difficult to provide, and hospitals are short of medicines and diagnostic and surgical resources.[19] The humanitarian situation in Gaza has brought international condemnation against Israel, but the Israeli government continues to attempt to isolate Hamas, citing ongoing rocket attacks and the refusal of Hamas to make political concessions.

In the meantime, the considerable international support that has been extended to Fatah in the West Bank has not yielded any progress on an Israeli–Palestinian peace. The fundamental issues dividing Israelis and Palestinians continue to plague efforts at establishing a formula for a lasting settlement. Despite a growing awareness in the U.S. government that the Israeli–Palestinian conflict both is central to Middle East peace and continues to fuel Islamic extremism and anti-Americanism in the region, efforts by the United States to broker even an interim agreement between the Palestinian Authority and the government of Israel have failed. Saudi and Egyptian efforts have met with a similar lack of success. At times, the magnitude and scope of the dispute seems overwhelming. Land, borders, Israeli settlements, religion, violence, the wall or security barrier, the status of Jerusalem, Palestinian refugees, and now a divided Palestinian leadership are all obstacles in the path of conflict management efforts. The future will bring new challenges but also new opportunities, and we must dare to hope that an agreement and ultimately a resolution can be found. This may require a committed international political intervention, especially by the U.S. government and the Obama administration. This, at least, is one thing on which most Israelis and Palestinians can agree.

DIPLOMACY AND CONFLICT MANAGEMENT IN NORTHERN IRELAND

The conflict in Northern Ireland has its origins in the Protestant English conquest of Catholic Ireland in the early 17th century. It has since become a conflict involving nationality, sovereignty, and self-determination. English dominance in Ireland was secured by William of Orange at the Battle of the Boyne in 1690. Catholic resistance and revolt through to the early 20th century (including the famous Easter Rising in 1916) increased sentiment in England for Home Rule in Ireland. Protestants opposed this idea as a recipe for absorption into the Catholic majority. After the Irish Civil War (1919–21) between the British and the Irish Republican Army (IRA) ended in a truce and the independence of Southern Ireland in 1922, sectarian violence in the North continued between Catholic Nationalists or Republicans, who wanted the six counties of Northern Ireland united with the South, and Protestant Loyalists or Unionists, who wanted Northern Ireland to remain under British rule.

The period between 1922 and 1969 was relatively calm, but sectarian violence returned in what has been called the modern "time of troubles" in which more than 3,200 people have been killed. The revived IRA began a campaign of violence against Protestants, and the British Army returned to Northern Ireland to restore stability. However, after the shooting of unarmed protestors in Londonderry in 1972 (known as "Bloody Sunday") and the imposition of direct rule from London, the British Army was regarded as an occupying force by most Catholics. Bombings and shootings by the IRA and extremist Protestant organizations continued through to the early 1990s. As with so many conflicts, most people and parties in Northern Ireland wanted a peaceful settlement, but extremist violence polarized the two sides and made compromise and reconciliation difficult. Many diplomatic efforts were made to resolve the conflict, but they foundered because one or more of the parties refused to negotiate or because acts of violence derailed peace initiatives.

A new round of peace talks began in 1996, under the mediation of U.S. Senator George Mitchell. Present were the Irish and British governments, and after the IRA announced a ceasefire and came to the table in 1997, all the major parties were present. Working under a deadline imposed by Mitchell, a diplomatic breakthrough occurred on April 10, 1998. The settlement was called the Belfast Agreement, but it is commonly called the Good Friday Agreement. The agreement included the following: Northern Ireland would remain a part of Great Britain as long as a majority of people wanted it; an assembly would be established in Northern Ireland for self-governance; institutions would be established to develop more cooperation between Northern Ireland and the Republic of Ireland; and the civil rights of Catholics would be established and protected. The agreement went to a referendum and passed by a large majority. Elections were held for the new assembly in June. However, violence continued in the form of bombings, assassinations, and attacks on property. Tensions rose during the infamous "Orange Marches," which commemorate the Battle of the Boyne. In late 1999, the implementation of the Good Friday Agreement stalled, and the British government suspended the new assembly when the IRA refused to disarm.

Attempts to revitalize the Good Friday Agreement in 2000 and 2001 were not very successful. Each side accused the other of noncompliance with the Agreement, and after a number of political resignations and the suspension of power-sharing negotiations between Republicans and Unionists in the new Northern Ireland assembly it seemed as if the process had failed.[20] However, in the wake of the September 11 attacks, the IRA was under increased pressure to meet its commitments to decommission its weapons and disarm.[21] The window of opportunity was lost amid revelations that the IRA had been spying on the Irish government (the case subsequently collapsed and one of the defendants was found to be a British agent). This scandal, and the very slow pace of IRA disarmament, once again led to the suspension of power-sharing negotiations and the assembly. In an effort to save the peace process, the British and Irish governments issued joint declarations in October 2003, calling on all sides to restore the momentum behind the Good Friday Agreement by disarming, halting violence, and establishing a power-sharing arrangement between republicans and unionists. In 2004, the IRA became increasingly isolated as its refusal to disarm and continued acts of violence committed by its members alienated the Irish public, including most Catholics. In July 2005 the IRA announced it was forsaking violence. In October 2006 the body established to observe IRA disarmament reported that this task had been completed. Although staunch unionists remained skeptical of IRA assurances, elections for the Northern Ireland Assembly took place in March 2007. In May, the leaders of the rival factions reached a historic power-sharing agreement and local government finally came to Northern Ireland. In 2008, the ten-year anniversary of the Good Friday Agreement, Northern Ireland was at peace and reconciliation efforts were under way to try to slowly heal the wounds of decades of sectarian violence.

However, in January 2009 a proposed plan to compensate the families of those killed in the "troubles" encountered stiff resistance, because many families believed it unjustly extended the same compensation to the families of dead "terrorists" as it did to the families of the "victims." In March 2009 gunmen shot dead two soldiers and wounded several civilians in an attack on a military base. These events are an illustration of the fragility of the peace and the ongoing enmity and hostility that endures in Northern Ireland.

The cases of the Israeli–Palestinian conflict and the Northern Ireland conflict illustrate the enormity of the challenges facing diplomatic efforts to resolve violent disputes in global politics. For diplomacy to be a successful conflict management instrument, the parties to a dispute must prefer a negotiated settlement to other available alternatives (such as war or achieving no settlement at all). This is not always the case, and if one or more parties to a dispute are not interested in negotiations or bargain in bad faith or refuse to compromise on certain issues, diplomacy stands little chance of success. Even when there is a commitment from all parties to achieving a settlement, they may have difficulty controlling extremist elements in order to implement the results of negotiation. As a result, the outcomes of diplomatic conflict management efforts may be many and varied. Results can include an improved climate between the parties to a dispute, the establishment of a basis for further negotiation, the creation of a short-term agreement to settle an immediate problem, or the establishment of a firm basis for a lasting peace. However, results can include the creation of an agreement that becomes a point of dissatisfaction or humiliation for one of the actors or a breakdown in negotiations and the collapse of diplomatic efforts. Diplomatic outcomes will not necessarily eliminate the possibility of future disputes between the parties, but diplomatic effort is a crucial instrument for resolving conflicts in global politics. Without it, recourse to armed struggle is often the consequence.

DISARMAMENT AND ARMS CONTROL

The main assumption behind disarmament and arms control efforts is that weapons contribute to the outbreak of war, a position juxtaposed with the realist view that peace and stability can be attained only through balances of power or through preparation for war.[22] Advocates of disarmament and arms control argue that the frequency of war can be reduced by eliminating threatening or destabilizing weapons, preventing arms races that increase tensions and hostility and absorb financial resources, promoting mutual trust and confidence, and limiting the destructiveness of war if it does occur. In certain periods in history, the idea of disarmament and arms control has been well received. The destructiveness of World War I led to several arms control efforts. After World War II, the development of the atomic bomb and the nuclear arms race between the superpowers led to increasing antinuclear and antiwar sentiment. Strong peace movements in many countries sponsored rallies, marches, and concerts dedicated to ending the arms race.

At this point, an important distinction must be made. Disarmament efforts seek to drastically reduce or eliminate weapons as an important step toward the elimination of war itself. Arms control efforts seek to reduce stockpiles of existing weapons or prevent their use—not to eradicate weapons or eliminate the threat of war, but to reduce the risk of war through stabilizing the status quo, building confidence between states and groups, encouraging the peaceful dispute resolution, and discouraging the use of force. Therefore, disarmament efforts are more transformative in their ambitions. As one analyst observes, "arms control is fundamentally a conservative enterprise. Disarmament seeks to overturn the status quo; arms control works to perpetuate it."[23] Not surprisingly, only a few historical examples of disarmament efforts exist. In sixth-century B.C.E. China, several states formed a disarmament league that contributed to a century of peace. In 1817, Great Britain and the United States signed the Rush–Bagot Treaty which demilitarized the Canada–U.S. border. At the end of World War I, U.S. President Woodrow Wilson called for national disarmament to the lowest point consistent with domestic safety (a provision later watered down to disarmament to the lowest level consistent with national safety, which could mean almost anything). The League of Nations sponsored a World Disarmament Conference in 1932, which attempted to ban offensive weapons, but foundered on the definition of which weapons were defensive and which were offensive. Finally, the UN has sponsored a number of special sessions on disarmament since its inception in 1945, although these efforts have yielded limited results.

In contrast, the historical record of arms control agreements is vast and varied. In almost all cases, arms control efforts have attempted to ban the production or deployment of a specific weapon (or a variant of a weapon) or to restrict the number of weapons a signatory is allowed to possess. For example, in the 11th century an effort was made by the Second Lateran Council to ban crossbows, and in 1868 the St. Petersburg Declaration banned explosive bullets. The 1899 and 1907 International Peace Conventions at The Hague banned a number of weapons (including poisonous gas). At the Washington Naval Conferences (1921–22), the United States, Great Britain, Japan, France, and Italy agreed to fixed ratios for the number of capital ships in their battle fleets, a production moratorium on new ones, and the scrapping of a significant number. During the Cold War, two broad types of arms control agreements existed. The most prominent of these were the bilateral agreements established by the two superpowers. In addition, several multilateral arms control agreements involving other countries were established. Some of these multilateral arrangements were directly related to the Cold War, while others were intended to have a wider, universal effect. Many of these agreements survive to this day and form the foundation of contemporary efforts to address contemporary security issues.

ARMS CONTROL IN GLOBAL POLITICS

Contemporary arms control efforts are focused largely on preventing the proliferation of weapons (see Chapter 6) and banning the use, production, or stockpiling of specific weapons systems. Some new agreements have been established to meet new concerns, but for the most part older Cold War agreements have been revisited in an effort to adapt them to new international conditions (see Profile 7.1). Nuclear weapons have been a special focus of arms control efforts since the end of the Cold War. The immediate priority was nuclear arms reductions and securing the nuclear arsenal of the former Soviet Union. After the collapse of the U.S.S.R., the Russian government either did not, or simply could not, account for all of the nuclear weapons on Russian territory, and it certainly could not negotiate on behalf of the former republics of Ukraine, Belarus, and Kazakhstan, which suddenly possessed weapons on their own territories. After a period of intense negotiation (in particular with Ukraine, which had a powerful domestic constituency favouring the retention of nuclear weapons), all three countries agreed to eliminate all nuclear weapons on their territories and sign the Non-Proliferation Treaty (NPT). They have now joined South Africa as the only states to dispossess themselves of nuclear weapons. In June 1992, at a summit in Washington, President Bush and President Yeltsin surprised the world by agreeing to a Joint Understanding under the START agreement that would reduce the nuclear arsenals of the superpowers by 60 percent—to 3,000 warheads for Russia and 3,500 warheads for the United States—by the year 2003 (later 2007). This understanding was formalized as a Treaty in the START II Agreement in January 1993. On May 24, 2002, U.S. President George W. Bush and Russian President Vladimir Putin signed the Strategic Offensive Reductions Treaty (SORT). The treaty restricts each country to possessing no more than 1,700 to 2,200 strategic warheads by December 31, 2012. While significant, the

PROFILE 7.1 — Major Multilateral Arms Control Treaties and Agreements

DATE	AGREEMENT	PRINCIPAL AIMS
1959	Antarctic Treaty	Prohibits military use of the Antarctic, including nuclear weapons testing
1963	Limited/Partial Test Ban Treaty	Prohibits testing nuclear weapons in the atmosphere, underwater, and in outer space
1967	Outer Space Treaty	Prohibits testing or stationing any weapons in space, and bans military manoeuvres in space
1967	Treaty of Tlatelolco	Creates Latin American nuclear weapons—free zone
1968 (1995)	Nuclear Non-Proliferation Treaty	Prohibits transfer of nuclear weapons and technology to non-nuclear states
1971	Seabed Treaty	Prohibits deployment of weapons of mass destruction (including nuclear weapons) beyond a 12-mile (20-kilometre) coastal limit
1972	Biological Weapons Convention	Prohibits production and stockpiling of biological weapons
1977	Environmental Modifications Convention	Bans use of technologies that can alter weather patterns or ecology
1981	Inhumane Weapons Convention	Prohibits or restricts certain fragmentation weapons, incendiary weapons, and treacherous weapons
1985	South Pacific Nuclear Free Zone (Rarotonga Treaty)	Prohibits testing, acquisition, or deployment of nuclear weapons in the South Pacific
1986	Confidence Building and Security Building Measures and Disarmament in Europe (CDE) Agreement	Requires prior notification and onsite inspection of military exercises
1987	Missile Technology Control Regime (MTCR)	Restricts export of ballistic missiles and technology
1990	Conventional Forces in Europe (CFE) Treaty	Limits numbers of five categories of weapons in Europe (extended to former Soviet Union states in 1992)
1992	Open Skies Treaty	Permits surveillance and verification flights over signatory countries
1993	Chemical Weapons Convention	Requires all stockpiles and production facilities to be destroyed within 10 years
1993	UN Register of Conventional Arms	Calls on states to submit sale and receipt information on seven categories of conventional arms to a central registry
1996	Comprehensive Test Ban Treaty	Requires all signatories not to test nuclear weapons
1997	Global Land Mines Treaty	Requires all signatories to destroy stocks of land mines and not produce or export them
2008	Cluster Munitions Convention	Requires all signatories to eliminate the use, production, stockpiling, and transfer of all existing and future cluster bombs

treaty did not address warhead destruction or reductions in nonstrategic (sometimes called "tactical") nuclear warheads. Nevertheless, if fully implemented, SORT will result in further cuts to the nuclear arsenals of the United States and Russia (see Figure 7.1 for a comparison of the number of nuclear warheads held by the United States and Russia under START and SORT).

Another immediate concern after the Cold War was securing Russia's nuclear warheads, fissile material, and nuclear weapons infrastructure. The collapse of the Soviet Union left the security and safety of vast numbers of nuclear warheads in doubt. Many Soviet nuclear scientists and weapons technicians were suddenly unemployed, raising fears that they would accept jobs developing nuclear weapons in other countries. In 1991, the United States passed the Nunn–Lugar Act, otherwise known as the Cooperative Threat Reduction Program. This program, initiated with the cooperation of the Russian government, provides U.S. financial assistance to Russia for the identification, securing, and destruction of Russian nuclear (and chemical) weapons, as well as assisting Russian nuclear scientists to find work in peaceful industries. Among other accomplishments, in the first 10 years of the program, 6,212 warheads were removed from their missiles and many were dismantled and the fissile material secured.[24] As concerns over the security and safety of Russia's nuclear weapons has receded in recent years, the concern over worsening relations between Russia and the West have renewed calls for more aggressive nuclear arms control efforts, including nuclear disarmament. In 2007 several former high-ranking U.S. officials called for a world free of nuclear weapons.[25] In July 2009 U.S. President Barack Obama and Russian President Dimitry Medvedev met to discuss how to move forward on a new strategic arms reduction treaty. The results of this process will be watched eagerly by arms control advocates.

While reductions in nuclear stockpiles remains an important objective of arms control efforts, today the focus of nuclear arms control is on proliferation. Two agreements figure

Figure 7.1 Reductions in Strategic Nuclear Weapons Under the START and SORT Processes

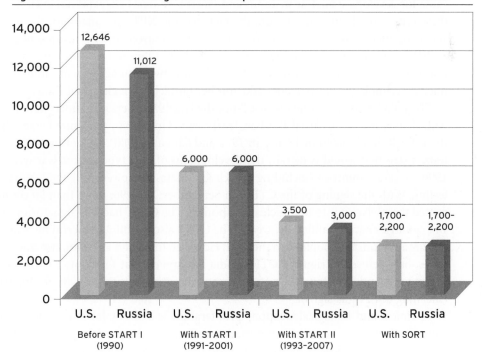

SOURCE: CENTER FOR DEFENSE INFORMATION AND FEDERATION OF AMERICAN SCIENTISTS.

prominently in the global effort to control the spread of nuclear weapons: the Non-Proliferation Treaty (NPT) and the Comprehensive Test Ban Treaty (CTBT). The NPT, signed in July 1968, is the most important international treaty on the issue of nuclear proliferation, binding its signatories to several provisions. Nuclear-weapons states are obligated not to transfer nuclear weapons or related technology to non-nuclear-weapons states. In turn, non-nuclear-weapons states are obligated not to try to acquire nuclear weapons or related technology. Materials related to nuclear energy are exempt from these provisions, because the NPT was originally designed to facilitate the spread of peaceful nuclear technology. For the same reasons, "peaceful" nuclear explosions were permitted. All signatories to the NPT pledge to work toward universal nuclear disarmament. The International Atomic Energy Agency (IAEA) is charged with verifying compliance with the NPT through constant monitoring of nuclear facilities in signatory countries and the use of onsite inspections.

The NPT has been the subject of considerable criticism. First, as an international treaty it binds only its members, and not all nuclear-weapons states are signatories (Israel, Pakistan, and India are not members of the NPT, and North Korea withdrew in 2003). Despite the efforts of the IAEA, some non-nuclear-weapons states have managed to build significant nuclear weapons development programs. For example, Iraq possessed a sophisticated program during the 1980s, which was exposed after the end of the 1990–91 Gulf War. North Korea managed to develop a nuclear bomb while a member of the NPT. Iran has conducted a number of clandestine nuclear activities that violate the terms of its agreement with the IAEA. These examples fuel accusations that the IAEA is ineffective as a **verification** and compliance mechanism because it lacks (among other things) sufficient resources and an enforcement capacity. Furthermore, the NPT and the IAEA are criticized for their role in encouraging the spread of nuclear energy. This role has raised environmental concerns, and civilian reactor programs can be the first step in acquiring a bomb. Finally, countries such as India have argued that the NPT also obligates nuclear states to work for disarmament, and in the absence of progress on nuclear disarmament, it is hypocritical of nuclear-weapons states to criticize countries such as India for developing nuclear weapons and violating a treaty they did not even sign. However, these criticisms should not obscure the fact that the NPT does maintain the norm that the spread of nuclear weapons is dangerous and should be avoided. This norm is nearly universal: as of 2009, 189 countries were signatories to the NPT (Taiwan has also signed on, though it is not formally recognized as a state). Along with a network of agreements among suppliers of nuclear technology, the NPT does add another obstacle to nuclear ambitions.[26]

The CTBT also has a long history. Since the late 1950s, periodic efforts have been made to ban all nuclear tests. A Partial Test Ban Treaty signed in 1963 by the United States, Britain, and the U.S.S.R. (and joined by France in 1974 and China in 1980) did not include underground tests, a step that would constrain the development of new types of nuclear weapons. In the 1990s, several countries (including the United States) followed unilateral moratoriums on testing. With the signing of the CTBT on September 24, 1996, more than 90 countries committed themselves not to test nuclear weapons.[27] The CTBT had 178 signatories in 2008 with 144 countries having ratified the treaty. The CTBT also prohibits peaceful nuclear explosions, closing an important loophole in the NPT. However, India and Pakistan, two nuclear-weapons states, have refused to sign the CTBT. India has argued that the treaty provisions violate its sovereignty, and Pakistan will not sign until the security situation in South Asia changes (meaning until India signs).

Chemical and biological weapons proliferation is another focus of contemporary arms control efforts. The two most important mechanisms designed to address the problem of chemical and biological weapons proliferation are the Chemical Weapons Convention (CWC) and the Biological Weapons Convention (BWC). The CWC was signed in January 1993 and entered into force in April 1997. It is an ambitious and forward-looking treaty, aimed at disarmament rather than arms control. The CWC was an especially complicated effort, since many chemicals used in weapons are "dual use" chemicals also used in industry and agriculture. The signatories to the CWC are obligated to complete the destruction of all of their chemical weapons and production facilities within 10 years of the treaty coming into force. Signatory countries must declare whether they possess chemical weapons or manufacturing facilities and provide a precise inventory of both, along with plans for their destruction. Signatories are also obligated to declare whether they have received chemical weapons from another country or whether they have transferred them to another country. The CWC also has a complex verification system in which countries may mount challenge inspections in other countries to verify compliance. As of 2008, 184 countries had signed the CWC (180 had ratified the treaty). However, once again the CWC binds only its signatories, and the ease with which chemical weapons can be manufactured has led to suspicion that clandestine chemical weapons facilities might evade the attention of the world community.

The BWC was signed in 1972 and came into force in 1975. It prohibits the development, production, and stockpiling of biological weapons, although it does not explicitly ban their use since the 1925 Geneva Protocol for the Prohibition of the Use in War of Asphyxiating, Poisonous, or Other Gases and of Bacteriological Weapons of Warfare had already done so. However, the BWC has been heavily criticized for lacking a verification system and allowing signatories to continue research into biological weapons and protective measures for defensive purposes. In recognition of the limitations of the BWC and the increasing threat posed by biological weapons, in 1995 an Ad Hoc Working Group of governments began discussions to strengthen the BWC. Over six years later, the working group drafted a proposed protocol to the BWC that would require signatories to declare the existence and location of treaty-relevant facilities, and put in place a system of verification inspections. However, in 2001 the United States rejected the draft protocol, arguing that it did not cover enough relevant facilities, would be applied mostly to Western states and not those states most suspected of developing biological weapons, and might be used as an instrument of industrial espionage against U.S. biotech companies. The U.S. rejection of the proposed protocol met with a great deal of criticism and condemnation, with supporters of the treaty inside the United States and around the world dismissing the concerns of the U.S. government as unwarranted and even inaccurate. However, the U.S. rejection of the protocol effectively erased any hopes for strengthening the BWC. As of 2008, 161 states had signed the BWC, and 147 had ratified.

As concern over the spread of conventional weapons has increased, greater attention has been placed on establishing controls over such weapons. Some prominent examples are the Conventional Forces in Europe (CFE) Treaty, the Missile Technology Control Regime (MTCR), and the UN Register of Conventional Arms. The CFE Treaty was signed by 23 European states in November 1990. The treaty entered into force in 1991 and was extended to include the newly independent states of the former Soviet Union in 1992. The treaty classifies weapons into five broad categories of Treaty Limited Equipment (TLE) in a geographic area from the Atlantic Ocean to the Ural Mountains in Russia (the so-called Atlantic to the Urals, or ATTU, zone). All countries have allowable limits in TLE, which they cannot exceed, although in practice most countries maintain arsenals lower than they are permitted under the CFE. The CFE treaty has recently become a victim of the deteriorating relationship between Russia and NATO. In July 2007, the then Russian President Vladimir Putin announced that Russia was suspending its observance of the treaty. The Russian government is upset with a variety of issues from NATO enlargement to plans for the deployment of a U.S. missile defence system in Eastern Europe, and is also seeking changes to the treaty that will allow Russia more flexibility in deploying military forces in the ATTU zone.

The MTCR is an informal arrangement designed to control the spread of **ballistic missile** technology. As such, it is not a treaty, nor is it legally binding on its membership. Formed in 1987 by seven producers of ballistic missile technology, the MTCR initially covered nuclear-capable missiles and was later expanded in 1993 to include chemical-capable and biological-capable missiles as well. The MTCR now comprises 34 states. However, because the MTCR is not a treaty, compliance is voluntary. In 1993, China (which had pledged to abide by the provisions of the MTCR) was found to have transferred ballistic missile components to Pakistan. India, Pakistan, Iran, and North Korea continue to develop their ballistic missile programs, and all have received at least some international assistance in doing so. On the other hand, the MTCR has contributed to the cancellation of some ballistic missile development programs, by making it difficult to acquire certain technologies or creating a political environment that condemns such efforts. Brazil, South Korea, Taiwan, Argentina, Egypt, and South Africa have all stopped or suspended ballistic missile development efforts. In 2002, the International Code of Conduct Against Ballistic Missile Proliferation was established. This agreement is non-binding, and calls for restraint in the production, testing, and export of ballistic missiles. With 119 signatories, the Hague Code of Conduct has a wider number of signatories but weaker provisions than the MTCR, which remains an export control group of producing countries.

The UN arms register was created in 1991 by a UN General Assembly resolution. The register is an attempt to establish an information service to track arms shipments around the world in seven categories of weapons: tanks; armoured combat vehicles; heavy artillery; combat aircraft; attack helicopters; warships; and missiles and missile systems. Ideally, states will submit information to the register on any exports and imports of weapons. It is hoped that this information will increase the transparency of arms transfers around the world and so reduce the secretive nature of arms transfers and the tensions and suspicions this secrecy can create. Critics of the registry argue that it places no real limits on the transfer of weapons and is entirely dependent on the willingness of states to provide information about their arms sales and purchases. In addition, the register can compile information only on the open arms trade and has no capacity to address the covert arms trade.

In addition to these mechanisms, other arms control instruments do exist, but they are unilateral, or measures agreed to by relatively small groups of states. In other words, they lack the near-universal quality of global arms control treaties. In the Western Hemisphere, 20 countries have signed the Inter-American Convention on Transparency in Conventional Weapons Acquisitions, which requires signatories to report their regional weapons sales and purchases. States can impose arms embargoes against other states, and impose arms sales codes of conduct on their domestic producers. Groups of states can agree not to transfer certain technologies to other states: for example, the 40 countries of the Wassenaar Arrangement on Export Controls for Conventional Arms and Dual-Use Goods and Technologies have agreed to exchange information on certain weapons transfers to encourage the responsible transfer of weapons and related technologies. All of these mechanisms have their limitations, and the challenges facing arms control agreements in general have raised questions about the effectiveness of arms control efforts.

CRITICS OF ARMS CONTROL

Both disarmament and arms control efforts have been subjected to heavy criticism. This criticism has varied with the nature of agreement under discussion, but several critical themes have emerged consistently over time:

- Arms control is risky and even dangerous because success depends on trusting one's opponents not to cheat.

- Because the word of one's opponents is not to be trusted, arms control compliance has to be verified, a complicated and difficult task.

- Arms control agreements will be violated in times of crisis or war.

- Weapons cannot be effectively banned, because the knowledge to manufacture them exists.

- The specific weapons banned or restricted may have little military utility and not be considered useful.

- Arms control agreements succeed only in channelling arms competitions into weapons-system types that are not banned or restricted, furthering legitimizing the highly lucrative arms trade.

- Technological developments can render arms control agreements obsolete or ineffective.

- Making agreements with authoritarian governments is ill advised, because they are more apt to cheat and are able to conceal this cheating with greater effectiveness.

- Arms control agreements bind only signatories, not nonsignatories, who may proceed with arms buildups or the manufacture of certain banned weapons.

In response to these criticisms, advocates of disarmament and arms control maintain that states and groups have entered into arms control negotiations with deceitful purposes; in other words, arms control has not been given the chance it deserves. States have used it to gain an advantage over an opponent. In some cases, they have made arms control proposals while they are ahead in an arms race. In other cases, states have sought to use arms control to permit weapons and capabilities where they have advantages and to restrict weapons and capabilities where they are at a disadvantage. At times, arms control has been used to sub-jugate other states. Many arms control advocates also suspect that states enter arms control arrangements as public relations exercises. Until governments around the world are committed to the idea of disarmament and arms control for the mutual long-term benefit of all, the capacity of disarmament and arms control measures to live up to their promise of a more peaceful world will be limited, and there is not much optimism that this will happen soon, for several reasons.

First, governments continue to direct more resources toward researching and developing new weapons than to attempts to control weapons. Second, military and political leaders remain wary of disarmament and arms control as a means of strengthening their security. As a result, military preparedness remains a primary instrument of state security. Third, leaders are reluctant to engage in arms control either because they want to attain a certain military capability (whether nuclear weapons or ballistic missiles) and are unwilling to commit themselves to an agreement not to acquire it, or because they possess a superiority in a certain military capability and see no reason why they should accept constraints on it. Fourth, many developing states view the effort to prevent the spread of certain weapons as discriminatory acts by the rich nations anxious to perpetuate their military superiority. Fifth, a growing number of states are becoming capable of developing and manufacturing sophisti-cated weapons systems, making the process of reaching an arms control agreement among a larger and larger number of states an increasingly difficult proposition. Sixth, the war in Iraq (fought largely on false allegations of Iraqi weapons of mass destruction) has complicated global diplomacy on arms control by undermining the credibility of subsequent allegations against suspected treaty violators.[28] Finally, arms control cannot be regarded as a panacea, for true international security "depends not as much on arms or arms control as on reducing as much as possible the sources of conflict in international situations and on finding effective nonviolent means of resolving the conflicts that remain."[29]

HUMAN SECURITY AND ARMS CONTROL

We introduced the concept of *human security* in Chapter 6, but expand on it here because much of the human security agenda is in fact a conflict management agenda. Human security is an idea that calls for a shift in thinking on security matters from the level of the state to the level of the human individual. In essence, human security proposes a new global hierarchy of security priorities, placing the security of individuals above state sovereignty and territorial integrity, particularly if a state proves unwilling or unable to provide for the human security of its population. Human security was first articulated in the UN Human Development Report in 1994. The report argued that "human security can be said to have two main aspects. It means, first, safety from such chronic threats such as hunger, disease and repression. And second, it means protection from sudden and hurtful disruptions of daily life—whether in homes, in jobs, or in communities."[30] Former Canadian Foreign Affairs Minister Lloyd Axworthy was one of the leading advocates of the human security approach. Axworthy defined human security as "security against economic deprivation, an acceptable quality of life, and a guarantee of fundamental rights … [this] requires that basic needs are met, but it also acknowledges that sustained economic development, human rights and fundamental freedoms, the rule of law, good governance, sustainable development, and social equity are as important as arms control and disarmament."[31] The human security concept did attract some governments, such as Canada and Norway, who made it a prominent component of their foreign policies. A Human Security Network was established, which currently consists of 13 states. Human security attracted many NGOs in the arms control, humanitarian, and aid communities, and governmental and NGO cooperation became a signature of the human security approach in practice, realized in such initiatives as the 1997 Treaty to Ban Landmines.

The concept of human security has been criticized, most notably for a lack of precision. "Human security" is by nature a very vague term that covers a wide range of issues and topics. While this makes it politically useful, it also makes it is a poor guide for establishing priorities. As Roland Paris argues, "Human security is like 'sustainable development'—everyone is for it, but few people have a clear sense of what it means."[32] The vagueness and scope of the term also create contradictions: there are material and moral consequences to intervening on behalf of human security, just as there are material and moral consequences of not intervening. In Canada, the human security concept was accused of being "pinchpenny diplomacy" (diplomacy on the cheap) and "pulpit diplomacy" (preaching morality while alienating allies).[33] Nevertheless, human security did establish a role and a voice for Canada.[34] Human security was also a driving intellectual force behind a number of concrete initiatives that culminated in international treaties or agreements, most notably the Ottawa Treaty (see Profile 7.2). Other initiatives that human security can claim as policy offspring are the International Criminal Court and diplomatic initiatives on child soldiers.

In a significant development for human security and arms control advocates, on May 28, 2008 an agreement was reached to ban cluster bombs, a weapon which disperses small "bomblets" over a wide area. Arms control advocates had been calling for a ban for years, arguing that many of these bomblets fail to explode immediately and become a hazard to civilians days, weeks, and months later. The Cluster Munitions Convention was signed by 111

PROFILE 7.2   Weapons Proliferation and Human Security: The Global Land Mines Problem

The Ottawa Treaty. The signing of the Convention on the Prohibition of the Use, Stockpiling, Production and Transfer of Antipersonnel Mines and on Their Destruction, December 3, 1997. From left are International Campaign to Ban Landmines representative Jody Williams, President of the International Committee of the Red Cross Cornelio Sommaruga, UN Secretary-General Kofi Annan, Foreign Affairs Minister Lloyd Axworthy, and Prime Minister Jean Chrétien. (Tom Hanson/CP Images.)

Anti-personnel land mines (APLs) are designed to explode automatically in response to pressure or tripwires. Because they are easy to make and deploy, and are cheap (as little as $3 to $15 for simpler mines), they have become very common in intrastate wars. In the mid-1990s, an estimated 60 million to 110 million land mines were buried in 64 countries. More mines were laid every year, while extraction rates were low: every year UN or private de-miners took out 10,000 mines. The human costs of land mines were horrific: land mines killed or wounded an estimated 26,000 people a year through the late 1980s to mid-1990s. It is estimated that there are currently 250,000 "mine amputees." Mine injuries are painful and crippling, involving costly treatment and lengthy rehabilitation. They are also an obstacle to post-hostilities recovery and development, rendering land unusable for crops or grazing and preventing safe passage on roads or trails. Mines are indiscriminate: they kill men, women, children, combatants, and non-combatants (as well as livestock), in many cases long after the war in which they were laid is

over. Land mines represent a serious threat to human security in countries such as Cambodia, Angola, Bosnia-Herzegovina, Mozambique, and Afghanistan.

Efforts to ban the stockpiling, production, and export of land mines grew in the 1990s. A UN resolution called for a moratorium on land mine exports (with then Secretary-General Boutros Boutros-Ghali giving the matter his personal attention), and NGOs such as the International Committee of the Red Cross and the International Campaign to Ban Landmines increased their pressure on governments. By 1996 Canada had begun to exert international leadership on this issue, imposing a unilateral moratorium on the production, export, and operational use of antipersonnel land mines. In 1997 Canada led a successful campaign to conclude a global antipersonnel land mine treaty, which was signed in Ottawa on December 2, 1997. The treaty bans the use, production, transfer, and stockpiling of anti-personnel mines and obligates signatories to destroy their stock of mines. The government of Canada contributes funds for mine clearance, medical treatment, rehabilitation, and artificial limbs. However, key countries have not signed the treaty, including the United States, Russia, China, India, Pakistan, Israel, and Iran. Nevertheless, the treaty was a major diplomatic and arms control success and a significant breakthrough for the human security concept. In 2008, 156 countries had acceded to the treaty, and land mine use has declined. Production of land mines has fallen, de-mining efforts continue, and the number of victims per year has declined.

SOURCES: UNITED NATIONS DEPARTMENT OF HUMANITARIAN AFFAIRS, "THE UNITED NATIONS AND MINE CLEARANCE," OVERVIEW, JUNE 1995, INTERNATIONAL MEETING ON MINE CLEARANCE, GENEVA, JUNE 5–7, 1995; "ARMS CONTROL ASSOCIATION FACT SHEET: THE OTTAWA CONVENTION: SIGNATORIES AND STATE PARTIES" (WASHINGTON, DC: THE ARMS CONTROL ASSOCIATION, 2004); AND INTERNATIONAL CAMPAIGN TO BAN LANDMINES, *LANDMINE MONITOR REPORT 2003: TOWARD A MINE-FREE WORLD* (NEW YORK: HUMAN RIGHTS WATCH, 2003).

states. The United States, China, Russia, Israel, India, and Pakistan (all major producers of the weapons) refused to attend the treaty conference or sign the agreement, arguing that the weapons were needed for military operations. Nevertheless, advocates of the ban were pleased with the result, and hoped that the ban would have a similar effect as the 1997 Ottawa Treaty, which reduced land mine use even by countries that had not signed it. Human security and arms control advocates also hope to develop arms control agreements on the proliferation of small arms and light weapons. Human security will continue to have a place in the policy initiatives of some states and NGOs. The lasting significance of human security may well be the entrenchment of the idea that security cannot, and should not, always be defined in state-centric terms.

INTERNATIONAL LAW AND CONTROLS ON WAR

Efforts to prevent or control war through international law have concentrated on two issues: the prohibition of war as an instrument of policy, and the imposition of rules and regulations to establish lawful conduct in war. Many efforts have been made to prohibit war, although many of these efforts were qualified in some way. The Hague Conventions of 1899 and 1907, for example, bound signatories to seek a peaceful resolution to their disputes before resorting to force. Presumably, if no peaceful resolution could be found, war was permissible. The Bryan Treaties of 1913–14 banned declarations of war by one state against another before an arbitration committee had met to consider the circumstances of the conflict. The Covenant of the League of Nations bound League members to renounce aggression, and the signatories to the 1928 Kellogg–Briand Pact forfeited the right to go to war (see Profile 7.3). The Charter of the UN (Article 2/4) prohibits the use or threat of force in the international system, and a 1974 General Assembly resolution banned aggression. However, none of these efforts has succeeded in achieving the real goal of eliminating war.

Partly because of the historical record of attempts to prohibit war, much of the body of international law on war concerns its conduct. As early as 1400 B.C.E. agreements had been established concerning the treatment of prisoners, and poisoned weapons were outlawed in India in 500 B.C.E. Modern legal efforts to control war are founded on the Geneva Conventions of 1948, and the additional Protocols of 1977. This body of law, sometimes referred to as the

---

PROFILE 7.3 ## The Kellogg–Briand Pact

The Kellogg–Briand Pact, formally known as the Treaty Providing for the Renunciation of War as an Instrument of State Policy, was originally agreed to by the governments of the United States and France in 1927. U.S. Secretary of State Frank B. Kellogg and French Foreign Minister Aristide Briand agreed to outlaw war between their two states. The enthusiasm of the U.S. government led to an open offer to other governments to sign the treaty; by 1934, 64 states (most of the states in the world at that time) were signatories. However, the hopes of the treaty were never realized. Most signatories placed caveats on their commitment to the renunciation of war; Japan, for example, insisted on the right to wage war in self-defence, while Great Britain insisted on its right to intervene militarily in areas of the world of interest to it (meaning its colonies). The treaty contained no enforcement mechanism and was unable to respond to acts of aggression. The treaty was also signed by states that had clear expansionist or revisionist ambitions. As a result, the treaty has been derided as an example of the emptiness and futility of efforts to outlaw war.

SEE R. FERRELL, *PEACE IN THEIR TIME: THE ORIGIN OF THE KELLOGG–BRIAND PACT* (NEW HAVEN: YALE UNIVERSITY PRESS, 1952).

laws of war or International Humanitarian Law (IHL), has focused on establishing rules of conduct that include distinguishing between combatants and noncombatants (civilians), the treatment of prisoners of war, establishing what is considered an indiscriminate attack, restrictions on carpet bombing, extrajudicial executions, and the establishment of war zones. International law has also focused on defining war crimes such as genocide (see Chapter 9), and on the prohibition or restriction of specific types of weapons.[35] Modern efforts at the latter are largely derived from two special UN conferences on conventional weapons held at Lucerne in 1974 and Lugano in 1976. These conferences laid the foundation for the three protocols of the 1981 Inhumane Weapons Convention, which banned different types of weapons systems. Protocol I covers fragmentation weapons, banning the use of toxic fragments and fragments that are undetectable by X-ray. Protocol II covers treacherous weapons, prohibiting booby traps, the use of mines against civilians, the placement of mines, and the recording of minefields. Protocol III covers incendiary weapons, prohibiting attacks on the natural elements (unless they are used as cover for military movements) and the use of incendiary weapons against civilians.

Despite the letter of international law, these provisions are frequently violated. Many states and substate groups violate IHL because they are unaware of the law or they choose to violate it knowing the chances of enforcement are slim. Few, if any, enforcement mechanisms exist to support the observation of international law in war. Nonstate actors such as the International Committee of the Red Cross and Red Crescent Societies have filled this gap, but can only call attention to violations of war law and lack the formal or practical capacity to enforce it. The efforts to build and apply war law—the Nuremberg and Tokyo war crimes trials and the international tribunals on atrocities committed in the former Yugoslavia and Rwanda—have been criticized as victors' justice, imposed on the losers of a conflict by the winners (see Chapter 9). International law also has difficulty keeping up with technological developments and many new weapons systems are not covered by international law. Nevertheless, international law on war establishes norms of conduct and seeks to ban certain weapon systems that are especially inhumane; to violate these norms is to invite international condemnation and the loss of legitimacy.

INTERNATIONAL ORGANIZATIONS AND CONFLICT MANAGEMENT

As liberal institutionalists remind us, IOs perform several tasks and roles that are both directly and indirectly related to conflict management. IOs can act as a forum for debate and discussion, reducing the chances of misunderstanding or misinterpretation. IOs can also act as a steam valve for international conflict and crises, permitting political leaders to accuse and condemn their opponents without resorting to violence. This ability can be particularly useful when public opinion back home demands some form of response, especially in cases in which doing nothing best serves the interests of peace. Of course, governments can be accused of avoiding substantive action on an issue by raising it in an international forum but doing little else. IOs can also provide third-party mediation services in times of crisis or war. Because they are established actors with a permanent location and membership, they can provide physical facilities, staff, and diplomatic support for negotiations. Other members of an IO can also encourage the parties to a dispute to come to a settlement and offer rewards and threats to that end. IOs can establish fact-finding and information missions designed to obtain more objective sources of evidence and information. In other cases, the staff or leadership of the organization itself (such as the UN Secretary-General) may become involved in facilitating an agreement. Finally, with the agreement of the parties to a dispute, IOs may act as arbitrators.

IOs can also provide legitimacy to the policies of a state or a group of states, and can serve to constrain unilateralism. To act as a collective, IOs require the consensus of their membership (depending on the voting procedure of the organization). If states or groups want to act as a collective, with the advantages of added legitimacy that joint action provides, then some states or groups will have to compromise or alter their positions so that a common stance can be reached. Therefore, organizations can help alter outcomes in such a way as to enhance peace by inhibiting or restraining certain members from aggressive actions. The Iraq War proved that in some cases states will act unilaterally or collectively without the legitimacy provided by an IO (in this case, the UN). However, the relatively low level of international support for the United States–led war is in part attributable to the lack of a UN Security Council resolution authorizing the invasion.

IOs can promote peace and stability by establishing norms and principles of conduct and governance among their members. Members must often commit to the rejection of aggression and military force as means of resolving disputes. Over time, this norm of nonviolence may become so pervasive that governments and substate groups will no longer regard military force as an option in the conduct of their affairs with each other. Karl Deutsch referred to such groups of countries as "security communities," which share common values, predictability of behaviour, and mutual responsiveness (the capability and willingness to respond quickly to one another).[36] The European Union (EU) is an example of an IO that can be described as a security community. In addition, IOs often seek to promote domestic values and systems of governance that are regarded as stabilizing and nonaggressive. Examples include the **Organization for Security and Co-operation in Europe (OSCE)**, which is built on the promotion of the principles of democracy and the protection of human rights, and the Organization of American States (OAS), which maintains a unit for the promotion of democracy. Of course, a realist would remind us that these organizations are nothing more than the creations of states and will act only when states agree to act. In contrast, the Marxist perspective would reject security communities and democracy promotion as yet another example of Western imperialism.

In recent years, emphasis has shifted toward regional organizations as conflict management instruments. The hope is that they may contribute to regional peace and security by encouraging and facilitating cooperation among their members, establishing norms for the peaceful resolution of disputes, and acting as conduits for regional efforts to manage conflict. Among the many examples of the involvement of regional organizations in conflict management efforts are the following:

- *The North Atlantic Treaty Organization (NATO).* Founded in 1949 to defend Western Europe against a Soviet attack, NATO has altered its political purpose to the maintenance of stability and has changed its military structure to respond to crises. The Alliance has expanded to include 28 members, and has created a number of consultative instruments to strengthen cooperation between its members and neighbouring states. NATO troops enforced the peace in Bosnia between 1995 and 2004. NATO launched an air war against Serbia in 1999 over the issue of human rights violations in Kosovo, and maintains a security presence in the troubled territory. In August 2003, NATO assumed command of the International Security Assistance Force (ISAF) in Afghanistan. Although political tensions and disagreements are common in the Alliance, it remains the most militarily powerful IO in the world.

- *The Organization of American States (OAS).* Founded in 1948, the OAS was preoccupied with the issue of the spread of communism to Latin America during the Cold War. Since the end of the Cold War, the central tasks of the OAS have been the promotion of mutual security, regional economic and social development, nonintervention and sovereign equality, the peaceful settlement of disputes, and democracy and human rights. In 1994, the OAS initiated the Summit of the Americas process, designed to bring the 34 member states together to solve regional issues. The OAS was involved in the termination of several insurgency conflicts in Central America in the 1990s. In 2001, the OAS adopted the Inter-American Democratic Charter, aimed at promoting democracy in the region. Subsequent Summits have focused on economic development and good governance.

- *The Organization of African Unity (OAU).* Established in 1963, the OAU was built on the concept of Pan-Africanism and the effort to encourage decolonization and economic development. The OAU had some success in mediating conflicts. However, it has failed to address more complex interstate and intrastate disputes such as the Nigerian Civil War, the Ethiopia–Somalia War, and the civil wars in Angola and Mozambique. In 2002, the OAU was replaced by the **African Union** (**AU**), which has deployed peacekeeping missions in Burundi, Darfur, and Somalia. An AU force restored stability to the Comoros in 2008. However, the peacekeeping efforts in Somalia and Darfur have been characterized by inadequate troop contributions and a lack of equipment and financial resources, and in 2008 the AU struggled to respond effectively to a developing political and economic crisis in Zimbabwe. Another African regional organization, the **Economic Community of West African States** (**ECOWAS**), dominated by Nigerian participation, has had mixed results in its efforts to manage the conflicts of West Africa.

- *The Arab League.* Formed in 1945 and now consisting of 22 states, the Arab League was designed to promote cooperation between Arab countries on economic and social affairs, communications, culture, and health. Egypt was expelled for making peace with Israel in 1979 but was readmitted in 1987. As a mechanism for conflict management, the Arab League has not been very successful; most of its proclamations and plans have gone unheeded. It was unable to broker a resolution in the events leading up to Iraq's invasion of Kuwait and ended up authorizing its member states to cooperate with the United States–led coalition against Iraq in 1990–91. Tensions over this decision led several states to boycott the League. Subsequent disagreement over the maintenance of sanctions against Iraq kept the League divided. The League has been criticized for its failure to respond effectively to the Iraq War, and it has had little or no impact in resolving interstate or intrastate conflicts among its members.

- *The Association of Southeast Asian Nations (ASEAN).* ASEAN was formed in 1967 and now consists of 10 member states. Formally a mechanism for regional cooperation, ASEAN has addressed a widening range of issues from trade liberalization to refugees to the drug trade. ASEAN has moved slowly into the realm of security issues. It played a significant role in ending the Vietnamese occupation of Cambodia. Today, ASEAN is the basis for regional political and security arrangements, including joint military exercises. ASEAN members are involved (often as a collective) in larger Pacific-wide cooperation initiatives, such as the Asia-Pacific Economic Cooperation (APEC) arrangement. In 1993, ASEAN expanded its security role with the creation of the ASEAN Regional Forum (ARF). However, there has been little progress on deepening security cooperation in this forum.

In part, this trend toward regionalism in conflict management is due to the perennial challenges facing the UN (see Chapter 5). Short of money and resources, the UN has found it increasingly difficult to maintain its current obligations and programs and even harder to undertake new operations and tasks. However, the turn to regional organizations is also a function of the belief that they are more effective as conflict management instruments within their respective regions than universal organizations such as the UN. Indeed, the UN Charter calls explicitly for cooperation between the two levels.

Regional organizations do have advantages when addressing crises or wars within their own region. First, their members will be more familiar with local disputes and tensions and will place the conflict in the hands of locals rather than in the distant headquarters of the UN. Second, regional organizations may not be constrained by disagreements among countries at the UN. To the extent that a regional consensus exists on a response to a crisis or conflict, a local mechanism may prove more capable of a response than a divided UN Security Council (or General Assembly). Third, regional organizations, by virtue of their geographic proximity, are better able to respond quickly than the UN is, particularly if a peacekeeping or intervention force is required. In some cases, regional organizations may have better capabilities than the UN and a more streamlined political and military decision-making structure (this is certainly the case with NATO).

However, regional organizations also have some drawbacks. First, the fact that local actors are involved may lead some of these actors to pursue their own interests in the crisis or conflict. Similarly, the parties to a dispute may feel that local actors and regional organizations lack the requisite neutrality and impartiality to act as mediators or facilitators. Second, regional organizations are often incapable of offering sufficient rewards (such as economic aid) or acting on threatened punishments (such as economic sanctions). Most regional organizations lack the economic resources and military capabilities to undertake significant action. In many cases they are unable under their respective charters to undertake such actions, and they are unable to enforce their will on states by any means other than moral appeal. Third, most regional organizations in the world do not have a high level of political or military cohesion. The members of such organizations are often deeply divided, and a meaningful consensus is often very difficult to achieve. Nonetheless, the potential certainly exists for regional organizations to play an increased role in conflict management, especially in cooperation with other organizations.

FROM UNITED NATIONS PEACEKEEPING TO HUMANITARIAN INTERVENTION

From its inception, the UN was first and foremost a security institution, designed to establish peace and security in the post–World War II world. As stated in the first sentence of the Preamble to the Charter, the UN was intended to "save succeeding generations from the scourge of war."[37] The UN was designed as a collective security system, and the UN Charter committed member states to resolve their differences peacefully and refrain from the use of force.[38] However, the UN Charter also recognized the limitations of collective security as experienced by the League of Nations. Under Article 51 of the Charter, UN member states retain the right of self-defence, and under Article 52, member states retain the right to engage in regional arrangements (such as alliances) to protect their security.

The conflict management provisions of the UN are found in Chapters 6 and 7 of the UN Charter. Chapter 6, entitled "Pacific Settlement of Disputes," calls on member states to resolve their disputes through "negotiation, enquiry, mediation, conciliation, arbitration, judicial settlement, resort to regional agencies or arrangements, or other peaceful means of their own choice." Chapter 7, entitled "Action with Respect to Threats to the Peace, Breaches of the Peace, and Acts of Aggression," is the heart of the collective security function of the UN. In Article 40, the UN Security Council may call on the parties to a dispute to abide by Security Council resolutions concerning the conflict. In Article 41, the UN Security Council can then call on member states to observe measures directed at the parties to a dispute that do not involve the use of force (these are commonly sanctions in some form). Finally, if these measures prove inadequate, the Security Council can invoke Article 42, which reads

> Should the Security Council consider that measures provided for in Article 41 would be inadequate, it may take such action by air, sea, or land forces as may be necessary to maintain or restore international peace and security. Such actions may include demonstrations, blockade, and other operations by air, sea, or land forces of Members of the United Nations.

Chapter 7 also specifies the obligation of member states to provide forces, facilities, and transit rights for such operations.

During the Cold War the UN was unable to perform its collective security function because of disagreements between the United States and the Soviet Union in the Security Council. Only the Korean anomaly (see Chapter 3) stands as an example of UN collective security in action during the Cold War. As a result, the most visible and significant conflict management role performed by the UN since its creation has been peacekeeping. Between 1948 and 2008, the UN created 63 peacekeeping operations, a remarkable achievement considering that peacekeeping was an improvisation and is not even mentioned in the UN Charter. The origin of UN peacekeeping lies in the use of observer and truce supervision missions, a tradition drawn from the experience of the League of Nations.[39] The UN established observer missions in 1947 during the Greek Civil War, in 1948 after the Arab–Israeli War, and in 1949 after a war between India and Pakistan. However, the term "peacekeeping" was not coined until 1956, when the Suez Crisis prompted (under the suggestion of Canadian Secretary of State for External Affairs Lester B. Pearson) the creation of the first United Nations Emergency Force (see Profile 7.4).

PROFILE 7.4 **The United Nations Emergency Force**

The Suez Crisis was precipitated by the nationalization of the Suez Canal by Egypt on July 26, 1956. Three months later, Israel, France, and Great Britain invaded Egypt. Israel sought to damage the Egyptian military in a preemptive war, while France and Great Britain were attempting to seize the canal. The invasion was widely condemned by the international community, including the United States. Under pressure from domestic opposition and from Washington, the warring parties agreed to a ceasefire on November 6–7. In previous weeks, Canada had proposed the creation of a UN force and had supplied a draft resolution and presented it to the General Assembly for approval. The creation of the United Nations Emergency Force (UNEF) satisfied many interests. France and Great Britain were spared some of the embarrassment of being forced to obey the United States; the United States achieved an end to the war without direct intervention. Canada prevented a serious rift between the United States and Great Britain; Egypt secured the canal; and Israel obtained a ceasefire after damaging the Egyptian armed forces. Launched on November 4, 1956, under a UN General Assembly resolution, the mission was mandated to secure and supervise the cessation of hostilities and facilitate the withdrawal of France, Great Britain, and Israel from Egyptian territory, and to serve as a buffer between Egyptian and Israeli forces. UNEF began to deploy after the ceasefire was in place. It reached a strength of 6,000 personnel, from Brazil, Canada, Colombia, Denmark, Finland, India, Indonesia, Norway, Sweden, and Yugoslavia. UNEF I was the beginning of the prominent role Canada would play in UN peacekeeping missions throughout the Cold War. However, UNEF I was expelled from Egypt in 1967, and another Arab–Israeli war soon followed.

Patrolling the Green Line. A British soldier with the United Nations Force in Cyprus walks the Green Line between the Greek- and Turkish-controlled parts of the island. This part of the Green Line, which runs through the Old City in Nicosia, is only three metres wide. In April 2004, Greek Cypriots rejected a UN-brokered peace plan to reunite the island. (CP Photo/Jeff McIntosh/STRJMC.)

These early experiences laid the foundation for UN peacekeeping during the Cold War. Over time, a set of conventions about the composition, aims, and tasks of peacekeeping operations emerged, which were for the most part consistently followed in most UN peacekeeping operations. The conventions of what came to be called "traditional" peacekeeping included:

- *Impartiality.* No side should be favoured by UN peacekeepers. Unlike Chapter 7 collective security operations, UN peacekeeping did not identify an aggressor (although an individual's acts could be condemned and blame assigned).

- *Nonhostile and lightly armed personnel.* As UN peacekeepers were not present to engage in offensive military operations and could not appear to be a coercive presence, UN peacekeepers were unarmed or lightly armed (generally with service rifles and side arms) for self-defence only.

- *Consent.* Respect for state sovereignty required the UN to obtain the consent of the parties to a dispute before a UN force could be dispatched. The UN presence also depended on host consent to remain in place.[40]

- *Keep, but don't make, the peace.* UN peacekeepers could not create the conditions for their own success. A peace had to be in place before the peacekeeping operation was deployed. Put simply, there had to be a peace to keep.

- *Military personnel.* UN operations were carried out primarily by individuals with military status.

- *Proper authorization.* UN peacekeepers had to be dispatched under UN authorization (or by organizations authorized to do so by the UN). In practice, this has generally meant the Security Council (although some early missions were authorized by the General Assembly), which also established the mandate for the mission (the legal and operational boundaries of the mission) and the rules of engagement (the legal and operational boundaries of the personnel in the mission).

- *Reliance on member states.* As the UN had no army, UN peacekeeping operations were entirely dependent on contributions of money, personnel, and equipment from member states.

- *Nonterritoriality.* Peacekeeping personnel patrolled a zone or line that had been negotiated by the parties to a dispute. They had no legal claim to that territory, nor did they exercise sovereignty over it.

The tasks of traditional UN peacekeeping included interposing between belligerents, gathering information and facts, observing ceasefire lines and reporting violations, supervising the withdrawal of belligerent forces, defusing tensions, preventing or controlling the outbreak of violence, assisting in the maintenance of order, acting as mediators and buffers between the parties to a dispute, and engaging in humanitarian tasks. For the most part, UN peacekeeping operations during the Cold War conformed to the above principles and tasks. UN peacekeeping operations thus occupied a middle ground between Chapter 6 and Chapter 7 of the UN Charter, leading to their description by former UN Secretary-General Dag Hammarskjöld as "Chapter Six-and-a-half" operations. By the end of the Cold War, peacekeeping had established itself as one of the most visible and respected of UN functions, and UN peacekeepers were collectively awarded the Nobel Peace Prize in 1988.

However, the character and qualities of peacekeeping operations began to change by 1990–91 for several reasons. First, intrastate conflicts dominated the international security agenda, and these conflicts were often identified as threats to international peace and security. The UN (and specifically the UN Security Council) therefore became engaged to an unprecedented degree in communal, intrastate conflicts. Second, the Security Council, freed from the constraints of the Cold War, was more capable of reaching agreements on the creation of peacekeeping forces. Third, there was much optimism that the UN would be able to perform as the instrument of international peace and security, as the drafters of the UN Charter had intended. This optimism was reflected in *An Agenda for Peace*, a document prepared in 1992 by Secretary-General Boutros Boutros-Ghali, in which he proposed to enhance the role of the UN in international peace and security:

> In these past months a conviction has grown, among nations large and small, that an opportunity has been regained to achieve the great objectives of the Charter—a United Nations capable of maintaining international peace and security, of securing justice and human rights and of promoting, in the words of the Charter, "social progress and better standards of life in larger freedom." This opportunity must not be squandered. The Organization must never again be crippled as it was in the era that has now passed.[41]

As a result, the number of peacekeeping operations mounted by the UN surged. In 1988, the UN was operating five missions, consisting of a total of 13,000 personnel, at a cost of US$266 million. However, by 1994 the UN was operating 17 missions, with 76 500 personnel deployed, at a cost of over US$3.3 billion.[42] Peacekeeping had become the preferred method of responding to the many intrastate conflicts that confronted UN member states in the early to mid-1990s. Not only did UN missions experience a surge in frequency, the missions themselves experienced a number of qualitative changes.[43] These changes included:

- *Increased size.* The size of many UN operations increased dramatically. The big three UN operations of the post–Cold War period—the United Nations Transitional Authority in Cambodia (UNTAC), the United Nations Protection Force in the Former Yugoslavia (UNPROFOR), and the second United Nations Operation in Somalia (UNOSOM II)—all deployed more than 20,000 personnel at their peak. During the Cold War, only the UN Operation in the Congo (ONUC) approached this size. Several other UN operations also deployed more than 6,000 personnel each.

- *Deployment within states.* Most post–Cold War UN peacekeeping operations have been conducted within the borders of states. As a result, while peacekeeping personnel may still perform missions associated with traditional peacekeeping, such as supervisory and observer tasks, they are doing so not between states but between warring parties within states. Often, there is no clear boundary between the combatants, and therefore no clear "line" to be patrolled.

- *Lack of consent.* Many UN peacekeeping operations took place in states experiencing intrastate war characterized by a humanitarian crisis and violations of human rights (see Chapter 6). In these cases, consent was difficult to obtain because governments were either nonexistent or opposed to UN action. Often the UN sought consent from the next-highest level of authority: the warring communal groups and factions themselves. However, this often proved difficult to achieve in negotiations if one or more parties opposed UN intervention. As a result, the UN faced a dilemma: Should it deploy a mission without consent or fail to respond to a humanitarian crisis? As a result, peacekeeping missions were often deployed without the consent of one or more of the warring factions.

- *Operations in hostile environments.* Many post–Cold War UN peacekeeping missions were deployed in areas in which there was no peace to keep. Negotiated arrangements among the warring factions were either nonexistent or fragile. As a result, UN contingents attempting to facilitate the delivery of humanitarian relief or to establish safe areas for refugees have encountered obstruction and threats, and have come under armed attack both from organized communal groups and from lawless bands of armed individuals not under firm political control.

- *Increased use of force.* The UN has also demonstrated a greater willingness to employ force and the threat of force during peacekeeping missions, in part because of the erosion of the principle of consent. The UN was widely criticized (particularly in UNPROFOR and UNOSOM II) for standing by while humanitarian relief supplies were blocked, human rights abuses were perpetrated, and UN personnel were obstructed and abused. In response, the UN employed a greater level of force against warring parties, and UN contingents became more heavily armed. However, this placed UN peacekeepers at risk of retaliatory attacks and undermined the impartiality of the UN force.

- *Proliferation of mission tasks.* The scope of UN missions has also changed. UN contingents now perform a much wider range of mission tasks. These include electoral support or management (Cambodia), judiciary and policy reform (El Salvador), refugee resettlement (Mozambique), facilitation of the delivery of humanitarian relief supplies (former Yugoslavia), disarmament of warring factions and weapons cantonment (former Yugoslavia), mine clearing and education (Cambodia), and protection of safe areas (former Yugoslavia). As a result, UN operations now include a wide variety of functional experts, such as civilian police, electoral personnel, human rights experts, and information specialists, and often involve close cooperation with aid and humanitarian relief agencies.

- *Peacebuilding and national reconstruction.* Many of the above tasks have a long-term objective: the reconstruction of a viable, stable country, including the repair of infrastructure, the creation of democratic political processes, and the entrenchment of law and civil society. This ambitious process is based on the belief that establishing ceasefires and a peace arrangement is not enough; the underlying conditions for peace must be created if a UN effort is to be successful over the long term. As Boutros-Ghali put it, "UN operations now may involve nothing less than the reconstruction of an entire society and state. This requires a comprehensive approach, over an extended period. Security is increasingly understood to involve social, economic, environmental, and cultural aspects far beyond its traditional military dimension."[44] This objective has transformed UN peacekeeping operations from almost exclusively military operations to missions coordinating a vast aid and development effort.[45]

As a consequence of the changing nature of peacekeeping operations and the different environments in which they were operating, UN peacekeeping experienced what can only be described as a time of troubles in the post–Cold War period. Highly publicized UN failures in the former Yugoslavia, Somalia, and Rwanda revealed the mismatch between traditional peacekeeping and the intrastate communal conflicts of the post–Cold War world.

Yugoslavia. The UN experience in Yugoslavia was, at best, mixed. Although the UN Protection Force (UNPROFOR) succeeded in facilitating the delivery of humanitarian relief to the civilian population, the UN failed to end hostilities in Bosnia-Herzegovina. UN personnel were the targets of intimidation and harassment, and were shot at and taken hostage. All sides during the Bosnian war routinely defied the UN. In one incident that has become a symbol of UN futility in Bosnia, Dutch peacekeepers protecting a UN safe area around Srebrenica found themselves outgunned by the Bosnian Serbs and withdrew, leaving the Muslim inhabitants to their fate (an estimated 7,000 Muslim men were subsequently massacred). It was the shifting nature of the military balance on the ground, the intervention of NATO, and the use of air strikes that prompted the signing of the Dayton Agreement in 1995. The implementation of the settlement was facilitated by the deployment of 60,000 NATO troops.

Somalia. The UN experience in Somalia was almost a complete failure. UNOSOM I was initially deployed to facilitate the delivery of humanitarian relief supplies. The obstruction of UN and aid agency efforts and the continued fighting in Somalia prompted the creation of the United States–led Unified Task Force (UNITAF), authorized under Chapter 7 of the UN Charter. While UNITAF was initially successful in achieving order, it became involved in a shooting war against one of Somalia's factions. Because of casualties to U.S. forces, UNITAF was deactivated and replaced by UNOSOM II. However, the failure to establish a peace settlement and the continued fighting in Somalia led to the withdrawal of UNOSOM II in March 1995. Although many lives were saved, Somalia is no closer to political stability today than it was before UN intervention.

A sad return. Roméo Dallaire, right, with a Rwandan security guard in Kigali, April 5, 2004, the 10th anniversary of the beginning of the Rwandan genocide (see Chapter 9). Dallaire is the retired Canadian general whose UN peacekeepers had to stand by helplessly as the slaughter unfolded. Dallaire, who went into suicidal depression because of his experiences in Rwanda, was on his first visit back to the country. Now a Senator in the Canadian parliament, he has emerged as one of the leading public proponents of humanitarian intervention in Sudan and elsewhere. (AP Photo/Sayyid Azim//CP Archive.)

Rwanda. The call for the creation of a UN force for Rwanda came on the heels of the Somalia imbroglio. A conflict between the Hutu government and the Tutsi-led Rwandan Patriotic Front (RPF) had been raging for decades. A peace settlement (the Arusha Accords) was signed in August 1993, and the United Nations Assistance Mission for Rwanda (UNAMIR) began deploying later that year. However, in 1994 an orchestrated genocide began in Rwanda. The UN force commander, Canadian General (and now senator) Roméo Dallaire, has often argued that if he had been given more troops and an appropriate mandate, he could have prevented the worst of the genocide. In fact, neither was forthcoming, and UN member states (remembering the Somalia experience) refused to acknowledge that genocide was under way, and actually reduced the size of UNAMIR. By then, at least 500,000 people had died, and many more would die as the world watched and did nothing.[46]

The story of post–Cold War UN peacekeeping is not entirely one of failure. The UN made some progress in reinforcing peace in Cambodia (UNTAC) and Angola (UNAVEM). Mozambique (UNOMOZ) is widely regarded as a success, and the UN has made some progress in restructuring the police and the judiciary in El Salvador (ONUSAL). However, these relative successes have been obscured by the high-profile failures in Yugoslavia, Somalia, and Rwanda. Because of these failures, the credibility of the UN as an effective conflict management instrument has been called into question. Much of the criticism has been directed at the UN itself. Former UN Assistant Secretary-General for Political Affairs Giandomenico Picco argued that "neither the post–Cold War climate nor civil wars can rightfully be blamed for the failures that have beset the United Nations since 1991. One must look to the workings of the United Nations itself."[47] Saadia Touval argued that

> It is increasingly apparent that the United Nations possesses inherent characteristics that make it incapable of effectively mediating complex international disputes. It does not serve well as an authoritative channel of communication. It has little real political leverage. Its promises and threats lack credibility. And it is incapable of pursuing coherent, flexible, and dynamic negotiations guided by an effective strategy.[48]

The UN has also been criticized for its inability to manage the peacekeeping operations it has mounted. UN peacekeeping missions have been plagued by a variety of operational problems, including poor communication with UN headquarters in New York; a shortage of long-range transportation and tactical airlift; the uneven quality of troop contributions and incompatibility of equipment; little or no capacity to gather information or intelligence; and slow reaction times, with as much as six months passing before a UN operation is ready to be deployed. A situation faced by Canadian General Lewis Mackenzie while serving with UNPROFOR in the former Yugoslavia dramatically illustrates UN shortcomings. The General, requiring a decision from UN headquarters in New York, was unable to contact anyone on the telephone because he placed his call after office hours!

While much of this criticism is justified, blaming the UN is somewhat misleading. Certainly, the organization struggled to manage the increase in peacekeeping operations, and there are bureaucratic and structural shortcomings within the UN system. However, it is member states that authorize peacekeeping missions (or refuse to do so), provide the mandates for those operations, provide the resources and troops and diplomatic support for those missions, and decide whether those missions are to be renewed or increased or decreased. Often, blaming the UN is a tactic states use to evade responsibility for their actions or inactions. The capacities of the UN are largely dependent on the commitment of member states, and so the UN can hardly be held solely accountable for failures in peacekeeping. As early as 1993, Boutros-Ghali warned: "Our renaissance remains in question; demands made upon the United Nations are not being matched by the resources to do the job."[49] Nevertheless, in the latter half of the 1990s the increased costs and risks involved in peacekeeping made governments increasingly cautious about supporting the creation of new missions or contributing to UN peacekeeping. This caution, in turn, compromised the ability of the UN to mount successful operations.

In the face of such problems, some attempts have been made to improve the capacity of the UN to create and deploy peacekeeping missions. The Department of Peacekeeping

Operations (DPKO) has created a 24-hour situation centre that provides UN headquarters with command, control, and communications capabilities. In 1992, a Humanitarian Early Warning System was created. In 1993 a UN Standby Arrangements system established a list of forces member states were willing to contribute to UN operations. A logistics base stockpile was established at Brindisi, Italy. Prompted by a Canadian study conducted after the failure in Rwanda, in 1995 the UN established a rapidly deployable peacekeeping headquarters designed to react swiftly in times of need. The long-standing suggestion that the UN should possess its own army continues to founder because of opposition from most member states who fear the creation of a military instrument under UN control and because of the prohibitive costs of such a venture. In August 2000, the UN released the *Report of the Panel on UN Peacekeeping Operations*, otherwise known as the Brahimi Report. As a result, DPKO has been restructured and in June 2007 a new Department of Field Support was established to strengthen the logistics support available to UN field missions. The UN introduced a new operational guidance document in 2008 to establish formal norms and rules governing peacekeeping.[50] These reform efforts have all had some positive impact, but due to monetary shortages and political opposition they must be described as relatively modest developments.

With the UN increasingly regarded as unsuited to the challenges of major regional conflicts and gross violations of human rights, states have turned to regional organizations or "coalitions of the willing" that are unburdened by the constraints of the UN system. Operating with UN authority (this is sometimes called "contracting out") or without UN authority, the regionalization of peacekeeping has diminished the role of the UN. In such cases, the UN no longer exerts direct control over the military mission or the political process, and in effect becomes a legitimating device for the coalitions or regional organizations that are conducting the operation through their own means and according to their own counsel. Nevertheless, UN peacekeeping continues to make a valuable contribution to conflict management efforts worldwide. The past few years have seen an increase in the number of missions and the number of deployed peacekeepers. In January 2009, the UN deployed 16 peacekeeping missions with some 111,828 personnel (91,049 of them military), the largest number of deployed personnel in the history of peacekeeping. In the 2008–2009 UN fiscal year, the peacekeeping budget was approximately US$7.1 billion, a trifle compared to virtually any measure of world military spending but nevertheless the largest ever annual budget allocation for peacekeeping. As of January 2009, the largest UN peacekeeping missions (each deploying over 7,000 military, police, and civilian personnel) were in Liberia, the Congo, Lebanon, Côte D'Ivoire, Haiti, Sudan, and Darfur.[51]

However, peacekeeping continues to face daunting challenges. Operating 16 simultaneous missions has placed a heavy burden on the administrative capacities of the UN system. The UN continues to rely on member states for troops, equipment, and adequate funding, and these are not always forthcoming. Peacekeeping personnel deployed into unstable areas such as Darfur and the Congo have been threatened and attacked. Contributions of troops from rich, industrialized countries have declined: in January 2009 the leading troop contributors were Pakistan, Bangladesh, and India, and only one industrialized country (Italy) was in the top ten. Canada, with a long tradition of participation in UN missions, ranked 49th. In some missions, sexual misconduct and corruption has damaged the reputation of peacekeepers. In addition, the high-profile counterinsurgency operations in Iraq and Afghanistan, as well as the use of terminology such as "stability operations" and "peace support operations" has led to confusion over the distinction between counterinsurgency and peacekeeping. The effectiveness of peacekeeping in the future will be determined by at least three factors: (1) the careful consideration of the demands of a proposed mission and the mandates and capabilities required to carry it out; (2) the willingness of contributing states to offer money and resources, including troops; and (3) the willingness of the parties to a dispute to stop fighting and begin the process of building a peace.

It is in the area of peacebuilding that the UN has become increasingly active. Peacebuilding, as defined by the UN Security Council, "is aimed at preventing the outbreak, the recurrence, or continuation of armed conflict and therefore encompasses a wide range of political, developmental, humanitarian, and human rights programmes and mechanisms."[52] The emergence of peacebuilding coincided with the need to develop the means to consolidate the gains of peace settlements. What point was there to deploying costly and risky UN peacekeeping missions if the underlying causes of conflict were not resolved, and there was no basis for a lasting, self-sustaining peace? By the mid-1990s, the UN peacekeeping missions were engaging in demobilization, disarmament, and reintegration of militias; refugee return; democratization; restoration or introduction of market activity; institution building; promoting dialogue and reconciliation; police and judicial reform; trauma recovery; and development assistance. Peacebuilding is thus based on the promotion of liberal values in societies torn by war or deep social conflict, and assumes that a lasting peace can be achieved through the instruments of the liberal peace formula. In 2005, the UN established a Peacebuilding Commission and a Peacebuilding Fund to increase the ability of the UN to manage and coordinate post-conflict reconstruction. The Commission has been engaged in the peacebuilding effort in Burundi and Sierra Leone, while the Peacebuilding Fund has contributed to several contingencies, all in Africa.

However, peacebuilding has also been criticized. The premise that political and economic liberalization will lead to peace has been challenged as an attempt at "social engineering" that might in fact lead to more conflict in a society as "both democracy and capitalism encourage conflict and competition—indeed, they thrive on it."[53] Many countries in the developing world are suspicious of peacebuilding, worried that it could lead to intervention in the domestic affairs of a society. It also faces the same challenges as peacekeeping: if member states do not support peacebuilding efforts with diplomatic backing, funding, and adequate resources, then UN efforts to build sustainable peace in war-torn societies will be unsuccessful.[54] The sheer magnitude of the task is also significant, since it contemplates nothing less than rebuilding a viable and sustainable country out of the ashes of war and the trauma of violence. Peacebuilding efforts must promote economic and social development, good governance and institutional reform, and social reconciliation and justice, while at the same time dealing with "spoilers" who might wish to derail the peace efforts for their own gain.[55] Perhaps this is why early assessments of peacebuilding success are not encouraging.[56] Nevertheless, peacebuilding remains critically important. Without successful peacebuilding, international military forces will have to remain in war-torn countries for a long time (as has been the case in Cyprus), and the possibility of a return to violence will threaten long-term development efforts.

THE WAR IN LEBANON AND THE UTILITY OF PEACEKEEPING

The conflict in Lebanon is one of the many tragedies of Middle East politics. Since achieving independence at the end of World War II the country experienced long periods of peace and prosperity, developing a reputation as a centre of banking and tourism. However, Lebanon has also had a turbulent and often violent history as a crucible for conflict between the religious factions (Shia, Sunni, and Druze Muslims, and Christians) that inhabit the country. In particular, the Lebanese Civil War (1975–1990) devastated the economy and worsened the sectarian and political divisions in the country. To make matters worse, Lebanon has also served as a battleground for competing regional interests between the United States, Israel, Syria, and Iran, which have supported Lebanese factions to achieve their own objectives. Finally, the Palestine Liberation Organization (PLO) used Lebanon as a base of operations for attacks against Israel during the Lebanese Civil War, and Israel invaded and occupied Lebanese territory in 1978 and again in 1982. An uneasy stability returned to Lebanon after 1990 and economic development and national reconstruction saw the return of financial activity and a revival of the tourist trade.

Lebanon's tragedy continued in July 2006 when Hezbullah fighters attacked an Israeli military patrol, killing three soldiers and taking two others hostage. Hezbullah is a Shia Muslim political, social, and military organization based in Lebanon and supported by Iran. Hezbullah is at the same time a political party with representation in the Lebanese parliament and a military organization dedicated to advancing Shia interests in Lebanese politics and the destruction of Israel. Many Western countries, including the United States and Canada, consider Hezbullah a terrorist organization. In response to the attack and kidnappings, Israeli launched a military campaign in Lebanon, consisting of extensive air strikes and a naval bombardment of Lebanese infrastructure and Hezbullah installations in the south of the country. Hezbullah responded by firing over one hundred missiles per day into Israel (forcing the evacuation of 300,000–500,000 people in northern Israel). Hoping to achieve a decisive victory against Hezbullah, Israel launched a ground offensive into southern Lebanon. The Israeli army encountered stiff resistance from well-prepared and heavily armed Hezbullah fighters. In the meantime, the damage done to southern Lebanon by Israeli air strikes, increasing civilian casualties and the possible collapse of the Lebanese government in the face of the Israeli invasion brought more energy to international conflict management efforts.

When the war broke out there was considerable condemnation of Hezbullah within Lebanon and in Europe and the Middle East, as the kidnapping of the Israeli soldiers was seen as a foolish provocation. This condemnation created an opportunity for Israel (with the support of the U.S.) to continue the military effort to destroy Hezbullah. However, as civilian casualties and media images of human suffering and destroyed buildings and infrastructure in Lebanon increased, opinion turned against Israel and the United States. As hopes for a military victory faded, Israel and the U.S. became more interested in international conflict management efforts. Hezbullah, weakened by the fighting and losing political support in Lebanon, was also willing to consider a ceasefire. Negotiations resulted in a UN Security Council Resolution of August 11, 2006, calling for the withdrawal of Hezbullah and Israeli forces from southern Lebanon and the deployment of a new UN peacekeeping force. A truce between Hezbullah and Israel came into force on August 14. The 33-day war caused considerable human casualties and infrastructure damage. Approximately 1,140 Lebanese civilians (a third of them children) and 43 Israeli civilians were killed.[57] Heavy damage was inflicted on Lebanese infrastructure by the Israeli bombing campaign: thousands of homes and apartments were destroyed along with dozens of bridges, roads, and power facilities. Unexploded munitions and cluster bomblets posed a danger to hundreds of thousands of civilians returning to their homes.[58]

The United Nations Interim Force in Lebanon (UNIFIL) is a prime example of both the limitations and continued relevance of peacekeeping in global politics. The original UNIFIL mission had been deployed along the Lebanese-Israeli border since 1978, but was powerless (in both the legal and the military sense) to prevent the Israeli invasion of Lebanon in 1982. Similarly, when the July War broke out, UNIFIL was powerless to stop the ensuing war and five peacekeepers were killed observing the conflict and providing humanitarian assistance. However, when interest in a ceasefire grew all parties recognized the need for an impartial peacekeeping mission to facilitate and support the provisions of the truce agreement. As a result, when an agreement was approved the UN Security Council authorized the deployment of a larger UNIFIL (sometimes referred to as "UNIFIL II") to southern Lebanon. The new UNIFIL began deployment in mid-September, with French, Italian, and Spanish troops joining the contingents from Ghana and India already in place. As of January 2009 UNIFIL had 12,738 military, police, and civilian personnel deployed in southern Lebanon. Like its predecessor, the new UNIFIL will be unable to resolve the underlying causes of the conflict along the Israeli-Lebanese border, but it has proven once more the utility of peacekeeping as a conflict management instrument.

HUMAN SECURITY AND HUMANITARIAN INTERVENTION

The concept of human security has a complex and controversial relationship with the concept of humanitarian intervention. The genocide in Rwanda was a benchmark in the development of human security because of the recognition that at least 500,000 people were slaughtered while the international community stood by and did nothing. The lesson of Rwanda was that a relatively small military force could have conducted a humanitarian intervention that would have saved many of the lives that were lost. Of course, this would have meant intervening in the internal affairs of Rwanda, but as the human security concept suggests this is no crime if governments cannot protect the human security of their own population (or if governments were actively involved in the persecution of their own population, as was the case in Rwanda). The genocide prompted an effort to get the UN to grapple with the question of when violations of state sovereignty and armed interventions against states would be permissible in the cause of protecting people threatened by gross violations of human rights. However, there was limited enthusiasm for this venture in the UN, where the vast majority of states (especially those in the developing world) stood firm on the principle of sovereignty, arguing it was one of their few protections against interference from powerful states. This prompted an effort to develop a dialogue outside the UN system, which led to the **International Commission on Intervention and State Sovereignty**. This commission consisted of leading experts and practitioners, and with the support of several governments, including Canada, the commission published its final report in December 2001. The final report, titled *The Responsibility to Protect*, argued that

a. State sovereignty implies responsibility, and the primary responsibility for the protection of its people lies with the state itself.

b. Where a population is suffering serious harm, as a result of internal war, insurgency, repression or state failure, and the state in question is unwilling or unable to halt or avert it, the principle of nonintervention yields to the international responsibility to protect.[59]

In 2006, the UN Security Council passed resolution 1674 on the Protection of Civilians in Armed Conflict, for the first time affirming the "Responsibility to Protect" doctrine.[60]

Three prominent examples of humanitarian intervention (Serbia, East Timor), and another example in which intervention has been avoided despite widely acknowledged mass atrocities (Darfur), illustrate the controversies and moral dilemmas associated with the implementation of this concept.

NATO AND HUMANITARIAN INTERVENTION AGAINST SERBIA

Since the creation of Yugoslavia, Kosovo has been a predominantly ethnic Albanian province of Serbia. Tensions grew between the Albanian majority, which called for greater autonomy or outright independence, and the Milosevic government in Belgrade. Violence broke out between Albanian separatists (later called the Kosovo Liberation Army, or KLA) and the Serbian police in the early 1990s. The violence intensified in 1998 and 1999 as an increasingly indiscriminate government campaign aimed at suppressing the KLA escalated into ethnic cleansing disturbingly similar to the kind witnessed in the Bosnian War. Incidents of mass murder became ever more frequent, and a serious refugee crisis developed inside and outside Kosovo. NATO threatened Serbia with air strikes unless the campaign against ethnic Albanians stopped. The Serbian government agreed to attend talks at Rambouillet, France, but refused to sign a peace agreement that would have given Kosovo considerable autonomy and provided for a future referendum on independence. On March 24, 1999, NATO began a bombing campaign against Serbia that would last 78 days until, on June 10, the Milosevic government accepted NATO demands to withdraw its security forces from Kosovo. On June 12, NATO began deployment of Kosovo-force (K-FOR) to restore law and order, demilitarize the KLA, and assist the UN with the restoration of civilian authority.

NATO's campaign against Serbia remains controversial. Critics charge that NATO acted illegally, as no UN resolution was ever passed authorizing the air campaign (K-FOR did have UN approval). Critics also argued that not enough time or effort was given to diplomacy. The bombing campaign itself was criticized as excessive and more damaging to civilian targets than to the Serbian military. NATO had violated the rights of a sovereign state and had in effect severed Kosovo from Serbia by force. Supporters of the NATO campaign argued that Serbia had violated international law, rejected diplomatic overtures, and had engaged in ethnic cleansing, which demanded a swift reaction before more Albanians died and the region became destabilized. To do nothing, supporters argued, would allow ethnic cleansing to continue and risk human rights violations on the scale of those in Bosnia. The air campaign was conducted to avoid civilian casualties as much as possible, and in any case Milosevic could have stopped the bombing by agreeing to terms far earlier. Serbia may have been a sovereign state, but by committing violations of human rights, it had given NATO countries little choice and every right to intervene. The government of Canada was confronted with the decision of whether to contribute to the war, and Foreign Affairs Minister Lloyd Axworthy, who was a champion of human security, grappled with the conflicting morals of intervening and killing Serbian civilians, or not intervening and allowing ethnic cleansing to continue. In the end, Canada participated in the war.

The debate and conflict over Kosovo is a vivid illustration of the dilemmas associated with humanitarian intervention, the right of self-determination, statehood, and international law. The final status of Kosovo has been uncertain since the intervention left the province of Serbia a de facto protectorate of NATO. Since 1999 Kosovo has been governed though a UN administration in cooperation with elected Kosovar Albanian representatives. Efforts to resolve the final status of Kosovo stumbled on a key point: the government of Serbia maintained that Kosovo was part of Serbia while Kosovar Albanians wanted independence and statehood for Kosovo. Complicating the dispute was the existence of a Serbian minority in Kosovo (approximately 10 percent of the population) which largely refused to accept independence, and the periodic violence between Albanians and Serbians in Kosovo that inflamed tensions between the two groups. The refusal of either party to compromise led to years of diplomatic stalemate. In 2006 a UN Special Envoy (former Finnish President Martti Ahtissari) acted as a third-party mediator to facilitate a diplomatic settlement between the Serbian government and the Kosovar Albanian leadership. Ahtissari's efforts failed and in the end he submitted a plan to the UN Security Council in March 2007 which called for the independence of Kosovo.

The Ahtissari plan was heavily criticized by the government of Serbia, which argued (correctly) that Kosovo was legally a province of Serbia and any forced independence of the province would violate Serbian sovereignty and constitute a breach of international law. On the other hand, the Ahtissari plan was welcomed by the Kosovo Albanian leadership, which argued that Kosovo Albanians clearly wanted self-determination and could not be expected to live in Serbia after the atrocities of 1999. UN Security Council Resolution 1244 (which ended NATO's military campaign against Serbia in 1999) complicated matters, for it recognized the sovereignty of Serbia but also called for a final settlement based on the will of the people! This classic demonstration of the inherent tension between the rights of sovereignty and the rights of self-determination caused international debate and conflict between Russia (which supported its traditional ally, Serbia) and most Western democracies, which supported Kosovo's independence. Russia used its Security Council position to block proposed resolutions on Kosovo's independence. In the absence of an agreed-upon international framework, Kosovar Albanians took matters into their own hands and declared independence on February 17, 2008. A month later, 28 countries (including Canada, after a period of awkward indecision) had recognized Kosovo's independence. A major international presence led by the UN, NATO and the European Union is assisting the fledgling state with its institutions and with internal security. However, the long-term stability of Kosovo is very much in question.[61]

AUSTRALIA AND HUMANITARIAN INTERVENTION IN EAST TIMOR

East Timor was a Portuguese colony for almost 500 years. In 1975, it was invaded by Indonesia and subjected to a brutal occupation that saw at least 200,000 deaths between 1975 and 1980 alone from executions, starvation, and military operations. East Timor became a symbol of the world's failure to respond to such human rights disasters. In 1998, a leadership change in Indonesia opened the way for a UN-supervised referendum on independence. However, violence perpetrated by pro-Indonesian militias supported by the Indonesian Army required the postponement of the referendum. Finally, on August 30, 1999, an extraordinary 98 percent of registered voters went to the polls despite threats of physical violence. Almost 80 percent voted against remaining tied to Indonesia. The pro-Indonesian militias reacted with a campaign of violence and intimidation, which rapidly escalated into the pillaging of East Timor. Faced with a humanitarian crisis, an Australian-led coalition developed plans for an intervention force to restore order and protect the East Timorese people. The proposed force received UN approval on September 15, and on September 20, an Australian-led force of 8,000 personnel began arriving in East Timor with the grudging consent of the Indonesian government. The force moved quickly to establish order and forced the militias out of East Timor. In February 2000 the Australian-led force withdrew and was replaced by a UN peacekeeping force. On May 20, 2002, East Timor became fully independent and changed its name to Timor-Leste, and joined the United Nations as the 191st member state.

It is difficult to find a critic of the Australian-led humanitarian intervention in East Timor because of the circumstances of the intervention, which included a clear moral purpose, UN authorization, and the consent of the Indonesian government. In this case, the circumstances were quite different from those confronted by NATO in Kosovo. However, some critics wonder why it took so long for the international community to respond to Indonesia's brutality in East Timor (which had lasted for almost 25 years). For most of that time, governments traded with Indonesia, participated in IOs with Indonesia, and held summits with Indonesian leaders. It took a change in East Asia's security environment (a consequence of the end of the Cold War), a change in the Indonesian government, the collapse of the Indonesian economy in the Asian financial crisis, and another humanitarian crisis to create the conditions for the outside world to respond to one of the longest-lasting human rights outrages in the world.[62]

Many welcome the idea of humanitarian intervention as a positive development, because it represents a willingness to act in support of human rights and international humanitarian law and against those regimes that perpetrate atrocities against groups of people. The alternative—to stand by and do nothing or wait for sanctions to work—is simply unacceptable. The big question then becomes one of resources: humanitarian intervention (or intervention of any kind) requires globally deployable military forces, and these are in increasingly short supply and have to be buttressed if humanitarian interventions are to be conducted in the future.[63] Critics argue that humanitarian intervention is seldom purely humanitarian, is selectively and inconsistently applied, and often results in the deaths of innocent civilians and the destruction of civilian infrastructure. The legal, moral, and political terms of this debate are now an important part of the debate over humanitarian intervention in Darfur.

HUMANITARIAN INTERVENTION IN DARFUR

Sudan has experienced numerous civil wars rooted in regional inequality, grievances over access to land and resources, culture and religion, and population movement and climate change. The war in the North, West, and South Darfur provinces (collectively referred to simply as "Darfur") has received considerable international attention, a reflection of the scale of human suffering, the spread of the conflict to neighbouring Chad and the Central African Republic, and the spotlight the Beijing Olympics has cast on China's support for the Sudanese government. The conflict in Darfur broke out in 2003, when two political movements composed of local African tribal groups rebelled against the government. In an effort to defeat the rebellion, the Sudanese government armed and supported an Arab "Janjaweed" militia that conducted an ethnic cleansing campaign against the African population of Darfur. According to most estimates, approximately 300,000 people in Darfur have been killed, and over two million have been displaced.[64] Villages throughout the region have been destroyed, and massacres and rape have been commonplace. Many humanitarian and aid organizations referred to the conflict as a genocide, a description echoed by U.S. President George Bush in June 2005.[65] The situation has been complicated by the evolution of the conflict, as noted by the International Crisis Group: "The Darfur conflict ... has evolved from a rebellion with relatively defined political aims to a conflict increasingly overshadowed by shifting alliances, defections, regional and international meddling and a growing, complex tribal dimension."[66]

Efforts to stop the conflict in Darfur have met with limited success largely due to the inability of the Sudanese government and rebel groups to reach a negotiated settlement, and the reluctance of the Sudanese government to accept international involvement without significant constraints. UN sanctions imposed on the country in 2004 and 2005 failed to stop or reduce the level of violence. In 2004, negotiations between the Sudanese government and the AU resulted in the deployment of a 7,000-strong African Union Mission in Sudan (AMIS). However, AMIS was unable to quell the violence due to a lack of military capacity (especially transport) and the reluctance of the government and the rebels to stop fighting. As the conflict began to spread to neighbouring countries (most notably Chad) and rebel factions began to fight among themselves, international efforts to mediate an end to the war increased. After seven unsuccessful attempts at negotiation since 2003, a peace agreement was signed between the government and one of the main rebel factions in May 2006. However, the settlement quickly broke down and violence resumed across Darfur, with frequent attacks on civilians, aid workers, and AMIS personnel. As a result, the Sudanese government came under intense international pressure to agree to the deployment of a UN peacekeeping force in Darfur to support AMIS. The government finally agreed to accept such a force in June 2007 and a UN Security Council Resolution on July 31 established the United Nations/African Union Mission in Darfur (UNAMID), a hybrid mission jointly operated by the two organizations. As conceived, UNAMID is supposed to deploy close to 20,000 troops (mostly from African

Soldiers of the United Nations/African Union Mission in Darfur (UNAMID) drive through the Kalma refugee camp in 2008. UNAMID has been criticized for failing to adequately protect civilians in Darfur, but it remains under-strength and short of vital equipment. (AP Photo/Sarah El Deeb/CP Archive.)

counties) as well as 6,000 police and a large civilian peacebuilding component, making it one of the largest peacekeeping missions ever mounted. However, contributions of troops and equipment have been slow to materialize, and the Sudanese government has been uncooperative and continues to receive diplomatic support from China, Russia, and some Arab states. Meanwhile, the violence in Darfur continues and now threatens stability in the Central African Republic and Chad.

The conflict in Darfur has provoked international outrage and calls for a humanitarian intervention to stop the violence. Advocates of more forceful humanitarian intervention have drawn parallels to the meek and wholly inadequate international response to the Rwandan genocide. The hope that the "Responsibility to Protect" framework might help avoid a repetition of genocide has been dashed by the events in Darfur. Of course, an intervention there would be no easy matter. The Sudanese government would not welcome such an intervention, and would cast it as yet another invasion of a Muslim country by the West. Any intervention force would have to be large and very well equipped to stabilize a territory almost as large as France. It would also undercut the efforts of the AU to take the lead on Darfur. And because Sudan is supported by China (which imports oil from Sudan), it is unlikely that any intervention would have the approval of the UN Security Council. Of course, all of these political constraints are of little solace to the civilians of Darfur, who have suffered horribly since 2003. As of late 2009, UNAMID had still not reached its full authorized strength and was trying to carry out its mission tasks even as the war and attacks on civilians and humanitarian aid workers continued.

SANCTIONS AND CONFLICT MANAGEMENT

Economic sanctions are "deliberate government actions to inflict economic deprivation on a target state or society, through the limitation or cessation of customary economic relations."[67] Economic sanctions, therefore, are coercive instruments. Nevertheless, they have been employed as instruments of conflict management in the international system. Economic sanctions may take several forms, including trade boycotts, embargoes, or restrictions on financial interactions (such as access to overseas assets or international financial institutions). Sanctions may be imposed unilaterally by one state, or multilaterally, by a group of states (or by the membership of an IO). When sanctions are imposed, the sending or initiating countries might have a number of possible goals or aims:

- *Compliance:* "to force the target to alter its behaviour to conform with the initiator's preferences"
- *Subversion:* "to remove the target's leaders or overthrow the regime"
- *Deterrence:* "to dissuade the target from repeating the disputed action in the future"
- *International symbolism:* "to send messages to other members of the world community"
- *Domestic symbolism:* "to increase its domestic support or thwart international criticism of its foreign policies by acting decisively"[68]

The use of sanctions has deep historical roots. In his history of the Peloponnesian War, Thucydides describes a trade embargo put in place by Athens against Megara, a Spartan ally. Under Napoleonic domination, most of continental Europe limited grain sales to Great Britain. However, the use of sanctions increased dramatically in the 20th century. One study found that since World War I, economic sanctions have been used 120 times, with 104 of those examples occurring since World War II.[69] The increased use of economic sanctions as an instrument of policy can be explained by the attractiveness of sanctions as a policy choice. Diplomatic measures, although they may carry the weight of the displeasure of one country against another or the force of global or world opinion, tend not to have the same strength as other instruments for two reasons: (1) the leverage one can exert against a target state is limited; and (2) the sending or initiating countries incur few costs, so diplomatic measures are less credible as expressions of will or commitment. On the other hand, military measures are both costly and risky. Therefore, sanctions are often an attractive option because although costs are involved (the severing of some or all economic ties with the target state), they do not carry the costs of military action and have more credibility than mere diplomatic measures.

Despite the frequency of their use, the effectiveness of economic sanctions in achieving their goals has been limited at best. The consensus is that when results are measured against goals and objectives, economic sanctions usually fail and often harm the most vulnerable people in target states. One study found that between 1914 and 1989, "although sanctions were successful in 34 percent of 115 cases ... success has become increasingly elusive in recent years.... The success rate among [the 46] cases begun after 1973 was a little less than 26 percent."[70] Several possible explanations exist as to why the success rate of economic sanctions is so low:

- The target state is usually able to find alternative sources of supply or markets for its exports (for this reason, unilateral sanctions are frequently ineffective, and most sanction efforts are multilateral in nature).

- In target states, sanctions may provoke nationalist sentiments and a willingness to sacrifice in the name of resistance against outside interference.

- Sanctions may do the most harm to the very people they are supposed to benefit. Authoritarian rulers who care little for the economic hardships of their people will not be swayed by sanctions. The people will suffer for the actions of their leadership. As Jim Hoagland has observed: "The logic of the policy seems to be to make unarmed citizens desperate enough to rise up and throw off the brutal regimes that other powers are not willing to use the world's best armies to topple."[71]

- Sanctions are often undercut by the actions of domestic companies, the companies of other countries, or by foreign governments. The longer sanctions last, the greater the likelihood that they will erode and collapse.[72]

- The imposition of sanctions can actually increase the power of undesirable political elites in the target country, as the sanctions can be used to justify their increased control over the country, or to create a lucrative environment for black market activity. Sanctions can also create a "rally around the flag" effect that can boost the popularity of an authoritarian leader.

- Sending or initiating countries can have inflated expectations about the utility of sanctions. Economic deprivation has never been a reliable means of forcing political change; the political context is usually a more important factor in the political outcome.[73]

The success of sanctions appears to depend on several variables. First, the relationship between the state (or states) sending the sanctions and the target is very important. If the target state is less economically powerful than the sending states, or is a close trading partner, economic sanctions will have a greater effect on the target country. Second, when countries impose sanctions quickly and decisively, and when sanctions do not involve significant economic hardships for sending countries, the sanctions will have greater credibility because they will be sustainable over time. Third, clear conditions must be established for the lifting of sanctions. In other words, it must be clear to the target country why the sanctions were imposed and what actions they must undertake to have them lifted. Furthermore, if objectives are broad and general, sanctions will not have the same chance of success as if the objectives are specific and clearly defined. Sanctions should, therefore, be imposed to give the target country an incentive to change certain specific policies rather than as a

---

PROFILE 7.5 Sanctions

QUALIFIED SUCCESS AND THE CASE OF SOUTH AFRICA

The South African apartheid regime was a prominent human rights issue during the Cold War. Apartheid institutionalized racial separation and discrimination against the black majority in South Africa, and to end this system sanctions were imposed on South Africa from a variety of sources. The UN imposed a voluntary arms embargo against South Africa in 1963, and this was made mandatory in 1977. Many other countries, including Canada, began to impose stronger unilateral sanctions against South Africa as well. In addition, campaigns in many countries led many corporations and social institutions (such as universities) to divest themselves of their interests and operations in South Africa. However, stiffer multilateral sanctions against South Africa could not be imposed because of the opposition of Great Britain and the United States. Both countries argued that sanctions would hurt only the black African majority in South Africa. Critics charged that the United States was being soft on South Africa because of its importance as a source of raw minerals and its opposition to communism in Africa. However, in 1985 Congress overrode a presidential veto and imposed harsh economic sanctions against South Africa. In 1989, F. W. de Klerk came to power in South Africa, intent on reform. He released the long-time jailed leader of the **African National Congress (ANC)**, Nelson Mandela. In 1993, apartheid was dismantled.

Sanctions were lifted, and South Africa was no longer an isolated country.

Did sanctions succeed in this case? The consensus is that they played a role. The South African economy was certainly damaged by sanctions, as trade fell, debt rose, loans were not renewed, foreign investment declined, and growth rates declined. Two questions remain: How much of this economic damage was due to sanctions, and how much was due to falling world prices for gold (a key South African foreign-exchange earner)? What would have happened had a hard-line South African leader determined to resist sanctions come to power, instead of the reform-minded de Klerk? In any event, the South African example stands as a success story for sanctions.

QUALIFIED FAILURE AND THE CASE OF IRAQ

When Iraq invaded Kuwait in 1990 the international community responded with diplomatic expressions of opposition and economic sanctions. These sanctions were organized through the United Nations and included a total ban on imports and exports to and from Iraq, with the exception of humanitarian imports such as medicine and some foodstuffs. Iraq was a vulnerable target, as its main export was oil, and it was heavily dependent on food imports. The stated goal of sanctions was to compel Saddam Hussein's government to withdraw from Kuwait. However, military force was eventually used to eject Iraqi forces from Kuwait.

(continued)

PROFILE 7.5 Sanctions (*continued*)

After the end of the Gulf War, sanctions remained in place against Iraq. The goal of the sanctions was to compel Saddam Hussein to cooperate with United Nations Special Commission (UNSCOM) weapons inspectors seeking to destroy Iraq's weapons of mass destruction program. Between 1991 and 1998, UN inspectors continued their work of compiling information on Iraq's programs and destroying the weapons and weapons-related infrastructure they found, all in the face of Iraqi efforts to hide evidence and obstruct the inspectors' work. However, the sanctions became increasingly controversial. Critics charged that the sanctions were causing extensive human suffering inside Iraq due to shortages of medicine, food, and basic industrial needs. On the other hand, supporters argued that sanctions remained the only lever available (other than the use of force) to pressure Iraq to give up its WMD and to prevent more aggressive behaviour by the Iraqi regime. International support for the sanctions began to waver, and public protests against sanctions grew in many countries. In an effort to reduce the human impact of sanctions, the UN authorized the delivery of humanitarian supplies (including food) to be paid for by authorized sales of Iraqi oil (which was otherwise under embargo by the sanctions). By August 1998, Iraq announced that it would no longer cooperate with the inspector teams, which were withdrawn in November. American and British air strikes followed, and a renewed weapons inspections program was mounted by the creation of the United Nations Monitoring, Verification, and Inspection Commission (UNMOVIC) in 2001. Meanwhile, the "food for oil" program was never successful in striking a balance between sanctions and human suffering in Iraq, and it was abandoned in 2001. By then, several countries were openly calling for an end to sanctions. It is unlikely that sanctions would have worked in the case of Iraq, but ultimately we can never be sure, as the 2003 Iraq War ended the sanctions debate.

general punishment for a broad range of actions. Finally, sanctions will be more effective if an internal faction exists within the target state that supports the imposition of sanctions and can exert domestic pressure against the government using sanctions as a political argument for changing a policy; this was certainly an instrumental factor in the case of apartheid South Africa (see Profile 7.5). Overall, sanctions will likely continue to be a frequently used instrument in conflict management. They remain a valuable tool to signal disapproval and are an important alternative to the use of military force. However, the controversy associated with their use may lead to an evolution of sanctions policy toward targeting political and economic elites rather than entire societies. Whether such "smart sanctions" will be successful is uncertain.[74]

A DEMOCRATIC PATH TO PEACE?

The idea that democracies are inherently peaceful forms of government is not unique to the post–Cold War era. Immanuel Kant suggested that constitutional governments and their respect for international law would be a constraint on war; we explore this line of thought in greater length in the section on liberalism in Chapter 1. However, the idea of a democratic peace took on a new significance after the Cold War. A belief prevails in most Western countries that democracies rarely, if ever, fight one another (although they do fight nondemocratic states). It follows that if you expand the number of democracies in the world, you will increase the chances of peace. This was one of the pillars of U.S. foreign policy during the Clinton administration, which promoted the concept of "enlargement of the world's community of market democracies" as a replacement for the Cold War strategy of containment.[75] According to former U.S. President Bill Clinton, "enlargement" is in the interests of the United States because "democracies rarely wage war on one another."[76]

The argument that democracies do not fight one another is based on two assumptions. First, the domestic institutional structures of democratic states act as a constraint on war. Democracies must answer to their citizens, and the financial and human costs of war might result in a government losing the next election. In addition, there are constraints on leaders in democracies. The checks and balances that exist in parliamentary and republican systems will help prevent warlike or renegade leaders from coming to power. Authoritarian governments, in contrast, have fewer constraints, and are thus more likely to engage in aggressive or warlike behaviour. Second, the norms of democratic governance promote the peaceful resolution of disputes. Democracies are governed by the rule of law and principles that seek to establish a balance between the rights of the individual and the common good. As a result, democracies use **adjudication** and bargaining to avoid violent conflict. Advocates of the democratic peace theory argue that democratic states will be more likely to negotiate, adjudicate, and bargain when disputes arise between them. As Bruce Russett suggests, "the culture, perceptions, and practices that permit compromise and the peaceful resolution of conflicts without the threat of violence within countries come to apply across national boundaries toward other democratic countries."[77] Michael Doyle agrees, suggesting that democracies that "presume foreign republics to be also consensual, just and therefore deserving of accommodation."[78]

However, the idea of a democratic peace has been challenged. First, critics argue that institutional constraints will not necessarily prevent wars between democracies. If they did, they would prevent democracies from going to war against any kind of opponent. The fact that democracies have often gone to war (although not necessarily with other democracies) raises doubts about the salience of democratic constraints on war. Public opinion has, in fact, often favoured war: American public opinion favoured war with Spain in 1898, and according to popular historical accounts, the publics of Europe enthusiastically welcomed war in 1914. Second, democracies have nearly gone to war with each other on numerous occasions. In one study, Christopher Layne argues that in four cases of near-war between democracies (the United States and Great Britain in the Trent Affair of 1861; the United States and Great Britain in the Venezuela Crisis of 1895–96; France and Great Britain in the Fashoda Crisis of 1898; and France and Germany in the Ruhr in 1923), war was avoided only because one side backed down due to fears that a war would end in defeat or quagmire.[79] Third, there have been very few democracies in history, and as a result there have been fewer opportunities for conflict and warfare between them. Furthermore, most states are rarely at war, so it should be no surprise that democracies are rarely at war.[80] Fourth, democracies have actually fought one another. Or have they? Here the problem is the definition of democracy. World War I saw democratic states fight one another. However, some debate exists as to whether Germany was a democracy and how democratic any of the combatants were in the realm of foreign policy decision making.[81] In another ambiguous case, the U.S. Civil War was a war that occurred within a democracy. Although this war has been dismissed as only a civil war, the War Between the States did have the character of an interstate conflict. In any case, why did the democratic institutions of the United States not save the country from civil war?

The debate over the idea of a democratic peace has profound policy implications. For example, should Canada support the spread of formal democracy in the hope that it will lead to a more peaceful world? Is it not possible that the effort to encourage or promote democracy will drag Canada (or other countries) into interventions and even wars in the cause of a democratic peace, thus increasing global insecurity? After all, one of the stated objectives of the U.S.-led Iraq War was to democratize the country, and similar language is used to justify continued intervention in Afghanistan.

CONCLUSIONS

This chapter has explored some of the conflict management instruments available to actors in global politics. As we have seen, conflict management efforts are plagued by several obstacles, most notably the interrelated problems of compliance, trust, and self-interest. Many actors sign international agreements or take on obligations but do not abide by them. Other actors refuse to engage in bilateral or multilateral conflict management efforts because they do not trust other countries to live up to their obligations. Many conflict management instruments founder because global actors do not believe it is in their best interests to pursue such a course. Conflict management is by its very nature a cooperative enterprise, and as we have seen, cooperation in a world that is at least in part anarchic is problematic. Despite the less-than-illustrious history of conflict management, some cause for optimism remains. Emerging transnational security issues may compel international actors—especially states—to increase their efforts to establish more rigorous and effective conflict management mechanisms in the future.

Endnotes

1. *Human Security Report 2005* (Oxford: Oxford University Press, 2005), 146.
2. G. Dyer, *War: The New Edition* (Toronto: Vintage Canada, 2004), 2.
3. C. Jönsson, "Diplomacy, Bargaining, and Negotiation," in W. Carlsnaes, T. Risse, and B. A. Simmons, eds., *Handbook of International Relations* (London: Sage, 2002), 121.
4. See A. Faizullaev, "Diplomacy and Self," *Diplomacy and Statecraft* 17, no. 3 (September 2006), 517.
5. G. Mattingly, *Renaissance Diplomacy* (Baltimore, MD: Penguin, 1964), 244.
6. See J. Melissen, "Introduction," in J. Melissen, ed., *Innovation in Diplomatic Practice* (London: Macmillan; New York: St. Martin's Press, 1999).
7. A. L. George, *Forceful Persuasion: Coercive Diplomacy as an Alternative to War* (Washington, DC: United States Institute of Peace Press, 1991).
8. For a highly readable and general text on negotiation, see R. Fisher and W. Ury, *Getting to Yes: Negotiating Agreement Without Giving In* (Boston: Houghton Mifflin, 1981). For studies of diplomacy and conflict management see: B. G. Ramcharan, *Preventive Diplomacy at the United Nations* (Bloomington, IN: Indiana University Press, 2008); and S. Hideo, *Containing Conflict: Cases in Preventive Diplomacy* (Tokyo and New York: Japan Center for International Exchange, 2003).
9. See K. Boulding, *The Three Faces of Power* (Newbury Park, CA: Sage, 1990); and W. Habeeb, *Power and Tactics in International Negotiation: How Weak Nations Bargain with Strong Nations* (Baltimore: Johns Hopkins University Press, 1988).
10. See J. Berkovitch, ed., *Resolving International Conflicts: The Theory and Practice of Mediation* (Boulder, CO: Lynne Rienner, 1996).
11. J. Pressman, "Visions in Collision: What Happened at Camp David and Taba?," *International Security* 28 (Fall 2003), 44–77.
12. For a study on the El-Aqsa Intifada, see H. Gordon, R. Gordon, and S. Taher, *Beyond Intifada: Narratives of Freedom Fighters in the Gaza Strip* (Westport, CT: Praeger, 2003).
13. For a discussion of the U.S. role in the Middle East, see S. Telhami, *The Stakes: America and the Middle East* (Boulder, CO: Westview Press, 2002).
14. For a discussion of the unravelling of the peace process, see N. Kozodoy, ed., *The Mideast Peace Process: An Autopsy* (San Francisco: Encounter Books, 2003). See also B. Wasserstein, *Israel and Palestine: Why They Fight and Can They Stop?* (London: Profile Books, 2003).
15. For a discussion of the issues surrounding the security fence, see J. Rynold, "Israel's Fence: Can Separation Make Better Neighbors?," *Survival* 46 (Spring 2004), 55–76.
16. Rynold, 56.
17. G. E. Robinson, "The Fragmentation of Palestine," *Current History* 106, no. 704 (December 2007), 421–422.
18. See International Institute for Strategic Studies, *Strategic Survey 2007* (New York: Routledge, 2007), 238.
19. From United Nations Office for the Coordination of Humanitarian Affairs (OCHA), *Gaza Humanitarian Situation Reports*, January–March 2008. http://www.ochaopt.org/?module=displaysection&section_id=11&format=html (accessed April 18, 2008), and Robinson, 423.

20. For an overview, see S. Wolff, "The Peace Process Since 1998," in J. Neuheiser and S. Wolff, eds., *Peace at Last? The Impact of the Good Friday Agreement on Northern Ireland* (New York: Beghahn Books, 2002).

21. M. Fitzduff, *Beyond Violence: Conflict Resolution Process in Northern Ireland* (Tokyo: United Nations University Press, 2002).

22. See R. Johansen, "Swords into Plowshares: Can Fewer Arms Yield More Security?," in C. Kegley Jr., ed., *Controversies in International Relations Theory: Realism and the Neoliberal Challenge* (New York: St. Martin's Press, 1995), 224–44.

23. J. Kruzel, "Arms Control, Disarmament, and the Stability of the Postwar Era," in C. Kegley Jr., ed., *The Long Postwar Peace* (New York: HarperCollins, 1991), 249.

24. Remarks by Senator Richard G. Lugar, Chairman, Committee on Foreign Relations, at the Chemical and Biological Arms Control Institute Tenth Anniversary Symposium, November 19, 2003. (Washington, DC: Bureau of International Information Programs, U.S. Department of State, 2003).

25. See G. P. Schultz, W. J. Perry, H. A. Kissinger, and S. Nunn, "A World Free of Nuclear Weapons," *The Wall Street Journal*, January 8, 2007.

26. For a discussion of the issues facing the NPT, see J. Dhanapala, *Multilateral Diplomacy and the NPT: An Insider's Account* (Geneva: United Nations Institute for Disarmament Research, 2005). See also *Arms Control Today: Atoms for Peace Anniversary Issue* 33 (December 2003).

27. See R. Johnson, "The In-comprehensive Test Ban," *Bulletin of Atomic Scientists* 52 (November/December 1996), 30–35.

28. See W. Sidhu and R. Thakur, eds., *Arms Control After Iraq: Normative and Operational Challenges* (Tokyo: United Nations University, 2006).

29. Kruzel, 268.

30. United Nations Development Programme, *Human Development Report, 1994* (New York: Oxford University Press, 1994), 22.

31. L. Axworthy, "Canada and Human Security: The Need for Leadership," *International Journal* 52 (Spring 1997), 184.

32. R. Paris, "Human Security: Paradigm Shift or Hot Air?," *International Security* 26 (Fall 2001), 88.

33. See R. K. Nossal, "Pinchpenny Diplomacy: The Decline of 'Good International Citizenship' in Canadian Foreign Policy," *International Journal* 54 (Winter 1998–99), 88–105; and F. O. Hampson and D. Oliver, "Pulpit Diplomacy: A Critical Assessment of the Axworthy Doctrine," *International Journal* 53 (Summer 1998), 379–407.

34. F. O. Hampson, N. Hillmer, and M. A. Molot, eds., *The Axworthy Legacy: Canada Among Nations 2001* (Oxford: Oxford University Press, 2001).

35. For examinations of war law, see R. Gutman et. al., eds., *Crimes of War 2.0: What the Public Should Know*, rev. upd. ed. (New York: W. W. Norton, 2007), and R. B. Byers, *War Law: Understanding International Law and Armed Conflict* (Vancouver: Douglas and McIntyre, 2005).

36. See K. Deutsch, *Political Community and the North Atlantic Area* (Princeton: Princeton University Press, 1957).

37. See *Charter of the United Nations and Statute of the International Court of Justice* (New York: United Nations), 1.

38. See Article 2/4, *Charter of the United Nations and Statute of the International Court of Justice*, 4.

39. For case studies of peacekeeping before the creation of the UN, see A. James, *Peacekeeping in International Politics* (New York: St. Martin's Press, 1990).

40. For more discussion of these principles and their interrelated nature, see F. T. Liu, *United Nations Peacekeeping and the Non-Use of Force*, International Peace Academy Occasional Paper Series (Boulder, CO: Lynne Rienner, 1992).

41. *An Agenda for Peace: Preventive Diplomacy, Peacemaking, and Peacekeeping* (New York: United Nations, 1992), 1–2.

42. Data from UN Department of Public Information and Global Policy Forum, http://www.globalpolicy.org/security/peacekpg/index.htm (accessed June 26, 2004).

43. For discussions of the changing nature of peacekeeping, see I. Rikhye, *The Politics and Practice of United Nations Peacekeeping: Past, Present, and Future* (Toronto: Brown Book Company, 2000); and O. P. Richmond, *Maintaining Order, Making Peace* (New York: Palgrave, 2002).

44. B. Boutros-Ghali, "Beyond Peacekeeping," *New York University Journal of International Law and Politics* 25 (Fall 1992), 115.

45. See E. Newman and O. P. Richmond, eds., *The United Nations and Human Security* (New York: Palgrave, 2001).

46. See R. Dallaire, *Shake Hands with the Devil: The Failure of Humanity in Rwanda* (Toronto: Vintage Canada, 2003). Most estimates put the number of deaths at 800,000.

47. G. Picco, "The UN and the Use of Force: Leave the Secretary-General Out of It," *Foreign Affairs* 73 (September/October 1994), 14.

48. S. Touval, "Why the UN Fails," *Foreign Affairs* 73 (September/October 1994), 45.

49. Quoted in P. Lewis, "United Nations Is Finding Its Plate Increasingly Full but Its Cupboard Is Bare," *The New York Times*, September 27, 1993, A8.

50. See *United Nations Peacekeeping Operations: Principles and Guidelines* (New York: United Nations, 2008).

51. Peacekeeping data from the United Nations Department of Peacekeeping Operations, http://www.un.org/ Depts/dpko/dpko/bnote.htm (accessed February 6, 2009). For a review of UN peacekeeping efforts after the 1990s, see *Annual Review of Global Peace Operations* (Boulder: Lynne Rienner, 2006).

52. See United Nations Security Council, S/PRST/2001/5, February 20, 2001.

53. R. Paris, "Peacebuilding and the Limits of Liberal Internationalism," *International Security* 22 (Fall 1997), 56.

54. See E. M. Cousens, C. Kumar, and K. Wermester, *Peacebuilding as Politics: Cultivating Peace in Fragile Societies* (Boulder, CO: Lynne Rienner, 2001).

55. See S. J. Steadman, "Spoiler Problems in Peace Processes," *International Security* 22 (Fall 1997), 5–53.

56. A. G. Sens, "From Peacekeeping to Peacebuilding: The United Nations and the Challenge of Intrastate War," in M. W. Zacher and R. M. Price, eds., *The United Nations and Global Security* (New York: Palgrave Macmillan, 2004), 141–60.

57. "Timeline of the July War 2006," *The Daily Star Lebanon* February 21, 2008.

58. For a compilation of facts and figures from various sources from the July War, see "Middle East Crisis: Facts and Figures," *BBC News*, http://news.bbc.co.uk/2/hi/middle_east/5257128.stm (accessed May 6, 2008).

59. *The Responsibility to Protect: Report of the International Commission on Intervention and State Sovereignty* (Ottawa: International Development Research Centre, 2001), xi.

60. United Nations Security Council Resolution 1674, S/RES/1674, April 28, 2006.

61. See "Kosovo's First Month," *International Crisis Group Europe Briefing No. 47*, March 18, 2008. See also B. Posen, "The War for Kosovo: Serbia's Political-Military Strategy," *International Security* 24 (Spring 2000), 3–50; W. Arkin, "Smart Bombs, Dumb Targeting?," *Bulletin of the Atomic Scientists* 56 (May/June 2000), 46–54; and A. Roberts, "NATO's Humanitarian War over Kosovo," *Survival* 4 (Autumn 1999), 102–23.

62. See J. Cotton, "The Emergence of an Independent East Timor: National and Regional Challenges," *Contemporary Southeast Asia* 22 (April 2000); and James Traub, "Inventing East Timor," *Foreign Affairs* 79 (July/August 2000), 74–89.

63. M. O'Hanlon and P. W. Singer, "The Humanitarian Transformation: Expanding Global Intervention Capacity," *Survival* 46 (Spring 2004), 77–100.

64. See International Institute for Strategic Studies, *Strategic Survey 2007* (New York: Routledge, 2007), 263.

65. J. VandeHei, "In Break with UN, Bush Calls Sudan Killings Genocide," *The Washington Post*, June 2, 2005.

66. "Darfur's New Security Reality," *International Crisis Group Africa Report No. 134* (November 26, 2007), 27.

67. D. Leyton-Brown, "Introduction," in D. Leyton-Brown, ed., *The Utility of International Economic Sanctions* (New York: St. Martin's Press, 1987), 1–4.

68. J. Lindsay, "Trade Sanctions as Policy Instruments: A Re-Examination," *International Studies Quarterly* 30 (June 1996), 153–73.

69. See G. Hufbauer, J. Schott, and K. Elliott, *Economic Sanctions Reconsidered: History and Current Policy*, 2nd ed. (Washington, DC: Institute for International Economics, 1990).

70. K. Elliot, "Sanctions: A Look at the Record," *Bulletin of the Atomic Scientists* 49 (November 19), 32–35.

71. See J. Hoagland, "Economic Sanctions Sometimes Do More Harm Than Good," *The State* 11 (November 1993), A12.

72. See Hufbauer et al., *Economic Sanctions Reconsidered*, 100–01.

73. Ibid., 94.

74. See J. M. Farrall, *United Nations Sanctions and the Rule of Law* (Cambridge: Cambridge University Press, 2007), and R. Eyler, *Economic Sanctions: International Policy and Political Economy at Work* (New York: Palgrave Macmillan, 2007).

75. Anthony Lake (Former U.S. National Security Advisor), "From Containment to Enlargement," *Dispatch* 4, no. 39 (Washington, DC: United States Department of State, Bureau of Public Affairs, September 1993), 3.

76. W. Clinton, "Confronting the Challenges of a Broader World," *Dispatch* 4, no. 39 (Washington, DC: United States Department of State, Bureau of Public Affairs, September 1993), 3.

77. B. Russett, *Grasping the Democratic Peace: Principles for a Post–Cold War World* (Princeton: Princeton University Press, 1993), 31.

78. M. Doyle, "Kant, Liberal Legacies and Foreign Affairs: Part One," *Philosophy and Public Affairs* 12 (Summer 1983), 205–35, 230.

79. C. Layne, "Kant or Can't: The Myth of a Democratic Peace," *International Security* 19 (Fall 1994), 5–49. See also A. Geis, L. Brock, and H. Müller, eds. *Democratic Wars: Looking at the Dark Side of Democratic Peace* (Basingstoke and New York: Palgrave Macmillan, 2006).

80. D. Shapiro, "The Insignificance of the Liberal Peace," *International Security* 19 (Fall 1994), 50–86.

81. Layne, 40–44.

Suggested Websites

Arms Control Association
http://www.armscontrol.org

Center for Defense Information
http://www.cdi.org

Federation of American Scientists
http://www.fas.org

Global Policy Forum
http://www.globalpolicy.org

Human Security Network
http://www.humansecuritynetwork.org

United Nations
http://www.un.org

Globalization, Marginalization, and Regionalization in the World Economy

If present trends continue, economic disparities between industrial and developing nations will move from inequitable to inhuman.

—James Gustave Speth, UN Development Programme Administrator[1]

INTRODUCTION: THE GLOBAL ECONOMY TODAY

Our convergence/divergence theme is perhaps best illustrated by an examination of the state of the global economy today. While more people enjoy a higher standard of living than at any time in human history, there has been a discernibly widening gap between rich and poor states and rich and poor people since 1945. Convergence can be seen in the form of increased world trade and financial flows, regional economic integration (especially in Europe and North America), bilateral free trade agreements between states, and the World Trade Organization (WTO), which in 2008 boasted 153 members. Divergence can be seen in the persistence of trade disputes, the division of the world into trade blocs, imbalanced investment flows, and the vastly different life experiences of low-income people from those of economic elites. All of these long-term developments and trends took place within the context of a global recession that began in earnest in 2008 and threatened to linger well into the 2010s.

The enormous gap in the quality of life, health, education, and general welfare remains a prominent reality in global politics, and indications are that while overall or aggregate wealth continues to increase, economic disparities remain as wide as ever. The majority of the world's wealth is controlled by a group of countries with 16 percent of the world's population; these countries accounted for 73 percent of world GDP in 2006, down modestly from almost 80 percent in 1992. Per capita GDP in high-income countries was 16 times higher than GDP per capita in low-income countries in 2006.[2] The richest 20 percent of the world population accounted for 75 percent of global consumption, while the poorest 20 percent accounted for just 2 percent of consumption.[3]

Perhaps the gap between rich and poor countries can be best illustrated using the Human Development Index (HDI) employed by the UN. In 2007, Canada (a "high human development" country) ranked fourth in the world on the HDI with a "score" of 0.968, behind

Iceland, Norway and Australia (the U.S. was ranked twelfth). Canada achieved this rank due to (among other things) a high life expectancy of 80.3 years, a literacy rate of over 99 percent, a 99 percent primary and secondary enrolment rate, and a GDP per capita of US$33,375. In contrast, Niger ranked 174th on the HDI list, with a "score" of 0.374, with life expectancy at 55 years, a literacy rate of 28.7 percent, primary and secondary school enrolment of 22.7 percent, and a GDP per capita of US$781.[4]

Such blatant inequality fuels the ongoing debate about the human impact of globalization, a term we attempt to define later in this chapter. Some economists argue that globalization and liberal development strategies are having, or will soon have, a widespread positive impact on the standard of living in typically impoverished states. For example, in his latest book *The World Is Flat: A Brief History of the 21st Century*, Thomas Friedman takes a rather rosy view of globalization, suggesting that the removal of barriers to competition are the key to further economic and thus human development.[5] In one sense this is undeniable: more people around the world have higher incomes and a better quality of life than ever before. However, a large number of states and people are being left behind, unable to take advantage of the bounty others enjoy. One of the most popular recent books on global inequality is Paul Collier's *The Bottom Billion: Why the Poorest Countries Are Failing and What Can Be Done About It.* In the book, Collier (winner of the prestigious 2008 Lionel Gelber Prize) argues that the 50-odd "failed states" at the bottom of the economic tree are the main issue facing contemporary global politics. For Collier, the world needs a new, concerted approach to poverty, as globalization is actually making the situation in these countries worse. Suggested remedies include preferential trade policies and the elimination of corruption (by international intervention if necessary).[6]

Many other voices are considerably less sanguine than Friedman, or even Collier.[7] The international system has simply not been responsive to the issue of chronic disparities in wealth and well-being, and the global recession of the late 2000s will only exacerbate this disparity, as the poorest countries are expected to suffer the worst drops in economic growth and living standards. We are certainly not on track toward achieving any of the Millennium Summit Goals (discussed later in this chapter), although some progress has been made according to the UN's *Millennium Development Goals Report of 2006*. While the total number of people affected by chronic hunger has risen to approximately one billion, there are pockets of actual improvement in some of the traditionally worst-hit areas in sub-Saharan Africa and South Asia. School enrolments have increased, though a gender gap persists in many regions. HIV/AIDS prevention efforts are proving effective in some areas, but in others infection rates and related deaths are still on the increase. Tuberculosis rates have risen dramatically.[8]

There is also increasing concern about the stability of the global economy. Financial crises have become commonplace: Mexico, Argentina, India, and Russia all experienced crises in the 1990s. The 1997–98 Asian financial crisis had a ripple effect throughout the world economy. In 2009 the world was again in the grip of an economic recession, caused by a serious credit crisis in the United States that spread around the globe (see Chapter 13). All of these crises revealed how foreign investors and currency speculators have come to play a decisive role in the daily economic life of countries, and when they remove their money amid concern over its safety the chaos can be immediate and long-lasting. At the same time, a sudden rise in the price of oil caused by increased demand and stock speculation contributed to commodity and food price increases that threatened the well-being of millions of people. These crises remind us that the global economy is far from shock-proof despite the existence of institutions designed to prevent crises.

A number of global economic issues are likely to be important subjects of ongoing discussion and debate. One persistent issue is the debt crisis. Some states have managed to reduce their debt burdens. Canada, for example, managed balanced budgets between 1997 to 2007, although it began to run budget deficits in 2008–2009 in an effort to counter the recession. However, debt has soared in other countries, especially in the United States. The costs of the Iraq War and the trillion-dollar stimulus packages implemented by the Bush and Obama administrations in response to the global recession will result in historic levels of national debt. However, developing countries have faced overwhelming debt for many decades, and have suffered the financial and social consequences of high interest payments and debt-restructuring policies. The politics of debt reduction and debt forgiveness will continue to be a feature of development diplomacy. New research has identified another global economic issue: women of all ages have become even more integrated with the modern production process than ever before. However, this is often occurring under exploitative conditions, most notably in the infamous "sweatshops" in many developing countries that produce goods for export for MNCs or locally owned businesses. Another issue is the increasing demand for energy, especially fossil fuels. Energy production remains a central issue of geostrategic importance, and oil politics are likely to become more and more significant. The attempts to manage the global economy, from the shelved **Multilateral Agreement on Investment (MAI)** to the meetings of the WTO (including the failed Doha Round) have met with increasing opposition from protest groups and governments concerned with the impact of globalization on societies, cultures, the workplace, employment, and the environment. Finally, technological innovations such as **genetically modified organisms (GMOs)** have further complicated trade negotiations, international law, intellectual property rights, and the agenda of protest groups and bioethicists. In short, the global economy has become more complex than anyone could have envisioned when the principles and institutions of the world economy were established during and immediately after World War II.

This chapter begins with a reexamination of the central perspectives of international political economy introduced in Chapters 1 and 4, placing greater emphasis on more contemporary global economic issues as well as concerns over the role of women in the world economy and environmental problems. We discuss the conceptual and policy challenges posed by globalization. The relationship between globalization, economic activity, and politics is illustrated through an examination of the role of multinational corporations (MNCs) in the world economy. Next, we discuss what other critics argue is the main problem with globalization: marginalization and the perpetuation of extreme poverty. The chapter then examines what some critics consider the main counterpoint to globalization: regionalization. Is the world economy globalizing or regionalizing? Finally, we reflect on the role of energy politics in IPE, particularly the politics of oil, which will continue to have a dramatic impact on the global economy.

FROM THEORY TO PRACTICE IN THE CONTEMPORARY GLOBAL ECONOMY

In Chapter 4, we examined the different theoretical perspectives in the study of IPE, and noted that the architecture—the principles, structures, and institutions—of the global economy is based largely on liberal economic theory. However, there is validity in competing theoretical perspectives as well. First, recall that realists see world politics as a struggle between states for self-preservation and the enhancement of state power. In IPE, realists argue that economic nationalism (or neomercantilism) will prevail (see Chapter 4). Governments are primarily concerned with the health and security of the nation-state itself, and economic power is simply a means to maintain or increase that power. Realists point to the maintenance of protectionist trade barriers, the provision of subsidies and tax benefits to crucial (and politically powerful) industries and economic sectors, the disagreements between states in world and regional trade talks, and the existence of trade disputes (such as the U.S.–EU conflict over genetically modified foods) as evidence that the world economy is a competitive arena in which states pursue their interests. Thus we can expect only limited progress from world and regional trade talks (the "Doha Round" of the WTO may have proved this point), or from financial institutions and trade organizations that are controlled by self-serving states. This is especially notable when state capital journeys abroad, purchasing access to natural resources, expanding export markets, or buying important real estate, or when states dedicate substantial resources to development in globally competitive sectors. Robert A. Isaac argues that, "[a]lthough the Cold War has ended, the primacy of insecurity—of the infinite striving for security—has not. Where military security prevails, such as in most of the industrialized democracies, there has merely been a shift in the form of insecurity to the economic or psychological realms, as nations seek to increase economic competitiveness and to reduce unemployment."[9] The spoils of victory will include industrial supremacy, technology and information leadership, and the economic capacity to sustain a modern military. The losing states will face the problems created by reduced fiscal resources: unreliable economic growth and a smaller economic pie; permanent relegation to the ranks of the resource extraction, branch plant, or cash-crop economies; second-rate technology and information systems; and a lack of the economic means to escape a cycle of poverty. The economic war between states is, therefore, cast in zero-sum terms; that is, gains for one side are seen as a loss for the other (see Profile 8.1).

Where the economic nationalist sees states struggling to survive or prosper in the world economy, liberals see individuals, households, and firms maximizing their opportunity

---

PROFILE 8.1 Survival of the Smartest: Geoeconomic Warfare

Many realists have predicted an increase in economic nationalism in the global economy. In particular, in 1993 Edward Luttwak suggested that "geoeconomics" would come to dominate international economic relations and trigger a "global war for economic power." Luttwak was writing long before the onset of the global recession in 2008–2009, but his predictions may have greater significance now than they did in 1993. Luttwak made the following arguments to support his case:

- Geoeconomics is spreading and becoming the dominant phenomenon in the central arena of world affairs, but not all states are equally inclined or equally capable of participating in the new struggle.

- Small but well-educated countries can be much more successful in geoeconomics than they could ever be in world politics,

where size always counts and may alone be decisive.

- States will tend to act geoeconomically simply because of what they are: territorially defined entities designed precisely to outdo each other on the world scene.

- When there is no strategic confrontation at the centre of world affairs that can absorb the adversarial feeling of the nations, those ill feelings may be diverted into the nation's economic relations.

- The emerging geoeconomic struggle for high-technology industrial supremacy among Americans, Europeans, and Japanese is eroding their old alliance solidarity. Increased geoeconomic activity will characterize their economic relationship, as opposed to free trade economics.

SOURCE: EDWARD LUTTWAK, "THE COMING GLOBAL WAR FOR ECONOMIC POWER," *THE INTERNATIONAL ECONOMY* 7 (SEPTEMBER/OCTOBER 1993), 20. REPRINTED WITH PERMISSION.

to pursue mutually beneficial exchange in the global marketplace. Through comparative advantage, a world adhering to the principles of free trade will reap the benefits of the efficient use of capital and resources. The institutions of the world economy were built by states in accordance with these liberal economic principles, and through tariff reduction, nondiscrimination, national treatment, and the harmonization of regulations, a rules-based trade and financial system has emerged. Through greater cooperation and economic interdependence a wealthier and less warlike world can be built. However, there is considerable debate between liberals on the role of the state and regulation in the world economy. Some liberals, adhering to classical liberal approaches but often referred to today as "neoliberals," argue that states should play a minimal managerial role in economic affairs. More state intervention will only create more obstacles to market activity. A typical neoliberal agenda would extract the state from as much of the economic realm as possible, and indeed many of those who espouse globalization believe state interference is but a hindrance to a more rational, less nationalist global society. Liberal institutionalists believe rational actors will converge in common institutions and regimes (see Chapter 5) to facilitate this process. This is the heart of the liberal "global governance" approach: a postnationalist international society can emerge with deliberate cooperation and institution building, but the global marketplace should not be subject to extraordinary controls or be responsible for the redistribution of wealth. There is, however, a great deal of variation among liberals on the influence such institutions or regimes should have.

In contrast, liberals in the Keynesian tradition (see Chapter 4) argue that there needs to be more intervention by states in the global economy, and especially more of an effort to manage the global economy in the interests of poor countries and poverty reduction. They argue that the world economy has been driven into disaster by the neoliberal agenda, which has captured international financial institutions and allied itself with the interests of big corporations. Keynesian liberal criticism of neoliberal economic philosophy has been especially strong in the wake of the U.S. financial crises that precipitated the global economic recession. In particular, Keynesian liberals argue that the recession was due at least in part to weak government regulation and oversight of large banks and other financial institutions on Wall Street. As a result, relying on profit-seeking financial institutions for economic growth is seen as an error in domestic public policy, while relying on international institutions following similar neoliberal assumptions is seen as an error in global governance and development policy. Today, this intra-liberal debate between neoliberals and Keynesians is one of the key features of the dialogue on globalization, with authors such as Joseph Stiglitz and George Soros stimulating dialogue on how the principles of liberal economics should be put into practice. The recent responses to the global economic recession suggest that considerable government intervention, especially in the form of stimulus spending and regulation of the banking system, will characterize the economic management strategies of most countries in the coming years.

Meanwhile, the Marxist perspective offers important insights into the state of the global economy. It rejects both mercantilist and liberal diagnostics and prescriptions: these interpretations are seen as mere shadows or reflections of the real structure of economic power. The global economy is characterized by the spread of world capitalism, which is defined by a class system in which economic elites dominate and exploit the poor. This class structure has spread to global proportions and works to keep the majority of people poor while the rich few, protected by the instruments of the state system and international investment and property protection mechanisms, get richer. This system has produced a transnational economic elite, which includes exploitative classes in postcolonial states. The social impact of globalized mass production, cash-crop agriculture, and exploitation of cheap labour has led to increased calls for alternative economic approaches at both the global and local levels. Today, Marxist thought is a powerful contributor to more transformative programs for political and economic change, and remains an ideological approach that to varying degrees has a sympathetic audience in some antiglobalization movements. The neo-Gramscian perspective, introduced in Chapter 1 and developed by scholars such as Robert Cox and Stephen Gill, retains its allure for graduate students and academics interested in understanding the intersections between empire, intellectual hegemony, and industrial (and postindustrial) production. Some of this work overlaps with postmodern and constructivist calls for a reexamination of economic theory, the principles on which it is based, and the assumptions that make these principles seem legitimate for some but illegitimate for many others.

Feminist and "gendered perspectives" have focused on the role of women in the world economy and what this means for global economic management and the social impact of globalization. More women are participating in the formal workforce than ever. Between 1997 and 2007, 200 million women joined the global labour force (an increase of over 18 percent), and in 2007 there were 1.2 billion women in paid work (in contrast to 1.8 billion men). However, women are more concentrated in informal, subsistence, and vulnerable employment than men, and on average earn 17 percent less than men globally. The global labour force is increasingly feminized, with approximately 60 to 90 percent of the labour-intensive component of the production of fresh produce and clothing in the developing world performed by women.[10] More women are now employed in the service sector worldwide than in agriculture, and they are the main labourers for outsourced corporate services such as call centres. Women are considered desirable workers in such industries because they are extended fewer benefits, are given lower pay, are less likely to form unions, and cannot find better work due to discrimination. While this employment may appear as progress to some, freeing women from the constraints of rural life and offering higher pay than could otherwise be obtained, others argue it amounts to a form of gender-discriminatory slavery, since the women work long hours and are paid very little for their efforts.

Many other challenges are faced by women in the global economy. The increasing trend toward the outsourcing or subcontracting of work to home labourers (referred to as "informal" work) leaves women highly vulnerable to poverty. Another challenge comes in the form of the proliferation of **export processing zones (EPZs)**, special territorial enclaves created by governments for industrial and trade activity by domestic and international corporations. These EPZs are exempt from national labour and environmental laws, and are having a negative impact on all workers but especially women workers. Millions of women work in the over 3,000 EPZs in over 120 countries worldwide, and therefore fall outside the jurisdiction of whatever minimal labour rights for women might exist in the host country.[11] None of this means the work many women do in the global economy is unimportant. Women grow much of the food consumed locally in most societies and care for the children and elderly in addition to paid work. However, feminists argue that the work many women do has been systematically undervalued in society and by governments and employers, and much of that work violates domestic and/or international labour and human rights law. Finally, global trafficking in women (especially for the large international sex trade which relies primarily on female labour) is a feature of the contemporary global economy, and is characterized by kidnapping, deception, and brutal coercion. While gathering data on the number of women affected by international trafficking is extremely difficult, according to the UN there were over 21,400 recorded victims of sexual trafficking in women in 2006.[12] However, this figure is likely to represent only a small fraction of the women actually involved: the European Union has noted that as many as 700,000 women and children are moved across international borders by trafficking rings every year.[13]

Meanwhile, the workforce in industrialized states has undergone significant demographic change since women began working in factories during the world wars. Many economies have shifted to a service and information orientation (see Chapter 12), putting more women in positions of decision-making power. Governments have often supported or encouraged this transition with employment equity programs. From a liberal feminist perspective, then, progress has been made—though just how much progress is still a matter of considerable debate. Among academics and politicians alike, much more attention has been paid in recent times to the role of women in development. Countries such as Canada have made women central players in their development assistance programs, though with mixed results. This is part of a more general, and welcome, move away from large infrastructure projects designed to bring Western-style growth to impoverished areas and toward focusing instead on smaller-scale development that involves local communities. International agencies, such as **UNICEF (United Nations Children's Fund)**, have been involved with acquiring bank loans for women in small-business sectors in countries such as Egypt and Pakistan. In many Southern states, women have organized cooperatives, income-producing businesses that range from garment production to food processing; the International Labour Organization (ILO) and many regional banks have promoted what is referred to as women's entrepreneurship development; and many successful microfinancing (small-loan) programs, such as the Grameen Bank founded in Bangladesh by 2006 Nobel Peace Prize winner Mohammed Yunus, have lifted tens of thousands of women out of absolute poverty.[14] Still, the majority of the malnourished and undereducated children in the world are female. Among the Southern regions, only in Latin America do women's literacy rates even approach those of men.

Ecofeminists, meanwhile, argue that despite all the media attention paid to the environment, industrialized Western society still does not understand the link between violence against women and environmental exploitation. The world economy remains heavily

Women have made great strides in terms of economic equality, but feminists argue that many problems remain. For example, large-scale production in a globalized economy often exploits women and children. The match factories of Tamil Nadu, India, rely almost exclusively on female labour working 12-hour days for 15 rupees (less than 50 cents) per day. (AP Photo/Cindy Andrew/CP Archive.)

dependent on the extraction of large amounts of resources, for both fuel and products, while violence against women remains a widespread phenomenon, especially in times of war, as witnessed in the former Yugoslavia in the early 1990s and the Congo and Sudan in the mid-to-late 2000s. Ecofeminists argue we need to stop both types of violence together and rethink our approaches to gender and ecology, our tendency to answer complex problems with technical solutions, our tendency to violent confrontations with each other and nature (a heritage of the liberal utilitarian perspective that sees nature and something to be conquered, tamed, and exploited), and our tendency to monoculture in terms of both agricultural production and intellectual diversity.[15]

While the type of deep change ecofeminists call for is a long way off, economists are recognizing the importance of the environment as both a causal variable and an ongoing concern in their work. The most widely publicized endorsement of the importance of the environment was the 1987 report of the Bruntland Commission, titled our *Our Common Future*.[16] This was followed by the environmental focus of the United Nations Conference on Environment and Development in Rio de Janeiro in 1992 (see Chapter 10) and subsequent meetings in Johannesburg, Copenhagen, and elsewhere. There is no doubt that the environment is now accepted as a crucial component of the study of the global economy and IPE.[17] Indeed, concerns over the gender dynamic in the international workforce, and the environmental problems resulting from large-scale industrialization and agriculture, are now well reflected in contemporary debates on the meaning, implications, and sustainability of globalization. We turn now to a brief discussion of this widely used but little understood term.

WHAT IS GLOBALIZATION?

Globalization is often accepted, without much examination, as an inevitable evolutionary feature of the world economy. But when did we begin thinking about a borderless world in which transnational forces, spurred on by technological developments (especially in the field of communications), are shrinking the globe? One might argue this has been a long-term project that commenced when humans first began communicating; some feel it will end only with the global domination of liberal democracy and capitalism, or a truly global marketplace. Indeed, the state-run economies that formed the "Second World" during the Cold War have largely collapsed. Although some states, such as China and Cuba, retain the rhetorical vestiges of socialism, they too have turned to what we might loosely label **marketization** (characterized ideally by the introduction of private property, free competition between firms, and the acceptance of foreign investment). Seen this way, globalization may be the logical end of history: other stages (the city-state system, feudal Europe, the nation-state system) of global development have merely been the means to this end. Others, however, might reject such a teleological approach or see the current era as the beginning of a

Can we measure globalization simply by the amount of goods and services traded from port to port? By cross-national investment flows? Or is there a deeper cultural meaning to the question? (AP Photo/Nick Ut/CP Archive.)

new history, marked by the spread of Western culture around the globe, resistance to it, and continued disparities in wealth and opportunity.[18] Some even suggest that global capitalism, driven by its own "manic logic," is creating an inhumane world based on internationalized predatory capitalism.[19]

Perhaps the most succinct definition of globalization is offered by Malcolm Waters in his short but fascinating book on the topic. As a sociologist, Waters is more interested in the relationships inherent in global shifts. He defines globalization as a "social process in which the constraints of geography on social and cultural arrangements recede and in which people become increasingly aware that they are receding."[20] Waters believes globalization has always been taking place, proceeding through the "fits and starts of various ancient imperial expansions, pillaging and trading oceanic explorations, and the spread of religious ideas." This path was interrupted by the European Middle Ages, a period of "inward-looking territorialism" but then picked up again in the 15th and 16th centuries, when the Copernican revolution convinced humanity that it occupied a globe (instead of a flat, endless plain) and when European expansion took the ideas that today still shape the global economy—market-based trade, for example—to distant lands where people had previously lived in "virtually complete ignorance of each other's existence."[21]

Others, such as the renowned Canadian international political economist Robert Cox, argue that the analysis of what Cox terms the "globalization thrust" must ultimately begin with an understanding of the internationalization of production:

> The internationalizing process results when capital considers the productive resources of the world as a whole and locates elements of complex globalized production systems at points of greatest cost advantage. The critical factor is information on how most profitably to combine components in that production process.... Producing units takes advantage of abundant, cheap, and malleable labour where it is to be found, and of robotization where it is not.[22]

While Waters's explanation rests more on the spread of ideas, Cox relies more on a materialist explanation (stressing the political implications of economic forces). Cox also takes a Gramscian approach, suggesting the hegemonic nature of globalization's ideology reflects the preferences of the structurally advantaged.

The debate over globalization has lost none of its intensity in the past few years. Globalization is most often associated with a borderless world, a world in which the conventions and norms of the Westphalian system of states are increasingly irrelevant and anachronistic. Globalization is often regarded as beyond the immediate control of state actors, or as an external force, to which actors in the international system must respond. This view suggests that we must, perhaps grudgingly, accept the fact that many people will be harmed by globalization even as others gain. After all, this has been a consistent theme in the evolution of economic systems: change tends to harm one part of a society even though society as a whole might benefit. However, another view argues that globalization is hardly an inevitable, impersonal force, but was created and driven forward by the policies of governments, in turn encouraged by financial actors. According to Jeffry A. Frieden, "[Globalization] is a choice made by governments that consciously decide to reduce barriers to trade and investment, adopt new policies toward international money and finance, and chart fresh economic courses. Decisions made by each government are interconnected; international finance, international trade, and international monetary relations depend on the joint actions of national governments around the world."[23] The Canadian government, for example, has been very proactive in seeking increased trade opportunities abroad, though its reaction to foreign investment in Canada has differed over time.

In general, international relations theorists have very mixed reactions to the assertion that we are in a new stage of world history. Realists point to the stubbornness of the institution of state sovereignty. Anyone travelling across a border and dealing with the officials stationed there to protect it realizes very quickly that borders still exist, and if anything border controls have become tighter after September 11, 2001. Although the functionalist school (see Chapter 5) believed international institutions would eventually supplant the state, they did not have the multinational corporation (MNC) in mind. For their part, Marxists would interpret globalization as the continuation of older forms of **imperialism**. In fact, they would be apt to wonder what all the fuss is about, since this process has been a constant feature of economic and political life since the beginning of the expansion of the ruling elite in ancient societies. The fallen socialist bloc did not stop imperialism, but merely and temporarily stalled its spread. The periphery of the world system continues to be a location for disciplined production and the exploitation of human labour, integrated by core financial institutions and marketplaces, feeding the voracious appetite of global capitalism. For Marxists, global recessions are empirical evidence of the fragility of the world economy and its predatory and merciless character.

Beyond these debates are questions about the important cultural implications of increased trade, investment flows, and telecommunications capacity, a theme to which we return in Chapter 12. In terms of globalization's cultural impact, some would no doubt argue that globalization is the modern equivalent of what development theorists earlier referred to as **modernization**. The latter term was harshly criticized because it implied that only Western states were modern and that those developing states that had failed to reach the point of mass consumption societies were "unmodern," perhaps because of geographic, cultural, or even personality traits prevalent in their societies. Thus, one might argue that the pressure to globalize, to become even further involved with the world economy and its regimes, is a destructive one that implies that non-Western societies have no choice, if they want to experience economic growth and development, other than to adopt the conventional attributes of the West: capitalism, commercial culture, secular governance, and an emphasis on the present. Opposition to this cultural set of values is of course common in many regions, and even Western states are concerned about the intrusion of external cultural influences. Canada and France frequently seek to protect culture in world trade talks, for example. For indigenous peoples around the world, the stakes are high: the intrusion of external cultural influences may threaten their very existence. The cultural destruction of Indigenous persons (which we discuss as a human rights issue in the next chapter) was an earlier variant of the wide-scale Westernization we see taking place today. And many religious leaders in the Middle East and elsewhere have sought to curb Western influences through an assertion of theocratic power.

Some would insist that the very concept of globalization, and its continual promotion by the corporate elite, belittles the strong cultural differences that exist today. One author argues that the world is still fundamentally divided into at least eight civilization groupings, the Chinese (Confucian–Taoist–Buddhist), Hindu, Islamic, Japanese (Shinton–Buddhist–Confucian), Latin American syncretist, Islamic, non-Islamic African, and Christian.[24] Does a secular vision of globalization, based on markets and investment and common values, do justice to the inherent diversity of humanity? What about the major split, presented as axiomatic by some analysts, between the Eastern and Western, or Islamic and Christian, communities? What about the differences within every nation-state, between rich and poor, between ethnic groups, between male and female? In short, can the forces of globalization overcome the realities of human diversity and environmental diversity? Perhaps **homogenization** is further off than a simplified vision of proliferate Western products and advertisements would have us believe.

Yet the belief in the magic of the marketplace to create wealth still reigns in influential circles. John Williamson coined the term *Washington Consensus* in 1990 to describe a set of policies designed by international financial institutions (IFIs) based in Washington to stimulate economic growth and development in Latin America.[25] The phrase is now generally used (or, as Williamson himself has argued, misused) to describe the so-called neoliberal approach to economic development, stressing the need for governments to pursue fiscal discipline, cutbacks to nonproductive sectors, lower taxes, and the relaxation of controls over interest rates. They should also allow their currencies to float on international financial markets, lower tariffs and encourage trade as well as foreign investment, privatize state-owned industries, deregulate industry and agriculture, and protect the private ownership of property. This agenda, which has been harshly criticized by social activists and others as placing far too much faith in the marketplace, has guided development assistance policies and the terms of the "structural adjustment" loans offered by the World Bank and the IMF. Many liberals see this "conditionality" as the necessary counterpart to loan guarantees to developing countries: it makes little sense to lend money to countries that are not following sound fiscal and economic policies. However, critics argue that this means governments have been forced to adopt a set of fiscal and economic policies that may be harmful to the most vulnerable sectors of their society, and may result in lower government spending on education, health care, environmental protection, and general welfare. A further criticism is that none of the advanced capitalist states have followed the rules themselves: they run deficits, protect their markets, and (as a government funding scandal in Canada demonstrated in early 2004) have their own corruption problems.

The rise of **currency and commodity speculation** adds more fuel to antiglobalization viewpoints. Various currencies have experienced great instability, and commodity prices are often artificially inflated, due to speculative investment, which is arguably an inherent element of what Susan Strange termed the "casino capitalism" of the West.[26] This has led to calls for measures to moderate these activities and generate revenue from them for international charitable projects. In fact, more than 24 years ago, economist James Tobin suggested that a tax be levied on international currency exchanges.[27] A "Tobin tax," it is often argued, would not only raise hundreds of billions of dollars which could be used for international humanitarian purposes, such as paying for peacekeeping operations or AIDS relief or climate change adaptation, but would also discourage speculation itself. However, it would be difficult to convince market-oriented governments that this type of intervention is justified, and, as an article in *The Economist* points out, unless every state participated, "trading would simply shift to tax-free havens. Also, financial wizards would quickly devise tax dodges: rather than trade yen for dollars, say, they might agree to swap Japanese government bonds for American Treasuries."[28] Finally, the increasing use of the **Internet** for commercial transactions would make such a taxation scheme even more difficult to implement.

One thing remains fairly clear: if the market has won over the hearts and minds of a transnational economic elite, it may not have done so among the millions of people who continue to forge their own path of development somewhere else. It would be a gross overgeneralization to argue that all that is left on the economic menu is global capitalism with minimal state interference. From the quiet fields of agrarian communities around the world, to the streets of the bustling megacities, people are engaged in forming their own substate arrangements and interpersonal relationships. For example, female workers formed many cooperative ventures to produce textiles in Guatemala; women in Kenya founded the Green Belt movement, planting millions of trees to stop **desertification**; artistic communities in many Northern states have formed mutually supportive networks; people rose in widespread protests to halt the privatization of water provision in South and North America and Africa; and unique resource-sharing regimes in environmental management are being forged as we grapple with problems of the commons. There is much more to the global political economy than the amorphous entity we refer to as the market, and though the conventional path of authoritarian state socialism may well be dead, with its stench of economic failure and political repression, a new, community-centred one may be emerging, built on the survival strategies implemented by people in both hemispheres.[29] However, there is little doubt that the marketplace, as defined by neoliberal ideology, retains a special place in the hearts and minds of those who benefit most greatly from globalization. This is best demonstrated with reference to a peculiarly 20th-century innovation with deep consequences, the multinational corporation.

THE CENTRAL ROLE OF MULTINATIONAL CORPORATIONS

Perhaps one of the most remarkable characteristics of the contemporary global economy is the expansive rise of the MNC. MNCs (also sometimes referred to as *transnational corporations*, or *TNCs*) are businesses with extensive investments or operations in more than one country. Typically, MNCs are headquartered in a home country, and own and operate affiliate businesses in other countries around the world. Larger MNCs may control large product lines and brand names, acquired through strategic corporate alliances, mergers, purchases of other companies, or hostile takeovers. Largely through the operations of MNCs, world production has become increasingly globalized, as production facilities have been constructed and/or relocated overseas and product components are assembled in a wide variety of countries. While some companies are major competitors, MNCs also cooperate extensively, often sharing production facilities and forming partnerships with local firms. American, European, and Asian MNCs are generally the largest and most powerful. As early as the 1960s, the power of MNCs led to questions about the primacy of the nation-state.[30] In particular, the dominance of American multinationals has caused Canadians, Europeans, and South Americans to worry about the influence of American corporate commercialism on their cultures (in the Canadian case, a short-lived spate of Canadian nationalism arose out of these concerns).[31] MNCs are regarded either as necessary suppliers of investment and technical knowledge or as predatory entities that perpetuate the underdevelopment of poor countries. In either conception, their influence is substantial (see Profile 8.2).

The sheer size of modern MNCs is intimidating. The Toyota Motor Corporation, for example, has manufacturing facilities in 27 countries and employs approximately 316,000 people worldwide. Some MNCs have a large number of subsidiary corporations. For example, Yum! Brands Inc. owns A&W, Pizza Hut, Taco Bell, Long John Silver's, Wingstreet, and Kentucky Fried Chicken, and operates 36,000 restaurants in 110 countries and territories, generating over US$11 billion in revenues in 2008. Yum! Brands Inc. was formerly Tricon Global Restaurants, itself a spinoff from PepsiCo in 1997. Corporate mergers and acquisitions have accelerated the growth of many MNCs: in 2000, the French car manufacturer Renault took over Nissan; in the pharmaceutical sector Glaxco Wellcome merged with SmithKline Beecham in an effort to capitalize on the drug potential of the human genome project; and America Online merged with Time Warner, creating a company with a market value of US$340 billion (although the drop in tech stocks in the latter half of 2000 reduced this figure by $140 billion). In 2004, Royal Dutch Petroleum Co. merged

PROFILE 8.2 The Debate over MNCs: Do They Exploit Low-Income Countries?

YES

1. MNCs decapitalize less-developed countries (LDCs). MNCs take more money in profit out of LDCs than they invest.

2. MNCs are obstacles to social progress. The profit motive makes MNCs unresponsive or opposed to progressive political change.

3. MNCs contribute to inequality. MNCs create an elite socioeconomic class in LDCs, isolated from the poor majority.

4. MNCs discourage indigenous development. They oppose efforts by LDCs to industrialize, as this would create domestic competition.

5. MNCs create dependence. LDC economies come to depend on MNCs for investment, technology, and markets.

6. MNCs use LDCs as sources of raw materials. MNCs extract raw materials for a low price and manufacture products abroad, forcing LDCs to purchase expensive finished products.

NO

1. MNCs provide investment. MNCs invest a lot of their own money and also attract foreign investors.

2. MNCs support peaceful domestic environments. MNCs require peace to operate effectively, and therefore have an interest in long-term stability.

3. MNCs create jobs. They have an interest in a capable workforce and provide training and education.

4. MNCs promote development. MNCs help create modern infrastructure and share technology and technique, therefore creating conditions conducive to domestic growth.

5. MNCs increase fiscal resources of LDCs. MNCs create royalties and tax revenues for LDCs.

6. MNCs give LDCs access to world markets. They provide a channel to markets for products as well as markets for purchase, enabling LDCs to access the global marketplace.

with Shell Transport and Trading Company, and in 2006 AT&T Inc. merged with BellSouth Corporation. Each of these corporate mergers and acquisitions had transaction values of over US$70 billion.

MNCs are extremely powerful economic entities, and their significance in the global economy has grown as world trade has expanded. In 2007, there were over 79,000 MNCs worldwide, with over 790,000 affiliates (often called "subsidiaries"). These MNCs accounted for 11 percent of world GDP and one-third of world exports.[32] It is striking that when the annual revenues of the largest MNCs in the world are compared with the annual GNP of states, more than one-third of the world's largest economic units are MNCs. Even more stark is the fact that while the UN regular budget is approximately US$1.9 billion, over 45 of the largest MNCs have annual revenues over US$100 billion. MNCs are also significant because of their numbers: few countries in the world do not host an MNC or a subsidiary within their territorial boundaries. Furthermore, MNCs have a great deal of control over the global capacity to manufacture products, sell services, and provide finance, and they are leading developers of technology and services. Most of the largest MNCs are in the manufacturing sector (Mitsubishi, Toyota), oil (Exxon, Royal Dutch/Shell Group), and electronics (IBM, AT&T). In other sectors, financial corporations such as the Industrial and Commercial Bank of China (ICBC), Bank of America, Citigroup Inc., and J. P. Morgan Chase are among the world's largest MNCs. The service sector also has many large MNCs, including McDonald's and Walmart, that can change the entire commercial and aesthetic landscape in the towns where they locate, often forcing small businesses into bankruptcy.

MNCs' influence can be measured by the familiarity with which we recognize the household names IBM, Hitachi, Microsoft, General Electric, Du Pont, PepsiCo, Eastman Kodak, Toyota, Mitsui, Volkswagen, Bayer, Renault, Michelin, Ciba-Geigy, Seagram, Thomson, Fiat, Philips, Unilever, and others. Billions of dollars are spent on advertising in home and foreign markets so that the products, logos, and advertising campaign themes of these corporations have become part of popular rich-world, largely Western culture. As these products are marketed around the world, they become visible reflections of Western presence, or what critics would term instruments of **cultural imperialism**.

Obviously, the role played by MNCs in the global economy is a controversial one. Some see MNCs as agents of their home states, used by states to further their own economic and even political interests in the world. Indeed, some MNCs have become deeply involved in the politics of host countries, even to the point of engineering the overthrow of governments. A famous example of this is the involvement of International Telephone and Telegraph (ITT) in the events that led to the overthrow of the Allende government in Chile in 1973. Others see MNCs as essentially benign actors, acting in the interests of their shareholders and motivated by profit, and essential to the efficient development, production, and distribution of goods and services in the global economy. Still others see MNCs as exploitative actors, preying on cheap labour markets and raw materials, and selling the resulting products at huge profit margins. For example, in the early 1990s, many Nike shoes were manufactured in Indonesia, where the typical worker was paid $1 a day in 1991 (minimum-wage legislation and labour rights are seldom enforced in Indonesia). In 2008 some 20,000 Vietnamese Nike workers went on strike to protest their $59 per month wages. Meanwhile, a pair of Nike shoes can easily cost more than $150 in Canada.

For critics of MNCs, situations like this are repeated in all economic sectors in poor countries around the world. Indeed, critics often charge that MNCs do not just take advantage of poverty, but with their limited investment in human development, lax environmental standards, and outsourcing of labour, help to create it as well. This has led to an effort to develop strategies for **corporate social responsibility** to encourage MNCs to adopt voluntary codes of conduct with respect to working conditions, environmentally sustainable practices, and a variety of other concerns. In 1999, the then UN Secretary General Kofi Annan called for the creation of a Global Compact to bring companies together with UN agencies and NGOs to encourage linkage between economic activity and human rights and environmental principles. For example, the International Council on Mining and Metals brings together industry and NGOs to promote discussion of sustainable mining practices. Many corporations also cooperate with NGOs to certify their products as "fair trade" or environmentally sustainable. While some activists are hopeful that such programs can make a real difference, others are concerned that the corporate bottom line is based solely on profit maximization and voluntary codes of conduct are no substitute for laws and strict enforcement.

Certainly, MNCs are major players in many people's lives today, in both the North and the South. But the causes and extent of poverty are much more complex than the dynamics of MNC activity, as our next section will demonstrate.

THE GREAT DIVIDE: THE POLITICAL ECONOMY OF THE RICH AND THE POOR

The gap between the rich and the poor peoples of the world is enormous, whether measured in terms of economic statistics or quality of life. This gap is often described in terms of a generally rich Northern Hemisphere and a generally poor Southern Hemisphere. In practice, however, there are significant exceptions to this generalization. For example, North Korea is relatively poor, while Australia is relatively rich. Nevertheless, issues surrounding poverty and development are often cast in terms of a North–South debate. Countries are also classified along "rich" and "poor" lines, with the countries of the developed world having attained a high level of wealth through industrialization and technological development, relatively equitable levels of income distribution, and high standards of living in stable, civil societies. In contrast, countries of the "developing world" have lower levels of wealth, agricultural or subsistence economies, and inequitable income distribution in societies dominated by small elites. From this distinction has grown the term **less-developed country (LDC)**. These supposedly polar opposites—rich and poor, North and South, modern and traditional—are, by and large, misleading caricatures. Indeed, poverty is a serious problem in all of the world's leading industrialized economies, and an extravagantly wealthy upper class is often visible in most lower-income countries. Furthermore, some groups—especially minority groups and working-class women—tend to be more marginalized than others from the benefits of the economy.

If we define the South as including the majority of lower-income states, we find the Northern Hemisphere contains one-quarter of the world's people but consumes three-quarters of its goods and services, while the Southern Hemisphere contains three-quarters of the world's people but consumes only one-quarter of its goods and services. Of the US$23 trillion world GDP in 1993, US$18 trillion (or over 78 percent) was in the "high-income economies." By 2002, world GDP had climbed to well over US$32 trillion, with US$26 trillion of this total in the high-income states (or over 81 percent).[33] The UNDP *Human Development Report* of 2003 contained many striking facts about global inequity. For example, some 54 states actually had less income and net worth in 2002 than they had in 1990; more malnutrition was recorded in 21 states; infant mortality (the death rate for those under five years of age) had increased in 14 states, and primary school enrolment rates fell in 12 states. The report observed that the

---

PROFILE 8.3 The "Third World"

Throughout this text, we have often avoided using the term *Third World* where it is usually employed. The term has been criticized as demeaning to lower-income states. However, although obvious ethnocentricity has been involved in labelling the developed capitalist states the *First World*, the term *Third World* was first used to indicate a non-American, non-Soviet path of political and economic alignment. Over time, however, it slipped into general usage as meaning the Southern states with low GNPs, and here it quickly began to make less sense, not only because there are large discrepancies in GNP figures across these states, but because, with the end of the Cold War, there is no longer a distinct Second World of communist states. Alternative phrases have proliferated over the years, such as *developing states*, *less-developed states*, *underdeveloped*

states, the *periphery*, the *South*, the *global South*, and the *Majority World*. The broader question is not really which is appropriate, since they all derive from political perspectives, but whether any sort of label is appropriate, given the diversity of states and peoples in the developing world. Enormous differences exist between states in wealth, income distribution, political systems, social structure, and economic organization. In the past, some scholars have suggested differentiating states in the developing world by creating additional categories, such as the Fourth World, the Fifth World, or the least developed of the less-developed countries (LLDCs). Nevertheless, terms such as *North–South* and *developing world* remain widely employed in diplomatic language, especially in the context of UN-sponsored forums.

richest 5 percent of the world's people receive 114 times the income of the poorest 5 percent, while the richest 1 percent receive as much income as the poorest 57 percent.[34] In 2008, another UN study revealed that the richest 1 percent of adults owned 40 percent of the world's wealth, while the bottom half of the world's adult population owned just 1 percent of global wealth.[35] The study estimated that a person in the top 1 percent of the world's population was 2,000 times richer than a person in the bottom half of the world's population. In 2008, the World Bank estimated that the richest 10 percent of the world's population was responsible for almost 60 percent of world consumption, while the poorest 10 percent was responsible for less than 1 percent.[36]

The relationship between these grim economic figures and quality of life is direct and real. While measures based on monetary shares cannot tell the whole story (some societies with very low per capita GNP rates nevertheless are successful in providing for basic human needs), the human dimension of these economic statistics is appalling. At the aggregate level, and at the individual level, global inequality has taken a devastating toll on the human condition in much of the world. According to the UNDP *Human Development Report* of 2007–2008, one billion people live in abject poverty on an income of less than US$1 per day, without access to basic nutritional requirements, health care, waste disposal, or adequate housing. Over a quarter of children in the developing world are suffering from malnutrition. Every year approximately 10 million children die before the age of five, one child every three seconds, mostly from poverty and malnutrition. Infectious diseases claim millions

---

PROFILE 8.4 The Millennium Summit Goals

In 2000, Secretary-General Kofi Annan hosted the Millennium Summit in New York, attended by most heads of state and other officials. He set out a series of challenges, which received a warm welcome and expressions of support from the gathered politicians. However, despite the earnest desire to curb the ill effects of poverty, it would be foolish to suggest we are anywhere near the accomplishment of these goals; the *UN Millennium Development Goals Report of 2006* states that some 824 million people are affected by chronic hunger. Can the global economy possibly achieve these goals without significant or perhaps radical change?

FREEDOM FROM WANT: THE MILLENNIUM DEVELOPMENT GOALS

- *Eradicate extreme hunger and poverty.* Target for 2015: Halve the proportion of the world's people (currently 22 percent) whose income is less than one dollar a day and those who suffer from hunger.

- *Achieve universal primary education.* Target for 2015: Ensure that all boys and girls complete primary school.

- *Promote gender equality and empower women.* Target for 2015: Eliminate gender disparities in primary and secondary education.

- *Reduce child mortality.* Target for 2015: Reduce by two-thirds the mortality rate of children under the age of five.

- *Improve maternal health.* Target for 2015: Reduce by three-quarters the number of women dying in childbirth.

- *Combat HIV/AIDS, malaria, and other diseases.* Target for 2015: Halt, and begin to reverse, the spread of HIV/AIDS, malaria, and other diseases, providing at least 95 percent of young people with access to HIV-prevention services.

- *Ensure environmental sustainability.* Target for 2015: Integrate principles of sustainable development, improve drinking water, improve conditions of slum dwellers.

- *Develop a global partnership for development.* This would involve governments, IOs, civil society, and the private sector

A girl sits with her brother in a poor township in the outskirts of Jammu, India. India has the largest food-insecure population in the world, with 200 million people who are chronically hungry according to the India State Hunger Index in 2008. (AP Photo/Channi Anand/CP Archive.)

of lives each year, with one million fatalities alone due to malaria. Over 40 million people worldwide are infected with HIV/AIDS and 3 million die each year from this disease.[37] Meanwhile the majority of the people living in abject poverty are women, and 99 percent of maternal deaths occur in low-income countries.[38] The UN has developed a program of action, known as the Millennium Development Goals, aimed at reducing these and other shortfalls in human well-being by 2015 (see Profile 8.4), but progress has been frustratingly slow.

In light of these statistics, it might be useful to reflect on how Canada compares to the rest of the world. The UN employs a measure called the Human Development Index, which is based on achievements in basic human capabilities across states. The HDI is measured by life expectancy, educational attainment, and income (GNP per capita). In the 1999 report, Canada ranked number one in the world (as it had since 1992), though it has slipped in more recent years, finishing fourth in 2007–2008, behind Iceland, Norway, and Australia. (Of course, fourth out of over 190 states is still a rather positive assessment of the quality of life in Canada!) These high rankings do not mean that Canada does not face problems associated with poverty, homelessness, or the economic and political marginalization of certain groups in society. Nevertheless, it should give Canadians pause to consider what ethical obligations they might have to work to alleviate global inequalities.

INTERNATIONAL RESPONSES TO GLOBAL INEQUITY AND POVERTY: TOO LITTLE, TOO LATE?

Before discussing contemporary multilateral efforts to ease the plight of the poor, some background is in order. In Chapter 2 we examined how the European empires expanded around the world and how non-European empires also expanded and conquered territories abroad, imposing alien systems of economic and political organization. Many of the problems that beset the Southern states have their origins in the nature of this colonial rule. As we have seen, these empires began to collapse after World War II, and many states gained their political independence. However, the end of colonial rule left most of these former colonies woefully unprepared to govern their political, economic, or social affairs. Although some colonies were better prepared for independence than others, in general the colonies lacked individuals trained or involved in the administration of independent government. Furthermore, the arbitrary nature of colonial borders left many new independent states with complex mixtures of ethnicities, languages, religions, and clans, many of which had historical animosities. The effort to build nationalism around loyalty to the state, as opposed to loyalty to ethnicity or clan, was never very successful, as we saw in our discussion of ethnic conflict in Chapter 6. Finally, a postcolonial dependence lingered: Southern states needed Northern capital, while Northern states continued to exploit Southern natural resources and labour. The legacy of imperialism had left the former colonies with the illusion of political freedom but the reality of economic subjugation, which in turn left them vulnerable to political interference and domination. Concern over the North–South split increased during the 1960s and 1970s, and became a major issue at the UN (where it is still an issue today). Southern states were now stuck in a cycle of underdevelopment, one that they felt was perpetuated by the investment activities of large corporations, the accumulation of external debt to the North, and the unequal trading arrangement of the world economy. Liberals counter that many of these states have followed poor economic practices and suffer corrupt leaders and economic elites more interested in personal enrichment than the welfare of their people. Under such circumstances, states cannot be expected to develop.

Efforts to address Southern poverty began at the Bandung Conference in 1955, a meeting of 25 Asian and African states that condemned colonialism. In 1964 a group of developing states in the UN formed the **Group of 77 (G-77)**, which called for the development of favourable terms of trade for developing countries in GATT. The G-77 did succeed in creating the pressure behind a **Generalized System of Preferences (GSP)**, an arrangement whereby rich states would permit certain products from the developing world to enter their economies on favourable terms (that is, lower tariff barriers). But this concession was not the decisive or major step the developing world sought. In 1974, the G-77 called for the establishment of a **New International Economic Order (NIEO)** that would give Southern states a better position in the world trading system. Many developing states had evolved into what economists have referred to as "one-commodity countries." Some examples include Bolivia (natural gas), Colombia (coffee), Venezuela (petroleum), Botswana (diamonds), Niger (uranium), Zaire (copper), and Fiji (sugar). The price of such items is susceptible to sudden and dramatic shifts in demand, and if the price drops, the country suffers. The NIEO called for commodity agreements that would free states highly dependent on a few products from suffering the effects of wild price fluctuations. It also called for an increase in economic aid from Northern states; debt relief by forgiving or postponing repayment; the provision of preferential treatment for exports from developing countries; transfers of appropriate technology to the South; and greater Southern influence on the boards of the main financial institutions, such as the IMF and World Bank Group. These demands, and others associated with the NIEO movement, called for heavy state intervention in the global economy, thus contradicting the principles of free trade on which the GATT trade system was slowly evolving. Despite a modest effort to bolster developing countries' trade through the European Economic Community in 1975 in the **Lomé Convention** (which currently covers trade with over 70 **African, Caribbean and Pacific [ACP] states**), the overall thrust of the NIEO plan was so anti-market and demanding from the North's perspective that it never had a serious chance of being implemented. Today, the G-77 countries (which now number more than 120) continue to press for changes to the international trading system, but their profile is no longer what it once was.

As efforts to decisively change the global trading system foundered and foreign direct investment proved insufficient, the developing world increasingly relied on financial aid for development. This aid came from three primary sources: loans from the World Bank Group and the IMF, private capital markets, and Official Development Assistance. Today, the World Bank Group includes the International Bank for Reconstruction and Development (IBRD), the **International Development Association (IDA)**, the **International Finance Corporation (IFC)**, and the Multilateral Investment Guarantee Agency (MIGA), and the International Centre for Settlement of Investment Disputes. Together, the Group extended US$24.7 billion in financial assistance commitments in 2007. The money in the bank comes from governments (which pay according to a quota) and from borrowing on private financial markets. Loans are extended by a vote, with countries that contribute most to the funds of the Group having increased voting weight. As a result, the United States has disproportionate influence, and the rich countries dominate the voting. The IBRD approves only hard loans, that is, loans that have a good prospect for obtaining returns (repayment with interest). The IFC acts as a bridge between the developing world and private investors and financial institutions, while the IDA assists the world's poorest countries in obtaining soft loans, with easier terms of repayment and lower rates of interest. The IMF has become a crisis lender to governments in immediate need of funds to balance their payments or compensate for a drop in commodity prices, and it has recently convened the Multilateral Consultation on Global Imbalances.

The institutions of the World Bank Group and the IMF have received considerable criticism. Critics charge that the world's richest countries control these institutions (through **weighted voting**), and as a result the institutions lend based not on the need of the developing world but in the interests of capital lenders. The terms of the loans of the World Bank are little better than those from private institutions, and the amount of money dispensed by the Group has never been sufficient to make a decisive difference in the position of the developing world. Finally, the World Bank Group and especially the IMF are criticized for imposing extensive and often harsh conditions for loans, conditions that critics argue are based on the flawed formula of the Washington Consensus (discussed earlier in this chapter). The **structural adjustment programs (SAPs)** recommended by the IMF and World Bank demand reductions in public spending (which hurt the poor the most) and a focus on trade liberalization and the exportation of natural resources, which harm the environment and curtail more diverse economic development. These measures can increase hardship in developing states and often create political instability.[39] Liberals argue that conditionality on Bank or IMF loans is put in place to ensure that the money is used properly and in accordance with sound economic practices. Otherwise, liberals argue, the money would be wasted on inefficient government-run industries, or due to corruption would not reach the people who need it most.

Through the IFC or through private negotiations, governments in the developing world also obtain finance from private lending institutions, primarily the major international banks. In the late 1960s and through the 1970s, private banks extended massive loans to the developing world. They were more than willing to offload heavy investments from the oil-exporting Arab states, but in the process flooded developing states with short-term infusions of often mismanaged cash. Many of the projects built with these loans failed to yield the expected economic returns, and by the late 1970s and early 1980s, many Southern states were facing massive debt crises. Defaults on interest charges began to occur, and many loans were extended or simply written off. As a result, today private lending institutions are very careful about lending money to the developing world, compounding the capital shortage in poor countries, and paying off the debt has dominated domestic policy decisions. Indeed, many poverty activists have long argued that debt relief is a vital first step to help Southern states escape the vicious cycle of repayment; in 2006, the total external debt of developing countries was still over 2.1 trillion dollars.[40] Yet many of the Southern states that are in great debt, such as Brazil, Argentina, and Nigeria, remain strong regional military powers, spending valuable resources on military equipment often supplied through the Northern states.

The third primary source of finance is Official Development Assistance (ODA), which consists of government grants or loans specifically intended for economic development, often used (as during the Cold War) for outright geopolitical purposes. ODA is extended on a bilateral basis or a multilateral basis (through an international organization), and much of it is in fact "tied aid," requiring the funds to be spent on products from the contributing country. Although the countries of the North agreed in 1970 (and again in 1992) to maintain ODA targets of 0.7 percent of GNP, they have fallen far short of that goal. Beyond the ethics of tied aid and the dilemmas inherent in fostering further dependence, ODA can also reinforce the power of undesirable regimes. It is hard to find a more glaring example of this than Sudan (whose leader is accused of genocide by the International Criminal Court). The Sudanese government routinely calls for and receives international food aid (despite being a leading African exporter of several crops) while people starve in the conflicted Darfur.[41] Other questions are raised about the long-term applicability of aid, suggesting the north is as addicted to it as the south. For example, China and India remain prodigious recipients of aid. While poverty is a serious problem in these two countries, China has sent a man into space and India has developed a large nuclear weapons program. Are these countries in need of aid, or is the market for aid-related goods a force of its own?

Further, leaders from developing countries complain of the reverse transfer of technology, or "brain drain," that has often occurred. Developed countries and MNCs have been reluctant to establish research and development and other facilities that employ and train local skilled labour, but they are often willing to take the brightest and hardest-working and train them in the North. One study suggested that, between 1960 and 1976, more than 300,000 people migrated from developing countries to work as engineers, scientists, physicians, surgeons, and other technical workers in the United States, Canada, and the United Kingdom alone (see Chapter 11).[42] The loss of these highly skilled workers makes it even more difficult to develop indigenous technological capabilities. This increases the dependence of Southern states on the North, and there is no indication that the trend is reversing. Indeed many AIDS activists complain bitterly that qualified doctors and nurses are being drained into states such as Canada, when they are badly needed at home to help with the pandemic.

Alternatives do exist to the formal economies largely controlled or regulated by states. Indeed, the real growth area in many parts of the world is in the informal sector, characterized by low-paying jobs that offer no form of formal social protection but are often supported by networks of family and friends. The informal sector includes a wide array of economic activity such as street vendors, rickshaw drivers, roadside barbers, garbage collectors, sweat shop workers, and unregistered businesses that are outside the realm of full time, stable, regulated and protected work. In the developing world, as much as one-half to three quarters of all non-agricultural employment is in the informal sector, including 51 percent in Latin America, 65 percent in Asia, and 72 percent in Sub-Saharan Africa.[43] In times of economic hardship the informal sector tends to expand, so we can expect the global recession of the late 2000s will only accelerate this trend as the ranks of the unemployed grow across the globe. We have already mentioned the tremendous amount of domestic work, usually performed by women, that offers little monetary compensation but can provide for family needs through local agriculture or barter. Similarly, small

The Nobel Peace Prize for the Grameen Bank of Bangladesh, 2006. Accepting for the bank is Ms. Mosammat Taslima Begun and the bank's founder, Muhammad Yunus. The bank lends to over 7.5 million people in Bangladesh, 97 percent of them women. Loan recovery rates are 98 percent. The bank's model is now increasingly employed worldwide to provide credit and capital to poor populations, especially in rural areas. (Kurt Peredersen/Stella Pictures/Abacapress.com/CP Images.)

communities work to support each other without the help of formal state and international institutions, and we should not overlook this. Furthermore, the development of microcredit or microfinance lending has enabled millions of poor women to access modest amounts of capital for small business projects. In particular, the Grameen Bank in Bangladesh has had extraordinary success, and is now a model employed worldwide. We must also recognize the fact that transnational organized criminal activity will generate employment as well (see Chapter 6), ranging from illicit drug production to prostitution to weapons smuggling. Although Northern states want to deal with these human security issues, which often threaten their own countries, there is reluctance to engage in the kind of sweeping economic reform and development programs that would encourage people to seek livelihood in the formal, rather than informal or black market, economy. For example, in Afghanistan, it is far more lucrative for farmers to grow poppies for drug production than to grow legitimate food crops, and many farmers have their lives and the lives of their families threatened if they do not grow poppies. In a similar situation, what choice would you make? To change this situation will require a combination of economic development, access to markets for legitimate products, security for people against threats, and a significant drop in demand for goods such as drugs and services such as prostitution. Small initiatives will make a difference for some people in the poor parts of the world, but not for all.

Some have suggested that major reforms in international trade rules could offer long-term solutions for the cycles of economic poverty described above, while others contend that more trade liberalization is a possible panacea. Whether or not one accepts the reformist position or the neoliberal premise, recent developments in world trade negotiations are not encouraging. As we saw in Chapter 4, the push toward freer trade continued through the successive negotiation rounds of the General Agreement on Tariffs and Trade (GATT), culminating with the conclusion of the Uruguay Round in 1994. The Uruguay Round agreed to establish a new international organization to manage world trade, and in 1995 the World Trade Organization (WTO) was created. The WTO is an international organization headquartered in Geneva, staffed by a modest secretariat of 629 people; it inherits all of the results of the GATT negotiation rounds. In effect, the WTO replaces GATT, and therefore the organization is built on the principles of liberal trade theory: comparative advantage, tariff reduction, nondiscrimination, national treatment, and regulatory harmonization. The WTO is the central forum for world trade negotiations, and WTO agreements reflect the ability of the 153 member states to reach agreement on trade liberalization. Biannual ministerial meetings are supposed to dictate WTO direction, and this ministerial council has subsidiary working bodies to administer WTO agreements in specialized areas of trade such as goods, services, the environment, and intellectual property. Countries accused of unfair trading practices must answer to the council, and other states are legally permitted to impose countervailing sanctions and to receive whatever compensation the WTO panel judges deem appropriate (see Profile 8.5). This dispute management system is a significant development, since GATT outcomes were often ignored. However, this process does give rise to complaints (by both economic nationalists and antiglobalization activists) that the WTO represents the subordination of national sovereignty to an international organization without accountability to the citizens of individual states.

The WTO is entering a crucial phase in its short history. The current round of trade negotiations launched in November 2001, known as the Doha Round, have proven acrimonious and divisive. In August 2008 the Geneva meetings of the WTO collapsed without an agreement on relaxing trade barriers and lowering agricultural subsidies in wealthy states in order to better assist Southern states to engage in world commodity exchanges. This is no small matter: government subsidies given to farmers in the OECD countries have averaged over

PROFILE 8.5   The WTO and Canada: Good News, Bad News

Decisions made by the WTO will help some governments achieve their goals while hampering others. It will become increasingly difficult to promote free trade in some products and yet remain protectionist with others. Compare the two accounts below for an idea of how the WTO will sometimes give but sometimes take away.

CANADA AND THE JAPAN LIQUOR TAX CASE

In October 1996, the WTO Appellate Body requested that Japan change its liquor tax regime to remove barriers to imports of a wide variety of distilled liquor products (ranging from whiskey to gin). In Japan, imported distilled liquor is taxed at significantly higher rates than competing Japanese distilled spirits such as *shochu*. Canadian, European, and American distillers want to sell their products in Japan at what they consider fair prices. This was the first Appellate Body ruling involving Canada and was the second complaint involving Japanese barriers to imported liquor. (In 1987 a panel under GATT upheld a complaint by the European Commission that Japan's liquor tax law gave a competitive advantage to Japanese distilled liquor. Although Japan changed its law, *shochu* continued to receive preferential tax rates.) Under WTO rules, the Appellate Body report must be adopted within 30 days of being circulated to WTO members. Japan would then have 30 days to notify the WTO Dispute Settlement Body of its plans for implementing the report's recommendation. "I am very pleased with this ruling, a first for Canada," said Art Eggleton, Canada's international trade minister at the time. "It will end a long-standing dispute, and we expect that it will lead to higher Canadian exports to the Japanese distilled liquor market. I urge Japan to carry out the ruling quickly." Japan did not carry out the ruling quickly, but

began lowering taxes and tariffs on imported liquor in 1998.

CANADA AND THE MAGAZINE CASE

In January 1997, a WTO panel ruled that the Canadian government's efforts to support the Canadian magazine industry violated world trade rules, finding that Ottawa was at fault for preventing the sale of magazines containing mostly U.S. editorial content. The case was filed by the Office of the U.S. Trade Representative at the Geneva-based WTO and followed a prolonged effort by Time Warner Inc. to establish an edition of *Sports Illustrated* magazine in Canada. The decision was regarded as a serious blow to Canadian government efforts to protect the cultural sector from Americanization. The decision by a WTO panel rejected Ottawa's attempts to prevent *Sports Illustrated* from publishing a Canadian edition with mostly U.S. editorial content. However, this was only part of the ruling, since the three-member panel also struck down key policies that supported the entire Canadian magazine industry and protected it from all-out competition, including preferential postal rates, a tariff restriction, and an up to 80 percent tax on split-run magazines. "We lost," said a Canadian governmental official. Canada now faced a choice of either implementing the WTO ruling or allowing Washington to establish trade barriers against Canadian products equivalent to protectionist measures directed against U.S. magazines. Although the Canadian government vowed to fight the ruling, in 1999 the two governments announced an agreement improving the access of U.S. publications to the Canadian market.

SOURCES: (LIQUOR LAWS) DEPARTMENT OF FOREIGN AFFAIRS AND INTERNATIONAL TRADE, NEWS RELEASE, OCTOBER 4, 1996; (MAGAZINES) D. FAGAN AND L. EGGERTSON, "CANADA LOSES MAGAZINE CASE," *THE GLOBE AND MAIL*, JANUARY 17, 1997, A1.

US$300 billion per year in recent decades, undercutting foreign producers who cannot hope to compete against such massive support. The reduction of tariffs on farm goods would allow developing states' agricultural products to enter the rich countries' markets at a lower price to the consumer, the elimination of agricultural export subsidies by rich states would make developing states' products more competitive, and the reduction in industrial tariffs on certain

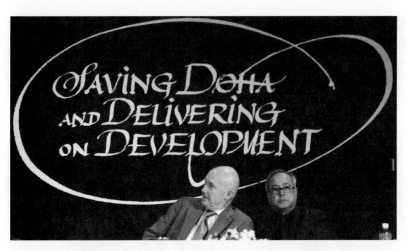

Looking for answers. The Director General of the World Trade Organization, Pascal Lamy, and Indian External Affairs Minister, Pranab Mukherjee, during a conference in New Delhi in March 2007. The aim of the conference, and many others like it, was to save the Doha Round. (AP Photo/Saurabh Das/CP Archive.)

products (especially textiles) would stimulate industrialization and economic growth in poor countries as their products could get better access to rich markets. The Doha agenda also promised liberalization in the trade of services, and would have established new global rules on the four "Singapore Issues" raised at an earlier WTO meeting: competition, investment, government procurement, and trade facilitation.

What went wrong? Put simply, in round after round of negotiations, countries in both North and South were unwilling to make the concessions and politically difficult sacrifices necessary to reach agreements. The EU has refused to eliminate export subsidies, and the United States has offered unacceptably low reductions in its own subsidy programs. India argued that it had not agreed to discuss new rules on the Singapore Issues. Japan has refused to contemplate reductions in its tariffs on rice. A group of states led by China, Brazil, and India has insisted on unrealistically deep cuts to agricultural subsidies and liberalization of farm trade by rich countries. Other countries, especially in Africa, are less enthusiastic about liberalizing farm trade, as they believed this would threaten the preferential access they already enjoyed with Europe. Other African countries wanted to see the United States eliminate its cotton subsidies, which amount to US$3 billion a year, making the U.S. the world's biggest exporter of cotton and the source of low world prices for that commodity. The prominence of the "most-favoured-nation status" principle means that a WTO state has to trade with other members as they would with their most favoured partners, and this is especially difficult for many states to swallow with the inclusion of states such as China, who have dubious records related to intellectual property and other contentious issues.

Many people—from environmentalists to trade unionists—resent the idea that global trade negotiations and a disconnected body in Geneva can make decisions that have such a large impact on national development issues (see Profile 8.6). Similar opposition, spread through the Internet, was discernible during the failed OECD negotiations for the establishment of the Multilateral Agreement on Investment (MAI), which would have taken the basic principles of trade agreements such as NAFTA and internationalized them, protecting international investors from government interference.[44] At any rate, it is clear that poverty will not be eradicated through trade liberalization alone; even the most successful trading states have great poverty in their midst. Much remains to be done, at all levels, to fight the scourges associated with impoverishment.

REGIONALIZATION IN THE WORLD ECONOMY

Partly as a result of the slow process characteristic of global trade negotiations, states have created a number of regional trade agreements with terms of trade that are preferential to those found in the WTO. That is, the member states of regional trade agreements have negotiated lower tariffs and more liberalized nondiscrimination and national treatment regulations

PROFILE 8.6 | The Battle in Seattle

A group of Seattle police officers stand in a cloud of smoke near WTO protestors in downtown Seattle, November 30, 1999. Demonstrators temporarily succeeded in delaying the opening session of the WTO. This scene resembles a war zone, or police state, more than a liberal democracy. Is the conflict over trade liberalization leading to further divides in domestic as well as international social structures? (AP Photo/ Beth Keiser/CP Archive.)

Civil disobedience is a time-honoured method of expressing one's opposition to government policies. An estimated 40,000 people took to the streets in Seattle in 1999 to register their opposition to the WTO as a regulatory body. Their main concern, although they had an impressive variety of concerns overall, was that the WTO was being granted too much power—the ability to make key decisions affecting people's health, environment, employment, and other issues. For many, the WTO represented the dark side of globalization. The sheer number of protestors surprised local authorities, and when a small minority became violent, the police responded with arrests and tear gas. Inside the WTO meetings, the ministers of member states were unable to reach a consensus on the issues that divided them. The meeting broke up with little in the way of substantive agreements. The protestors had made their point, and the governments of the world could not make the WTO meetings a success, possibly because of the increased public awareness brought about by the debate over globalization. Similar, though less violent, protests were mounted during the IMF annual meeting in Washington in April 2000 and the Summit of the Americas in Quebec City in April 2001. Seattle, Washington, and Quebec City were just the beginning of a global campaign of protest against the institutions promoting globalization, and major summits and meetings of these institutions now regularly attract large protests and "alternate summits."

than those that exist at the world (WTO) level. This has raised the possibility that the future of trade liberalization rests not in the global arena through the WTO, but in various regions through regional trade agreements.

Much of the free trade debate is, in fact, oriented toward the relative merits of regional trade agreements. These agreements are sometimes called preferential trade agreements, because they represent regions, or zones, of preferred terms of trade among participating countries. In Europe, a process of economic integration has been under way since the 1950s. In 1957, the European Economic Community (EEC) created a **customs union** covering all products among its members. In 1967, The EC marked the successful elimination of most of the remaining impediments to the free flow of goods, labour, and capital across the borders of member states. In 1993, the EC became the European Union (EU) after the **Maastricht Treaty** was ratified. The EU enlarged to a total of 25 member states as of May 1, 2004. Under the terms of the Maastricht Treaty, member states developed a monetary union which resulted in the establishment, and partial implementation, of a common currency, the **euro**.

Predictably, the process of integration in Europe has provoked protest over the loss of state control over national economies, social institutions, and culture. These concerns continue to plague the operation of the EU and the ability of governments to reach common policies on controversial issues. In particular, efforts to coordinate political and military policy through the EU have not been particularly successful. In 2005, a new constitution treaty for the EU which envisioned much deeper political and economic cooperation among member states was rejected in referendum votes in France and the Netherlands. This was considered a blow to further integration in Europe, and a statement by European voters that political and economic integration was proceeding too quickly and without due regard for national sovereignty on a host of economic, cultural, and political issues. In 2007, member states signed the Lisbon Treaty, designed to streamline economic and political decision making in the EU. However, in August 2008 Irish voters rejected the treaty in a referendum vote, casting more doubt on the future of the European integration process. These failed efforts illustrate the gap between EU advocates and government officials and many European publics who are concerned that decisions taken at the EU headquarters in Brussels are having too much of an impact on their lives. Nevertheless, the EU is the most highly integrated and institutionally developed of the world's trading areas, leading some to argue that the EU might one day become a supranational organization, perhaps even a "United States of Europe." In reality, the EU is far from this since member countries remain politically sovereign, although they have agreed to share decision-making responsibility and place some of the authority to make decisions in the hands of the EU. This strategy is sometimes called **pooled sovereignty**. The economic power of the EU (centred on the economic strength of a united Germany) is felt throughout Europe, and it acts as a centre of gravity for economic activity across the continent.

The present EU, however, has moved beyond efforts at economic integration and toward monetary union as well. Other EU members tired of relying principally on the German economy and its central bank, the Bundesbank, which tends to raise interest rates quickly whenever inflation becomes a possibility.[45] As of 2010, the euro is common currency in Belgium, Germany, Greece, Spain, France, Ireland, Italy, Luxembourg, the Netherlands, Austria, Portugal, Finland, Slovenia, Cyprus, Slovakia, and Malta. In other words, the euro is the currency in all EU states except the United Kingdom, Denmark, Sweden, and some of the new member states that joined the EU on May 1, 2004, including the Czech Republic, Estonia, Latvia, Lithuania, Hungary, and Poland. This movement toward monetary union is a huge step, but one unlikely to be repeated elsewhere. For example, it would be difficult to imagine the Federal Reserve of the United States and the Bank of Canada allowing some other agency to determine monetary policy for both states, though it is obvious that American monetary policy has a tremendous impact on the Canadian economy. However, the rise of the euro's value raises the prospect that it might eventually replace the American dollar as the preferred currency of international trade.

Whether or not the euro comes into effect across the expanded EU, the changes that have characterized European integration have set landmarks in the transition of world politics from a state power focus to a transnational economic focus. Genuine concerns exist about the viability of the project, but no one can deny that despite centuries of animosity among the great powers of Europe, there is a higher level of policy coordination, trust, and communication and travel than ever. However, we should be very careful about using the EU as a prototype for future regionalism. In fact, it is a common criticism of the neo-functionalist school that it uses European examples as a standard that simply cannot be exported elsewhere: Europe has a very high standard of living (though there are differences within the region, which the EU is supposed to attempt to rectify); it has global connections in both trade and diplomacy; and it has been under the military protection of the United States for much of its recent history.

At the same time, we can argue that there is a noticeable trend toward regional integration in trade and investment and the creation of political mechanisms to facilitate this in other parts of the world as well. Examples include the **North American Free Trade Agreement (NAFTA)** and the **Association of Southeast Asian Nations (ASEAN)** Free Trade Area. These efforts present a potential tri-regional model of the future world economy centred on the Americas, Europe, and Asia. Other regional trade arrangements also exist, including the Common Market of Eastern and Southern Africa and the Southern Common Market (also known as MERCOSUR). However, there has also been resistance to these regional trade agreements in member states. A plan to create a Free Trade Area of the Americas (FTAA) floundered amid domestic opposition to such an agreement in many countries and the opposition of several governments.

A regionalized model of trade contrasts in style and ultimately in purpose with the more global approach encouraged by the WTO. Those liberals who argue that peace follows commerce might be concerned that dividing the world into three large trade zones will encourage a tripolar mentality that might even lead to military conflict as the interests of the three areas begin to be incompatible. Liberals would also point out that a world largely managed by three regional blocs would in effect exclude most poor countries. The success of the WTO is therefore regarded as crucial, for the alternative is the greater isolation of the developing world from the rich world. Others, especially those from the Marxist tradition, contend that each area will be a political empire of the dominant power and its capitalist classes. Thus, imperialism continues in a highly integrated fashion, and imperial powers inevitably come into conflict as resources grow scarce and expansionism becomes the driving norm (this was, partially, Lenin's explanation of World War I).

Some of globalization's proponents might argue that regional integration is just a step along the road to a harmonized global economy. It occurs simultaneously as the world economy develops as well; the two processes reinforce rather than challenge each other. And, as regional organizations form, the political machinery of multilateralism is created. Though it has become almost habitual among students of international political economy to refer to the EU as the primary example of regional neo-functionalism, other situations exist in which states are engaging. A famous example, of course, is NAFTA, which includes Canada, the United States, and Mexico, and may soon include several Latin American countries as well. The Canada–U.S. Free Trade Agreement was signed in January 1989, between the two countries that exchange more goods and services than any other two in the world. This bilateral arrangement was expanded in 1992 with the addition of Mexico. NAFTA provides for the increased flow of goods and services across the borders of these states, especially in agriculture, automobile products, and clothing and textiles. The agreement was not without considerable controversy. There were many concerns in Canada that NAFTA was a threat to Canadian sovereignty and culture and that NAFTA might threaten safety regulations and environmental protection in Canada, as well as social programs such as health care (such concerns continue today). Others were concerned that jobs would leave Canada and head to Mexico, where salaries are lower. Advocates of NAFTA responded that Canadian sovereignty, social programs, and standards were protected under NAFTA. (And these advocates point out today that there is little or no evidence to suggest that NAFTA has led to job losses in Canada.) Similar concerns about jobs were voiced in the United States, while in Mexico some expressed fears about becoming an economic colony of the United States.

Two side agreements accompanied NAFTA, one on labour and one on the environment. These were made largely to counter opposition on the grounds that NAFTA would promote the degradation of labour standards, wages, and the environment. The environmental agreement created the Commission for Environmental Cooperation (or CEC, headquartered in Montreal), and it has filtered funding to many NGOs that have developed projects related to sustainable development. Examples include a project by the Air and Waste Management Association (Ottawa) to advance air quality in Hamilton, Ontario, and Monterrey, Mexico; the development of non-wood forest products in Oaxaca, Mexico; and water quality-monitoring project for Colonia residents in El Paso County/Valle de Juarez. However, critics charge that NAFTA, by encouraging investment along the U.S.–Mexican border, is designed primarily to keep Mexicans there (and not migrating northward) and will inevitably result in a lessening of environmental protection in the already heavily polluted region. The CEC has been criticized as an ineffective watchdog, having no real power to force any of the states to improve environmental standards.

In Asia, Japan is the regional leader, although the rise of China as the dominant economic power poses an obvious threat to that distinction. In Asia, however, regionalism is far less defined and far less institutionalized. In part, this difference is due to the tradition of bilateral economic diplomacy in Asia, as well as fear of Japanese and/or Chinese political hegemony (with the memory of World War II still fresh in people's memories). Nevertheless, some regional arrangements have taken shape, most notably ASEAN, established in 1967 to promote economic, political, and social cooperation among its members. ASEAN now comprises 10 countries. The Asian financial crisis of 1997, in which many of the large economies in the region suffered meltdowns (huge withdrawals of foreign investment and the crash of currencies, which began in Thailand and spread throughout the region) slowed Asian growth somewhat, but overall this area (and especially "socialist" China) retains the image of a capitalist boom.

More broadly, perhaps the most visible development in the world economy in the past few decades has been the emergence of the Pacific Rim as a major trading area. The Asia-Pacific Economic Cooperation forum (APEC) was founded in 1989 and currently involves 21 countries that touch the Pacific Rim, states as diverse as Australia, Brunei, Canada, Indonesia, South Korea, Japan, Malaysia, China, Thailand, New Zealand, the Philippines, Singapore, Mexico, Hong Kong, Taiwan, Chile, the United States, and Papua New Guinea. At its third ministerial meeting in Seoul, Korea, the Seoul Declaration stated four common objectives: to sustain growth and development of the region, to enhance positive gains resulting from increased trade, to further develop and strengthen the multilateral trading system, and to reduce barriers to trade in goods and services among participants. In 1993, at Bill Clinton's suggestion, the conference met with official heads of state in attendance. This brought the leaders of China, Taiwan, and Hong Kong together for the first time (although this did not change the PRC/Taiwan/Hong Kong relationship: Taiwan continues to be denied state status by the Chinese, and Hong Kong became Chinese territory in 1997). In the longer term, analysts foresee the formation of a PAFTA (Pacific Area Free Trade Agreement) that would tie Asian, North American, and South American states together, though such an arrangement remains speculative at present. The 1997 APEC meeting took place in Vancouver, and it was dominated by concerns over economic instability in some key Asian states and, outside the conference, concerns with human rights violations, by both dictatorial states such as Indonesia and by the Royal Canadian Mounted Police, who used pepper spray on protestors (with or without the prime minister's blessing). In total, members of APEC account for 40 percent of the world's population and 54 percent of the world's GDP. The organization does go beyond trade, making periodic forays into techno-logical, environmental, and cultural issues. However, it has not yet emerged as a significant political coalition in global politics.

Will these economic regions coalesce into antagonistic trade blocs? Many fear that political and economic friction between countries, as well as pressure from disaffected publics, will promote protectionism and provoke trade wars between regions. Economic regionalism will turn into political regionalism, and the world will become Balkanized and divided in a scenario not dissimilar to the interwar experience. Others are more optimistic, arguing that economic regions are beginning to overlap in their membership and that virtually all countries have a stake in the continued health of the global economy.

While it is impossible to forecast the long-term outlook of the world economy, we can say that both the trend toward regional integration and the broader trend toward global-ization will continue in the near future, though it has certainly been interrupted by global recession. Canada, for example, has signed bilateral free trade agreements with Colombia, Peru, Costa Rica, Chile, and Israel. Barring a major military confrontation, which is always a possibility, trade among nations will probably increase as economic growth continues, which will please most liberals, some economic nationalists, few environmentalists, and even fewer neo-Marxists. Ironically, one of the more widely hailed benefits of international commerce—the idea that with increased trade comes increased mutual vulnerability and understanding, and thus the reduced likelihood of warfare—is often challenged by those who argue globalization is simply redirecting conflicts between states into the realm of eco-nomics. Regardless of the shape of the architecture of the world economy, however, there are several factors that will inevitably have a tremendous impact on its evolution. We explore many of them in subsequent chapters, but one is so fundamental we elect to introduce it here: the price of energy.

THE POLITICAL ECONOMY OF ENERGY PRODUCTION AND CONSUMPTION

The world economy is powered by a vast infrastructure of energy production, distribution, and consumption; without it, the wheels of the global economy would grind to a halt. The pri-mary sources of energy today remain oil (approximately 34 percent of global energy supply), coal (approximately 26 percent), and natural gas (approximately 20 percent). It is clear that fossil fuels are by far the largest energy sources at present: combustible renewables and waste (10 percent), nuclear power (6 percent), and hydroelectricity (2 percent) make up relatively small shares of world supply.[46] This reliance on fossil fuels continues to have a major impact on global politics in the form of conflict over oil, disparities in energy access and consump-tion, and growing concern over the environmental damage caused by large-scale energy pro-duction and consumption. While fossil fuels are most often associated with environmental effects (especially with respect to climate change), hydroelectric dams are notorious for cre-ating environmental damage and nuclear power has proven expensive and produces highly radioactive waste. Global energy consumption patterns are characterized by high levels of disparity. The rich industrialized countries account for almost 50 percent of consumption. Citizens in North America consume far more energy resources per capita than all but a very few countries in the world.[47] Consumption is also very high per capita in Western Europe,

Japan, and Australia. By comparison, citizens in South Asia and Africa consume very little energy on an individual basis, but China's unparallelled increase in demand has had a major impact on both oil prices and projections of climate change.

Oil remains synonymous with power and wealth. It is relatively cheap (if environmentally dangerous) to transport; it provides exporters, including Russia, Mexico, Venezuela, Canada and Nigeria, but especially the Persian Gulf states (Kuwait, Saudi Arabia, Iran, the United Arab Emirates, Qatar, Bahrain, Oman, and Iraq), with hard currency. To ensure a steady supply of oil from the Middle East, the area was colonized by the Europeans early in the 1900s and inundated with American MNCs after that. As we saw in Chapter 4, OPEC's oil price increases brought on worldwide confusion and **recession** in the early 1970s and 1980s. Though the George H. W. Bush administration in the United States and the UN Security Council emphasized the importance of protecting Kuwait's sovereignty, it is quite clear that dependence on Middle Eastern oil was an important contributory factor in causing the West to go to war against Iraq in 1991, and oil access was also a factor (though not the only factor) in the decision to invade Iraq in 2003.

As Hanns Maull writes, the two chief concerns regarding the control of oil are price stability and access:

> Price stability does not necessarily mean stable prices; it implies only that prices move smoothly, without drastic jumps, roughly in line with world inflation and towards the cost of alternative sources of energy. Access is defined as the availability of supplies in sufficient quantities over time without major disturbances.[48]

The chairman of Exxon, one of the world's largest oil multinationals, once complained that predicting oil prices was much like "trying to paint the wings of an airplane in flight."[49] When OPEC was founded in 1960, the price of oil was determined by that of Saudi Arabian light, a medium-density oil used as a standard for crude-oil prices until 1980. The price then

A meeting of the OPEC ministers at the organizations headquarters in Vienna, Austria, in September 2008. The 13-nation organization was meeting to consider cuts to oil production amid falling prices in late 2008. (AP Photo/ Ronald Zak/CP Archive.)

was about US$2 per barrel. An Arab oil embargo after the Middle East war of 1973 caused widespread panic buying, and OPEC was able to raise the price of crude to $11.50 a barrel by 1974. By January 1980, after the Iranian revolution induced further panic buying, Saudi Arabian light was selling for as much as $36 a barrel. These prices not only contributed greatly to the recession of that time but also forced Western states to focus on alternative sources (such as North Sea oil) and conservation. World crude oil demand rose in the 1990s by nearly 12 percent, driving world prices for crude oil to nearly $40 a barrel in late 2000, a price that resurfaced in mid-2004. In the summer of 2008, oil soared to nearly $150 a barrel. For Canadians, this meant paying near $1.50 for a litre of gas (over $4 a gallon for Americans). The price rose due to a number of factors, including political instability in the Middle East, Nigeria, and Venezuela; an enormous boom in oil speculation in world markets; concerns over global warming; and the simple fact that it is becoming more and more difficult to profitably extract oil from the ground. Indeed, Canada is now the largest exporter of oil to the United States, not through conventional drilling techniques, but because of the huge tar sands projects displacing large swaths of the boreal forest in Alberta. The Harper government in Ottawa has referred to Canada as an "energy superpower," but the environmentally costly tar sands remain a contentious topic in both Canada and the United States. Although oil prices fell in the latter part of 2008 due to economic recession, the increase in oil prices in mid-2008 was a reminder of the political and economic impact of high energy costs.

It is difficult to overestimate the significance of a future severe spike in the price of oil, since the global economy is so reliant upon it. While upheaval in rich countries will probably remain confined to protests (such as the protests over fuel prices across Europe in May and July 2008) and the disruption of some industrial production, in many countries violence is possible as high oil prices undermine fragile economies and family incomes and help put food prices out of reach. Others suggest that the record profits recorded by big oil companies are reflective of the predatory capitalism that characterizes the global economy, permitting widely differentiated levels of capital accumulation and human suffering. There is also a demonstrable link between human rights violations and oil, a link reinforced in recent years by China's relationship with Sudan and the activities of Shell Oil in Nigeria. Others remind us of the link between resource scarcity and armed conflict and predict that states will continue to jostle for access to oil. As a result, the price spike in oil in 2008 served as a reminder of the global economic and political significance of this resource.

Looking to the future, the World Energy Council suggests that by 2020, more than 90 million barrels of oil will be consumed daily and that coal output will almost double to seven billion tonnes. So, too, will natural gas demand double, reaching four trillion cubic metres. This huge increase in energy demand will result from the increasing industrialization of the Latin American and, especially, Asian regions.[50] China, the world's sixth-biggest oil producer (ahead of Venezuela), became a net oil importer at the end of 1993. It will have to rely heavily on the Middle East and Africa for its supply, further complicating regional geopolitics in places such as Sudan, and on the prospect of oil deposits in the heavily contested South China Sea. Furthermore, China's energy future is crucial to efforts to control global warming (see Chapter 10).

Ultimately, many analysts believe that a global conversion toward alternative fuel sources must take place, and in particular to the renewable resources such as wind, geothermal, and solar power that many environmentalists have advocated for decades. This conversion is especially important for developing countries: in India, for example, two million small power plants are turning cow dung into electric power and cooking fuel.[51] Efforts to switch to "biofuels," however, have fuelled more debate than cars. Although such programs have been successful in some countries (such as Brazil's sugar-cane-to-fuel system) it is phantasmal to think the millions of cars in North America will run on corn any time soon. Moreover, the rush toward biofuel production helps drive food prices upward and raises serious questions about the ethics of producing food for fuel in a world where billions are malnourished.

Optimistically, the push for increased efficiency by environmentalists and managerial elites alike will force states such as China and the United States to mitigate the potential excesses of development and further explore renewable energy sources. Technological improvements and even lifestyle changes in the West have, in some cases, reduced energy consumption, though overall it continues to rise. Most states have an avenue toward energy self-sufficiency; Canada has huge oil and natural gas reserves, for example, though its heavy reliance on tar sands oil production is based largely on revenue related to American consumption. But the current pace of industrialization around the world and the uncertainties associated with oil prices make it difficult to suggest that the more advanced industrialized states have achieved any form of everlasting energy security; one might argue that their dependence (and resulting vulnerability to both supply disruption and the effects of climate change) has increased.

Finally, fuel for human movement—the food which sustains and powers us as living organisms—is also rising in price at an alarming rate. There are many reasons for the increase in food prices, including increased demand for meat in the rapidly expanding economies in Asia, increases in oil prices which drive production and transportation costs upward, speculative bidding on food futures markets, and the displacement of food crops for the production of biofuels. Rising food prices harm the poor, increase political instability, and force governments and people alike into further debt. Efforts to respond were slow. Governments, relief agencies, and international organizations such as the World Bank responded with increased food aid and emergency financing. The agricultural sector in many countries has responded by increasing the area of land under cultivation. However, none of these measures addresses the root causes of the global food crisis, which are found in the structure of the global economy itself.

CONCLUSIONS

This chapter has reinforced the central paradox of global politics. While the global economy displays a trend toward *convergence* in the form of increased trade between countries and peoples, increased levels of global and regional economic cooperation and management, and growing financial interdependence and levels of transactions across state borders, one can also identify trends of *divergence*, in the form of the regionalization of the global economy, the persistence of economic nationalism, and the widening gap between the rich and poor peoples of the world.

All the key variables discussed above, as well as many others, will continue to affect the development of the world economy. We should also keep in mind that the other topics discussed in this text, such as resource scarcity, overpopulation, international organization and law, and military spending, will further affect economic outcomes. Indeed, from the vantage point of 2009, it appears that we can expect much more turmoil and hardship in the global economy of the near future as an unprecedented global recession takes root. It is unlikely that the promise of liberal economics and short-term Keynesian spending can possibly overcome these challenges, leaving us with the question of how the global economy can be reformed or transformed to enhance social stability and improve the human condition. Ultimately, this is a question pertaining to the quality of human life and dignity, a topic to which we turn in our next chapter.

Endnotes

1. Quoted in *The Globe and Mail*, July 17, 1996, A10.

2. See *Development and Globalization: Facts and Figures 2008* (New York and Geneva: United Nations Conference on Trade and Development, 2008), 2.

3. *2008 World Development Indicators* (Washington, DC: The World Bank, 2008), 4.

4. *Human Development Report, 2007/2008* (New York: United Nations Development Program, 2007), 229, 232.

5. T. Friedman, *The World Is Flat: A Brief History of the 21st Century* (New York: Farrar Straus and Giroux, 2006). See also J. Bhagwati, *In Defense of Globalization* (New York: Oxford University Press, 2004); and M. Wolf, *Why Globalization Works* (New Haven: Yale University Press, 2004).

6. P. Collier, *The Bottom Billion: Why the Poorest Countries Are Failing and What Can be Done About It* (Oxford: Oxford University Press, 2007).

7. For example, see A. McGrew and N. Poku, eds., *Globalization, Development and Human Security* (Cambridge: Polity, 2007), and B. Milanovic, *Worlds Apart: Measuring International and Global Inequality* (Princeton: Princeton University Press, 2005).

8. See *The Millennium Development Goals Report 2006* (New York: United Nations, 2006), http://mdgs.un.org/unsd/mdg/Resources/Static/Products/Progress2006/MDGReport2006.pdf (accessed August 15, 2008).

9. R. Isaac, *Managing World Economic Change: International Political Economy*, 2nd ed. (Englewood Cliffs, NJ: Prentice Hall, 1995), 30. As Michael Mastanduno argues, "Even if nation-states do not fear for their physical survival, they worry that a decrease in their power capabilities relative to those in other nation-states will compromise their political autonomy, expose them to the influence attempts of others, or lessen their ability to prevail in political disputes with allies and adversaries." See M. Mastanduno, "Do Relative Gains Matter? America's Response to Japanese Industrial Policy," *International Security* 16 (Summer 1991), 78.

10. *Who Answers to Women? Gender and Accountability. Progress of the World's Women, 2008/2009* (New York: United Nations Development Fund for Women, 2008), 53–58. See also International Labour Organization, *Global Employment Trends for Women* (Geneva: International Labour Office, 2008), 2, http://www.ilo.org/global/About_the_ILO/Media_and_public_information/Press_releases/lang--en/docName--WCMS_091225/index.htm (accessed March 13, 2009).

11. *Who Answers to Women? Gender and Accountability*, 61.

12. United Nations Office on Drugs and Crime, *Global Report on Trafficking in Humans* (February 2009), 10.

13. *Trafficking in Women: The Misery Behind the Fantasy: From Poverty to Sex Slavery: A Comprehensive European Strategy*, European Commission, Department of Justice and Home Affairs, http://ec.europa.eu/justice_home/news/8marsen.htm#a1 (accessed March 14, 2009). See also United Nations, *The World's Women 2000: Trends and Statistics* (New York: UN Publications, 2000), 158, and K. Kempadoo, *Global Sex Workers: Rights, Resistance and Redefinition* (London: Routledge, 1998).

14. See J. Bystydzienski, ed., *Women Transforming Politics: Worldwide Strategies for Empowerment* (Bloomington: Indiana University Press, 1992); on microfinance, see http://www.microfinancegateway.org; see also M. Yunus, *Banker to the Poor: Micro-Lending and the Battle Against World Poverty* (New York: Perseus, 2007). For a review of feminism and globalization see M. E. Hawkesworth, *Globalization and Feminist Activism* (Lanham, MD: Rowman and Littlefield, Publishers, 2006).

15. See V. Shiva, *Staying Alive: Women, Ecology, and Development* (London: Zed, 1998); B. Cook, *Women Writing Nature: A Feminist View* (Lanham: Lexington Books, 2007); and R. Ruether, *Integrating Ecofeminism, Globalization, and World Religions* (Lanham: Rowman and Littlefield, 2005); and for a critical analysis, see Janet Biehl, *Finding Our Way: Rethinking Ecofeminist Politics* (Montreal: Black Rose Books, 1991).

16. The World Commission on Environment and Development, *Our Common Future* (Oxford: Oxford University Press, 1987). In fact, an entire subfield, referred to as *ecological economics*, has emerged in recent decades. See also R. Paehlke, *Democracy's Dilemma: Environment, Social Equity, and the Global Economy* (Cambridge, MA: MIT Press, 2003).

17. An important work in this direction was J. MacNeil, P. Winsemius, and Taizo Yakushiji, *Beyond Interdependence: The Meshing of the World's Economy and the Earth's Ecology* (Oxford: Oxford University Press, 1992), 32.

18. For an expanded treatment of this section, see P. Stoett, *Human and Global Security: An Exploration of Terms* (Toronto: University of Toronto Press, 2000), 97–118.

19. See W. Greider, *One World, Ready or Not: The Manic Logic of Global Capitalism* (New York: Simon and Schuster, 1997); J. Gélinas, *Juggernaut Politics: Understanding Predatory Globalization* (London: Zed Books, 2003); J. Petras and H. Veltmeyer, *System in Crisis: The Dynamics of Free Market Capitalism* (London: Zed Books, 2003); and T. Smith, *Globalisation: A Systematic Marxian Account* (Boston: Brill, 2006). For discussions of the relationship between globalization and social change see B. Barber, "Jihad vs. McWorld." *Atlantic*, March 1992, 53–63; R. White, *Global Spin: Probing the Civilization Debate* (Toronto: Dundurn, 1995), 127. See also A. Linklater, "Globalization and the Transformation of Political Community," in J. Baylis and S. Smith, eds., *The Globalization of World Politics: An Introduction to International Relations*, 2nd ed. (Oxford: Oxford University Press, 2001), 617–34; and U. Schuerkens, ed., *Globalization and Transformations of Local Socioeconomic Practices* (New York: Routledge, 2008).

20. M. Waters, *Globalization* (London: Routledge, 1995), 3.

21. Ibid., 4.

22. R. Cox, "The Global Political Economy and Social Choice," in D. Drache and M. Gertler, eds., *The New Era of Global Competition: State Policy and Market Power* (Montreal/Kingston: McGill-Queen's University Press, 1991), 335–49, 336.

23. J. Frieden, *Global Capitalism: Its Fall and Rise in the Twentieth Century* (New York: W. W. Norton and Company, 2006), xvi–xvii. For explorations of globalization, see A. MacGillivray, *A Brief History of Globalization: The Untold Story of Our Incredibly Shrinking Planet* (London: Robinson, 2006); S. Dasgupta and R. Kiely, eds., *Globalization and After* (Thousand Oaks, CA: Sage Publications, 2007); L. W. Pauly and W. D. Coleman, eds., *Global Ordering: Institutions and Autonomy in a Changing World* (Vancouver: UBC Press, 2008); and R. Munck, *Globalization and Contestation: The New Great Counter-Movement* (New York: Routledge, 2007).

24. V. Kavolis, "Contemporary Moral Cultures and 'the Return of the Sacred,'" *Sociological Analysis* 49, no. 3 (1988), 203–16.

25. J. Williamson, "What Should the World Bank Think About the Washington Consensus?" (Washington DC: Institute for International Economics, July 1999).

26. S. Strange, *Casino Capitalism* (NY: Blackwell, 1986). On today's currency trade, see A. Balakrishnan, "Daily Currency Trade Equal to Germany's Annual Output," *The Guardian*, September 26, 2007.

27. See M. ul Haq, I. Kaul, and I. Grunberg, eds., *The Tobin Tax: Coping with Financial Volatility* (Oxford: Oxford University Press, 1996).

28. "Floating the Tobin Tax," *The Economist*, July 13, 1996, 84.

29. See, for example, J. Goodman, *Protest and Globalisation: Prospects for Transnational Solidarity* (Annandale: Pluto Press, 2002).

30. R. Vernon, *Sovereignty at Bay: The Multinational Spread of U.S. Enterprises* (New York: Basic, 1971); R. Barnet and R. Muller, *Global Reach: The Power of Multinational Corporations* (New York: Simon and Schuster, 1974). For studies on the role of multinational corporations in world affairs, see S. D. Cohen, *Multinational Corporations and Foreign Direct Investment: Avoiding Simplicity, Embracing Complexity* (New York: Oxford University Press, 2007); L. Cuyvers and F. De Beule, eds., *Transnational Corporations and Economic Development: From Internationalization to Globalization* (New York: Palgrave, 2005); and O. de Schutter, ed., *Transnational Corporations and Human Rights* (Oxford: Hart, 2006).

31. See, for example, K. Levitt, *Silent Surrender: The Multinational Corporation in Canada* (Toronto: Macmillan, 1970).

32. *World Investment Report 2008: Transnational Corporations and the Infrastructure Challenge* (New York and Geneva: United Nations Conference on Trade and Development, 2008), xvi. See also *World Investment Report 2007: Transnational Corporations, Extractive Industries, and Development* (New York and Geneva: United Nations Conference on Trade and Development, 2007), xvi.

33. UNDP, *Human Development Report, 1996* (New York: Oxford University Press, 1996), 2; World Bank figures obtained from WB Indicators Database, http://www.worldbank.org/data/databytopic/GDP.pdf (accessed April 24, 2004).

34. Figures are from the UNDP's *Human Development Report, 2003*, http://hdr.undp.org/reports/global/2003/pdf/hdr03_complete.pdf (accessed April 24, 2004). For explorations of international development issues, see T. Addison, T. Shorrocks, and A. Swallow, eds., *Development Agendas and Insights: 20 Years UN-WIDER Research* (Helsinki: United Nations University, 2005) and J. S. Saul, *Development After Globalization: Theory and Practice for an Embattled South in a New Imperial Age* (Blackpoint, NS: Fernwood Publishers, 2006).

35. J. B. Davies, S. Sandström, A. Sharrocks, and E. N. Wolff, *The World Distribution of Household Wealth*, United Nations University—World Institute for Development Economics Research Discussion Paper No. 2008/03 (February 2008), 7.

36. *2008 World Development Indicators* (Washington, DC: The World Bank, 2008), 4.

37. *Human Development Report, 2007/2008* (New York: United Nations Development Programme, 2007), 25.

38. *Maternal Mortality in 2005: Estimates Developed by WHO, UNICEF, UNFPA, and the World Bank* (Geneva: World Health Organization, 2005), 1.

39. See T. Lairson and D. Skidmore, *International Political Economy* (Fort Worth, TX: Harcourt Brace, 1993), 65–66; S. George, *The Debt Boomerang* (Boulder, CO: Westview Press, 1992); and S. George, *A Fate Worse Than Debt* (Harmondsworth: Penguin, 1988).

40. See World Resources Institute, *Earthtrends*, http://earthtrends.wri.org/searchable_db/index. php?theme=5&variable_ID=229&action=select_countries (accessed March 10, 2009).

41. See J. Gettleman, "Darfur Withers as Sudan Sells a Food Bonanza," *International Herald Tribune*, August 10, 2008.

42. UNCTAD Secretariat, *Technology: Development Aspects of the Reverse Transfer of Technology*, Report of the Secretariat (New York: United Nations, 1979), para. 6.

43. See *Women and Men in the Informal Economy: A Statistical Picture* (Geneva: International Labour Office, 2002), 10.

44. There is a Canadian connection here, since the Council of Canadians, an antiglobalization coalition, was the organization that initially circulated a copy of the proposed MAI over the Internet in April 1997. See T. Clark and M. Barlow, *MAI: The Multilateral Agreement on Investment and the Threat to Canadian Sovereignty* (Toronto: Stoddart, 1997), 21–22.

45. One of the reasons some EU members were fond of the more flexible euro concept is that the Bundesbank has had such a strong anti-inflationary agenda that it has resulted in a "single-minded fixation on price stability [that] has left Europe facing a long-term crisis of joblessness." James Laxer, "Germans Are Creating a Monetary Quagmire," *Toronto Star*, July 21, 1996, F3. More generally on regionalization, see A. Hülsemeyer, *Globalization in the Twenty-First Century: Convergence or Divergence?* (New York: Palgrave Macmillan, 2003).

46. All data from 2006, in International Energy Agency, *Key World Energy Statistics 2008* (2008), 6, http://www.iea.org (accessed March 11, 2008).

47. See "Energy Consumption: Consumption per Capita," Energy and Resources database, World Resources Institute, http://earthtrends.wri.org (accessed June 27, 2004); and recent Human Development Index Reports.

48. H. Maull, "The Control of Oil," *International Journal* 36, no. 2 (1981), 273–93. For a review of the politics of oil, see F. R. Parra, *Oil Politics: A Modern History of Petroleum* (New York: I. B. Tauris, 2004) and T. Shelley, *Oil: Politics, Poverty and the Planet* (New York: Zed Books, 2005).

49. Quoted in *The Globe and Mail*, March 15, 1994.

50. "Survey," *The Economist*, June 18, 1994, 1–6.

51. P. Sampat, *World Watch*, November/December 1995, 21–23.

Suggested Websites

APEC
http://www.apec.org

Canadian Free Trade Agreements
http://www.international.gc.ca/trade-agreements-accords-commerciaux/agr-acc/index.aspx?lang=en#free

European Union
http://www.europa.eu.int

International Chamber of Commerce
http://www.iccwbo.org

International Institute for Sustainable development
http://www.iisd.org

International Monetary Fund
http://www.imf.org/external/index.htm

Link to Women's Studies/Women's Issues WWW Sites
http://research.umbc.edu/~korenman/wmst/links.html

NASDAQ Stock Market
http://www.nasdaq.com

Oneworld.Net
http://www.oneworld.net

United Nations Development Program
http://www.undp.org

World Bank
http://www.worldbank.org

World Trade Organization
http://www.wto.org

Human Rights and Human Security

No one shall be subjected to torture or to cruel, inhuman or degrading treatment or punishment.

—*Universal Declaration of Human Rights, 1948, Article 5*

There is little evidence to suggest that mankind has advanced much beyond [the] level of jungle morality.

—*Robert Gilpin[1]*

INTRODUCTION: CAN WE INSTITUTIONALIZE ETHICS ON A WORLD SCALE?

Violations of human rights occur throughout the world on a daily basis. Some of these violations are well documented and draw the condemnation of many international institutions, governments, and human rights organizations. In particular, grave violations of human rights (such as genocide, mass deportations or ethnic cleansing) often draw international attention and can spark international crises and confrontations between the perpetrators of these crimes and the outside world. Other violations pass unnoticed or ignored, lost behind more publicized events or subordinated to more urgent political priorities or national interests. Humanitarian and human rights law (introduced in Chapter 5) is more developed than ever, but as a mechanism to prevent and respond to human rights violations and humanitarian crises it still faces serious challenges: the privileged position of states over individuals; the continued resort to force by both state and nonstate actors; the impact of globalization on economic and social rights; and the erosion of civil liberties by counterterrorism policies. This chapter will reflect on human rights issues from a global politics perspective. Human rights issues continue to exert influence on the security, economic, and sustainable development agendas, and reflect the themes of convergence and divergence in global politics. Although we have discussed human security in many other chapters, we will also give it explicit attention here, since the promotion and protection of human rights is a fundamental aspect of the provision of human security, and humanitarian intervention remains one of the most daunting issues on this agenda.

In March of 1995, Canadians mourned the death of Professor John Peter Humphrey, the founder and first director of the United Nations Human Rights Division, a post he held for 20 years. He also founded the Canadian Human Rights Foundation and the Canadian branch of Amnesty International, a nongovernmental organization dedicated to protecting citizens from state human rights abuses. However, Professor Humphrey will be most widely remembered for his contributions to the writing of the Universal Declaration of Human Rights.[2] Most observers consider it a largely symbolic work, albeit one of great significance; as a declaration, it does not carry the status of international law attributed to a convention or treaty. This is but one example of the general frustration with international law encountered by those who would aspire to produce a more standardized world order or human rights regime. As discussed in Chapter 5, some wonder whether law can even be said to exist if there is no formal, coercive mechanism to enforce it. Indeed, if we need reliably effective enforcement machinery to establish law, we do not have international law. Though states will often engage in punitive measures to attempt to enforce trade agreements, or to punish gross violations of human rights such as the institutionalization of apartheid by the former South African government, it is another thing entirely to speak of a systematic law applied consistently across the globe.

However, others argue that the absence of an enforcer does not imply that international law, in a less strict sense, does not exist. One might argue that outside the confines of a domestic legal system, a law that relies on force alone for its legitimacy is essentially tyrannical and bound to be short-lived. International law is a system in which consent-granting state leaders choose to participate not because they have to—though no one would deny the fact that some pressure does exist—but because they believe that it will ultimately benefit them. For realists, this is the explanation for the existence of international law: it is an example of self-interested cooperation in an anarchic international system. The Roman and British empires spread law throughout many lands, but it was the law of empire, not of consensual states. When Hugo Grotius published his *De jure belli ac pacis* (*On the Law of War and Peace*) in 1625, he was writing in an age when the dominant European colonial powers were defining international law and imposing it on the rest of the world (see Chapter 5). The periods of decolonization that followed, especially after World War II, have at least in part changed this perception.

Formal state sovereignty, and its protection in documents such as the UN Charter, ensures that international law is not something imposed by Romans or Europeans but something that has gained the acceptance of self-determining members of the international community. It might be argued that the participation of states in international legal arrangements reflects an even stronger incentive to comply than if that system of law were coercive or imposed. However, one of the problems with this perspective is that in many areas of international law, including questions about human rights, the people most threatened by abuses are the citizens of states, and not those who control the government in power. The principle of territorial sovereignty does not distinguish between democratically elected leaders and tyrants, and many citizens are victims of human rights abuses by authoritarian governments who refuse to respect international human rights law, and then reject international pressure to change their behaviour as interference in their domestic affairs. Another problem is that conceptions of human rights vary, on both philosophical and political grounds. This variation raises the tricky question of whether the international community has an obligation, or for that matter the ability, to institutionalize conceptions of justice, law, and human rights on an international level. However, recent movements toward individual accountability under international law, such as the development of the International Criminal Court, suggest we may be moving toward a system characterized by both state voluntarism and a potentially viable, if highly controversial, effort to hold state leaders responsible for the more egregious crimes against humanity. We expand on these questions below when we discuss human rights law more specifically. For now we will examine the essential divisions of opinion on human rights.

International Days and Weeks Declared by the United Nations Related to Human Rights

PROFILE 9.1

Note that most of the days and weeks declared by the UN celebrate some sort of human-rights-related issue. But does all this celebration really advance these causes?

January 27	International Day of Commemoration in Memory of Victims of the Holocaust	August 9	World's Indigenous People Day
February 21	International Mother Language Day	First Monday of October	World Habitat Day
March 8	International Women's Day	October 10	World Mental Health Day
March 21	International Day for the Elimination of Racial Discrimination	October 16	World Food Day
March 21–28	Week of Solidarity with the Peoples Struggling against Racism and Racial Discrimination	October 17	International Day for the Eradication of Poverty
March 22	World Water Day	October 24	United Nations Day
March 23	World Meteorological Day	October 24–30	Disarmament Week
April 7	World Health Day	November 6	Day for Preventing the Exploitation of the Environment in War and Armed Conflict
May 3	World Press Freedom Day	Week of November 11	International Week of Science and Peace
May 15	International Day of Families	November 20	Universal Children's Day
May 17	World Telecommunications Day/World Information Society Day	November 20	Africa Industrialization Day
May 31	World No-Tobacco Day	November 29	International Day of Solidarity with the Palestinian People
June 4	International Day of Innocent Children Victims of Aggression	December 1	World AIDS Day
June 5	World Environment Day	December 3	International Day of Disabled Persons
June 20	World Refugee Day		
June 26	International Day against Drug Abuse and Illicit Trafficking	December 5	International Volunteer Day for Economic and Social Development
July 11	World Population Day	December 10	Human Rights Day
September 8	International Literacy Day	December 18	International Migrants Day
Third Tuesday of September	International Day of Peace	December 20	International Human Solidarity Day
October 1	International Day of Older Persons		

As we noted above, serious philosophical differences of opinion exist regarding human rights. The first debate concerns the subject matter and its definition: Do we focus on the political rights of the individual or the socioeconomic rights of the collective? The tension between the two has been the source of considerable political controversy in global politics and a mainstay of heated debate. A second debate revolves around the question of whether human rights is a relative or a universal concept. Some charge that the prevalent approach to human rights is an imposed Western idea, and that civilizations, societies, peoples, and groups have different conceptions of the term. Others argue that basic human rights are universal for all peoples. A third debate concerns the usefulness and effectiveness of international laws to protect and promote human rights and human security. As you might anticipate, each theoretical perspective on global politics that we have introduced in this book regards the issue of human rights very differently.

INDIVIDUAL VERSUS COLLECTIVE CONCEPTIONS OF HUMAN RIGHTS

During the Cold War (see Chapter 3) it became standard for the two opposing camps to each present their vision of human rights as morally superior. The West insisted that the individual is the most important component of any political system, and that an individual's rights must be protected from encroachment by the state. The Soviet Union naturally rejected this definition of human rights, arguing that collective rights, or those of entire populations, had to come first. The communist parties of the East rejected the right to private property, long taken as a fundamental right in the West. They also rejected the right to practise religion freely, which remains a highly contested right in some societies today where a single religion is instituted as that of the nation-state, such as in Iran. Even in Western states, repetitious references to God and country by political leaders raise concerns about protecting religious diversity and tolerance.

We are engaging in what some might consider excessive dichotomization here. Every society needs some sort of balance between the individual and collective conceptions of rights, such as the right to individual liberties and the right to be free from life-threatening poverty. Individual rights can be superseded in the most liberal states by the need to protect collective rights; for example, in many parts of the United States, a self-declared bastion of civil liberty, the state can still kill people who are found guilty of treason or other crimes. Sometimes, the logic of group rights can lead to divisive debate. For example, the Universal Declaration states that "the family is the natural and fundamental group unit of society and is entitled to protection by society and the State" (Article 16/3). This statement remains open to interpretation and can be used to challenge the legitimacy of same-sex marriage. In Canada, there are competing conceptions of which should take precedence, the individual or groups such as francophones in Quebec or First Nations peoples. States such as Malaysia have argued that Western notions of individual liberty are fine, but they should not be imposed on non-Western states that emphasize collective rights. Human rights groups such as Amnesty International argue that there are some things all individuals should be protected from, including repression and **torture** at the hands of the state. This helps form the basic argument that in international law, *jus cogens* (preemptory norms that override all treaties or agreements), universally agreed standards, and protections from the more extreme violations of human rights, do in fact exist. This leads however to our next topic: Beyond the right to life itself (and even this is highly controversial in the abortion debate), which norms or belief systems should receive universal protection?

RELATIVISM VERSUS UNIVERSALISM IN HUMAN RIGHTS

In the African country of Ghana, a few isolated communities still practise an ancient Ewe custom, shared by other communities in Togo, Benin, and southwest Nigeria. The custom holds that for serious crimes against the community such as murder, rape, or theft, "the spirits can be appeased only by the enslavement of young [female] virgins from the offender's family in the shrines of traditional priests." This enslavement of girls as young as 12 includes the expectation that the girls will participate in sexual acts with the priests. Many Ghanaians are campaigning against the practice, which is said to have enslaved "as many as 10,000 girls." But in the Ghanaian coastal village of Tefle, many of the village men insist they have the right to practise what they consider to be a vital custom.[3] This is an extreme case; others, such as child labour, invoke similar feelings of horror among Westerners accustomed to a different set of principles. However, many Africans and South Americans consider the Western tradition of putting older citizens into retirement facilities instead of keeping them at home with extended families to be equally barbaric, and the lack of care for the homeless in major urban centres is viewed with similar disdain. So we realize that there are cultural differences between different societies, as there have always been. The question is whether some practices, often claimed as integral to those cultures, should be universally condemned.

As suggested above, we have to ask also whether it is even appropriate to condemn some states for human rights violations: What gives anyone, or another state, the right to make such pronouncements? Some postmodern theorists reject the premise of a universal moral order, arguing that norms and principles are subject to a specific time and place. In other words, what is morally acceptable today may not be tomorrow; this is certainly the case with some widespread institutions, such as that of slavery in the Americas. It has been suggested that as we progress toward a more civilized world order, we are redefining certain types of behaviour as illegitimate. As described in Chapter 5, the institutionalization of this process of redefinition has been specifically referred to as the social construction of global prohibition regimes: they are guided by norms that "strictly circumscribe the conditions under which states can participate in and authorize these activities and proscribe all involvement by nonstate actors."[4] Once we have made some sort of collective decision regarding the immorality of an act or even a sociopolitical system, such as the former apartheid in South Africa, or the current state repression in Burma, then we should make an attempt to universalize this decision and spread it around the world, through education or outright coercion.

To many, this sounds rather confusing, for while it may have the most progressive of foundations (such as outlawing slavery, for example), it also implies that the majority (or perhaps merely the strong) has the moral right (or even duty) to impose its will on others. Is this much different from what the imperial powers did during the dark years of colonial administration? Does this simply replace the old political and economic dominance of the West with a new form of cultural imperialism?[5] This term usually refers to the imposition of one society's values on another, through either the force of law (as in direct colonialism) or the less overt manipulation of minds through the media (television, radio, newspapers, or even the Internet). However, when it comes to standards of international law and human rights in particular, the promotion of Western values with aid policies designed to award liberal democratization are equally suspect, as are rhetoric-laden UN resolutions, which can be seen as the soft law of cultural imperialism.

The idea behind cultural relativism is that ethical values (ostensibly the root cause of governments' human rights policies) vary from place to place and over time. As R. J. Vincent writes, this means "that moral claims derive from, and are enmeshed in, a cultural context which is itself the source of their validity."[6] In other words, beyond condemning the most brutal of practices such as slavery and torture (and even these are subject to relativist definitions), it is intrinsically unfair to criticize the ethical positions of others, since they arise out of the specific conditions faced by them at the time. Japan has always had a strong dependency on seafood, for example; perhaps we should not be surprised or outraged that some Japanese still sell whale meat in restaurants in Tokyo and elsewhere. Amsterdam's "red light" district, where prostitution is on open and legal display, would appear distinctly unethical in many other areas of the world. While the United States often condemns states for engaging in repressive policies, many point to the increasing use of the death penalty and the disproportionately high incarceration of minorities in that country as an indication of regressive public ethics. The role of women has changed rapidly in Western societies, but does this imply that all states should adopt similar legal provisions for women's rights? Since no states are without human rights problems and controversies, it may not be just cultural imperialism to force one's own values onto the international stage; it may be nakedly hypocritical as well.

Even the more obvious cases can become complicated with a close look. For example, the right to food is often used as an example of a universal human right.[7] However, we must ask whether people have a simple right to adequate amounts of food, or even equitable amounts of food within their own societies (few, if any, states would pass that test). We might argue that the right to environmental security should be universally applicable, and that all people should be able to live in a local environment free from profound ecological threats. However, any attempt to ensure this right would not only challenge sovereignty as an institution but also in many cases require the redistribution of resources within societies. At the same time, cultural relativism can become a cloak behind which abusers of basic rights can hide, and we should not let it stop us from analyzing controversial issues. Or, in the words of the distinguished scholar Fred Halliday,

> While an awareness of relativity and difference is essential to an explanation of how and why systems of domination originate and are maintained, such a recognition need not necessarily lead, out of a misplaced anthropological generosity, to denying that forms of oppression do exist and recur in a wide range of societies and historical contexts.[8]

A yet broader issue concerns whether questions of ethics and morality should even be part of the study of international relations.[9] If state sovereignty is sacrosanct, states really have no right to comment on what goes on in other states in the first place. If this were the case, the ethical responsibilities of government leaders would not extend beyond the borders of their own countries.[10] Since the most fundamental principle of international law is state sovereignty, international law reinforces, rather than challenges, this perspective. However, leaving questions of permanence aside, states are almost invariably involved in each other's domestic economies; they often share transnational cultural understandings; and much migration has occurred in the past two centuries. All of this leads us to suggest that, whether they like it or not, government leaders do bear some measure of ethical responsibility for what occurs outside their borders and for what their citizens do outside them as well. While this responsibility has always pertained to the actions of soldiers, it includes the actions of civilians. For example, the Canadian government has joined several other states to make it possible to prosecute Canadians who purchase sex with children when abroad. Similarly, activists have campaigned for MNCs to adopt ethical guidelines, or codes of conduct, when operating in low-income regions (see Chapter 8). When a government provides low-cost insurance for firms investing in conflict zones, it is making an ethical decision on the implications of investing there. In fact, most questions related to foreign policy, as well as our own individual policies when we interact with the world, involve the realization and implementation of ethical standards, even if we don't habitually agonize over our choices.

As Sidney Bailey and Sam Daws write, "from a moral point of view, human rights are about the behaviour of individuals. From a legal point of view, human rights are about the responsibilities of governments."[11] Until roughly the mid-to-late 19th century, human rights concerns were regarded as within the domestic jurisdiction of rulers. Campaigns to abolish the slave trade and to provide humanitarian care for wounded soldiers helped break this confinement, although the principle of nonintervention maintains its prominent place in the UN Charter today. The human rights field has expanded considerably in scope since the end of World War II, the cataclysmic event that so horrified the world that the international community began to gradually accept the notion that international law might play a role in avoiding future holocausts. Where the human rights issue-area departs most noticeably from conventional international legal matters, however, is that it forces us to look beyond the usual tradition that defines international law as law for, and by, states. Even in the World Court, states are still recognized as the sole actors in international law. This distinction becomes more difficult to maintain as global human rights movements, conventions and agreements, and the ICC continue to evolve. Increasingly, governments are regarded as having responsibilities beyond their borders. As Kenneth Roth argued in his introduction to the 2009 *Human Rights Watch World Report*, "A government's respect for human rights must be measured not only by how it treats its own people but also how it protects rights in its relations with other countries."[12] Human rights and human security are ultimately about protecting people, not the relatively abstract conceptions we call states.

In recent decades, human rights issues have become increasingly prominent concerns for governments, international organizations, and publics. Why has this happened? In the first place, awareness has increased. Global communications, travel, and print and television media have made us more aware of what goes on in other countries (see Chapter 12). States are no longer as capable of controlling information flows across their borders as they once were, though Marxists argue that media sources are still controlled by elites. Economic interdependence and global communications have provided governments, groups, and individuals with the means to act to promote human rights, through mechanisms such as trade restrictions, boycotts, and public information campaigns and protests. For example, consumer boycotts of MNCs have had some success, as many consumers resist buying products produced by victims of repression. Consumer awareness campaigns directed at Heineken, Carlsberg, British Home Stores, and Liz Claiborne compelled those MNCs to leave Burma. Campaigns have also been mounted against Royal Dutch/Shell for its operations in Nigeria, Total and Unocal in Burma, Nike in Indonesia and Vietnam, Disney in Haiti, and Zenith and General Motors for gender discrimination in Mexico.[13] A long record of human rights abuses directly and indirectly related to economic activity continues to drive calls for more robust corporate social responsibility provisions and "global intergovernmental standards" on business activity and human rights.[14]

The growth of human rights groups has also given interested individuals the opportunity to devote more time and effort to the cause of human rights. Such nongovernmental organizations (NGOs) include Amnesty International, Human Rights Watch, the International League for Human Rights, and the International Commission of Jurists. As we discussed in Chapter 5, these NGOs work to create awareness and persuade governments to act on human rights issues. As a result, governments are no longer regarded as the primary means of advancing human rights. In fact, governments are increasingly regarded as serious obstacles to progress. Nevertheless, they remain an essential piece of the effort to develop more effective legal instruments and responses to human rights issues, and as a result human rights groups attempt to raise public awareness to create pressure on governments for change.

PROFILE 9.2 Human Rights and Nobel Peace Prize Winners

Former U.S. President Jimmy Carter right, waves alongside Cuban President Fidel Castro at the airport in Havana, Cuba, May 17, 2002. Carter wrapped up a historic visit after seeking to bring Cuba and the United States closer by challenging both countries to change after more than four decades of enmity. (AP Photo/Gregory Bull/CP Archive).

Shirin Ebadi, winner of the Nobel Peace Prize, right, holds up the hand of Narges Mohammadi, wife of Taqi Rahmani, a prominent jailed political activist, during a gathering at the Amir Kabir University in Tehran, Iran, October 29, 2003. In her most biting criticism of the ruling hard-line Islamic establishment yet, Ebadi said she owes the award to Cyrus the Great, king of ancient Persia, and those Iranian writers and intellectuals who have been jailed for political reasons. (AP Photo/ Vahid Salemi/CP Archive.)

The Nobel Peace Prize has often been awarded to outstanding members of the human rights community; the assumption is that true peace is impossible without freedom and dignity for all. In 2003, Shirin Ebadi of Iran won the esteemed prize for her work on women's rights and democracy in Iran. She was born in Tehran in 1947, and served as the president of the city court of Tehran, as one of the first female judges in Iran, in the 1970s. After the 1979 revolution, she was forced to resign. She now works as a lawyer and teaches at the University of Tehran; as an activist and researcher she has lobbied for increased rights for refugees, women, and children. She represents a movement called Reformed Islam, and argues for a new interpretation of Islamic law that is in harmony with vital human rights such as democracy, equality before the law, religious freedom, and freedom of speech. She uses Islam as her starting point to promote peaceful solu-

tions, and promotes new thinking on Islamic terms. She has displayed great personal courage as a lawyer defending individuals and groups who have fallen victim to a powerful political and legal system that is legitimized through what many consider an inhumane interpretation of Islam. Ebadi has shown her willingness and ability to cooperate with representatives of secular as well as religious views. Critics charge that she received the prize precisely because her views are in line with Western critiques of Iranian theocracy, but this overlooks her commitment to Islam and her many personal achievements. In 2008 Ebadi argued that the human rights situation in Iran was regressing. She continues to receive death threats against herself and her family.

In contrast, the Nobel Peace Prize winner of 2002 was well known around the world: former U.S. President (1976–80) Jimmy Carter. Carter has long been active since his defeat by Ronald Reagan in undertaking various peace diplomacy missions, with mixed results; in 2004 he was involved in efforts to calm the Haitian crisis. However, one could as plausibly argue that his Peace Prize reflected the international communities' respect for his work in the human rights field. Founded

(continued)

Human Rights and Nobel Peace Prize Winners (*continued*)

in 1981, the Carter Center is an Atlanta-based organization devoted to global peace and social justice. Carter has travelled around the globe monitoring elections, promoting human rights, and providing health care and food to the world's poor; the Carter Center is also involved in providing low-cost housing to the poor in the United States. There is always some controversy about the Nobel Peace Prize; some critics felt that a former U.S. president was not a sound choice, given that state's mixed record on promoting human rights abroad. Most, however, felt the Norwegian Nobel Committee got it right this time, rewarding a stalwart defender of rights for the poor and a reliable voice for calm, even if the publication of his recent book, *Palestine: Peace Not Apartheid* (New York: Simon and Schuster, 2006) caused many to criticize his views on the Middle East peace process. See also the website for The Carter Center at http://www.cartercenter.org.

HUMAN RIGHTS AND GOVERNMENTS

States and governments continue to perpetuate abuses and often fail to act on human rights abuses at home or abroad. Violations of human rights by states and governments occur across a broad spectrum of political, economic, social, and cultural issues, and rights advocates often assert that no state is exempt from criticism. According to Freedom House, 43 countries and eight territories in the world in 2007 were described as "Not Free and whose citizens endure systematic and pervasive human rights violations." The very worst violators were identified as Burma, Cuba, Libya, North Korea, Somalia, Sudan, Turkmenistan and Uzbekistan, and the territories of Chechnya (in Russia) and Tibet (in China).[15] Living conditions in the West Bank and the Gaza Strip have provoked international condemnation against Israel. China has been accused of widespread human rights violations in Tibet. Canada has been condemned for its treatment of indigenous (First Nations) peoples. Amnesty International catalogues a wide range of human rights violations based on the rights enshrined in the Universal Declaration. Cases of torture and cruel or inhumane punishment were documented in 81 countries in 2007. At least 23 countries have laws that specifically discriminate against women, while 15 countries have laws discriminating against migrants, and 14 have laws discriminating against minorities. In 2007, at least 1,252 people were executed under death penalty legislation in 24 countries around the world (although 104 countries did vote in favour of an international moratorium on the death penalty that year). Unfair trials were held in 54 countries in 2007, and at least 77 countries restricted the freedom of expression and the press.[16]

Governments were slow to react to the human rights abuses in the former Yugoslavia and to the genocide in Rwanda. Governments in Angola and Cambodia have extended amnesty to human rights abusers. The Japanese government remains unwilling to formally compensate for the treatment of approximately 200,000 "comfort women" used as sex slaves for the Japanese military in World War II. Many other countries are struggling with political opposition to the investigation of human rights abuses, and some governments attempt to intimidate human rights advocates, harassing many, imprisoning some, and killing others.[17] The record of governments in human rights issues is, therefore, rather poor; although governments can be important agents of progress, all too often they are obstacles, or the very source of the problem. This fact complicates related diplomatic initiatives. For example, at least two highly murderous regimes have had nonpermanent seats on the Security Council (Cambodia, then called Kampuchea, in the mid-1970s; and Rwanda in 1994) even while massive campaigns of genocide were carried out back home. And we should stress the relationship between political power, military control, and human rights abuses: the brutality displayed by the military government led by Robert Mugabe in during elections in Zimbabwe in the summer of 2008, the repression following the controversial election in Iran in June of 2009, and the reluctance of the Burmese (Myanmar) government to permit foreign emergency aid to reach the hundreds of thousands of victims of Cyclone Nargis in early May of 2008, are two highly visible examples. This depressing overview illustrates the scale and scope of the human rights situation in the world and the outrages to human dignity that are committed by states on a daily basis.

Human rights are an always controversial factor in foreign policy decision making. Many governments have participated in efforts to build international law and international regimes to promote them, and they have responded to human rights abuses with diplomatic protests and (often limited) economic sanctions (such as those directed against apartheid South Africa and against China after the June 1989 Tiananmen Square massacre in which the Chinese military crushed a pro-democracy protest). Other governments have also taken steps to improve human rights in their own societies by prosecuting abusive officials and exposing the stark legacies of their past. For example, the Truth and Reconciliation Commission in South Africa undertook an investigation that implicated top-level officials in the former South African government in the apartheid-era state violence. The Guatemalan government acknowledged past abuses and purged the military and the police of the worst human rights offenders. The government of South Korea has convicted two former presidents for their role in a 1980 massacre of civilians by the South Korean military. The newly formed government of Iraq hanged former leader Saddam Hussein on December 30, 2006, after charging him and his surviving leadership with crimes against the Iraqi people.

Governments have often displayed inconsistency and a lack of commitment on human rights issues. In particular, governments around the world (including the government of Canada; see Profile 9.3) appear consistently willing to subordinate human rights concerns to their desire for trade and investment opportunities. Governments have defended this approach by arguing that trade, investment, and interdependence will generate social change in countries with human rights problems and that interdependence will create leverage that can later be used to promote human rights. This "constructive engagement" strategy has angered critics, who charge that it amounts to a facade of a human rights policy rather than any genuine commitment.[18] Governments also tend to exert human rights pressure on poor states while not doing the same with economically attractive states, and great powers have often continued to provide Official Development Assistance (ODA) and even military aid to some abusive regimes. Governments have also obstructed efforts to reveal the involvement of their own officials in human rights abuses. The U.S. government, for example,

Standing up for liberty. In this now-famous photograph, an anti-government protestor stands in front of advancing tanks in Beijing's Tiananmen Square on June 5, 1989, at the height of the pro-democracy protests. Deng Xiaoping is believed to have given the final orders for the military suppression of the 1989 Tiananmen Square pro-democracy protests, which claimed hundreds, perhaps thousands, of lives. Though China has partially liberalized its economy, the Communist Party continues to hold an iron grip on political representation, has actively repressed spiritual groups such as the Falun Gong, and continues its tyranny over Tibet. The 20th anniversary of Tiananmen was celebrated with stony official silence and denial in June of 2009. (AP Photo/Jeff Widener/CP Archive.)

PROFILE 9.3 Talisman and Sudan

The concept of human security was put to an interesting test in the recent dispute over a Canadian oil firm's investment and operations in the North African state of Sudan. Civil war has raged in that country for almost 50 years, and reports of mass displacement and military attacks continue in 2004. The northern Arab-dominated National Islamic Front government has been fighting the Christian and animist southern region in a brutal confrontation that has killed some 1.5 million southerners and has seen the use of food as a weapon, concentration camps, and reports of southern villagers being taken into slavery by northern militias. (Western Christian groups have engaged in so-called redemption programs, literally buying back slaves from their oppressors, but this has been criticized as well, since it drives up the price of slaves.)

In October 1998 Talisman Energy acquired Arakis Energy for C$200 million. This gave Talisman a 25 percent share in the Greater Nile Oil Project, a consortium with China and Malaysia. In southern Sudan, huge oil fields are being drilled and a major pipeline to Port Sudan is planned. The project employs 2,000 Sudanese, and more than 100 Canadians have helped train them. However, the southern rebels, in particular the Sudan People's Liberation Army, consider this collaboration with the northern government an affront to their territorial sovereignty and have declared such installations legitimate military targets. As a result the Sudanese government, which takes a share of the revenue generated by the oil extraction, employed military forces to protect the Canadian workers and installations.

Critics charged that a Canadian firm was helping to fund a genocidal war. In response, the Canadian government sent African expert John Harker to investigate the situation, and his report was largely condemnatory. In early 2000 the Canadian government decided that no sanctions would be imposed against Talisman but that the company should be encouraged to carefully monitor the situation and perhaps create a trust fund to help southerners after the conflict is over. Human rights activists, who argue that the conflict will not end as long as the Sudanese government is funded by oil revenues, expressed dismay at this decision. The decision also angered the United States, which has imposed tough sanctions (with some notable exceptions) on Sudan because of suspected terrorist connections. Should the Canadian government have taken steps to force Talisman out of Sudan, or is business just business? Finally, in response to shareholder concerns over human rights abuses, and an American threat to delist the company from the New York Stock Exchange, Talisman agreed in March 2003 to sell its 25 percent stake in Sudan's Greater Nile Oil Project to an Indian state-owned oil company called ONGC Videsh. Indeed, Talisman profited from the sale! The episode heightened awareness of the potential impact of foreign investment, and raised questions about the human costs of promoting "business as usual."

SOURCES: A. NIKIFORUK, "OIL PATCH PARIAH," *CANADIAN BUSINESS*, DECEMBER 10, 2000, 69; *HUMAN SECURITY IN SUDAN: REPORT OF A CANADIAN ASSESSMENT MISSION PREPARED FOR THE MINISTER OF FOREIGN AFFAIRS* (OTTAWA: DEPARTMENT OF FOREIGN AFFAIRS AND INTERNATIONAL TRADE, JANUARY 2000); S. KOBRIN, "OIL AND POLITICS: TALISMAN ENERGY AND SUDAN," *NEW YORK UNIVERSITY JOURNAL OF INTERNATIONAL LAW AND POLITICS* 36 (2004): 425–456.

has been reluctant to release documents related to the activities of the Central Intelligence Agency (CIA) in Haiti, Honduras, and Guatemala, obstructing the human rights investigations in progress in those countries.

HUMAN RIGHTS AND THE UN SYSTEM

In June 1993, the UN-sponsored World Conference on Human Rights in Vienna declared that "the promotion and protection of all human rights is a legitimate concern of the international community."[19] Similar sentiments had been expressed at previous UN conferences and forums. Yet such declarations conflict with the principle of sovereignty enshrined in the UN Charter. As Stephen Marks has observed, "Human rights in the United Nations has been, to a large extent, the story of tension between the principle that the United Nations cannot intervene in the domestic affairs of states and the principle that states must act with the United Nations to realize fully all rights."[20]

PROFILE 9.4 · Selected UN Human Rights Instruments

Note: After each convention appears the year it was opened for signature and the year it came into force (note that many of these conventions have yet to come into force).

GENERAL HUMAN RIGHTS

International Covenant on Civil and Political Rights, 1966, 1976

Optional Protocol to the International Covenant on Civil and Political Rights, 1966, 1976

International Covenant on Economic, Social and Cultural Rights, 1966, 1976

UN World Conference on Human Rights: Vienna Declaration, 1993

RACIAL DISCRIMINATION

International Convention on the Elimination of All Forms of Racial Discrimination, 1965, 1969

International Convention on the Suppression and Punishment of the Crime of Apartheid, 1973, 1976

International Convention Against Apartheid in Sports, 1985

RIGHTS OF WOMEN

Convention on the Political Rights of Women, 1952, 1954

Convention on the Nationality of Married Women, 1957, 1958

Convention on Consent to Marriage, Minimum Age for Marriage and Registration of Marriages, 1962, 1964

Convention on the Elimination of All Forms of Discrimination against Women, 1979, 1981

SLAVERY AND RELATED MATTERS

Convention for the Suppression of the Traffic in Persons and of the Exploitation of the Prostitution of Others, 1949, 1951

Slavery Convention of 1926, as amended in 1953, 1953, 1955

Protocol Amending the 1926 Slavery Convention, 1953, 1955

Supplementary Convention on the Abolition of Slavery, the Slave Trade, and Institutions and Practices Similar to Slavery, 1956, 1957

REFUGEES AND STATELESS PERSONS

Convention on the Reduction of Statelessness, 1949, 1951

Convention Relating to the Status of Refugees, 1951, 1954

Convention Relating to the Status of Stateless Persons, 1954, 1960

Protocol Relating to the Status of Refugees, 1966, 1967

OTHER

Convention on the Prevention and Punishment of the Crime of Genocide, 1948, 1951

Convention on the International Right of Correction, 1952, 1962

Convention on the Non-applicability of Statutory Limitations to War Crimes and Crimes Against Humanity, 1968, 1970

Convention Against Torture and Other Cruel, Inhuman or Degrading Treatment or Punishment, 1984, 1987

Convention on the Rights of the Child, 1989

International Convention on the Protection of the Rights of All Migrant Workers and Members of Their Families, 1990

Draft Declaration on the Rights of Indigenous Peoples, 1992

While the UN Charter does call explicitly for international cooperation on economic, social, cultural, and humanitarian matters, and the promotion of human rights and fundamental freedoms (Articles 4 and 55, respectively), it is the Universal Declaration of Human Rights, adopted by the General Assembly in 1948, that has the most impact on legal thinking regarding the obligations of states toward their citizens. More than 60 other human rights instruments have been adopted by the General Assembly since 1948, including the International Covenant on Civil and Political Rights and the International Covenant on Economic, Social and Cultural Rights. These two international covenants and the Universal Declaration of Human Rights are collectively known as the International Bill of Rights. Despite considerable dissension, the UN-sponsored World Conference on Human Rights in Vienna (the first in a quarter-century) concluded with a commitment to the idea of universal human rights, and established the post of a UN High Commissioner for Human Rights. The Commissioner helps coordinate the work of the 53-member Commission on Human Rights (a subsidiary body of ECOSOC), and in 2004 a well-respected Canadian jurist, Louise Arbour, was appointed to this demanding post, which she held until the summer of 2008.

In addition, many other bodies in the UN address human rights issues. These include the Committee on the Elimination of Racial Discrimination, the Commission on the Status of Women and the Committee on the Elimination of Discrimination Against Women, the High Commissioner for Refugees, the High Commissioner for National Minorities, the International Labour Organization, and the Crime Prevention and Criminal Justice Division in Vienna.

HUMAN RIGHTS AND REGIONAL ORGANIZATIONS

In addition to efforts to promote human rights through the UN, regional IGOs have also made similar efforts, though with varying degrees of commitment and concrete results. In Europe, the foundation for the large body of human rights legislation and institutions is the 1953 European Convention for the Protection of Human Rights and Fundamental Freedoms, drafted to prevent a recurrence of the Nazi crimes against humanity. Two institutions in Europe have built on the principles of the European Convention. The **Council of Europe** maintains the European Court, which, among other cases, has heard charges against the British government alleging that the laws enacted to suppress the Irish Republican Army (IRA) violated the human rights provisions of the European Convention. The Organization for Security and Co-operation in Europe (OSCE), established in 1994 as a replacement for the Conference on Security and Cooperation in Europe (CSCE), was built on the principles of the Helsinki Final Act of 1975, which provided for the protection of human rights by all signatory governments across Europe (including the U.S.S.R.) and North America (including Canada and the United States). In 1990, the Charter of Paris committed members to observe the human rights provisions of the CSCE Final Act (and any subsequent amendment) and proclaimed human rights as a "legitimate concern" of all signatory governments. The OSCE mounts periodic fact-finding missions to investigate human rights concerns. In addition, much of the European Convention on Human Rights is reflected in the local laws of several EU member states, the most recent being that of Britain.

The Organization of American States (OAS) Charter of 1948 has a Declaration of the Rights and Duties of Man, and in 1978 the American Convention on Human Rights (with an Inter-American Court of Human Rights) came into force. In Africa, the 1981 African Charter on Human and Peoples' Rights (the Banjul Charter) was adopted by the OAU. In Asia, the Association of Southeast Asian Nations (ASEAN) possesses a human rights commission, and the Asia-Pacific Economic Cooperation (APEC) forum possesses a Human Resources Development Working Group. However, while most of these regional human rights efforts are staffed by dedicated and hard-working personnel, and while many of them perform important roles and tasks on a variety of human rights issues, all of them suffer from the problems of limited financial and human resources and the intransigence (and sometimes the resistance) of member governments.

CONTEMPORARY HUMAN RIGHTS ISSUES

Before looking at specific examples of human rights issues, we should mention the difficulty involved in choosing such examples. As space constrains us from embarking on anything approaching a comprehensive survey, we have chosen several issues that have had a high public profile in the press in recent years. Although this selection is of course arbitrary, we hope we have covered issues of concern to most contemporary students and encourage you to look elsewhere for information on other pertinent topics, such as freedom of speech, the right to food and education, and gay and lesbian rights. In addition, we have not included a discussion of the refugee crisis (which many consider the most pressing and perhaps challenging human rights issue of our time) in this chapter because we deal with it at length in Chapter 11 on population and population movements. We deal with reproductive rights in that chapter as well.

ETHICS AND CONSTRAINTS ON WAR

We include a discussion of the ethical reasoning behind war efforts because war is, at heart, a human rights issue. If war is justified, then killing individual human beings to win one may be justified, and this justification is subject to all the dilemmas inherent in the universal/particular split mentioned above. Have we established a universal code of ethics that tells us when national leaders should declare war on other states, thus risking the lives of their own citizens as well as endangering those of others? The relationship between war and ethics has been a complex one.[21] Most of the world's ethical systems (heavily influenced by religion) deplore the act of killing as a general principle. And yet virtually all ethical systems establish sets of conditions under which such killing is justified or permissible. Ethicists, theologians, and philosophers have established the foundations for the ethical rejection of international violence and war, while at the same time their arguments have been used to support or justify international violence and wars; for example, in the name of national liberation or humanitarian intervention.

There is also the sentiment that war is a distinct human activity in which ethics have no place. *Inter arma silent leges*: "In times of war the law is silent." Despite this ethical debate, moral condemnation of the ethics of war tends to be *utilitarian* in nature; that is, the benefits and costs of any act must be judged in moral and ethical terms. As a result, war can be justified in certain cases, such as resisting and punishing aggression, although such wars must still be fought in accordance with certain ethical principles. The problem with utilitarian approaches is that states and groups will manipulate ethical principles to sanction the use of violence, at which point utilitarian ethics may erode into apologies or justifications for the very worst acts of war. *Absolutist* ethics, however, maintain that nothing can justify a certain act, which forms the foundation of the beliefs of pacifists, who maintain that international violence and war are never justified, no matter what the circumstances. The problem with absolutist ethics is that a refusal to use violence or go to war may permit the most horrible acts to take place; inaction itself can be morally bankrupt.

Those who advocate a "just war" doctrine attempt to constrain warfare by establishing the conditions under which it is just to enter into a war and by establishing what level of violence is considered acceptable in the prosecution of that war. This hinges on the distinction between **jus ad bellum** (the justice of a war) and **jus in bello** (the justness of the manner in which a war is fought). In his writing on *jus ad bellum*, Michael Walzer argues that only aggression can justify war, and that wars fought in self-defence are just.[22] The aggressor, once defeated, is to be punished, for punishment will deter future aggression. In society, we punish criminals to deter criminal violence; internationally, aggression is punished to prevent future aggression. From this basic principle are drawn the criteria by which just wars are measured:

- A just war is a war of last resort; all other means of resolution must be explored.
- A just war must be authorized by a legitimate authority, either the state or an international organization.
- A just war must be waged for a just cause, not for aggression or a desire for vengeance.
- A just war must have a good chance of successfully achieving a desirable outcome, and wars fought for good causes that are ultimately hopeless are not justifiable.
- A just war must end in a peace that is preferable to the situation before the outbreak of war.

Jus in bello maintains that a war may also be just or unjust in the manner in which it is fought. A war may have just origins, but it cannot be fought unjustly. Two measures determine the just conduct of a war:

1. A just war must be fought in ways consistent with the principle of proportionality. The potential positives deriving from military activity (such as a bombing campaign) must outweigh the negatives of destruction and death. Military methods must also be limited to the level of violence required to achieve the mission at hand, and any risk to civilians must be proportionate to the military value of the target.
2. A just war must discriminate—combatants and noncombatants must be treated differently. Civilians cannot be the intentional targets of military operations, and civilian casualties must be minimized when this is possible.

Just war doctrine thus argues that wars should be limited and that the conduct of war is (and should be) governed by rules of behaviour and conduct. It is important to remember that in practice few wars meet all of these criteria, and so debates about the justness of a war generally revolve around examples of when certain principles might have been violated or argue to what extent a war can be considered just.

Nuclear weapons, and in particular nuclear deterrence, pose a challenge to ethical constraints on war. During the Cold War, most secular and religious ethicists agreed that nuclear weapons are by their very nature indiscriminate and disproportionate, and so nuclear war was generally regarded as inherently unjust. However, nuclear deterrence, the deployment of nuclear weapons in an effort to deter their use, was more controversial. Is it legitimate or just to threaten an action that would be immoral or unjust if it were carried out? The legitimacy of nuclear deterrence was justified on the grounds that it is necessary to avoid a greater evil (aggression by an enemy or subjugation of the free world at the hands of totalitarianism). However, many argued that the arms race invalidated the moral basis of deterrence as a temporary measure; nuclear deterrence was endangering peace, not contributing to it. So, for example, the United Methodist Council of Bishops argued that "the moral case for nuclear deterrence, even as an interim ethic, has been undermined by unrelenting arms escalation. Deterrence no longer serves, if it ever did, as a strategy that facilitates disarmament. Deterrence must no longer receive the churches' blessing."[23] Although the prominence of this issue has receded somewhat, the ethical status of nuclear weapons remains a subject of intense debate, particularly in the context of proliferation and post–Cold War efforts to ban nuclear weapons.

Critics of just war doctrine charge that since the judges of whether a war is just tend to be the very states, governments, or peoples engaged in the violence, a natural tendency exists to frame whatever one side does in good or just terms and to frame everything the opposition does in bad or unjust terms. Nevertheless, to reject just war doctrine outright would be to invite the separation of morality and war. Furthermore, opposition to war is generally founded on judgments of what is considered just. Opposition to the Vietnam War in the United States was largely built on the view of many that the war was unjust, both in terms of its conduct and its origins. Before the Gulf War, extensive efforts were made by governments to convince public opinion that the cause was just; this has proven rather more difficult during and after the U.S.–Coalition invasion of Iraq in 2003. While many people were willing to accept the war in Afghanistan as a just response to the terror attacks of 9/11, the proffered causes for the Iraqi operation—that Saddam Hussein was a viable threat to Western states, capable of developing and using weapons of mass destruction in the near future—were rejected by many as either the consequence of a trigger-happy Bush administration or disinformation. To the extent that support for a war is a function of the extent to which it is just, the criteria of just war doctrine would seem to have some value. Furthermore, just war doctrine is a significant part of the debate over humanitarian intervention, which we turn to later in this chapter.

GENOCIDE AND WAR CRIMES

Few words are as connotative as *genocide*. That the term refers to mass murder is common knowledge; less well known but equally important is that it refers to mass murder perpetrated by a state or a nonstate actor against a specific group of people.[24] This definition is important not only because it recognizes a form of collective rights (freedom from discriminatory murder), but also because it implies that the state—traditionally the guarantor of citizens' rights—can at times become the worst enemy of the people. The Convention on the Prevention and Punishment of the Crime of Genocide (1948) grew out of the recognition of three types of crimes during warfare: crimes against humanity, crimes against peace, and war crimes.

After World War II, trials were held in which the losers—Germany and Japan—were judged by the victors. At the most famous of these trials, the **war crimes trials** in Nuremberg held from 1945 to 1949 (the Tokyo war crimes trials are less well known), **crimes against humanity** were considered to be murder, extermination, enslavement, deportation, imprisonment, torture, rape, or persecutions on political, racial, or religious grounds committed against any civilian population (including one's own). The term was first introduced in the London Agreement of August 8, 1945 (issued by the United States, the U.S.S.R., Great Britain, and France). **Crimes against peace** included planning, preparing, initiating, or waging a war of aggression and participating in a common plan or conspiracy for the accomplishment of war crimes. Nazi aggression was considered a crime against peace, though its chief architect, Adolf Hitler, had killed himself before the bitter end of the struggle in Berlin, thus escaping trial. **War crimes** were considered murder, ill treatment or deportation to slave labour, killing of hostages, and plunder and wanton destruction with no military necessity.

Obviously some measure of overlap exists in these crimes, but they are considered important legal precedents. Polish jurist Raphael Lemkin coined the word "genocide" during the implementation of Hitler's "final solution." Lemkin had a wide awareness of the atrocities being waged across Europe largely on racial grounds and affecting one ethnic group in particular, the European Jewish community. Thus, he introduced a new term "to denote an old practice in its modern development," derived from the Greek word for race or people, *genos*, and the Latin *caedere* (-cide), which means to kill.[25] The Holocaust is still widely considered the ultimate example of genocide. Estimates vary, but at least six million Jews—and many others, including Gypsies, prisoners of war, and German "undesirables," such as people with disabilities and homosexuals—were killed.[26] Due to the massive numbers involved, and the administrative efficiency of such systematic murder, the Holocaust remains a singular event in history, but many examples of genocide exist, such as the murder of millions of Armenians by the Ottoman Turks during World War I.

Two events in the 1990s brought the term "genocide" and the mechanism of the war crimes trial back into public view (and others, such as the continuation of hostilities in Sudan, keep it there). The first was the outbreak of war in the former Yugoslavia (see discussion in Chapter 6) and the "ethnic cleansing" (the forced expulsion of particular ethnic groups), concentration camps, mass murders, and rape that characterized the conflict. The second was the outbreak of the carnage in Rwanda in the spring and summer of 1994. This orchestrated campaign of genocide shocked the Western world with images of dismemberment, displacement, starvation, and bloated corpses floating down the Kagera River entering Uganda and Lake Victoria. As a result of just two months of intense violence, UN officials estimated the death toll of unarmed civilians in Rwanda at approximately 800,000.[27] State-employed Hutu militia men are thought responsible for much of the killing, which began after Hutu President Juvenal Habyarimana was killed in a rocket attack on his plane. Rwanda has been plagued with violence, before and after its achievement of independence from Belgian rule in 1962; indeed, it was a massacre of Tutsis in 1959 that originally created an exiled Tutsi community in Uganda, remnants of which returned to Rwanda in an unsuccessful invasion in 1990 and again in 1994 with the currently governing Rwanda Patriotic Front. But nothing in known African history has equalled the recent bloodbath in terms of its scope and, as chilling, the speed with which events took shape.[28] The repercussions of these events spread through the African Great Lakes region in 1996 and 1997, in the form of massive refugee flows and the fall of the long-time president of Zaire, Mobutu Sese Seko, and an escalation in the subsequently established Democratic Republic of the Congo, where millions have died as a result of civil war and related displacement as well.

In 1993, the UN Security Council created the International Tribunal for the Prosecution of Persons Responsible for Serious Violations of International Humanitarian Law in the Territory of the Former Yugoslavia since 1991 (known as the ICTY, or International Criminal Tribunal for the former Yugoslavia). The ICTY is located at The Hague in the Netherlands. In 1995 the Dayton Agreement which ended the war called for the parties to the conflict to cooperate with the tribunal (this has been less than forthcoming, however). After the fall of Slobodan Miloševi's regime in 2000, he was put on trial at The Hague, where he erratically defended himself until his death in March of 2006. In July 2008, former Bosnian Serb leader Radovan Karadzic (who, along with a military general, is held responsible for the massacre of some 8,000 men in the small Bosnian town of Srebrenica) was captured after 12 years of hiding in Belgrade posing as an alternative medicine practitioner. Karadzic was extradited to the Netherlands to face the ICTY on charges of genocide, war crimes, and crimes against humanity.

In 1994, the Security Council created the International Criminal Tribunal for Rwanda (ICTR). This tribunal operates in Arusha, Tanzania, though it has tried only a tiny fraction of those responsible for the genocide: the governmental elite. The others captured by the Rwandan Patriotic Front in 1994 have certainly suffered a worse fate, as some 80,000 were crammed into a prison system built for 13,000. Many of them were children at the time and are now fully grown men and still imprisoned awaiting trial in 2010 (though efforts to utilize a village justice system in its place, wherein prisoners can return home if their home communities elect to forgive them, show some remarkable progress at this stage). The objective of both of these tribunals is to bring the perpetrators of war crimes, crimes against humanity, and genocide to justice. The progress of the tribunals has been slowed by financial problems, the active opposition of those who fear exposure and retribution, and an inability to physically apprehend many of those charged. Nevertheless, the tribunals have been active and have secured convictions. The international community, especially the United States, saw both tribunals as an effort to compensate for the relatively lacklustre response to the carnage that occurred in the Balkans and Rwanda. The establishment of a permanent International Criminal Court (discussed later in this chapter) was a response to the crimes committed in the former Yugoslavia and Rwanda and an effort to respond to the weaknesses of the ICTY and ICTR.

On a broader scale, one might argue that "genocide" can be used to describe the manifestations of structural violence as well.[29] Murder, including state murder, takes many forms: the deliberate starvation of entire communities and the use of food as a weapon in general; the lack of clean water supplies in the slums of major cities; the destruction of East Timor by the Indonesian military, or of Tibet by the Chinese, or of parts of Indochina by the Americans, or of political opponents of various Soviet regimes; or the drainage of marshes in southern Iraq. All these cases involve mass death inflicted with obvious intent. By such an expanded definition, war itself could be seen as an inherently genocidal project. Cultural destruction that has a physical component, commonly called *ethnocide*, is a type

A place of death. A Christian figure stands between human skulls, August 2003 at the Ntarama church in Nyamata (south of Kigali) where up to 5,000 people were killed during the 1994 Rwanda genocide, which claimed the lives of approximately 800,000 Tutsis and moderate Hutus. (AP Photo/Karel Prinsloo/CP Archive.)

of genocide, the destruction of the indigenous peoples in the Americas after 1492 being a prime example; similarly, the construction of large-scale dams that displace millions of people, the Himalayan deforestation that has caused floods, and other forms of *ecocide* (see Chapter 10) might be called genocidal when death results. Most lawyers and scholars reject this expanded concept, with good reasons, but we should not ignore the large-scale death and destruction that results from conflict and change that has not been branded genocide according to the 1948 Convention.

The advent of the nuclear age takes us further toward an alternative and expanded perspective on genocide. It can be argued that nuclear deterrence, based on the threat of mass annihilation, was based on the threat of implementing the ultimate genocidal policy. Of course, one might argue that the threat of nuclear war introduced a new concept to the lexicon, that of *omnicide*. However, since nuclear strategy was predicated on the destruction of a specific enemy, omnicide was not contemplated (though it did not take a considerably bright individual to predict it would result). It is this element of intention, or even incitement, that can lead to the labelling of the nuclear arms race as genocidal. If, as UN officials have insisted, we can consider the Rwandan slaughter an instance of genocide because, for example, a Hutu official had given a speech in 1992 in which he "explicitly called on Hutus to kill Tutsis and dump their bodies in the rivers,"[30] then what are we to make of a system of national defence

---

The Canadian Global Human Rights Commissioner

Former chief UN war crimes prosecutor and UN High Commissioner for Human Rights Louise Arbour speaks to the press after she was decorated with the Order of Canada, October 2008. (CP Archive/ Jacques Boissinot.)

In 1992 the Security Council of the UN created a Commission of Experts to investigate and report on "the evidence of grave breaches of the Geneva Conventions and other violations of humanitarian law in the territory of the former Yugoslavia" (Res. 780, 1992). After the taking of an interim report, which clearly indicated that mass murder had taken place, the Security Council established an international tribunal for the prosecution of individuals responsible (UN Doc. S/Res/808, 1993). In March 1996 Canadian Justice Louise Arbour was appointed chief prosecutor for the International Criminal Tribunals for the former Yugoslavia and Rwanda. She had previously been a member of the Court of Appeals for Ontario. The term of chief prosecutor runs four years and is renewable after that; Arbour left for the Supreme Court of Canada in September 1999 and was replaced by Carla Del Ponte of Switzerland. In early 2004, Arbour was appointed UN High Commissioner for Human Rights, a position she held amid great controversy for her stands on many issues, including her condemnation of Israel and relative silence on Russia and China. She retired as High Commissioner in July 2008, and was awarded the Order of Canada in October.

that called on thousands of soldiers to take part, if necessary, in the complete annihilation of hundreds of millions of civilians? Or does international, as opposed to civil, war justify such technique? While The Hague Convention[31] merely states that the "right of belligerents to adopt means of injuring the enemy is not unlimited," it is certainly difficult to argue that the use of hydrogen bombs would be limited in any real manner.[32]

FEMALE GENITAL MUTILATION

One of the more complex human rights issues involves the practice commonly called *female genital mutilation*, also often called *female castration, circumcision,* or *genital cutting*. It refers to the practice in many countries of removing or altering parts of the female genitalia at a certain age as a rite of passage. As you can tell, even the question of which name we assign to this practice is highly controversial, for each carries a strong connotation regarding the legitimacy of the act. Two forms of genital mutilation remain prevalent among certain segments of African women: infibulation, the severing of the clitoris and labia while the two sides of the vulva are sutured (tied together); and clitoridectomy, the partial or complete removal of the clitoris or the removal of both the clitoris and the labia minora. Either procedure comes under severe criticism from many quarters, while it is defended as a cultural priority in others. Several Western states, such as Canada and the United States, have made it illegal for doctors to perform the procedure. This law is not insignificant, since large numbers of recently arrived African women live in both states. No strong opposition to the practice exists at the international level, though UN agencies such as the World Health Organization generally oppose it. According to the United Nations Children's Fund (UNICEF) approximately 70 million girls or women aged 15 to 49 in 27 countries in Africa and the Middle East have undergone this practice.[33]

The medical case against female genital mutilation is a very strong one: it can result in excessive bleeding, infection, and even death when improperly performed; and the after-effects include the risk of childbirth complications and of developing obstetric fistulae—holes between the vagina and the bladder, the rectum, or both. Beyond this, however, it represents to many women an act of oppression because it involves removing part or the entire clitoris and thus denies women a basic form of sexual pleasure.[34] Thus, the issue has become a rallying cry for the feminist movement in general. Some Islamic customs, such as *purdah* (the segregation of the sexes and the covering of the female body) have come under intense criticism by Western feminists, but genital mutilation remains the most widely condemned. The international implications of this condemnation can be seen in Canadian refugee policy, which has periodically adopted the inclusion of women fleeing persecution based on discrimination against their sex as a valid reason to seek asylum. However, most women who undergo the procedure are quite young and are unable to leave their native countries on their own.

Howard French, in an article written for *The New York Times* that explores the issue within the context of the question of cultural relativity, writes about a small group of women in Sierra Leone who are working to ban the practice. One of the group's leaders argues that stopping the practice must be done in as culturally sensitive a manner as possible. For example, genital cutting was traditionally the culmination of a months-long retreat, known as *Bondo*, to mark the passage into womanhood, when older women would share their wisdom with the young. As the years passed, the retreat withered into an increasingly shorter ceremony and was finally represented almost solely by the cutting. Trying to restore the full value of *Bondo* might lead to a greater acceptance of the idea that the circumcision is part of a larger process and may eventually be discarded for hygienic reasons. For many, of course, this approach is far too timid. However, stronger appeals can lead to almost immediate condemnation by religious groups; for example, when a Freetown newspaper published a series of articles critical of the custom, "it became the target of a hostile protest movement by a group of women sworn to defend the rite."[35]

As an issue that forces us to examine the universal/relativist, as well as the gender-related discussions above, female genital mutilation, circumcision, or genital cutting will continue to outrage many communities. However, those who are campaigning to stop it are in a difficult bind: the harder they work, especially when they manage to publicly question or challenge the legitimacy of the practice, the more the pro-traditional forces will be inspired to resist change. Governments will have to seriously consider this matter when directing development assistance toward health programs abroad, and when determining their own operational definition of refugee status.

HEALTH AS A HUMAN RIGHT: HIV/AIDS

It is often argued that one of the most fundamental human rights is access to decent health care. This issue forces the divide between those willing to accept the need for societies to redistribute resources and those who reject this need. In the case of HIV/AIDS (see Chapter 11), questions of equal access to health care have come to represent severe human rights questions because many of the antiretroviral drugs that can mitigate the effects of the disease are still not widely available, especially in sub-Saharan Africa where millions suffer and hundreds die every day from AIDS, despite the relatively low death rates in the West, where such drugs are widely obtainable. Efforts to force pharmaceutical companies to dispense the drugs at cheaper cost met with resistance, but declarations by states such as Brazil and South Africa that they would proceed, despite international patent laws, with their own generic versions of the drugs, have gradually shifted Western perceptions on the matter.

Beyond this particular North–South dispute, there are other human rights issues associated with the spread of deadly disease. AIDS victims, in particular, are often subject to ostracism (this is doubly tragic for women who have acquired HIV/AIDS after being raped, which is not uncommon in Rwanda and elsewhere). Many of the fundamental human rights of people living with HIV/AIDS—such as the right to nondiscrimination, equal protection and equality before the law, privacy, liberty of movement, work, and equal access to education, housing, health care, social security, assistance, and welfare—are often violated on the basis of their known or presumed HIV/AIDS status. It can also be argued that people living without access to decent health care and related education are more susceptible to acquire the disease in the first place; this would include those caught in the global sex industry, where worker protection is all too often the last of concerns. Other serious health concerns, such as malaria, malnutrition, amputation (common in areas such as Angola and Cambodia where land mines were used extensively during conflicts), and psychological problems, severely hamper the human development of millions, even billions, of people today. Is the achievement of freedom from these problems to be seen as an essential human right, or a privilege obtainable by only a few? We return to this issue in Chapter 11, where we discuss global public health.

TORTURE

The word *torture* is derived from the Latin word *torquere*, which means "to twist." As a means to ensure the compliance of the people to a ruler's wishes, torture is as old as governance itself. When we mention torture, we are referring essentially to acts committed by governments, though it is clear that nongovernmental forces in wars and even terrorist and resistance groups resort to it as well. Torture is an old and tested technique that can be employed to get people to confess to just about anything, whether or not they have committed the act in question. Historians write of the unspeakable brutality inflicted by Ivan the Terrible and the Spanish Inquisition burnings, both during the 1500s. Torture was an accepted form of public punishment during the early development of the European penal systems, and it was employed as a device to facilitate slavery and colonialism.

PROFILE 9.6 Stephen Lewis, Tireless and Eloquent

Stephen Lewis, former UN special envoy for HIV/AIDS in Africa, speaking at conference in 2007. (CP Archive/ Larry MacDougal.)

Canadian Stephen Lewis is the former UN Secretary-General's Special Envoy for HIV/AIDS in Africa. Lewis previously served as Deputy Executive Director of the United Nations Children's Fund (UNICEF) from 1995 to 1999, former Canadian Ambassador to the United Nations, and leader of the New Democratic Party of Ontario. Five key objectives for the global anti-AIDS campaign include preventing the epidemic's further spread, reducing mother-to-child HIV transmission, providing care and treatment to all, delivering scientific breakthroughs, and protecting the vulnerable, especially orphans. Lewis has been a tireless campaigner, employing his well-known eloquence, and celebrities such as Oprah Winfrey and U2's Bono, to chide the Northern states to do more for Africa's 11 to 14 million AIDS orphans, and to provide affordable, lifesaving drugs to the poor. *Maclean's* chose him as Canadian of the Year in 2003:

> At the beginning of 2003, frustrated and disheartened by Western nations' willingness to ignore the crisis and commit "mass murder by complacency" while they devoted billions to ousting Saddam Hussein, Lewis agonized over whether he could continue. But he decided to turn his despair and anger to advantage, and push all the harder. "I'm still at the end of my rope because I find myself not handling things well when I travel. I get too distraught, too quickly," says Lewis. "But what is my emotional disarray compared to the hell that is happening? I'm in a great rage now, as I understand how many lives we have lost. But I don't want to leave until I see the breakthrough"....
>
> At home, he has started the Stephen Lewis Foundation (www.stephenlewisfoundation.org), devoted to providing small-scale funding to communities dealing with the ravages of AIDS. In nine months, it has raised close to $900,000, mostly from individual donations. In Namibia, the money will pay for funerals and coffins; in Kenya, for home care for the dying; in Zambia for a prevention program. Lewis says he has been humbled and revitalized by the outpouring of support. "If our governments were one-tenth as generous as average Canadians, the problem would be solved," he says. "Truthfully, when I see what we can accomplish with money on the ground, it's the only time in my life I have wished I was Bill Gates."

SOURCE: "MACLEAN'S 2003 CANADIAN OF THE YEAR: STEPHEN LEWIS," *MACLEAN'S*, QUOTED AT HTTP://WWW.THECANADIANENCYCLOPEDIA.COM/INDEX.CFM?PGNM=TCE&PARAMS=M1ARTM0012546 (ACCESSED JUNE 13, 2009). REPRINTED WITH THE PERMISSION OF *MACLEAN'S* MAGAZINE.

The 1789 French Declaration of the Rights of Man forbade torture "forever" and the U.S. Bill of Rights forbade "cruel and unusual punishment." As incarceration in prisons began to replace torture as the chief means of punishing criminals (though many would equate imprisonment with torture as well), it became a less acceptable means of enforcing law and order or extracting confessions. However, torture was still widely practised throughout the world, and during World War II was employed by the Nazi Gestapo and the Japanese military (among other organizations). The Soviet state under Stalin was renowned for its willingness to punish dissidents with psychological torture. In fact, it would be difficult, if not impossible, to find a society where some form of state-sanctioned torture has not occurred at some time.

Torture continues to be employed as a means of extracting knowledge from political participants, and is often administered by people who have been specially trained as torturers; the act takes place as a means to something else, be it the suppression of popular dissent or the acquisition of information deemed important by government bureaucrats. Though some individuals involved in its application are no doubt sadistic themselves, they are merely employees in a larger project. This definition helps us distinguish torture in the political sense from that in the criminal sense. Obviously, however, the very definition of torture leaves a great deal open to interpretation. Though the international community has signed many agreements[36] that make the use of torture by governments against the convention of international law, the principle of nonintervention requires that states avoid interfering in the domestic affairs of other states.[37] During the Cold War, many dictatorial or military regimes practised torture, and this was largely ignored for the sake of maintaining alliances (both Western and Eastern). Several Latin American regimes, most notably that of Augusto Pinochet in Chile in the 1970s, were infamous for their human rights abuses and torture techniques, and we should note the complicity of the superpowers themselves in many of these cases. In the post–Cold War era, when the old bloc system can no longer be used to justify the toleration of such excesses, some Western governments are moving toward making the receipt of donor assistance contingent on the pursuit of democratic institutions, which would (one might hope) by definition preclude torture. However, critics have pointed out that the Bush administration's "War on Terror" employed torture in various forms, including the incarceration of so-called unlawful combatants at Guantanamo Bay, the use of waterboarding, and the well-publicized and -photographed mistreatment of some prisoners of war in Iraq by U.S. soldiers.

INTERNATIONAL LAW AND THE GLOBAL "WAR ON TERROR"

The post–September 11 years have been trying times for international law. In particular, the integrity of international war law and international humanitarian law has been called into question by the U.S. "global war on terror." Of course, war law and humanitarian law have been violated in the past by many states. However, U.S. violations have caused special concern because they have had a global impact and because America's support for international law is seen as vitally important. In the wake of the September 11, 2001 attacks on the United States, the Bush administration made a number of decisions that have had far-reaching impact not only on international law but also on the legitimacy of American counterterrorism efforts. As Roy Gutman, David Rieff, and Anthony Dworkin argue, "In a very short time, the United States went from being the guarantor of the regime of humanitarian law to becoming a major violator of it."[38]

The Bush administration's repeated sidestepping of Supreme Court rulings on the validity of torture and the legitimacy of the Guantanamo Bay prison for "enemy combatants" captured in Afghanistan (including a Canadian, Omar Khadr, who was a child soldier at the time of his apprehension) has also caused concern about the eroding observance of U.S. domestic law. In particular, the Central Intelligence Agency has come under criticism for continuing interrogation and detainment practices found to be unacceptable by U.S. courts.[39] The administration argued that captured terrorists (broadly defined) were "unlawful combatants" and were therefore not protected under the provisions of the 1949 Geneva Conventions on the Laws of War. This unilateral "reinterpretation" of the Geneva Conventions set the stage for systematic abuses, including secret detentions and long-term imprisonment without trial in facilities such as Guantanamo Bay, a U.S. naval base on Cuba that remained under American control after the Cuban Revolution in 1959. U.S. interrogators have used torture (including "waterboarding," which simulates drowning) to extract information. In a procedure called "extraordinary rendition" the CIA used secret flights to transfer detainees to other countries for interrogation under torture. Several European countries have been accused of permitting these flights to transit through their airspace or territory. As the 2008 *Annual Report* of Amnesty International noted, "With breathtaking legal obfuscation, the US administration has continued its efforts to weaken the absolute prohibition against torture and other ill-treatment."[40]

Indeed, a central theme in the human rights debates of the past few years has been the relationship between civil liberties and the U.S. "global war on terror." The violent and disturbing images from the Abu Ghraib prison, which depicted the torture and sexual humiliation of Iraqi prisoners by American military guards, shocked many, but for many more (especially in the Middle East) simply confirmed the belief that the American military enterprise in Iraq was anything but benevolent in intent. The subsequent military tribunals convened to investigate and prosecute these crimes were limited to low-ranking soldiers only, and ignored the wider political and senior military leadership's role in fostering a culture of indifference and contempt toward human rights and international law.[41] According to Amnesty International, in 2007 the United States had detained 600 persons without charge, trial, or judicial review in Afghanistan and as many as 25,000 in Iraq.[42] Meanwhile, questions have also been raised about the global war on terror and its impact on civil liberties in the U.S. and other liberal democracies. The U.S. Patriot Act of 2001 has raised many concerns about the increased powers of law enforcement and intelligence agencies to conduct surveillance, searches, and detainment of citizens and foreign nationals living in America.

Does the record of the past few years mean that international war law and international humanitarian law have suffered permanent damage? There are encouraging signs despite the seriousness of recent violations. International law has been held as the standard of acceptable behaviour and by violating those standards the U.S. government has paid a political price. Belatedly, the U.S. government began to recognize the cost of these policies to its legitimacy and how they have served to undermine counterterrorism efforts. The Bush administration came under increasing pressure to close Guantanamo and reassert its commitment to the Geneva Conventions. President Obama will have an important role in deciding whether America will uphold the principles of international law on these matters. In his first 100 days, President Obama pledged to close Guantanamo Bay and banned the practice of waterboarding (although rendition was still permissible under certain circumstances). Meanwhile, many Canadians have expressed concern that Prime Minister Stephen Harper has not acted to have Canadian Omar Khadr removed from Guantanamo and sent to stand trial in Canada. Canada has also been criticized for violating the Geneva Conventions in Afghanistan (see Profile 9.7).

HUMAN SECURITY AND HUMANITARIAN INTERVENTION

As we have seen in this text, most of the violent warfare of the latter half of the previous century occurred at the intrastate level, and much human suffering took place at the hands

PROFILE 9.7 Canada, Human Rights, and Detainee Transfer in Afghanistan

In November 2007 an Amnesty International report accused Canada of complicity in torture. Canadian soldiers fighting in Afghanistan had transferred captured Taliban combatants to Afghan government facilities, where they were subsequently tortured by Afghan military and intelligence personnel (there appear to have been approximately 30 cases involved). Critics in Canada charged that this violated international law, as the Geneva Conventions forbid the transfer of prisoners of war to parties known to use torture. Critics also charged that the Canadian government agreed to a detainee transfer agreement with the government of Afghanistan in 2005 that had very weak visitation or oversight measures (unlike similar British or Dutch agreements), and therefore Canadian officials had few avenues to observe the treatment of transferred detainees. Why were Taliban detainees transferred to Afghan authorities under these circumstances? Did senior Canadian officials and military officers neglect the detainee transfer issue because it was considered a low-priority concern? Did Canadian officials lack sympathy for captured Taliban fighters and turn their backs on how they might be treated? Or did Canadian officials sympathize with U.S. legal interpretations of the rights of detainees and were consequently unconcerned with the Geneva Conventions? There are no clear answers to these questions, but the episode caused controversy in Canada and reminded Canadians of our own obligations under international law. In April 2007 the Canadian government signed a new detainee transfer agreement with Afghanistan that many consider a model agreement; one wonders why such an agreement was not signed in the first place.

of the state. Outside the sporadic cases of communal violence, most instances of mass killing have been cases of "death by government."[43] In other cases, rebel groups inflict great harm on innocent civilians. Either way, the question that often faces the international community is whether, and when, and how, to intervene (see Profile 9.8). The 2001 *Report of the International Commission on Intervention and State Sovereignty*, which has heavy Canadian influence, claimed that the international community has the "Responsibility to Protect" citizens in complex humanitarian emergencies. How do we draw the line between intervention for the sake of protecting human rights, and intervention that is a thinly veiled effort to assert state interests, such as geopolitical dominance in a certain region? How do we ensure that the impact of intervention does not create a worse situation for those we are attempting to aid? We discussed this topic at length in Chapter 7, but revisit it here because it is central to the challenge of protecting human rights and human security.

One need not be a hard-core realist to accept the proposition that state policies will, by and large, reflect the self-perceived national interests of those who make key foreign policy decisions. Though this may change with time, interests are a vital component of international commitments, and we would be wrong to assert that we can expect states to contribute valuable resources and, more importantly, potential lives, to humanitarian missions if there was nothing at stake. This is why the problem of "selective intervention" will always be with us. Humanitarian interventions will tend to be mounted in contingencies where both interests and values are engaged. Interventions will be less likely to occur when interests are not engaged to the same extent. This explains why NATO intervened in Bosnia and Kosovo, but did not in Albania and Algeria. Some have suggested that this is why the UN needs its own army, an independent military force that could be called into action at the UN's request. Of course, even if such a UN army existed (and it is highly unlikely that it will in the near future) it would be called into action only under Chapter 7 of the UN Charter—in other words, when all of the permanent five members agreed it was either necessary or did not challenge their

PROFILE 9.8　A Case for Humanitarian Intervention? The LRA

Unfortunately, there are all too many examples of large-scale atrocities being perpetrated today. The international community must struggle with the question of when to intervene, and how. Ten years after the Rwandan genocide, we are arguably no closer to consensus on this most delicate of issues. One case where a strong argument can be made concerns the Lord's Resistance Army (LRA), led by Joseph Kony, a self-proclaimed messiah who wants to establish his kingdom of God on earth. The LRA operates mostly in Northern Uganda, attacking from bases in Sudan; it has been alleged that the Sudanese government has aided it in the past. Uganda and Sudan had for years exchanged accusations of backing each other's rebels until they struck a deal in March 2002 allowing Ugandan forces to pursue the LRA into Sudan. Most notoriously, the LRA has abducted thousands of boys and girls and terrorized them into slavery as soldiers and concubines: more than 6,000 were abducted in 1998 alone. More than 500,000 people have been displaced in Northern Uganda due to the fighting there between the LRA and government troops. The attacks on sleeping villages have involved slaughter and abduction on a large scale and are a constant source of fear and anxiety in towns such as Kitgum, where 48 people were hacked to death on July 25, 2002. The Ugandan army has been unable to defeat the LRA, and repeated attempts to negotiate a peace have been unable to reach a settlement.

While it is clear that the LRA is embedded in a complex civil war in Northern Uganda involving different ethnic groups, the central government (itself a dubious provider of human security for its civilians, hundreds of thousands of whom live in unprotected refugee camps), and the Congo and Sudanese governments, this complexity alone does not explain the inability to stop the LRA. One reason humanitarian intervention would be difficult is that the LRA is so enmeshed in the countryside. Another is that in order to stop them, killing hundreds of child soldiers might be inescapable. Yet a well-trained and well-equipped force would be able to decisively eliminate Kony and his top aides if the international community gave this high priority and the Ugandan government permitted it. As always, the dangers and morals of intervention have to be weighed against the dangers and morals of failing to intervene. Meanwhile, Kony's indictment by the ICC in 2007 (initially requested by the Ugandan government, then rescinded) has only served to steel his resolve to avoid capture and peace, and has helped ignite a debate (fuelled further by the indictment of the Sudanese president) about the proper role of the ICC in ongoing conflicts.

SOURCES: GLOBALSECURITY.ORG, HTTP://WWW.GLOBALSE CURITY.ORG/ MILITARY/WORLD/PARA/LRA.HTM (ACCESSED MAY 30, 2004); AND BBC NEWS, HTTP://NEWS.BBC.CO.UK/1/HI/ WORLD/AFRICA/2982818.STM (ACCESSED MAY 30, 2004).

interests. Even in cases when humanitarian motives were a significant factor in a decision to use military force—such as the NATO air war against Serbia in 1999—interests were engaged, in particular the desire to prevent the conflict from reigniting a wider war and a consensus that Slobodan Miloševi had to be removed from power. However, not everyone was convinced of the sincerity of the humanitarian motive: critics saw it as yet another expression of NATO power, and another effort to generate increased military spending in the United States and elsewhere.[44] In other cases, humanitarian rationales can be virtually absent: justifying the wars in Afghanistan and Iraq as humanitarian interventions requires a great stretch of the imagination. These wars were motivated by interests, and while humanitarian rationales may have been a small part of the motivation, or were used to obtain political support, it is highly unlikely either of these wars would have been mounted on humanitarian grounds alone. Even the Russians claimed they were acting on humanitarian grounds when they bombed parts of Georgia in 2008.

And yet, there are cases in which the humanitarian argument is certainly a strong one. In Somalia in 1992 a drought and a murderous war between clan factions precipitated starvation and human suffering on a large scale. As we saw in Chapter 7, states responded with a troubled and ultimately unsuccessful intervention that was primarily based on humanitarian impulses. However, in Rwanda, where chaos and genocidal violence created a bloody inferno, an intervention would certainly have been warranted. A similar argument might be made for intervention in the Darfur region of Sudan. It would also have been warranted as a response to violence in the Democratic Republic of the Congo. And yet, as of 2009 only UN peacekeeping operations with limited resources and mandates were mounted in either of these cases. Much intervention is thinly veiled self-interest, such as the United States in Colombia, or Russia in Georgia, where interests are engaged. The UN will then be called upon to clean up the mess or to take over when the dirty work of military action is over. Alternatively, postconflict security might be provided by private security companies, which are increasingly prominent actors in global politics (see Profile 9.9). There are, of course, notable exceptions to this, as our discussion of the recent liberation of East Timor indicated. More frequently, however, intervention reflects state leaders' perceptions of opportunity or opportunity costs. India's interventions in West Pakistan (now Bangladesh) and Sri Lanka, Tanzania's invasion of Uganda (overthrowing the notorious Idi Amin), the Vietnamese invasion of Cambodia (stopping the murderous Khmer Rouge regime), and Nigeria's engagement in West Africa are all examples of interventions in which local powers perceived interests as well as opportunities. Although it might be argued that all these actions (most of which occurred outside the parameters of UN diplomacy) had positive effects, we cannot expect interests to be separated from the humanitarian intervention equation; they will remain an important part of any decision whether to intervene in humanitarian crises. Further, the immensely complex and expensive process of nation building in postconflict contexts remains at best an experimental process that can be seen as a cross between humanitarian assistance and cultural imposition; it can be no substitute for local institution building and recovery.

Therefore, the need for conflict prevention through the pursuit of human rights—including minority rights and sustainable development—is paramount in the quest for a more humanitarian world. In other words, the best way to avoid the need for humanitarian intervention, and the debates that surround it, is to avoid the need to intervene in the first place. This is yet another "easier said than done" prospect, but one worth pursuing for the sake of those who have perished and those who might perish in future conflicts.

CHILD LABOUR

As mentioned earlier in this chapter, the international community has condemned slavery for some time, beginning with the major European powers at the Congress of Vienna in 1815. By 1880 more than 50 bilateral treaties on the subject had been concluded. At the Brussels Conference in 1890, an antislavery act was signed and later ratified by 18 states. This act instituted a number of mutually-agreed-upon measures to suppress the slave trade both in Africa and on the high seas, including the right of high-seas visits and searches, the confiscation of ships engaged in the trade, and the punishment of their masters and crew. Though slavery is still reported in some parts of the world, such as in the Sudan, it is generally considered a criminal activity.

However, some would argue that the international community has done much less, and should do much more, to suppress another form of economic activity that many feel is the modern-day equivalent to slavery: the exploitation of child labour. It is impossible to provide accurate estimates of the number of children working in the world because of disputes over

PROFILE 9.9 The Return of the Mercenary?

Observers have noticed a trend in many recent military operations: the employment of private military companies (PMCs). The *mercenary* (a soldier who fights for pay and profit) is an age-old fixture in global politics. Mercenaries have been used by rulers, states, and armed groups to supplement their own military capability. Today, private companies specializing in various aspects of military and police operations are increasingly important actors in armed conflicts and peace and stability missions. Private security contracting is big business in world affairs, with major firms from the United Kingdom, United States, South Africa, and elsewhere engaged in hundreds of operations worldwide. There are over 200 PMCs in the world, providing services that include provision of food and maintenance of equipment, translation and interrogation, land mine clearance and education, personal security, military and police training, guarding installations, and supporting military operations. In the past, companies such as Executive Outcomes and Sandline provided combat capacities (both companies no longer exist). Today, no PSC openly offers combat services, although the U.S.-based company Blackwater has indicated it could provide a battalion of peacekeepers if authorized by the UN. Frequently, these companies are hired by governments and armed forces, but corporations and NGOs also hire PMCs to protect assets and individuals. Although PMCs are active across the world, they are heavily employed in Iraq, where companies such as Blackwater, DynCorp, Erinys, Global Risk Strategies, and many others employed over 20,000 personnel in 2006 (the second-largest contingent after the U.S. military).

PMCs have been a source of debate and controversy in global politics. Many consider such companies little more than mercenary organizations, a charge PMCs vigorously deny. The accountability of PMC employees has also been called into question. The laws of war generally cover regular military personnel, and there have been numerous cases of PMC employees committing crimes and escaping punishment because no legal mechanisms exist to prosecute them. In Iraq and Afghanistan, security company personnel were immunized against local prosecution, which has made it difficult if not impossible to ensure employees are held accountable for their actions. The use of such personnel has also generated a political debate. PMCs may be effective contributors of personnel and capacity in situations where governments and international organizations are unwilling to contribute adequate resources to peacekeeping and stability missions. On the other hand, PMCs are less subject to control and oversight, making them potentially a liability. For example, in Iraq the careless or blatantly illegal actions of some PMC employees have alienated locals and damaged the efforts of United States and other officials to gain public support.

Perhaps the growth of PMCs in global politics should not surprise us, as there has been a shift toward privatized security within many states for several decades: there are more private armed security guards in the United States or Africa than there are police, and even more controversially, many prisons are run as for-profit enterprises.

SOURCES: S. PERCY, *REGULATING THE PRIVATE SECURITY INDUSTRY*, ADELPHI PAPER 384 (OXFORD: ROUTLEDGE, 2006); M. BARSTOW, "SECURITY COMPANIES: SHADOW SOLDIERS IN IRAQ," *THE NEW YORK TIMES*, APRIL 19, 2004, A1; AND P. SINGER, *CORPORATE WARRIORS: THE RISE OF THE PRIVATIZED MILITARY INDUSTRY* (ITHACA, NY: CORNELL UNIVERSITY PRESS, 2003).

what constitutes exploitative labour and because many countries refuse to participate in surveys. UNICEF and the International Labour Organization (ILO) estimate that approximately 218 million children are working in exploitative conditions, but this figure excludes domestic work.[45]

In itself, child labour is nothing new; one might argue that it is only Western notions of adolescence that make the phenomenon recognizable. In other words, before we had

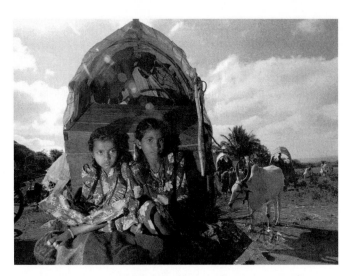

Malova, left, and her sister Bharti sit together on the road near Saundatti in Southern India on their way to be initiated as devadasis, young girls dedicated to a Hindu goddess. In modern times the religious trappings have all but disappeared, and the *devadasi* system has become a network for recruiting child prostitutes in India. (AP Photo/Sherwin Crasto/CP Archive.)

anything resembling high school, teenagers simply worked in the fields and factories. It is, therefore, a Western notion of industrial progress that helps us see child labour as abhorrent. However, in some cases we might argue further that there is an unusual level of exploitation involved, since children as young as six are toiling away at repetitive and physically demanding jobs in Africa, Asia, and South America. In Malaysia, some children work up to 17-hour days on rubber plantations enduring insect and snake bites. In Tanzania and Kenya, they pick coffee, inhaling pesticides. In Cote d'Ivoire, young boys (many from neighbouring Mali) have been brutally exploited in the cocoa trade, enduring slave-like conditions to ensure chocolate production.[46] In Portugal, children as young as 12 work on construction sites. In Morocco, they sew carpets for export. In the United States, children are exploited in sweatshops. Many children end up working to pay off their parents' debts, and their opportunities for education and an escape from the cycle of poverty are virtually nonexistent. Many young female workers (and some young male workers as well) have to often endure the additional burden of sexual abuse, including the sexually transmitted diseases associated with prostitution.

The products of child labour, many of which are in the textile industry and include clothing and rugs, often end up for sale in North America and Europe. In Bangladesh, textile and clothing exports to the United States have doubled since 1990. As a result of American pressure, some 30,000 children were removed from the country's textile industry between 1993 and 1995. However, one problem that Western governments will have an even harder time addressing is that many of these children do not end up in school (indeed, many of them are from regions where school is a luxury for the privileged few) but end up on the street, engaging in begging and prostitution to make a living. As an *Economist* editorial suggested, corporate codes of conduct regarding child labour may not end it at all, but "merely shift it to shadier areas of the economy that are far harder to police."[47] Foreign investors are often criticized for exploiting local labour, which usually includes child labour. In response, Levi Strauss provides schooling for child workers in its suppliers' plants in Bangladesh. This raises yet another ethical dilemma, since one can argue the company is merely reinforcing dependence on it and reaping profits in the process. However, without this schooling, what type of future would the children have?

The question of child labour poses one of the harshest challenges to the concept of universal human rights and human security. Although it may be possible for people in the West to look on child labour as an awful thing, and it is condemned by the ILO and the widely signed UN Convention on the Rights of the Child, people in impoverished regions do not force children to work because they derive pleasure from it (sadly, there are exceptions to this, in both the North and the South); rather, they do so because they have to ensure the survival of a family. The economic conditions of the underprivileged seem to be worsening, not improving, as time moves on and markets become increasingly global (see Chapter 11).

It is difficult to conceive of an end to child labour in light of this fact. Consider the remarks of a mother (a sweeper and latrine cleaner) from India:

> Nearly all our girls work as sweepers. Why should I waste my time and money on sending my daughter to school where she will learn nothing of use? … So why not put my girl to work so that she will learn something about our profession? My elder girl who is fifteen years old will be married soon. Her mother-in-law will put her to cleaning latrines somewhere. Too much schooling will only give girls big ideas, and then they will be beaten up by their husbands or abused by their in-laws.[48]

The split is pronounced between the North and South on the general issue of labour standards. The United States and some other Western countries have expressed a desire to use the WTO to fight child labour, unfair (i.e., too low) wages, "union-busting," and other practices that they argue may give other countries an unfair advantage in a world moving toward free trade. Southern politicians and economic representatives argue that this effort is really just old protectionism in new clothing. The ILO has tried to implement a universal code of conduct regarding conditions of employment, but it is up against opposition in the South and North. Consumers everywhere can investigate the origin of their products and refuse to purchase those made with child labour, but without simultaneous advances in poverty eradication it is of limited use.

SELF-DETERMINATION

To give a more rounded assessment of the concept of collective rights, we turn now to a discussion of the principle of self-determination. *Self-determination* can be defined as either the right of all peoples to choose their own government or the right of all peoples to independence and sovereign statehood. As we will see, this issue-area presents all sorts of headaches for national leaders, and cuts to the root of the problems inherent in maintaining a status quo international system while attempting to institutionalize ethics on a global scale.

In 1996, the Nobel Peace Prize was awarded to Bishop Carlos Belo and Jose Ramos Horta of East Timor. They had both worked to restore the right of self-determination to the

---

PROFILE 9.10 Canada and Child Labour

Prompted by child rights activists, Western governments are starting to speak loudly about the continued problem of child labour. In 1996, the Canadian government made a contribution of $700,000 to the ILO's International Program for the Elimination of Child Labour. In August 1996 in Stockholm, then–Minister of Foreign Affairs Lloyd Axworthy, Senator Landon Pearson, and the Honourable Hedy Fry attended the World Congress Against the Commercial Sexual Exploitation of Children, along with 700 representatives from 119 countries, more than 100 participants from other international organizations, 500 NGOs and youth delegates, and 500 media representatives. On April 18, 1996, Bill C-27 was tabled, proposing amendments to the Criminal Code to allow for the prosecution of Canadian citizens and permanent residents who engage in commercial sexual activities with minors while abroad—a practice commonly known as "sex tourism."

SOURCE: LLOYD AXWORTHY, CANADIAN MINISTER OF FOREIGN AFFAIRS, ADDRESS BEFORE THE PARLIAMENTARY SUB-COMMITTEE ON SUSTAINABLE HUMAN DEVELOPMENT OF THE STANDING COMMITTEE ON FOREIGN AFFAIRS AND INTERNATIONAL TRADE, OTTAWA, OCTOBER 2, 1996.

people of East Timor, which has been occupied by Indonesia for more than two decades. This dedication shows how strong the ethic of self-determination remains today, even if it is still unrecognized in many parts of the world. Woodrow Wilson emphasized the right to self-determination in his famous "Fourteen Points" speech following World War I. It was, and still is in many parts of the world, seen as the principle that would guide the way out of colonial domination. States such as the United States were born of revolution and war; states such as Canada found their way gradually, eventually achieving the self-determination necessary to become recognized (in the Canadian case, in the League of Nations) as a sovereign state. More recently, the dissolution of the Soviet empire can be seen also as the achievement of self-determination by the peoples of the former U.S.S.R. and the former Warsaw Pact countries. Some of them, like the Czechs and Slovaks, decided to split even further. Others, such as the Chechens, have become military targets of Moscow instead. Recently, the East Timorese elected to establish full independence, finally ending years of brutal rule by Indonesia; after protracted and intense conflict, a UN-sponsored Australian peacekeeping team entered the country to try to maintain order despite the opposition of some elements of the Indonesian military (see Chapter 7), and the Timorese have finally obtained independence.

The concept of self-determination remains so difficult, however, because of the collective nature of the right. It raises the further question of just who has the right to self-determination. In the Canadian case, two groups, First Nations peoples and Quebec separatists, argue that they should have the right to self-determination; some of them demand a sovereign state of their own. Even the seemingly monolithic United States has separatist movements emerging in idyllic Hawaii (see Profile 9.11), Puerto Rico, and Texas. The problem is much more acute in areas such as the former Yugoslavia, where pronouncements of sovereignty (and their recognition by the international community) have given rise to ethnic conflict

PROFILE 9.11 Hawaiian Sovereignty?

We usually think of Hawaii as only a popular and expensive tourist destination, but an independence movement there has gained strength over the years. Dozens of pro-sovereignty organizations have appeared, and in 1993 the state legislature passed several laws and resolutions acknowledging sovereignty as a long-term goal. An article in the *Boston Globe* explained the roots of the movement:

> In 1920, 20 years after the islands were annexed as a territory and 39 years before statehood, the U.S. Congress passed legislation to which many historians trace the situation today. The Hawaiian Home Act carved out 203,500 of the island's 4.1 million acres—including some of the least productive and poorly situated land—for use by natives. Most of the remaining land was held by private interests or placed under state control, while the U.S. military signed 99-year leases, at $1 each, for several large, strategically located parcels of land. The Indigenous people, known in their language as *kanaka maoli* and defined as those with at least 50 percent Hawaiian blood, have since experienced many of the same difficulties many native peoples face: lower income, higher-than-average alcoholism rates and health problems, and resentment over their "colonization." Their fight for independence continues in 2004, including campaigns by the Hawaii Nation to educate American tourists, who are often blissfully ignorant of the fact that Hawaii is in effect an occupied territory. For more information, see the website of the "Hawaii Nation": http://www. hawaii-nation.org.

and cleansing. Observers remain concerned that the unilateral declaration of independence from Serbia by Kosovo in late winter of 2008, recognized with approval by many Western governments such as the United States and (belatedly) Canada, but firmly rejected by Russia and China, could spark renewed ethnic violence in the region. Russia's military intervention or invasion of Georgia in August of 2008 (condemned by Western governments) was linked to Russian support for secessionist movements in South Ossetia and Abhkazia, two regions of Georgia seeking independence. One can argue that the right to self-determination, while acting as a vehicle toward freedom for colonized peoples in the past, invariably creates conflict within, and (just as importantly), among states.

HUMAN RIGHTS AND THE SPECIAL ROLE OF NGOS

By now you are no doubt aware that one of the trickiest aspects of human rights work is that the perpetrators of crimes are so often the same people or institutions that are supposed to uphold and enforce them—in other words, the state itself. For this reason, many people argue that it is short-sighted to trust governments, and that nongovernmental organizations without formal ties to governments can do a better job of providing information about and evidence of human rights violations. For example, many NGOs have participated in the work of the War Crimes Commission of Experts in the former Yugoslavia, including Amnesty International, the International Committee of the Red Cross, Physicians for Human Rights, Médecins sans Frontières, Helsinki Watch, the International League of Human Rights, the Union for Peace and Humanitarian Aid to Bosnia and Herzegovina, the International Criminal Police Association, the National Alliance of Women's Organizations, and the International Centre for Criminal Law Reform.[49]

The most prominent NGO involved in the human rights issue-area is Amnesty International, which was started in London in 1961 as a campaign by several lawyers and writers. Peter Berenson drew attention to the campaign with an article in London's *Observer Weekend Review*, in which he suggested that the revulsion we often feel regarding human rights violations could be put to good use: "If these feelings of disgust all over the world could be united into common action, something effective could be done."[50] Amnesty now has more than 1 million members, subscribers, and donors in more than 150 countries, and it seeks to publicize the plight of people who are held as political prisoners around the world. Other groups, such as Americas Watch, Asia Watch, and Africa Watch, monitor human rights adherence by governments, including their foreign policy activities. Church groups are often involved as well, especially in Latin America. The International Committee of the Red Cross is also a prominent player in the human rights issue-area.

NGOs use a wide variety of strategies to call attention to their efforts.[51] They campaign in local settings, exhort members to participate in letter-writing campaigns to pressure public officials to reverse certain decisions, and occasionally participate in protests that result in media coverage as well. Information technology, discussed at greater length in Chapter 12, offers newfound opportunities also. In Thailand, people have referred to the "cellular phone revolution" in which students protesting against the government were joined by relatively affluent Thais with modern phones and fax machines. Protestors used mobile phones to keep in touch after an army crackdown in 1992.[52] During and after the infamous Tiananmen Square massacre of 1989, the Chinese government made a concerted effort to control the flow of information in and out of China. Police monitored incoming faxes, but students were able to use electronic mail on the Internet for some time before authorities detected this and began shutting down computers as well. Indeed, a quick Internet search under the phrase "human rights" will produce a bewildering variety of NGO-sponsored websites and media reports.

PROFILE 9.12   A Human Rights Advocate: Aung San Suu Kyi

Holding a poster of Myanmar's pro-democracy leader Aung San Suu Kyi, a protestor denounces the Myanmar government at a rally in Seoul, South Korea, in 2008. (AP Photo/Lee Jin-man/CP Archive.)

Myanmar is a small Southeast Asian state, known as Burma before a military coup in 1988. Its military dictatorship, self-labelled as the State Peace and Development Council, is known as one of the most oppressive governments on earth, severely curtailing freedom of expression and movement and accused of using the forced labour of its citizens. It has actively suppressed opposition with military means, including the beating and imprisonment of protesting monks, whose colourful robes gave rise to the name "Saffron Revolution" in 2007. Most infamously the government denied any substantial emergency aid to victims of the Cyclone Nigris in the Irrawaddy Delta in the spring of 2008. In this context, Aung San Suu Kyi, daughter of Aung San, the founder of the Anti-Fascist People's Freedom League, has arisen as the key

representative of a democratic voice. She has also been consigned to house arrest and had her movements curtailed. However, she was the winner of the Nobel Peace Prize in 1991, and her status as an international figure has restrained the government from more violent methods of limiting her influence. Aung San Suu Kyi's father was killed in 1947, after leading the struggle for Burmese independence, and she lived in India with her mother and attended Oxford University in England in the late 1960s and 1970s before returning to Burma for the last open multiparty elections there in 1990. Her party won the elections but the government refused to recognize the results. She has never left Burma since and refuses to cease her condemnation of the regime. Sadly, her husband, Michael Aris, died of prostate cancer in London in March 1999, and she was unable to see him. He was denied entry to Burma, and she feared that if she were to go to him, she would not be allowed back in the country to resume her struggle. Thus are the hardships those committed to such demanding causes must endure. On-and-off "house arrests" have become routine events for this activist, and though she survived the cyclone of 2008 and the subsequent political unrest in the country, as late as 2009 there was uncertainty about her safety as she was again arrested and sentenced to yet more "house arrest," based on what are considered bogus charges.

SOURCE: SEE AUNG SAN SUU KYI, *FREEDOM FROM FEAR AND OTHER WRITINGS*, ED. M. ARIS, 2ND ED. (NEW YORK: PENGUIN, 1995).

The increased participation of women in international affairs is obvious, especially if one looks at the proliferation of women's groups active in the transnational context.[53] Though many feminists argue that women have yet to influence the real citadels of power in a meaningful way, women's groups have successfully brought women's rights issues on to the agenda of international institutions and have played a role in the creation of many international legal instruments designed to protect women's rights. In particular, women's groups have often worker through UN mechanisms. In 1946, the 45-member Commission on the Status of Women was established to collect data on women's rights and make recommendations. It had an immediate impact as the Declaration of Human Rights was being drafted; the original text, borrowing ideas from the American Declaration of Independence, had begun, "All men are brothers"; the Commission on the Status of Women objected to this sexist language and the draft was amended to read, "All human beings are created free and equal in dignity and rights."[54]

Eleanor Roosevelt, the widow of American President Franklin Roosevelt, played a key role in the writing and passing of the Declaration itself.

In the 1970s ECOSOC (the UN's Economic and Social Council) created the International Research and Training Institute for the Advancement of Women (INSTRAW). As well, the UN Development Fund for Women (UNIFEM), part of the UN Development Programme, was established in 1976 to provide direct support to women's projects. In 1979 the General Assembly passed the Convention on the Elimination of All Forms of Discrimination against Women (CEDAW), and 23 experts were appointed to oversee that convention's implementation. In 1985, the UN Division for the Advancement of Women was set up following the important outcome of a conference in Nairobi, Kenya, a document called *The Forward Looking Strategies for the Advancement of Women to the Year 2000*. The UN has an active Commission on the Status of Women, a 45-member intergovernmental body that meets annually in New York and prepares reports for ECOSOC. On March 8, 1993, International Women's Day, the Commission on Human Rights adopted by consensus a resolution aimed at integrating the rights of women into UN human rights mechanisms; in December of that year, the UN adopted a Declaration on the Elimination of Violence Against Women. In September 1995, the UN Fourth World Conference on Women was held in Beijing, and drafted a Platform for Action for women's empowerment. The "Beijing Platform" is aimed at removing obstacles to women's participation in all aspects of public and private life, through a full and equal share in economic, social, cultural, and political decision making.[55] The Beijing Platform has been reviewed and expanded in two subsequent conferences held in 2000 and 2005. All of these initiatives were characterized by the active engagement of human rights and women's NGOs.

It is obvious that NGOs, including women's groups, will continue to develop their role in the human rights issue-area. They form part of an expanding and increasingly influential network. However, it is unrealistic to assume that such organizations can battle the very real power of states that continue to grossly violate their citizens' rights; that takes concerted international efforts as well as change from within. The fall of apartheid in South Africa is a brilliant example of how that combination can succeed, but the continuation of poverty and violence there is indicative of the long road ahead.

THE QUESTION OF JUSTICE

Many of the issue-areas discussed above lend themselves to a discussion of preventive measures. Although it may be impossible to avoid child labour without eradicating poverty or to stop genital female mutilation without a radical change in cultural perspective, it can be argued that crimes against humanity, such as genocide and torture, can be avoided by pursuing what domestic legal experts and judges call the *power of deterrence*. In other words, if state and military leaders have reason to fear retribution, be it through domestic or international means, they may refrain from excessive atrocities. This was the initial idea behind the Nuremberg war crimes trials, discussed above, and it is one of the main justifications for the two international criminal courts described above, as well as the new International Criminal Court.

Both of the extant courts have received mixed reviews. The International Criminal Tribunal for the Former Yugoslavia has more than 1,000 staff members from more than 75 countries, and an annual budget of more than US$90 million. As of September 2008, it has tried 115 accused and had 46 ongoing trials for various war crimes, including grave breaches of the 1949 Geneva Conventions, violations of the laws or customs of war, genocide, crimes against humanity, and sexual offences. Several individuals have been found guilty, but of course they have the right to appeal and have done so. Slobodan Milošević died while on trial, raising concerns about the pace of the court's proceedings. However, the ongoing relevance of the court was illustrated by the summer 2008 capture and extradition of Radovan Karadžić. Similarly, the International Criminal Tribunal for Rwanda has become a fairly major operation, with 28 completed cases, including the former prime minister as well as all senior military leaders and high-ranking government officials, several of whom have been convicted for genocide and crimes against humanity, and many more awaiting trial. While fairly widespread support for both courts exists, they face many problems regarding acquisition of both the indicted and evidence; they are often viewed as partial courts, in which guilty verdicts are inevitable (and thus they are equated with Nuremberg, largely viewed as a "victor's court"). Maintaining adequate funding is an ongoing concern as well; these tribunals were intended as temporary institutions, yet their work is far from complete more than decade after they were established.[56]

The need for a more permanent tribunal was central to many NGO and state demands in the mid-1990s. States and NGOs met in Rome in 1998 to hammer out a treaty to establish an International Criminal Court (ICC), based partly on the ICTY and ICTR experience but also as an effort to deter future acts of state genocide and torture. The resulting Rome Statute was ratified on July 1, 2002, when the required 60 **ratifications** were obtained. Canada ratified the Rome Statute in July 2000, but several key states, including Russia and China, refused to sign. The United States initially refused to sign, did so in December 2000, and rescinded its participation on May 6, 2003. The ICC focuses only on the most egregious crimes, such as genocide, crimes against humanity, war crimes, and aggression (when an agreeable definition of the term is found). Many disputes influenced the adoption of the statute: the permanent members of the Security Council insisted that the Council had ultimate control over the Court, while others wanted a strongly independent chief prosecutor's office. During negotiations, the Americans expressed three main reservations, which determined their decision not to ratify. They felt the ICC would be an untamed animal, with unchecked prosecutorial power, despite the statute's built-in principle of complementarity (ensuring that the ICC is the court of last resort); they believed that the ICC's pledge to be apolitical would undermine the influence and integrity of the Security Council; and they claimed that the ICC threatens American sovereignty. Thus, the United States succeeded in persuading several states to enter impunity agreements that would prevent U.S. nationals accused of genocide, crimes against humanity, or war crimes from being surrendered to the ICC. Nonetheless, the Court was established and, under the leadership of the current President, Canadian Philpee Kirsch, and an aggressive Prosecutor, Argentine Luis Moreno-Ocampo, it has begun the trials of several individuals apprehended from Africa and made highly controversial indictments of others.

For "security reasons," the UN-backed tribunal on war crimes in Sierra Leone is trying former Liberian leader Charles Taylor at The Hague instead of in Africa. The ICC has also indicted the leader of the Lord's Resistance Army in Uganda, Joseph Kony. While this might be seen as a progressive step for international criminal law, the ICC indictment is controversial, because Kony refuses to further negotiate a peace settlement with the Ugandan government while the indictment stands. In July 2008 the Prosecutor of the ICC accused Sudanese President Omar al-Bashir of genocide, war crimes, and crimes against humanity. The ICC prosecutor went further in March 2009, when the ICC issued an arrest warrant for President Bashir for war crimes and crimes against humanity, marking the first time a sitting head of state has been indicted by the ICC. However, the decision has revealed the limitations of international law in general and the ICC in particular. The ICC has no means of enforcing its indictment or physically arresting President Bashir in Sudan itself. Many African and Arab governments have called on the ICC to suspend the indictment for a year, arguing that

The prosecutor of the International Criminal Court, Luis Moreno-Ocampo, speaks at press conference as Deputy Prosecutor Fatou Bensouda looks on. In July 2008 the ICC filed charges of genocide against Sudanese President Omar al-Bashir. As a result, the Sudanese government expelled badly needed aid organizations from the region, further fuelling debates over the optimal extent of the ICC's actions. (AP Photo/Fred Ernst/CP Archive.)

the ICC decision endangers peace talks between the Sudanese government and resistance movements in Darfur. Human rights advocates argue that many African and Arab governments are wary of the indictment, because they are fearful of being indicted for their own human rights violations. In many countries (especially Sudan), the ICC decision has been framed as an example of Western imperialism and interference in the domestic affairs of a country. The immediate Sudanese government reaction was to expel UN and humanitarian aid NGOs from Sudan, with potentially catastrophic consequences for over one million war-affected people in Darfur who are dependent on international agencies for water, food, and health care. As a result, the ICC indictment has caused great controversy and raised questions about whether it was helpful or harmful.[57] These cases are vivid reminders of the tension that can exist between the need to cooperate with leaders of groups or states to establish peace and deliver humanitarian aid and the need to achieve justice for grave violations of human rights.

Another means to achieve justice is unilateral action, and the case of General Augusto Pinochet of Chile provides a promising, but cautionary, tale. Pinochet assumed control of Chile in a brutal coup in 1973 (the former leader, socialist Salvador Allende, was killed; thousands of opponents were jailed and tortured, many of them disappearing altogether during Pinochet's lengthy rule). Chileans rejected his bid to be installed as president-for-life in 1988, but for the plebiscite on this to take place, an agreement was reached that he would be retained as head of the army and that criminal charges would not be laid against members of his regime. While in London for back surgery in October 1998 he was arrested by British authorities, who planned to extradite him to Spain. The Spanish wanted to charge him with various crimes (in the end these were reduced to the charge of torture) against Spanish nationals during his reign. The international community was quite divided over this issue, since it is highly irregular to detain a former head of state who can claim diplomatic immunity. Eventually, British authorities (the Home Secretary), concerned with Pinochet's failing health, decided he had the right to return to Chile, where he could have faced charges brought on by his own country. However, his health seemed to fail whenever such a prospect loomed, and he died in December 2006.

At any rate, this was an interesting development, because it involved a former head of state. Other developments (and especially the Sudan case described above) suggest such people will not be immune from prosecution in the future. A judicial investigation has been initiated in Senegal, at the request of a coalition of human rights groups, against the former President of Chad, Hissein Habré, for alleged crimes under international law, including torture, committed during his 1982 to 1990 rule. After initial efforts by the European Union to extradite Habré to Belgium for trial were rejected, Senegal took steps to amend its constitution and legal system to put Habré on trial. As of 2008, evidence was still being gathered by Senegalese authorities. Of course, it could be a chaotic situation if every head of state is brought to justice for crimes committed during his or her rule; few would be exempt, depending on one's definition of crimes. The difficult task of moving on—in Chile's case, difficult indeed, as thousands of relatives and friends of present-day Chileans suffered

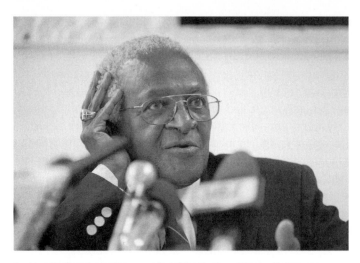

Seeking truth and opening wounds. Of the Truth and Reconciliation process, Chair of the TRC Anglican Archbishop Desmond Tutu wrote in the final report that people "risked opening wounds that were perhaps in the process of healing." (AP Photo/Sasa Kralj/CP Archive.)

under Pinochet's iron-fisted rule, or in the case of Cambodia, where over a million citizens were murdered by the infamous **Khmer Rouge** in the late 1970s—remains a challenge for victims and their families.

Another path suggests that South Africa's Truth and Reconciliation Commission (TRC) is a superior way to mend the pain of the past while bringing the negative into the open.[58] However, the effectiveness of the truth-and-reconciliation-commission model is dependent on political conditions and the willingness of both past oppressors and victims (who may prefer to try to forget and move on) to expose themselves to the community at large. Furthermore, many commissions are mandated to extend amnesty to those who participate, which is often opposed by victims and their families. In South Africa, the Commission included three committees. The Human Rights Violations Committee investigated human rights abuses that took place between 1960 and 1994, established the identity of and located the victims, and referred them to the Reparation and Rehabilitation Committee. A President's Fund, funded by parliament and private contributions, was established to pay urgent interim reparation to victims in terms of the regulations prescribed by former President Nelson Mandela. Finally, and most controversially, the Amnesty Committee considered applications for amnesty from those accused of human rights violations. Applicants could apply for amnesty for any act, omission, or offence associated with a political objective committed between March 1, 1960, and December 6, 1993 (the cutoff date was later extended to May 11, 1994). Archbishop Desmond Tutu chaired the Commission, lending his considerable moral weight to the proceedings. Between early 1996 and mid-1998, the commission heard more than 20,000 people give evidence, including members of the ruling ANC party who had resorted to violence during the struggle against apartheid.

This process was, no doubt, constructive for many. Although one might have a hard time equating appeals for amnesty with repentance, and most of the major administrators of apartheid never appeared before the commission (they do not believe they did anything wrong), it was a progressive step to air old animosities and, importantly, cases in which black South Africans had engaged in abuse were given equal footing. Even Mandela's own party, the ANC (African National Congress), tried to block the final Report's publication in 1998, concerned about allegations of ANC atrocities committed outside South Africa. At the same time, such a public step could unleash a swell of demands for compensation the state cannot possibly provide, and it might inflame an already volatile country. It was certainly a risk, though in South Africa's case it appears to have been worth it. Whether this could be a means used elsewhere, however, is uncertain. For example, it will be difficult for Indonesia to come to terms with the legacy of the Suharto dictatorship, even if his family is forced to pay back some of the hundreds of millions of dollars he effectively stole from the country, since the old political machinery is still largely in place in Indonesia. Cambodia's promise to hold a similar truth committee has been criticized as too little, too late by many; and the trial of Saddam Hussein in Iraq was rejected as "victor's justice" by many in the Arab world—as Milosevic's unfinished trial at The Hague was seen by many Serbians.

The call for justice and reconciliation will continue to ring out as long as gross human rights violations take place. Students of international relations will remain interested in how the international system responds to human rights violations, and how, in turn, these responses will shape the ability of international organizations and foreign policies to pursue the objectives of human security.

CONCLUSIONS

Although the split between two competing conceptions of human rights (those that protect the individual and those that seek to protect the collective) remains a strong one, governments no longer have the Cold War to blame for ignoring gross human rights violations. One might argue that the current debate centres on the legitimacy of a universal approach that seeks common ethical themes we can apply across the globe against a relativist conception of rights that argues each state has its own right to make its own domestic laws and apply them as each deems necessary. As we have seen, human rights as an issue-area covers a diverse range of topics, but they all point up the difficulty of applying any sort of universal barometer of human well-being at the global level, and the difficulties of ensuring human security in a world largely securitized by the state.

We also examined the important role played by NGOs and women in the evolution of an international human rights regime. While NGOs are still relatively powerless compared with the states they seek to monitor, they can publicize cases that may otherwise remain hidden from the international community. Likewise, while the feminist movement has not altered the fundamental discrepancy in power between men and women, women have made considerable progress in popularizing their causes in international forums such as the UN. What remains to be seen, however, is whether this progress can be sustained as the economic forces of globalization take precedence in government thinking. We looked also at various efforts to affect post-atrocity justice, including international criminal tribunals and courts, unilateral prosecution, and truth and reconciliation commissions. We should note also, however, that many analysts and activists argue that real justice must involve economic factors as well: that the world is still divided between the very affluent, the middle class, and the very poor, and that the international system encourages rather than presents an obstacle to this trend. Further, human rights are of little benefit without a survivable environment in which to enjoy them. We turn to the theme of environmental security in global politics in the next chapter.

Endnotes

1. *War and Change in World Politics* (Cambridge, UK: Cambridge University Press, 1981), 224.
2. For J. P. Humphrey's obituary, see *The Globe and Mail*, March 16, 1995, A20. Interestingly, Humphrey was not originally credited with writing the Declaration: "French human-rights activist Rene Cassin, who claimed authorship of the declaration, was honoured with a Nobel Peace Prize in 1968. Yet when researchers pored over Prof. Humphrey's papers at the McGill library [in Montreal], they discovered the original copy in his handwriting."
3. H. French, "Africa's Culture War: Old Customs, New Values," *The New York Times*, February 2, 1997, E1.
4. E. Nadelmann, "Global Prohibition Regimes: The Evolution of Norms in International Society," *International Organization* 44, no. 4 (1990), 481–526.
5. Note, however, that it can be argued that racist conceptions of universal morality delayed the spread of a universalized conception of human rights. Asbjorn Eide reminds us that "there was a long debate in Spanish

theological and philosophical discourse on whether the Indians had a soul. This was also the period in which the theories of racism were gaining ground in Europe. From the simplest efforts at classification of human groups by Kant, Linneaus, and Buffon, to full-fledged racist ideologies like that of Gobineau (mid-1850s), these were obstacles to the evolution of universal human rights, as distinct from the Western 'natural rights' which for a long time was limited to the male Caucasian." See "Linking Human Rights and Development: Aspects of the Norwegian Debate," in I. Brecher, ed., *Human Rights, Development and Foreign Policy: Canadian Perspectives* (Halifax: Institute for Research on Public Policy, 1988), 5–30, 27*n*6.

6. R. J. Vincent, *Human Rights and International Relations* (Cambridge, UK: Cambridge University Press, 1986).

7. See K. Tomasevski, ed., *The Right to Food: Guide through Applicable International Law* (Dordrecht, Netherlands: Martinus Nijhoff, 1987).

8. F. Halliday, *Rethinking International Relations* (Vancouver: UBC Press, 1994), 167.

9. See R. Niebuhr, *Moral Man and Immoral Society* (New York: Scribner's, 1947); and T. Nardin, *Law, Morality, and the Relations of States* (Princeton: Princeton University Press, 1983).

10. Hence the title of Stanley Hoffmann's important book, *Duties Beyond Borders* (Syracuse, NY: Syracuse University Press, 1981).

11. S. Bailey and S. Daws, *The United Nations: A Concise Political Guide*, 3rd ed. (London: Macmillan, 1995), 87.

12. *Human Rights Watch World Report 2009* (New York, Human Rights Watch, 2008), 1.

13. *Human Rights Watch World Report 1997* (New York: Human Rights Watch, 1996), xxi.

14. *On the Margins of Profit: Rights at Risk in the Global Economy* (New York: Human Rights Watch and the Center for Human Rights and Global Justice, 2008), 3.

15. See *The Worst of the Worst: the World's Most Repressive Societies, 2008* (New York: Freedom House, 2008), 1.

16. Figures from Amnesty International, *Amnesty International Report 2008* (London: Amnesty International, 2008).

17. *Human Rights Watch World Report 1997*, xxvi.

18. *Human Rights Watch World Report 1997*, xiii.

19. World Conference on Human Rights, *Vienna Declaration and Programme of Action*, Part I, Para. 4.

20. Stephen P. Marks, "Social and Humanitarian Issues," in *A Global Agenda: Issues Before the 51st General Assembly of the United Nations* (Lanham, MD: Rowman and Littlefield, 1996), 173. See also J. Mertus, *The United Nations and Human Rights* (London: Routledge 2005).

21. For an important early treatment of this subject, see Q. Wright, "The Outlawry of War and the Law of War," *American Journal of International Law* 47 (1953), 365–76.

22. Michael Walzer, *Just and Unjust Wars*, 2nd ed. (New York: Basic Books, 1992).

23. See United Methodist Council of Bishops, *In Defense of Creation: The Nuclear Crisis and a Just Peace* (Nashville, TN: Graded Press, 1986).

24. Article II of the Genocide Convention defines genocide as "any of the following acts committed with intent to destroy, in whole or in part, a national, ethnical, racial, or religious group, such as (a) Killing members of the group; (b) Causing serious bodily or mental harm to members of the group; (c) Deliberately inflicting on the group conditions of life calculated to bring about its physical destruction in whole or in part; (d) Imposing measures intended to prevent births within the group; (e) Forcibly transferring children of the group to another group." The last two are clearly related to the policies employed by the Nazi regime regarding forced sterilization and a program to transfer Aryan-looking children into Aryan families.

25. See his landmark *Axis Rule in Occupied Europe* (Washington, DC: Carnegie Endowment, 1944), 79.

26. R. Hilberg, *The Destruction of the European Jews* (New York: Holmes and Meier, 1983); see also H. Fein, *Accounting for Genocide: National Response and Jewish Victimization During the Holocaust* (New York: Free Press, 1979).

27. A United Nations report by three African jurists concluded that the killings were part of a larger plan aimed at exterminating the Tutsis; they also noted that "some reliable estimates put the number of victims at close to one million, but the world is unlikely ever to know the exact figure." *The Globe and Mail*, December 3, 1994, A13. Most experts accept 800,000 as the most likely figure now.

28. See, for example, A. Destexhe, "The Third Genocide," *Foreign Policy* 97 (Winter, 1994–95), 3–17; and A. Des Forges, *Leave None to Tell the Story: Genocide in Rwanda* (New York: Human Rights Watch, 1999). The entire Congo region (formerly known as Zaire) has erupted into violent conflict in the years following the 1994 genocide, and the neighbouring state of Burundi has an equally distressing political past and may be on the verge of similar chaos.

29. See P. J. Stoett, "This Age of Genocide: Conceptual and Institutional Implications," *International Journal* 50, no. 3 (1995), 594–618.

30. *The Globe and Mail*, December 3, 1994, A13.

31. Article 22 of the regulations annexed to the Hague Convention of 1907.

32. To quote two international legal experts: "In light of the multifarious effects of hydrogen-bombs, and particularly the area of devastation from 'fall-out' with its unpredictable genetic effects, it could not be said that a belligerent in resorting to thermo-nuclear weapons was adopting a means of injuring the enemy which was 'limited' in any sense of the word." N. Singh and E. McWhinney, *Nuclear Weapons and Contemporary International Law*, 2nd ed. (Dordrecht, Netherlands: Martinus Nijhoff, 1989), 115–16.

33. *The State of the World's Children, 2009: Maternal and Newborn Health* (New York: United Nations Children's Fund, 2008), 34.

34. See A. Walker and P. Parmar, *Warrior Marks: Female Genital Mutilation and the Sexual Blinding of Women* (New York: Harcourt Brace, 1993).

35. H. French, "Africa's Culture War: Old Customs, New Values," *The New York Times*, February 2, 1997.

36. The most important of which are the Universal Declaration of Human Rights and the Convention Against Torture and Other Cruel, Inhuman or Degrading Treatment or Punishment.

37. Note also that if torture takes place during war, it is considered a crime against humanity.

38. R. Gutman, D. Rieff, and A. Dworkin, eds., *Crimes of War: What the Public Should Know*, rev. and upd. (New York: W. W. Norton and Company, 2007), 10.

39. See *Human Rights Watch World Report 2008* (New York: Human Rights Watch, 2008), 540–544.

40. "Foreword," *Amnesty International Report 2008* (London: Amnesty International, 2008), 5.

41. For a harrowing account of the experience of serving at Abu Ghraib see P. Gourevitch and E. Morris, "Exposure: The Woman Behind the Camera at Abu Ghraib," *The New Yorker*, March 24, 2008, 44–57.

42. Figures from *Amnesty International Report 2008*.

43. R. Rummel, *Death by Government* (New Brunswick, NJ: Transaction Books, 1994). See also I. Horowitz, *Genocide: State Power and Mass Murder* (New Brunswick, NJ: Transaction Books, 1976); T. Weiss, *Humanitarian Intervention: Ideas in Action* (Cambridge: Polity Press, 2007); M. Finnemore, *The Purpose of Intervention: Changing Beliefs About the Use of Force* (Ithaca: Cornell University Press, 2003); and A. Bellamy, "Humanitarian Responsibilities and Interventionist Claims in International Society," *Review of International Studies* 29, no. 3 (2003): 321–340.

44. For a controversial treatment, see Diana Johnstone, *Fool's Crusade: Yugoslavia, NATO and Western Delusions* (New York: Monthly Review Press, 2002). More broadly, see N. Wheeler, *Saving Strangers: Humanitarian Intervention in International Society* (Oxford: Oxford University Press, 2000); E. Newman, "Humanitarian Intervention: Legality and Legitimacy," *The International Journal of Human Rights* 6, no. 4 (2002), 108–30; C. Lu, *Just and Unjust Interventions in World Politics: Public and Private* (New York: Palgrave Macmillan, 2006); and S. Hoffman, *The Ethics and Politics of Humanitarian Intervention* (Notre Dame, IN: University Press, 1996).

45. United Nations Children's Fund, *Child Protection Fact Sheet: Child Labour* (May 2006). See also United Nations Children's Fund, *The State of the World's Children 1997* (Oxford: Oxford University Press, 1997), 26.

46. For a detailed account, see C. Off, *Bitter Chocolate: Investigating the Dark Side of the World's Most Seductive Sweet* (Toronto: Random House, 2006). The chocolate industry, much like the diamond industry, has promised to try to eliminate child labour, but the problem persists.

47. "Child Labour: Consciences and Consequences," reprinted in *The Globe and Mail*, June 5, 1995, A17.

48. N. Burra, *Born to Work: Child Labour in India* (New Delhi: Oxford University Press, 1995), 211.

49. As well, four Canadians participated in a team of 11 women lawyers, sponsored by the Dutch government, who went to the former Yugoslavia to interview victims of sexual assault and collect evidence for the related military tribunals. See also B. Allen, *Rape Warfare: The Hidden Genocide in Bosnia-Herzegovina and Croatia* (Minneapolis: University of Minnesota Press, 1996).

50. P. Berenson, "The Forgotten Prisoners," *Observer Weekend Review*, May 28, 1961, 21.

51. See, for example, V. P. Nanda, J. Scarritt, and G. Shepherd, eds., *Global Human Rights: Public Policies, Comparative Measures, and NGO Strategies* (Boulder, CO: Westview, 1981).

52. See P. Shenon, "Mobile Phones Primed, Affluent Thais Join Fray," *The New York Times*, May 20, 1992, A10.

53. See S. Shreir, ed., *Women's Movements of the World: An International Directory and Reference Guide* (Essex, England: Longman, 1988). See also Women, Law, and Development International's website, http://www.wld.org

54. Bailey and Daws, 90.

55. The United Nations Fourth World Conference on Women Platform for Action, Beijing, China, September 1995, http://www.un.org/womenwatch/daw/beijing/platform/plat1.htm#statement (accessed March 21, 2009).

56. Both courts have websites: see http://www.un.org/icty and http://www.un.org/ictr; for the ICC, see http://www.icc-cpi.int. For slightly outdated but comprehensive treatments of the state of international criminal law, see S. Ratner and J. Abrams, *Accountability for Human Rights Atrocities in International Law: Beyond the Nuremburg Legacy*, 2nd ed. (Oxford: Oxford University Press, 2001); A. Cassese, *International Criminal Law* (Oxford: Oxford University Press, 2003), and Y. Beigbeder, *Judging War Criminals: The Politics of International Justice* (New York: St. Martin's Press, 1999).

57. See "The ICC Indictment of Bashir: A Turning Point for Sudan?," International Crisis Group website, http://www.crisisgroup.org/home/index.cfm?id=5959&l=1 (accessed March 17, 2009); and N. MacFarquhar and M. Simons, "Bashir Defies War Crime Arrest Order," *The New York Times*, March 5, 2009, http://www.nytimes.com/2009/03/06/world/africa/06sudan.html?_r=1 (accessed March 17, 2009).

58. For an analysis, see C. Moon, *Narrating Political Reconciliation: South Africa's Truth and Reconciliation Commission* (Lanham, MD: Lexington Books, 2007).

Suggested Websites

Amnesty International
   http://www.amnesty.org

The Carter Center
   http://www.cartercenter.org

Hawaii Nation
   http://www.hawaii-nation.org

Human Rights Watch
   http://www.hrw.org

Human Rights Web
   http://www.hrweb.org

International Centre for Human Rights and Democratic Development
   http://www.dd-rd.ca/site

International Criminal Court
   http://www.icc-cpi.int

Montreal Institute for Genocide and Human Rights Studies (MIGS)
   http://migs.concordia.ca

Research Guide to Human Rights
   http://www2.spfo.unibo.it/spolfo/HRLAW.htm

Women, Law, and Development International
   http://www.wld.org

Witness
   http://www.witness.org/index.php

Directions

In this final section, we look forward and examine some of the big issues likely to dominate the study of global politics in the 21st century. All these challenges are familiar ones, including environmental degradation and climate change; population growth, migration, dislocation, and health; and the impact of information technology on global politics. However, we contend that these issues will loom larger than most on the canvas of international relations in the near future. What will the future hold? Will climate change and natural resource depletion make human sustainability increasingly untenable? Will population growth and movement place insurmountable burdens on the world's food supply and other natural resources and cause increased social friction? Will epidemics of infectious disease sweep across the planet? Will information technology provide opportunities for human and social well-being, or exacerbate existing economic and social problems? Although the prognostications can at times be bleak, the fact that the human race has survived so many centuries of war, plague, and hardship offers some comfort! As we discussed in preceding chapters, societies and governments have proved capable of cooperating and addressing political problems. Of course, the prospects for conflict and failure exist as well. The pivotal question in the future of global politics will be whether humanity can respond collectively, and effectively, to the global challenges we face.

Global Ecopolitics: Crises and Change

The whole point of being a doomsayer is to agitate the world into proving you wrong or into doing something about it if you are right.

—Les Kaufman, 1993[1]

It is time to understand "the environment" for what it is: the national security issue of the twenty-first century.

—Morton Kaplan, 1994[2]

... human society has been built using the planet as an endless debit account.

—Clive Doucet, 2007[3]

INTRODUCTION: CAN WE SUSTAIN OURSELVES?

The earth has endured centuries of human population growth, agricultural development, resource extraction, landscape-ravaging wars, and industrial pollution. As we watch the polar ice caps melt with unprecedented speed, the Amazon jungle continue to burn, and the oceans empty of fish by industrial harvesting, we have to wonder whether we have entered this millennium under such a dark ecological shadow that there is no escape. Species extinction is caused primarily by the destruction of habitat. Viewed from a distance, one might conclude that human society has been committing collective suicide over the past century with an unrelenting assault on its own habitat, the biosphere of the planet. Though some believe in the almost unlimited store of the earth's resources and the innate ability of humankind to adapt, many see the current situation as reflective of human folly and greed. The symptoms of the environmental stresses placed on the earth range from the global, such as the depletion of the ozone layer and climate change, to the local, such as the erosion of soil that has been overworked in small African communities and the collapse of the cod fishery off Newfoundland. Two major reports, the Millennium Ecosystem Assessment (2005) and the Global Environmental Outlook (2007), have highlighted the broad range of environmental issues facing human society.[4] These issues include:

- *Biodiversity loss and habitat destruction.* Sixty percent of our ecosystems have been degraded, and resource exploitation has caused irreversible damage to the earth's natural processes. About 35 percent of the world's mangrove forests have been lost since 1980. The species extinction rate is now 100 to 1,000 times above the background (or natural) rate.

- *Land stress and degradation.* The conversion of land to agriculture and the widespread use of pesticides and fertilizers are altering the land surface of the earth more rapidly than at any time in human history, and climate change is altering both polar and arid regions.

- *Ocean stress.* Fisheries resources are being overexploited, with all major commercial fisheries now fully or over harvested. In the past 20 years, 20 percent of the world's coral reefs have been destroyed, and climate change is accelerating this process.

- *Freshwater stress.* The quality of aquatic ecosystems continues to decline, a function of increased demand for freshwater as well as the increased threat to safe supplies from pollution and invasive species.

This is far from a complete list of the environmental issues facing human society, and this chapter can only hope to present a partial description of the global politics involved with these problems. However, we should note that—as both liberal institutionalists and critical theorists stress—crises present opportunities for cooperation; environmental diplomacy, transnational activism, and corporate activity are often aligned with public concern to combat these problems. The question we face is whether, given intransigence, competitiveness, and the sheer reliance on a fossil fuel–based economy in countries such as Canada—where tar sands oil production has sent greenhouse gas (GHG) emissions soaring—we can collectively overcome

Industrialization and environmental destruction: till death do they part? A spectacular column of smoke and fire rises beside the derrick as the first oil and gas is flared at Imperial Oil's Leduc No. 1 on February 13, 1947, in Alberta, Canada. The initial daily production was about 1,000 barrels; by 2008, daily production of oil from the Albertan tar sands operations exceeded 1.1 million barrels. (CP Photo.)

these problems, or continue along the path of inequity described in Chapter 8. We discussed the relationship between various environmental issues and poverty in that chapter as well. Keep this theme in mind as you read on.

Ecological challenges have had a major impact on IR theory. While it was once possible to relegate environmental issues to a second tier of priorities in the discipline, today even realists acknowledge that the environment is pertinent to national security, geopolitical thinking, and international political economy. For example, due to climate change the Arctic will soon become navigable on a year-round basis, provoking political tension amongst circumpolar states over territorial and resource claims. The development of the numerous international environmental regimes discussed in this chapter pushed liberals to think harder about cooperative solutions to problems of the global commons, and the maintenance and effectiveness of related institutions. Many other theorists, especially ecofeminists, began their analytical assumptions with concern over the biosphere foremost in mind, but even those who did not, such as most neo-Marxists, have had to incorporate ecology into their thinking about the evolution of the world system. And constructivists of all stripes would agree that one of the most important social conventions in any community, be it a small village or the global one, is the set of dominant assumptions and attitudes we have constructed to rationalize our approach to nature.[5]

Global ecopolitics is where ecological concerns meet international political theory and action, and this must be viewed from both local and global perspectives today. We address the more specific issue of overpopulation and the movement of peoples, as well as the spread of infectious diseases, in Chapter 11. Here, we will focus on how environmental problems are a source of both convergence and divergence in global politics, moving from a discussion of the main actors and governance structures involved, to problems of the commons and climate change, the oceans, land degradation, and species impoverishment. We then discuss transboundary issues, before visiting the ongoing debate over the linkages between environmental degradation and violent conflict. What emerges is a complex political landscape full of challenges and opportunities that simply must be faced if human society is to survive its own onslaught on the earth.

GLOBAL ECOPOLITICS: THE ACTORS AND STRUCTURES

One of global ecopolitics' distinctions is the sheer level of complexity involved, which can be demonstrated with reference to the many actors/agents in the field. Obviously, the state remains a central player. Most of the environmental diplomacy we discuss below was conducted by state agents, often representing the executive branch of government but also departments and agencies. In Canada (see Profile 10.1), these include the departments of Environment, Foreign Affairs and International Trade, and Natural Resources, as well as the Public Health Agency. To confuse matters somewhat, we often see other levels of government (for example, the Premiers of Canadian provinces, or Governors of American states) taking decisive action on international agreements. Indeed, national government leaders from federal states often find themselves playing two-level games at international talks, dealing with other state officials in negotiations while faced with the daunting prospect of going home and actually implementing agreements that may challenge the jurisdictional authority of other levels of government in their own country. For example, in 1997 the Canadian government negotiated and signed the Kyoto Protocol on climate change, committing Canada to reducing its greenhouse gas emissions (GHGE) by 6 percent from its 1990 levels. This met with open disdain by several provincial governments, who under the Canadian constitution have authority over many of the areas that need to be changed in order to achieve such goals (indeed, Canada's performance on target meeting has been rather dismal, as we discuss later in this chapter). Representatives from the supranational European Union face a similar dilemma.

At the international level state cooperation has given rise to what some have called *global environmental governance*. In 1972 the UN sponsored the Conference on the Human Environment (UNCHE) in Stockholm, where the UN Environment Programme (UNEP) was created. Its secretariat, based in Nairobi, attempts to coordinate all the UN bodies involved in environmental areas. One of UNEP's most important tasks was to aid in the setup of the UN Conference on Environment and Development (UNCED), held in Rio de Janeiro, Brazil in June 1992, under the leadership of Canadian Maurice Strong. UNCED was the largest diplomatic summit ever, and it generated a great deal of press coverage around the world. It established the UN Commission on Sustainable Development (CSD), the "Rio Declaration," a framework for action labelled Agenda 21, as well as several landmark agreements discussed in this chapter. A "Rio + ten" summit was held in Johannesburg in 2002, and we can expect something similar in 2012. But none of these initiatives have even come close to solving the ecological crises we are watching unfold today; and most of them have yet to receive the necessary funding for full implementation.

PROFILE 10.1 Selected Canadian International Environmental Commitments

1909	Treaty Between the United States and Great Britain Relating to Boundary Waters
1916	Convention Between the United States and United Kingdom for the Protection of Migratory Birds in Canada and the United States
1946	International Convention for the Regulation of Whaling (Canada withdrew in 1982)
1963	Treaty Banning Nuclear Weapons Tests in the Atmosphere, in Outer Space, and Under Water
1971	Convention on Wetlands of International Importance
1972	Canada–U.S. Great Lakes Water Quality Agreement Stockholm Declaration on the Environment London Convention on the Prevention of Marine Pollution by Dumping of Wastes and Other Matter Convention Concerning the Protection of World Cultural and Natural Heritage
1973	Convention on International Trade in Endangered Species of Wild Fauna and Flora
1978	Protocol on the International Convention for the Prevention of Pollution from Ships
1979	Convention on Long-Range Transboundary Air Pollution (LRTAP)
1982	UN Convention on the Law of the Sea (ratified 2003)
1985	Vienna Convention on the Protection of the Ozone Layer Canada–U.S. Agreement Concerning Pacific Salmon
1986	Canada–U.S. Agreement on the Transboundary Movement of Hazardous Waste
1987	Montreal Protocol on Substances That Deplete the Ozone Layer
1989	Basel Convention on the Control of Transboundary Movements of Hazardous Wastes and Their Disposal
1991	Canada–U.S. Air Quality Agreement NOx Protocol to the 1979 LRTAP Convention/Declaration on the Protection of the Arctic Environment
1992	UN Framework Convention on Climate Change Convention on Biological Diversity Agenda 21 "Rio Declaration" Statement of Guiding Principles on Forests
1993	North American Agreement on Environmental Co-operation
1994	International Tropical Timber Agreement Protocol to LRTAP on Sulphur Emission Reductions
1995	UN Agreement on Straddling Fish Stocks and Highly Migratory Fish Stocks
1996	Comprehensive Nuclear Test Ban Treaty
1997	Kyoto Protocol on Climate Change (ratified 2002) Canada–Chile Agreement on Environmental Co-operation
2000	Biosafety Protocol for Biodiversity Convention (signed but not ratified)
2004	Stockholm Convention on Persistent Organic Pollutants
2004	Rotterdam Convention on the Prior Informed Consent Procedure for Certain Hazardous Chemicals and Pesticides

When it comes to the environmental impact of the role played by the major development players in the UN system, many analysts are highly critical. In particular, the International Bank for Reconstruction and Development (IBRD or World Bank) and the International Monetary Fund (IMF) have come under fire for promoting large-scale industrialization and structural adjustment programs that encourage the depletion of natural resources for export. We should note, however, that initiatives such as the Global Environmental Facility, administered by the World Bank, UNEP, and UN Development Programme (UNDP) are contributing to the advancement of less harmful environmental technologies. Meanwhile, suggestions to establish a World Environmental Organization, which would supersede the UNEP and be placed on an equal footing with the WTO or IMF, have not been realized.

Perhaps just as importantly, however, the private sector plays a large role in any form of environmental policymaking, be it a supportive or oppositional one. The extractive industries (those that take natural resources from the earth for redistribution at a profit elsewhere) are self-evidently major actors; this includes the energy industry (oil and natural gas, coal, and uranium) and mining, forestry, and fishing. As our previous discussions of MNCs have made clear, these are extraordinarily powerful industries, though they are not free from the vagaries of the marketplace or geopolitics. Increasingly, they are being forced to adapt to the environmental agenda, but they are often accused of engaging in public relations campaigns that "greenwash" their actual negative contribution or "ecological footprint." Private-sector actors are also playing a major role in funding research and implementing renewable energy sources (such as wind, geothermal, and solar power) and advancing recycling technology, to name but a few areas. Efforts to privatize water and other elements of the commons are more controversial. While there is often a wide divide between the proglobalization, market liberal approach to environmental challenges (which suggests that the solution lays in further economic growth and market-based decisions) and those who believe either a strong state (a "green leviathan") or a socialist one is necessary, most analysis today accepts the significance of private-sector participation in locating achievable solutions.[6]

Many observers would claim that NGOs have been the principal instigators all along, since they played a large role in forcing states to take environmental concerns seriously in the first place. NGOs have often assumed a watchdog role, reporting on the activities of MNCs and governments for the general public; they can also influence policy formulation at the national level. For example, Greenpeace members are included in the official American delegation to the International Whaling Commission, where the United States has consistently opposed lifting the global moratorium on commercial whaling now in place (controversially, it insists Alaskan Inuit and First Nations peoples should have the right to whale, but not Japanese or Norwegian coastal fishermen). NGOs also influence the operations of multilateral forums, contributing to World Conservation Union meetings and their outcomes. At times, they are criticized for insisting on a Western environmentalist ethic, even in local situations where people are more attuned to living on the land than most NGO members have ever been, and for focusing on a few key issues, including ones that can aid in fundraising appeals. No doubt, this is a cause of some friction, as the debate over the Canadian seal hunt suggests. Groups such as the International Fund for Animal Welfare (IFAW) strongly oppose the hunt, which in 2009 was allocated a quota of 280,000 seals. Sealers argue they are engaging in a vital aspect of their livelihood in economically depressed regions, and that urban environmentalists neither understand nor care about them. (Though taking baby whitecoat seals is banned, harp seals over two weeks old can be killed, which enrages those who campaign tirelessly against this hunt.) With some exemptions, seal products remain banned in the United States and were banned in the European Union in May of 2009, but new markets have emerged in Asia and Russia. The best way to influence the Canadian government on such issues, it is often suggested, is by campaigning abroad so as to embarrass it.

We should add a few words here as well about the vital role played by science in global ecopolitics, in issues ranging from the debates over the impact of genetically modified organisms (see Profile 10.2), to concerns with the implementation of nanotechnology, to discrepancies over the remaining populations of endangered species. However, nowhere is the relationship between science and politics more evident than on the issue of climate change. From a political

PROFILE 10.2 Genetically Modified Organisms (GMOs)

Genetic engineering refers to a variety of techniques aimed at deliberately changing the genetic makeup of a cell or organism. Scientists have been able to modify the genes of many crops, including tobacco, tomatoes, corn, soybeans, canola, squash, potatoes, and cotton. Some crops, such as the Flavr Savr tomato (which is designed to prolong freshness) have been available in North American markets for many years. The tomato (along with a wide range of other GM crops) is FDA-approved, but critics have argued that the long-term effects on health and cross-pollination and contamination scenarios are unknown. Many plants have been modified to increase their resistance to weed killers, insects, viruses, or fungi. Researchers can also genetically engineer many food animals, including fish, cows, goats, sheep, and pigs. This can be combined with cloning techniques to produce identical animals, which can be used for research into human health issues and even for organ transplants. Critics are concerned about the ethical implications of modifying

nature and possible accidents. The powerful biotechnology industry, much of it located in the United States and Japan, wants the EU and others to open their markets to GMOs, while the EU—reflecting public opinion there—is reluctant to do so. The industry and GMO advocates argue that such technology improves crop yields and holds the promise of eliminating or reducing world hunger and nutritional deficiencies. However, concerns remain about the tendency of large firms to force farmers to use their products (especially in the Southern Hemisphere) and the lack of labelling identifying GMO products in supermarkets. NGOs such as Greenpeace have made GMOs part of their platform. While the Biosafety Protocol of the Convention on Biological Diversity dealt with the issue to some degree, it remains a contested trade, public health, and ethical issue.

FOR A CANADIAN PERSPECTIVE, SEE S. MULLIGAN, "CANADA AND THE GENE REVOLUTION IN AGRICULTURAL BIOTECHNOLOGY," IN C. GORE AND P. STOETT, EDS., *ENVIRONMENTAL CHALLENGES AND OPPORTUNITIES: LOCAL-GLOBAL PERSPECTIVES ON CANADIAN ISSUES* (TORONTO: EMOND MONTGOMERY, 2009), 43–70.

perspective, the series of conclusions published by the Intergovernmental Panel on Climate Change (IPCC) could be a vital step toward achieving the type of collective action such global problems demand, confirming what many political analysts have suggested: science is playing an increasingly large role in galvanizing political action, even at the international level. Scientific consensus was certainly integral to the process of negotiating an international regime to curb the destruction of the ozone layer. However, there is a fine line between the necessary use of science to protect human and ecological health, and the adoption of a technocratic approach to governance that would put inordinate power in the hands of "scientific experts," many of them employed by large corporations with their own commercial interests.

Finally, there is the individual—as consumer, as voter, as taxpayer, as political animal. This is one subfield of global politics where we can without equivocation say that the actions of each of us make a difference, and that our own thinking about the environment and change will impact our broader local and ultimately global communities. As David Suzuki and Holly Dressel have argued, a growing environmental consciousness is emerging at the local and community level, exerting pressure for positive change on governments, corporations, and societies.[7] Though the ecological and political problems we discuss below seem insurmountable, in ecopolitics positive action often begins at the kitchen table.

PROBLEMS OF THE COMMONS

Global environmental problems are often characterized as problems of the commons, or more technically, international common pool resources. According to Wilfred Beckerman, this "refers to situations in which nobody can be excluded from the use of an asset—such as common grazing land, or fishing grounds, or the atmosphere [but] one person's use of the asset reduces the amount available to other potential users' unrestricted use of the asset and can easily lead to over-use, so that only if some voluntary or enforcement mechanism is introduced can the supply be matched to the demand."[8] One example of an international common pool resource is the moon, though most resources are rather more accessible! The essential problem is that everyone has an incentive to conserve the commons together but also has an individual incentive to exploit them: cooperation is necessary to balance these counterincentives. Or, as Stephen Krasner puts it, "the basic challenge for states is to overcome market failure, the situation in which individual rational self-interested policies produce outcomes that leave each state worse off than it might otherwise have been."[9] The added dimension of environmental degradation demands we move beyond asking simply how states can share resources to asking how they can simultaneously conserve or preserve them.

Solutions to typical problems of the commons are rather elusive. Many have argued that the privatization of land or other resources will increase the sense of environmental responsibility or stewardship by rights holders. This proposition is debatable enough in a domestic context, but is even less clear when it comes to the international arena, where privatization is akin to territorialization. For example, the 1982 UN Convention on the Law of the Sea (UNCLOS) designated new 200-nautical-mile (approximately 370-kilometre) exclusive economic zones (EEZs) in which coastal states would have not only resource rights but also inherent environmental responsibilities. The hope was that inside the 200-mile limit, increased coastal authority by individual states would lead to better management. Instead, "coastal countries such as Canada and the United States displaced overseas fleets from Europe and Japan with new programs and subsidies to build up their domestic fleets [then] scooped up cod and salmon on both coasts with alarming speed, and disastrous results."[10] Relying on the responsibility or stewardship of rights holders (be they individuals or states) may not be the best approach to protecting the environment. Furthermore, the entire principle of private property and legal ownership of resources is far from universal, and some peoples, such as indigenous groups, would reject this concept as an imperialistic imposition. Yet the creation of strong governance structures to overcome individual inclinations is viewed with equal concern by states and corporations.

Indeed, one of the central ecopolitical questions that concerns scholars is how dealing with the commons affects national sovereignty, the core principle of the UN Charter, and the key operative concern of the realist perspective. Does the rise of transboundary pollution problems justify infringements on the sovereignty of states, as do cases of extreme international security concerns and genocide? Does the need to avoid the tragedies of the commons demand a pooling of sovereignty in certain issue-areas? Has the creation of institutions designed to mitigate environmental damage threatened the long-term future of the nation-state as predicted by the older functionalist school (see Chapter 5)? It is quite clear, in the legal sense, that the principle of sovereignty remains sacrosanct. In 1962, the UN General Assembly adopted a resolution that referred to the "inalienable right" of all states to freely "dispose of their natural wealth and resources."[11] Malaysia made particular reference to this precept during the forestry negotiations leading up to UNCED in 1992. This is a common North–South sticking point as Southern state elites claim that any global environmental agenda infringes on their national sovereignty. Principle 2 of the Rio Declaration asserts that "states have the sovereign right to exploit their own resources pursuant to their own environmental and developmental policies."

There is also the question of cost distribution, or who should pay for international efforts to save the commons. On issues such as ozone-layer depletion and global warming, there is a large divide between the developed and the developing world on burden sharing. The collective decision to protect the ozone layer (which shields us from the sun's ultraviolet radiation) from volatile chemicals known as **chlorofluorocarbons (CFCs)** used in refrigeration, industrial production, and aerosol cans set an important precedent. CFCs, along with carbon and other so-called greenhouse gases, prevent infrared radiation from escaping the earth's atmosphere. The result is not only increased global warming potential but also increased rates of skin cancer and eye problems and adverse agricultural effects. But the vast majority of states affected by this potential crisis do not even use CFCs in their industries. The Montreal Protocol to the 1985 Vienna Convention on the Protection of the Ozone Layer established a cost-sharing agreement to help less-industrialized states develop alternatives to CFC production; by mid-2007, the Fund had supported the transfer of technology and capacity building through about 5,500 projects and activities in 144 low-income countries. Environmental diplomat R. E. Benedick concludes, "As a consequence of the ozone issue, the richer nations for the first time acknowledged a responsibility to help developing countries to implement needed environmental policies without sacrificing aspirations for improved standards of living."[12] However, one might argue that the Montreal Protocol, a fairly demanding document reached in a relatively short time, was successful because remarkable scientific consensus existed regarding the causes of ozone depletion, as did genuine international fear of the consequences. This type of cohesion of knowledge and expectation has yet to be reached in many other areas related to the environment.

Another example of relative success in managing the commons is Antarctica, which is in essence the world's largest wildlife sanctuary, home to some 100 million birds, including the famous penguin, six species of seals, fifteen species of whales, and ice sheets that offer unique windows on geophysical history. The Antarctic Treaty, in many ways a landmark, was signed in 1959.[13] Though several nations have laid (and maintain) claim to specific parts of Antarctica, they all agreed to adhere to a common management scheme. Both of the Cold War superpowers signed, and Antarctica became the world's first nuclear-free zone. Antarctica has maintained its nonmilitarized status since. The treaty provides onsite verification measures on research conducted in the region, and it opened the door for nonclaimant nations to establish research facilities on the continent. Canada participates in the Antarctic Treaty System (ATS) as a nonconsultative party (i.e., it has no voting rights in ATS meetings but can attend as an observer). The ATS involves other management regimes, such as the Convention on the Conservation of Antarctic Marine Living Resources (CCAMLR), well known for its ecosystem approach to resource management. But this example of success must be tempered by several facts. Many would rather see a global, UN-based approach to managing this common area. Realists point out the lack of access to resources or military value of Antarctica, suggesting it is an anomaly. And the Antarctic ice sheet, which contains close to 90 percent of the world's ice, is beginning to collapse due to climate change. It is to that much more stubborn and complex issue that we turn next.

CLIMATE CHANGE

The logic of the greenhouse effect is well understood: human activity is causing an increasing buildup of greenhouse gases (GHGs) in the earth's atmosphere, preventing more and more heat absorbed from the sun from escaping back into space. Carbon dioxide accounts for about half of the greenhouse effect; methane, nitrous oxide, ozone, and chlorofluorocarbons make up the rest. As global temperatures continue to increase and more of these gases are released into the atmosphere by modern society, the greenhouse effect has evolved from contentious theory to established reality. This has led to increased calls from the scientific community

Threatened by climate change. A polar bear mother and her cubs walk along the shore of Hudson Bay near Churchill, Manitoba. In 2007 the United States government decided to place the polar bear on the threatened species list due to the impact of climate change on the arctic environment. (CP Archive/Jonathan Hayward.)

and environmental groups (and increasingly governments as well) for mitigation strategies to reduce GHG emissions. Meanwhile, extreme weather events, such as hurricanes (including Hurricane Katrina, which devastated New Orleans in 2005), and the movement of environmental refugees from Pacific islands such as Vanuatu due to rising sea levels, force us to think about the potential damage climate change could cause to all life forms, and what adaptation measures can be taken to adjust to the climate change that is already occurring.

Our heavy reliance on the burning of fossil fuels (coal, oil, and natural gas) releases billions of tonnes of GHGs into the atmosphere every year, and deforestation, livestock, cement production, and other activities add millions more. Unusual warming has also shifted the distribution and seasonal appearance of vector-borne diseases such as malaria, dengue fever, and schistosomiasis; and invasive species, such as the zebra mussel and pine beetle in Canada, are encouraged by warmer temperatures to spread their assault on local ecosystems. Circumpolar states such as Canada and Russia will face special challenges and opportunities as the Arctic passages become ice-free on a year-round basis, encouraging shipping and oil drilling. In the face of growing climate change effects, awareness and calls for action have increased. The 2007 Human Development Report focused on the pressing issue of how low-income states can adapt to climate change. In 2007 Al Gore and the IPCC won the Nobel Peace Prize for their work on publicizing and better understanding the issue (and Gore's documentary film, *An Inconvenient Truth*, won an Oscar). An estimated two billion people watched some part of the Live Earth concert televised worldwide on July 7, 2007. Increasingly, large corporations (including Alcoa, Caterpillar, Duke Energy, Du Pont and General Electric) are calling for laws mandating greenhouse cuts. "Going green" has become fashionable, and national and local governments are passing emissions reductions regulations and incentives. This concern and action is both a validation of earlier environmentalists' concerns and a central challenge to conventional approaches to economic activity.

In 1992, a Framework Convention on Climate Change (UNFCCC) was signed at the UNCED in Rio, committing the signatory states to reductions in their emissions of greenhouse gases, most notably carbon dioxide; but it was not until a conference of the Rio signatories in Kyoto, Japan, took place in December 1997 that states committed themselves to more strict emissions controls. The exact formula was different for each state: Canada, for example, pledged to reduce emissions to 94 percent of the 1990 level by 2010, though it did not ratify the Kyoto Protocol until 2002. However, Canada has in fact increased its emissions by as much as 30 percent since 1990, and the implementation of the Protocol was complicated by the objections of several provincial governments and a change in federal government. The Kyoto Protocol calls for more than cuts to GHG emissions: it permits industrialized states to gain credit for investing, either as donors or as partners, in conservation measures through the Clean Development Mechanism (CDM) and Joint Implementation; it calls for the establishment of an international carbon trading system, which would price carbon then allow states that exceed their targeted cuts to sell quotas to overproducing states; and it calls for an Adaptation Fund, to help assist those hardest hit by climate change who can least afford to adapt or pay. Unfortunately, none of these measures has been implemented to the extent necessary to meet the challenges of climate change.

The Kyoto Protocol came into force on February 16, 2005, following the long-awaited ratification by Russia. As of May 2008, 181 countries have ratified it, although one of the key greenhouse gas producers, the United States, remains a non-signatory, and several large emitter states such as China and India are presently exempt from targets (see Profile 10.3). However, in the past few years international pressure for more immediate and meaningful cuts in greenhouse gases has increased. This pressure flows from three factors: the recognition that very few if any states will successfully meet their Kyoto greenhouse gas reduction goals by the target dates of 2008–2012; growing evidence that global warming is having a more

---

PROFILE 10.3 | **Carbon Dioxide and National Responsibility**

The growth rate of carbon emissions worldwide tripled in the first four years of this decade as compared with the rate in the 1990s, surpassing even the most significant increases suggested in recent United Nation's climate reports. China has surpassed the United States as the largest emitter, though we should bear in mind that from a per capita perspective it is far behind most states.

CARBON DIOXIDE EMISSION RATES FOR 2006

	COUNTRY	TOTAL EMISSIONS (MILLIONS OF TONNES)	PER CAPITA EMISSIONS (TONNES)
1.	China	6017.69	4.58
2.	United States	5902.75	19.78
3.	Russia	1704.36	12.00
4.	India	1293.17	1.16
5.	Japan	1246.76	9.78
6.	Germany	857.60	10.40
7.	**Canada**	**614.33**	**18.81**
8.	United Kingdom	585.71	9.66
9.	South Korea	514.53	10.53
10.	Iran	471.48	7.25
11.	Italy	468.19	8.05
12.	South Africa	443.58	10.04
13.	Mexico	435.60	4.05
14.	Saudi Arabia	424.08	15.70
15.	France	417.75	6.60
16.	Australia	417.06	20.58
17.	Brazil	377.24	2.01
18.	Spain	372.61	9.22
19.	Ukraine	328.72	7.05
20.	Poland	303.42	7.87

SOURCE: UNION OF CONCERNED SCIENTISTS, U.S. DEPARTMENT OF ENERGY, HTTP://WWW.UCSUSA.ORG/GLOBAL_WARMING/SCIENCE_AND_IMPACTS/SCIENCE/EACH-COUNTRYS-SHARE-OF-CO2.HTML (ACCESSED JUNE 2009).

significant and more immediate impact on the environment than previously estimated; and an increasing consensus that the provisions of the Kyoto Protocol are insufficient to prevent accelerating global climate change.

In 2007 the IPCC released its Fourth Synthesis Report, which contained the direst warnings yet of the impact of human activity on the climate. The report concluded that "[w]arming of the climate system is unequivocal, as is now evident from observations of increases in global average air and ocean temperatures, widespread melting of snow and ice and rising average global sea level."[14] The report attributes the increased concentrations of the four principal GHGs (carbon dioxide, methane, nitrous oxide, and halocarbons) to human activity. Global GHG emissions increased by 70 percent between 1970 and 2004, or from 28.7 gigatonnes in 1970 to 49 gigatonnes in 2004. Energy supply accounted for 25.9 percent of global greenhouse gas emissions, with industry (19.4 percent), forestry (17.4 percent), agriculture (13.5 percent) and transport (13.1 percent) making up the other major sources of emissions. While some industries (such as the automobile industry) are moving rapidly toward technological adjustments to reduce carbon footprints, others (such as aviation and cement) are having a much harder time.

A wide number of issues related to global warming are now at the forefront of the global politics agenda. For example, the impact of the Asian Brown Cloud (see Profile 10.4) may be even more profound than previously thought. Scientists are now claiming that in combination with greenhouse gas emissions, the haze is accountable for the rapid retreat of the Himalayan glaciers. This loss of ice will have severe consequences for the hundreds of millions of people in Asia who live near the mountain range, since it will induce flooding in the short term and will result in drought in the long term.[15] As mentioned above, scientists have also warned that the ice sheets in Antarctica and Greenland, and other Arctic ice sheets at the north pole, are

---

PROFILE 10.4 The Asian Brown Cloud

In early 1999 scientists were startled to discover a brown haze covering most of the South and Southeast Asian regions, as well as large swaths of the Indian Ocean—a haze covering approximately 10 million square kilometres. This was at first attributed to forest fires (most deliberately set to clear brush for agriculture), but it is now believed to be the consequence of a mixture of pollutants, including fossil fuel combustion. According to the United Nations Environment Programme (UNEP), "Simulations with global climate models indicate that the haze could have major impacts on the monsoon circulation, regional rainfall patterns and vertical temperature profile of the atmosphere." Combined with greenhouse gases the cloud is thought to account for the retreat of the Himalayan glaciers.

One of the most interesting things about the haze, which since 2004 has been identified as drifting into the Middle East as well, is that it is probably misnamed. One atmospheric scientist at the Scripps Institution of Oceanography at the University of California, Veerabhadran Ramanathan, said the major contributors to this worldwide circle of pollution were Los Angeles, Delhi, Bombay, Beijing, and Cairo: "Pollution in the eastern United States can go in four or five days to Europe and in a week it goes from Europe to South Asia. This is fast transport which converts a local problem into a regional and global problem," the Indian scientist said. Ramanathan said he suspected the effect of the shroud of pollution across the globe would be to dry the planet. The brown cloud demonstrates both the problems of scientific inquiry into such large-scale problems and the urgent need to protect the commons.

SOURCES: UNEP/EARTHSCAN, *GLOBAL ENVIRONMENT OUTLOOK 3: PAST, PRESENT AND FUTURE PERSPECTIVES* (LONDON: EARTHSCAN, 2002), 222; A. HAMMOND, "SCIENTIST SAYS 'ASIAN BROWN CLOUD' THREATENS GULF," *ENVIRONMENTAL NEWS NETWORK*, FEBRUARY 25, 2004, HTTP://WWW.ENN.COM/NEWS/2004-02-25/S_13447.ASP (ACCESSED MAY 26, 2004).

beginning to collapse. Combined with warmer, expanding water, this might lead to increases in sea levels sufficient to force hundreds of millions of evacuations from coastal areas world-wide during hurricanes such as Ivan in 2008.

Indeed, as sea levels increase the very existence of some states will be threatened. Some low-lying countries (such as the Netherlands) have the resources to adapt and protect their populations, while others (such as Bangladesh) do not. The coastal dwellers of one south Pacific island, Vanuatu, have had to be moved inland, giving them the title of the world's first climate change refugees. The melting of Arctic ice intensifies the global warming process, since ice normally reflects ultraviolet rays back into space: the less ice there is to reflect the sun's radiation, the more ultraviolet is absorbed and trapped in the atmosphere. Furthermore, the melting of permafrost will release unknown quantities of methane, a more intense greenhouse gas than carbon dioxide. The severity of extreme weather events, such as Hurricane Katrina, may be linked to global warming, although the disproportionate suffering of the poor in that city may be more firmly linked to racial inequality. In another example of linkage, the over-fishing crisis will only be magnified as sea warming causes acidification and the destruction of coral reefs, which in turn threatens to cause accelerated marine mammal extinction. Threats to global food security are also linked to climate change: food prices are rising because of a number of factors, including the price of oil (a reflection of continued turmoil in Iraq and rising demand in China, India, and elsewhere), speculation on futures markets for food, the use of arable land for biofuel production, and the land degradation related to agricultural overproduction and climate change. These environmental and social factors resulted in several large-scale humanitarian emergencies in 2008, requiring a response from many agencies such as the World Food Program.

There is widespread recognition that international cooperation will be required to meet the challenges of climate change in the area of mitigation (reducing emissions) and adaptation (adjusting to a warmer world), including the recent "Stern Report" written by a British economist who makes dire warnings about the potential economic costs of not taking strong action.[16] In the wake of Kyoto, the UNFCCC process continues, though without much substantive success. At the Vienna meeting of the UNFCCC in 2007 the parties agreed to "consider" emissions cuts of 25 to 40 percent below 1990 levels to try to hold global temperature increases below two degrees. Similarly, no binding agreement on GHG emissions cuts could be reached at the Bali climate change conference later that year. In September 2007 the United States began its own "climate summit" process, with 16 countries in attendance. This process was largely regarded as an empty gesture by the U.S. government, as none of the provisions agreed to were considered binding. The European Union, which has emerged as a leader on this front, has announced plans to pursue a 20 percent reduction below 1990 greenhouse gas emissions levels by 2020. Emissions trading plans are entering into effect in several areas, and may be the centrepiece of the Obama administration's climate change policy. However, we have yet to achieve an international carbon trading system, while carbon taxes are being applied at other levels of government (for example, the provincial governments of British Columbia and Quebec). While some states participate in the CDM, which grants carbon credits for contributions to energy conservation measures in less-industrialized states, others are reluctant to commit to what they see as a redistribution of wealth on an international scale. Similarly, the carbon trading system strikes some as a mechanism to permit polluting as usual, while rewarding states that have defunct economies for reasons other than pollution abatement.

Why has it proven so difficult to secure a binding international treaty on climate change, and even harder to achieve compliance? First, governments are concerned that rigorous emissions regulations or taxes will damage economic growth and competitiveness. This has been

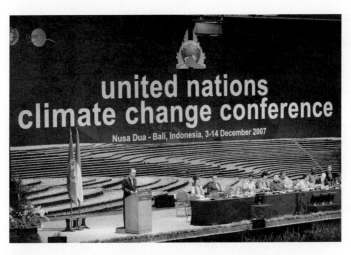

Hoping for results. UN Secretary General Ban Ki-moon addresses the delegates to the UN Climate Change Conference on December 17, 2007 in Nusa Dua, Bali, Indonesia. (AP Photo/Ed Wray/CP Archive.)

a major reason why the U.S. government has been reluctant to agree to any climate change mitigation process that does not involve China and India. Second, it is difficult to secure a climate change treaty among many states with divergent interests. Any negotiated agreement will be the product of the lowest common denominator among the participants, and is therefore likely to be watered down to meet a minimally acceptable standard. The UNFCCC negotiations at Bali failed to achieve agreement on binding cuts because some states (especially the U.S.) refused to agree to such a policy. Climate change is often seen through the lenses of the broader north–south debate about responsibility and the need to ensure that human rights and development are not compromised in any mitigation efforts. Third, there is the familiar problem of compliance and enforcement. Governments may sign treaties binding them to emissions cuts (such as Kyoto) but then fail to live up to their commitments with little or no international repercussions. Finally, domestic politics can drive government negotiation positions. For example, in Canada the Conservative minority government has a strong constituency base in Alberta, and its obvious reluctance to seriously pursue Canada's Kyoto commitments is often attributed to this domestic political reality. Furthermore, the priorities of governments at home (economic growth, employment) and political vulnerability (electoral politics, coalition governments) also influence their positions in climate change negotiations. For these reasons, securing an international agreement on climate change in the future will be a daunting challenge. The scientific evidence of accelerating climate change continues to accumulate, and with it the urgency of progress on mitigation and adaptation measures at the UNFCCC Copenhagen Summit in December 2009.

Given the media exposure and diplomatic activity surrounding this issue-area, it is tempting to focus entirely on climate change as the main ecopolitical debate of our time. But we should remember that many other issue-areas, all of which are linked in one way or another to climate change, demand similar attention. Organizations of states and nonstate actors have developed around these issues, many of them located in Montreal (see Profile 10.5). We turn now to brief discussions of several of these issues, beginning with what might well be the most dramatic: the fate of the oceans.

THE OCEANS IN CRISIS

June 8, 2009 was the first UN-declared World Oceans Day, and the resulting publicity about the plight of the oceans could not have come soon enough. In retrospect, it may be understandable that the oceans were viewed as an inexhaustible commons. After all, they cover over two-thirds of the earth's surface, and have been supplying humanity with food and other resources for all of history. Yet the oceans have endured a relentless assault in recent centuries, one that threatens our own existence. As Sylvia Earle wrote in 1995, the "living ocean drives planetary chemistry, governs climate and weather, and otherwise provides the cornerstone of the life-support system for all creatures on our planet, from deep-sea starfish to desert

PROFILE 10.5   The Montreal Connection

Montreal is world-renowned for its old-world charm, cosmopolitanism, and summer jazz festival. But given its location next to the once-heavily-polluted St. Lawrence River, few would expect Montreal to also become a magnet for international organizations dealing with environmental problems; yet, with the support of the federal government (no doubt influenced by continued fears over separatism), Montreal has attracted a great deal of expertise and officialdom to the area. In fact, one can take a cursory glance at the extent of multilateral action on environmental issues with a survey of the bodies that have located there. The following organizations are already located in Montreal:

- The Secretariat of the Multilateral Fund of the Montreal Ozone Protocol

- The North American Commission for Environmental Cooperation (a North American Free Trade Agreement institution)

- The Secretariat of the United Nations Convention on Biological Diversity

- The Montreal office of the World Conservation Union

- The Network of Expertise for the Global Environment

- The International Secretariat for Water

Montreal lost a bid for the Desertification Secretariat, which was located in Bonn, Germany.

sagebrush.… Our future and the state of the oceans are one."[17] But just as we are all connected to the oceans, their fate is inextricably connected to global politics.

Historically, the seas have been viewed as a commons, and in fact "freedom of the seas" has long been an accepted legal term. This freedom involved not just the right to travel, but to harvest resources and pollute. Restrictions on all of these rights have been slowly developing with the establishment of related international regimes. The UNCLOS took nine years to negotiate (1973–82), and 159 states and other entities initially signed the Convention. In November 1993, Guyana became the 60th state to deposit its instrument of ratification with the UN, and the Law of the Sea officially became effective in November 1994. It established an International Seabed Authority that would facilitate the sharing of deep-sea resources, particularly any derived from deep-sea mining, among all states. This notion of sharing proceeds from resource extraction was opposed in the United States (and some other Western states), which argued that such revenue sharing would undermine the profitability of deep-sea mining. As a result, many Western states have signed the Law of the Sea but have not ratified it. Canada did not ratify the Law of the Sea until November 2003; there were 158 ratifications as of May 2009. Nonetheless it has become largely accepted as the most authoritative international legal instrument on ocean issues, and firmly establishes the norm that coastal states have EEZs extending from their shorelines.

Yet UNCLOS has had very limited impact on curtailing what has become known as the global oceans crisis. There are many interlinked threats facing the oceans today, and we have space to address only a few of them here.[18] Overfishing is perhaps the most visible, as ever-greater numbers of people compete to catch dwindling supplies of edible fish stocks. There are limits to sustainable yield harvests, and we have surpassed them in most popular fish stocks. Previously, the world witnessed the near-extinction of many species of whales due to an underregulated regime, advanced technology that gave whalers the decided edge, and the urge to capitalize on investments before stocks ran out completely. This galvanized the NGO and scientific community to protest whaling practices, and in 1982 the International Whaling Commission adopted a zero-quota commercial catch limit on all species of whales, a prohibition still in place today (limited aboriginal and so-called scientific whaling still takes place, and whale meat is still sold in some Asian markets). This was and remains a highly controversial story in ecopolitical history, pitting different conceptions of human-nature relations and animal rights against each other and raising sharp diplomatic conflicts between former whaling states such as the U.S. and Australia against contemporary whalers such as Japan and Norway.[19] The important point, however, is that many of the great whale populations have made recoveries, even if they now face different, climate-oriented threats, and the pressure to resume commercial whaling remains.

There has been no such success with fish, which have less charismatic appeal, and are of course widely eaten across the earth. By 2000, it had become apparent that global fish catches had been declining for over a decade, and the Food and Agriculture Organization (FAO) declared that three-quarters of major species stocks were either fully exploited or nearing collapse. In 2007, the FAO estimated that over 80 percent of global fish stocks were fully exploited or overexploited, and required "effective and precautionary management."[20] The sheer size of discarded bycatch (i.e., the non-targeted fish species, including marine mammals, that are killed in the process and then simply dumped back into the sea) is also a tremendous problem, as is bottom trawling and the use of lengthy driftnets that collect everything in their miles-long path (these are banned in most cases but are still used; some become detached from fishing vessels and roam the sea as indiscriminate "ghostnets"). Most ocean fishing is governed by sovereign states with exclusive rights to coastal waters, but many states sell the right to fish in their marine territory; and illegal fishing is very common in areas where coastal states have limited enforcement capacities.

While there are numerous regional agreements to regulate certain fisheries in specific areas (see Profile 10.6), and a series of UNCLOS-related agreements on overfishing and the use of driftnets as well as a soft-law FAO Code of Conduct for Responsible Fisheries, there is no effective enforcement of such provisions.[21] An FAO International Plan of Action to Deter, Prevent and Eliminate Illegal, Unreported, and Unregulated Fishing has had some success in Asia and elsewhere, but it is of course impossible to ascertain its impact.[22] While there was once optimism that aquaculture—for example, the farming of fish such as Atlantic salmon in salt water, and the huge shrimp industry in southeast Asia—would provide some relief, environmentalists are concerned with the ecological impact of introducing new fish species to ecosystems and the salinization of marshlands and other vulnerable ecosystems.[23] Despite the immensity of challenges, we would be extremely hard pressed to support over seven billion people without the protein supplied by fish stocks. The collapse of the world's fisheries present an unprecedented challenge to global food security, and the ethical and legal obligations that follow from this premise make it clear than we must act quickly and responsibly.[24]

The second most visible threat is that of pollution, and it would take a text almost the length of the one you are reading just to list the many forms of ocean pollution that exist. Spectacular accidents, such as the Exxon Valdez oil spill off of Alaska in 1989, are dramatic and highly publicized events. Yet far more pernicious is the daily legal and illegal dumping of discharged oil and other wastes at sea by ships. Though the International Maritime Organization (IMO) has negotiated a Convention on the Prevention of Pollution from Ships (MARPOL), its implementation remains a serious problem. Pollution from persistent organic pollutants (POPs), which are transported through the atmosphere, also affects ocean health, and these pollutants are extremely difficult to source. Again, a convention is in place to limit the production and use of certain POPs, but this has had limited effect, especially in the more fragile Arctic and Antarctic Ocean ecosystems. Coastal pollution remains a grave threat to the health of fish and marine mammals as well. Despite decades of progress in human sanitation systems, raw sewage and agricultural runoff are still primary sources of pollution, and sewage-borne invasive pathogens such as cholera are serious threats to human security

PROFILE 10.6 — Canada Gets Aggressive: Defending Migratory Fish Stocks

Managing international fisheries has often proven to be one of the more complex diplomatic tasks. The so-called cod wars between Iceland and Britain in the 1960s and 1970s provide a historical example of potential conflict over dwindling resources, but Canadians have a more recent example on which to reflect. The case involved the Spanish fishing fleet and an uncharacteristically assertive Canadian government. The Spanish Basques were fishing off the coast of Newfoundland as early as 1530, and by the 1580s, French Basque ships were returning from the area loaded with cod and, eventually, whale oil. In 1994, the multilateral Northwest Atlantic Fisheries Organization (NAFO) had set limits on the total allowable catch of Greenland halibut (or turbot), allocating national quotas for this resource. The European Union, pressured by Spain and Portugal, rejected the quotas as unfair.

Canada imposed a unilateral moratorium, concerned with the depleting turbot stocks, and eventually seized the Spanish fishing vessel *Estai*, claiming that the trawler was not only violating the quota rules but also using illegal fish nets in the process. Since the vessel was on the high seas, Canada was, in effect, breaking international law. Canada's seizure of the Spanish trawler led to international tension, because Canada's international legal jurisdiction stops after the 200-nautical-mile (1 nautical mile = 1,852 metres) EEZ provision of UNCLOS. Thus, the fishery dilemma quickly became a foreign policy problem. Eventually, Canada passed legislation that would make it legal (in the domestic context, if not in the international) to physically stop ships from fishing near the exclusive economic zone. A subsequent international agreement on straddling stocks was hammered out in New York, giving coastal states the right to inspect ships fishing near such areas. Is the lesson here that Canada had to break international law to make it? Or that realists are right, that states will only take serious international environmental action if their national interest is directly at stake?

FOR A SUCCINCT ANALYSIS OF THE CANADA–SPAIN "FISH WAR," SEE ANDREW COOPER, *CANADIAN FOREIGN POLICY: OLD HABITS, NEW DIRECTIONS* (SCARBOROUGH, ON: PRENTICE HALL ALLYN AND BACON, 1997), 142–72.

in many southern regions. The dumping of excessive nutrients through nitrogen fixation (fertilizers entering the oceans through sewage and agricultural runoff) and industrial and vehicle emissions is exacerbated by the destruction of "natural interceptors" such as coastal wetlands, coral reefs and mangrove forests; these fall victim to coastal development, but as a result leave shorelines more vulnerable to extreme storm surges. This in turn adds to the natural process of eutrophication (excessive plant growth and decay) and toxic blooms, which kill fish and drive away birds and mammals. Further, the human alteration of river systems and estuaries has increased the level of sedimentation entering the oceans, depriving ocean species of needed sunlight. Invasive alien species are dumped from the ballast water of cargo ships. And nonbiodegradable litter is scattered throughout the seas, killing countless marine mammals and birds.

All of this occurs in the context of global warming, and the oceans play a key role in maintaining atmospheric balance; the concerns is that polar warming and ice cap melting, which has been accelerating in recent years, will slow down the global atmosphere/ocean "heat engine," which could alter the flow of major ocean currents and affect atmospheric temperatures (perhaps even causing an ice age). While this sounds more like the stuff of science fiction (and has been the source of inspiration for several such films), it is a serious long-term concern, along with the sea-level rises and extreme weather events discussed in the preceding section. But the impact of climate change is not limited to the weather. For example, the exotic coastal reefs are particularly vulnerable ecosystems, and not only is the acidification

Seized ship: a victory for conservation, or piracy? Onlookers watch the Spanish trawler *Estai* arrive at St. John's on March 12, 1995. A Canadian fisheries patrol vessel fired the first salvo in what became the Great Turbot War between Canada and the European Union. (CP Picture Archive/Fred Chartrand.)

of the oceans bleaching them to death, but higher concentrations of carbon dioxide in the oceans impairs the growth of their limestone skeletons. Compounded with the effects of sedimentation, irresponsible tourism, and overfishing, the reefs are in danger of extinction, despite the vital role they play in regulating the ocean ecosystems in the Indian ocean, Southeast Asia and the far-western Pacific.[25] There is no international agreement designed specifically to protect the coral reefs, though such protection is arguably enshrined in the UNCLOS and other conventions. Coral reefs generally fall within the EEZs of states, so they are not in the strict sense considered part of the global commons; yet their key natural role prompts many to argue they should be treated as such. Climate change is also affecting the eating, reproductive, and migratory patterns of marine mammals, birds, fish stocks, and plankton, and it facilitates the spread of dangerous invasive species that are transported across oceans by commercial shipping lines.

The oceans crisis is one of the most urgent issues we face: here we have a true problem of the commons, and the complex patchwork of governance efforts has thus far failed to reduce the severity of the problem. One of the biggest challenges scientists, industry, and politicians alike face in the near future is responding to the crisis facing the oceans.

DEFORESTATION AND LAND DEGRADATION

Another serious global problem is the impact of human activity on the land surface, in particular the removal of the world's forests and the decreasing availability of arable land. Deforestation has become an increasingly popular and public issue in the past three decades, not least because of its link to climate change. For example, what has become known as REDD—Reducing Emissions Caused by Deforestation and Degradation—figured prominently at the Copenhagen conference in 2009. While tropical rain forest depletion has gathered the most attention, it is important to remember that wetlands, boreal forests, and temperate rain forest depletion are all serious problems. According to the Food and Agriculture Organization of the United Nations between 1990 and 2005 over 125 million hectares of forest cover was lost worldwide, about 3 percent of the world total in 1990.[26]

International efforts to curb deforestation have, predictably enough, generated sustained political friction. Low-income countries see these efforts as inimical to their own economic development: industrialized countries, having exploited much of their own forests, are now trying to prevent them from exploiting their own. However, tropical rain forest depletion is especially severe; every year, an area the size of Belgium is cleared of rain forest, often by slash-and-burn methods. In Central and South America, 64 million hectares of forest cover (about 7 percent of total forest cover in the two regions) was destroyed between 1990 and 2005.[27] In Brazil's Amazon Basin, more than 11 percent of the jungle has been destroyed since 1975 (an area the size of Morocco). Deforestation has continued at even higher rates: in June 2003, the deforestation rate in Brazil's Amazon increased by 40 percent. According

Deforestation in Indonesia. A worker cuts down a tree in Riau Province in central Sumatra, Indonesia, 2008. The World Wildlife Fund estimated that 10.5 million acres (about 4.25 million hectares) of tropical forest and peat swamp had been destroyed in Riau Province alone over the past 25 years. (AP Photo/Achmad Ibrahim/CP Archive.)

to Environmental News Network, figures released by the Brazilian environment ministry showed "deforestation in the Amazon jumped to 9840 square miles last year—the highest since 1995—from 7010 square miles in 2001."[28] Tropical rain forest is also being depleted in Indonesia, Colombia, Thailand, and the Philippines. In Haiti, more than 90 percent of the country's rain forest has disappeared. Rain forest depletion occurs for many reasons, including a local desire for pastureland, export crops, fuel, and lucrative foreign markets for hardwood.

Another tragedy of rain forest depletion is the impossibility of full regeneration. Old-growth timber areas (in both tropical and temperate zones) possess ecosystems and biodiversity developed over thousands of years. Although they cover less than 10 percent of the earth's surface, it is estimated that tropical forest ecosystems may contain up to 90 percent of all species. Replanted or second-growth regions never achieve this level of biodiversity.[29] In addition, because in many cases forests are cleared for pastureland or cropland, the delicate soil is often exhausted after a few years. As a result, the forest cannot regenerate because the land cannot support it. The subsequent loss of trees reduces the capacity of the earth to produce oxygen and absorb carbon dioxide, which in turn contributes to climate change (as does the carbon released when felled trees are burnt or converted to charcoal). Rainfall patterns are affected, and soil erosion increases because of a lack of root structures, contributing to deadly floods in states such as Bangladesh.

In addition to loss of forest cover, land and soil degradation is a serious environmental problem (see Profile 10.7). Land and soil degradation comes in many forms, including soil erosion, nutrient depletion, water scarcity, salinity, and disruption of biological processes. At the Johannesburg Earth Summit in 2002, soil degradation was estimated to affect some two billion hectares worldwide, and about two-thirds of the world's agricultural land. Much of this

---

PROFILE 10.7 **The Causes of Land Degradation**

Note: Causes are listed in order of magnitude of impact, according to estimates by the Food and Agriculture Organization (FAO) report *Our Land Our Future* (Rome: FAO, 1996).

1. *Overgrazing.* Over 20 percent of pasture and rangelands have been damaged, most severely in Africa and Asia.

2. *Deforestation.* Large-scale logging, clearance for farming, and urban use.

3. *Agricultural mismanagement.* Water erosion, soil salinization, waterlogging.

4. *Fuelwood consumption.* Wood remains a primary energy source in the Southern Hemisphere, and the use of biofuels for energy will only increase this land pressure.

5. *Industry and urbanization.* Road construction, mining and industrial development, suburban developments.

SOURCE: COMPILED FROM *UNEP GLOBAL ENVIRONMENTAL OUTLOOK 3* (LONDON EARTHSCAN: 2002), PAGE 64. REPRINTED WITH PERMISSION OF EARTHSCAN.

degradation is once again caused by human activity: deforestation, overgrazing, and agricultural mismanagement. In severe cases, soil degradation can result in desertification and complete loss of land productivity. Because it takes thousands of years to form a few centimetres of topsoil, this problem has severe implications for the world's food supply. Further, poorly designed irrigation systems and aquaculture (described in the preceding section) can cause salinization and other problems, and the use of pesticides and herbicides, a major interest of MNCs involved in agribusiness, can cause many long-term problems for both ecology and human health. Others worry that the introduction of GMOs and new biotechnology will further homogenize crops, lowering food security in the long run and harming poor farmers who are forced to buy biotech products (see Profile 10.2); and that any substantive shift toward using biofuels such as ethanol to power vehicles will put even more pressure on limited land and further increase food prices.[30]

Taken together, deforestation and land degradation represent a serious assault on the earth's land mass. A UN Convention to Combat Desertification was signed after the Rio Summit of 1992, and there are two major international initiatives to govern world forestry, the International Tropical Timber Organization of 1983 and the Tropical Forestry Action Plan launched in 1985 (later renamed the Tropical Forestry Action Programme, and largely considered a failure). Unquestionably, forestry practices in countries such as Canada and the United States have improved in recent decades, and public concern over the fate of forest ecosystems remains a strong stimulant. But overall, global deforestation, as well as the desertification of arable land and wildlife habitat destruction, continues at an unsustainable pace. In the meantime, as our next section indicates, we are fundamentally changing the evolutionary path of the world's species, altering some, and finishing others altogether.

SPECIES IMPOVERISHMENT

The physical division of the earth into nation-states is contrary to the flow of nature, and this becomes most apparent when we consider the fate of migratory mammals that do not recognize borders and have their paths disrupted by such constructions. This issue raises a broader question: Are the many species of animals and plants that are currently endangered part of the commons, regardless of where they live? From an ecological viewpoint, the crisis presented by dwindling whale and tiger populations and current attempts to save them is really one of biodiversity, or, put more emphatically, what M. Brock Fenton and others call *species impoverishment*.[31] Though there is nothing unnatural and certainly nothing new about extinction, the 20th century in particular saw more extinctions in the wild world than ever before. Scientists are still debating the causes of the late Cretaceous extinction, in which the large dinosaurs were rendered extinct, about 65 million years ago. This is a question partly of effect, for as David Jablonski notes in a fascinating essay on the topic, the late Cretaceous extinction is a very complex phenomenon: "Tropical marine groups were more severely affected than temperate or polar ones; open-ocean plankton and larger swimmers, such as the mosasaurs, were affected more than bottom dwellers; and large land dwellers more affected than small ones, even though some larger forms survived as well."[32] Whatever caused this extinction, it did not kill off all the species on earth at the time, nor did it even come close to doing so. And the key difference: it was, by any account, not preventable with human effort (humans weren't around, according to most scientists!). Humans are believed to be at least partially responsible for the large extinction of land animals in the Pleistocene period, but the development of agriculture so fundamentally changed the human–nature relationship that we have been able to affect a myriad of ecosystems, even the biosphere, with our economic activities.

The human tendency to overhunt constitutes a principal threat to biodiversity today. Columbus discovered the Caribbean monk seal, the single tropical pinniped, in what was called the New World. It has not been seen since 1922. The Steller's sea cow was spotted by a Russian hunting expedition in 1741 in the Aleutians; it was regarded as extinct by the late 18th century. More recently, we have witnessed massive fish extinctions—more than 200 species—from Lake Victoria in Africa. These extinctions had many causes, including overfishing, pollution, and the introduction of alien species, such as the Nile perch. Les Kaufman has referred to Lake Victoria as the "Hiroshima of the biological apocalypse."[33] The reduction of species populations will, of course, have a severe impact on their reproductive health. While this may increase the chances of survival for some, since there is less competition for limited resources, it may lessen the chances of survival for the group as a whole. An important element here is the gene pool, which itself must be sufficiently diverse for healthy populations to thrive: "Gene pools are being converted into gene puddles vulnerable to evaporation in an ecological and evolutionary sense."[34] Other crises will have direct impacts on human survivability; for example, tropical deforestation may steal from future generations remedies for serious diseases, and the recent decline of pollinating global honeybee populations reduces our food security.

The loss of genetic diversity may well be the most serious long-term threat to our environment. As James Scarff notes,

> [the] elimination of a species reduces the genetic capacity of the ecosystem to respond to perturbations or long-term changes in the environment. Such a loss may also initiate irreversible ecological adjustments which destabilize the ecosystem leading to further extinctions. Economically, the extinction of a species represents the permanent loss of a renewable resource of unknown value [as well as] potential uses for medicine, scientific research, human food, education, and recreation.[35]

The international community has taken steps to limit the degradation of wildlife species. There are numerous fisheries agreements and institutions in place, such as the previously mentioned Northwest Atlantic Fisheries Organization and the International Whaling Commission. Early organizations included the International Council for Bird Preservation (1909) and the International Congress for the Protection of Nature (1913). As early as 1886 a Treaty Concerning the Regulation of Salmon Fishing in the Rhine River Basin was signed by Germany, Luxembourg, the Netherlands, and Switzerland. The first international agreement to conserve a marine mammal was in all likelihood the Fur Seal Convention of 1911, signed by Japan, Russia, Great Britain (for pre-independence Canada), and the United States. Another groundbreaking agreement was the U.S.–Great Britain Migratory Birds Convention, signed in 1916, which was a precursor to a range of contemporary transborder agreements.[36]

What Robert Boardman has called the "linchpin of the system"[37] was originally formed in 1948 as the International Union for the Protection of Nature, now known as the **International Union for the Conservation of Nature (IUCN)**. The IUCN is a unique umbrella organization that covers intergovernmental and transnational conservation activity, often working laterally with a plethora of other organizations—both state multilateral and nongovernmental in composition—that have achieved global significance. Its biannual World Congress (held in Barcelona in October 2008) attracts thousands of experts and advocates involved in conservation efforts from around the world. The Convention on International Trade in Endangered Species of Wild Fauna and Flora (CITES) is often heralded as a diplomatic success; it resulted

Facing an uncertain future. A Silverback mountain gorilla in Virunga National Park in the eastern Congo. Deforestation, war, disease, and poaching have reduced the gorilla population in the Virunga reserve to just 200. (AP Photo/Jerome Delay/CP Archive.)

in the controversial international ivory trade ban of 1989 (periodically lifted to allow sales of stockpiled ivory from three southern African states to Japan). But CITES is torn between Northern states demanding complete protection of species and Southern states wanting to trade in animal parts as part of a broader conservation strategy. The role of opposing NGOs lobbying CITES delegations is interesting as well, as they compete to have their worldviews accepted by state delegates. The Convention on Biodiversity (CBD), signed in Rio de Janeiro in 1992, further committed states to preserving biodiversity and committed the North to paying the South for use of genetic material found in the latter. The treaty, signed by more than 160 countries in 1992 (the United States signed after Bill Clinton's election later that year, but has not ratified the treaty), went into effect in 1993. Delegates from all the signatories form a conference of parties, which meets every year to review progress made toward the three central thrusts of the treaty: the conservation of biodiversity, the sustainable use of biological resources, and the equitable sharing of the benefits arising from such use. An additional Biosafety Protocol for the Convention on Biological Diversity (CBD) was negotiated in 2000.[38]

Another major threat to biodiversity is the rise of Invasive Alien Species (IAS), which excel at surviving in new environments because of the lack of natural predators. Though bio-invasion is nothing new IAS today pose severe challenges to ecological integrity, economic security, environmental philosophy, and international modes of governance. Both unintentional and purposive introductions of alien species have often proven disastrous to local ecologies, and the incidental spread of IAS as a result of international trade is a pervasive problem; one author refers to them as "pathogens of globalization."[39] In addition, the symbioses between globalization and global warming are increasing the likelihood of bio-invasions at both the microbial and species levels, causing shifts in pathogenic virulence, as discussed in the section on climate change earlier in this chaper.[40] Beyond the question of climate change, however, IAS are a conceptual challenge, because the mode of their introduction varies considerably, from intentional to incidental, and they are to some extent a normal natural phenomenon. They are a governance challenge because they cross borders, and often result from trade and other factors, such as the introduction of genetically modified organisms, that rely on other governance mechanisms. They also raise ethical challenges, because the costs of dealing with them are not always shared among those who cause this risk, and environmental ethicists struggle with the idea of killing large numbers of one species to protect others.

Various bilateral, and often voluntary measures have been instituted, for example to deal with Great Lakes ballast water and the fear of the voracious Asian Carp; there are numerous multilateral agreements that touch upon IAS, such as the CBD; and in 1997 the Global Invasive Species Programme (GISP) was founded. It produced the Global Strategy on IAS, which is not an international legal instrument but may emerge as the basis for future global governance efforts, albeit with other agreements on trade, investment, and biosafety. Indeed, this is an area where global governance is just beginning to take shape, and it will face large obstacles, not the least of which is the political economy of trade and the apparent supremacy of the WTO in relation to environmental matters. Yet without hard work in this area, species such as the black jellyfish, the Asian tiger mosquito, the yellow crazy ant, the European shore crab, and many other varieties of aggressive shrubs, trees, insects, seaweed, and other species will choke local ecosystems and diminish biodiversity in their wake.

However, global governance efforts to preserve biodiversity are meaningless if the broader problem, the preservation of habitat, is not addressed. This task requires much more than the regulation of fishing fleets or the ban on alligator-skin purses or the confiscation of exotic plants at borders. It requires creating the conditions in which humankind no longer has the perceived need to destroy natural habitat. Despite encouraging conservation programs around the world, we are a long way from environmental sustainability, and many scientists are already resigned to the need to begin cloning endangered species to ensure the continuation of their gene pools. Scientific understanding of the fundamental interconnectivity of all things natural, long a fundamental principal of indigenous knowledge, means that we have no excuse.[41]

TRANSBORDER ENVIRONMENTAL ISSUES

Transborder pollution flows from one country into another, through rivers, streams, lakes, air, and even underground. Since power differentials usually exist between neighbouring states—one is often more industrialized or has a geographic advantage, such as being upstream—realists argue that transborder pollution will be the cause of future violent conflict. However, many states—Canada and the United States with their International Joint Commission (IJC) are often used as an example—co-manage their mutual frontiers on an ongoing basis. Even so, the potential for conflict exists: Canada and the United States argued for years over the effects of **acid rain** that came to Canada from southern industrial regions and continue to dispute the co-management of the Pacific salmon stock, the prospects of drilling for oil in the Arctic Wildlife Refuge in Alaska, the diversion of water from Devil's Lake outlet in North Dakota, and other points of contention.

Aftermath of ecological calamity. Workers who constructed the cement sarcophagus covering Chernobyl's deadly reactor in 1986 pose with a banner reading: "We will fulfill the government's order!" Thousands of workers who took part in the cleanup of Chernobyl have died from the after-effects suffered during the work, according to information from the Union-Chernobyl-Ukraine, and their children have suffered severe health problems, including thyroid cancer, congenital birth deformities, and leukemia. The area remains cordoned today. (AP Photo/Volodymyr Repik/CP Archive.)

Perhaps the most famous case of transborder pollution resulted from an accident at the Chernobyl nuclear reactor in Ukraine in April 1986 (at the time, Ukraine was still part of the Soviet Union). A meltdown in a reactor unit caused an explosion and fire that spread airborne radioactivity as far away as Italy and Sweden. Soviet leaders made matters worse by initially shrouding the event in secrecy, not even informing neighbouring states of incoming radioactivity. In Scandinavia, nomadic Laplanders were severely affected as their reindeer herds ate toxic grass. Leaks of radioactive inert gases and iodine from a reactor near St. Petersburg in the 1990s have accentuated the fear that more Chernobyls are waiting to happen. Throughout the Cold War, Eastern Europe had served as a captive market for the Soviet nuclear industry, and Soviet-designed reactors (located in Czechoslovakia, Hungary, Bulgaria, and Eastern Germany) did not always include sufficient emergency core cooling systems or containment vessels. Since the unprecedented nuclear disaster at

Chernobyl, a new customary norm has emerged in international law: states have an obligation to inform bordering states if a disaster with such far-reaching consequences has occurred.

Other transborder pollution problems have resulted from industrialization. Several regional agreements aim at reducing acid precipitation (acid rain), which damages forests and lakes. For example, in 1988, 24 European states signed a treaty to limit nitrogen oxide emissions to 1988 levels by 1995, and Canada and the United States have a bilateral agreement that was the result of many years of protracted bargaining.[42] However, without funding for effective scrubbers for smokestacks for industries burning lignite (a highly sulphurous coal), acid rain will continue to be a major problem, particularly in Eastern Europe.

Yet another transborder environmental issue is the circulation of pesticides, an issue that illustrates the complexity of both modern science and the world economy. For example, in 1990 U.S. manufacturers exported more than 24 million kilograms of pesticides such as DDT, dieldrin, toxaphene, endrin, ethyl parathion, and other compounds that were banned, restricted, or unregistered for use in the United States. Most of these were shipped to Southern states, such as Argentina, Colombia, Ecuador, and the Philippines, though a significant amount went to Belgium, Japan, and the Netherlands. The Stockholm Convention on **Persistent Organic Pollutants** (POPs), which went into force in 2004, has limited this trade. Nevertheless, in his excellent study of pesticide regulation, John Wargo draws attention to the difficulty of regulating such international commerce in products that are highly hazardous to both human and ecosystem health:

> An active ingredient produced in the United States may be shipped to Switzerland where it is combined with other ingredients and shipped to Egypt. In Egypt, it might be applied as an insecticide to cotton. Cottonseeds may then be harvested and sold to a commodity broker in Israel, who then sells them to a manufacturer of cottonseed oil in Italy. The Italian firm may then sell the oil, perhaps mixed with other oil from seeds grown in Guatemala with the help of another pesticide, to an American food processing company.[43]

Another local and regional environmental issue is access to freshwater. Though recent events, such as flooding in India, Bangladesh, and Mozambique, suggest that the problem of water is one of overabundance, water scarcity is also a growing concern. Only about 3 percent of the world's water is fresh, and much of that is frozen in the polar ice caps. In effect, less than 1 percent of the world's water is easily accessible freshwater. Heated debates have ensued over whether the privatization of water is a violation of basic human rights, since it is generally considered a common public good. Global water use doubles every 21 years, and water use now exceeds sustainable consumption limits. Astoundingly, about 1.1 billion people, or 18 percent of the world's population, lack access to safe drinking water, and 2.5 billion are without proper sanitation. If present trends continue, by 2025 1.8 billion people will be living in regions or countries suffering from acute water scarcity, and as much as two-thirds of the world's population could be under water stress.[44]

Aquifers (underground water supplies) in many of the world's regions are running dry or becoming contaminated with seawater, arsenic, and other dangerous chemicals. Many major rivers are mere streams when they reach the coast due to diversion of water for irrigation. The demand for freshwater comes from agriculture (66 percent of the total consumption), industry (25 percent), and human consumption (9 percent). In some regions, the increased rate of water use has had dramatic consequences. A stark example can be found in the Aral Sea

PROFILE 10.8 Canada's Freshwater Supply

Canada has a large supply of freshwater, and this is expected to be a growing issue in its relations with the United States. In both countries, water demand continues to increase, making successful management all the more important in the future. According to a 2001 report, Canadians rank "a dismal 28th out of 29 OECD nations in water consumption per capita, with only Americans consuming more water. The amount of water consumed in Canada has increased by 25.7%" between 1980 and 2001.

Other factors to consider:

- Between 1972 and 1991, Canada's water usage increased from 24 billion cubic metres per year to over 45 billion cubic metres per year—a rise of more than 80 percent; in the same period, population increased only 3 percent.

- Freshwater lakes, rivers, and underground aquifers hold only 3.5 percent of the world's water. By comparison, saltwater oceans and seas contain 95.1 percent of the world's water supply.

- Canada has about 9 percent of the world's fresh renewable water supply, compared with 18 percent for Brazil, 9 percent for China, and 8 percent for the United States.

- The Great Lakes constitute one of the largest systems of freshwater reservoirs on earth, with 18 percent of the world's fresh surface water.

- About 7.6 percent of Canada is covered by freshwater in lakes and rivers—755,165 square kilometres. To this can be added 195,059 square kilometres of perennial snow and ice.

There is increasing pressure on provincial governments to begin bulk water exports to the increasingly dry United States, but this is a highly sensitive subject to Canadians. One can reasonably expect this pressure to increase, however.

SOURCES: D. BOYD, *CANADA VS. THE OECD: AN ENVIRONMENTAL COMPARISON* (VICTORIA, BC: UNIVERSITY OF VICTORIA, 2001); ENVIRONMENT CANADA, HTTP://WWW.EC.GC.CA/WATER (ACCESSED MAY 26, 2004).

region of Central Asia. During Soviet rule, massive quantities of water were diverted from the river systems feeding the Aral Sea to irrigate a huge agricultural project. The flow of water to the Aral Sea slowed to a trickle, and as a result the Sea has now shrunk by one-half. Not only has this devastated the local fishing industry, but the dry sea salt is swept up by winds into dust storms, which deposit salt over a wide area, poisoning land and people.[45] Within a geopolitically contested region, the reduced flow of water in the tributary rivers of the shrinking Sea has been a major cause of concern for the states of the former Soviet Union, though they have established an intergovernmental commission for water coordination.

In fact, a new term has been coined to refer to conflicts over water resources: *hydropolitics*.[46] Water conflict has been an acute problem in areas with arid climates, such as northern Africa and the Middle East (see Profile 10.9). As water consumption increases alongside population and economic growth, the quest for sources of freshwater becomes more dramatic and has already been the cause of conflict between several states. There are 261 river basins shared by two or more states, including the Nile, Jordan, Euphrates, Amazon, Mekong, Rhine, Ganges, Indu, Colorado, and others. They are all potential sources of both conflict and cooperation. As we discussed at the beginning of this chapter, water scarcity will not automatically lead to protracted and perhaps violent future conflict. Some argue that shared resources can bring out the best in states, promoting their ability to cooperate when they must to achieve mutual benefits. Thomas Homer-Dixon argues that, though there are historical examples of wars caused by the quest for nonrenewable resources (such as oil and minerals), "the story is different for renewables like cropland, forests, fish and freshwater. It is hard to find clear historical or contemporary examples of major wars motivated mainly by scarcities of renewables."[47] This analytic caution is certainly warranted, but it does not really contradict the claim that

PROFILE 10.9 — Water and Interstate Conflict in North Africa and the Middle East?

THE NILE

The Nile River is one of the most famous and historic rivers of the world. It is also a river of tremendous regional economic importance. The Nile is the primary source of water for both human consumption and agriculture in Northeast Africa, in particular Egypt and the Sudan. In fact, almost all of Egypt's water is drawn from the Nile. However, almost all of the source water of the Nile originates outside Egypt, in the seven countries that straddle the Nile River Basin: Sudan, Ethiopia, Kenya, Rwanda, Burundi, Tanzania, and Zaire. The exploitation of water resources in these countries would reduce the flow of water to the Nile and to Egypt. To the Egyptian government, this is a major security concern, prompting former Egyptian president Anwar Sadat and former Foreign Minister Boutros Boutros-Ghali to warn that conflict over water might result in Egypt going to war. In 1999, the Nile Basin Initiative was signed, and there are hopes that this can help manage the situation as well as promote development in the region.

THE JORDAN RIVER BASIN

The Jordan River Basin is a valley in the central Middle East that collects most of the rainwater that falls on the region. Syria, Lebanon, Israel, Jordan, and the West Bank are heavily dependent on the Jordan Basin for their water supplies, and since the creation of Israel in 1948 access to this water supply has been a factor in the Arab–Israeli conflict. In fact, approximately 40 percent of Israel's groundwater originates in the territories occupied by Israel in 1967. Water demands in Israel are rising as the population increases, and this has resulted in an increased dependence on water drawn from the Jordan Basin. Israel has also drawn water from groundwater aquifers, which are becoming saline from overuse. Israel runs a water deficit, drawing out more water than nature replaces. Water has become a crucial point of discussion and dispute between Israel and the Palestinian people (who have had their access to water restricted by the Israeli government), as well as between Israel and neighbouring Arab states. Conflict over water could easily spark a wider conflagration in a region already beset with conflicts and high levels of tension, and resource sharing must be part of any future peace negotiations.

SEE M. LOWI, *WATER AND POWER: THE POLITICS OF A SCARCE RESOURCE IN THE JORDAN RIVER BASIN* (CAMBRIDGE, UK: CAMBRIDGE UNIVERSITY PRESS, 1993).

conflicts over resources are potential causes of international and civil warfare, as well as factors in long-range geostrategic thinking and trade policy, as water-rich states such as Canada contemplate bulk water exports.

Water is not the only resource that might spark future conflicts, but given the increasing consumption and decreasing availability of this vital resource, water may become as much a factor in war between states as oil and strategic minerals have been in the past. In the longer term, these stresses are expected to worsen. According to one estimate, by 2075 the number of people living in regions with chronic water shortages could be as high as three to seven billion, while the number of people living in regions with high water stress could be as high as four to nine billion, depending on the scenario. As a result, the danger of conflict over water scarcity, especially in combination with population growth and climate change, cannot be ignored.[48]

ENVIRONMENTAL DEGRADATION AND MILITARY CONFLICT: AN ONGOING CIRCLE

The link between military preparation and environmental degradation has been increasingly regarded as a security issue in the study of international relations. However, the conceptualization of the environment as a security problem is not without its detractors. Skeptics argue that it is inappropriate to characterize environmental issues as security issues because the environment is not an enemy and environmental issues cannot be addressed through traditional military means. Others argue that little hard evidence exists to support the link between environmental degradation and conflict and war.[49] However, we would argue that there is often a vicious circle at play when it comes to military conflict and the environment. War can cause severe environmental destruction, which contributes to resource scarcity, which in turn contributes to structural conditions conducive to conflict and more war. We will deal with each turn of the circle in this section.

On November 5, 2003, the UN declared that each November 6 would be recognized as the International Day for Preventing the Exploitation of the Environment in War and Conflict. While it may seem self-evident, the fact that war is bad for the environment is often overlooked. The environment can be harmed incidentally, a function of strategic necessity or negligence; it can be harmed deliberately, as a strategy in itself often referred to as *ecocide*; and it can be harmed in the course of military preparation, not only in terms of munitions/weapons testing, but also in terms of the atmospheric pollution, chemical spills, and radioactive waste emitted by the military-industrial complex.[50] Invariably, military strategy and tactics, offensive and defensive, involve a good deal of environmental assault and modification. As early as 2400 B.C.E., Entemenar—the ruler of Sumer—modified the land by constructing a canal that diverted water from the Tigris to the Euphrates watershed, which ceased Sumer's dependence on the Kingdom of Umma. As Fred Roots has pointed out, the groundwater rose with this construction, which caused a rapid increase in salinity, impoverishing Umma. Eventually, however, Sumer suffered as well, as its own overirrigated desert soils were leached. Roots concludes that by 2200 B.C.E., "mighty Sumer was easy prey for upstart Babylon, which had less wealth and poorer technology but a clean environmental base." On a further note, Roots cites the most famous Biblical example of environmental modification for military purposes, the parting of the Red Sea by Moses: "The mechanism by which Moses accomplished this rapid environmental modification is not clear to ordinary mortals today, but presumably he did it all by triggering tectonic movements. Certainly the geological structure and accumulated crustal stress in the Red Sea graben makes this a good potential location … if God is on your side."[51]

An incomplete list of major ecologically disruptive wars stretches back to the Persian–Scythian War of 512 B.C.E. (as the Scythians retreated they hindered Persian pursuit with a scorched-earth policy, a theme found frequently over the long years of military history). The Peloponnesian War (431–404 B.C.E.), made famous by Thucydides, saw the annually repeated destruction of Athenian grain crops by the Spartans. At the end of the Third Punic War, the Roman victors polluted the farmland around Carthage with salt. Genghis Khan, leading the Mongols through Asia and Eastern Europe, destroyed irrigation works located along the Tigris River in Mesopotamia. The Dutch flooded their own land to keep away French troops in the Franco–Dutch War of 1672–78. Destruction of agricultural land, intended to starve rebellious states into the Union, was routine policy during the last years of the American Civil War. The Chinese used scorched-earth tactics to put down the Taiping Rebellion (1850–64). The Portuguese used herbicides to destroy crops during the Angolan War of Independence (1961–75). Water and water-related facilities have often been targeted in times of war. In the ancient period, wells were poisoned to deny water to the enemy, a practice that continued for centuries. In the 20th century, hydroelectric dams were targets during World War II and the Korean War. Irrigation systems in North Vietnam were bombed by the United States during the Vietnam War, and Syria and Israel had violent clashes over water in the mid-1960s. In the Gulf War, Kuwaiti desalination plants were destroyed by Iraq, while coalition bombing largely destroyed Iraq's water supply system, both in 1991 and in 2003.

In North America and Europe, concerns with the environmental impact of war first became pronounced in the 1960s. It became apparent that, with the advent of nuclear weapons, it was now possible for military conflict to destroy most of the biosphere. Perhaps the most widely read account of such Armageddon-like forecasting was Carl Sagan's discussion in the widely read journal *Foreign Affairs* of the possible climatic catastrophe—nuclear winter—that would follow even small-scale nuclear war. Atmospheric nuclear tests in the 1950s created radioactive fallout that travelled thousands of kilometres, raising public concern over the discovery of cesium-137, strontium 90, carbon 14, and various isotopes of plutonium in the environment. An earlier book by Jonathan Schell received a popular reaction, and public awareness of the ill effects of nuclear testing (including the discovery of iodine in breast milk) was partly responsible for the eventual acceptance of the Partial Test Ban Treaty in 1963.[52]

The end of the Cold War and the deliberate burning of an estimated 500 million barrels of oil in Kuwait after the Gulf War of 1990–91 provoked a shift from an understandable nuclear preoccupation to concerns over how conventional warfare has harmed ecosystems and caused related population displacements in various regions of the world. However, the U.S. military probably inflicted the largest single wartime assault on an ecosystem during the Vietnam War. The destruction of large areas of Indochina's forests using herbicides was intended to remove the forest cover concealing the location and movement of enemy forces and to deprive them of their food supply. Many chemical herbicides were used, especially the infamous Agent Orange (2,4-D and 2,4,5-T), Agent White (2,4-D and Picloram), and Agent Blue (Cucodylic Acid). In addition to the landscape alteration wrought by the infamous Rome plough (which tore up entire fields to destroy farming capability), more than 17,000 square kilometres of South Vietnam were damaged by herbicides, and over 1,500 square kilometres of ecologically sensitive mangrove forest was completely destroyed. This campaign generated understandable moral outrage in the United States itself, and while some 10,000 affected U.S. veterans won $180 million in damages in a civil suit against Dow, Monsanto, and other manufacturers, the Vietnamese have never been compensated.[53] The Vietnam War coincided with a growing domestic environmentalist movement in the United States, and was probably the first military campaign that was heavily criticized in some quarters for its environmental impact. Richard Falk wrote in 1973: "surely it is no exaggeration to consider the forests and plantations treated by Agent Orange as an Auschwitz for environmental values, certainly not from the perspective of such a distinct environmental species as the mangrove tree or nipa palm."[54] In the 1999 military intervention in Serbia, NATO bombing "destroyed fertilizer plants and oil refineries located on the tributary of the Danube river, resulting in fires and the release of petroleum byproducts and other carcinogens into the water. Additional bombs … released large amounts of PCBs and liquid mercury into other Danube tributaries, posing severe danger to human life."[55]

Toxic conflict. A U.S. soldier from the 1st Marine Expeditionary Force stands guard at a burning oil well at the Rumeila Oil fields in Iraq, March 23, 2003. Several oil wells were set ablaze by retreating Iraqi troops in the Rumeila area, the second-largest offshore oil field in the country, near the Kuwaiti border. (AP Photo/Ian Waldie/Pool/CP Archive.)

Despite a treaty designed to curb the deliberate damage of the environment during warfare in 1977 (the Convention on the Prohibition of Military or Any Other Hostile Use of Environmental Modification Techniques, or ENMOD), it is clear that ecocide continues to be employed in war. In Colombia, the so-called War on Drugs has seen widespread spraying of "broad spectrum herbicides in ecologically fragile areas. In a single two-week period in 2000, approximately 25,000 hectares were fumigated from the air with a glyphosate-based chemical agent."[56] Is this spraying meant simply to stop narcotics production, or is it an instrument of war against rebels? In Mexico, Zapatista rebels have "denounced what they consider to be hostile environmental modification aimed at stopping their insurgency. According to villagers in Zapatista regions, the government's massive spraying of pesticides to control the Mediterranean fruit fly has deliberately hit food crops, ruining them. The villagers say the spraying is a thinly disguised attempt to destroy the food security of farming communities suspected of harbouring rebel sympathizers. The Mexican government of Ernesto Zedillo, while admitting that the Army played a role in fruit fly control, insisted that spraying was purely for phytosanitary reasons." The same communities suspect local forest fires could be deliberately set as well, a theme repeated by the Yanomami in the Brazilian Amazon, and indigenous peoples in Kalimantan, Indonesia.

The use of such techniques has long-term consequences. The German Army first used liquid chlorine (which inflames the lungs, causing those exposed to drown in their own exudation) near Ypres, Belgium in April 1915. In June 1916, the Allies first used the even deadlier phosgene during the famous Battle of the Somme. According to Robert Harris and Jeremy Paxman, "Long after the initial bombardment had occurred, an area which had been contaminated by mustard gas was liable to remain dangerous. The liquid formed pools in shell craters.... It polluted water. In cold weather it froze like water and stayed in the soil: mustard used in the winter of 1917 poisoned men in the spring of 1918 when the ground thawed."[57] Land mines destroy people and arable land long after they are planted as well. Similarly, areas near many of the nuclear weapons production plants in the United States and Russia are contaminated by various chemical hazards and radiation, and Canada continues to lament the chemical residue left by the long-abandoned Cold War Distant Early Warning System in the North. Today, we are more likely to worry about whether there will be a long-lasting health impact from depleted uranium (DU) projectiles fired by U.S. tanks and planes to penetrate Iraqi and Serbian armour. We can safely predict that there will be similar instances and long-term problems in the future so long as states do not take the ENMOD convention seriously. Military research projects involving even more ambitious environmental modification techniques, such as cloud seeding and other forms of weather modification, have been ongoing. Research in even more exotic fields, such as nanotechnology and the ionosphere, will also have military applications.

However, our circle does not end here. Military violence and political instability can lead to increased environmental scarcity and, thus, enhance the prospects for more military conflict. The hypothesis that environmental degradation is a cause of conflict in the international system is built on the logic of scarcity. Both renewable and nonrenewable resources are finite in quantity. As the population of the planet increases, and as industrialization and consumption continue to grow and spread, the scarcity of resources will become increasingly acute for three main reasons:

1. Human activity will increasingly consume more resources, degrading the quality and availability of resources.

2. Population growth will increase the number of people making demands on a shrinking resource pie.

3. Resources will not be distributed equally, and the concentration of resources in a small segment of the population will decrease the availability of that resource to the rest of the population.

As available resources deteriorate or are depleted, competition for access to these resources will increase. Spontaneous conflict and organized war over resources might well be result. Indeed, some would argue that this process has already begun. A major Canadian-led international research project on environmental scarcity and violent conflict reached the following conclusion:

> Scarcities of renewable resources will increase sharply. The total area of high quality agricultural land will drop, as will the extent of forests and the number of species they sustain. Coming generations will also see the widespread depletion and degradation of aquifers, rivers, and other water resources; the decline of many fisheries; and perhaps significant climate change ... environmental scarcities are already contributing to violent conflicts in many areas of the world. These conflicts are probably the early signs of an upsurge of violence in the coming decades that will be induced or aggravated by scarcity.[58]

A number of different environmental issues have been cited as causes of existing or future conflicts:

- The degradation and loss of arable land, with consequent implications for crop and livestock production
- The destruction of forests and consequent loss of forestry-related employment, revenue, topsoil, and species diversity
- The depletion and degradation of freshwater supplies
- The depletion of strategic minerals, including oil
- The overexploitation and consequent depletion of fisheries resources

An illustration of the link between environmental degradation, resource scarcity, and political upheaval and violence can be found in the plight of Haiti. A combination of population growth, land shortages, and corrupt leadership bent on expropriating available wealth has left Haiti the poorest country in the Western Hemisphere. Haiti's forests have virtually disappeared, cut down to create more land for cultivation. Poor Haitians move up the mountainsides, clearing more forests and exhausting the land. The loss of the forest contributes to soil erosion, which has rendered almost half of the countryside unsuitable for farming. This, coupled with population growth, has led to a fall in per capita incomes. People have migrated to the cities, especially Port-au-Prince, a teeming city dominated by enormous slums. Many others have fled Haiti as refugees. Political instability and civil strife have characterized recent Haitian politics as the rich political classes use increasing levels of force and repression to maintain their control over the country. In 1986 the "Baby Doc" Duvalier regime collapsed, and international intervention restored civilian rule. Political instability in Haiti in the early 1990s resulted in the creation of a UN peacekeeping mission that helped to restore order, but the environmental and economic problems of the country were never resolved. In 2004 violence erupted as President Aristide was pushed from power. The UN has returned to Haiti again, and order is always a tentative prospect in this troubled state. Indeed, the severity of environmental degradation in the country raises doubts about the prospects for long-term economic and political stability.

In Brazil, fears persist that the unequal distribution of land and wealth could create domestic instability and increasingly violent conflict in the future. Although Brazil ranked ninth in the world in gross domestic product in 1996, the distribution of wealth in Brazil is highly unequal. In fact, the poorest 40 percent of the Brazilian population receives only 7 percent of total income. Land distribution is even more unequal, with less than 1 percent of all landowners controlling almost half of Brazil's privately held land. As a result, Brazil has some 12 million landless peasants while more than 180 million hectares of farmable land lie unused. Many of these peasants have migrated to the cities, feeding Brazil's expanding urban slums. Lack of housing, jobs, and access to government services, as well as extreme poverty, have contributed to a soaring crime rate. Recently, there has been a move to return to the land, in the form of squatting and occupying unused tracts of land. This has brought the landless peasants and the Landless Workers' Movement, the organization that represents them, into conflict with local landowners and the police. This confrontation has not always been peaceful: more than 1,700 people have been killed in the past decade. More radical organizations committed to armed struggle have grown rapidly. Unless meaningful land reform is enacted over the opposition of the politically powerful landowning class, a violent conflict over land distribution may be in Brazil's near future.

As was discussed in Chapters 6 and 8, many would argue that access to oil was a major factor in the 2003 invasion of Iraq. But there are many other, less-well-known examples. The dispute over the Spratly and Paracel Islands in the South China Sea carries the potential for interstate conflict over the right to exploit oil and mineral deposits on the seabed. The Spratly Islands are a group of 500 small islands situated in the South China Sea. Six states lay claim to some or all of the Spratly Islands or their territorial waters: Brunei, China, Malaysia, the Philippines, Taiwan, and Vietnam (see Chapter 6). Although most of the islands are mere outcroppings of rock or coral, they possess strategic value for three reasons: they are located in the middle of an important international sea lane, their territorial waters are rich in fish stocks, and their seabeds contain oil and mineral deposits. The Spratly Islands dispute has had a violent dimension, particularly between Vietnam and China. These two countries have clashed over some of the islands in 1974, 1982, 1988, and 1992. Most countries that lay claim to some or all of the islands maintain military garrisons on selected islands, and all maintain an air force and naval presence in and around the islands. Despite calls for a regional conference on the future of the islands, and the opening of talks between China and Vietnam, the Spratly Islands remain a subject of intense interstate dispute. There are concerns that this dispute, and many others with similar profiles, could result in armed conflict at any time.

Perhaps the greatest challenge to those who wish to avoid future resource wars relates to the disproportionate impact of climate change, which is sure to breed resentment and instability. Beyond the overwhelming scientific evidence that we face serious problems, and the inherent complexities of global governance efforts, we stress the ethical obligation to take action. In the case of climate change, the inequality of cause and effect here is startling. For example, "the average U.S. citizen dumps as much greenhouse gas into the atmosphere as nine Chinese … eighty Bangladeshis … [and] and over five hundred citizens of Ethiopia, Chad, Zaire, Afghanistan, Mail, Cambodia, and Burundi."[59] The need to pursue greater global equality has never been stronger.

CONCLUSIONS

In this chapter, we have discussed the main agents and structures in global ecopolitics; problems of the commons, including climate change, the crisis of the oceans, land degradation and deforestation, and species impoverishment; transborder pollution, military activity, and resource conflicts. All these problems are interrelated and require concerted international action to meet the challenges they pose. It may be the case that we are on the verge of civilizational collapse, and that this crisis (or, rather, this set of interlinked crises) will spur unprecedented innovations as various political communities struggle to adapt.[60] As Thomas Friedman warns us, "The world … is getting hot, flat, and crowded. That is, global warming, the stunning rise of middle classes all over the world, and rapid population growth have converged in a way that could make our planet dangerously unstable."[61]

This should impose an obligation on states and individuals to seek mitigation and adaptation norms that embrace global environmental justice. Indeed, as Michael Mason suggests, it is the "intersection of individual rights and responsibilities with (inter)state obligations that offers concrete possibilities for citizen participation in global decisionmaking."[62]

The steps taken from here, such as a serious effort to reduce greenhouse gas emissions, the provision of adequate funding for global climate change adaptation, and the sound management of the world's land, oceans, freshwater, and atmospheric resources, will largely determine your future. It is clear that a momentous effort lies before us all, in our capacities as researchers, teachers, policymakers, global citizens, consumers, family members, and individuals. Though controversies abound, what emerges from the scientific and legal community is an emphasis on adopting the precautionary principle in environmental management. The principle, which is endorsed in the Rio Declaration of 1992, Agenda 21, the UNFCC, the CBD, and a plethora of other international agreements, insists that, in the absence of scientific certainty regarding the future impact of human activity, we should err on the side of caution.[63] Today, the precautionary principle seems more logical a path to take than ever.

Endnotes

1. "Why the Ark Is Sinking," in L. Kaufman and K. Mallory, eds., *The Last Extinction*, 2nd ed. (Cambridge, MA: MIT Press, 1993), 1–46, 12.

2. M. Kaplan, "The Coming Anarchy," *Atlantic Monthly*, February 1994, 58.

3. C. Doucet, *Urban Meltdown: Cities, Climate Change and Politics as Usual* (Gabriola Island, BC: New Society Publishers, 2007), xvii.

4. See *The Millennium Ecosystem Assessment* (Washington, DC: Island Press, 2005) and *Global Environmental Outlook GEO4: Environment for Development* (New York: UNEP, 2007).

5. The relationship between understandings of IR and ecology is explored in much greater depth in E. Laferrière and P. Stoett, *International Relations Theory and Ecological Thought: Towards a Synthesis* (London: Routledge, 1999). See also M. Mies and V. Shiva, *Ecofeminism* (Halifax: Fernwood Publications, 1993); N. Choucri, ed., *Global Accord: Environmental Challenges and International Responses* (Cambridge, MA: MIT Press, 1993); R. Eckersley, *The Green State: Rethinking Democracy and Sovereignty* (Cambridge: MIT Press, 2004); M. Paterson, *Understanding Global Environmental Politics: Domination, Accumulation, Resistance* (Basingstoke: Macmillan, 2000); S. Dalby, *Environmental Security* (Minneapolis: University of Minnesota Press, 2002); P. Dauvergne, ed., *Handbook of Global Environmental Politics* (Cheltenham, UK: Edward Elgar, 2005); and E. Laferrière and P. Stoett, eds., *International Ecopolitical Theory: Critical Approaches* (Vancouver: University of British Columbia Press, 2006).

6. See J. Clapp, "Global Environmental Governance for Corporate Responsibility and Accountability," *Global Environmental Politics* 5, no. 3 (2005), 23–34; and J. Clapp and P. Dauvergne, eds., *Paths to a Green World: the Political Economy of the Global Environment* (Cambridge: MIT Press, 2005).

7. D. Suzuki and H. Dressel, *Good News For a Change: How Everyday People Are Helping the Planet* (Vancouver: Greystone Books, 2003). See also P. Wapner, *Environmental Activism and World Civic Politics* (Albany, NY: SUNY Press, 1996).

8. W. Beckerman, "Global Warming and International Action: An Economic Perspective," in A. Hurrell and B. Kingsbury, eds., *The International Politics of the Environment* (Oxford: Clarendon Press, 1992), 253–89.

9. S. Krasner, "Sovereignty, Regimes, and Human Rights," in V. Rittberger, ed., *Regime Theory and International Relations* (Oxford: Clarendon Press, 1993), 139–67. See also P. M. Wijkman, "Managing the Global Commons," *International Organization* 36, no. 3 (1982), 511–36; S. Buck, *The Global Commons: An Introduction* (Washington, DC: Island Press, 1998); E. Ostrom, *Governing the Commons: The Evolution of Institutions for Collective Action* (Cambridge, UK: Cambridge University Press, 1990); E. DeSombre, *Global Environmental Institutions* (New York: Routledge, 2006).

10. M. M'Gonigle and D. Babicki, "The Turbot's Last Stand?," *The Globe and Mail*, July 21, 1995, A19.

11. General Assembly Resolution 1803 (XVII), December 14, 1962. See N. Schrijver, *Sovereignty over Natural Resources: Balancing Rights and Duties* (Cambridge, UK: Cambridge University Press, 1997).

12. R. E. Benedick, *Ozone Diplomacy: New Directions in Safeguarding the Planet* (Cambridge MA: Harvard University Press, 1991), 207. See also K. Litfin, *Ozone Discourses: Science and Politics in Global Environmental Cooperation* (New York: Columbia University Press, 1994).

13. For the complete text, see *Antarctic Journal of the United States* (Natural Science Foundation) 26, no. 4 (December 1991). See also O. S. Stokke and D. Vidas, eds., *Governing the Antarctic: The Effectiveness and Legitimacy of the Antarctic Treaty System* (Cambridge, UK: Cambridge University Press, 1996).

14. IPCC, *Climate Change 2007: Synthesis Report—An Assessment of the Intergovernmental Panel on Climate Change*, 30.

15. See "Asian Brown Clouds Intensify Global Warming," *Environmental News Service*, August 1, 2007, http://www.ens-newswire.com/ens/aug2007/2007-08-01-02.asp (accessed June 1, 2008).

16. N. Stern, *The Economics of Climate Change: The Stern Review* (Cambridge: Cambridge University Press, 2007); T. Flannery, *The Weather Makers: Our Changing Climate and What It Means for Life on Earth* (New York: Penguin, 2006); G. Monbiot, *Heat: How to Stop the Planet from Burning* (Toronto: Doubleday Canada, 2006); and W. Burroughs, *Climate Change: A Multidisciplinary Approach* (New York: Cambridge University Press, 2007).

17. S. Earle, *Sea Change: a Message of the Oceans* (New York: Fawcett Columbine, 1995), xii. See also A. Mitchell, *Sea Sick: The Global Ocean in Crisis* (Toronto: McClelland and Stewart, 2009).

18. Much of the following information is taken from the UNEP's *Global Environmental Outlook 3* (New York: UNEP and Earthscan, 2002), pp 180–209.

19. See P. Stoett, *The International Politics of Whaling* (Vancouver: University of British Columbia Press, 1997). On the impact of whaling on the oceans, see J. Estes, ed., *Whales, Whaling, and Ocean Ecosystems* (Santa Cruz: University of California Press, 2006).

20. See *The State of World Fisheries and Aquaculture 2000* (Rome: Food and Agriculture Organization, 2001) and *The State of World Fisheries and Aquaculture, 2008* (Rome: Food and Agriculture Organization, 2009), 7.

21. See E. Allison, "Big Laws, Small Catches: Global Ocean Governance and the Fisheries Crisis," *Journal of International Development* 13 (2001), 933–950; L. Juda, "Rio Plus Ten: The Evolution of International Marine Fisheries Governance," *Ocean Development and International Law* 33 (2002), 109–144.

22. See K. Riddle, "Illegal, Unreported, and Unregulated Fishing: Is International Cooperation Contagious?," *Ocean Development and International Law* 37 (2006), 265–297.

23. For a Canadian perspective, see J. Volpe and K. Shaw, "Fish Farms and Neoliberalism: Salmon Aquaculture in British Columbia," in C. Gore and P. Stoett, eds., *Environmental Challenges and Opportunities: Local-Global Perspectives on Canadian Issues* (Toronto: Emond Montgomery, 2009), 131–158.

24. See R. Rayfuse, "The Challenge of Sustainable High Seas Fisheries," in N. Schrijver and F. Weiss, eds., *International law and Sustainable Development: Principles and Practice* (Netherlands: Martinus Nijhoff, 2004), 467–499.

25. See C. Wilkinson, ed., *Status of Coral Reefs of the World* (Townsville: Australian Institute of Marine Science, 2000).

26. Data from *State of the World's Forests, 2009* (Rome: Food and Agriculture Organization of the United Nations, 2008).

27. *State of the World's Forests 2009*, 35.

28. See A. Bugge, "Amazon Destruction Jumps; Environmentalists Are Shocked," *Environmental News Network*, http://www.enn.com/news/2003-06-27/s_5841.asp (accessed May 27, 2004).

29. See United Nations Department of Public Information, "Press Release of the Secretary-General's Report on Implementing Agenda 21," Johannesburg Summit 2002, http://www.johannesburgsummit.org/ html/ media_info/pressreleases_factsheets/press_summary_sg_report2801.pdf (accessed May 27, 2004).

30. On GMOs, see R. Falkner, ed., *The International Politics of Genetically Modified Food: Diplomacy, Trade and Law* (Houndmills, UK: Palgrave, 2007), 138–54; for Canadian perspectives, see P. Andrée, *Genetically Modified Diplomacy: The Global Politics of Agricultural Biotechnology and the Environment* (Vancouver: UBC Press, 2006) and S. Mulligan, as in Profile 10.1. On biofuels, see C. F. Runge and B. Senauer, "How Biofuels Could Starve the Poor," *Foreign Affairs* 86, no. 3 (May/June 2007).

31. M. B. Fenton, "Species Impoverishment," in J. Leith, R. Price, and J. Spencer, eds., *Planet Earth: Problems and Prospects* (Montreal/Kingston: McGill-Queen's University Press, 1995), 83–110. See also P. Ehrlich and A. Ehrlich, *Extinction* (New York: Wiley, 1986); N. Eldredge, *The Miner's Canary: Unravelling the Mysteries of Extinction* (New York: Prentice Hall, 1991); and P. Colinvaux, *Why Big Fierce Animals Are Rare: An Ecologist's Perspective* (Princeton: Princeton University Press, 1978). For an excellent Canadian text, see S. Bocking, *Biodiversity in Canada: Ecology, Ideas, and Action* (Peterborough, ON: Broadview Press, 2000).

32. D. Jablonski, "Mass Extinctions: New Answers, New Questions," in L. Kaufman and K. Mallory, eds., *The Last Extinction*, 2nd ed. (Cambridge, MA: MIT Press, 1993), 47–68, 52.

33. "Why the Ark Is Sinking," in L. Kaufman and K. Mallory, eds., *The Last Extinction*, 2nd ed. (Cambridge, MA: MIT Press, 1993), 1–46, 43. See also Kaufman's "Catastrophic Change in Species-Rich Freshwater Ecosystems: The Lessons of Lake Victoria," *Bioscience* 42, no. 11 (1992), 846–58; Y. Baskin, "Africa's Troubled Waters: Fish Introductions and a Changing Physical Profile Muddy Lake Victoria's Future," *Bioscience* 42, no. 7 (1992), 476–81; and the controversial Hubert Sauper 2004 film *Darwin's Nightmare*.

34. T. Foose, "Riders of the Last Ark: The Role of Captive Breeding in Conservation Strategies," in L. Kaufman and K. Mallory, eds., *The Last Extinction*, 149–78.

35. J. Scarff, "Ethical Issues in Whale and Small Cetacean Management," *Environmental Ethics* 2, no. 3 (1980), 241–80, 244n., 14.

36. See R. Boardman, *The International Politics of Bird Conservation: Biodiversity, Regionalism and Global Governance* (Northampton, MA: Edward Elgar, 2006).

37. R. Boardman, *International Organization and the Conservation of Nature* (Bloomington: Indiana University Press, 1981).

38. See P. Stoett, "Wildlife Conservation: Institutional and Normative Considerations" in N. Schrijver and F. Weiss, eds., *International Law and Sustainable Development: Principles and Practice* (Leiden, Netherlands: Martinus Nijhoff, 2004), 501–518; and same and P. Le Prestre, "International Initiatives, Commitments, and Disappointments: Canada, CITES, and the CBD," in K. Beazley and R. Boardman, eds., *Politics of the Wild: Canada and Endangered Species* (Toronto: Oxford university Press, 2001), 120–21; and G. Rosendal, "Impact of Overlapping International Regimes: The Case of Biodiversity," *Global Governance* 7, no. 2 (2001), 95–117.

39. C. Bright, "Invasive Species: Pathogens of Globalization." *Foreign Policy*, Fall 1999: 50–58; see also P. Stoett, "Counter-Bioinvasion: Conceptual and Governance Challenges," *Environmental Politics* 16, no. 3 (2007), 433–452.

40. See A. Price-Smith, *The Health of Nations: Infectious Disease, Environmental Change, and Their Effects on National Security and Development* (Cambridge: MIT Press, 2002).

41. An important contribution to this awareness was the famous text by R. Carson, *Silent Spring* (Boston: Houghton Mifflin, 1962).

42. See D. Munton and G. Castle, "Reducing Acid Rain, 1980s," in D. Munton and J. Kirton, eds., *Canadian Foreign Policy: Selected Cases* (Scarborough: Prentice Hall, 1992), 367–80. Critics charge that the G. W. Bush administration (2001–2009) slowly dismantled the Clean Air Act of 1972, thus harming this bilateral agreement as well.

43. J. Wargo, *Our Children's Toxic Legacy: How Science and Law Fail to Protect Us from Pesticides* (New Haven: Yale University Press, 1996), 281. Note that there is an energetic debate between those who wish to ban DDT outright and those who claim the pesticide is still necessary to kill disease-spreading mosquitoes in Africa.

44. See United Nations Department of Public Informaton, "Johannesburg Summit Secretary-General Calls for Global Action on Water Issues," Johannesburg Summit 2002, http://www.johannesburgsummit.

org/html/media_info/pressrelease_prep2/global_action_water_2103.pdf (accessed May 27, 2004), and *Global Environmental Outlook 4: Environment for Development* (New York: United Nations Environment Programme, 2007), 125. Water-related diseases include malaria, severe diarrhea, intestinal worms, trachoma (which causes blindness), cholera, and schistosomiasis.

45. See W. Ellis, "A Soviet Sea Lies Dying," *National Geographic*, February 1990, 73–93.

46. See L. Ohlsson, ed., *Hydropolitics: Conflicts over Water as a Development Constraint* (London: Zed, 1995). See also M. Lowi, *Water and Power: The Politics of a Scarce Resource in the Jordan River Basin* (Cambridge: Cambridge University Press, 1993); and the award-winning book by K. Conca, *Governing Water: Contentious Transnational Politics and Global Institution Building* (Cambridge, MA: MIT Press, 2006).

47. T. Homer-Dixon, "The Myth of Global Water Wars," *The Globe and Mail*, November 9, 1995, A23. He adds that the alarmist concern with inevitable water wars "distracts the public's attention from the real results of water scarcity. Shortages reduce food production, aggravate poverty and disease, spur large migrations and undermine a state's moral authority and capacity to govern. Over time, these stresses can tear apart a poor society's social fabric, causing chronic popular unrest and violence."

48. M. Falkenmark, A. Berntell, A. Jägerskog, J. Lundqvist, M. Matz, and H. Tropp, *On the Verge of a New Water Scarcity: A Call for Good Governance and Human Ingenuity*, SIWI Policy Brief (Stockholm: Stockholm International Water Institute, 2007), 6.

49. See, for example, M. Levy, "Is the Environment a National Security Issue?," *International Security* 20 (Fall 1995), 35–62; S. Dalby, op. cit.; and Astri Suhrke, "Environmental Change, Migration, and Conflict: A Lethal Feedback Dynamic?," in C. Crocker, F. Osler Hampson, and P. Aall, eds., *Managing Global Chaos: Sources of and Responses to International Conflict* (Washington, DC: United States Institute of Peace Press, 1996), 113–27.

50. See W. Thomas, *Scorched Earth: The Military's Assault on the Environment* (Philadelphia: New Society Publishers, 1995); N. Gleditsch, "Armed Conflict and the Environment," in P. Diehl and N. P. Gleditsch, eds., *Environmental Conflict* (Boulder, CO: Westview Press, 2001), 251–72; and S. Lanier-Graham, *The Ecology of War: Environmental Impacts of Weaponry and Warfare* (New York: Walker and Company, 1993); N. Brown, "Climate, Ecology and International Security," *Survival* 31 (1989), 519–32.

51. E. F. Roots, "International Agreements to Prohibit or Control Modification of the Environment for Military Purposes: An Historical Overview and Comments on Current Issues," in Bruno Schiefer, ed., *Verifying Obligations Respecting Arms Control and the Environment: A Post Gulf War Assessment* (Saskatchewan: University of Saskatchewan, 1992), 13–34, 13.

52. C. Sagan, "Nuclear War and Climatic Catastrophe: Some Policy Implications," *Foreign Affairs* 62 (Winter 1983/84), 257–92; J. Schell, *The Fate of the Earth* (New York: Knopf, 1982). See also C. Caufield, *Multiple Exposures: Chronicles of the Radiation Age* (London: Secker and Warburg, 1989).

53. See P. Robinson, *The Effects of Weapons on Ecosystems* (Toronto: Pergamon for UNEP, 1979), 15; and A. Westing, ed., *Herbicides in War* (London: Taylor and Francis, 1984). For a fascinating legal and sociological discussion of the reactions of American Vietnam veterans to Agent Orange, see J. Jacobs and D. McNamara, "Vietnam Veterans and the Agent Orange Controversy," *Armed Forces and Society* 13, no. 1 (1986), 57–80; and F. Wilcox, *Waiting for an Army to Die: The Tragedy of Agent Orange* (New York: Random House, 1983).

54. R. Falk, "Environmental Warfare and Ecocide: Facts, Appraisal, and Proposals," *Bulletin of Peace Proposals* 4, no. 1 (1973), 84.

55. E. DeSombre, *The Global Environment and World Politics: International Relations for the 21st Century* (London: Continuum, 2002), 46.

56. All quotes in this paragraph are from S. Pimiento Chamorro and E. Hammond, "Addressing Environmental Modification in Post–Cold War Conflict," paper presented to the Civil Society Conference to Review ENMOD and Related Agreements on Hostile Modification of the Environment, Amsterdam, May 2001, The Sunshine Project, http://www.edmonds-institute.org/pimiento.html (accessed May 30, 2004).

57. R. Harris and J. Paxman, *A Higher Form of Killing: The Secret Story of Gas and Germ Warfare* (London, UK: Chatto and Windus, 1982), 27. This is a fascinating book for anyone interested in the evolution of chemical and biological weapons.

58. T. Homer-Dixon, "Environmental Scarcities and Violent Conflict: Evidence from Cases," *International Security* 19 (Summer 1994); see also his *Environment, Scarcity, and Violence* (Princeton: Princeton University Press, 1999).

59. R. Timmons and B. Parks, *A Climate of Injustice: Global Inequality, North-South Politics, and Climate Policy* (Cambridge, MA: MIT Press, 2007), 146.

60. For an engaging read on this theme, see T. Homer-Dixon, *The Upside of Down: Catastrophe, Creativity, and the Renewal of Civilization* (Toronto: Alfred Knopf, 2006).

61. Thomas L. Friedman, *Hot, Flat, and Crowded: Why We Need a Green Revolution—and How It Can Renew America* (New York: Farrar, Straus and Giroux, 2008), 5.

62. M. Mason, "Citizenship Entitlements Beyond Borders? Identifying Mechanisms of Access and Redress for Affected Publics in International Environmental Laws," *Global Governance* 12, no. 3 (2006), 283–304, 285.

63. D. Freestone, "The Precautionary Principle," in R. Churchill and D. Freestone, eds., *International Law and Global Climate Change* (London: Graham and Trotham, 1991), 21–39. The debate over GMOs is especially indicative of the debates that can ensue over the implementation of this principle, as proponents argue the benefits of genetic manipulation outweigh the contested risks feared by opponents.

 ## Suggested Websites

Climate Action Network Europe
http://www.climnet.org

Energy and Environment Links
http://zebu.uoregon.edu/energy.html

EnviroLink
http://www.envirolink.org

Global Environmental Facility
http://www.gefweb.org

GreenNet
http://www.gn.apc.org

Intergovernmental Panel on Climate Change (IPCC)
http://www.ipcc.ch/index.htm

National Geographic (Environment)
http://environment.nationalgeographic.com/environment

TRAFFIC
http://www.traffic.org

UNEP
http://www.unep.ch

Union of Concerned Scientists
http://www.ucsusa.org

Worldwatch Institute
http://www.worldwatch.org

Population Growth, Movements, and Global Health

To couple the concept of freedom to breed with the belief that everyone born has an equal right to the commons is to lock the world into a tragic course of action.

—Garrett Hardin[1]

The existence of refugees is a symptom of the disappearance of economic and political liberalism. The basic real solution of the refugee problem, real or potential, is necessarily therefore related to the solution of the great problems of economic and political adjustment in the contemporary world.

—Sir John Hope Simpson, 1938[2]

INTRODUCTION

The preceding chapters on human rights, human security, and global ecopolitics are linked by the shared concern with the impact of population growth and population movements, as well as the quest to provide for human health needs. While the spectre of an overcrowded world is unsettling, the image of hundreds of millions of migrants and desperate refugees provokes even more anxiety. Some analysts insist these problems are exaggerated, and are only defined as "problems" because of a Western or rich-world bias. Others argue that population growth remains the gravest threat to the future of humanity. While this debate rages, refugee movements continue to challenge national sovereignty and human rights laws, and international surveillance of infectious disease is one of the key roles of many international organizations and global governance efforts today. As always, we are left wondering what types of international responses, national policies, and transnational activism can have a positive impact on the challenges posed by population growth and population movement.

Liberal institutionalists argue that governments should create regimes and strengthen international organizations and law to help us cope with these issues. In contrast, realists predict that states will respond to population movements and related problems by strengthening their laws to restrict immigration and increasing border security. Neo-Marxists have argued that both international organizations and state security are in effect further entrenching a global apartheid system whereby the poor and sick are neglected, marginalized, and perhaps even quarantined, to protect the relatively wealthy and healthy from potential harm. Feminists have long argued that the debate over population control has been a masculine moral construction that does not always take into account women's reproductive health and rights, and that migration's dark side—global trafficking for the sex trade—needs more serious treatment. Constructivists point out that much of the debate over population movement has become securitized; that is, it is seen as a security problem to be addressed by using instruments such as the police, border guards, and the army. Instead, the focus should be on the socioeconomic factors that actually drive population-related issues.

This chapter begins by asking whether overpopulation itself is the main problem we face. While population growth remains a serious global challenge, we are as concerned today with consumption patterns per capita as we are with sheer numbers of people. Furthermore, many states are more preoccupied with the effects of an aging population than a growing one. Next, we examine one of the more visible manifestations of population growth and movement, the increasing urbanization of our world, which (along with the climate change issue) is enhancing the political importance of the governance of cities in world affairs. We then discuss immediate concerns with population control measures, most notably their potential impact on women's reproductive health and rights.

From population issues themselves we move to populations on the move. We begin by discussing the causes and consequences of international migration, including efforts to protect international migrants, and the myriad human security threats associated with refugee movements. These include political persecution, the link between environmental degradation and population movements, the often invisible plight of the internally displaced, and the global sex trade. Finally, we close with a discussion of a topic that is intrinsically linked to all of these factors, namely the spread of infectious diseases, such as **HIV/AIDS**, **SARS**, the swine flu, and the avian flu.

THE OVERPOPULATION DEBATE

It is, in retrospect, hard to imagine a world in which overpopulation was not a topic for heated discussion, yet this has been the case for most of human history: the leaders of most political units (from villages to city-states to modern nation-states) have viewed population increases as a source of military and economic power. At the end of the last Ice Age, when people began migrating to the area we now know as the Americas, the entire earth probably supported fewer than 10 million people. By 1930, the population of the planet had reached 2 billion and by 1972, 3.85 billion. According to the UN Population Division, global population reached 6.7 billion in 2006. Predictions suggest the population of the planet will exceed 9 billion by 2050, an increase of 2.5 billion people (equivalent to the entire population of the planet in 1950) in just 43 years.[3]

Demographers liken population growth rates to large cargo ships: one can stop the engines, but it will be some time before the boat stops. Because so many women in the world today are of child-bearing age, even if fertility rates fall from the global average of 2.55 children per woman in 2006, world population will still increase dramatically until 2050. This population growth comes at a time when a major food crisis may be looming on the horizon. During the 1960s and 1970s, the so-called green revolution increased crop yields through the use of irrigation, pesticides, and fertilizer. This is a less viable option today, when almost all prime arable land has been put to use, the excessive use of pesticides has often caused more problems than it has solved, and the conversion of food crops to biofuel continues in many areas. The promise of GMOs (see Chapter 10) remains politically and scientifically contentious. Though enough food is available to feed everyone now, and malnutrition and undernourishment are largely a consequence of inadequate distribution, this may not be the case when we have nine billion people to feed. Current trends indicate that the distribution of food continues to be uneven, creating some areas of overindulgence and others of severe malnutrition. A sudden increase in food and commodity prices in 2008 made even basic foodstuffs unaffordable for millions of people worldwide, providing a warning of how fragile food security can be in a world of increasing demand, high energy costs, and growing reliance on non-local food sources.

Population growth is also distributed unevenly across the world's regions. The so-called **demographic transition** experienced by the industrialized countries involved the decline of both death and birth rates as medical technology reduced infant mortality and extended life spans. People also became less likely to raise large families due to a combination of birth control and advances in the economic and social status of women. As a result, many developed countries have birth rates below population replacement levels, raising a set of issues related to the "greying" of societies and debates over immigration. However, in many regions this demographic transition has not taken place. High infant mortality rates encourage parents to have more children since infant survival is less certain. With more limited economic or social opportunities, women tend to have more children at an earlier age. Larger families provide parents at least some prospect for care in old age in the absence of government social safety nets. Therefore, most of the population growth in the future will take place in lower-income states, with serious consequences for food security, environmental sustainability, employment opportunities, and provision of health care, education, and other social services (see Profile 11.1).

PROFILE 11.1 **The 20 Most Populous States, 2009**

Note: As with all statistics, we must be cautious about accepting population figures; they are at best crude estimates, based on government census data that often exclude the homeless and those living in remote rural areas, and that are subject to sudden changes due to war, pandemics, and natural disasters.

1. China 1,346,000,000
2. India 1,198,000,000
3. United States 315,000,000
4. Indonesia 230,000,000
5. Brazil 194,000,000
6. Pakistan 181,000,000
7. Bangladesh 162,000,000
8. Nigeria 155,000,000
9. Russian Federation 141,000,000
10. Japan 127,000,000
11. Mexico 110,000,000

12. Philippines 92,000,000
13. Vietnam 88,000,000
14. Egypt 83,000,000
15. Ethiopia 83,000,000
16. Germany 82,000,000
17. Turkey 75,000,000
18. Iran (Islamic Republic of) 74,000,000
19. Thailand 68,000,000
20. Dem. Republic of the Congo 66,000,000
    Canada 33,504,680

SOURCES: POPULATION DIVISION OF THE DEPARTMENT OF ECONOMIC AND SOCIAL AFFAIRS OF THE UNITED NATIONS SECRETARIAT, *WORLD POPULATION PROSPECTS: THE 2008 REVISION* (NEW YORK: UNITED NATIONS, 2009), TABLE A3, 11, HTTP://WWW.UN.ORG/ESA/POPULATION/UNPOP.HTM (ACCESSED MARCH 28, 2009); STATISTICS CANADA ESTIMATES FOR JANUARY 2009, HTTP://WWW.STATCAN.GC.CA/START-DEBUT-ENG.HTML (ACCESSED MARCH 28, 2009).

In China and India, each with well over one billion citizens, it is doubtful any sort of transition can stem massive population increases. Many argue that China's one-child policy, while a threat to individual liberty (and to the lives of consequently unwanted children—usually female), was a necessary step that should be followed elsewhere to avoid a global "population bomb." The idea of a population bomb was popularized in the 1970s by writers such as Paul and Anne Ehrlich, who argued that massive increases in population threatened not just the standard of living of people around the globe, but human life itself.[4] In what has become a classic piece of **neo-Malthusian** literature, "The Tragedy of the Commons," professor of human ecology Garrett Hardin argued that we simply cannot afford to allow population increases to continue to grow, and that to ensure our future collective survival the freedom to reproduce must be limited.[5]

Of course, many dismiss this as an extreme position. Some argue population growth will level off with economic prosperity as economic development ushers in a demographic transition similar to that experienced by the industrialized countries. State control of reproduction is certainly viewed as an infringement on civil liberties in most countries, and contradicts the conventions espoused by most religions. Others suggest that high populations themselves are not to blame for global environmental problems. These problems are caused by the high consumption patterns and large ecological footprints of people in the high-income world. According to a classic formula developed in the 1960s, the environmental impacts of population size, affluence (i.e., consumption), and technology are interrelated.[6] This formula suggests that while absolute increases in population do put added strains on ecosystems, what that population consumes (and how it does so) is just as important. However, while the industrialized countries have clearly contributed more to global warming and other environmental problems than lower-income countries, one cannot ignore the substantial environmental and consumption impact that millions more people have on the planet each year. It should be clear, then, that both the North and the South have an important role to play in decreasing the negative effects of population growth.

China's one-child policy, which began in the early 1990s, has been the most controversial with respect to the ethics of government imposed birth control. Renamed the Population and Family Planning Law in 2002, the policy in fact limits reproduction to one child for each couple in the cities, and two for those who live in rural areas and whose first child is a girl. Families of ethnic minorities are allowed to have two or three children. This demonstrates some sensitivity to the problems of gendercide and ethnocide the original policy entailed. The Chinese government claims that the policy has led to 300 million fewer births to the world's biggest population and it has vowed to maintain the policy in order to achieve its goal of controlling the population at the 1.6 billion level by 2050. Inducements to comply include charging fees for services for second children that were free for the first and rewarding single-child couples with promotions at work and free university education for the child. Abortions are strongly "encouraged" in the advent of a second pregnancy. In some cases, this policy has resulted in **infanticide**: since baby boys are more highly valued than girls, couples intent on having a son may resort to murder should a girl be produced. Similarly, families in India, China, and elsewhere have used prenatal amniocentesis and ultrasound scanning to discover the sex of fetuses, and then aborted the females.[7] During the 1970s, China's fertility rate fell from 6 children per woman to about 2.5. Despite this drop, most people would agree that China still has a tremendous overpopulation problem. However, the ethical questions remain and will become only more pronounced as governments and international aid agencies struggle with continued population growth.

While a UN Conference on Population and Development in Cairo in 1994 did produce a vague plan to prevent world population from exceeding 7.2 billion people by 2015, the plan relies entirely on the ability and political will of states to invest in development measures, and it remains to be seen whether states will actually commit the resources this entails. We should also bear in mind that some states, such as Canada, are more concerned with aging populations and actually seek to raise birth rates in the short term. Ultimately, it is up to individual governments to stem poverty and provide family-planning possibilities and the record so far is not encouraging. Two of the more visible outcomes of the population explosion are urbanization and the demand for family-planning policies in crowded states.

URBANIZATION

One of the most pronounced effects of population growth and movement is urbanization.[8] The world passed a demographic milestone in 2008, when it was estimated that half of the world's population (or approximately 3.3 billion people) lived in urban areas.[9] In recent years, increased attention has been devoted to the challenges of urbanization, especially with respect to governance, poverty and slums, the provision of services, and environmental sustainability. With the number of people living in cities expected to reach six billion (two-thirds of the world's population) in 2050, this is likely to be one of the growing areas of study in global politics. The city has often been viewed as a primary indicator of "modernity"; urbanization followed industrialization, which meant that **gross national product (GNP)** was increasing and society was advancing toward the Western ideal. Cities came to symbolize a certain notion of progress, but do the steel and glass highrises of Bangkok and Shanghai offer positive proof of the development of Thailand and China? Or do they merely put a glittering face on the detrimental effects of rapid economic growth? Is the quality of life in burgeoning Mexico City an improvement over life in rural Mexico?

The pure logic behind the quest for the city is clear. Big cities with high population densities reduce the unit costs of infrastructure: it becomes cheaper to supply essential services (such as water, electricity, and education) to people if they live closer together. Companies are more likely to invest in cities, where both labour pools and urban middle-class markets are more easily accessible than they are in remote areas. Employment opportunities, and the image of a better life, attract migratory labour. And since all this activity is highly concentrated, it can be regulated by government and, to the extent possible under a market economy, urban planning can facilitate a more humane, less alienating centre of human life. For example, some cities favour an "eco-density" approach to urban planning and public transport that is con-

A universal problem: A homeless man eats his lunch in his make-shift shelter along the Paris ring road, 2008. (AP Photo/Remy de la Mauviniere/CP Archive.)

sidered more environmentally sustainable than sprawling suburbs served by highways, and many cities have joined climate change initiatives and made other efforts to reduce their ecological footprint. However, if cities produce more pollution than can be safely managed, if traffic congestion not only creates smog but also actually impedes transportation, if neighbouring land is degraded because of waste disposal needs and excessive demands on natural resources, and if most rural–urban migrants end up in unsanitary and politically marginalized shantytowns, is urbanization really a step in the right developmental direction? Increasingly, analysts of sustainable development cast rapid urbanization in a negative light. This view is tied, of course, to population growth. Most dramatically, the spectre of rising **megacities**, great centres of sprawl, chaos, and pollution, looms over many countries around the world (see Profile 11.2). The air quality at the summer 2008 Olympics in Beijing was perhaps a startling revelation for viewers of the games, but experts have long lamented the impact of rapid urbanization on human and environmental health. Interestingly, the megacity is itself an important actor in national and global politics (see Profile 11.3).

PROFILE 11.2 Megacities

Generally, *megacities* or *urban agglomerations* are defined as those with more than 10 million inhabitants. Below we list the world's megacities in 1975 and 2007, and the projected populations of these megacities in 2025. Of course, by 2025 many new cities will be counted as megacities.

Note: It is very difficult to compare estimates of city size, since different surveys include different areas as part of city centres. For example, if we exclude the suburban areas around New York, Los Angeles, or Tokyo, their population would be considerably reduced. In addition, the homeless often go uncounted. Finally, cities can have an incentive to exaggerate their numbers for purposes of obtaining funding.

All numbers below are in millions.

MEGACITIES, 1975	MEGACITIES, 2007	PROJECTED 2007 MEGACITY POPULATIONS, 2025
Tokyo, Japan 26.6	Tokyo 35.7	Tokyo 36.4
New York, USA 15.9	New York 19.0	New York 20.6
Mexico City, Mexico 10.7	Mexico City 19.0	Mexico City 21.0
	Mumbai (Bombay), India 19.0	Mumbai 26.4
	São Paulo, Brazil 18.8	São Paulo 21.4
	Delhi, India 15.9	Delhi 22.5
	Shanghai, China 15.0	Shanghai 19.4
	Kolkata (Calcutta), India 14.8	Kolkata (Calcutta), 20.6
	Dhaka, Bangladesh 13.5	Dhaka, 22.0
	Buenos Aires, Brazil 12.8	Buenos Aires, 13.8
	Los Angeles, USA 12.5	Los Angeles, 13.7
	Karachi, Pakistan 12.1	Karachi, 19.1
	Al-Qahirah (Cairo), Egypt 11.9	Al-Qahirah (Cairo), 15.6
	Rio de Janeiro, Brazil 11.7	Rio de Janeiro, 13.4
	Osaka/Kobe, Japan 11.3	Osaka/Kobe, 11.4
	Beijing, China 11.1	Beijing, 14.5
	Manila, Philippines 11.1	Manila, 14.8
	Moskva (Moscow), Russia 10.5	Moskva (Moscow) 10.5
	Istanbul, Turkey 10.1	Istanbul 12.1

PROFILE 11.3 **An Emerging Global Megacity System?**

Here is an interesting scenario: As globalization reduces the importance of the nation-state, the megacity replaces it as the primary means of expressing political power and conducting global interaction. The trend toward the megacity is evident in Ontario, where the provincial government amalgamated the different districts of Toronto into one big administration, and in Montreal, where the same thing happened in 2003 (neither effort proceeded without controversy). Business today is conducted largely between cities, not countries. Likewise, travel is from metropolis to metropolis. As cities increase in size and wealth, devouring more of the countryside around them, the megacity may become the most important political unit. This is not without historical precedent: in the period 800 to 322 B.C.E., a Greek city-state system flourished. The population of the cities varied: larger states such as Syracuse, Acragas, and Athens had around 50,000 citizens, while smaller cities, such as Siris and Thourioi in Sicily, had but several

thousand. Eventually, Athens formed a far-reaching empire that kept other cities under domination; this move was opposed by Sparta and other cities in the Peloponnesian League. War between the two alliances broke out in 431 B.C.E., and the entire system fell to Philip of Macedonia later that century. Might we see a world where dominant cities such as New York, London, and Tokyo battle it out for commercial and cultural supremacy? While this is an interesting scenario, most states retain tight control over borders in the post–September 11 era, and large cities are especially vulnerable to terrorist attack. This suggests that if megacities are to rise as the new centres of autonomous political power, they will have to usurp the traditional, jealously guarded security role played by the national state apparatus first, which is unlikely.

SEE K. HOLSTI, *INTERNATIONAL POLITICS: A FRAMEWORK FOR ANALYSIS*, 7TH ED. (ENGLEWOOD CLIFFS, NJ: PRENTICE HALL, 1995), 36; THE AUTHOR ALSO CITES K. FREEMAN, *GREEK CITY STATES* (LONDON: METHUEN, 1948). SEE ALSO G. MODELSKI, *WORLD CITIES: –3000 TO 2000* (WASHINGTON, DC: FAROS, 2003); AND P. KING AND P. TAYLOR, EDS., *WORLD CITIES IN A WORLD-SYSTEM* (CAMBRIDGE, UK: CAMBRIDGE UNIVERSITY PRESS, 1995).

It is clear that the combination of urbanization, poverty, poor services, and lax regulations can have disastrous environmental effects. Katmandu, Nepal, a city designed for some 40,000 occupants, now has more than 710,000, and the famous Katmandu Valley is covered by a blue haze of pollution from cars, wood fires, kilns, and construction, which forces pedestrians and cyclists to wear cloth masks (a scene common in Mexico City as well as many other urban centres). The rapid urbanization of Bhopal, India was what made the 1984 industrial accident in that city so disastrous in terms of human casualties, as leaked gas from a Union Carbide pesticide plant descended on the sleeping occupants of a nearby shantytown, killing thousands. Only 2 percent of Bangkok is connected to city sewers. Violence is common in many urban centres throughout the world, as are illicit forms of economic activity; schooling is relatively inadequate, and there are fewer social opportunities for restless youth. In Kibera, Kenya, the biggest slum in Africa, where population density can exceed 89,000 per square kilometre (mostly without sanitation or electricity systems), the government has been bulldozing shantytown dwellers' shacks into the ground, leaving them homeless. The sorry list goes on and on: infrastructure unable to meet city demands; unequal access to the available infrastructure; and lack of precautions against the environmental risks, both natural and industrial, that face certain segments of city populations.[10] Rural populations, meanwhile, have to play the role of provider to the large city, not only servicing it with food, wood, textile resources, and other commodities, but also absorbing the pollution and waste expelled.

However, none of this guarantees that megacities must become violent, overcrowded dystopias in the future. Many cities are coping well with growth, adopting cleaner environmental standards and recycling programs that lower the total waste burden, pursuing urban agriculture, attracting tourists with their historical importance while protecting cherished monuments, and diversifying their economic activities to avoid the traps inherent in dependent development. Large cities are centres of commerce and culture, and they continue to play a leading role in defining the nation-state (New York is inextricably linked to the U.S., London to the U.K., and Tokyo to Japan) while revealing the reach of globalization (most major retail and entertainment outlets can be found in cities as diverse as Paris, Shanghai, and Mexico City). The dangers are that urban growth will spiral out of control, marginalized urban populations will continue to suffer, and urban bias will lead to the further neglect and exploitation of the rural countryside. But, as we will now see, efforts to control population growth are in inherently controversial and often quite dangerous.

WOMEN'S RIGHTS AND BIRTH CONTROL

If we do accept the proposition that overpopulation is a real and urgent problem, we must ask next what we can do about it and what ethical implications will be raised. Birth control has been the technological cause of reduced fertility in the industrialized North, combining with higher education levels and higher standards of living to reduce reproductive rates. As mentioned earlier, China's highly controversial "one-child" policy has been credited with lowering birth rates, but critics charge it has made unfair demands of parents, especially mothers, and has even resulted in the infanticide of girls and forced abortions. In the South, irreversible female sterilization is often the most common form of birth control. Concerns have been raised about the health impact of new birth control technologies, such as a drug called quinacrine, which is in fact an antimalarial drug that causes scar tissue if placed directly in the womb. The scarring causes the fallopian tubes to become permanently blocked. Quinacrine also damages DNA in bacteria, so experts worry it might cause cancer in women. It was banned in India in 1998, but remained in use in West Bengal, Chile, the Philippines, Venezuela, Vietnam, and elsewhere.[11]

Beyond immediate health concerns, many raise questions regarding the ethical appropriateness of encouraging women—largely rural, uneducated women in developing countries—to submit themselves to birth control measures (men are also encouraged to pursue vasectomies). A common complaint is that the population issue, when it gets into the hands of government leaders and international bureaucrats at the UN and elsewhere, becomes a quantified issue or a numbers game. Groups such as the International Planned Parenthood Federation promote birth control as a means toward greater societal stability but thus deflect attention from women's sexuality and reproductive freedom.[12] The abortion issue is even more divisive, since many religious representatives refuse to deal with policies that they think legitimize abortion-on-demand. During the Reagan and both Bush administrations, the United States refused to fund Planned Parenthood programs because of their acceptance of abortion and contraception; the Obama administration has once again reversed this policy. Yet the health impacts of unsafe abortion practices pose a major threat to women in many regions today.

Others argue that instead of focusing on reducing sheer numbers, policies designed to limit population increases should concentrate on infant mortality and women's health. The lack of access to health care is a primary factor here. A 2005 study released by the **World Health Organization (WHO)** estimated that 536,000 women die from pregnancy-related causes each year, almost all these deaths (99 percent) occurring in low-income states.[13] In the developing countries, complications associated with pregnancy are often the leading causes of death among women of child-bearing age. In 2005, maternal mortality rates in low-income states averaged 450 in 100,000 births. In contrast, the maternal mortality rate in the higher-income states averaged just 9 in 100,000. The maternal mortality rate was highest in Sub-Saharan Africa at 900 deaths per 100,000 births.[14] Many families are further burdened with the growing transference of diseases such as HIV/AIDS to newborns.

We should also consider the words of Mahbub ul Haq, a famous Pakistani economist and former special advisor to the administrator of the UN Development Programme (UNDP) who passed away in 1998. While he was the minister of planning and finance in Pakistan (1982–88) he worked hard, aided by a **USAID** grant, to "saturate the villages with condoms." Nonetheless, "it was my greatest policy disaster. Despite the campaign, the population growth rate actually went up, from 3 to 3.1 percent. What went wrong? The answer is that female literacy in the villages was only 6 percent. Without investing in educating women, it was naïve to expect investment in condoms to yield any effective results. If I had to do it all over again, I would put almost all that money into boosting female literacy."[15] These are hard-learned lessons, and there simply is not enough development funding to afford repeating such mistakes. Of course, birth control is the responsibility of men as well. Millions of men have undergone vasectomies in the past two decades, and medical advances may make it possible for men to take a birth control pill themselves. Failing this, the good, old-fashioned condom is a safe and reliable way to avoid unwanted pregnancy and to protect partners from sexually transmitted diseases.

We now turn to one of the more pronounced effects of a heavily populated world: the rise in mobility of people in the form of both migrants and refugees. One of the primary stimulants to migration has always been employment opportunity, so we begin with a brief look at the contemporary context.

MIGRATION AND GLOBAL POLITICS

People have always been on the move, for the purpose of escape, enrichment, or just plain adventure. As Sidney Klein has demonstrated, mass migrations "go back millions of years," long before the advent of the modern nation-state.[16] To name just a few examples, early movements in Mesopotamia of Assyrians and Hittites, and of Indo-Europeans into India, date back to 2000 B.C.E. The people who developed Greek civilization filtered down through the Balkan peninsula to the shores of the Aegean Sea about 1900 B.C.E., undermining the older Cretan civilization, and around 1150 B.C.E. other Greek-speaking tribes invaded from the North. The Greeks would go on to form the city-states, such as Athens and Sparta, which many historians view as the beginning of the international system (see Chapter 2).

Many generations later, the industrializing states of Europe used the emigration of tens of millions of Europeans to head off a looming overpopulation problem in the 19th and early 20th centuries; they encouraged immigration in the post–World War II period to provide the labourers needed for reconstruction. In fact, Europe's burgeoning cities would have suffered from unprecedented overpopulation between 1840 and 1940 were it not for the migration of almost 60 million people from Europe to countries such as the United States, Russia, Argentina, Canada, Brazil, and Australia. The great European exodus was caused by a combination of push and pull factors. Politically, the age of individual liberalism meant that people were for the first time literally free to move. Europeans were pushed out of Europe by rises in population and scarcity of work; in an extreme case, millions fled the famine in Ireland in 1846. As usual, technological advances played a decisive role as well. The steamship made it easier, and cheaper, to cross the sea (an experience enjoyed previously only by the very rich or by sailors). Railroads were instrumental in distributing people to and from ports. Some people were fleeing from political persecution. On the pull side, many of the receiving states actively campaigned to attract Europeans as valuable labourers and farmers (exceptions to this pattern were Australia and New Zealand, which discouraged the importation of cheap labour).

Today, economists still consider migration (the crossing of borders for temporary or permanent stay) the result of push–pull factors. Unemployment, low wages, environmental deterioration, warfare, and other negatives push migrants (or, in more extreme cases, refugees), while the promise of employment, higher wages, education for children, and other positive expectations pull them into big cities and across borders. Employment has always been the central concern for economists dealing with migration and, until recently, it may be argued that migration was largely considered an employment-related phenomenon. The world's labour force is projected to grow by almost one billion during the next two decades, mostly in countries hard pressed to generate anywhere near an adequate number of jobs. Already, the human traffic within countries like China is startling, and the global recession which began in 2008 is only exacerbating this phenomenon. Policymakers also have to grapple with the question of what to do about this movement when international boundaries are involved. Despite the rhetoric of proponents of globalization, borders remain very relevant in immigration, refugee, and migrant worker policy. The efforts of the United States and the European Union to control migration are important examples.

The migration of peoples, in all its forms, has become much more prominent in global politics in the last few years. In 2008, there were over 200 million migrants worldwide, meaning that about 3 percent of the global population lives outside its country of birth. Most migration remains stimulated by economic motives, and most of it is legal; only approximately 10 to 15 percent of the global migrant population is unauthorized or illegal (see Profile 11.4).[17] The economic impact of migration is far from insignificant. Remittance money (sent home by migrants) is an important source of income for families and for developing countries.[18] In fact, the annual amount of remittances (estimated at over US$337 billion in 2007) is more than the annual amount of foreign aid flows.[19] While the predominant image of an economic

---

PROFILE 11.4 Migrants and Refugees: What Is the Difference?

Generally speaking, the difference between "migrants" and "refugees" is that the former leave their country voluntarily, while the latter are forced to do so. Migrants are individuals who cross international borders with the aim of settling in another country (tourists and business travellers are not considered migrants). On the other hand, refugees have fled their country of origin due to persecution (or fear of persecution) based on race, religion, nationality, or political beliefs, and as a result are unwilling to return to their home country. However, the distinction between voluntary and involuntary movement of peoples is necessarily fuzzy. Many migrants and refugees are fleeing economic hardship or political instability. Verifying the accuracy of claims of

persecution or fear of persecution is difficult. Anthony Richmond prefers the terms *proactive* and *reactive* migration. We should note also the existence of another category of migrants who are usually labelled *unauthorized*, *illegal*, or *nondocumented* migrants or aliens. According to the Program of Action of the International Conference on Population and Development (ICPD), documented migrants are "those who satisfy all the legal requirements to enter, stay and, if applicable, hold employment in the country of destination." By this definition, all others are "illegal." See also Profile 11.6 on Civil War refugees and Canada.

See A. Richmond, *Global Apartheid: Refugees, Racism, and the New World Order* (Oxford: Oxford University Press, 1994).

migrant is an individual who comes from a low-income country and settles in a high-income country, in fact about 40 percent of migrants move to another middle-income or lower-income country. Migration is generally beneficial to the recipient country (particularly those countries with ageing populations), since some migrant workers have skills that may be in short supply in fast-changing economies, while others are willing to do jobs considered unde-sirable. On the other hand, while remittances can be economically valuable for developing countries, "brain drain" is a serious problem in many countries struggling to retain their skilled workers, professionals, health providers, and scientists.

It is also important to understand that ethnicity and population movements are often closely connected. Two terms frequently used to reflect this are *irredenta* and *diaspora*. Irredenta are "territorially based minorities contiguous to a state controlled by their co-ethnics," people who often call for the right to self-determination.[20] Hitler used Germans living abroad to encourage acceptance of his expansionist foreign policy. A Malay–Muslim majority inhabits Thailand's four Southern provinces, though Malaysia and Thailand have maintained fairly good relations over the last few decades. Irredenta are created by shifts in political geography—the movement of borders induced by occupation or annexation, for example. Diaspora, however, are created by migration; they are groups of people who live outside their area of ethnic origin. Many diasporas have been very influential because of their cosmopolitan orientation, diverse language skills, and commercial contacts. Examples include Jews and Greeks in the Ottoman Empire, Germans in Tsarist Russia, and Chinese in many Asian states, including Thailand and Malaysia. Other diaspora are linked more directly to population movements induced by the opportunity of working abroad, such as Algerians and Senegalese in France, Jamaicans and Pakistanis in Great Britain, and Mexicans and Filipinos in the United States. These groups often become permanent citizens, and, as in the case of the American Cuban community, they can be quite vocal in political terms.

Despite the economic value of migration, there is a growing public backlash in many developed countries against illegal immigration, refugees, and asylum seekers. For example, the 2007 election campaign of French President Nicolas Sarkozy was openly hostile to foreigners. Italian politicians blamed migrants for the death of a woman in Rome in 2007, touching off a series of violent attacks against migrants, and the reelected Italian prime minister, Silvio Berlusconi, has made migrant crime a major issue. In much of Europe, there is concern that Muslim immigrants in particular have not integrated into society and hold values inconsistent with social norms. Violence against immigrants has become common in Europe, while protests against discrimination have taken place since 2005, with some protests turning violent. In the spring of 2008, nearly 50 migrant workers were killed in South Africa. In the United States, where 12 million illegal migrants live, opposition to immigration has grown steadily. An immigration-reform bill failed to pass Congress despite the support of President Bush and Republican and Democratic Party leaders. An increasing number of people worldwide are worried that migrant workers will take jobs or will change the character of a society. Governments are more likely to view migrants as an economic burden or a security threat (especially in the context of international terrorism). As pressure grows for governments to adopt more stringent rules for immigrants, refugees, and asylum seekers, illegal immigration and forced expulsions might become even more frequent.

If the world had no sovereign nation-states and no borders, there would be few political constraints on population movements. According to a simple economic model, labour follows capital. In other words, a truly borderless world would mean that people would flock to sources of employment, wherever they might be. However, there would be other constraints on popu-lation movements. Access to transportation would be a key factor, as it has been throughout history, and although it is now possible to travel long distances, by plane, ship, or train, with modest financial means, rising fuel prices might reintroduce this constraint for most people. Another constraint would be family ties and cultural affinity, perhaps most importantly the link between people and the land on which they were born and raised. Another constraint on movement is a rather difficult thing to measure: contentment. If people are relatively satisfied with the standard of living they enjoy, they will not see a need to move on. The Europeans who flooded the United States and Canada in the late 19th century were leaving in search of a better life, just as many migrants from developing states are doing today when they move toward wealthier societies, sometimes under illegal and perilous conditions. In a world divided between rich and poor, there is more pressure than ever for economic migration, and were it not for the immigration controls afforded by borders, the flow would presumably be much greater. We do not, however, live in a borderless world (despite what some of the more assertive advocates of globalization have been telling us). In fact, the migration and refugee issue-area reinforces the concept of the state system based on territory and sovereignty, for much of the world lives behind relatively closed borders, and states are increasingly protecting their own citizens before admitting others.

Realists would argue that increased population pressure and migration, far from encouraging convergence and cooperation, will be a source of divergence and conflict in the world system. As migration increases states will take ever more desperate measures to protect their borders from foreign intrusion. This fact is most evident in the **immigration** and border control policies of states. Trade liberalization encourages capital mobility, but there has not been a commensurate opening of borders to labour migration. If anything, the opposite has occurred as governments in the rich world increase entry requirements and attempt to lure only those migrants who can clearly afford to pay their own way or possess the means to contribute to or invest in the economy. Nowhere is this as acute as in Europe, where the fall of the Soviet Union and Eastern bloc states led to one wave of **emigration** (see Profile 11.5), while in recent years a second wave of migrants from North Africa and the Middle East have caused growing concern in EU countries. While labour mobility is famously fluid within the EU, it is another thing to get into the EU from the outside. As opposition to migrants increases in Europe, governments have placed more emphasis on border controls. The EU has established a border security organization known as Frontex, which is responsible for (among other things) preventing illegal immigration into the EU using patrol boats, spotter aircraft, and radar. We need not stop at Europe, however, for a look at contemporary efforts to control migrant flows. America's border with Mexico is guarded by walls and fences and patrolled by 36,000 border guards equipped with infrared and motion detectors

An uncertain future. Migrants wait for instructions from Spanish authorities off the Canary Island of Tenerife, Spain. In June 2008, the European Union approved a new set of common rules for expelling illegal immigrants. (AP Photo/Arturo Rodriguez/CP Archive.)

PROFILE 11.5 Mass Migration and the Former Soviet Union

Few areas have experienced the type of turmoil brought on by the dissolution of the Soviet Union in the late 1980s. One of the more pronounced effects of this political transformation was a huge exodus of ethnic groups across the region. After 1989, more than nine million people left their homes because of ethnic tension or environmental disasters. This figure means that 1 out of every 30 residents of the former Soviet Union migrated! Many of them were Russians moving back into Russia from former republics such as Ukraine, Latvia, and Belarus. They had originally moved as part of Moscow's efforts to "Russify" outlying areas, but after the fall of the Soviet Union they felt relatively unsafe outside Russia. In other cases it is clear that people were forced to migrate: some 3.6 million refugees have fled from the Armenia–Azerbaijan war and the fighting in Chechnya in the mid-1990s alone. Many of the migrants were trying to return to ancestral homelands after their previous forced evacuation during the Stalin era. Slavs moved in large numbers from the five new states of Central Asia—Turkmenistan, Uzbekistan, Kazakhstan, Tajikistan, and Kyrgyzstan. The severe environmental decay of the Aral Sea in Central Asia, radiation in the Semipalatinsk nuclear testing range, and the infamous Chernobyl meltdown (see Chapter 10) also forced citizens to move themselves and their belongings to other areas. Given the economic crises Russia faced, many educated and highly skilled people sought employment elsewhere, leading to a severe "brain drain" crisis. In addition, a very disturbing trend has emerged involving the emigration of Russian women who are being trafficked into the global sex industry: tens of thousands of women have left the former Soviet Union under these circumstances since 1990. The economic crisis in the late 2000s can only exacerbate the trend.

SOURCES: R. EVANS, "MASS INTERNAL MIGRATIONS UNSETTLE FORMER SOVIET STATES," *THE GLOBE AND MAIL*, MAY 23, 1996; AND T. HELENIAK, MIGRATION INFORMATION SOURCE OF THE MIGRATION POLICY INSTITUTE, "MIGRATION DILEMMAS HAUNT POST-SOVIET RUSSIA," HTTP://WWW.MIGRATIONINFORMATION. ORG/PROFILES/DISPLAY.CFM?ID=62 (ACCESSED APRIL 28, 2004).

and spotter drones, helicopters, and all-terrain vehicles. India is completing construction of a 4,100-kilometre fence along its border with Bangladesh to keep out migrants from that country. Physical border security is not the only mechanism used to prevent illegal migration. The United Kingdom is introducing identity cards for foreigners, and France is planning to use DNA tests to verify that migrant families are in fact related. The EU has a fingerprint database for asylum seekers, and in the United States every detained illegal immigrant is fingerprinted and entered into a database available to law enforcement agencies, while an electronic system called E-Verify allows employers to check whether workers are authorized to be in the country. Similar measures are likely to be introduced in Canada. These measures have drawn criticism from human rights advocates and fuelled charges of racism and **xenophobia** (a fear or hatred of others not in one's social or ethnic group).

Will tighter border controls work? Interceptions of illegal migrants have fallen in recent years in Europe and the United States, and some claim this as evidence of the success of more heavily guarded borders. However, the sheer volume of migrants guarantees that some will always manage to pass even the most heavily guarded borders. There is evidence that organized criminal groups are benefiting by charging huge sums to transport migrants into the EU or the U.S. The harder the journey, the more these criminal groups benefit. Furthermore, increasingly desperate migrants are attempting more dangerous routes into Europe and America, crossing turbulent seas in flimsy craft, trekking through desert, or travelling in cargo containers. As a result, thousands die every year. Ironically, tight border controls discourage migrants from leaving: the tougher the border, the more likely a migrant is to stay permanently and have their family attempt to join them. Finally, there is the reality that rich economies need foreign labour, even as public attitudes toward migrants have become more negative.

For these reasons, alternatives to fences and surveillance have been put forward. One idea is called *circular migration*: migrants are let into a country for a specific period of time and then are required to return after that time has expired. This has been attempted in Spain to accommodate seasonal labour demand in the agricultural and tourism sectors. Another alternative is the active recruitment of migrant workers by employers in rich countries, with the assistance of governments in both rich and poor states. It is unclear if such measures, long practised in Canada, Germany, and elsewhere, have resolved the problem of migrants refusing to return home and disappearing into the local diaspora, or reduced the social hostility toward migrants that favours tight border controls. Finally, there is the question of citizenship, and establishing a legal basis by which unauthorized or illegal migrants can become legal residents. This has proved controversial in the United States, where a Bush administration plan to offer a way for unauthorized migrants to become legal while also tightening border controls was rejected by public pressure and Congressional opposition. Critics of the plan felt that amnesty arrangements for illegal migrants would penalize legal migrants and encourage more illegal entries. Ultimately, migration is a challenge to the concept of citizenship and nation, and an important reflection of the tension between a world of sovereign, territorial states and the eternal push and pull factors that drive population movements.

Migration has become an increasingly important subject for international diplomacy. Since 2001, the International Organization for Migration (IOM) has conducted a dialogue process designed to promote an exchange of views and cooperation on migration issues. In July 2007 the first Global Forum on Migration and Development was convened in Brussels to promote international dialogue and cooperation on migration. The forum, which consisted of 43 countries, the EU, and a large number of civil society actors and international organizations, emphasized the relationship between migration and development, and promoted legal migration as an opportunity for development in both origin and destination countries. The central topics of discussion were labour mobility, remittances, and policy coherence across countries and international institutions. Human rights and gender-sensitive policies were also recognized as key components of the migration dialogue.[21] While the intent of the forum was to develop international cooperation on migration and share different experiences and strategies, there were few expectations that the forum would lead to significant change in national and regional migration policies.

PROTECTING MIGRANT WORKERS

Protecting migrant workers has been a special area of emphasis in international diplomacy and cooperation on migration issues. Migrant workers often end up in vulnerable positions and are perceived as needing additional, international protection.[22] However, this is a very sensitive issue area, since it falls within the jurisdiction of individual states to govern their own domestic labour laws. Previous work by the International Labour Organization (ILO) helped form the basis for what is arguably the most important UN General Assembly resolution dealing with migrant labour, the International Convention on the Protection of the Rights of All Migrant Workers and Members of Their Families. This is a comprehensive document that, at present, has not been signed or ratified by the majority of UN states, including Canada. It requests governments to pursue nondiscriminatory practices regarding migrant employees, including undocumented migrants, and their families. It is, in essence, an attempt to guarantee migrant workers the same rights that are already enshrined in the Universal Declaration of Human Rights (1948) and the subsequent International Covenants on Human Rights. For example, Article 10 states that "No migrant worker or member of his or her family shall be held in slavery or servitude"; Article 12 calls for their right to "freedom of thought, conscience and religion," including the right to "ensure the religious and moral education of their children in conformity with their own convictions"; and Article 18 gives migrants "the right to equality with nationals of the State concerned before the courts and tribunals."

At a much more visible level, the UN Conference on Population and Development at Cairo (1994) was precedent-setting in that it included migration on its agenda. The most significant outcome was the establishment of the Program of Action of the International Conference on Population and Development (ICPD). Canada pushed strongly to include migration on the ICPD agenda. Chapters IX and X of the ICPD Program of Action discuss contemporary migration pressures, assuming a broad scope on the topic, including the role of development, documented and undocumented migrants, refugees, asylum seekers, and displaced persons. The program suggests that the North–South gap in wealth be reduced; that migrants' remittances be facilitated and channelled into productive investment in developing states; that discriminatory practices that harm migrants, including current outbreaks of racism and xenophobia be stopped; that family reunification of migrants be promoted; that the exploitation of undocumented migrants be prevented; and, related to the latter, that international trafficking in migrants (especially for the purpose of prostitution) be prevented. As with all such sweeping statements, most of this is a lot easier said than done, and like the UN General Assembly Convention described above, progress has been slow in the face of governments reluctant to commit to migrant worker protection and anti-migrant worker sentiment in destination countries.

Another multilateral effort to aid migrants has been the work of the aforementioned IOM, which has assisted in many efforts to help refugees but also helps migrants settle in new areas and acquire needed job skills. By 1976 the IOM had permanent offices in Indonesia, Malaysia, Singapore, and Thailand. In the 1980s the IOM became increasingly involved in migration and refugee assistance in Latin America and in 1991 was entrusted by the UN Disaster Relief Coordinator to organize the **repatriation** of foreigners stranded in the Gulf region after Iraq's invasion of Kuwait; this amounted to some 200,000 repatriations.[23] The IOM was also involved extensively with the U.S.–Haitian refugee situation, helping with the interview process of migrants and refugees in Port-au-Prince (the in-country refugee processing system); Miami (facilitating domestic transportation for approved refugees); and Kingston, Guantanamo, and the Turks and Caicos Islands. The IOM prepares case files, coordinates interviews with American immigration officers, arranges for departure assistance, and aids resettlement in the United States for approved refugees.[24] More controversially, the IOM has become involved in the repatriation process as well. The IOM is often criticized for promising more than it can deliver, and since it is dependent on receiving states for funding, it is often accused of being an organization that merely fulfills the wishes of the United States and other donor countries.

Many multilateral organizations and countries have put migration somewhere on their policy agendas, if not front and centre. For example, the G-8 states which hold annual summits and lesser-publicized ministerial-level meetings to discuss economic and political coordination, often deal with migration issues. However, migration has yet to become a focus of G-8 deliberations, despite the fact that it is obviously intrinsic to the often-discussed questions of economic growth and unemployment. The OECD surveys migration trends as well, and as discussed earlier the EU has a variety of mechanisms designed to both facilitate labour movement within the Union and limit migration into it. Canada has been participating in the Intergovernmental Consultations on Asylum, Refugee, and Migration Policies in Europe, North America, and Australia (commonly referred to as either the IGC or the Informal Consultations) based, with its own small secretariat, in Geneva. At present,

15 governments take part in the consultations, which began in 1985, and generate documentation on issues such as temporary protection, asylum procedures, trafficking in illegal aliens, and unaccompanied minors. The **UN High Commissioner for Refugees (UNHCR)** and IOM both participate in the process, though it has a rather closed-door image. Since the consultations are among countries of destination only, they have been criticized for what one analyst believes is a self-protective focus on "removals, prevention of asylum-seeking, and individuals seeking asylum in order to avoid asylum shopping."[25] However, we should not exaggerate the IGC's ability to realize its goal, since most states—including Canada—remain reluctant to lose their ability to be flexible on asylum, refugee, or migration policies.

REFUGEES

According to the Universal Declaration of Human Rights, "Everyone has the right to seek and enjoy in other countries asylum from persecution."[26] While legal migration makes up the largest part of global migration patterns, refugees and internally displaced persons are also a permanent concern. Refugees are created when people facing persecution flee their circumstances, individually or in groups, or are forcibly expelled from their home state. Though we usually envision the former when we think of refugees, we should also keep in mind that mass expulsions have been common forms of policy throughout history: some 15 million Africans were forced overseas into slavery before 1850 and massive forced movements were notable before, during, and after World War II.[27] During the Cold War, the West often considered some refugee movements (often referred to as political defections when this involved individuals or small groups of people fleeing from the Soviet Union or other Eastern-bloc countries) to be political priorities. However, today most refugee populations receive a less than urgent response. Although many states such as Canada have maintained fairly liberal refugee acceptance policies, international refugee assistance is clearly underfunded and lacking political support.

It is, of course, extremely difficult to measure the number of refugees worldwide, especially if one seeks to include people who have been displaced within their home state. When G. J. van Heuven Goedhart was appointed the first UN High Commissioner for Refugees in 1951, there were 1.25 million refugees. In 1976, with Sadruddin Aga Khan as High Commissioner,

Finally returning home. A Rwandan family reaches their home-town of Luhondo in November 2008. The family fled Rwanda in 1994 and had stayed in a refugee camp in Zaire for almost 14 years. (CP Photo/Paul Chaisson.)

there were 2.8 million recognized refugees; by 1980, almost 8.5 million. In 1992, by contrast, there were almost 18 million. Between the end of 2005 and the end of 2006 alone, the UNHCR reported that there were 9.9 million refugees in the world. However, the numbers of "persons of concern" (which includes refugees, returnees, stateless and internally displaced persons) rose from 21 million to 32.9 million, an incredible 54 percent increase in one year.[28] The largest sources of refugees are, not surprisingly, from states where prolonged and severe conflict has occurred. However, along with the unprecedented increase in refugee numbers in the early 1990s, a much more complex understanding of refugee and migration issues evolved. While armed conflict continues to be a primary cause of refugee and IDP flows, the social upheavals caused by globalization create a range of push and pull factors that induce refugee movements. Human rights violations in countries or regions provoke individuals to seek asylum in other countries. Natural disasters, whether they are tsunamis or droughts, create migratory flows out of affected areas. The creation of large refugee camps and settlements can cause friction between local populations and refugee populations, complicating humanitarian aid efforts.[29] While political refugees were once regarded as "the tragic product of an incompatible juxtaposition, whether of faction, class, religion, ideology, or nationality,"[30] other factors such as the environment, lack of development, and overpopulation play major roles today, necessitating even more complex models. We should note also that there are legal and philosophical disputes about who should qualify for refugee status; we turn to one of those disputes now, but add that, no matter how well managed and liberal a refugee policy might be, there will always be a certain percentage of applicants who make false claims, and this further stigmatizes claimants with legitimate refugee status.

ENVIRONMENTAL REFUGEES AND ECOPOLITICAL VIOLENCE

In the previous chapter we discussed the links between political violence and environmental degradation. The latter is also expected to be a leading cause of migration in the future, primarily due to shoreline erosion, coastal flooding and agricultural disruption. There is considerable debate over the use of the term "environmental refugee" because under international law refugees must be fleeing persecution and must cross an international boundary. This is far from a matter of semantics, because under international law governments have obligations to provide protection to political refugees and there is resistance to extending those same rights to people fleeing environmental degradation. With some estimates placing the number of environmental "refugees" at 50 million by 2010 and 200 million by 2050, this debate is likely to intensify.[31]

Many analysts have drawn a disturbing connection between environmental degradation, failed states, armed conflict, and refugee flows. Environmental degradation and resource scarcity increase demands on government finances and services. For example, shortages of water require expensive dams or new irrigation systems. The loss of rural incomes from environmental degradation provokes migration to cities, increasing demands for transport, energy, water, sanitation, food, and health care. As economic activity is affected by environmental degradation, government revenues decline, reducing the ability of governments to maintain services and order. As Thomas Homer-Dixon argues, "A widening gap between state capacity and demands on the state, along with the misguided economic interventions such a gap often provokes, aggravates popular and elite grievances, increases rivalry between elite factions, and erodes a state's legitimacy."[32] As a result, conflict between communal groups within a state, or conflict between governments and disaffected communal groups, will intensify as competition to control resources and wealth grows. In many cases, political elites will hoard whatever surplus wealth is produced, and use it to maintain their power and their privileged lifestyles. The rest of the population will struggle for what share of the resource pie is left, or they will seek to overthrow the political elites. The overall result is the erosion and collapse of social order, and the disintegration of the state as different factions and groups do battle over a shrinking economic base, often destroying what little in the way of resources, facilities, or livelihoods remained to them. This condition of near anarchy exacerbates environmental degradation and economic deprivation. Where there is no government or system of order, there are no regulations or laws governing the use of natural resources. Conservation and preservation become impossible. In the worst cases, these factors can converge into a horrific blend of violent conflict, crime, poverty, disease, and starvation and malnutrition. All of this occurs in those areas of the world least equipped to respond to such crises or to manage them effectively.

In the face of such conditions, a natural reaction of people is to flee to escape the violence of war or the hardships of economic deprivation. Environmental degradation and environmentally induced social instability or armed conflicts can thus create large refugee movements. These movements in turn are identified as another source of potential conflict, for refugee movements create tensions and disputes in the regions or countries that receive them. As Nazli Choucri has argued, "The masses of forcefully uprooted persons ... might become a key element in the lethal feedback dynamic between environmental degradation and violent conflict."[33] Refugee movements can create or spread conflict because the influx of a large number of refugees can alter land availability and distribution patterns, disturb economic relations, alter the political and social climate, and upset the local ecological balance. This can provoke communal conflicts between migrant peoples and the peoples in the receiving region. This is true of both international refugees (those who cross state borders) and internally displaced refugees (those who flee from one area of a country to another). In the Canadian study on environmental degradation and violent conflict discussed in Chapter 10, Homer-Dixon argued that "there is substantial evidence to support the hypothesis that environmental scarcity causes large population movement, which in turn causes group identity conflicts."[34] Similarly, Nazli Choucri claimed that "environmental degradation forces people to move, sometimes across borders, and most assuredly to impinge on and ultimately challenge [host] populations."[35]

However, because migrations and the effects they produce are influenced by a wide variety of factors, the link between environmental refugees and the spread of conflict is not an automatic one. In fact, according to Astri Suhrke, conflict will occur "only under conditions of zero-sum interaction—whether actual or perceived. The alternative is a value-added model, where migrants are incorporated into the host society without collective strife, typically by providing needed labour and skills. Nor does ethnic differentiation between host population(s) and newcomers necessarily make the incorporation process conflictual."[36] There are also constraints on the capacity of refugees to create conflict. Refugee populations may be isolated in refugee encampments in relatively remote regions. They may be too weak or disorganized to be regarded as a threat. In many cases, refugee movements that are regarded as a threat have the support of a neighbouring state, and therefore the refugees are seen as an instrument of foreign interference. Nonetheless, there are many examples of environmentally induced refugee movements provoking political and social upheaval and violence. Refugee flows from Bangladesh into Northeast India (arising largely from population growth and land scarcity) have provoked communal conflict between migrant and Indigenous peoples. In Assam, the Lalung peoples have reacted angrily and sometimes violently against the Muslim Bengali migrants, whom they accuse of appropriating scarce farmland. In Tripura, Tripuris conducted an eight-year insurgency over access to land, which was in short supply due to a massive influx of refugees from Bangladesh. Efforts by the Indian government to return dispossessed land and stop the flow of migration have met with mixed success in the face of continued environmental stresses on land resources in the region. In Africa, refugees fleeing environmental degradation and armed conflict in Somalia and Darfur have created tensions in neighbouring countries.

More generally, it is quite logical to assume that increasing environmental degradation will lead to more people being forced to move for survival reasons. At present, the Convention of Refugees would not automatically qualify them as refugees, and many would argue this is unfair, since the ecological destruction forcing their departure is so often caused by elements beyond their control, such as drought, the construction of large dams, and the industrialization of agriculture. Global warming, which could raise sea levels and flood hundreds of millions out of coastal zones, and submerge entire island states, is perhaps the biggest threat here.

As things are, however, one must be fleeing abject political persecution and cross a border to either qualify as a refugee or seek asylum. It is unlikely this will change in the future, as industrialized states fear it would open the doors to hundreds of thousands of asylum seekers to include categories such as economic migrants and environmental refugees in the official definition. We turn now to a brief discussion of the international refugee regime.

MULTILATERAL RESPONSES TO REFUGEE CRISES: EFFORTS AND DILEMMAS

Usually, asylum seekers will arrive at an airport, or cross a border, by themselves or with their family. They can apply for asylum with local authorities, and the process of refugee determination will begin. They will be assisted by a lawyer, UNHCR representatives, or others who can support their claim, while the refugee determination board involved will face the difficult task of determining whether or not the applicant would suffer unacceptable persecution if returned home. However, in many cases (especially where conflict has forced people to flee) refugee arrivals number in the tens of thousands, making the asylum process impossible to implement. At the international level, the UNHCR remains the principal organization whose mandate is to aid and assist refugees. The UNHCR is constantly employed today in all the major regions of the globe. While its primary mandate relates to caring for those Convention refugees who cross borders, it is increasingly dealing with internally displaced persons as well—but can do so only when requested by the Security Council, General Assembly, or host country. The UNHCR budget, which is derived from voluntary contributions (largely from states but also from nongovernmental organizations and individuals), is divided into funding for general programs (basic projects for refugee aid and durable solutions, the most important of which is repatriation) and special programs, which include responses to sudden emergencies such as the outflow of more than one million Rwandans from that troubled state in 1994. As the UNHCR was designed to solve what was in 1945 considered a temporary problem—the relocation of people displaced by World War II in Europe—it was not created as a permanent agency. As such, it needs to have its mandate renewed every five years, and to beg states and private donors for funding on a continual basis.

Several other UN bodies are involved in refugee protection and assistance. Most notably, the United Nations Relief Works Administration (UNRWA), another voluntary, contribution-based international organization, was established in 1949 to deal with the refugees generated by the first Arab–Israeli War, and its operations have expanded to include health care and education provision. It had more than 4.1 million people registered in 2004, located in Jordan, Syria, Lebanon, the West Bank, and the Gaza Strip.[37] The UNRWA, with more than 18,000 Palestinian employees, is the single largest operating program within the UN system. Despite the political uncertainty in the region, it "carries on a thankless task, criticized for not doing more while financial contributors grow restive in support of a relief operation that has no end in sight."[38] A Canadian-led international committee, the Refugee Working Group, has toured Jordanian refugee camps for Palestinians, with an aim toward incorporating the refugee question into the broader Middle East peace process. However, Israeli governments have been reluctant to put the right of Palestinian refugee return on the bargaining table (see Chapter 7).

There is a long tradition of humanitarian aid organizations predating World War II, but most of the extant organizations today can trace their roots directly to that epic confrontation. The UN Relief and Rehabilitation Administration (UNRRA) was established by the Allies in 1943 to follow them into liberated areas at the close of World War II to provide immediate relief to victims of the war, including concentration camp survivors. The UN International Children's Emergency Fund (UNICEF) was established in 1946, and in 1953 moved into longer-term programs beyond Europe and Asia. UNICEF delivers aid to drought- and war-stricken regions and works with WHO to help meet the nutritional requirements of refugee children. WHO is also involved with assessing the nutritional requirements of refugee populations. For example, in 1988 an international conference, Nutrition in Times of Disaster, met at WHO's headquarters in Geneva. More broadly, the UNHCR works in conjunction with the World Food Programme in many cases of unexpected refugee flows.

The UNHCR also consults with some 300 NGOs that play roles in relief operations. In 1993, more than one-quarter of the UNHCR budget went to NGOs. The most significant NGO partner is the International Committee of the Red Cross (ICRC), and, in Islamic countries, the International Committee of the Red Crescent. The history of the ICRC dates back to 1859, and it was charged in 1864 with overseeing the implementation of the first Geneva Convention. In 2009 the ICRC had offices in 80 countries and had a total of over 12,000 staff. A considerable portion of its operations involve refugee assistance: examples are El Salvador and Nicaragua, Sudan, Angola, Mozambique, Uganda and Somalia, Afghanistan, Pakistan, the Thai/Cambodian border, and the territories occupied by Israel. The ICRC represents displaced civilians to governments and armed movements; actively protects them through its ability to achieve legal access (occasionally denied) to refugee and internment camps; provides medical, food, and material assistance; and runs the Tracing Agency, which seeks to reunite displaced and separated families.[39]

The ICRC and UNHCR have some overlap in their mandates, but a general division of labour has evolved: the ICRC assumes primary responsibility for persons displaced within a country during wartime, while the UNHCR has exclusive responsibility for refugees in countries of temporary or first asylum. This distinction, however, is not permanent, as was evidenced with the ill-fated Safe Haven plan in Bosnia-Herzegovina, when the UNHCR was used to protect and feed internal displaced persons. In an African case, a UN pullout left the ICRC to service genuine cross-border refugees as well.[40] Though it might appear as if these two agencies overlap considerably, it is essential that each exist independent of the other. The Red Cross is involved with warfare-related situations exclusively, while the UNHCR is not. The Red Cross operates independently from the UN system (although it has observer status in the General Assembly), while the UNHCR does not. The Red Cross is willing to go where

---

PROFILE 11.6 Civil War Refugees

In 1996, Canada issued new guidelines that reduce the confusion over who can be admitted as a refugee during a civil war. The chair of the Immigration and Refugee Board, Nurjehan Mawani, said these guidelines reflect what many board members were already doing, as well as the precedents set by the Federal Court of Appeal. People fleeing civil war are judged by the risk of persecution they face. Individuals do not have to be personally singled out. If they are members of a large, persecuted group, they are considered refugees under the United Nations refugee convention, which includes persecution based on race, religion, nationality, or membership in a social group. Civilians caught in indiscriminate shelling or looting are not considered refugees unless they are members of an ethnic or religious group that is a target. However, they must show that they cannot flee to another part of their home country or that another group cannot protect them. Of course, they also have to make it to Canada somehow, not an easy feat for someone with no income trapped in a war zone. It is far more likely that the UNHCR and other multilateral organizations will be the relevant interventional body in most cases where war is involved, and Canada's financial contributions to them are as important as its own refugee policies.

SOURCE: LILA SARICK, "GUIDE ON CIVIL-WAR REFUGEES ISSUED," *THE GLOBE AND MAIL*, MARCH 8, 1996, A7.

the UNHCR is not, and the UNHCR does things the Red Cross cannot. Both are desperately needed today; unfortunately, both are entirely dependent on the voluntary contributions of states and individuals for funding, which is habitually meagre.

Meanwhile, humanitarian relief organizations can find themselves in terrible ethical and practical dilemmas. Should they accept the military protection of forces active in the area, including international intervention forces, and thus risk losing the perception that they are impartial? Without this protection they are in effect intriguing targets for kidnapping and theft; with it they may be seen as enemies by at least one side of the conflict. Should they cooperate extensively with occupying powers, such as the coalition forces in Iraq? Should they aid refugees who are clearly violent criminals? The latter question surfaced most markedly after hundreds of thousands of Hutus fled the Rwandan Patriotic Front after the genocide in Rwanda in 1994; many of them had participated in the genocide before crossing into Zaire, and even used the camps as recruitment grounds for raising a possible retaliatory force. This ultimately caused some groups, such as Médecins sans Frontières (Doctors Without Borders), to pull out of the camps, even though this entailed abandoning thousands of innocent women and children in dire need of medical assistance.[41] It might also be argued that aid agencies contribute to structural violence, merely by seeking a return to "normalcy" in crisis situations. For example, Mark Duffield argues that the problem with helping the displaced Sudanese is not the rush to cope with emergency situations, or complicity in perpetuating the civil war in Sudan, but rather the fact that efforts to obtain peace can result in the continuation of prior relations of exploitation and, by extension, genocidal policies not directly linked to the civil war effort. As he puts it, "goal-oriented humanitarianism in the transition zone can be argued to have reinforced those everyday relations that denote 'peace.' In other words, aid agencies have strengthened and tacitly supported those economic and political relations of desocialisation, subordination and exploitation that constitute normal life. In the transition zone, since the Dinka are enmeshed in such relations, aid policy has been complicit in their oppression."[42] Similarly, the UNRWA might be accused of perpetuating the status quo in Israeli–Palestinian relations. However—and here is the hard part—these concerns must be weighed against the cost of nonintervention in immediate human suffering, lack of education for youth, chronic long-term malnutrition, and other problems.

Other NGOs play important roles in emergency humanitarian assistance as well. Notably, the Save the Children Fund has played a key role in many refugee relief situations (more than half the world's refugees are children) in places as diverse as Russia, Hungary, Korea, Algeria, Jordan, Gaza and the West Bank, Cambodia, Laos, Central America, Iraq, Rwanda, Zaire, Nepal, and Bangladesh. The Save the Children Fund was founded in 1919 by a British schoolteacher named Eglantyne Jebb, who would draft the Declaration of the Rights of the Child in 1923, adopted by the League of Nations in 1923 and, much later, redrafted as the 1989 UN Convention on the Rights of the Child. In 1979 various national units came together under the umbrella of the Geneva-based International Save the Children Alliance (ISCA), which now has 27 members.[43]

On a global level, the refugee situation is particularly acute. If the world community, and especially the primary donor states, wants the UNHCR to deal with emergency refugee flows, then it will have to increase funding for this highly strained organization. For example, Canada currently funds overseas emergency refugee assistance through the International Humanitarian Assistance (IHA) budget of the **Canadian International Development Agency (CIDA)**; however, this traditionally amounts to a small percentage of the IHA budget. As for the idea that giving aid to refugees will foster dependence and corrupt the initiative of refugees themselves, this has been widely disputed by scholars such as David Keen.[44] What matters is the way in which emergency aid is delivered: though it is a highly demanding policy, agencies and governments must struggle to preserve human dignity and cultural uniqueness as far as possible. Sometimes, this is just a matter of conducting sound preliminary research. But in times of severe crisis, it is difficult to prepare for the unexpected. More than ever, diligent observation of political developments, including armed conflicts and social unrest, government and rebel-group aggression and persecution, and environmental impact assessment are vital tools in the fight against harm.

THE INTERNALLY DISPLACED

As indicated above, social and environmental problems, including poverty, resource scarcity, and warfare, can induce large-scale refugee movements. However, most displaced people do not cross national borders. There are millions of "involuntary migrants" who are victims of political violence and environmental degradation but are not officially considered refugees because they do not step, sail, drive, or fly over an imaginary line that distinguishes one state from another. With notable exception, their plight is still considered purely one of domestic policy. Rural–urban migration; population displacement caused by large-scale development projects, deforestation, and soil degradation; and even forced expulsions between regions within states are still considered the domestic affairs of sovereign states, and although outside funding agencies can certainly wield influence in directing governments away from these processes, stopping them altogether is not a distinct possibility under the present circumstances. It is important to stress that such movements are often quite orchestrated, and not the byproduct of natural disasters beyond the control of governments. Whether the consequence of ethnic cleansing, industrialization, ecocide, or inadequate responses to disasters that marginalize certain sectors of society, such population movements are both human rights dilemmas for the international community and major sources of destabilization for national and local governments alike. In 2007, there were an estimated 26 million **internally displaced persons (IDPs)** in 52 countries worldwide.[45]

The government of Indonesia has orchestrated one of the largest internal movements of people in history. In an effort to reduce overcrowding on the main Indonesian island of Java, some six million people have been moved to outlying islands such as Sumatra, Kalimantan, Sulawesi, and Irian Jaya. Most of those resettled work in agriculture and many now actually own their own land. Lately, the migrants have found work in other areas, such as rubber and coffee plantations, fishponds, and seaweed processing plants. However, despite reforestation projects in Eastern Kalimantan, environmentalists complain about the widespread deforestation caused by this mass migration to formerly remote areas, and many of the migrants are living in dire poverty in their new locations. Violence has frequently erupted between the newcomers and previous inhabitants (though this can be attributed to larger patterns of sectarian violence in the region). Nonetheless, the program continues, as Jakarta, the main city on Java, continues to grow, with over nine million inhabitants in 2008.[46]

Two categories of IDPs exist: those who have fled warfare or extreme environmental degradation, and those who have been moved by their governments for the purposes of economic development. In either case, it is still a matter of considerable debate whether the UNHCR or any other body should be permitted to interfere in the internal affairs of a state to help internally displaced people.[47] When Russian forces caused people to flee the war zone in Chechnya, Russia asked the UNHCR to assist in the care of the internally displaced. However, this request was an exception to the rule. Even before the devastating cyclone of 2008, there were probably hundreds of thousands of internally displaced people in Burma. After the cyclone the number of displaced increased by tens of thousands and the UNHCR has no ability to aid them without the permission of the military regime (see Chapter 9). There are millions of displaced persons in other countries, such as Sudan and Colombia, who receive little or no assistance either. More generally, millions of internally displaced people in the next few decades will have a difficult time integrating with the rest of the societies in which they live. This difficulty will in turn increase outward, cross-border migratory pressure as well.

GENDER, THE SEX TRADE, AND TRAFFICKING IN MIGRANTS

Within the subfield of migration studies, several other issue-areas are receiving increasing attention. The question of gender is foremost among them. Women migrants and refugees face a unique set of obstacles as they resettle in new countries.[48] They are often the victims of outright repression in their home states, and, in fact, several states—Canada among them— have gone so far as to accept such women as legitimate Convention refugees.[49] This applies particularly to women who have fled states where they have legitimate fear that they will be punished for avoiding traditions such as female genital mutilation (see Chapter 9). More generally, however, women migrants face special challenges when moving to new areas where they may have a more difficult time than men obtaining employment that can adequately support them and their children. Single women, particularly, and unaccompanied minors are certainly vulnerable to harm, especially sexual abuse, in refugee camps. Many children have lived their entire lives in what were supposed to be temporary refugee camps and consequently received little if any formal education.

As the result of destitution or outright coercion, many women and children migrants become involved in the international sex-trade industry (see Profile 11.7). This represents not only a shameful aspect of the failure to provide basic human rights to those affected but also increases the health risks associated with such work. Most notably, of course, the spread of HIV/AIDS, which is virtually uncontrollable in many regions of the world today, is undeniably accelerated by prostitution, which often assumes the form of a global operation, complete with resorts attracting men from North America, Europe, and Asia. The international community has often dealt with this issue; even the long-defunct League of Nations had a Committee on the Abolition of White Slavery (terminology largely discarded today) and before that there was an international Agreement for the Suppression of the White Slave Traffic and related conventions in 1904 and 1910, respectively. It is impossible, therefore, to argue that this issue is too new to deal with. Yet we need more global attention to stop or at least limit this flagrant form of exploitation, as well as domestic legislation discouraging the practice.[50] However, until this issue becomes more prominent and is addressed with more energy, little will be done, and the stark reality is that some government officials are accomplices in the growth of the sex industry.

The illegal trafficking in migrants is of growing concern worldwide, affecting some 700,000 people on a yearly basis, despite measures such as the Convention on the Rights of the Child, which states, "State parties shall take measures to combat the illicit

Internally displaced in the Sri Lankan civil war, September 2008. Ethnic Tamils sit outside a UNHCR compound in a protest against a government decision to order aid agencies out of rebel-held areas. (AP Photo/ CP Archive.)

PROFILE 11.7 Transnational Prostitution: A Resolution

A large traffic in women and children for the purpose of prostitution remains, according to a resolution adopted by the United Nations General Assembly in 1995. In it, the UN condemned the illicit and clandestine movement of persons across national and international borders, largely from developing countries and some countries with economies in transition, with the goal of forcing women and children into sexually or economically oppressive and exploitative situations, for the profit of recruiters, traffickers, and crime syndicates, as well as into other illegal activities related to trafficking, such as forced domestic labour, false marriages, clandestine employment, and false adoption. What is necessary, however, is a full-frontal attack on the demand side of this equation: without an eager market, sex traders would have no incentive to engage in their activities.

SOURCE: UN RESOLUTION A/RES/49/166, FEBRUARY 24, 1995; SEE ALSO THE UNESCO TRAFFICKING STATISTICS PROJECT, HTTP://WWW.UNESCOBKK.ORG/INDEX.PHP?ID=1022.

transfer and non-return of children abroad."[51] A recent seminar sponsored by the IOM on the trafficking of migrants concluded that it was part of a much broader pattern of transnational criminal activity and could be dealt with only as an element of an internally coordinated strategy to eliminate that sector.[52] However, this is much easier said than done, for a wide variety of reasons that space does not permit us to explore here, such as government corruption, coercive techniques by traffickers, the stimulus of poverty, demand for cheap labour and prostitution, and many other factors. In addition, there is the question of the rights of illegal migrants, which is a particularly visible issue in the United States. The Migrant Worker's Convention outlined above would apply to these people as well, and this explains some of the overwhelming reluctance among industrialized states to even sign the agreement.

Discrimination against migrants, especially female migrants, takes many forms around the globe.[53] It might be argued that one of the greatest difficulties involves encouraging governments to accept the idea that all migrants, be they permanent (settlers), temporary contract workers, temporary professional transients, clandestine or illegal workers, asylum seekers, or genuine refugees as defined by the 1951 Convention, are entitled to the same rights. This is simply not an acceptable formula; it would imply, for example, that temporary workers and even illegal migrants would have the right to vote and receive the same social services as regular tax-paying citizens. And yet their contributions to society certainly imply they deserve no less than the full protection of the law.

POPULATION MOVEMENT, THE SPREAD OF INFECTIOUS DISEASE, AND GLOBAL HEALTH

One of the most dangerous elements of population movement is that people can carry diseases with them when travelling. Epidemics are restricted to geographic and temporal boundaries; pandemics, on the other hand (such as malaria, tuberculosis, and HIV/AIDS) know no such boundaries. We may live in an age of pandemics, but it can be easily argued that human security has always faced its most prevalent and enduring threat from microorganisms. The bubonic plague, or Black Death, first struck Europe in 1348 and wiped out entire towns and villages. The plague bacillus was carried by the rats that infested the overcrowded, unsanitary towns. Between the hundreds of thousands of fatalities caused by the plague and those caused by the Hundred Years' War (England versus France, 1337–1453), the population of Europe did not recover until the 1500s. After the expansion of European civilization into colonized areas such as the Americas, indigenous peoples around the world suffered from the sudden introduction of foreign microbes; it is often charged that some of the diseases were deliberately spread. The Spanish flu of 1918–1919, spread as soldiers returned from war, was the most deadly of all, killing an estimated 20 to 30 million people (though some estimates are closer to 50 million), many in their late teens and twenties. The historical record aside, some experts argue that the problem is getting worse, not better, despite the advancement of science. The rapid spread of the HIV/AIDS virus, and highly publicized events such as the outbreak of the pneumonic plague in Surat, India in 1994, the Ebola virus in Zaire in 1995, SARS in Canada and elsewhere in 2003, and the swine flue pandemic in 2009, have alerted governments and citizens to the importance of infectious disease, and the understandable panic they can cause among both local and distant populations.[54]

For example, in 2003 the discovery of "mad cow disease" (bovine spongiform encephalopathy, BSE) in a single Canadian-born cow residing in the United States set off a national agricultural panic and a trade dispute with the U.S. BSE is a fatal disease that causes progressive neurological degeneration in cattle. In 1996, following outbreaks of BSE among British cattle, scientists found a possible link between BSE and a new variant of CJD (Creutzfeldt-Jakob disease), a rare disease similar to BSE that occurs in humans. Millions of cattle were slaughtered in Britain; and millions of chickens, mostly in Asia but also in British Columbia, have been slaughtered over concerns with the spread of avian flu in 2003–04. These pathogens have had relatively little impact on human populations due to such precautionary measures (they might prompt us to rethink our dependence on large-scale meat production, but that is another issue), but there is widespread concern among epidemiologists that certain strains of avian flu (notably H5VN1, which killed some 250 people between 2003 and 2008, mostly in Asia), might at some point escape the confines of its current transmission path and become able to spread from human to human. The disease has spread from Asia to Turkey and northern and southwestern Africa. Given the impact of the so-called Spanish flu at the tail end of World War I (1918–1919), when some 50 million people were killed, it is feared that such a massive pandemic could kill hundreds of millions of people. Other experts are concerned that extreme weather events, said to be characteristic of climate change, will add to the spread of disease.

Another quite modern pathogen is the West Nile virus. West Nile is a mosquito-borne virus that can cause a range of illnesses, such as acute encephalitis (inflammation of the brain), or meningitis (inflammation of the membranes and fluid surrounding the brain and spinal cord). Birds are the main reservoir of the virus: when a mosquito bites an infected bird, the mosquito can spread the virus by biting another bird or another animal, such as a human. West Nile was first located in 1937 in Uganda. Later it was found in Asia, Europe, and the Middle East; it was not until 1999 that it was discovered in New York. Preventive measures include using insect repellent and reporting dead birds to local health workers. Though it has had limited impact in terms of taking human life, West Nile is another indication of the perils of modern travel, since the pathogen was probably delivered by way of transported infected mammals or people.

Much more dramatic was the rise of severe acute respiratory syndrome (SARS), a deadly form of pneumonia that emerged from China in November 2002, most likely linked to the practice of eating the masked palm civet and the raccoon dog in certain regions of that country. Much to the consternation of city officials, the World Health Organization (WHO) issued a global alert in March 2003, warning travellers to avoid certain regions, including Toronto, where SARS was most prevalent. SARS has all the characteristics of a pandemic

On the front line: A health worker at Hong Kong International Airport checks the temperature of a departing passenger during the city's SARS outbreak, May 20, 2003. Hong Kong saw a dramatic drop in tourist and business arrivals, which prompted the city's flagship airline to cancel numerous inbound and outbound flights. (CP Photo/Adrian Brown.)

disease: it is easily spread, transmitted by coughing or sneezing at close range, and it is lethal—though infected persons can survive if the disease is detected in time. The virus can also spread when a person touches a surface or object contaminated with infectious droplets and then touches his or her mouth, nose, or eyes; it is particularly dangerous for healthcare workers because of their increased likelihood of exposure. During the outbreak of 2003, at least 8,098 people worldwide became sick, and some 774 died, 38 in Canada.[55] The outbreak provoked a closer look at how healthcare infrastructures can respond to sudden outbreaks. In contrast, the international response to the outbreak of what has been termed Mexican swine flu (H1N1) in winter 2009 has been much more efficient and coordinated. It was declared a pandemic by the WHO in June of 2009, although the overall numbers of deaths worldwide at that time were surprisingly low.

Though many infectious diseases are spread by mosquitoes, food, drinking water, and other vectors, some are spread by direct human contact, and this is often exacerbated by international travel. For example, a major cause of HIV/AIDS in sub-Saharan Africa is prostitution centred on the trucking routes of the region; another is the impact of military personnel having unprotected sex (or, in worst cases, engaging in rape) when stationed abroad. Similarly, many intravenous drug users who contract the disease do so when living as transients in large urban centres, such as Amsterdam and Vancouver. The fact that the earliest genetic traces of HIV proto-DNA was taken from a male who died in Zaire in 1954 is testament to how rapidly this pathogen has spread to almost all regions of the earth. Though it is impossible to give an accurate figure, an estimated 33 million people were living with HIV/AIDS in 2007, and as many as two million died as a result in that year alone. Sub-Saharan Africa is the region most affected: over 22 million people, or 5 percent of the population, are infected with HIV. According to these estimates, 2.7 million new infections occurred in 2007, with over 1.9 million of them in Sub-Saharan Africa.[56]

AIDS stands for *acquired immune deficiency syndrome* and it is caused by HIV, the human immunodeficiency virus. HIV and AIDS have no known cure or vaccine, though antiretroviral drugs are effective in mitigating its worst effects. Our immune systems fight off infections, and AIDS destroys this capacity. Thus, people with AIDS are highly susceptible to other sicknesses as well, such as the common cold. HIV-positive people will have antibodies to HIV, which can be discovered with a simple blood test. The most common prescription for avoiding HIV is to refrain from engaging in unprotected sex and from sharing intravenous needles. Intrauterine devices (IUDs), oral contraceptives, male and female sterilization, and natural family-planning methods such as rhythm and withdrawal provide no protection against sexually transmitted diseases (STDs). HIV/AIDS has reached epidemic proportions in areas of Africa (where two-thirds of all HIV/AIDS victims live) and Asia (where the sex industry has proliferated in the past few decades). In addition to the suffering AIDS has brought to Africa, the economies of some countries are already being affected. However, there are current concerns that the disease is rapidly progressing in other parts of the world such Eastern Europe, Russia, and Central Asia. International cooperation on HIV/AIDS continues:

the 17th Annual International AIDS Conference, held in Mexico City in August 2008, high-lighted a wide range of cooperative efforts from prevention to treatment. The struggle to distribute urgently needed antiretroviral drugs continues, as states such as Brazil and South Africa begin to dispense generic drugs to their citizens. Gradually, Northern pharmaceutical firms are being persuaded to either abandon patent protection laws and allow generics to be distributed or lower significantly the cost of their drugs for easier distribution elsewhere (see our profile on Canadian Stephen Lewis in Chapter 9). But this has been too little, too late for millions of people.

There are a plethora of diseases and serious health issues affecting sub-Sarahan Africans: malaria, hepatitis B, micronutrient malnutrition, iodine and vitamin-A deficiency, syphilis, gonorrhea, genital herpes, and other sexually transmitted diseases, to name but a few. But HIV/AIDS is so prevalent, and so deadly, that it is actually transforming the social profile of entire societies, resulting in an unprecedented number of orphans, and a continuous crisis in the public sector. More broadly, it can be argued that such infectious diseases are threatening the state's capacity to govern in many countries. In a provocative and careful study, Andrew Price-Smith concludes that "since increasing disease prevalence destroys or debilitates national populations and compromises both productivity and governance, infectious disease may be correctly seen as both a direct and an indirect threat to the national security of seriously affected states," and it can also "compromise the ability of transitional states (e.g., Russia and South Africa) to consolidate democratic and effective systems of governance."[57] It also results in the social isolation of the infected, and entire states, such as Haiti, have become known for its prevalence. Though a great deal can be done with improved health care and education, we can be sure that HIV/AIDS and other pandemics will continue to spread as long as people are able to travel.

Dennis Pirages argues four major transformations are under way that "seem to be strengthening the microbes' hands." Rapid population growth and urbanization lead to situations conducive to the rapid spread of disease, especially in the teeming megacities of the South, where adequate health care is seemingly beyond reach for the majority of citizens, and in areas where overpopulation has led to mass movements. Many of the refugees fleeing violence in Rwanda in 1994 died from cholera in the resulting overcrowded refugee camps. Population pressure is forcing people to inhabit previously wild areas, and this has had two consequences: new inhabitants are bringing new diseases into these areas, harming the indigenous people and wildlife; and the newcomers themselves are exposed to new diseases, which are then spread into the general population. Pirages writes also of changes in human behaviour, such as the so-called sexual revolution of the late 1960s and 1970s in the United States and the global spread in the use of drugs, which facilitated the spread of disease. Cramped prison conditions, which help spread tuberculosis, result from policy shifts and increases in crime often linked to poverty. Third, the environment itself is changing in a way that makes it more difficult to control the spread of disease. Sudden or gradual climate change may give a temporary advantage to resident microbes. For example, Pirages suggests that a fatal outbreak of hantavirus in the desert Southwest of the United States may have been triggered by sudden rainstorms that increased population growth among the virus-carrying rodents. In each summer since 1999, the West Nile virus has surfaced in mosquitoes in New York, prompting massive pesticide sprays in the city; this may be related to climate change. Finally, Pirages refers to technological innovations that have increased, rather than decreased, the ability of microbes to travel, such as the invention of the airplane: "Aircraft cabins are an excellent place for a rendezvous with cosmopolitan world-traveling viruses and bacteria."[58] A virus that causes hemorrhagic fever is said to have found its way to Baltimore from Seoul by way of wharf rats that made the journey in cargo ships. These viruses seem to understand what many global politics analysts do as well:

a truly interdependent and interconnected world economy presents as much opportunity as it does danger.

Not surprisingly, analysts are divided on the conceptual implications of global health issues such as the spread of infectious disease, the rise in global cancer rates, and the effects of climate change on human health. Liberals tend to believe these common threats will contribute further to convergence as humanity struggles together to solve these problems and limit their impact. Realists will believe states will close their borders and take additional measures of self-protection; and critical theorists will emphasize the disproportionate suffering borne by the marginalized peoples we discussed at some length in Chapter 8. Scholars of all stripes are also concerned with the security implications of the possible deliberate spread of disease for military or terrorist purposes, as discussed in Chapter 6.[59] One thing is certain: international efforts to monitor these diseases are crucial, as are efforts to ensure we avoid new forms of biological apartheid by sharing medical technology, prevention programs, and treatment efforts. Beleaguered international institutions such as the WHO have key roles to play here, but so do national governments, multinational pharmaceutical firms, and NGOs.

CONCLUSIONS

This chapter has covered many topics, and we must stress how interrelated they are, in theory and practice. While avoiding simplistic linear explanations, it can be plausibly argued that population growth can lead to increased population movement, massive urbanization, challenges to women's reproductive health and rights, drains on natural resources, political violence, increased opportunities for sexual exploitation, and increased opportunities for the spread of infectious disease. In both debates over population control measures and questions about the protection of refugees, North–South splits as well as gender issues are evident. This comes at a time when migration policies among the industrialized Northern states have, by and large, emphasized the closure, and not the liberalization, of borders.[60]

However, it is safe to say that it is impossible to stop migratory pressure. Georges Tapinos notes this with regard to NAFTA: its initial success might absorb some of the surplus of Mexican labour resulting from industrialization and a decrease in agricultural subsidies, "but the majority will seek employment in the United States. It is a straightforward illustration of the fact that [trade and investment] liberalization between countries with significant differences in size, endowments, and production patterns cannot in the short run simultaneously achieve two objectives: an increase in the standard of living, and a decrease in the propensity to emigrate."[61] Globalization hardly seems the solution to the crises generated by population growth and movement; indeed, overconsumption of resources and skilled workers by the North—those who have arguably benefited most from globalization—is part of the problem, not the solution. Realists would not be surprised that states have yet to develop an overarching ethos that permits responsive and systematic cooperation on these questions, while liberals suggest we are slowly on the way to creating institutions that may well do so in the future, providing individual rights are protected in the process. Neo-Marxists emphasize the links between exploitation, production, and migration, while feminists argue that a patriarchal world system is bound to result in many of the problems we have discussed in this chapter. Constructivists suggest that the way we look at and think about these issues is the result of years of thinking within narrow boxes defined by nationalism, borders, and citizenship, and we need to forge a new understanding of human identities to escape these old patterns. The fear of global apartheid (or, if the potential of pandemics is realized, global bio-apartheid) remains a central theme among constructivist theorists.

In this chapter we have examined issues related to the large population increases experienced in the 20th century, including the question of responsibility for promoting sustainable development, urbanization, birth control, voluntary and involuntary population movements (including environmental refugees, victims of the global sex trade, and people fleeing disease). There can be little doubt that the increase in population puts additional strain on the natural ecosystems on which we all ultimately depend, and that overconsumption in both the North and the South exacerbates the environmental problems discussed in Chapter 10. If high populations are a reflection of poverty, so are large population movements. In this chapter, we discussed the push–pull factors involved in migration and then looked at the contemporary refugee crisis, with an emphasis on multilateral responses. It should be apparent that these interlinked themes, held together by our interest in security, political economy, and policy analysis, offer what is often contradictory evidence to those pursuing the convergence/divergence theme of this textbook. And we can be sure that the global population will continue to rise in the future. The realistic question is not whether things will be moving in this direction, but how we will cope with unprecedented numbers of people, millions of whom will be on the move, presenting the threats associated with population displacement and disease. In the midst of all this humanity, can compassion survive?

Endnotes

1. Garrett Hardin, "The Tragedy of the Commons," *Science* 162 (December 1968), 1243–48.
2. John Hope Simpson, *Refugees: Preliminary Report of a Survey* (London: Chatham House, 1938), 193.
3. United Nations Department of Economic and Social Affairs, Population Division, *World Population Prospects: The 2006 Revision* (New York, United Nations, 2007), vii, http://www.un.org/esa/population/publications/wpp2006/WPP2006_Highlights_rev.pdf (accessed August 5, 2008).
4. See P. Ehrlich and A. Erlich, *The Population Explosion* (New York: Simon and Schuster, 1990).
5. Hardin, "The Tragedy of the Commons."
6. This formula is usually expressed as follows: $I = PAT$: impact is equal to population size, multiplied by per capita consumption (affluence), multiplied by a measure of the damage done by the technologies chosen to supply each unit of consumption.
7. Amniocentesis uses a sample of amniotic fluid from a pregnant woman's uterus to diagnose possible genetic defects and reveals the gender of the fetus in the process. See N. Kristof, "Peasants of China Discover New Way to Weed Out Girls," *The New York Times*, July 21, 1993, A1. It was the main cause, the critics alleged, of the high ratio of 117 boys born to every 100 girls in China, compared to the world average of 106 to 100.
8. Parts of this section are taken from P. J. Stoett, "Cities: To Love or to Loathe?," a review article based on J. Kasarda and A. Parnell, ed., *Third World Cities: Problems, Policies, and Prospects* (London: Sage, 1993), and J. Hardoy, D. Mitlin, and D. Satterthwaite, *Environmental Problems in Third World Cities* (London: Earthscan, 1992), which appeared in *Environmental Politics* 3, no. 2 (1994), 339–42.
9. *State of the World Population 2007: Unleashing the Potential of Urban Growth* (New York: United Nations Population Fund, 2007), 1.
10. See Kasarda and Parnell, *Third World Cities*; Hardoy, Mitlin, and Satterthwaite, *Environmental Problems*; and P. Gizewski and T. Homer-Dixon, "Urban Growth and Violence: Will the Future Resemble the Past?," *Project on Environment, Population and Security* (Toronto: AAAS and University College, University of Toronto, 1995); on Kibera, see J. Vasagar, "Residents Left Scrambling as Kenya Clears Shantytowns," *The Globe and Mail*, April 23, 2004, A12.
11. See R. Biswas, "Banned Drug Still Used on Women," *India Tribune*, January 25, 2004, http://www.tribuneindia.com/2004/20040125/herworld.htm#2 (accessed May 30, 2004).
12. See B. Hartmann, *Reproductive Rights and Wrongs: The Global Politics of Population Control and Contraceptive Choice* (New York: Harper and Row, 1987). For an excellent essay dealing with the transnational alliances and networks that have evolved related to population control issues, see B. Crane, "International Population Institutions: Adaptation to a Changing World Order," in P. Haas, R. Keohane,

and M. Levy, eds., *Institutions for the Earth: Sources of Effective International Environmental Protection* (Cambridge, MA: MIT Press, 1994), 351–96.

13. *Maternal Mortality in 2005: Estimates Developed by WHO, UNICEF, UNFPA, and the World Bank* (Geneva: World Health Organization, 2005), 1. This represents an improvement over the 585,000 average deaths estimated by the UNFPA (United Nations Population Fund) in 1995. See "Maternity: Greater Peril?," *Populi: The UNFPA Magazine* 23, no. 1 (1996), 4–5. This suggests medical procedures and equipment may be improving at the global level.

14. *Maternal Mortality in 2005: Estimates Developed by WHO, UNICEF, UNFPA, and the World Bank* (Geneva: World Health Organization, 2005), 1.

15. "Hard Lessons in Population Planning," *Our Planet* 6, no. 3 (1994), 32.

16. *The Economics of Mass Migration in the Twentieth Century* (New York: Paragon House, 1987). See also Stephen Castles and Mark Miller, *The Age of Migration: International Population Movements in the Modern World* (New York: Guilford, 1993).

17. Data from the International Organization for Migration, "Global Estimates and Trends," http://www.iom.int/jahia/about-migration/facts-and-figures/global-estimates-and-trends (accessed March 30, 2009).

18. *Global Economic Prospects 2006: Economic Implications of Remittances and Migration* (Washington, DC: World Bank, 2006), xi.

19. Data from the International Organization for Migration, "Global Estimates and Trends," http://www.iom.int/jahia/about-migration/facts-and-figures/global-estimates-and-trends (accessed March 30, 2009). See also "A Special Report on Migration," *The Economist*, January 5, 2008, 11.

20. L. Hossie, "Migration Increases as Search for Good Life Grows," *The Globe and Mail*, June 22, 1993, A10; 2000 estimate from http://www.un.org/esa/population/publications/ittmig2002/press-release-eng.htm (accessed May 28, 2004). Of course, these figures are highly imprecise, given the large numbers of illegal immigrants who escape governmental detection. According to Statistics Canada's census, in 1991, 16.7 percent of the Canadian population was foreign-born; in 2001 the figure had risen to 18.8 percent, and it was over 19 percent by 2006. Between 1995 and 2000, Canada accepted 845,000,000 immigrants; between 2001 and 2006, some 1.1 million immigrants entered Canada. The main source countries were China, India, the Philippines, Pakistan, the United States, and South Korea. See Citizenship and Immigration Canada's annual reports, http://www.cic.gc.ca/english/pub/#reference (accessed May 28, 2004 and August 15, 2008).

21. *Report of the First Meeting of the Global Forum on Migration and Development*, Belgium, July 9–11, 2007, http://www.gfmd-fmmd.org/en/system/files/2080096_FORMON_UK_BAT.pdf (accessed on August 7, 2008).

22. Parts of this section are taken from P. J. Stoett, "International Mechanisms for Addressing Migration," *Canadian Foreign Policy* 4, no. 1 (1996), 111–38.

23. For a concise history of the IOM and discussion, see R. Appleyard, *International Migration: Challenge for the Nineties* (IOM: Geneva, 1991).

24. *IOM News* 7 (1994), 2.

25. Nazare Albuguerque-Abell, "The Safe Third Country Concept: Deflection in Europe and Its Implications for Canada," *Refuge* 14, no. 9 (1995), 1–7, 5.

26. Universal Declaration of Human Rights, 1948, Article 14.

27. The postwar expulsion of millions of Germans from various regions following the Potsdam Treaty is particularly notable, though it is often ignored in popular histories of the war. See Alfred-Maurice de Zayas, "International Law and Mass Population Transfers," *Harvard International Law Journal* 16, no. 2 (1975), 207–58.

28. *Statistical Yearbook 2006: Trends in Displacement, Protection and Solutions* (New York: The United Nations High Commissioner for Refugees, 2007), 23–24.

29. See Office of the United Nations High Commissioner for Refugees, *The State of the World's Refugees 2006: Human Displacement in the New Millennium* (Oxford: Oxford University Press, 2006).

30. E. Buehrig, *The United Nations and the Palestinian Refugees: A Study in Nonterritorial Administration* (Bloomington: Indiana University Press, 1971), 3.

31. See Oli Brown, *Migration and Climate Change*, IOM Migration Research Series, No. 31 (Geneva: International Organization for Migration, 2008), 11.

32. T. Homer-Dixon, "Evidence from Cases," *International Security* 19, no. 1 (1994) 5–40. For a good case study, see C. Kahl, "Population Growth, Environmental Degradation, and State-Sponsored Violence: The Case of Kenya, 1991–93," *International Security* 23, no. 2 (1998), 80–119.

33. N. Choucri, "Environment, Development, and International Assistance: Crucial Linkages," in S. J. Brown and K. M. Schraub, eds., *Resolving Third World Conflict: Challenges for a New Era* (Washington, DC: United States Institute of Peace Press, 1992), 101.

34. Homer-Dixon, "Environmental Scarcities and Violent Conflict," 20.

35. Choucri, "Environment, Development, and International Assistance," 101. See also N. Myers, *Ultimate Security* (New York: Norton, 1993).

36. A. Suhrke, "Environmental Change, Migration, and Conflict: A Lethal Feedback Dynamic?," in C. A. Crocker, F. O. Hampson, and P. Aall, eds., *Managing Global Chaos: Sources of and Responses to International Conflict* (Washington, DC: United States Institute of Peace Press, 1996), 116. There is a voluminous literature on environmental refugees; see, for example, A. Nash, "Environmental Refugees: Consequences of Policies from a Western Perspective," *Discrete Dynamics in Nature and Society* 3 (1999), 227–38.

37. Palestinian refugees in Israel were initially under the care of the UNRWA, but Israel assumed that responsibility in 1952. See A. Bligh, "From UNRWA to Israel: The 1952 Transfer of Responsibilities for Refugees in Israel," *Refuge* 14, no. 6 (1994), 7–10, 24; and UNRWA, "Switzerland and UNRWA to Host Major Conference on Humanitarian Assistance to Palestine Refugees," press release, http://www.un.org/unrwa/news/releases/pr-2004/hqg-0404.pdf (accessed June 22, 2009).

38. R. Riggs and J. Plano, *The United Nations: International Organization and World Politics* (Belmont, CA: Wadsworth, 1994), 230.

39. F. Maurice and J. de Courten, "ICRC Activities for Refugees and Displaced Civilians," *International Review of the Red Cross* 280 (1991), 9–21.

40. This occurred in northwest Somalia, in 1990–91, where the ICRC extended its operations in aid of Ethiopian refugees after the World Food Programme and UNHCR suspended their activities for security reasons. The ICRC also found itself without proper military protection in Bosnia during the civil war there.

41. On this heart-wrenching decision, and others, see MSF staffer Fiona Terry's book, *Condemned to Repeat? The Paradox of Humanitarian Action* (Ithaca: Cornell University Press, 2002); on the Rwandan genocide, see P. Gourevitch, *We Wish to Inform You That Tomorrow We Will Be Killed with Our Families: Stories from Rwanda* (New York: Farrar Straus and Giroux, 1998).

42. M. Duffield, *Global Governance and the New Wars: The Merging of Development and Security* (London: Zed Books, 2001), 205.

43. For an excellent essay on the Save the Children Fund in Britain and its constant interaction with the UNHCR, World Food Programme, and other UN bodies, see A. Penrose and J. Seaman, "The Save the Children Fund and Nutrition for Refugees," in P. Willetts, ed., *"The Conscience of the World": The Influence of Non-Governmental Organizations in the UN System* (Washington, DC: Brookings, 1996), 241–69.

44. D. Keen, *Refugees: Rationing the Right to Life* (London: Zed Books, 1992), 55.

45. Data from the International Organization for Migration, "Global Estimates and Trends," http://www.iom.int/jahia/about-migration/facts-and-figures/global-estimates-and-trends (accessed March 30 2009). For reviews of the IDP challenge, see R. Cohen, *Human Rights Protection for Internally Displaced Persons* (Washington, DC: RPG, 1991); and F. Deng, *Protecting the Dispossessed: A Challenge for the International Community* (New York: Brookings, 1993).

46. S. Mydans, "Indonesia Resettles People to Relieve Crowding on Java," *The New York Times*, August 25, 1996, 4. For a report on a similar situation in Thailand, see D. Hubbel and N. Rajesh, "Not Seeing the People for the Forest: Thailand's Program of Reforestation by Forced Eviction," *Refuge* 12, no. 1 (1992), 20–21.

47. See R. Plender, "The Legal Basis of International Jurisdiction to Act with Regard to the Internally Displaced," *International Journal of Refugee Law* 6, no. 3 (1994), 345–61.

48. See S. Martin, *Refugee Women* (Oxford: Lexington Books, 2004).

49. See N. Spencer-Nimmons, "Canada's Response to the Issue of Refugee Women: The Women at Risk Program," *Refuge* 14, no. 7 (1994), 13–18. We should note also the role played by the Canadian Working Group for Refugee Women, a subgroup of the NGO-based Canadian Council for Refugees.

50. In 1996 Canada joined Sweden, Norway, Denmark, France, Belgium, Germany, Australia, the United States, Finland, Iceland, and New Zealand in passing legislation making it possible to charge citizens abroad who purchase sex from minors. J. Sallot, "Canada Targets Overseas Child Sex," *The Globe and Mail*, April 4, 1996, A4.

51. UN Resolution A/RES/44/25, November 20, 1989, Article 11.

52. "International Response to Trafficking in Migrants and the Safeguarding of Migrant Rights," *International Migration* 32, no. 4 (1994), 593–603. On the surge of this trade from the former Soviet bloc, see V. Malarek, *The Natashas: The New Global Sex Trade* (Toronto: Viking 2003); see also J. Vocks and J. Nijboer, "The Promised Land: a Study of Trafficking in Women from Central and Eastern Europe to the Netherlands," *European Journal on Criminal Policy and Research* 8 (2000), 379–388. For an interesting critical article, see J. O. Davidson, "Will the Real Sex Trade Please Stand Up?," *Feminist Review* 83 (2006), 4–22.

53. In the 1990s, the question of discrimination against migrants seeking employment was brought home to Canadians, as it was suggested that non-white Canadians were having a difficult time finding overseas jobs teaching English. "Asian Schools Avoid Non-White Canadians," *The Globe and Mail*, March 28, 1996, A1. For an interesting treatment of seasonal migrant workers in Canada, see T. Basok, *Tortillas and Tomatoes: Transmigrant Mexican Harvesters in Canada* (Montreal: McGill-Queen's University Press, 2002).

54. Two popular books were R. Preston, *The Hot Zone* (New York: Random House, 1994), and L. Garrett, *The Coming Plague: Newly Emerging Diseases in a World out of Balance* (New York: Farrar, Straus, and Giroux, 1994). See also F. Cartwright, *Disease and History* (New York: Thomas Crowell, 1972), and W. McNeill, *Plagues and Peoples* (London: Doubleday, 1976); and especially A. Cosby, *Ecological Imperialism* (Cambridge, UK: Cambridge University Press, 1994).

55. See "SARS Death Toll Rises to 38 in Toronto," CBCNews, http://www.cbc.ca/stories/2003/06/22/sars_030622 (accessed May 28, 2004). Though the disease was well-contained after its initial period, there are reports that it has resurfaced in China in April 2004.

56. Data from *UNAIDS Annual Report: Knowing Your Epidemic* (Geneva: Joint United Nations Programme on HIV/AIDS, 2008), 8, and *AIDS 2008 Fact Sheet: HIV/AIDS*, http://www.aids2008.org/admin/images/upload/732.pdf (accessed August 7, 2008).

57. A. Price-Smith, *The Health of Nations: Infectious Disease, Environmental Change, and Their Effects on National Security and Development* (Cambridge, MA: MIT Press, 2002), 172. Price-Smith also presents an excellent chapter on how climate change can increase the range of pathogens, a topic we discuss in Chapter 10.

58. Dennis Pirages, "Microsecurity: Disease Organism and Human Well-Being," *Environmental Change and Security Project Report* (Woodrow Wilson Center), 2 (1996), 9–14, 10; see also L. Garret, "The Return of Infectious Disease," *Foreign Affairs* 75, no. 1 (1996), 66–79.

See M. Zacher and T. Keefe, *The Politics of Global Health Governance: United by Contagion* (New York: Palgrave Macmillan, 2008); R. Dodgson and K. Lee, "Global Health Governance: A Conceptual Review," in R. Wilkinson and S. Hughes, eds., *Global Governance: Critical Perspectives* (London: Routledge, 2002); D. Fidler, *SARS, Governance and the Globalization of Disease* (Basingstoke: Palgrave Macmillan, 2004); A. Kelle, "Securitization of International Public Health: Implications for Global Health Governance and the Biological Weapons Prohibition Regime," *Global Governance* 13 (2007), 217–235, and WHO (World Health Organization), *WHO Guidelines for the Global Surveillance of SARS: Updated Recommendations, October*, WHO/CDS/CSR/ARO/2004.1 (Geneva: WHO, 2004).

60. For a survey, see D. Kubat, *The Politics of Migration Policies: Settlement and Integration, the First World into the 1990s* (New York: Center for Migration Studies, 1993).

61. "International Migration and Development," *Population Bulletin of the UN* 36 (1994), 1–18, 12.

Suggested Websites

International Committee of the Red Cross
http://www.icrc.org/eng

International Organization for Migration
http://www.iom.int/jahia/Jahia/lang/en/pid/1

Médecins sans Frontières
http://www.msf.org

The Population Council
http://www.popcouncil.org

Refugees International
http://www.refugeesinternational.org

United Nations High Commissioner for Refugees
http://www.unhcr.org/home.html

UNESCO Trafficking Statistics Project
http://www.unescobkk.org/index.php?id=1022

World Food Programme
http://www.wfp.org

World Health Organization
http://www.who.int/en/

Global Politics and the Information Age

Technology is now, for better or for worse, the principal driving force behind the ongoing rapid economic, social, and political change. Like any irrepressible force, the new technology can bestow on us undreamed of benefits but also inflict irreparable damage.

—Wassily Leontief, economist[1]

We, the representatives of the peoples of the world ... declare our common desire and commitment to build a people-centered, inclusive and development-oriented Information Society, where everyone can create, access, utilize and share information and knowledge, enabling individuals, communities and peoples to achieve their full potential in promoting their sustainable development and improving their quality of life....

—Declaration of Principles of the World Summit on the Information Society[2]

INTRODUCTION: GLOBAL POLITICS AND SOCIAL REVOLUTIONS

The development of human society is often conceptualized in terms of stages or revolutions. Each stage represents a significant leap forward in human development, and lays the foundation for successive revolutions. In each of these forward leaps, a close relationship exists between technological developments and the evolution of political, economic, and social organizations. For example, the **Agricultural Revolution** greatly increased food production in 18th-century Europe through a combination of mechanical innovations, cropping techniques, and changes in landholding practices. The **Industrial Revolution** represented a shift from agrarian-based economic activity to manufacturing, which profoundly altered the character of society. The very concept of work was transformed, and the social relations that sustained manufacturing became the subject of historians such as Karl Marx and authors such as Charles Dickens. Years later, the **Green Revolution**, stimulated by the mechanization of agriculture and the development of new fertilizers, pesticides, and seeds, had a global impact in the form of increased food production as well as concerns over the safety of chemicals in the food supply. Today some argue we are in the midst of a Revolution in Military Affairs

(RMA) that reflects the profound impact of technology on weapons systems and military capabilities.

The phenomenon of human development can also be seen in terms of waves stimulated by technical advances. In the 1920s, Russian economist Nikolai Kondratieff identified waves in the world economy approximately 50 to 60 years long. Each cycle was characterized by a surge in economic growth and productivity. In 1939, economist Joseph Schumpeter explained these waves in terms of clusters of technical inventions, innovations (the development of new techniques and products from these inventions), and diffusion (the spread of these techniques and products around the world). Each wave of inventions, innovations, and diffusion stimulates a surge in economic activity, after which economic growth slows as all the potential from new inventions is realized. Schumpeter characterized these waves as "creative gales of destruction" because they would sweep old industries aside and replace them with new ones. Following Schumpeter's reasoning, four such waves have been identified: the 1780s to 1840s, driven by the steam engine and innovations in textiles and iron; the 1840s to 1890s, and the era of the railway; the 1890s to 1930s, driven by electric power, chemical technologies, and improved steels; and the 1930s to 1980s, driven by the automobile and petroleum energy.[3]

The development of the computer began discussions of another potential revolution or wave in the evolution of human society. In 1980, Alvin Toffler's book *The Third Wave* argued that the transition from an agricultural society (the first wave) to an industrial society (the second wave) was being followed by a transition to an information society (the third wave).[4] In the same year, a study on the impact of computers argued that "the computer is not the only technological innovation of recent years, but it does constitute the common factor that speeds the development of all others. Above all … it will alter the entire nervous system of social organization."[5] Today, we do not have to stretch our imaginations to argue that the computer and the information revolution constitute another wave in social development. This new information age is built on the advances in microelectronics that have vastly increased the processing power of computers while reducing cost and bulk. Improvements in storage capacity and retrieval have led to an explosion in the gathering, storing, processing, and analysis of information, which has become increasingly vital to political and economic activity.

More importantly for the student of global politics, the development of improved communications technologies and the creation of many different international communications channels or "networks" have allowed computers and their users to transmit or disseminate information around the world. Information and data management is now the fastest-growing area of economic activity, prompting suggestions that the industrialized world is heading into a postindustrial and increasingly globalized society where new applications of information and communications technology (ICT) could actually transform social relations. As William J. Drake and Rikke Frank Jørgensen suggest, "the technologically enabled creation, distribution, and manipulation or application of information is becoming a key driving force and defining feature of social change worldwide.…"[6] As a result, global politics is increasingly characterized by the emergence of what the UN calls the "global information society." The UN has responded to the global implications of ICT by convening the World Summit on the Information Society (WSIS) in 2003 and 2005, and carrying out a series of related and ongoing projects through 2008.[7]

The development of ICT and the rise of the global information society have stimulated a lively theoretical debate. Realists argue that technological change is important because it has implications for the economic and military power of states. However, according to realists, technology will not have a structurally transformative effect on global politics, which has remained consistent across the social revolutions in human history. Liberals are more enthusiastic, suggesting the ICT and networks promote global interdependence by facilitating trade and financial flows and intercultural communication. Neo-Marxists charge that a global information society reflects and even exacerbates divergences in wealth and power, and is promoted by the economic liberalization theology underpinning globalization. However, neo-Marxists would also advocate using the technology to rally for change. Postmodernists warn that information is never neutral or autonomous from power, and is often manipulated in the interests of those who control it. At the same time, as constructivists would assert, ICT can change or challenge identities and belief systems and even create new cross-national constituencies. Feminists regard ICT as potentially liberating for women, enabling increased communication and networking. However, technology is embedded in male-dominated political and economic structures, reinforcing male power and dominance. Finally, some observers suggest we might be exaggerating the impact of the information age on global politics. As Christopher May argues, "these changes are not as profound as they are often presented."[8]

THE COMPUTER AND THE INFORMATION REVOLUTION

If any form of technological change has had a profound impact on the lives of millions of people in recent times, it is the advent of the personal computer (PC). The evolution of the modern computer began in 1946 with the development of the **ENIAC (electronic numerical integrator and calculator)**, widely regarded as the first electronic computer. Initially designed to calculate the trajectories of artillery shells, ENIAC was a remarkable accomplishment for its time. It could execute 5,000 arithmetic calculations per second. It was also 3 metres high, 30 metres long, and weighed more than 30,000 kilograms! ENIAC used 18,000 vacuum tubes and consumed 150,000 watts of power. With the invention of the transistor in 1947, computer design was liberated from the limitation of the vacuum tube. Through the 1950s and 1960s, large, centralized mainframe computers dominated the computer industry, and International Business Machines (IBM) became a dominant MNC in the 1970s. The combining of many miniature transistors on a single silicon chip (the integrated circuit) in 1959 and the development of the microprocessor (in essence a computer on a silicon chip) in 1971 profoundly altered the computer industry. Microchips rapidly became increasingly powerful. The 486 microprocessor, used in the early 1990s, could execute 54 million instructions per second, weighed only a few grams, and used less than two watts of electricity. By 2008, microprocessors were capable of executing 50,000 million instructions per second. The speed of microprocessors now doubles every 18 months, in a formula known as Moore's Law. The fact that this type of speed exists is amazing enough, but what is revolutionary, in political terms, is that so many people have access to it.

These advances in miniaturization, processing power, and cost-effectiveness made the PC practically and economically viable, putting unprecedented processing power in the hands of individuals. The first PCs were introduced in 1975, and contemporary personal computers are many times more powerful than the mainframe computers of the mid-1970s.

Fifty years of progress. Jan Van der Spiegel holds a microprocessor (the black dot at the lower right corner of the square pad in his hand) in front of about one-tenth of the 30,000-kilogram original electronic numerical integrator and computer (ENIAC), the world's first general-purpose electronic computer, on the 50th anniversary of the machine's construction, January 31, 1996. Professor Van der Spiegel's chip has about one-20th the computing power of ENIAC, which was operational on February 14, 1946. (AP Photo/William B. Plowman/CP Images.)

With the development of the PC, the number of computers in the world began to grow rapidly. In 1971, there were approximately 50,000 computers of all kinds in the world. In 2006, there were 885 million personal computers up from 275 million just ten years earlier.[9] The computer industry has also become increasingly important to the global economy. By 1985, the output of the global electronics industry equalled the output of the world automobile industry and exceeded the output of the world steel industry.[10] Today, there are few industries or economic sectors that do not employ computers in some aspect of their operations. However, the development of computers—their increased miniaturization and cost effectiveness, and increases in processing speed—was only one part of the computer revolution. We have entered a new stage in the evolution of the computer: the development of networks. As the 2001 Human Development Report argued, "Today's technological transformations are intertwined with another transformation—globalization—and together they are creating a new paradigm: the network age."[11]

In one sense, the idea of networks is not new. In 1833 the invention of Morse Code (by Samuel Morse) ushered in the development of the telegraph in 1837, and telegraph lines soon extended across continents. In 1876, the telephone was invented by Alexander Graham Bell, and television demonstrators were being shown as early as in the 1920s. Both inventions went on to become linked to vast networks of cables and transmission receivers around the globe. The networking of computers has had yet another profound impact, ushering in a new age of communications. Coupled with advances in communications technologies, users are increasingly linking their computers with others to facilitate business, communication, financial transactions, and access to information. While the most famous of these networks is the Internet, a wide variety of other computer networks exist, such as local area networks (LANs) and wide area networks (WANs), which facilitate links between the computers of a specified group of people (such as corporate employees, bank branches, or network games players). As information and communication networks continue to grow in size and capacity, the issues associated with the global information society have become more important in global politics. These issues include: the regulation of global communications networks; "e-governance" (the use of electronic media to develop and implement public policy); e-commerce and trade in information and communications services; freedom of speech, censorship, and privacy protection; cybercrime, hacking, and espionage; intellectual property and copyright protection; and the implications of ICT for lower-income states and marginalized people. As Jonathan Aronson has observed, "These technologically sophisticated networks are reshaping the landscape of politics and international relations, transforming global commerce, recasting societies and cultures, and altering policy formulation and implementation."[12]

THE INFORMATION AGE AND GLOBAL COMMUNICATIONS NETWORKS

Today, hundreds of millions of people have access to unprecedented communications links, including telephone, fax, e-mail, text messaging, social networking websites, television, and international radio services. We are able to communicate and exchange more information more frequently and at less cost than ever before. In the past, the speed of communication was essentially equivalent to the speed of transportation. With the exception of very basic signalling using flags or smoke, messages could travel only as fast as the messenger carrying them. In practice, this meant the use of human, animal, or mechanical transport. While some of these communications methods were relatively swift and effective (such as the pony express system of Imperial China and the use of carrier pigeons), it might take days, weeks, months, or even years to transmit messages or news over long distances. In the 18th century, a trip around the world took several years by sailing ship. Today, jet aircraft can fly around the world

You've come a long way, baby. Martin Cooper, chairman and CEO of ArrayComm, holds a Motorola DynaTAC, a 1973 prototype of the first handheld cellular telephone in San Francisco in this April 2, 2003 photo. (AP Photo/Eric Risberg/ CP Images.)

in less than a day carrying large parcels and other mail items. Bulk cargo ships are far faster than the merchant sailing ships of just 200 years ago. Trucks can haul large amounts of freight over expansive road networks.

However, the most remarkable advances have been in the area of electronic communications. As recently as 100 years ago, the idea of virtually instantaneous global communication would have been dismissed as an unrealistic dream. Today, it is a commonplace for an increasing number of people around the world. The scope of transnational communication flows is astounding. From the development of the telegraph to modern satellite communications in the 1990s, technological advancements have enabled millions of people to communicate almost instantaneously using telephones or electronic messages.[13] For example, international phone traffic has increased dramatically. The use of international telephone calls (measured in terms of minutes) jumped from 38 billion minutes in 1991 to an estimated 183 billion minutes in 2006.[14] In 1960, a transatlantic telephone cable could carry 138 conversations. Today's fibre-optic cables are a fraction of the size and are capable of carrying 1.5 million conversations. In 1980, a copper wire phone line could transfer data at a rate of approximately one page per second. Today, an optical fibre the width of a human hair can carry the equivalent of 90,000 volumes of an encyclopedia per second.[15] The use of satellites has freed global telephone traffic from reliance on undersea or underground cables linking continents and cities. Electronic messaging has grown dramatically: over nine trillion e-mails are sent every year.[16] Moreover, the cost of this communication has decreased dramatically. The cost of a three-minute telephone call between New York and London fell from US$244.65 in 1930, to US$31.58 in 1970, to US$3.32 in 1990, to US$0.35 in 1998 (in 1990 dollars).[17] An e-mail message from Calgary to Paris costs no more than an identical message from Calgary to Edmonton. Because of these developments, it is possible to speak of a communications revolution and the consequent "death of distance" made possible by the computer and the proliferation of networks around the world.

Another trend is clearly identifiable: the increasing use of wireless communications networks. With some exceptions, most communications in the 20th century required a hard link of some kind, usually in the form of a copper-based or fibre-optic cable. Increasingly, communications are wireless, using radio waves to transmit messages and data through the air (or space). Such technologies include cellular phones and satellite receivers and dishes, which enable people to communicate from remote areas or receive television broadcasts even when no physical link is available. Advances in wireless technology have been swift. The first-generation wireless phone was introduced in 1981 and was the size of a small suitcase! In 1991, second-generation wireless phones were handheld and offered messaging services. In 2001, third-generation wireless phones began to offer multimedia and networking capacities in a small handset. There has been an explosion in the use of mobile or cellular phones. In 1991 there were 16 million mobile phone subscribers in the world, but by 2007 the number of subscriptions had ballooned to almost 3.3 billion.[18] Wireless Internet access is now increasingly common worldwide, and new generations of wireless technologies are in development, promising faster access speeds and information services. We have only just entered the age of the "wireless" revolution.

The most significant ICT network in global politics is the Internet, which has its origins in a U.S. military communications project known as the Advanced Research Projects Agency

Network (ARPAnet). Developed in the 1960s, ARPAnet was established to ensure that communications between political and military leaders could be maintained even in the event of a nuclear attack. ARPAnet was transferred to the National Science Foundation, which renamed the network NSFnet. NSFnet was expanded to universities and government agencies in the 1980s and then turned over to private companies. The beginning of the explosion in Internet use occurred in the late 1980s, as more powerful computers emerged and the World Wide Web (WWW) was created. The WWW software, created by Tim Berners-Lee at the European Particle Physics Laboratory (CERN) in Switzerland in 1989, established the common user protocols for addresses, languages, file transfers, and browsers. The Web facilitated the use of the Internet through easier-to-use interface software (first introduced with Mosaic in 1993), enabling anyone with a computer, a modem, a browser, and the requisite interest to use the Internet. The growth of the Internet has been spectacular. The International Telecommunication Union estimates that Internet use increased from 4.4 million users in 1991 to almost 1.5 billion in 2007, roughly 22 percent of the world's population.[19] In 1995, there were just 18,000 websites online, a number that grew to over 172 million by 2008.[20] Today, Internet users are just clicks away from abundant information, services, and entertainment, through e-mail, e-banking, e-government, e-health, e-learning, and eBay.

Within the larger ICT revolution, something of a mini-revolution is occurring. The merger of the cell phone, handheld computer, and Internet is creating the conditions for a very different kind of connectivity across people and places, a connectivity with significant implications for global politics. In the past, Internet users were essentially tied to fixed or mobile computer technology and connectivity "hot spots." Mobile phone users were primarily engaging in voice communication. Combining the two technologies has combine the mobility of the cell phone with the information and networking capacities of the internet, creating a "nomadic" future.[21] This promises to transform work, travel, and relationships between space and people. It has already had a practical impact on world politics. Elections monitoring by international observers now makes extensive use of text messaging. Large-scale international protests are now planned and coordinated worldwide through the use of the cell phone and the Internet, with images and digital video complementing traditional text. Human rights abuses have been exposed and publicized through general-traffic websites such as YouTube and dedicated sites such as Witness. Responses to local and international epidemics have been facilitated by mobile phone technology that greatly increases the ability to gather and disseminate data.

Another mini-revolution under way is the integration of ICT and the internet with photographic or satellite imagery, in a fusion of physical geography and social science data. Google Earth provides virtually complete photographic images of the planet, overlaid with data provided by a combination of sources. Launched in 2005, Google Earth and other similar "geobrowsers" such as World Wind and Virtual Earth are all made possible by high-resolution satellite imagery, powerful computers, cheap data storage, and broadband Internet connections. Geobrowsers have had an increasing impact on global politics in ways that were not anticipated by their designers. The human rights situation in Darfur has been highlighted by data overlays of destroyed villages over the geographic maps of the area, naturally without the consent of the Sudanese government. This has increased awareness of the violence in Darfur and has been an important tool for human rights activists. After Hurricane Katrina struck New Orleans in 2005, Google Earth was used by relief agencies to coordinate their efforts. An American charity equipped indigenous tribes in the Amazon rainforest to use Google Earth to assert their territorial rights against logging and mining operations.[22] Insurgents in Iraq have used Google Earth to plan attacks on U.S. and other coalition bases in the country, prompting concerns about the utility of geobrowsers for warfare or acts of terrorism. Other concerns are related to individual or organizational privacy in a world where places (homes, businesses, medical clinics) can be spotted and located with relative ease.

Some feel the long-term impact of transnational communications networks will be to bring humanity closer together, in a global village or cyberworld in which national borders become irrelevant and a global awareness of a shared human identity and destiny will take shape. In other words, the Internet might be one of the most important instruments of convergence in human history. However, this enthusiasm must be tempered with some sobering realities. While the Internet has realized its enormous potential for business, personal communication, and access to information, its use remains dominated by the industrialized world (and the U.S. in particular). Most Internet users live and work in industrialized states, and the majority of people in the developing world have little or no Internet access. In fact, much of the world's population has never made a telephone call, despite the proliferation of cell phones described above. Furthermore, like television programming, the quality of the websites on the Internet varies widely. Some are reputable and of high quality; others are virtually useless and contain false or misleading information. The Internet offers a forum to any individual or group that can construct a website (including hate groups), which demands a careful critical perspective when viewing information on the World Wide Web. One of the fastest-growing sectors on the Internet is erotica and pornography, raising or renewing questions about censorship and access control and denial by governments, groups, or individuals, and the sexual exploitation of women and children.

Another serious issue raised by ICT and the Internet is the relationship between the individual and the state and privacy and free speech. While Web advocates cite the Internet's capacity to promote democracy, diversity, and the free flow of information, all information can be manipulated and controlled. One survey of 40 countries found that 26 of them practised some form of Internet *filtering*, stopping their citizens from viewing certain general subjects or specific websites.[23] As reporters covering the summer 2008 Olympics discovered, China operates the most rigorous filtering effort in the world, blocking access to a wide range of topics, with the compliance of major search engines such as Google (see Profile 12.1). Beyond this, and despite the great diversity of websites, the rich world dominates online content, and English is the dominant language. The fact that globally popular websites and Web-based services are themselves owned by large corporations raises questions of how their behaviour can be managed or regulated. The content of the Internet is heavily corporate, and money matters in terms of vying for viewers (a familiar phenomenon to advertising executives and political campaign managers). This leaves little space for political dissent or protest, as Gregory J. Walters points out: "The Internet has been almost completely incorporated into the corporate media and communications system, and the political left has been relegated to the margins of cyberspace."[24] The Internet also raises issues related to privacy (including the security of financial and medical information) and copyright (witness the debates over filesharing websites and content on YouTube). Finally, computer piracy and hacking have raised concerns about the security of computer systems and the challenges of responding to this problem in a world of governments with different legal systems. These and other issues serve as a reminder that the considerable promise of the global information society must be viewed with a healthy caution about the implications for global inequality and human rights.

THE INFORMATION AGE AND THE WORLD ECONOMY

The global economy is being transformed by the technological developments of the information age. As John Zysman and Abraham Newman argue, "[ICT] does more than just change the costs of transportation and communication: it alters the manner in which economic value

PROFILE 12.1 China and the Internet

China is a good example of a country attempting to embrace communications technology while exercising political control over information content. As part of a government plan in place since the early 1990s, China has been developing its communications infrastructure. Internet use has increased from 50,000 users in 1995 to over 200 million in 2008. However, the Chinese government continues to impose tight controls on the flow of information, fearing the consequences for the country's political system. As the late Chinese leader Deng Xiaoping once said, "When you open the window, the flies come in." The Ministry of Information Industry controls Internet traffic entering the country, blocking Western news websites such as the BBC as well as the websites of human rights organizations and Chinese dissident groups. However, users in China can bypass government controls that block access to certain domain names by finding a proxy server that provides a link to Western news websites under a different domain name. The difficulty is finding such proxy servers. E-mail is one way of providing such information to Chinese Internet users, but the Chinese government employs 30,000 people to scan e-mails entering and leaving China for this kind of information. Prison sentences have been handed out to Chinese citizens who violate domestic laws on the dissemination of information and protest material over the Internet. In 2006, the search engine company Google was widely criticized for creating a special search site for users in China that met the censorship guidelines of the Chinese government. These practices included blocks on searches for subjects such as "Tibet" or specific websites such as the news site of the British Broadcasting Corporation. Google's response (that removing some Google search results was better than providing no Google services at all) was seen as self-serving, given the corporation's battle with other search engines for a share of the lucrative Chinese market. As China becomes more connected to the world economy, and as the economic importance of information flow increases, the interaction will become a fascinating case study in the clash between the power of the state and the forces of an electronic and supposedly borderless world.

SOURCES: CLARK BOYD, "BYPASSING CHINA'S NET FIREWALL," BBC NEWS, UK EDITION, MARCH 10, 2004, HTTP://NEWS.BBC.CO.UK/1/HI/TECHNOLOGY/3548035.STM (ACCESSED MAY 31, 2004); RONALD DIEBERT, ET AL., EDS., *ACCESS DENIED: THE PRACTICE AND POLICY OF GLOBAL INTERNET FILTERING* (CAMBRIDGE, MA: MIT PRESS, 2008); AND *STATISTICAL SURVEY REPORT ON THE INTERNET DEVELOPMENT IN CHINA* (BEIJING: CHINA INTERNET NETWORK INFORMATION CENTER, JANUARY 2008), 9, HTTP://WWW.CNNIC.CN/UPLOADFILES/PDF/2008/2/29104126.PDF (ACCESSED JUNE 9, 2008).

is created, changes how international production is organized, and reopens basic societal bargains struck around individual liberty and economic rights."[25] As a result, ICT is often described as having a transformative impact on the world economy. The nature of work is changing in many societies as technology alters the nature of products, production, and productivity. Wealthy states are in transition from industrial or manufacturing-based economies to information or knowledge-based economies. The global economy is characterized by the increased mobility of capital and production made possible by ICT networks. As Jonathan Aronson has observed: "These technologically sophisticated networks are reshaping the landscape of politics and international relations, transforming global commerce, recasting societies and cultures, and altering policy formulation and implementation."[26] This economic transition is provoking intense political debate over the relationship between workers and employers, citizens and the state, and markets and regulation.

In the workplace, the impact of the computer and information revolution has been dramatic. By 1991, companies were spending more money on computer and communications equipment than on industrial, mining, farming, and construction equipment combined.[27] Businesses use computers for communications, data storage and retrieval, business administration, payroll, record keeping, and budgeting. Banking and financial industries are almost entirely dependent on computers and communications links. Manufacturing industries use computers to design new products, operate their production facilities, manage inventories, track shipments, and distribute raw materials, supplies, and parts. The architecture, fashion, and graphic design fields make wide use of computers. The increasing mobility of networked wireless technologies also means that the traditional divisions between home, leisure, and workplace have begun to erode: work is increasingly something we do rather than a place we go.[28] The ICT revolution has also affected the very nature of work in modern industrialized societies as a whole. In the 1950s the majority of workers in the industrialized world were involved in manufacturing or transporting material goods.[29] By 1996 the OECD concluded that there was a clear trend in affluent countries toward an economy in which more than half of the labour force was engaged in the production, distribution, and use of information.[30]

In many ways, the information age has transformed national and international economic activity, blurring the distinction between the two. Most money is stored and exchanged in electronic form. Physical cash now makes up a small portion of most countries' money supplies, and increasingly direct deposit and credit and debit cards dominate commercial transactions. Major credit cards such as Visa, MasterCard, and American Express are accepted worldwide (as well as for online purchases), and it is possible to withdraw local currency from an ATM machine connected to a global network such as Plus or Interac. The direct deposit of paycheques and electronic bill payments are the norm. As we saw in Chapters 4 and 8, international trade and financial agreements paved the way for huge sums of money to cross borders, change hands, and be exchanged from one currency to another, often instantaneously. This was done over a growing international financial system of institutions and banks, all linked by communications networks and common information protocols. This has had a profound impact on government policy: with so much money in motion, rigid currency controls became increasingly irrelevant, and most governments have abandoned them. Central banks struggle to defend currencies under pressure, so great is the volume of international currency flows. Individual or corporate investors and fund managers can move money in and out of markets with great speed, complicating governmental responses to domestic and international economic crises. This was certainly the case during the onset of the global economic recession in 2008. Technology facilitated the spread of toxic assets to banks and investment funds around the world, and in turn facilitated a market response characterized by mass panic as investors pulled their money out of banks, funds, and countries in an effort to preserve their assets. However, we should not blame the technology in isolation from political and ideological factors. Neoliberal economic views had dominated the financial sector for decades and contributed to a political consensus that the financial sector should be as free from regulation as possible. The global recession was brought about primarily because of extraordinary greed on the part of many financiers and bankers, unrealistic expectations of investment returns and debt servicing by large numbers of consumers, and poor regulatory oversight of large financial institutions in the United States and elsewhere.

Business has also been affected by the ICT revolution. In his book *The World Is Flat*, Thomas Friedman describes how businesses are redistributing various components of work around the world to where it can be done most efficiently and at the lowest cost.[31] ICT plays a crucial role in the offshore production of goods and outsourcing of services. Multinational corporations increasingly conduct business according to the principles of collaborative planning, forecasting, and replenishment. Suppliers and retailers cooperate to determine anticipated customer demand, which in turn informs production, shipping and stockpiling of products. ICT enables businesses at all points of the product cycle—development, production, transportation, and sales—to instantly share data to optimize the flow of goods and services. Furthermore, the Internet and the Web have precipitated an enormous increase in electronic commerce (or e-commerce). In effect, the Internet has removed personal travel from the process of purchasing goods and services. E-commerce also widens the range of choice for consumers, who can now roam across the world in search of products, including those that are restricted or banned in their own countries. While still dependent on traditional mail and courier services for the physical delivery of the product, consumers need not go to the local shopping mall: the global shopping mall has come to them. Virtually all companies, especially banks and software firms, have moved at least some of their services online.

The ICT revolution is intimately connected to increasing economic interdependence. Together, ICT and globalization are having a mutually reinforcing impact on global politics, accelerating the pace of change, the spread of information, and the forging of relationship networks, and presenting new challenges to cultural identity and political authority. As Michael J. Mazaar notes, "The Internet would have had a substantial effect on world politics under any circumstance. In the context of globalization, that effect is magnified many times."[32] The impact of ICT on the global economy has been the subject of an intense and emotional debate. Advocates of ICT have stressed the beneficial affects of the technology. As ICT lowers the costs of information and travel and increases access to diverse supplies of resources, capital and labour, economic activity is stimulated. In the liberal perspective, these are positive developments which promote comparative advantage and increasing wealth and prosperity. The editors of one supportive report have argued, "There is growing evidence that ICT is driving innovation by allowing creative-thinking and responsive problem-solving to provide the promise of never-before-seen opportunities for all."[33]

However, many argue that this postindustrial society will be one not of promise but of increased dislocation, unemployment, and economic hardship for many, if not most, people. Unemployment and stagnant or falling wages and household incomes are growing concerns worldwide. While these problems are now attributed to the global recession of 2009, many allege that the underlying cause is the ICT revolution, coupled with the growing globalization of the world economy. Increases in telecommunications, trade, and financial flows have increased international competition, prompting firms to "downsize" (the technical term for firing employees) and facilitating their efforts to shift production to low-wage countries. As a result, unemployment (and the social problems associated with it) is on the rise. In addition, those jobs that are created will be insufficient in number to replace the jobs lost, and many of them will be low-paying service-sector jobs with poor benefits and low job security (sometimes called "McJobs"). Globalization and technological change have driven employers and workers farther apart in many sectors of the economy: as profits rise and wages fall, the bulk of income and revenues will go to a few individuals, widening the gap between rich and poor. These conditions have led Ethan B. Kapstein to argue as follows:

> The global economy is leaving millions of disaffected workers in its train. Inequality, unemployment, and endemic poverty have become its handmaidens. Rapid technological change and heightening international competition are fraying the job markets of the major industrialized countries. At the same time, systemic pressures are curtailing every government's ability to respond with new spending. Just when working people most need the nation-state as a buffer from the world economy, it is abandoning them.[34]

Christopher May has contended that the axiomatic divisions in society have remained despite the allegedly transformed nature of the knowledge-based economy. Basic questions, such as who knows what, who possesses value, and who works for whom, continue to define the workplace and the economy. Employment policies are still controlled by managers, and intellectual property rights have extended ownership into the realms of information and knowledge.[35]

Critics also argue that ICT and globalization are undermining the capacity of states to manage and intervene in their own economies, to the detriment of the wider social good. The decentralized and globalized character of communication, finance, and production in the networked information-age economy makes it difficult for governments to exercise regulatory and legal oversight. Governments are finding it increasingly difficult to respond to the tax implications of evolving business practices, as well as maintaining effective fraud, privacy, labour rights, property rights, and financial transparency legislation. Government laws and regulations on financial activity are increasingly difficult to enforce in a world of global electronic commerce. The ability to move production and financial operations around the world enables businesses to find favourable regulatory environments abroad, avoid or minimize taxes, and escape government oversight. Corporations can also use the threat of relocation to leverage governments to change regulatory policies and laws on environmental protection and labour rights, creating a "race to the bottom" as governments compete to retain and attract business activities and investment by weakening social, environmental and labour laws.[36]

Alternatively, many argue that these fears are alarmist and that protestors are the equivalent of modern-day Luddites, a reference to the British workers of the early 19th century who smashed the machines that threatened their jobs. Advocates of the computer and information revolution argue that predictions that machines will cause unemployment and social dislocation have been common. In the 1930s, automation of manufacturing was blamed for increases in unemployment. In the 1940s, others predicted that computers would throw massive numbers of individuals into enforced idleness. Today, ICT is blamed for job losses and social dislocation, while its defenders argue that society benefits from technological innovation. Despite the increasing pace of technological change, and indeed because of it, employment, incomes, and living standards have risen steadily. Because computers and information systems enhance productivity, advocates maintain, they will increase real incomes, from either higher wages or lower prices. This increases the purchasing power of the average consumer, which stimulates other sectors of the economy. With respect to unemployment, innovation does not mean painful labour market adjustments will not occur, especially in the short term. The key is that these positions are in new sectors promising greater growth and social benefits, rather than in traditional employment sectors.

Others argue that the impact of ICT on societies and global economics has not been as significant as some predicted, due to the fact that many goods and services cannot be exchanged electronically.[37] It is also the case that states are far from irrelevant in the emergence of the information age. Governments create the rules and regulations which govern information flows. Governments promote or directly develop the infrastructure (such as satellites and communications facilities) that ICT requires. Governments pass laws protecting intellectual property rights and privacy. Governments have also taken an active role (along with corporations and citizens groups) in the social debate over ICT. Therefore, the state is very much alive and well in the information age. This debate is likely to continue, for it is an inescapable fact that many people in various economic sectors around the world felt less secure in their jobs even before the onset of the global recession. Furthermore, there is a general dissatisfaction with economic performance in the industrialized countries and concern over social problems caused at least in part by divisions between rich and poor. Whether the computer and information revolution is blamed (justly or unjustly) for these problems, responding to these conditions presents a major challenge to the economic and fiscal policies of the developed world, which could continue to pursue the opportunities of the information age while seeking to protect their societies against the worst of the economic dislocation that ICT, globalization, and recession might bring.

THE DIGITAL DIVIDE

The ICT revolution has serious implications for the problem of inequality in the global economy. On the one hand, information technology has the potential to make a significant contribution to economic development and the human condition of poor peoples around the world.[38] On the other hand, information technology also has the potential to widen the gap between rich and poor as wealthy societies stand to benefit most from new innovations. Information-age technologies and capacities are unevenly distributed around the world. As a result, a digital divide exists within as well as among states.[39] Some countries, regions and peoples remain marginalized and even excluded from the economic benefits of the information age. These persons are disconnected from the communications networks that most citizens in the relatively affluent states take for granted. It is estimated that in 2006, over 58 percent of the population of high-income countries used the Internet, as against just over 10 percent of the population of low-income countries.[40] Bridging this divide is a priority in national and international development strategies.

The promise and the limitations of ICT as an instrument of development can be illustrated by mobile telephone use in Africa. The mobile phone revolution has greatly expanded telephone use on the African continent. With a very low ratio of telephone landlines to population (3 fixed lines for every 100 Africans) the mobile phone has proven particularly valuable, with over 75 percent of African telephone users employing mobile cellular technology. Cellular phone subscribers in Africa have increased from over 37 million in 2002 to over 264 million in 2007, or 27 phones for every 100 Africans.[41] This is an impressive development, because mobile technology has enabled many Africans to circumvent the infrastructure requirements of traditional telephones. However, the problem of inequality remains. Despite the enormous increase in mobile phone use in Africa, the continent lags behind in the adoption of this technology. In the Americas, there are almost 72 phones for every 100 inhabitants, and in Europe there are more cellular phones than people. In 2007, the Connect Africa Summit established a set of goals to improve connectivity, access, and ICT skill development across the continent. Regarded as an integral part of the larger World Summit on the Information Society targets and the Millennium Development Goals, the Connect Africa Summit succeeded in raising pledges of US$55 billion to fund the effort.[42]

Critics suggest that real development will not come from cell phone use; that heavy demand for the minerals used in cell phones, such as cobalt, have contributed to resource wars in the Congo and elsewhere; and that we are still uncertain as to whether long-term cell phone usage actually creates health problems, especially for children. Nonetheless, there is no escaping the importance of technology in development efforts, since information is now a "basic resource needed for technico-economic activity, on a par with matter and energy."[43] However, there is a danger that too much emphasis might be placed on ICT as a panacea for economic development problems. As Anthony P. D'Costa observes, "past radical technological developments such as railways, telephone and television have not fundamentally transformed the economic structures of developing countries."[44] In a three-volume work on the information age, economics, and society, Manuel Castells argues that the world economy is now in an informational rather than an industrial mode of development. Castells observes that a new international division of labour has formed, and is "constructed around four different positions in the information/global economy: the producers of high value, based on information labour; the producers of high volume, based on low cost labour; the producers of raw materials, based

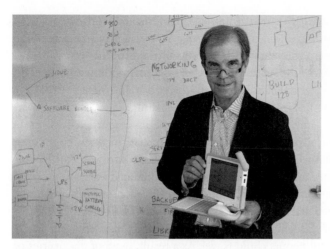

The promise of technology. Nicholas Negroponte, the head of the nonprofit One Laptop per Child project, holds the 100-dollar laptop designed for children in the developing world. (AP Photo/Namas Bhojani/CP Archive.)

on natural endowments; and the redundant producers, reduced to devalued labour."[45] The ICT revolution might help or hinder efforts to achieve greater global equality, but it will not be the only determinant of economic development. The digital divide is only one of many factors in the complex structure of the global economy.

If low-income countries hope to capitalize on the potential of ICT to escape from their disadvantageous positions in the international division of labour, they will have to make a major effort on a number of levels. They will have to improve their national communication and energy infrastructures to enable the adoption and effective use of computers and networks. Taking advantage of the potential of the Internet and e-commerce depends on the availability, accessibility, and affordability of this infrastructure.[46] Furthermore, appropriate and effective legal and financial frameworks must be in place for knowledge-based economic activity to operate.[47] Most importantly, developing countries will need the human capital required of information-age activity, in the form of knowledge workers and information literacy. Educational disparities are a critical variable when development emphasizes technology. Certainly, the technology aspects of development are inseparable from the human: the next generation of complex technology will increase wealth and opportunity for those with access to education. Can the digital divide be bridged? Technology and innovative methods may promise an answer: in Bangladesh, a bank issued microloans for the purchase of mobile phones to women, who then charged a cost for its shared use. This gave inexpensive phone access to millions of people.[48] The International Telecommunications Union has launched an effort to "connect the unconnected" by 2015, a recognition of the need for international cooperation if ICT is to fulfill its development potential for poor countries. If properly managed at both the local and international level, ICT might prove to be a potential source of liberation from poverty and hardship. If improperly managed, or not managed at all, ICT will almost certainly contribute to increased economic disparity.

THE DISSEMINATION OF TECHNOLOGY, INFORMATION, AND IDEAS

The computer revolution and the creation of expanding communications channels have led to an explosion in the availability of information. The volume of information available to us is extraordinary. Technology facilitates the creation, processing, accumulation, storage, and management of information on an unprecedented scale. Equally important is the decline in the cost of transmitting information. In 1970, the cost of transmitting a trillion bits of information across North America was US$150,000; by 2001, the cost had fallen to U.S.$0.12.[49] Desktop, laptop, and handheld computers can now process vast amounts of information and data and create spreadsheets, charts, and multimedia presentations. Single CD/DVD and digital recording devices can store volumes of books and images and music selections. Modern libraries are increasingly electronic, storing a growing amount of their information holdings in digital form and offering computerized access to their databases and to the databases of other libraries. Traditional media sources such as newspapers, magazines, and television programming all have online resources and archives that allow us to access a wide variety of news items, technical information, images, and music. Governments can receive information on domestic political events and international political events within minutes.

The availability and dissemination of ideas and information is having a dramatic effect on scientific discovery and innovation. Science can be a lonely enterprise; the image of the lone scientist toiling in a lab into the late hours of the night is an accurate one. However, scientific discovery is also a collaborative enterprise, as well as a competitive one. Scientists often seek out colleagues for assistance or advice. The process of scientific verification and review demands that experiments and discoveries be replicated and evaluated by scientific peer groups. The collaborative aspects of scientific discovery can thus be facilitated and accelerated by communications technology and the dissemination of information within **epistemic communities** of individuals dedicated to the common pursuit of ideas and objectives, regardless of their location or country of residence. In the past, innovations disseminated slowly, spreading only as fast as messages and people could travel. As a result, news of discoveries or innovations took a long time to come to the attention of those who could make use of them. In the television series *Connections*, host James Burke suggested that technological change was largely the result of inventors taking older discoveries, adding an innovation of their own, and applying it to the problem with which they were concerned. The result was a new way of doing things, inspired by the borrowing and adaptation of ideas. Today, the availability and dissemination of information allows would-be innovators to access a vast reservoir of information and ideas from around the world. New ideas and innovations appear almost daily, and those who are interested in certain scientific or technical pursuits can easily access the information they need. The potential for scientific and technical progress is therefore extraordinary.

However, the dissemination of scientific discovery and innovation is not always regarded as a good thing. In fact, many scientific discoveries and innovations are kept secret. The belief that national security may be put at risk is one rationale for preventing the spread of information. Another may be the commercial potential of the discovery and the desire to profit from it. Of course, there is an increasing trend toward using information networks for **industrial espionage** to steal information and data. This type of theft raises a number of questions about the security of personal information in an information age. Information about our financial situation, medical history, family records, and backgrounds increasingly resides in computers in electronic form. This is a growing problem for the privacy of the individual. There are similar concerns over the controversial introduction of "electronic voting" in the United States and elsewhere. In short, the dissemination of technology and ideas will continue to affect the global economy and the workplace. As James Rosenau argues, technology has "profoundly altered the scale on which human affairs take place, allowing people to do more things in less time and with wider repercussions than could have been imagined in earlier eras."[50] At the same time, technological advances and their economic implications will be jealously guarded in a world still full of competitive states, corporations, groups, and individuals.

THE MEDIA AND GLOBAL POLITICS

In the late 1980s, someone living in Canada interested in news and information from India, Brazil, or China would have to make do with limited television, radio, or newspaper reports supplemented by week-old newspapers and back issues of magazines purchased at specialty news stores. Letters written to friends or relatives took days or weeks to deliver and long-distance telephone calls were expensive. Today, that same person now has access to satellite television stations and online newspapers, magazines, and radio stations. E-mails and telephone calls are relatively inexpensive, as are social networking websites. The information age and the ICT revolution have greatly increased the availability of information and news from a wide range of sources around the world. In turn, this information is crucial to the impressions and opinions of events, peoples, and societies held by political and economic elites and a growing public audience throughout the world. How this information and news is gathered, packaged, and distributed is a matter of growing concern. As a result, the media (especially radio, television and Internet news services) are rightfully accorded special significance in the study of global politics.

The term "media" refers to three related aspects of information dissemination: the technological means of communication; the production and distribution of information; and the content received by audiences.[51] In the 1990s, satellite news services began to expand dramatically, and forged links with virtually all satellite and cable service providers around the world. The televised 24-hour coverage of the fall of communism in Eastern Europe, the collapse of the Soviet Union, and the 1990–91 Gulf War ushered in a new media age. German social theorist Jürgen Habermas suggested that "through the electronic media, these events were brought instantaneously before a ubiquitous public sphere. In the context of the French Revolution, Kant made reference to the reactions of a participatory public. At that time, he identified the phenomenon of a world public sphere, which today is becoming political reality for the first time in a cosmopolitan matrix of communication."[52] We are now accustomed to receiving news and information about events around the world virtually as they occur. As a result, we increasingly refer to a global media that delivers information, sounds, and images from political events (such as terrorist attacks), wars (such as Afghanistan and Iraq), natural disasters (such as earthquakes and hurricanes), and a wide variety of cultural and sporting events to a global audience. Because of this, global media have had a notable impact on the knowledge and attitudes of individuals, as well as on the policies of governments.

The power of the media and related industries is potentially enormous, for they are the source of much of the information that people receive about the world in which they live. What is reported and what is excluded is crucially important in how people perceive events and ideas. In the past, newspapers, magazines, radio, and "newsreels" (short news presentations shown before feature films) were the dominant forms of media. Radio was pioneered as a mass propaganda device by Joseph Goebbels and the Nazi Party of Germany in the 1930s, and it remains a powerful medium largely because it is easily accessible. There are more than two billion radios in the world, and in countries where illiteracy rates are high the radio is the primary source of information about national or international events. International shortwave radio broadcasts, such as Voice of America (VOA), the British Broadcasting Corporation (BBC) World Service, and Radio Canada International, reach into the remotest regions of the world to bring news items, political perspectives, and entertainment to those with shortwave receivers. Radio was also used extensively to deliver hate speeches in preparation for the genocide committed against the Tutsis in Rwanda in 1994. In conflicts such as Afghanistan and Iraq, as well as in many UN peacekeeping missions, establishing a "friendly" radio service is considered a priority.

Television is even more politically powerful, largely because of the impact images can have on human emotions and reactions. It brings a sense of immediacy, or presence, that other media do not possess. There are over 800 million television sets in the world, and an increasing range of channels is available to most consumers. As James Rosenau has argued, "Access to television has become sufficiently global in scope that it must be regarded as a change of [fundamental] proportions."[53] Cable channels and satellite television channels continue to proliferate, and in North America, some viewers have more than 100 channels to choose from. Like radio, television also has networks devoted to international broadcasting.

The U.S.-based Cable News Network (CNN), the British Broadcasting Corporation (BBC) and the British-based International Television Network (ITN) are the most prominent examples. CNN ushered in the age of the 24-hour news station in 1980, as a component of Turner Broadcasting System Inc.[54] Today, there has been a notable increase in international broadcasting aimed at projecting a national perspective into the global media arena, often in the language of the target audience. Many of these stations were established to counter the presence and presumed influence of CNN, the BBC, and ITN. This was a major motive for the creation of France 24. Stations such as Russia Today are in English, while the German network Deutsche Welle and the U.S. TV channel Al-Hurra broadcast in Arabic.

In the Arab world, the media environment has been turned upside down by a private satellite news channel, Al-Jazeera (which roughly translates as "the Peninsula"). Al-Jazeera began broadcasting in 1996 and operates out of Qatar.[55] The station has established itself in the Arab world as an alternative to highly censored state-owned television networks and has stimulated a growing number of private broadcasting stations in the Middle East. Al-Jazeera has gained attention in the West for its broadcast of videotapes by Al-Qaeda and Osama Bin Laden, but in the Arab world it is better known for its critical coverage of many Arab governments, as well as its coverage of the Israeli–Palestinian conflict and the wars in the region (particularly in Afghanistan and Iraq). This coverage is unabashedly critical of Israel and the United States. While U.S. media coverage of the invasion and occupation of Iraq, with its embedded journalists, was criticized for its failure to present a range of opinion and show the bloody consequences of the conflict, the United States has accused Al-Jazeera of showing little other than civilian casualties, while providing little information on the stated U.S. reasons for fighting. Nevertheless, the popularity of Al-Jazeera rests with its credibility in the region for broadcasting "news gathered independently by Arabs for Arabs and that sees events through *their* eyes."[56] In 2001, Al-Jazeera launched an Internet version of its news service, first in Arabic and then in English in 2006, which has brought the network and its perspective into the global arena.

The arrival of global media sources to the Middle East and the creation of Al-Jazeera have stimulated a debate about the transformative power of the media. Some argue the region is changing because of growing access to information delivered by global media sources, and Al-Jazeera is a reaction to this new reality. For example, Mohammed Jassim Al Ali (former managing director of Al-Jazeera) has argued: "Democracy is coming to the Middle East because of the communication revolution. You can no longer hide information and must now tell people the truth. If you don't the people won't follow you, they won't support you, they won't obey you."[57] Other observers are not so sanguine, arguing that media in the Arab world remain highly controlled by governments and rulers. As Mamoun Fandy argues, "The ownership of a given media outlet determines its coverage and the type of commentaries its airs.… The reality is that the Arab media's impact on transforming Middle Eastern societies is at best minimal."[58] Naomi Sakr agrees, arguing that editorial content in Arab media reflects the agendas of political and economic elites: political change causes change in editorial content, not the other way around.[59] This debate raises an interesting point about the global media. Certainly, there is very little critical coverage of Islamic Jihad, Hamas, or the Sudanese Islamic government in the Arab media. However, the same might be said when it comes to coverage of certain issues in U.S. or Western media. American news networks were notably uncritical of the war in Iraq and seldom make references to the reasons for the popularity of organizations like Hamas. Perhaps Al-Jazeera and other stations like it represent a new age in global media diversity, competition, and political debate.

However, we must be cautious when we proclaim that an age of global media is upon us. Perhaps it is more accurate to say that the potential for a global media is upon us, because the reality is that most programming in any given spot in the world is overwhelmingly local or national in its coverage. As Ted Magder suggests, "We may live in a world of globalization, but we do not yet live in the age of global news *per se*, either in the sense that audiences the world over pay attention to the same international stories on an everyday basis or even in the sense that audiences get more global (or foreign) news than in the past."[60] For the most part, citizens are interested in local news that directly impacts their lives, communities, and daily decisions. The economics of the media industry also play a role: local stories sell and are cheaper to produce, while international stories generally do not sell and are expensive to produce. When major events happen, media industries can mobilize rapidly, even sending their anchors to cover dramatic events—such as the fall of the Berlin Wall or the beginning of war against Iraq—from the scene. However, once the drama ends, and intensive or "special extended coverage" packages are no longer securing viewers, the old pattern of emphasis on local news returns. Furthermore, it is unclear just how much influence the media has on its audiences. Lived experiences and social frames of reference are difficult to challenge or alter. The volume of information available makes it difficult to assimilate complicated or contradictory messages. Media is also voluntary to the extent that a viewer can switch channels or websites (or even read a book!).

There is also a growing critical reflection on the role of the media that calls into question the existence of a new global media age. Some suggest that during the fall of the Berlin Wall, the collapse of the U.S.S.R., and the 1990–91 Gulf War, the media (and the public who watched it) were mere spectators, not actors or agents or participants in the events. Concerns that the media are manipulated by economic or political elites have also grown. The Vietnam War was a watershed for the news media: one of the turning points of the war was CBS news anchor Walter Cronkite's televised statements declaring the war a bloody stalemate in which victory was impossible. Coverage of the war brought the brutalities of the conflict to televisions in the United States, and this coverage was a major reason for the change in American public opinion. This first "living room war" prompted a change in the relationship between the military and the media; in the 1989–90 invasion of Panama and the 1990–91 Gulf War the media were tightly grouped into reporter "pools" and provided information in a controlled environment by way of daily news briefings from the U.S. military. Gone were the violent images, dead bodies, and expressions of disgust and discouragement by soldiers: instead, coverage was sanitized, bloodless, and homogenous. In the 2003 invasion of Iraq, the media were permitted to use so-called embedded reporters, who were assigned to U.S. units and whose coverage was heavily censored. The relationship between the military and news media has become so proximate that Daya Kishan Thussu and Des Freedman observe that "military and media networks have converged to the point where they are now virtually indistinguishable … media constitute the spaces in which wars are fought and are the main ways through which populations (or audiences) experience war."[61] In this media age, then, the trend may not be toward greater understanding and participation, but toward passive, uncritical absorption of managed information.

Making Al-Jazeera famous. In this television image broadcast on April 15, 2002, by Arab satellite station Al-Jazeera, Osama Bin Laden, right, listens as his top deputy, Ayman al-Zawahiri, speaks at an undisclosed location. (AP Photo/Al-Jazeera/APTN/CP Archive.)

Another concern is the concentration of international media in a shrinking number of large corporations. In the 1980s, the global media was concentrated in perhaps 50 corporations. Today, only a few companies dominate the global gathering, processing, and dissemination of news programming, led by the "Big Five" of Time Warner, Disney, Bertelsmann, Viacom, and News Corporation. Time Warner is an example of the extraordinary concentration of media services in large corporations. In 2008, Time Warner companies included America Online, Inc.; Time Warner Book Group; Time, Inc.; Time Warner Cable; Home Box Office (HBO); and the Turner Broadcasting System (which owns CNN). Critics charge that the global media is essentially controlled by major corporations, a consequence of the neoliberal economic model, which promotes deregulation, privatization, and commercialization. The dominance of this model (in the U.S. and the global economy) has facilitated the creation of corporate media monoliths that in turn are promoting the spread of market-oriented values in news, advertising, and entertainment.[62] However, it is also the case that media-sector markets are intensely competitive in the global and national arena, and new sources of news and information are constantly emerging. The presence of transnational media giants does not necessarily translate into influence or dominance in societies that often have trusted local and national media outlets. And to be successful, even the largest media companies have to adjust to local tastes and interests. This debate shows no sign of abating, even as the size of some media corporations continues to grow and new ones rise to prominence.

The global media is of particular concern to developing countries. The rich industrialized world's domination of the global media and information content on the airwaves and the Internet raises concerns about the ability of the developing world to have its voice heard, its concerns expressed, and its cultures and values protected. Many developing countries see the rich world's domination of the information age and the global media as another factor promoting modernization, imperialism, and globalization, thereby perpetuating the dependence of poor countries.[63] Of course, some of these concerns are shared by certain industrialized countries (such as France and Canada) worried about the intrusion of American cultural products into their own societies. In the 1980s, several leaders from the Southern Hemisphere called for the adoption of a New World Information and Communication Order (NWICO) that would establish limits on the domination of the media and information networks and create space for the voices of the South. This effort never overcame opposition from rich countries, but the struggle continues in the form of disputes over cultural protection and control of local independent media establishments around the world. Hopefully, in the future local media will become a tool for people in the developing world to make social change according to their own desires and visions, rather than act as instruments of government repression or foreign economic interests.

THE GLOBAL MEDIA AND POLITICAL DECISION MAKING

There is growing interest in the influence the media might have on the foreign policy decisions of governments. The predominant view is that the media must play an important and in some cases decisive role in foreign policy decision making. The leaders of governments and their key advisors may be personally influenced by current news coverage or had their views framed by previous media portrayals of the issue in question. The media can also influence public opinion, which can then exert pressure on governments through elected representatives, opinion polls, and protest. This connection between the media and governments is sometimes described as a cause-and-effect relationship: the media pressures government. However, this is a very simplistic formula. International events can compel governments to react for reasons that have little to do with media exposure, while governments may have particular foreign policy goals they want to achieve. Therefore, caution must be exercised when attributing government action in global affairs to the media. Another interpretation of the relationship between the media and foreign policy decision making involves the use or manipulation of the media by governments to gain public support for foreign policy decisions. From this perspective, the media is a propaganda tool of government or the dominant economic elites (which may be inextricably linked from a Marxist viewpoint). This manipulation can be direct (in cases when state-operated media is essentially an arm of the government) or indirect (when media coverage reflects a larger elite consensus or a misplaced sense of national loyalty or patriotism). The causal relationship is therefore reversed: government manipulates the media. A third perspective suggests that the relationship between the media and foreign policy decision making is mutually influential. Media–government relations consist of an ongoing "conversation" in which each influences the other.[64] Despite this debate, there is general agreement that the media can exert some influence over foreign policy decision making in the following ways.

Agenda Setting. The items on any government's foreign policy agenda are those that are considered important enough to demand government attention. The global media (and the domestic national media) play a role in this process by bringing issues to the attention of the public. In the process of reporting on certain issues (and not reporting on others) the media influence the agenda confronting decision makers, and in so doing create a dilemma. As Stig Hjarvard argues, "Under special circumstances, the power of such globalized public opinion poses a severe problem for even the mightiest of nations, because public opinion demands political action that either contradicts national policies or outstrips the diplomatic, economic, or military power of the nations involved."[65] Hjarvard cites the example of the massacre of pro-democracy protestors in China at Tiananmen Square in 1989: the world expressed outrage, but what could be done beyond the sanctions levelled against China? The media may also structure agendas by influencing perceptions of which issues should have a higher priority than others. If an issue is a public issue, then it becomes an issue for elected officials, who must be sensitive to the concerns of their constituents. In Canada and in other parliamentary democratic systems, an issue can be raised in the legislature, at a press conference, or at a public meeting. Elected officials are required to respond in an informed manner, with some explanation of the government's response. As a result, issues brought to the foreign policy agenda by the media become relevant to unelected officials as well. Bureaucracies and bureaucrats pay close attention to media reports, for they know that members of the legislature and the executive have to respond to these issues, and will turn to the bureaucracy for advice and assistance in preparing responses.

Influencing Decision Makers. In addition to exerting pressure on government through public opinion, the media can often have a direct impact on decision makers themselves. Elected and unelected government officials (including prime ministers and presidents) watch television, listen to the radio, and read newspapers. As a result, they can be directly affected by media stories and media portrayals of the issues. For world leaders, as for publics, news items from global television networks such as CNN or ITN are often the first indication that an event has occurred, and the first source of information on breaking events. Government officials will also monitor media coverage of their own actions and responses to see how their own policies are played out in the media and what reactions those policies are receiving from the public.

Shaping Perceptions. Just as the media can bring issues to public attention, the media can also influence public perceptions of these issues. Media (especially television) can transmit sounds, images, or narratives that engender a strong emotional reaction in the public. Pictures of famine victims, human rights abuses, brutality, and human suffering can put strong pressure on governments to do something to alleviate or stop these injustices. In many cases, the media story may blame certain individuals or groups for these injustices and highlight a possible course of action or target for government policy. As a result, not only is the public made aware of the issue but also the media story may influence public perceptions of what ought to be done. This can create policymaking problems, for if governments and those advising them feel that this public perception of what ought to be done is not feasible or even dangerous, they will be reluctant to act. Alternatively, governments may find another course of action more appropriate and face the task of selling this policy to a public that may have different perceptions of the issue. The media can also provide the public with a sense of how their own individual feelings about an issue are shared (or not shared) by society. Media coverage of mass protests, rallies, and marches can provide a perception of what the rest of society feels is important. And because many people, from news commentators to protestors to foreign policy experts, have their opinions on what ought to be done solicited and broadcast to the public, the government must respond to the various proposals for action put forward from a wide variety of individuals.

Embarrassing Governments. The ability of the media to discover and reveal events around the world often forces governments to face the consequences of their actions in the international realm. It is increasingly difficult for governments to hide or ignore unfavourable news or politically problematic issues. If governments make mistakes, or make what in retrospect are poor decisions, they will quite likely have to respond to critical reports and investigations in the media. On other occasions, current government policies may be subject to criticism. As a result, governments and politicians often find themselves faced with embarrassing (and potentially politically damaging) inquiries into why the government is pursuing its course of action. For example, the efforts of the Liberal government under Jean Chrétien to expand Canadian trade in Asia through the "Team Canada" missions met with criticism from human rights organizations that the government was not doing enough to promote human rights in Asia. This criticism was accompanied by media stories and images of poorly paid workers toiling for long hours under terrible working conditions.

Together, the ability of the media to pressure governments through agenda setting, influencing decision makers, shaping perceptions, and embarrassing governments has been described as the "CNN Effect" (see Profile 12.2). Some might conclude that the power of the media is decisive as a determinant in foreign policy decision making, but this is inaccurate. After all, even if the agenda is at least in part set by media reports, in practice governments have a lot of flexibility over how they might actually respond to an issue. When public pressure encourages governments to do something, it does not always specify what that something should be. Agenda setting is not policy setting. Although media stories may influence the public's perceptions of what their government ought to do, only rarely is public opinion unified on an issue. The fact that public opinion is often split or undecided allows governments considerable room to manoeuvre when making decisions. As for the media affecting government leaders and key officials directly, while this can happen, they are also surrounded by advisors and experts armed with secret intelligence or information, wider historical perspectives, and policy experience. This group enables decision makers to draw on more sources of information and ideas than those presented on television. And while it is harder for governments to escape the consequences of poor decisions, the unintended consequences of their decisions, or even criminal or unethical decisions, the media also provide governments with an unprecedented capacity to explain and defend their actions or even to apologize and acknowledge mistakes.

THE INFORMATION AGE AND THE FUTURE OF THE STATE

Will the information age may be the final blow to the supremacy of the state in international relations? According to liberals, the power of the state has been eroding due to increased

PROFILE 12.2　The "CNN Effect" and Global Politics

In 1992 the U.S. government led a coalition of countries (which included Canada) in a UN Security Council authorized intervention in Somalia, which had collapsed into communal warfare between rival clan factions. The objective of the operation was to establish order in the country and to facilitate the delivery of humanitarian relief to a population suffering from war and starvation. The prevailing explanation for this intervention was the extensive media coverage of human suffering in the weeks leading up to the intervention. As news reports and media images of starving and abused Somalis reached publics around the world, pressure built up on governments to respond. In the U.S. the coverage of the humanitarian crisis on CNN is said to have exerted a decisive influence on President Bush and the American public to intervene in Somalia. In Canada and other coalition governments, similar pressures were exerted through the media on government decision makers. In a *New York Times* editorial the famous American foreign policy elder statesman George Kennan argued that U.S. foreign policy was been led by the media, especially television. The link between media coverage and U.S. foreign policy was reinforced a few months later, when 18 U.S. soldiers were killed and their bodies dragged through the streets of the Somali capital of Mogadishu. The images of this act precipitated outrage in the U.S. public, and America withdrew from Somalia shortly thereafter. The phrase "CNN Effect" has since been used to describe a theory that policy making can be driven by media coverage rather than national interests. However, the accuracy of the "CNN Effect" has been challenged by the argument that the U.S. decision to intervene in Somalia was driven primarily by diplomatic and bureaucratic debates in the government about what to do in Somalia. These debates predated media coverage of the crisis, and when reporters became aware of these internal government debates they dutifully reported on them in the news. This phenomenon is referred to as "news indexing," which theorizes that the media tend to follow and report on what political elites are discussing and thinking of doing. As a result, some critics of the "CNN Effect" charge that the media did not influence the U.S. government to intervene in Somalia, but rather the U.S. government influenced the media to focus on Somalia. Others suggest that the government and the media influenced each other, driving the Somalia issue further up on the U.S. government's agenda. Nevertheless, the "CNN Effect" remains a compelling explanation of some government actions. In 2006, the news network Al-Jazeera provided graphic coverage of the July War in Lebanon. This coverage is said to have influenced political elites and publics in Saudi Arabia and Jordan to adopt more pro-Hezbullah positions than they might have otherwise. This link between coverage and foreign policy decision making was described as the "Al-Jazeera Effect."

SOURCES: PIERS ROBINSON, *THE CNN EFFECT: THE MYTH OF NEWS, FOREIGN POLICY AND INTERVENTION* (LONDON: ROUTLEDGE, 2002); PHILIP SEIB, ED., *NEW MEDIA AND THE NEW MIDDLE EAST* (NEW YORK: PALGRAVE, 2007); AND DEREK B. MILLER, *MEDIA PRESSURE ON FOREIGN POLICY: THE EVOLVING THEORETICAL FRAMEWORK* (NEW YORK: PALGRAVE MACMILLAN, 2007).

economic interdependence and globalization. Now, the information age has ushered in an era of relatively unfettered flows of ideas, transactions, and communications across the world, virtually unaffected by states and governments. The state is now losing its capacity to control or influence the flow of information within and across its borders, and over what its citizens see, hear, and think. Individuals, groups, and organizations are in increasing contact across state borders, creating new communications networks, channels for ideas and debate, business and financial links, and international civil society organizations. Some observers suggest that information and communication technologies are "reformatting politics" by enabling NGOs and civil society organizations to link local issues with global issues and in the process become more effective and influential actors in world affairs.[66]

Many governments, including the government of Canada, now make little or no effort to directly control this flow of information (though they will make efforts to manipulate it, and political parties use it extensively to sell their policy platforms). This is particularly true of those governments in politically open societies. The struggle over the interpretation and portrayal of ideas and events goes on daily. Domestic critics of government use their unprecedented access to information to criticize the government and its policies in the media. The most open of governments still keep much of their foreign and defence policy affairs (and many other areas as well) behind a veil of secrecy, which the media and citizens' groups often try to penetrate. Governments must continually grapple with issues related to the material content of information flows, as citizens' groups call for the ban or regulation of material they consider immoral or misleading.

For many governments, the free flow of information represents a threat to the power, and even the survival, of the regime. Ideas and information, particularly if they expose lies, abuses, or the controversial nature of ideological claims, can be politically powerful. During the Cold War, the Soviet Union and Eastern Europe jammed foreign radio broadcasts (especially Radio Free Europe, the Voice of America, the BBC World Service, and Radio Liberty) and foreign television broadcasts. Telephone links to the outside world were tightly controlled and monitored; as late as 1987, the Soviet Union possessed only 16 international long-distance telephone circuits.[67] Newspapers were heavily controlled and censored. Photocopy machines were not available to the public. Underground literature (called *Samizdat*) was replicated by hand, on typewriter, and passed from person to person. Today, countries such as North Korea, Sudan, Iran, and Myanmar impose draconian restrictions on information flows within and across their borders. And as we have seen in our discussion of the global media, Western governments have not escaped criticism about the control of the media either.[68] Despite such efforts, information and communications technologies can be powerful instruments of dissent, even in countries with highly authoritarian political systems. Audio and videotapes have played instrumental roles in the toppling of governments. In the years before the Iranian revolution, audiotapes recorded by the Ayatollah Khomeini in France and smuggled into Iran played a decisive role in the undermining of the Shah's regime and the enormous popularity of Khomeini on his return from exile. In the Philippines, the dictatorship of Ferdinand Marcos fell in part due to the circulation of videotapes showing the assassination of the Philippine opposition leader, Benigno Aquino. Telephone, fax, and computer networks have also played a role in political dissent. During and after the Tiananmen Square protests of 1989, protestors and sympathizers abroad made extensive use of fax machines and e-mail to gather and disseminate information on events at Tiananmen. In Thailand, protestors against the military government used telephone and fax lines to communicate and coordinate their efforts. When the government employed force to suppress the protests, cutting phone lines and shooting at the demonstrators, the opposition remained in communication using cellular telephones. In Serbia, street demonstrations broke out in protest of the government's cancellation of local election results in 1997. The protestors employed a radio station to combat government domination of the media. When this was shut down, the protestors communicated with each other and the outside world using the Internet. Antiglobalization organizations and anti–Iraq War protests have used ICT to plan their campaigns and disseminate their messages. As Isabel Vincent observes, "It used to be that guerrilla fighters lugged AK-47s and sent battlefield news in rolled-up scraps of paper, faithfully carried by couriers through treacherous jungles and mountain passes. Today's revolutionary carries a laptop, and plugs into the Net."[69] The Internet has also been used as an instrument of communication and activism by human rights advocates (see Profile 12.3).

PROFILE 12.3 Hacktivism at the University of Toronto

In the Munk Centre for International Studies at the University of Toronto is a facility known as The Citizen Lab. Established in 2001 through the efforts of Professor Ron Diebert, the Lab engages in what Dr. Diebert calls "hacktivism," a combination of traditional computer hacking and social and political activism. Dr. Diebert believes that understanding how technology works and what is behind it is essential to a liberal, democratic society: "Citizens can't just accept technology at face value. They need to open the lid, so to speak, understand how it works, beneath the surface." By bringing together a diverse group of faculty and students from computer science through political science, Dr. Diebert wanted to encourage the creation of a group of technically adept activists. The heart of Citizen Lab activities is the OpenNet Initiative, targeted at countries that attempt to block access to the World Wide Web.

"Hacktivists" at the lab attempt to identify what methods governments use to block access to certain websites. The Lab then develops techniques and software to help citizens in these countries circumvent the controls. The Citizen Lab also operates the Information Warfare Monitor in cooperation with the SecDev Group,

an international security think tank based in Ottawa. The Monitor is a research program exploring the use of cyberspace as an environment for the exercise of state power. In March 2009 it exposed a large Chinese-government cyber-espionage effort directed against the Tibetan community worldwide. The spying campaign, called GhostNet by the authors of the report, involved the infection of at least 1,295 computers in 103 countries with malware designed to provide full access to secret files and personal information, including those in the offices of the Dalai Lama.

How do target countries feel about the activities of the Citizen Lab? "Some authoritarian regimes obviously don't like what we're doing," says Diebert. "But I feel we're working in support of broader principles of human rights, so I don't mind the controversy. Sometimes it helps."

SOURCE: CLARK BOYD, "'NET NINJAS' TAKE ON WEB CENSORSHIP," *BBC NEWS*, WORLD EDITION, APRIL 18, 2004, HTTP://NEWS.BBC.CO.UK/GO/PR/FR=/=/2/HI/TECHNOLOGY/3632757.STM (ACCESSED APRIL 18, 2004); INFORMATION WARFARE MONITOR, *TRACKING GHOSTNET: INVESTIGATING A CYBER ESPIONAGE NETWORK*, MARCH 29, 2009, HTTP://WWW.SCRIBD.COM/DOC/13731776/TRACKING-GHOSTNET-INVESTIGATING-A-CYBER-ESPIONAGE-NETWORK; AND THE CITIZEN LAB WEBSITE, HTTP://WWW.CITIZENLAB.ORG. THE CITIZEN LAB IS RUN OUT OF THE MUNK CENTRE FOR INTERNATIONAL STUDIES AT THE UNIVERSITY OF TORONTO.

Despite the association of ICT with political freedom, governments can also harness the power offered by the information age. Does this new era of technology-induced freedom from state controls exist primarily in the minds of those who foresee a technological, transboundary world? Is the computer, information, and communications revolution overrated as an agent of change in global politics? After all, information has always been an important element of state power, and computers and communications technologies permit states to access, store, and use information as never before. States employ this information to their advantage in a number of ways. In their interactions with one another and with nonstate actors, information (or "intelligence") has always been a vital dimension of diplomacy and war. Negotiation, bargaining, and conflict management efforts are facilitated by virtually instantaneous communication and the increasing capability of states to gather information independently. The telephone has become a central tool of contemporary diplomacy and leaders and officials of states often communicate with each other simply by picking up the phone. States also employ information as an instrument of state power, by disseminating information into the international system in the form of radio broadcasts, information services, and statements in the media. Governments may also spread **disinformation** in a deliberate attempt to mislead other governments (or their own populations). The ability of computers to store and retrieve information offers governments an unprecedented capability to watch over the lives of citizens and keep files on suspected subversive elements. These technologies may therefore increase, rather than decrease, the power of the state with respect to the individual.

This raises the issue of information power. In the future, the states that are world leaders in computer development, information production, and communications technology will likely be the most powerful states in the international system. Just as past technical innovations increased the power of certain societies or states, the information age will increase the power of those states best able to develop and harness the potential of these new technologies. Many observers argue that the country best placed to increase its power and exert leadership in the information age remains the United States:

> Knowledge, more than ever before, is power. The one country that can best lead the information revolution will be more powerful than any other. For the foreseeable future, that country is the United States. America has apparent strength in military power and economic production. Yet its most subtle comparative advantage is its ability to collect, process, act upon, and disseminate information, an edge that will almost certainly grow over the next decade.[70]

State power in the information age will not be dependent on natural endowments of population or resources or geographic position, although these will still have relevance. Instead, power will depend on technological leadership, on political, economic, and social flexibility, and on education.

A GLOBAL CULTURE?

The relationship between transnational communications networks and culture is a growing topic in the study of global politics. Dramatic statements have been made on the impact of the information age in the industrialized world. Bill Gates, for example, argues that a "global interactive network will transform our culture as dramatically as Gutenberg's press did in the middle ages."[71] Of course, it is not so much the network that will have this impact but the content it is carrying. Today, the global impact of such networks on cultures worldwide is beginning to be understood. As with so many aspects of the information age, there are both encouraging and discouraging dimensions to this issue. Transnational communications technologies and the global media are shrinking the planet. Individuals around the world can watch the same news reports, listen to the same music, watch the same sporting events, see the same movies, eat the same food, and be exposed to advertising for the same consumer products. As a result, a global culture may be taking shape. To be sure, it exists only in very embryonic form today, if at all. And even if it does develop, the most of the planet will not share in this experience. However, we may be witnessing the beginning of a form of cultural integration or homogenization, borne on the pathways opened up by transnational communications technologies and the information revolution.

Sociologists interested in technology have introduced a convergence theory that is not unlike the idea of convergence as we have used it in this book. According to this theory, "the opportunities and demands presented by modern technology promote the convergence of all societies toward a single set of social patterns and individual behaviours."[72] In other words, the adoption of Western technology and science will lead to the establishment of political institutions and cultural environments similar to those in the advanced European and American worlds. Thus, globalization will inevitably be realized through technological standardization.

As a theory, however, this leaves some room for healthy speculation. One might point to the spread of capitalism as the source of this convergence instead of to the technology employed. Obvious cases exist where distaste for Western society has led to an assertion of anti-Western political change, such as the Iranian revolution that ushered into power the late Ayatollah Khomeini. Indeed, recent research indicates that there is a "contra-flow" of communication and cultural influences in much of the world which is a reaction to U.S. and Western cultural influences.[73] In a more general sense, one might argue that culture does not necessarily converge simply because of technological similarities. There are distinct patterns of social interaction within different societies despite a high rate of technological convergence. Japan, the United States, and Germany all have adopted industrial technology yet remain quite different in terms of cultural attributes. Though many would argue with this, we can even point out significant cultural differences between countries as similar in technological circumstances as the United States and Canada.

Television programming, movies, and music have become increasingly globalized. Audiences around the world can watch television programming from a wide variety of other countries. These programs can reveal the nature of life in other societies, and as a result television can be a powerful educational tool. However, television can also distort the perception of life in other countries. For example, exported Western soap operas have created the impression among many people in other societies that all North Americans and Europeans are wealthy. One of the most watched series around the world is *Baywatch*, and it features swimsuit models working on Californian sunny beaches. Another is *American Idol*, which has been replicated in many other states and depicts average citizens pursuing the American Dream of fame and monetary success. Children and family programming is also increasingly globalized, as suggested by the international success of the *Mighty Morphin Power Rangers* (dubbed into English from the original Japanese); the Canadian television series *Degrassi Junior High*; and the success of Japanese anime. Movies are also distributed internationally, as are music recordings. Quality cinema is shown at international film festivals (such as the famous Cannes Film Festival) and the international success of "Bollywood" films produced in India demonstrates the cross-fertilization of cultural influences. Classical musicians and conductors move routinely across national borders. In the genres of rock, jazz, and blues, tours are often international in scope. Some varieties of music are explicitly international in inspiration, and are sometimes referred to as "world music."

Sporting events have also become internationalized. The Olympic Games and the World Cup (to name only two) are major international events, watched by hundreds of millions of people. Virtually all athletic and sporting pursuits have some version of a world championship, whether it is in figure skating, ice hockey, or car racing. Many prominent sports teams, such as the Montreal Canadians, New York Yankees, Dallas Cowboys, and Manchester United, have international followings. Frequently, sporting figures will become international celebrities, famous throughout the world and connected to the global advertising capacities of major multinationals such as Nike or Adidas. Sports can create a sense of human community, and some suggest that sporting events can be a force for peace, unifying peoples in a shared activity. Of course, sports can bring out intense state or even ethnic nationalism, as people cheer for their national team or competitor. Sporting events can also take on a political dimension. For example, witness the intense rivalry of the Canada–Soviet Union hockey confrontations, and the undertones of some football (soccer) matches during the World Cup. However, sports bring people (both participants and spectators) together, and the increasing trend toward international competitions, visiting tours of sport teams, and exchanges and trips in youth sports is another example of the blurring of national boundaries.

The wide availability of food and consumer items from other countries (made possible by global trade) also has contributed to the globalization of culture. Many food and consumer products are indistinguishable from the culture that produced them: when one thinks of sushi, one thinks of Japan; when one thinks of Mercedes, one thinks of Germany; when one thinks of Marlboro, one thinks of the United States; when one thinks of Roots, one thinks of Canada. In addition, advertising has a powerful cultural dimension, as advertising increasingly links products and the multinational corporations that produce them with music, images, and international celebrities.

However, considerable concern remains that this global culture may in fact be less of a fusion, or integration, of cultures from around the world than the spread—or, worse, imposition—of Western (and especially American) culture; some would argue we are witnessing cultural imperialism. The global culture is dominated by the English language, the U.S. film and television industries, American and Western media networks, and advertising for Western-style consumption. For example, Hollywood dominates global cinema and the television programming industry; it supplies 80 percent of the world's demand for films and 70 percent of the world's demand for television shows. By the mid-1990s, Hollywood was making more than half its money abroad.[74] Icons of Western culture have spread dramatically, and some are approaching the status of global icons, such as the Golden Arches and Ronald McDonald of the American fast-food chain, or the omnipresent Coca-Cola sign. However, advertising also carries certain cultural values and messages, and can encourage Western-style consumerism and materialism, to the detriment of local businesses and traditions, and sometimes the very health of the local population. The dominance of Western cultural influences on the Internet is another reflection of this phenomenon. As a result, we are also witnessing a global cultural backlash, with populations increasingly suspicious and even hostile to foreign

McDonald's in the United Arab Emirates, 2004. Almost all of the world's brands are present in Dubai, which built the largest shopping mall in the world in 2005. Is this a meeting of cultures, or an imposition?
(© Amar Abd Rabbo/ABACA/CP Images.)

influences, although this rejection is likely to be selective: even as some influences are opposed others will be accepted.

WAR IN THE INFORMATION AGE: A REVOLUTION IN MILITARY AFFAIRS?

So far in this chapter we have explored how the rapid pace of technological change has affected (and perhaps even transformed) the global political economy, information flows, and financial markets, global cultural politics, the media, and the state. This rapid techno-logical change has also dramatically increased the capacities of modern weapons and the efficiency of military communications and information systems. Indeed, many observers of military affairs argue that we are witnessing a profound transformation in the effectiveness of military forces. This argument is based on a particular interpretation of military history, which argues that the development of military capabilities has not progressed in a steady, evolutionary fashion. Instead, increases in military capabilities have been characterized by sudden surges, or revolutions, in the effectiveness of weapons and military technique. These surges originate from technological, organizational, and larger social and economic innovations in certain countries. It can hardly be surprising that against the backdrop of the computer and information revolution, declarations have been made that we are experi-encing a parallel military revolution. For example, Alvin and Heidi Toffler argue that "as we transition from brute-force to brain-force economies, we also necessarily invent what can only be called 'brain-force-war.'"[75] This transition is now called the **Revolution in Military Affairs (RMA)**.

An RMA is the relatively swift onset of a qualitative transformation in the effectiveness of mil-itary technologies that fundamentally alters the conduct of military operations and the nature of the strategic environment. One key concept that distinguishes changes in military technologies, doctrines, and organizations (which are not rare) from revolutionary developments (which are rare) is discontinuity. That is, revolutions are characterized by transformations in the nature of the conduct of military operations such that previous technologies and techniques are rendered obsolete. Early RMAs have been associated with gunpowder, the rise of the national citizen armies of the Napoleonic period, and the Blitzkrieg warfare of World War II (see Chapter 2). It is worth emphasizing that technological developments are not sufficient indicators of military revolutions, although weapons developments are almost always central to any revolution that has ever been identified. Military revolutions are also based on organizational innovation and are grounded in larger economic, social, and political changes that impact on military capabilities.

What are the components of the current RMA? Advocates of this concept point to the following:

- A decrease in the relationship between distance and accuracy, made possible by modern electronics. Precision-guided munitions are now capable of hitting targets over long distances with a high probability of success (though not as high as is often advertised by weapons manufacturers and governments).

- The increased capacity of some weapons systems to act autonomously from human operators. These military versions of robots promise a transition from current semi-autonomous warfare (a human fires the weapon, which guides itself to the target) to fully autonomous warfare (the weapons system decides when and where to fire on the basis of its programming).

- The development of stealth technology, which renders some weapons systems extremely hard to detect by conventional radars.

- An increase in the capability to conduct surveillance and reconnaissance over the battlefield through the employment of remotely piloted vehicles, satellites, and signal-intelligence equipment.

- An increase in the capacity to store, analyze, and disseminate information in real time (no time delay) through communications and battle management systems, reducing the "fog of war."

- An increased capacity to fight at night and in all weather conditions with minimal degradation of effectiveness.

- An increased ability to engage in offensive information warfare to disrupt the opponent's military and civilian communications and thus influence the political and psychological dimensions of the conflict.

- The increased use of space.

- The development of doctrine and training and leadership skills assisted by realistic simulations.

- The potential to reduce civilian casualties and *collateral damage* associated with the use of military force.

As noted above, developing technologies also promise new methods of conducting information warfare, and managing the public relations and imagery of wars and interventions. In this sense, future wars will take place not only between combatants and their weapons systems, but also in the arena of public perception and opinion, the media, and in information and disinformation efforts mounted by governments, groups, and individuals.[76]

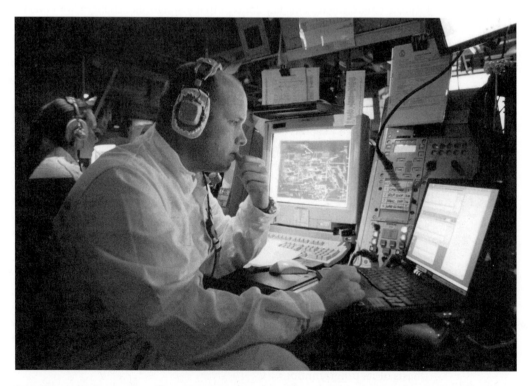

Computers and networks at war. The communications warfare officer at work in the Operations Room on board the British naval vessel HMS *Ocean* in the Persian Gulf. (Canadian Press STRPA/© PA Photos Limited 2002. All rights reserved.)

Not surprisingly, the leading proponents of the RMA concept work in the United States.[77] The objective is to ensure that the U.S. armed forces remain preeminent on the battlefield in the 21st century—a key element, realists would say, of maintaining U.S. hegemony.[78] Some U.S. allies (including Canada) are expected to try to remain as interoperable as possible with the U.S. military to ensure that their forces can cooperate effectively on the battlefield (a major issue in allied or coalition operations). However, few if any countries have the resources to implement RMA techniques and weapons with the enthusiasm displayed by America. Still, as we discussed in Chapter 6, as weapons technologies continue to diffuse through the international system, more countries are acquiring more modern weapons. They may not always be the most modern ones, but they are far more capable and destructive than previous generations of hardware and software. As a result, we can expect future interstate wars involving industrialized, information-age states to be fought with progressively more sophisticated technologies.

Considerable controversy is associated with the RMA.[79] Some security studies experts doubt that RMAs even exist, disputing the notion of historical discontinuities in the development of warfare.[80] Others point out that it is essentially an American enterprise and is, therefore, motivated more by the U.S. military and its corporate suppliers than by any sense of security requirements. Still others argue that the RMA is relevant to U.S. military requirements, but the danger is that the United States will move so far ahead of the rest of the world (including its key allies) in military capabilities that it will be less disposed toward multilateralism and more disposed toward unilateralism in the military realm. Why would the United States invite other countries to participate in multilateral military efforts when only a few countries can provide significant military contributions? The short answer is that America will still value its allies because coalitions will still impart a moral weight, or legitimacy, to U.S. actions. However, if most countries are contributing forces to U.S.-led efforts for purely symbolic purposes, and these military forces are not capable of meaningful military operations, what political influence or voice can these countries expect to have on U.S. policy? This is a particular concern in Canada, where the Canadian government has always tried to encourage the United States to pursue multilateral solutions to problems.

There is also the question of the effectiveness of the new technologies. For every measure there is a countermeasure, and even the most sophisticated weapons can be defeated using relatively simple techniques. Doubts exist as to whether RMA capabilities will be effective in forest or jungle terrain. During the bombing of Serbia, the Serbian military made wide use of decoys, which proved effective against many high-technology weapons. In other cases, controversies may erupt concerning the use of certain weapons. This has occurred with respect to the alleged health effects of depleted uranium munitions in the Gulf War and in the former Yugoslavia, and in the use of area-denial munitions and cluster bombs, some of which may fail to explode and thus represent a threat to civilians. Finally, some question the relevance of the RMA in an era where major war may be increasingly rare or even obsolete.[81] RMA capabilities will not enhance the ability of military forces to conduct peacekeeping missions or low-intensity conflicts, which are precisely the kind of operations militaries have been most frequently asked to perform. Certainly, the struggles of the U.S. and coalition forces to maintain order and fight insurgents in Iraq and Afghanistan exemplify the limitations of RMA technologies and doctrines in such operations. As Nigel Aylwin-Foster observed, "the US Army has developed over time a singular focus on conventional warfare, of a particularly swift and violent style, which left it ill-suited to the kind of operation it encountered as soon as conventional warfare ceased to be the primary focus in [Iraq]."[82] In Iraq and Afghanistan "theory has clashed with reality" and forced the U.S. military to focus more on counterinsurgency, stability, and peace support operations.[83]

This last point raises the question of whether the RMA is an effort to prepare for the wrong kind of war, and therefore we should not pay an undue amount of attention to it. The vast majority of recent and current wars are fought not with the high-technology weapons and techniques of the 21st century but with the low-technology weapons and techniques of the 20th. As we discussed in Chapter 6, almost all these wars have been fought between communal groups at the substate level. The character of war in the future is therefore likely to be bifurcated between two styles. First, wars or interventions involving advanced industrialized states will feature modern weapons systems, highly trained professional personnel, and the organizational techniques characteristic of information-age societies. Second, other wars (likely far more numerous) will feature armed groups using light weapons and the techniques of 20th-century warfare or insurgency conflicts. The war in the former Yugoslavia and the war in Liberia are examples of this kind of warfare. Interventions to stop such wars, or efforts to use peacekeeping forces to control them, will demand a capacity to meet this kind of combatant when the high-technology innovations of the RMA will be of little, or marginal, utility.

MISSILE DEFENCE

In the 1990s, advances in computer and information technology made the idea of missile defence—the ability to shoot down ballistic missiles in flight—appear more feasible. As we saw in Chapter 3, the idea of missile defences had been shelved during the Cold War (and essentially banned in the 1972 Antiballistic Missile Treaty) in the interests of maintaining the stability of deterrence and Mutual Assured Destruction (MAD). However, during the 1990s concern over the proliferation of ballistic missiles (possibly equipped with nuclear, chemical, or biological warheads) prompted several governments to conduct missile defence research. The U.S. research program was the most ambitious, driven by fears that America could be vulnerable to ballistic missile attack from an increasing number of countries. During the Clinton administration, a research program was already under way. In 1998 a Commission to Assess the Ballistic Missile Threat to the United States warned that America could be threatened by ballistic missile attack from Iraq, Iran, or North Korea within 5 to 10 years of any decision by these states to acquire such a capability.[84] The Commission was widely criticized for being alarmist, but the threat of ballistic missile attack from a "rogue state" was considered serious enough to warrant enhanced research. On December 17, 2002, President G. W. Bush announced that the United States would develop and deploy a ballistic missile defence system by 2004–05. A few days earlier, the Bush administration had announced its intention to withdraw from the ABM Treaty. Construction on the system began shortly thereafter. The ballistic missile defence system employs ground-based missile interceptors carrying hit-to-kill warheads. Any incoming ballistic missile warhead would be detected and tracked by radar stations in North America, Greenland, and the United Kingdom. The ballistic missile system would launch interceptors at the incoming warhead in hopes of hitting it and destroying it. In 2008, the system consisted of 24 ground-based interceptors at Fort Greely in Alaska and Vandenberg Air Force Base in California, as well as ship-based Aegis missile systems.

The U.S. deployment of a ballistic missile system is very controversial.[85] First, many critics argue that the system simply does not work. Testing of system components has been plagued with problems and failures, and the integrity of the testing program itself has been called into question. The technical challenge demanded of a successful intercept of an incoming warhead is considerable: both the interceptor warhead and the incoming ballistic missile warhead will be travelling at speeds in excess of that of a bullet out of the barrel of a gun. Second, critics argue that the system is too expensive in relation to its expected utility. In 2009 alone, the Bush administration requested US$12.3 billion for missile defence, and since 1985 successive governments have spent over US$120 billion on missile defence programs.[86] Critics argue that deterrence through punishment remains the best way of preventing attacks on North

America. Third, critics argue that the ballistic missile threat is rather low, and there are many other, cheaper ways of attacking the United States, as the September 11 attacks proved. Finally, critics argue that the United States has abrogated the 1972 ABM Treaty (inflicting a setback to the international arms control regime) and damaged its relationship with Russia and China (both governments had expressed opposition to the system).[87] However, advocates of the system argue that one cannot take chances and trust dictatorial regimes not to attack. If deterrence were to fail, there would be nothing between a rogue state missile and hundreds of thousands, perhaps millions, of American lives. Advocates of missile defence argue that defensive systems will improve with time as technology advances. As for other ways of attacking the United States, the ballistic missile system will not defend America from those threats, but then it is not designed to. Other measures will be put in place to defend the United States against other possible attacks. Meanwhile, other states are forced to respond to the plan, invoking domestic political debate. During the Canadian 2004 election campaign, the militarization of space became one of the few foreign policy issues on the agenda. The government subsequently declined to become involved in the U.S. missile defence system.

U.S. plans to deploy missile defence systems in Eastern Europe have added more fuel to the debate. In August 2008 the United States and Poland signed an agreement to base interceptors on Polish territory, while a radar system was to be based in the Czech Republic. The United States argues that this system is necessary to defend Europe against a possible ballistic missile attack from Iran. Not all European governments or publics are convinced a system is necessary or that it would work, and heated debates over missile defence have occurred in many European countries. There is strong public opposition to the U.S. plan in both Poland and the Czech Republic. The planned deployment of the U.S. system has also angered the Russian government, which claims the system is intended to intimidate or threaten Russia. Meanwhile, other states in other regions are also developing missile defences, often in cooperation with the United States. Israel has developed an antiballistic missile known as the Arrow. Japan has been engaged in missile defence research since 1998, and India also has an advanced research program. As computer and information technology advances, we can expect more controversy and debate on weapons system research and development in general and on missile defence in particular, a reminder of the link between technological change and global politics.

CONCLUSIONS

Where will the information age and developments in ICT take us? Innovation is very difficult to predict. New discoveries may open up completely new areas of human endeavour, much as the development of the computer has. The question for observers of global politics is how these innovations will affect the interaction of states, international organizations, MNCs, political and cultural groups, and individuals. As we have seen, the impact up to now has been profound. The majority consensus is probably that the information age will accelerate the erosion of the state and enhance global interdependence. Perhaps a new era of global communication promises improved international understanding and the establishment of new patterns of human interaction across state boundaries. However, the information age may also enhance the power of some states (and corporations) in the international system and serve to make us all more vulnerable in varying ways. The pervasiveness of certain cultures and perspectives on computer networks and in the global media may lead to a cultural backlash against transnational communication. We must not forget that many of the people on this planet are essentially untouched by the information age. What does it promise these people? The information age may be a force of convergence for many in the international system, but it is also a force of divergence, as so many past revolutions in human history have been.

Endnotes

1. Quoted in Charles W. Kegley Jr. and Eugene R. Wittkopf, *World Politics: Trend and Transformation*, 5th ed. (New York: St. Martin's Press, 1995), 554.

2. Geneva Declaration of Principles, World Summit on the Information Society, WSIS-03/GENEVA/DOC/4-E (December 12, 2003), 1.

3. See J. Goldstein, *Long Cycles: Prosperity and War in the Modern Age* (New Haven: Yale University Press, 1988); and C. Freeman, "Diffusion, the Spread of New Technology to Firms, Sectors, and Nations," in A. Heertje, ed., *Innovation, Technology, and Finance* (New York: Basil Blackwell, 1988), 38–70.

4. Alvin Toffler, *The Third Wave* (New York: Morrow, 1980).

5. S. Nora and A. Minc, *The Computerization of Society* (Cambridge, MA: MIT Press, 1980), 3.

6. W. J. Drake and R. F. Jørgensen, *Human Rights in the Global Information Society* (Cambridge, MA: The MIT Press, 2006), 1.

7. See *World Information Society Report 2007: Beyond WSIS* (Geneva: International Telecommunications Union, 2007).

8. Christopher May, *The Information Society: A Skeptical View* (Malden, MA: Blackwell, 2002). For a good discussion on the different interpretations of the information age, and how this relates to environmental reform, see A. Mol, *Environmental Reform in the Information Age: The Contours of Informational Governance* (Cambridge University Press, 2008).

9. International Telecommunications Union, *Key Global Telecom Indicators for the World Telecommunications Service Sector*, http://www.itu.int/ITU-D/ict/statistics/at_glance/KeyTelecom99.html (accessed May 19, 2008).

10. M. Castels and L. D'Andrea Tyson, "High Technology Choices Ahead: Restructuring Interdependence," in J. Sewell and S. Tucker, eds., *Growth, Exports, and Jobs in a Changing World* (New Brunswick, NJ: Transaction Press, 1988), 57.

11. United Nations Development Programme, *Human Development Report 2001* (Oxford: Oxford University Press, 2001), 27.

12. J. Aronson, "Global Networks and Their Impact," in J. N. Rosenau and J. P. Singh, eds., *Information Technologies and Global Politics: The Changing Scope of Power and Governance* (Albany, NY: State University of New York Press, 2002), 39.

13. See I. de Sola Pool, in Eli M. Noam, ed., *Technologies Without Boundaries: On Telecommunications in a Global Age* (Cambridge, MA: Harvard University Press, 1990).

14. International Telecommunications Union, *Key Global Telecom Indicators for the World Telecommunications Service Sector*, http://www.itu.int/ITU-D/ict/statistics/at_glance/KeyTelecom99.html (accessed May 19, 2008).

15. Alex Lightman and William Rojas, *Brave New Unwired World: The Digital Big Bang and the Infinite Internet* (New York, John Wiley and Sons, 2002), 9.

16. See R. Farnsworth et al., "Networks Changing the Way We Work, Live, Play, and Learn," in S. Dutta and I. Mia, eds., *The Global Information Technology Report 2006–2007: Connecting to the Networked Economy* (New York: World Economic Forum and Palgrave Macmillan, 2007), 27.

17. See *Global Economic Prospects and the Developing Countries* (Washington, DC: World Bank, 1992), and *Human Development Report 1999* (New York: United Nations, 2000).

18. International Telecommunications Union, *World Telecommunications/ICT Indicators*, http://www.itu.int/ITU-D/icteye/Reporting/ShowReportFrame.aspx?ReportName=/WTI/CellularSubscribersPublic&RP_intYear=2007&RP_intLanguageID=1 (accessed May 19, 2008). Note that all this radio-wave activity has given rise to related health concerns for children, adults, and nonhuman animals.

19. International Telecommunications Union, *World Telecommunications/ICT Indicators*.

20. See Netcraft Ltd. June 2008 Web Server Survey, http://news.netcraft.com (accessed June 2008).

21. A. Kluth, "Nomads at Last," *The Economist* 387, no. 8575 (April 12, 2008), 3–5.

22. See "The World on Your Desktop," *The Economist* 384, no. 8545 (September 8, 2007), 19.

23. See R. Faris and Nart Villeneuve, "Measuring Global Internet Filtering," in R. Diebert, et al., eds., *Access Denied: The Practice and Policy of Global Internet Filtering* (Cambridge, MA: The MIT Press, 2008), 5.

24. G. J. Walters, *Human Rights in an Information Age: A Philosophical Analysis* (Toronto: University of Toronto Press, 2001), 5.

25. J. Zysman and A. Newman, "Frameworks for Understanding the political Economy of the Digital Era," in J. Zysman and A. Newman, eds., *How Revolutionary Was the Digital Revolution?* (Stanford, CA: Stanford University Press, 2006), 4.

26. J. Aronson, "Global Networks and Their Impact," in J. N. Rosenau and J. P. Singh, eds., *Information Technologies and Global Politics: The Changing Scope of Power and Governance* (Albany, NY: State University of New York Press, 2002), 39.

27. See P. Pritchett, *The Employee Handbook of New Work Habits for a Radically Changing World* (Dallas: Pritchett and Associates, 1996), 4.

28. Farnsworth et al., 27.

29. P. Drucker, *Post-Capitalist Society* (New York: Harper Business, 1993), 40.

30. Dominique Foray and Bengt-Ålce Lundvall, "The Knowledge-Based Economy: From the Economics of Knowledge to the Learning Economy," *Employment and Growth in the Knowledge-Based Economy*, OECD Documents (Paris: Organization for Economic Cooperation and Development, 1996), 16.

31. T. Friedman, *The World Is Flat* (New York: Farrar, Straus and Giroux, 2006).

32. M. J. Mazaar, "Introduction: Information Technology and World Politics: The Growing Connection," in M. J. Mazaar, ed. *Information Technology in World Politics* (New York: Palgrave MacMillan, 2002), 2.

33. See S. Dutta and I. Mia, eds., *The Global Information Technology Report 2006–2007*, ix.

34. Ethan B. Kapstein, "Workers and the World Economy," *Foreign Affairs* 75 (May/June 1996), 16.

35. Christopher May, *The Information Society: A Skeptical View* (Malden, MA: Blackwell, 2002).

36. See A. Tonnelson, *The Race to the Bottom* (Boulder, CO: Westview Press, 2000).

37. See E. Brousseau and N. Curien, "Internet Economics, Digital Economics," in E. Brousseau and N. Curien, eds., *Internet and Digital Economics: Principles, Methods and Applications* (Cambridge: Cambridge University Press, 2007), 1–56.

38. E. G. Carayannis and C. M. Sipp, *E-Development Toward the Knowledge Economy: Leveraging Technology, Innovation and Entrepreneurship for "Smart" Development* (New York: Palgrave MacMillan, 2007), 4.

39. See J. James, *Bridging the Global Digital Divide* (Chattenham, UK: Edward Elgar, 2003), x.

40. International Telecommunications Union, World Telecommunications/ICT Indicators Database, http://www.itu.int/ITU-D/ict/statistics/ict/index.html (accessed July 4, 2008).

41. International Telecommunications Union, *World Telecommunications/ICT Indicators*, http://www.itu.int/ITU-D/icteye/Reporting/ShowReportFrame.aspx?ReportName=/WTI/CellularSubscribersPublic&RP_intYear=2007&RP_intLanguageID=1 (accessed May 19, 2008).

42. *Connect Africa Summit Outcomes Report*, http://www.itu.int/ITU-D/connect/africa/2007/finalreport.pdf (accessed July 22, 2008), 3.

43. J. Salomon and A. Lebeau, *Mirages of Development: Science and Technology for the Third Worlds* (Boulder CO; London: Lynne Rienner, 1993), 86. See also Paul Kennedy's *Preparing for the Twentieth Century* (New York: Random House, 1993).

44. A. P. D'Costa, "Introduction: Charting a New Development Trajectory?," in A. P. D'Costa, ed., *The New Economy in Development: ICT Challenges and Opportunities* (New York: Palgrave Macmillan, 2006), 10.

45. Manuel Castells, *The Information Age, Volume 1: The Rise of the Network Society* (Oxford: Blackwell, 1996), 147.

46. See M. Kagami, M. Tsuji, and E. Giovannetti, eds., *Information Technology Policy and the Digital Divide: Lessons for Developing Countries* (Cheltenham, UK: Edward Elgar, 2004).

47. See S. Roy, *Globalisation, ICT and Developing Nations: Challenges in the Information Age* (New Delhi: Sage Publications, 2005).

48. A. Lightman and W. Rojas, xii.

49. United Nations Development Programme, 30.

50. J. Rosenau, *Turbulence in World Politics* (Princeton: Princeton University Press, 1990), 17.

51. T. Flew, *Understanding Global Media* (New York: Palgrave Macmillan, 2007), 1–3.

52. J. Habermas, *Between Facts and Norms: Contributions to a Discourse Theory of Law and Democracy* (Cambridge, UK: Polity Press and Blackwell Publishers, 1996), 514.

53. J. Rosenau, *Turbulence in World Politics: A Theory of Change and Continuity* (Princeton, NJ: Princeton University Press, 1990), 339–43.

54. For a discussion of CNN's development, see D. Flournoy, "Coverage, Competition, and Credibility: The CNN International Standard," in T. Silvia, ed., *Global News: Perspectives on the Information Age* (Ames, IA: Iowa State University Press, 2001), 15–44.

55. See N. Miladi, "Mapping the Al-Jazeera Phenomenon," in D. K. Thussu and D. Freedman, eds., *War and the Media: Reporting Conflict 24/7* (London: Sage Publications, 2003), 149–160.

56. P. Seib, ed., *New Media and the New Middle East* (New York: Palgrave, 2007), xiii.

57. Quoted in M. Zayani, "Introduction: Al-Jazeera and the Vicissitudes of the New Arab Mediascape," in M. Zayani, ed., *The Al-Jazeera Phenomenon: Critical Perspectives on the New Arab Media* (Boulder, CO: Paradigm, 2005), 33.

58. M. Fandy, *(Un)Civil War of Words: Media and Politics in the Arab World* (Westport, CT: Praeger, 2007), 139, 142.

59. N. Sakr, *Arab Media and Political Renewal: Community, Legitimacy and Public Life* (London: I. B. Tauris, 2007), 6.

60. T. Magder, "Watching What We Say: Global Communication in a Time of Fear," in Thissu and Freedman, 33.

61. See D. K. Thissu and D. Freedman, "Introduction," in Thissu and Freedman, 7.

62. See L. Artz, "The Corporate Model from National to Transnational," in L. Artz and Y. R. Kamalipour, eds., *The Media Globe: Trends in International Mass Media* (Lanham, MD: Rowman and Littlefield, 2007), 141–161.

63. C. Sparks, *Globalization, Development, and the Mass Media* (London: Sage Publications, 2007), 189.

64. D. B. Miller, *Media Pressure on Foreign Policy: The Evolving Theoretical Framework* (New York: Palgrave Macmillan, 2007), 9.

65. S. Hjarvard, "News Media and the Globalization of the Public Sphere," in S. Hjarvard, ed., *News in a Globalized Society* (Gothenburg, Sweden: Nordicom, 2001), 18.

66. See J. Dean, J. W. Anderson, and G. Lovink, eds., *Reformatting Politics: Information Technology and Global Civil Society* (New York: Routledge, 2006).

67. A. Ramirez, "Dial Direct to Moscow and Beyond," *The New York Times*, May 20, 1992, D1.

68. Some argue that the media in advanced capitalist states are just as manipulative and that there is a connection between the owners of the media and pro–status quo forces in government. The most famous proponent of this view is Noam Chomsky; see for example Noam Chomsky, *Media Control: The Spectacular Achievements of Propaganda* (New York: Seven Stories Press, 1997).

69. I. Vincent, "Rebel Dispatches Find Home on Net," *The Globe and Mail*, June 11, 1996, A1.

70. J. Nye Jr. and W. Owens, "America's Information Edge," *Foreign Affairs* 75 (March/April 1996), 20.

71. B. Gates, *The Road Ahead*, 2nd ed. (London: Penguin Books, 1995), 9.

72. R. Volti, *Society and Technological Change*, 2nd ed. (New York: St. Martin's Press, 1992), 235.

73. See D. K. Thussu, "Mapping Global Media Flow and Contra-Flow," in D. K. Thussu, ed., *Media on the Move: Global Flow and Contra-Flow* (London: Routledge, 2007), 11–32.

74. "Star Wars," *The Economist*, March 22, 1997, 15.

75. A. Toffler and H. Toffler, *War and Anti-War: Survival at the Dawn of the 21st Century* (Boston: Little, Brown and Company, 1993), 10–11. See also R. Preston and S. Wise, *Men in Arms: A History of Warfare and Its Interrelationships with Western Society*, 4th ed. (New York: Holt, Rinehart, and Winston, 1979).

76. See Y. R. Kamalipour and N. Snow, eds., *War, Media, and Propaganda: A Global Perspective* (Lanham, MD: Rowman and Littlefield, 2004); D. Miller, ed., *Tell Me Lies: Propaganda and Media Distortion in the Attack on Iraq* (London: Pluto, 2004); and M. Ignatieff, *Virtual War* (Toronto: Penguin Books of Canada, 2000).

77. See R. O. Hundley, *Past Revolutions, Future Transformations: What Can the History of Revolutions in Military Affairs Tell Us About Transforming the U.S. Military?* (Santa Monica, CA: Rand, 1999).

78. For a cautious note, see B. R. Posen, "Command of the Commons: The Military Foundations of US Hegemony," *International Security* 28 (Summer 2003), 5–47.

79. For a discussion of the many issues surrounding the RMA, see B. Schreer and E. Whitlock, eds., *Divergent Perspectives on Military Transformation* (Berlin: Stiftung Wissenschaft und Politik, 2005), 30–36; C. S. Gray, *Strategy for Chaos* (London: Frank Cass, 2002); and T. Gongora and H. von Riekhoff, eds., *Toward a Revolution in Military Affairs? Defence and Security at the Dawn of the Twenty-First Century* (Westport, CT: Greenwood Press, 2000).

80. See P. L. Ritcheson, "The Future of Military Affairs: Revolution or Evolution?," *Strategic Review* 24 (Spring 1996), 31–40.

81. M. Mandelbaum, "Is Major War Obsolete?," *Survival* (Winter 1998/99), 20–38.

82. N. Aylwin-Foster, "Changing the Army for Counterinsurgency Operations," *Military Review*, November/ December 2005, 9.

83. *The Military Balance 2007* (London: International Institute for Strategic Studies, 2007), 15.

84. Executive Summary of the Report of the Commission to Assess the Ballistic Missile Threat to the United States, July 15, 1998, 1.

85. For a brief review of ballistic missile defences in context, see S. D. Sagan and K. N. Waltz, *The Spread of Nuclear Weapons: A Debate Renewed* (New York: Norton, 2003).

86. J. Tierney and S. Flynn, "Misguided Missile Defense," *The Boston Globe*, March 28, 2008, http://www.boston.com/bostonglobe/editorial_opinion/oped/articles/2008/03/28/misguided_missile_defense (accessed August 21, 2008).

87. C. L. Glaser and S. Fetter, "National Missile Defense and the Future of U.S. Nuclear Weapons Policy," *International Security* 26 (Summer 2001), 40–92.

Suggested Websites

Fairness and Accuracy in Reporting
http://www.fair.org/index.php?page=100

Freedominfo.org
http://www.freedominfo.org

Global Media Monitor
http://lass.calumet.purdue.edu/cca/gmm

International Telecommunication Union
http://www.itu.int/home/index.html

Media Reform Information Center
http://www.corporations.org/media

Netcraft
http://news.netcraft.com

Organisation for Economic Co-operation and Development
http://www.oecd.org/home

Wired News
http://www.wired.com

World Bank Group
http://www.worldbank.org

World Summit on the Information Society
http://www.itu.int/wsis/index.html

New Directions in Theory and Practice

Pessimism over the future of the world comes from a confusion between civilization and security. In the immediate future there will be less security than in the immediate past, less stability. But, on the whole, the great ages have been unstable ages.

—*A. North Whitehead[1]*

Society wills and acts collectively, as the output of systems (including law-making systems) which aggregate the willing and acting of individual human beings. But the intervention of those systems creates a new mind-world, a new form of human reality, a new form of human world. The public mind is society's private mind. The public mind of international society is the private mind of the human species.

—*Philip Allott[2]*

... to all other peoples and governments who are watching today, from the grandest capitals to the small village where my father was born: know that America is a friend of each nation and every man, woman and child who seeks a future of peace and dignity, and we are ready to lead once more.

—*Barack Hussein Obama[3]*

INTRODUCTION: THE FUTURE OF GLOBAL POLITICS

Predicting the future is a perilous enterprise. As Nicholas Rescher has argued, "The three most salient facts about the future are: that it does not (yet) exist, that it unavoidably will, and that we do—and can—have only very incomplete information about its nature, let alone achieve control of it."[4] Nevertheless, prediction is a vitally important part of global politics. For example, the debate over climate change and appropriate mitigation and adaptation strategies is largely based on scientific predictions of the impact of increasing greenhouse gas emissions and trends in observable phenomena such as melting ice sheets and rising sea levels. Efforts to prevent armed conflict through early intervention often depend on predictions of the imminent outbreak of violence, based on the observation of key indicators such as arms races, propaganda campaigns and inflammatory rhetoric, and lower-level violence.

Major economic decisions are made on the basis of predictions of economic performance by states or corporations and the direction of key economic indicators such as inflation, interest rates, and commodity prices. Naturally, being able to anticipate future events or conditions allows us to prepare for those eventualities, reduce risks, or take steps to prevent certain events from happening. As a result, despite the difficulties inherent in prediction, huge investments are made by governments, armed forces, corporations, investors, and scholars to devise the analytical equivalent of a crystal ball that will enable them to see into the future.

When predictions are made about the future of global politics, they are most often based on trends or identifiable patterns in the behaviour of actors or phenomena. While identifying such trends and projecting them into the future is the most important tool of prediction, identifiable trends can change. In the 1980s, economic trends led some analysts to suggest that Japan would supplant the United States as the world's largest economy, with political and military conflict between the two a distinct possibility.[5] However, Japanese economic growth rates stagnated in the 1990s, undercutting the basis for predictions about the future size of the Japanese economy, and fears of major Japanese rearmament proved unfounded. In addition, unanticipated events (such as the fall of the Soviet Union or the September 11, 2001 terrorist attacks on the U.S.) can alter the course of world affairs and confound predictions made under a very different set of circumstances. Our ability to predict must therefore be constantly questioned, and our predictions must be made with commensurate humility. David Staley suggests we should view the future in the same way we view the past, not through the prism of scientific prediction and certainty but through the historical lens of interpretation and context.[6]

In this concluding chapter, we will examine some of the most prominent predictions made about the future of global politics. We begin the chapter by exploring the future relevance of the issues raised in Part One of the book. How will IR theory evolve in the future, and what will be the forces driving theoretical innovation? What new ideas might emerge that will help us understand the world in which we live? We then turn to the power politics theme that was so central to our historical overview of major events and transitions from early civilizations to the Cold War. Though we are clearly in a new era, old questions remain: what distribution of power is emerging in our world? What is the significance of the rise of China? Is a new Cold War developing between the West and a resurgent Russia? And what will be the future of American power in the world, and the consequences for its allies, such as Canada? In Part Two of the book, we examined the challenges of international security, conflict management, and globalization. While we explored the possible origins of future wars throughout the text, is it possible that future wars will, in essence, be wars between "civilizations," and not states? In the age of globalization, what are the key issues facing the future of the global economy? In the realm of international organizations and international law, as we shall see, the future will present many new challenges to these instruments of global governance, dialogue, and cooperation. In Part Three, we examined the environment, population and health issues, and the information age. Can multilateralism succeed in meeting these challenges?

Three things seem certain at this point. First, these issues are not new. They have always been with us in some form and always will be, barring a cataclysmic event such as a global epidemic, a large-scale nuclear war, or a catastrophic meteor impact. Even if the state system as we know it were to crumble, we would still debate the distribution of power, the merits of trade, the risks and benefits of cooperation, the causes of friction between ethnicities, the prospects for equality and sustainable development, and other ageless themes. Second, we tend to interpret these issues through our embedded belief systems, lived experiences, and intellectual theories and frameworks (whether that entails a structural realist, liberalist, critical theory, or other perspective). Denying this is futile, but being imprisoned by it is not necessary either. Students should strive to apply other ways of thinking about global issues, even those that evoke intellectual discomfort, some of which we hope you have acquired through this textbook. Third, although there will be many developments in global politics that are successfully anticipated and many others that we fail to predict, we can be certain that the dynamic relationship between these events and our responses will continue, as long as people are genuinely interested in not only understanding the world but also forging a new one.

THE FUTURE OF THEORY

As this text has illustrated, meta-theoretical discourse—debate about theory—is important. Theory provides us with a framework for looking at the world, with structures for organizing and prioritizing the bewildering array of issues and events that constitute global politics. Although a claim could be made that certain perspectives (such as realism and liberalism) have had their moments of dominance in the field, there has never been a universally accepted theoretical framework describing the nature and dynamics of global politics. This is why so much disagreement exists on the issues covered in this book. We have introduced several contending perspectives, such as idealism, realism, liberalism, Marxism, feminism, and constructivism, among others. However, while these theories offer very different ways of looking at the world, there is considerable overlap between many of these theories on many issues. For example, one can be a realist with Marxist leanings; in fact, some interpretations of the foundational work of E. H. Carr suggest this was his persuasion.[7] One can be a structural realist based in a world systems theory of global politics, as the Argentinean author Carlos Escude's idea of peripheral realist foreign policy suggests,[8] While most feminists would reject a realist interpretation of events, many are quite willing to accept a liberal or Marxist one.[9] Regime theory is fairly strongly rooted in liberal suppositions about cooperation under conditions of self-interest, but there have been efforts to critically analyze the normative and socially constructed aspects of regimes.[10] Geopolitical theory can be analyzed from an environmentalist perspective.[11] Practical foreign policy questions, such as the wisdom of humanitarian intervention, are being revisited by philosophers of different persuasions.[12] Distinctions between theoretical perspectives are not hard boundaries, and theoretical innovation and flexibility is, arguably, much more common today than ever.

It may make more sense to speak of an epistemological division in the discipline, predicated on thinking about the nature of knowledge itself, rather than a division based on essentialist ideologies or theoretical perspectives. In other words, debates between positivists and post-positivists might have as much to tell us as disputes between the realists, liberals, and critical theorists.[13] Methodological issues are still very much part of the study of global politics. The discipline has been through several periods of self-examination in the past, pushing methodology in new directions. The study of global politics has moved from a historical discipline based on the analysis of leaders and military strategy to one fixated on the Cold War and game theory constructions. It has moved from a behaviouralist period, where quantification of data and rational choice assumptions regarding human nature led to efforts to model human behaviour at the international level, to a discipline concerned with the validity of its own prevalent assumptions and their impact upon the real world. Social constructivism, as developed by Alexander Wendt and others, is often seen as an effort to bridge the divide between rationalist approaches (neorealism, neoliberalism) and "reflectivist" approaches (postmodernism, some feminist theory, normative theory, and historical sociology).[14] While social constructivism certainly rose in prominence during the 1990s and 2000s, we suggest that the growing urgency around issues such as terrorism, climate change, and social injustice will enhance the theoretical attention paid to the role of human agency and belief systems in global politics.

While the split between positivists and post-positivists is still defining the work of many scholars in the field, it can be argued that both sides of this divide are more willing to listen to the other, and this is a good thing. On the one hand, the need for empirical data gathering is undeniable, and testing various hypotheses in the laboratory of distant and recent history gives us clues about patterns of behaviour, though we should always be cautious about using this to predict the future. On the other hand, the values and aspirations that guide the actors in global politics did not emerge from a vacuum; they are the product of social-norm construction and the ebb and flow of events, which are interpreted according to the intellectual prisms (some would use the word "prisons") from which we see the world. Finally, there is a place for **normative theory** in global politics, defined by Chris Brown as "that body of work which addresses the moral dimensions of international relations and the wider questions of meaning and interpretation generated by the discipline … the ethical nature of the relations between communities/states, whether [it is] focused on violence and war, or the new(er) agenda, which mixes these traditional concerns with the modern demand for international distributive justice."[15] Ethics are the topic of legitimate study in global politics, even among those who favour Machiavelli over Kant. It is our hope that future scholars in the discipline will approach global politics with a favourable attitude toward the many possibilities of synthesis and cross-pollination this vast field has undergone over the past 100 years.

In the future we can expect even greater diversity among students and scholars of global politics, as the interdisciplinary nature of the field continues to expand and sophisticated contributions increase from analysts around the world. Of course, to some degree this is already the case. Global politics as a discipline is itself globalizing. Some might argue that we have no right to call global politics a discipline, because of the breadth and scope of the subject matter, but we respectfully disagree. The study of the big issues facing us all cannot be properly achieved without an interdisciplinary approach that offers a large forum for the voices and concerns that must be heard. While it is clear that most IR textbooks emanate from either the United States or the United Kingdom (and, to a lesser degree, France), there are many notable exceptions and these exceptions will increasingly become the rule. This has happened: dependency theory originated in Latin America, and many development models were conceptualized in Africa. Much of the political economy and ecofeminist literature comes from India, reflecting postcolonial experiences in South Asia. In the future, we can expect more ideas and theoretical innovations to spread through the discipline from region to region, country to country, and scholar to scholar. An exposure to outside ideas is gradually translating into new ideas about global politics from previously silent sources. It is our hope that the decline in the Eurocentric character of the discipline will not only permit indigenous views to develop and become part of traditional dialogues and debates, but also expose Western scholars to alternative views.[16] Conferences in the Southern Hemisphere, Internet communications, and a wider audience of the curious and dedicated intellects from around the earth will further enrich the discipline in the years to come, unless we revert to fixed ideological lines and the suppression of alternative views, as was seen on both sides at various times during the Cold War. Ongoing security threats such as terrorism should give rise to thought-provoking treatments of the causes of terrorism, the use of state power, and new modes of conflict management. Further, continued concern with environmental degradation will engender more theoretical construction on issues of the commons, regime building, and the links between ecology, gender, violence, and cooperation.

Another reason we expect IR theory to become more dynamic is because more people than ever are aware of its importance. While there will always be limitations to the breadth of the discipline—for example, there are only so many jobs at universities and think tanks for professionals to pursue such questions as part of their occupations—the interest in global politics is widespread, and many people engaged in other academic disciplines now realize that global politics is a vital component of self and collective identification, economic prosperity and marginalization, environmental management, and migratory pressures. In short, global politics cannot be ignored. It has become a tired cliché to suggest that for many North Americans September 11 and the Iraq War brought world politics home, but it is certainly the case. Europeans, engaged in their ambitious and controversial project of political integration, are also forging new self-identities in the process. Protest movements around the globe, many in areas that we would never have heard of a few decades ago, are spawning fresh insights with their lessons learned, and their strategies to seek solidarity elsewhere with other transnational actors. Diasporas continue their struggles in their adopted societies, spreading awareness of far-off conflicts. Globalization can be viewed as a point of contention and division, but even here we have seen that there is considerable overlap amongst proponents and opponents.

While all of this diversification and widespread interest is a positive thing for IR theory, we would also suggest that the traditional questions raised by IR theory are alive and well. There are reliable continuities in global politics, age-old debates to which, it would seem, we are destined to repeatedly return. This text has suggested that we live in a world characterized by two forces: convergence and divergence. The simplistic question is, Which is the stronger? The answer, it seems, is neither: the two phenomena seem to exist side by side in the international system. We see convergence in the increasing interdependence between states, in the growth of IGOs and NGOs, in the awareness and action devoted to transnational issues such as the environment, and in the increase in contact, travel, and transactions between the peoples of the world. However, we see divergence in conflict between states, in the disintegration of some states, in intrastate wars and separation movements, in the increasing gap between rich and poor, and in the split between the technological haves and have-nots. At this point, identifying a dominant trend is impossible, although it is clear that for some convergence is the reality in their lives, while for others divergence is the more powerful influence. In Canada, we are very privileged in many ways, but we are not immune from these forces. Even as globalization links us to the world of trade, travel, and telecommunications, it stimulates national debates about our economic future, our culture, and public health. The enduring national unity debate is a reminder that we are not immune from the forces of divergence. Nor are we immune from broader conflicts between the United States and its proclaimed enemies. Indeed, the question of American dominance in world affairs is necessarily of primary importance to all states today, but this is nothing new: states were often forced to make a choice of allegiance during the Cold War as well.

The central questions asked by IR theory will continue to frame the debate to come: Is it still reasonable to view the world from a state-centric perspective? Are theories of grand evolutionary changes valid when explaining history, and if so where do they suggest we are heading? What types of subconscious learning processes are at work in the perpetuation of conflict, domination, and resistance? Is the spread of liberal democracy of inherent value, not only in terms of human development and freedom, but also in terms of the promotion of peace? Or is this simply another face on an old process, the structural growth of capital accumulation, accompanied by cultural imperialism? Perhaps the most basic question remains: When will we overcome the historically demonstrable urge toward organized violence? These, and many more, theoretical questions will remain salient to the people of this century.

THE FUTURE DISTRIBUTION OF POWER

In Chapters 2 and 3, we observed that changes in what realists call the distribution of power are an eternal feature of global politics. Historically, the rise and decline of civilizations, societies, states, and empires is accompanied by shifts in the patterns of interaction between these actors. These shifts in patterns of interaction can take a number of forms: threat perceptions might change as some states increase in power and others decline; balances in power will be destabilized; new alliances may form and old ones will weaken or disintegrate; patterns of diplomacy and trade will reflect new markets and new centres of growth and innovation; and some political units will fragment (like the Austro-Hungarian Empire) and others will amalgamate (the 13 American colonies) or be absorbed (Bavaria). Because shifts in the distribution of power can so profoundly alter the shape of global politics and the security and foreign policy strategies of states, trends in relative power distribution are watched very closely. As Richard Little observes in his excellent historical account of the balance-of-power idea, the concept is one of the most enduring theories in international relations literature, and certainly the most widely cited.[17]

However, the balance-of-power concept is far from a historical artifact. The concern over global and regional power balances is a prime example of how an idea grounded in historical observation can have an impact on how contemporary global politics is described and how states should conduct themselves. The balance of power is a central feature of contemporary debates on the future of global politics in general and U.S. foreign policy in particular. At the core of the general debate is whether global politics will retain its unipolar quality (with or without America acting as the hegemon) or whether a multipolar or other form of system is evolving as other countries (such as China) or other regions (such as Europe) rise in both absolute and relative power. At the core of the U.S. foreign policy debate is how American policy might—or might not—have an impact on America's hegemonic status and affect the future of the global balance of power. It is sobering to consider that the debate on the future of U.S. foreign policy highlighted in the 2008 election campaign was heavily influenced by a concept that has been in use for over 500 years. The balance-of-power concept is also relevant for the role it plays as a theory of regional power politics in Asia, while the consequences of the Iraq War (which include the weakening of the power of Iraq) have raised concerns about the future balance of power in the Persian Gulf and the Middle East.

Many observers of global politics have argued that a multipolar system is already emerging. In a striking observation, in 2004 the U.S. government's own National Intelligence Council noted: "The likely emergence of China and India as major new global players—similar to the rise of Germany in the 19th century and the United States in the early 20th century—will transform the geopolitical landscape, with impacts potentially as dramatic as those of the previous two centuries."[18] In a provocative book, Parag Khanna makes the observation that the world is now dominated by three empires: a declining United States; a rising but struggling China; and an increasingly powerful European Union. Khanna argues that "Big is back" in the study of global politics: it is inter-imperial relations that drive global politics, not international or intercivilizational relations.[19] Fareed Zakaria has argued that global politics is increasingly characterized not by the presumed decline of the West but the "rise of the rest," meaning the non-Western countries. This will usher in not an Asian century but a complex blend of Eastern and Western powers. For Zakaria, U.S. foreign policy in this transformed world must avoid hegemonic pretension and instead work to establish an inclusive multipolar global system.[20] Meanwhile, Robert Kagan argues that the post–Cold War delusions about the end of ideological conflict and the triumph of liberal democracy have been dashed. We now live in a world more analogous to the 19th century, a world divided between democratic states and autocratic states, with a single power (the United States) that is most influential but not dominant.[21] While all of these views speak to the existence of a multipolar world, some analysts have argued that we live in neither a unipolar nor a multipolar system. In a provocative article, Richard Haas has suggested that contemporary global politics is characterized by so many centres of power (Haas identifies six major state powers as well as numerous regional powers, organizations, companies, media outlets, and NGOs) that it is functionally "nonpolar."[22]

A common theme in the contemporary literature on the balance of power is the rise of China. The Chinese economy has quadrupled in size since the 1970s. China is a major manufacturing centre, has massive foreign reserves exceeding a trillion U.S. dollars, and is a growing diplomatic presence in Africa, Latin America, and the Middle East. Some suggest that China could become the world's largest economy in the next 20 years (although the global recession may frustrate such predictions); China's emergence is certainly challenging the current status quo in global politics. As a classical realist author, Hans Morgenthau, has argued: "The policy of the status quo aims at the maintenance of the distribution of power as it exists at a particular moment in history [and any] reversal of power relations" will be opposed.[23] Does the projected rise of China threaten the international balance of power? And will the United States, heavily dependent on Chinese investment, even be able to oppose it? Some American analysts argue that China is a rising revisionist state seeking to remake the international system. Economic power is the basis of military power, and a stronger China will exert itself regionally and globally to protect and promote its interests. As Richard K. Betts argued, "Should we want China to get rich or not? For realists, the answer should be no, since a rich China would overturn any balance of power."[24] However, other analysts dispute the notion that China represents this kind of threat. China's leadership is focused on internal development; China faces serious social and environmental problems; and China has joined a large number of international institutions and become further integrated into the global trade regime by joining the WTO. As Alastair Iain Johnston concludes, "it is not clear that describing China as a revisionist or non-status-quo state is accurate at this moment in history."[25] Others agree, pointing out that viewing China through the prism of balance-of-power theory might lead to erroneous assumptions, dangerous policies, and self-fulfilling prophecies.[26] This has sparked a debate on whether U.S. policy should engage or contain China.[27] Others suggest that confrontation is not inevitable. Mark Brawley has argued that the Chinese leadership fears U.S. preventive action against a rising China, and therefore will be cautious in rhetoric and action until Chinese economic and military power is more fully developed.[28] Furthermore, much of the world's behaviour toward China has sought to avoid isolating and alienating the country, although the row over the Beijing Olympics and the consequent rise of Chinese nationalism is seen as a worrying development.[29] Challenging the current international order would not be easy: it is deeply entrenched and supported by states other than America. As a result, G. John Ikenberry argues it is more likely that China will join the Western international order rather than oppose it.[30]

The rise of China is not the only point of debate in discussions about the future distribution of power in global politics. India is also a rising actor, with a growing economy and an increased presence in international trade and science and technology markets. However, India has significant challenges with respect to poverty, resources, and internal stability. It also faces growing regional tensions with Pakistan and China, as well as the ongoing troubles of Sri Lanka and Central Asia. Some speculate that the EU may become a counterbalance to the United States. The combined economies of EU members exceed the size of the American economy, and as European integration deepens and the EU takes on more of a foreign policy role, Europe could well become the new centre of power in world affairs. The problem with this projection is the high level of disagreement on foreign and security policy matters among EU members despite recent efforts to increase coordination and cooperation.[31] Furthermore, despite recent tensions between Europe and America on a wide range of issues from trade to the environment to the Iraq War, the political and security relationship between Europe and

America remains strong. The two continents are thus likely to remain friendly even as the relationship is redefined.[32] Japan is frequently mentioned in discussions of the contemporary balance of power, as its economy remains large and technologically advanced. However, Japanese economic growth has stagnated and Japan lacks the global diplomatic and military reach associated with hegemonic ambitions. Other countries that ranked in the top 15 in GDP in 2009—Brazil, South Korea, Canada, and Mexico—are not expected to increase in power to the point that they become new entrants to the great power order. The power politics of the future are thus likely to be relatively stable, characterized by a dominant United States, a rising but cautious and internally challenged China, a declining Japan, a prosperous but still divided Europe, and rising regional powers such as India and Brazil. However, the resurgence of Russia has added a new element to deliberations about the future of power politics, and we turn now to this topic.

A NEW COLD WAR?

The end of the Cold War was a world-changing event. However, in the past few years there has been a growing concern that a new Cold War has begun between a resurgent Russia on the one hand and America and Europe on the other. As Eugene B. Rumer has observed: "In Europe and the United States, the Russian resurgence in the international arena has been a matter of considerable and growing discomfort partly because Russia's newly confident voice has resonated with Cold War-like echoes.… The question of whether the West and Russia are heading into a new Cold War-style confrontation is being asked with increasing frequency on both sides of the Atlantic."[33] This concern has renewed interest in the origins and characteristics of the Cold War, in an effort to avoid repeating the mistakes of the past. As we discussed in Chapter 3, after the Cold War Russia faced enormous political, economic, and social problems. While many of these problems persist, under the former Russian President Vladimir Putin (who moved into the position of prime minister in 2008) Russia has returned to prominence in global politics. Putin enjoys widespread support in Russia. During his tenure as president the overall economy grew rapidly (largely due to surging oil and gas revenues), the quality of life improved for many Russians (though it declined for many as well), relative security and stability replaced the uncertainties of the 1990s, and Russia was once again an actor on the world stage. The Putin presidency and the resurgence of Russia have raised serious concerns about the domestic political direction of the country as well as a debate over the intentions and ambitions behind Russian foreign policy.

Observers of Russian domestic politics are now deeply concerned about the state of Russian democracy. The Russian leadership is dominated by ex–secret police and –security services associates of Putin and Russia's new economic elites. These two constituencies have collaborated to centralize political and economic power by dominating the state bureaucracy and regional governments and controlling Russia's natural resource wealth (particularly the energy sector). Some estimates suggest that as many as 70 percent of senior Russian civil servants had links to the Russian secret police and secret service at some point in their careers.[34] The media is heavily influenced (some critics would say controlled) by the state, and has become increasingly nationalistic. The actions of the West are heavily criticized and framed as part of a larger plan to isolate and marginalize Russia and interfere in the domestic affairs of the country. The activities of opposition parties are constrained, and citizen groups are carefully monitored. In 2006, the murders of Anna Politkovskaya, a prominent journalist and critic of the Putin government, and Alexander Litvinenko, an ex–secret service agent who accused the Kremlin of staging fake terrorist attacks in Russia to increase public support for military intervention in Chechnya, caused great concern among journalists and human rights activists worldwide. These are worrying developments, and Russia today is sometimes compared to the Weimar Republic in interwar Germany, when economic hardship, political humiliation, and a sense of national persecution created fertile ground for the emergence of authoritarian rule. The implications for the future of global politics are stark: an authoritarian, nationalistic Russia driven to restore its pride and place in the world is an uncomfortable thought. Some observers, such as Edward Lucas, suggest that a new Cold War is already under way between Russia and the West, driven by Russia's slide into authoritarianism.[35] However, others are not so willing to put the blame on Russia. For example, Stephen F. Cohen puts much of the blame for a new Cold War on Western (and especially U.S.) policy, which he argues has ignored Russia's legitimate security interests.[36]

Over the past several years the relationship between Russia and most Western industrialized states has deteriorated dramatically due to a number of ongoing disputes. First, the expansion of the North Atlantic Treaty Organization (NATO) to include countries in Eastern Europe and the former Soviet Union was regarded by the Alliance as an effort to build a wider post–Cold War security framework in Europe. However, the Russian government interpreted NATO expansion as an effort to encircle and threaten Russia. This issue intensified when NATO announced plans to consider NATO membership for the Ukraine and Georgia in 2008. Second, geopolitical rivalry centred on oil and natural gas resources and pipeline routes in Eastern Europe, Central Asia, and the Caucasus has caused considerable friction. The United States and Europe have become increasingly worried about the growing European dependence on oil and gas produced in Russia or transiting through Russian territory. Russia has used the interruption of oil supplies as an instrument of pressure in its disputes with the Ukraine and Georgia, and there are concerns that Europe might suffer a similar form of coercion. As a result, the United States and Europe sought to establish alternative pipeline routes carrying Central Asian and Caspian Sea oil that would avoid crossing Russian territory. The Russia government responded by making its own arrangements with supplier countries, arrangements that committed these suppliers to send their oil through Russia. Third, the issue of the independence of Kosovo (discussed in the update to Chapter 7) has pitted Russia against the United States and most of Europe. While Washington, Ottawa, and most European capitals have supported Kosovo's independence, the Russian government has opposed it on the grounds that Kosovo's independence is illegal and a violation of Serbian sovereignty. Fourth, the Russian military has resumed some practices that observers find provocative. The Russian navy has resumed oceanic training exercises and the Russian air force has resumed the kind of long-range bomber flights once considered routine during the Cold War, including flights close to Canadian Arctic airspace. Fifth, the planned installation of a U.S. missile defence system in Poland and the Czech Republic caused consternation in Russia, despite U.S. assurances that the system was aimed at defending Europe from possible missile attack from the Middle East. Finally, there has been considerable friction over Western democracy promotion in Russia and the countries of the former Soviet Union. In the United States and Europe, democracy promotion is regarded as a means of encouraging political freedoms and strengthening stability. However, the Russian government views democracy promotion as meddling in the internal affairs of Russia and the countries in which Russia has a direct security interest. In particular, Russian officials have been critical of Western support for democratic opposition movements in Serbia, Georgia, the Ukraine and (unsuccessfully) in Belarus. These efforts were actively resisted by Moscow.[37]

However, the tipping point in the relationship between Russia and the West may prove to be the conflict in Georgia. Relations between Russia and Georgia had already been poor after the collapse of the Soviet Union, but they deteriorated rapidly in 2004 as Russia began to reassert its influence in the perimeter around Russia known as the "near abroad." *The Economist* referred to this desire by Russia to reexert control over certain neighbouring countries as the "new Russian imperialism."[38] Georgia came under special pressure because of its strong relationship with the West, its desire to become a member of NATO, and the value of its territory as an alternative pipeline route for Caspian Sea oil. Russia cut trade ties with Georgia and severed transportation links and natural gas supplies to pressure the Georgian government. Tensions between the two countries were exacerbated by Russian support for two regions of Georgia that desired independence: Abkhazia and South Ossetia. South Ossetians wanted to unite with North Ossetia, a territory in Russia. Russian support for South Ossetian independence included offering Russian citizenship to South Ossetians and the deployment of Russian soldiers (described as "peacekeepers") to deter any Georgian effort to reassert control over the region. Open conflict broke out in August 2008 when the Georgian government sought to regain control over South Ossetia by force, an act that can only be described as a major miscalculation. Russia responded by invading Georgia and seizing South Ossetia and advancing deeper into Georgian territory. A peace agreement brokered by French President Nicholas Sarkozy brought an immediate end to the fighting but not a resolution of the roots of the conflict. The Russian actions prompted intense Western criticism and Russian, European, and American officials began to use rhetoric reminiscent of the Cold War. Many analysts expressed concern that Georgia was only the beginning of tensions between the West and Russia in the "near abroad" with the next conflicts likely to occur over the Crimea in the Ukraine.

Does this mean that a new Cold War is under way or is inevitable? The answer is no, for it is quite clear that there are significant differences between the situation today and the Cold War standoff. The ideological dimension of the Cold War (with the U.S. and the Soviet Union the self-appointed leaders of rival visions of the future of human society) does not exist today. There is no arms race between Russia and the United States of the kind that horrified a generation during the Cold War. Instead, the two governments signed a new nuclear arms control agreement in July 2009. On many issues, such as nuclear proliferation, terrorism, and climate change, Russia and most other industrialized states are in general agreement. Despite some inflammatory rhetoric and bellicose statements and actions, Russian resurgence may mean no more than the return of Russia to great-power status after the hiatus caused by the end of the Cold War.[39] Finally, there is the practical matter of the limits to Russian power. The gross domestic product (GDP) of Russia was approximately US$1.3 trillion in 2007, in contrast to U.S. GDP at US$13.8 trillion, the EU at US$13.8 trillion, and China at US$3.2 trillion, suggesting it does not possess the economic capacities required to carry out a new Cold War.[40] The new president, Dmitry Medvedev, is widely regarded as a political puppet of Putin, who will continue to rule through his chosen successor. However, within Russia there is concern that Putin's policies have put the country into a confrontation with the West, a confrontation that Russia is not powerful enough to sustain and that is bad for business. Russia needs good relations with the world even as it reasserts its great-power status and President Medvedev (with or without guidance from Putin) will have a choice of which path to follow.[41] Leaders in other countries will have choices as well, and as constructivists would remind us, it is these choices and not some inevitable fate that will determine whether a new Cold War emerges between countries that ought to know better.

THE FUTURE OF THE AMERICAN EMPIRE

In Chapter 4 we explored the concept of hegemony, hegemonic decline, and the debate over the decline of U.S. power. In many ways, these issues are more salient today than ever before, and we can expect debates about the role of America in the world to be a persistent theme in global politics in the future, because the implications of these debates are so enormous.

A growing number of people of varying ideological persuasions now feel comfortable referring to the "American Empire" as a fact of our time. However, the fate of that empire will be decisive in determining the character of global politics in the future. Are the days of American Empire numbered? There is certainly inconclusive evidence of U.S. hegemonic decline. First, the wars in Afghanistan and Iraq, and the massive economic stimulus packages and bailouts of financial institutions initiated in the wake of the financial crisis in 2008–2009, plunged the United States deep into debt. As of mid-2009, U.S. national debt exceeded US$10 trillion, and the U.S. government was adding to that debt at a fantastic rate. Obviously, there are only two ways to make up the difference between spending and revenues while avoiding high inflation rates, and that is through borrowing or raising taxes (a politically difficult task in the U.S.). However, at some point the debts will have to be paid, and budgets balanced. All the while, the money spent on defence and military adventure abroad is money not being invested in infrastructure upgrades, health care, education, and scientific innovation at home. Even though the U.S. economy is large and its private scientific and research base is enormous, the diversion of some government funds away from long-term economic development is worrisome to many U.S. analysts. The Obama administration is attempting to use generous economic stimulus spending to achieve some of these broader social objectives, but ultimately the economic health of the country depends on a recovery from recession.

Second, America's global legitimacy and credibility have been weakened. This is significant because according to hegemonic stability theory, a hegemon's status and preeminence depends on some loyalty from willing followers. If a hegemon provides public goods and establishes norms and rules for the governance of the system, much of the power derived from such privilege rests on the willingness of most states to accept these norms and rules. This willingness to follow is in essence the test of legitimacy in global politics (one faced by international institutions and law as well). However, some commentators suggest that the U.S. invasion of Iraq has damaged this vital aspect of American power. For example, G. John Ikenberry has argued that

> It is hard to think of another instance in American diplomatic history where a strategic wrong turn has done so much damage to the country's international position—its prestige, credibility, security partnerships and goodwill of other countries—in so short a time, with so little to show for it. A single-minded American campaign against terrorism and rogue states in which countries are either "with us or against us" and bullied into support is not leadership but a geostrategic wrecking ball that will destroy America's own half-century old international architecture.[42]

However, the invasion of Iraq was not the only reason for the decline in America's international credibility. U.S. government opposition to the Kyoto Protocol, objection to the ICC (among other U.S. government positions), and the often-bellicose rhetoric of the Bush administration all contributed to a growing skepticism of American leadership. Even erstwhile defenders of American power and righteousness became concerned about the implications of the anti-American backlash on U.S. power. In particular, the divide between America and Europe is troubling for those who have long regarded the strategic and political partnership of America and Europe as a bulwark of global peace and stability. In his reflection on the transatlantic divide, Robert Kagan observed that "it is precisely the question of legitimacy that divides Americans and Europeans today—not the legitimacy of each other's political institutions, perhaps, but the legitimacy of their respective visions of world order. More to the point, for the first time since World War II, a majority of Europeans has come to doubt the legitimacy of U.S. global leadership."[43] Others, like George Soros, were far more biting in their criticism of the Bush administration, not out of anti-American spite or a rejection of America's core values, but because they feel those very values are being betrayed.[44] The Obama administration has recognized this challenge, but it remains to be seen if America's legitimacy and credibility can be fully restored.

Third, others have suggested that U.S. foreign policy has overemphasized hard power, at the expense of an underappreciated American resource: soft power. Joseph Nye is the leading proponent of this view. For Nye, "This soft power—getting others to want the outcomes you want—co-opts people rather than coerces them. Soft power rests on the ability to shape the preferences of others."[45] Nye goes on to argue that "winning the peace is harder than winning a war, and soft power is essential to winning the peace. Yet the way we went to war in Iraq proved to be as costly for our soft power as it was a stunning victory for our hard power."[46] In the future, will American governments be more aware of the relationship between power, economics, and legitimacy? Will they recognize the significance of soft power and the importance of balancing the use of the military instrument within a larger political and diplomatic context? Will they recognize the value of multilateral action, and the fact that the United States has been uniquely fortunate since the end of World War II to face an environment in which most of the great powers of the world are its allies?

Of course, it will take more than American initiative to restore its legitimacy among its allies and its soft power around the world. America's allies must be willing to accept U.S. leadership to some extent. However, this may not be the reaction of other key states. States might form a grand alliance to counterbalance American power. Alternatively, states might form or strengthen regional trade and political organizations to undermine or reduce the influence of global institutions such as the WTO and the IMF. Transatlantic relations between Europe and the United States might break down over trade and political and security issues. If this happens, U.S. power will have to exert itself in a less favourable international environment than it has in the past. On the other hand, it is likely that the United States and its allies will reach accommodation more often than not. Shared interests and shared values will bring America and other countries together in cooperative efforts that may rebuild trust and confidence. As for U.S. decline, a note of caution is warranted. The decline of the Roman Empire is sometimes recorded as beginning with the end of the Antonine Emperors in 180 C.E.; the Vandals sacked Rome 275 years later. Decline, it would seem, is a slow process.

For other analysts, the reality of U.S. global dominance is unlikely to change and will continue to characterize the global distribution of military, economic, and diplomatic power. However, this "primacist" view seldom comes without the qualification that the U.S. government must act appropriately to preserve its dominant position. Barry Posen argues that "Unipolarity and U.S. hegemony will likely be around for some time."[47] However, this does not mean that the United States can sustain its position indefinitely. Posen argues that the United States can maintain its preeminence, but only if it maintains a disciplined approach to foreign policy. Niall Fergusson argues that the existence of an American "liberal empire" is evident by all economic, military and diplomatic measures. Fergusson argues that the threat to this empire comes not from rising rivals but from a failure of Americans to recognize the reality of their imperial status and exert the necessary leadership to maintain it. Americans, Fergusson notes, would rather "consume than conquer."[48] A supporter of the 2003 Iraq War (though a critic of subsequent postwar policy), Fergusson insists that U.S. primacy is a fact, and the continued existence of a U.S. liberal empire is desirable for the future of global politics.

Not all primacists arrive at the same conclusions as Fergusson. Joseph Nye has argued that U.S. military power, economic power, and ideological/cultural "soft" power will endure into the future, despite the neglect of soft power during the Bush administration, which Nye finds troubling. Nye suggests that the United States must combine its hard power and its soft power into a "smart power" strategy (a not-so-subtle implication that Nye feels the Bush administration was following a dumb-power strategy).[49] In a similar vein, Amy Chua has observed that successful empires maintain their longevity through co-optation or toleration. Political, religious, and cultural understanding and accommodation can encourage cooperation and a willing (though sometimes grudging) loyalty that helps preserve the power of the empire. Chua argues that the United States can maintain its power by following such policies in the future.[50] However, many analysts that accept U.S. hegemony as fact argue there are limits to what American policy can do to influence or counteract balance of power behaviour. Joseph Joffe and Julia Sweig have argued that America is unpopular and resented because it looks, acts, and talks like a hegemon and is therefore a natural magnet for resentment and hostility.[51] This argument—that antipathy is a corollary of dominance—implies that there will be limits to the success of any effort by the Obama administration to close the gap between its power and its legitimacy in the post-Bush era. Others have suggested that the United States must avoid hegemonic pretensions and alter its foreign policy strategy to accommodate balance of power behaviour. For example, Christopher Layne argues that U.S. grand strategy since the 1940s has been driven by the desire to achieve security through expanding its power and pursuing hegemony, particularly in Western Europe, East Asia, and the Persian Gulf. Layne argues that this approach cannot be successful because it will provoke balancing behaviour by other states (particularly China) and overstretch U.S. resources. Instead, Layne suggests the United States should pursue an "offshore balancing strategy" as the only alternative to seeking hegemony.[52] As Layne argues elsewhere, "US hegemony cannot endure indefinitely."[53]

A CLASH OF CIVILIZATIONS?

In a famous and controversial article published in the influential journal *Foreign Affairs* in 1993, the late Harvard professor Samuel Huntington argued that the primary source of conflict in the future would not be ideology, economics, or nationalism. Rather, future wars would occur between the world's civilizations: "Nation states will remain the most powerful actors in world affairs, but the principal conflicts of global politics will occur between nations and groups of different civilizations. The clash of civilizations will dominate world politics. The fault lines between civilizations will be the battle lines of the future."[54] As we discussed in our historical review, conflict between civilizations was a fixture of human history before the development of the modern Westphalian state system. Huntington suggested that with the state (and state nationalism) eroding and the great ideological battles over, we are returning to an era characterized by conflict between civilizations. He defined a civilization in the following manner: "A civilization is a cultural entity. Villages, regions, ethnic groups, nationalities, religious groups, all have distinct cultures at different levels of cultural heterogeneity … Arabs, Chinese, and Westerners, however, are not part of any broader cultural entity. They constitute civilizations. A civilization is thus the highest cultural grouping of people and the broadest level of cultural identity people have short of that which distinguishes humans from other species."[55] Huntington argued that there are eight major civilizations in the world: Western, Confucian, Japanese, Islamic, Hindu, Slavic-Orthodox, Latin American, and African. Many recent and current conflicts in the contemporary international system are taking place along these fault lines, in places such as the former Yugoslavia, Azerbaijan, Armenia and Georgia, the Horn of Africa, Russia and Chechnya, India and Pakistan, and India and China. Huntington predicted that the conflicts of the future will increasingly take place along the fault lines where these civilizations meet.

He offered several explanations as to why intercivilization disputes are growing and will become the basis for most future conflicts. First, civilizations are more basic than the state, for our self-identities owe less to the state than to the civilization to which we belong. Civilizations are differentiated by history, religion, language, culture, and tradition. Differences among civilizations are therefore fundamental and very enduring. As a result, differences among civilizations have generated the longest and most violent conflicts and will do so increasingly in the future. Second, increasing global interdependence, interaction, and contact between peoples of different civilizations is not contributing to understanding and accommodation, but rather is making more people aware of the differences between them. Interdependence and globalization are contributing to civilization-consciousness among the peoples of the world. Third, economic and social change around the world is altering the relationship between individuals and traditional social institutions. In particular, the state is in decline and religion is replacing it. The revival of religion around the world means a world increasingly united around the religious heritages of civilizations rather than the nationalist heritage of nation-states. Fourth, the spread and power of Western civilization is provoking a counterreaction in other civilizations. Civilization-consciousness is in part a reaction to the encroachment of Western culture and values on traditional belief systems. An anti-Western return to civilization roots is under way around the world, from Asianization in Japan to the Hinduization of India to the re-Islamization of the Middle East and the Russianization of Russia. Fifth, Huntington suggested that civilizational differences are less subject to change or flexible adaptation. Negotiations, compromises, and resolution of disputes that have a civilizational aspect are more difficult to achieve. Finally, Huntington argued that economic patterns are assuming civilizational forms and shapes. Civilization links will become more important factors in the creation of economic zones of activity, with peoples of shared heritage more disposed toward doing business with each other than they are with peoples of other civilizations.

Ultimately, Huntington warned that civilization identity is becoming increasingly important as an influence on the perceptions of peoples around the world. This influence will create an "us versus them" mentality, which will drive intercivilization differences on a whole range of international issues, from human rights, immigration, trade and commerce to the environment, the global spread of Western culture and power has already provoked a backlash against the West. The future may be one of "the West against the rest." This argument (as Huntington himself pointed out) is not an original one. Kishore Mahbubani has argued that the central axis of conflict in the world in the future will be between Western civilization and the non-Western civilizations of the world.[56] This conflict will take two forms: on the one hand there will be a struggle for military, economic, and institutional power. On the other hand, there will be a struggle over culture. The response of the non-Western world in this struggle will continue to be varied. Some non-Western states will adopt a policy of isolation, in effect sealing off their societies and economies from the West. Other states will join the West and adopt Western values and institutions, including democracy, law, and human rights. The difficulty with this course of action is that it involves the import of value systems that are very different from those shared by the majority (or a significant portion) of the population. This may create social and political unrest between those who want to Westernize and those who want to protect the history and culture of the society. A final option is to acquire military and economic power to resist the West and to make common cause with other non-Western peoples in this effort. The reaction of the West will also be crucial. In the long term, Huntington argued that the West must recognize that the dominance of Western civilization around the world is ending and that other civilizations will begin to reexert their place and influence on global politics. The West, along with all of the world's civilizations, will have to develop an increased understanding of the philosophical and religious differences between them. There will be no universal civilization but a world of civilizations.

Huntington's thesis has stirred considerable debate, and the attacks of September 11, 2001 and the subsequent "War on Terror" and the invasion of Iraq launched by the Bush administration added fuel to the controversy over the clash of civilizations thesis. In the United States and some other countries, the September 11 attacks and subsequent response have been cast as a civilization clash: the attacks were carried out by militant Islamic fundamentalists preaching hatred against the West in general and the United States in particular. Walter Laqueur argued that the motive of Islamic fundamentalist terrorism does not originate with poverty or repression, but the desire to destroy Western civilization.[57] Norman Podhoretz, one of the leading figures of the neoconservative movement in the United States, argues that America is fighting World War IV against "Islamofascism."[58] Meanwhile, in the Islamic world the wars in Afghanistan and Iraq are widely regarded as a Western crusade against Islam, part of a long history of Western oppression of Muslims. Anthony Pagden has argued that the history of the East and the West is a history of 2,500 years of struggle and conflict. In this context, Pagden suggests that "the 'clash of civilizations'—a crude but useful phrase—is the enduring reality of Islamic life, as it has always been a central feature of Islamic history."[59] These sentiments have been strengthened by strident rhetoric emanating from political and religious extremists in the West and the Islamic world.

However, there are serious limitations to this thesis. Huntington's critics argue that the boundary between civilizations is far from distinct and that conflict within a civilization—that is, intracivilization conflict—may be more common than clashes between civilizations. The future will thus be characterized as much by conflict within the Muslim world (between Muslim states or between Shia and Sunni Muslims) than wars between the Muslim and Christian civilizations. Others stress that states are a far more decisive force than Huntington suggests. Instead of civilizations motivating the actions of states, it is more accurate to say that states dominate civilizations and cultures. Huntington has also been criticized for overestimating the role played by culture in the world. Most peoples and governments are motivated not by cultural concerns but by concerns over economic growth. The world is characterized not by the triumph of religious and culturally oriented governments, but by the failure of such governments. The West remains a source of attraction for non-Western peoples, in particular the young, the poor, and the oppressed. Many people today would identity themselves with neither state nor culture, reflecting cosmopolitan values revolving around universal concerns such as ecology or human rights. Huntington's thesis is based on such broad generalizations that it is often decried as poor social science, closer to rhetorical incitement than serious analysis. However, it remains a serious point of discussion in the debate about the origins of the conflicts and wars of the future.

THE FUTURE OF GLOBALIZATION

Our discussion of the global economy suggests that economic issues have increased in importance in global politics. It is clear that this trend will continue into the future, with the dominant concerns revolving around the relationship between markets and regulation, the stability of the global trade and financial system, and the persistent inequities in wealth distribution. In the coming years the theoretical debate underpinning economic policy is likely to become more intense and antagonistic. We live in a world in which news and debates on economics, business, government fiscal policy (taxing and spending), government monetary policy (interest rates and money supply), and the decisions of international financial institutions such as the International Monetary Fund and the World Bank are dominated by liberal economic principles. In fact, if there is one foundation to the modern world economy, it is liberal economic theory translated into practice by decades of government policy and international negotiations. In recent decades, a variant of liberal economic thinking has emerged known as neoliberalism. The neoliberal agenda emphasizes the global freedom of capital and reduction of state intervention. Neoliberals argue that such policies are essential to foster economic growth and the improvement of living standards worldwide, and this view is reflected in the formula of the Washington Consensus and the operations of large financial institutions and corporations. Will the neoliberal agenda triumph? Some scholars, such as the neo-Marxist Stephen Gill, see the agents of the global economy representing an emerging system of global economic governance (a "disciplinary neoliberalism") based on a quasi-constitutional framework for the reconstitution of the legal rights, prerogatives, and freedom of movement for capital on a world scale (a "new constitutionalism").[60] Gill envisions a global system designed to promote the interests of capital first and foremost. Given how entrenched neoliberal thinking is many of the world's leading financial institutions, it is not hard to envision the kind of future Gill suggests.

However, the neoliberal agenda has come under growing pressure from critical economists and a variety of domestic and international groups and organizations as the drawbacks and failures of the neoliberal approach have become more evident in the wake of the credit crisis and the global economic recession. Keynesian or interventionist liberals are skeptical of the neoliberal ideology, arguing that markets require management and regulation if equitable distributions of wealth and social development are to be achieved. As George Soros has suggested: "To stabilize and regulate a truly global economy, we need some global system of political decision making. In short, we need a global society to support our global economy."[61] Soros envisions a global system of regulatory measures exerting control over the worst effects and excesses of the hidden hand of the market. Soros is far from alone in this vision, as the concern about the implications of globalization grows. There are those who feel their entire cultural identity is threatened by Westernization, and feel the need to defend their way of life. Labour and worker's rights organizations are concerned about the exploitation of labour. Environmentalists point to the link between globalization and damage to the ecology. Fair trade advocates make the case for increased balance in profit sharing. Anti-poverty organizations highlight the need for greater justice in the distribution of wealth, water and food, health care, and services. It is also the case that most governments do not subscribe to the neoliberal agenda, at least not in the form it takes in the United States. The question of whether neoliberal economic theory or more interventionist liberal economic theory becomes the guiding framework for the policies and practices of the world economy is one of the biggest questions of our time. Of course, the debate over globalization is largely an intra-liberal debate. Realists remind us that states act in their own narrow self-interest to promote their own economic power. For Edward Luttwak, the ability of states to meet the challenges of privatization, deregulation, and globalization—what he refers to as "turbo-capitalism"—will determine whether they will be winners or losers in the new global economy.[62] Meanwhile, neo-Marxists remind us that economic elites act to promote their own privilege over the marginalized and exploited. Evidence supporting these theoretical perspectives is visible in international economic affairs today. And so, while liberal economics is the orthodoxy and dominates economic debate and policy decisions, it does not have a monopoly on theory or practice and is not beyond criticism (or in some cases, outright opposition).

The magnitude of economic globalization is striking when aggregate statistics on economic growth and trade and financial flows are used as measures. According to the World Bank, the world's economic output totalled US$59 trillion in 2006.[63] Trade continues to be an important force in global economic growth. Merchandise exports accounted for 35 percent of world gross domestic product (GDP) in 2006, up from 10 percent in 1960. The value of merchandise trade alone was over US$12 trillion in 2006.[64] Investment flows have also increased steadily: the value of all foreign direct investment (FDI) inflows was over US$1.3 trillion in 2006.[65] Global financial flows are facilitated by big currency markets in New York, London, Zurich, Tokyo, and Hong Kong, among others. In 2007, the value of trade in global currency reached US$3.2 trillion per day, an increase of 71 percent since 2004.[66] The sheer volume of global trade and financial transactions raises questions about how (or if) these flows can be managed and regulated effectively. The history of the world economy discussed in Chapter 4 is far from irrelevant in contemporary debates about the future of global economic relations. The prevailing view today is that national boundaries will continue to erode in the face of an irresistible tide of globalization and the unstoppable expansion of trade, financial, and other economic activity. However, in the early 1900s people felt much the same way about the global economy: unprecedented levels of economic integration had developed over decades along with an international financial system. Nevertheless, it all came to a disastrous end in World War I. As Jeffry A. Freiden observes in his excellent history of the global economy, "the bases on which global capitalism rests today are not much different from what they were in 1900, and the potential for their disruption is as present today as then. Globalization is still a choice, not a fact."[67] Freiden's caution is especially pertinent in light of the global recession that began in 2008, and the accompanying concern that states might turn to protectionism and economic nationalism in response.

One trend in particular animates both proponents and opponents of globalization, and will continue to be a central point of ideological divergence: the privatization of the commons and the deregulation of public control over private commercial and industrial activity. This represents the continuation of a trend that began when capitalism took over as the dominant mode of production in Europe and eventually spread around the world. The acceptance of a culturally significant definition of private property was in direct conflict with many social norms in Asia, Africa, North and South America, for most of the past millennium. The process of appropriation of the commons for the pursuit of private and corporate gain remains the defining feature of global capitalism; it permeates every area of life, from resources, land, water, and the provision of previously public services to less tangible aspects of modern life, such as intellectual property rights, gene patents, and even the right to pollute. Water, in particular, will be the focus of great debate, as neoliberals argue that privatization will lead to more efficiency, while critics charge that this amounts to an appropriation of what was once considered one of the most basic human rights: access to water as a precondition for survival.[68] The biopolitics of the future will involve furious debates, in both national and multilateral forums, about the intersection between the ethics of genetic manipulation and genetically modified organisms and the profit factor in their development and dissemination.

The debate over development will continue as well. As Jeffrey Sachs points out, globalization can be a force for good, but it is simply not true that a rising tide lifts all boats.[69] Most scholars and activists engaged in the development issues of our time have largely forsaken "modernization" theory as a form of cultural imperialism, and dismissed the once-hegemonic belief that large-scale infrastructure development (dams, pipelines, highways, railroads) was the precondition for economic and political development. However, this model of development remains popular with key decision makers in donor states and most recipient states. This is due to a persistent belief in some circles that modernization through infrastructure development is the best path to development, and because this model of development creates opportunities for donor state corporations to secure large contracts with developing countries. Many recipient states also pursue the industrial and infrastructure model of development because industrialization is seen as synonymous with growth and economic power. Neo-Marxists would remind us of another explanation: elites in developing countries are looking after their interests above all else, and large industrial and infrastructure projects promise wealth and power for those that control them. It is likely that the infrastructure model of development will persist, and it would be inaccurate to dismiss it entirely: a very real problem in many developing countries is a lack of serviceable infrastructure. However, in the future we can expect development projects to take more of a local and community-based focus. This will place a greater emphasis on environmental sustainability, women in development, and microcredit arrangements consisting of small loans to individuals to start their own businesses.[70] Nevertheless, we will still witness a cultural divide between those societies that have largely accepted privatization and capitalism as the dominant mode of development, and those that either reject this model or are determined to fashion it in their own way. The latter approach (local adaptation and development) would seem to hold the most promise. Ultimately, the stark dichotomy between market and socialized life is a false one. Societies around the world have thrived on marketplace interactions. As William J. Bernstein observes, "Trade is an irreducible and intrinsic human impulse, as primal as the needs for food, shelter, sexual intimacy, and companionship."[71] It is also the case that even the most industrialized and free market states provide a wide range of public goods for their citizens, from health care to education to pensions. The broader question is what type of synthesis between public and private property rights will emerge in the long term.

Finally, the future of economic globalization itself is in question. The collapse of the Doha Round of the WTO talks, the persistence of trade disputes, the rising tide of opposition to economic integration in most parts of the world, and the global recession raise doubts as to whether increased progress on world trade liberalization is possible. Has globalization, economic interdependence, the implementation of liberal economic principles in the structure of the world economy and the institutions that govern it reached the pinnacle of what is politically possible? For most liberal observers, protectionism is likely to be the key issue in the management of the world economy in the future. The concern is that rising protectionist sentiment in governments and populations around the world will precipitate a new era of economic nationalism, reducing trade and stifling the international flow of capital. This in turn will worsen the global recession and precipitate a world economic downturn that will lead to greater economic hardship for people around the world. Faced with the inability to make progress in the WTO, states will turn instead to regional multilateral agreements to secure markets and access to resources, or to networks of bilateral trade agreements with select partners. The result will be an increasingly fragmented world economy, with little or no capacity for the global governance Soros and many others suggest is necessary if the global economy is to be managed effectively. The G-20 Summit in April 2009 and the G-8 Summit in July 2009 were dedicated to avoiding such a scenario, but while agreement was reached on many general principles and objectives it was unclear whether the participating governments would be willing or capable of following through on these commitments. For liberals, the fragmentation of world economic patterns and the rise in protectionism will lead to a world that is less prosperous, less respectful of individual liberties, and less peaceful in the future.

FUTURE CRISES IN THE GLOBAL ECONOMY

The global economy has suffered through numerous economic crises. The Wall Street Crash in 1929 and the ensuing Great Depression still resonates today. The oil shock of the 1970s caused economic turmoil worldwide. In the 1980s, the U.S. savings and loan crisis, the Japanese property crash, and the Latin American debt default crisis spread fear about the global financial system. The 1997 Asian financial crisis and the Russian financial crisis of 1998 shook confidence in globalization. The collapse of the "dot-com" companies' stock values in 2000–2001 revealed the influence of unfettered speculation in global stock markets. The frequency and severity of these crises has led to growing fears that the global economic system is unstable, prone to sudden shocks that can spread through an integrated world economy. Another example of this instability occurred in 2007–2008 in the form of the U.S. mortgage crisis, which destabilized financial markets worldwide. The roots of the crisis go back to 2005, when large numbers of low-income borrowers with poor credit histories took out long-term house mortgages (called "subprime" mortgages) with low initial interest rates. That is, to the borrowers the costs of purchasing a home looked affordable because initial interest rates payments (for the first two years or so) were quite modest. By 2006, 20 percent of all new mortgages in the U.S. were subprime.[72] However, through the neglect of the home buyer or the deliberate manipulation of the lenders, what was forgotten or concealed was that interest rates on the mortgage loan would jump dramatically after the initial two- or three-year period of low rates. When the interest payments on the subprime mortgages went up, it had devastating consequences for the home buyers' personal finances. In dramatically increasing numbers through 2007 and early 2008, people began to default on their loans and were forced out of their homes.

In the past, clients defaulting on their loans would mean that the lenders (banks, for the most part) would be saddled with the loss. However, most of these mortgages were financed by packaging them into financial products and selling them to other U.S. and foreign banks and investment funds. Why would anyone buy a package of debt? These mortgage products had value because of the promise of the repayment of the loan in full (the principal) along with the interest on that loan. If the loan was repaid in full along with the interest, the buyer of the loan package (a bank or investment fund) would make a considerable profit. Anticipating these profits, American and foreign banks and investment funds invested heavily in these mortgage financial products, often without a clear understanding of the risk. This is how the global financial system became involved in the crisis. When American home buyers were forced to default in large numbers, the value of the mortgage packages crumbled almost overnight, and banks and investment funds around the world lost billions of dollars. Banks alone announced losses of over US$60 billion in 2008, and by early 2009 some predictions of total global losses from the financial crisis exceeded US$2.2 trillion.[73] The shock reverberated through the global financial system. The financial losses from defaults on mortgage loans in Cleveland and Phoenix have impacted on the finances of investors in Asia and Europe. Some major banks and mortgage lenders (such as Bear Sterns, Fannie Mae and Freddie Mac in the U.S., and Northern Rock in the United Kingdom) went bankrupt and had to be bailed out by governments. In summarizing the cause of the disaster, *The Economist* made the following observation:

> For the critics of modern finance [the crisis] … was the inevitable consequence of the laissez-faire philosophy that allowed financial services to innovate and spread almost unchecked. This has created a complex, interdependent system prone to conflicts of interest. Fraud has been rampant in the sale of subprime mortgages. Spurred by pay that was geared to short-term gains, bankers and fund managers stand accused of pocketing bonuses with no thought for the longer-term consequences of what they were doing. Their gambling has been fed by the knowledge that, if disaster struck, someone else— borrowers, investors, taxpayers—would end up bearing at least some of the losses.[74]

By mid-2008, some observers suggested that the world was on the verge of a global financial pandemic.[75] By the end of 2008, the crisis had spread beyond the U.S. economy and beyond the global financial sector. How did the crisis spread? First, financial institutions worldwide became much more careful about lending and raised their interest rates. The result was a global capital shortage (often called a "credit crunch") that slowed economic growth because businesses and investors now longer had access to cheap capital through low-interest loans. Banks became reluctant to lend to each other (a common practice before the crisis), because they no longer trusted the each other's finances. Second, the housing market began to deflate in other countries when interest rates rose, credit dried up, and property values fell. Third, as a result of the crisis, the U.S. housing market was hit hard by a drop in home values and a slump in construction, dealing another blow to a U.S. economy already hit by a declining dollar, famously high levels of household debt, and higher fuel prices. U.S. business expansion slowed due to a lack of affordable credit. Unemployment began to climb as businesses downsized their workforces. As the U.S. economy slowed, American consumers bought less of the world's exported products, reducing global demand for goods, services, and raw materials. American consumer spending before the crisis totalled US$9 trillion per year, as against US$1 trillion in China and US$600,000 in India. This served as a reminder of the crucial importance of the U.S. economy (25 percent of the global total) and the familiar refrain that when the U.S. sneezes the world catches a cold. The IMF predicted that world economic growth would slow to one-half of a percentage point in 2009, the slowest rate of growth since World War II.[76] The worldwide impact of the U.S. mortgage crisis illustrates the continued vulnerability of the global economy to unexpected shocks and has provided more fuel to critics of the global financial system and even capitalism itself.

HUMAN RIGHTS AND INTERNATIONAL LAW

We have yet to establish a universal international human rights order. Establishing such an order is a priority for many human rights activists. However, others caution that any universal order would only be the result of coercion or cultural imperialism. What is more disturbing is the unseemly level of hypocrisy evident in the realm of human rights. The grand pronouncements of state representatives and international legal conventions seem meaningless as human rights abuses continue on a daily basis. Often, human rights abuses in one country attract a great deal of attention, while similar abuses in other countries are ignored. It is also the case that most governments are critical of human rights abuses in other countries while paying less attention to abuses at home. Whether it is the treatment of indigenous peoples in Canada and Australia, the incarceration without due process of thousands of Muslim men after September 11 in the United States, the denial of the right to education to women in many states, the passive acceptance of the international trade in human beings, or hundreds of other controversial practices, no states are immune from questions about their domestic and foreign policies on human rights. In the future, we can expect human rights violations (and erratic and inconsistent responses to them) to remain a prominent feature of global politics.

Can we expect a reasonable improvement in the global human rights situation? For all the lofty talk about the primacy of international law, the need to establish some sort of universal set of guidelines for the interaction between states, and the need to promote adherence to the founding principles of the United Nations, a world governed by law remains a hope, not a reality. While many states obey most international laws at least some of the time, they break those laws when decision makers feel it is in their interests to do so. Imagine, for example, telling a police officer that you were speeding down the highway because you had decided that following the law was not in your best interests that day! Imagine if most drivers on the road with you felt the same way and drove accordingly! There is no global culture of implicit acceptance of international law as the arbiter in disputes, and of course there is no police officer to enforce the law. Yet a world governed by law would promise much. For example, the American response to September 11 has been a heavily militarized one. While it quickly became apparent that the United States interpreted the attacks as an assault not only on America but also on the free world and civilization itself, others such as Mary Robinson, then the UN High Commissioner for Human Rights, suggested that it would be better to view the September 11 attacks as a crime against humanity. This would encourage a response to terrorism based not on statist reflexes and outright military power, but on a more liberal international effort to establish the rule of international law, strengthen the UN, coordinate law enforcement and intelligence-gathering institutions, increase financial regulation, use international courts, and lower the disparity between rich and poor. The turn to an excessively militarized strategy in the "War on Terror" may be viewed as a significant lost opportunity to strengthen international stability and order.[77] Whether or not this would have been politically palatable in the United States is, however, another matter. Recall also, from Chapter 10, that Canada once broke international law to enforce a fisheries conservation measure that would later become codified law, proving you sometimes need to break law to make it.

However, there is some cause for optimism. We have seen several developments that might well give rise to a new stage in the evolution of human rights and humanitarian law. South Africa's Truth and Reconciliation Commission represented a bold, if troubled, effort to permit a traumatized society to come to terms with its past. The establishment of the International Criminal Court, based loosely on the ad hoc tribunals for the former Yugoslavia and Rwanda, puts unprecedented emphasis on the accountability of individuals under international criminal law. The fact that court has tried individuals and indicted others shows that the court is taken seriously by at least some states. Given the historical record, it is likely that the court will be used only to prosecute individuals who have committed crimes against humanity in peripheral states and members of defeated military regimes. But the potential is there for a much more robust and lasting effort to take such criminals to task, including such often ignored crimes as rape as an instrument of war, ethnic cleansing, and genocide. Various ad hoc courts in places such as Sierra Leone, Cambodia, and Iraq, beset with their own unique difficulties, will further contribute to ending the culture of impunity. However, the ICC will have to determine its proper political role, as the controversial indictment of the Sudanese president has made clear.

For international law in general, the prospects are as exciting as they are daunting. Globalization is accompanied by the legal property rights regime that reflects Western institutions and corporate law, so there will no doubt be great opportunities for private international lawyers. International public law is also attracting increasing numbers of bright and ambitious students. The International Court of Justice will be used for its dual purpose: to hear cases based on disputes between states, in its role as arbitrator, and to pass judgment on questions of advisory opinion, such as the construction of the so-called security fence by Israel. These judgments do not always change the behaviour of states, but they do focus attention on the issues, and suggest that the real role for international law is not as an ordering device with definitive powers, but as an instrument of legitimacy and moral suasion with limited but real influence in global politics.[78]

HUMAN HEALTH, THE ENVIRONMENT, AND MULTILATERALISM

We have some major choices ahead of us regarding the future health of the planet. Our dependence on fossil fuels for energy is affecting the climate, contributing to conflict, and limiting the options for future generations. The immense byproduct of industrialization and urban concentration, and the sheer waste involved in the productive and consumptive processes of this era, is difficult to fathom. Overfishing and pollution threaten the oceans and marine life, and freshwater is becoming increasingly precious. The availability of land for cultivation is decreasing. The widespread use of chemical fertilizers has increased crop yields but also increased pollution. Mono-crop agriculture has marginalized traditional farmers. Deforestation is a consequence of population pressure and expanding agricultural, forestry, and mining industries, and is accompanied by the loss of global biodiversity and the threat to the livelihood and rights of indigenous peoples. In short, the price that has been paid for economic development, modernization, and globalization has been very high. Increased calls for the adoption of sustainable economic and environmental practices are likely to increase in the future.

The need for multilateral coordination to mitigate and adapt to these consequences is obvious. All liberals, and even many realists, would agree. However, whether adequate multilateral responses can be forged is still uncertain. Can a world still organized into sovereign territorial states organize itself to respond to truly global issues? Critical theorists remind us that the very multilateral institutions being constructed to "manage" such issues are products of the very states, companies, and household habits that have encouraged this type of development for many decades. Thus they argue transnational solidarity with those most affected is also necessary. We can expect the marginalized and disadvantaged to join in alliances in order to fight what they perceive as their unjust treatment by the international community. Despite the seemingly insurmountable obstacles to change, there is hope for the future. More and more people are becoming aware of environmental degradation, pollution, and climate change. As a result, environmentally friendly practices, products, and industries are gaining in size and popularity. Most societies and cultural traditions have some sort of stewardship principle, which suggests present generations have an ethical obligation to look ahead and consider the impact of their actions on the yet unborn. Taken together, this may manifest itself in a slow but steady movement toward the adoption of more sustainable practices and the increased universality of concepts such as the precautionary principle.

Beyond the ecological harm caused by industrialization, militarization, agribusiness, and consumption, there are many threats to human health related to the human population itself. Though the worst predictions of a "population bomb" expected a few decades ago have not come to pass, we are nonetheless living in a world with very close to seven billion people, and the figure continues to rise, adding to migratory pressures and the negative aspects of mass, rapid urbanization. It is a falsehood, however, to blame these problems on population growth itself as a variable, since human behaviour is at the core of the aggregate impact of human populations. Again, there is a need for multilateral assistance, market access, and freedom from repression and corruption in order to improve the conditions of life for the millions of undernourished and marginalized people. We can foresee an even larger role for the informal sector in the future as people are forced to rely less on the state and legal economic activity and more on their own survival strategies within a context of human insecurity. We can also foresee increased tensions within many countries in both the developing and developed worlds over the privatization and deregulation of everything from public space to water rights to health care. States intent on pursuing this course will face growing opposition and increasingly fractious domestic politics, while others will resort to oppressive measures, which will in turn threaten their own fragile legitimacy. And yet, this scenario too can be avoided if governments and international institutions turn away from an ideological fixation on market liberalization and boundless privatization toward a more balanced approach. There are signs this may already be happening: the Washington Consensus formula itself is under revision, and the IMF and the World Bank, among others, are increasingly cognizant of the social and environmental impact of economic policies. Perhaps the future will be characterized by a new consensus on achieving a harmony between the market and social and environmental sustainability. Constructivist and feminist theorists would contend that part of the problem has been the tendency to resort to blueprints, ready-made models that are supposed to apply everywhere, regardless of circumstances. This needs to change, not only because of large differences in culture, history, structural power, and other variables, but also because development and environmental management and population issues are not static, but fluid: priorities often change over even short periods of time.

Another threat to human security that has made numerous appearances in this text is the modern pandemic. HIV/AIDS has killed over 25 million people in the past three decades. As is the case with the uncountable deaths the world has witnessed due to malnutrition and easily preventable diseases, many HIV/AIDS victims in the poor parts of the world will die young because the medical services required to help them are absent or in short supply. This is indisputably harming the prospects of future generations as well. While there has been some progress made toward achieving the Millennium Goals (see Chapter 8), there is an urgent need to accelerate such action, and once again the costs of delay are as debilitating as they are heartwrenching. All the wireless networks we create, and renewable energy advances we pursue, and peace negotiations we conduct, will be in vain if the international community does not address these fundamental threats to human security. Every year billions of dollars are spent on military production, on combating the epidemic of obesity in high-income states, and on the production of goods and services that are simply not needed. Can the will and a way be found to devote the mere fraction of these resources that would be necessary to mitigate the intolerable harm done by disease and marginalization around the world?

The population of the planet will continue to increase. However, population growth rates have slowed in many areas, in some cases due to tragic circumstances, but in most due to active family-planning measures and changing perspectives on the utility and challenges of having several children. But we will face new demographic challenges in the future. In areas devastated with pandemics, especially in the HIV/AIDS context, states will have to cope with an unprecedented number of orphans and single-parent families. Areas affected with rampant violence will struggle with accompanying physical and psychological health problems, as well as the legacy of environmental destruction, land mines, and the need to overcome the past. And another health crisis is quickly looming: the economic impact of aging populations in both high-income Western states and many poorer non-Western states. This "greying" of society will have a profound impact on the workforce, perhaps stimulating relaxed migration policies and redefinitions of health itself.[79]

CANADA AND THE FUTURE OF GLOBAL POLITICS

In many ways, Canadians are extraordinarily fortunate. Canada is largely insulated from the full effects of war and instability abroad, and faces no direct military threat to its territory or society. Canada possesses the second-largest territory in the world (after Russia) with a population of just over 33 million people. The country is rich in freshwater, arable land, and mineral resources. The Canadian economy is the ninth-largest in the world, with a highly educated workforce and an advanced communications, transportation, and energy infrastructure. Canada ranks in the top 15 countries in the world in wealth per capita. The country is among the world leaders in key social health indicators such as infant mortality, adult literacy, and life expectancy. Canada consistently ranks among the top five countries in the world on the UN Human Development Index. By most accounts, Canada is one of the best places to live in the world. In some ways, this makes Canada strong, even though most Canadians do not tend to see the country this way. As Michael Byers has argued, "We are, believe it or not, the envy of the world. We are—take a deep breath and don't laugh—a powerful country."[80]

However, Canada's place and role in the world has been a subject of criticism and debate in recent years. A common theme is Canada's declining profile in global politics, and how Canada can capture, or recapture, a more influential role in world affairs. For example, Andrew Cohen has argued that "our vision is less broad today than it was in the past, especially in the decade or so after the Second World War. We are no longer as strong a soldier, as generous a donor, and as effective a diplomat, and it has diminished us as a people."[81] To recapture a worthy role in world affairs, Cohen suggests Canada increase the size and capacity of its military, increase foreign aid, diversify its trade, and reinvigorate the foreign service. In another popular book, Jennifer Welsh observed that "We find ourselves at a significant crossroads. Either we make the choices that will allow us to thrive on the North American continent and contribute actively in creating a better world, or we will cease to exist—in anything but name—as a sovereign country."[82] Welsh believes that Canada must choose what kind of society it wants to be in the future, and it must contribute leadership, money, ideas and people to create a working world. The message is consistent: because it can, Canada must exert itself in the realm of global politics.

But what should Canada's role be? What should be the priorities of the country in the global politics of the future? There is much less agreement on these questions among observers of Canada and Canadians themselves. Michael Byers suggests that "Canada should, as a country, be asserting itself as a 'global citizen,' shaping the international agenda and using its influence to secure positive, progressive change."[83] Drawing on liberal and constructivist themes, Byers supports the idea of Canada as source of new ideas and an agent of change in global politics. Others suggest that Canada's role in the world should be defined by its national interests, which according to Steven Kendall Holloway can be identified as: national security (including territorial sovereignty); political autonomy; national unity; economic prosperity; and principled self-image (identity).[84] This perspective, more akin to realism, is based on a self-professed sober reflection on Canada's capacities and power in the international system. On the other hand, feminist scholars point out the marginalization of women's voices in much of this debate, and call for a more inclusive approach to thinking about Canadian foreign policy and a broader vision of what that policy should be.[85] The lack of consensus on Canada's role in the world ensures that the debate over Canadian foreign policy will continue.

What challenges does Canada face in the global politics of the future? Climate change will have a growing impact on Canada in the form of warming temperatures and soil erosion, especially in the north. The Northwest Passage is expected to be clear of ice for longer periods in the future, raising the possibility that it will become an increasingly important sea lane. This in turn raises questions about Canadian sovereignty and the economic development of the North, and the place and role of Canada's northern First Nations and Inuit peoples. Arctic security is likely to become increasingly important, with possible disputes over territory and natural resource rights between Canada and Russia and other northern countries. Climate change will also impact on Canadian agriculture and fisheries. Canada's extensive energy sector will also come under increasing pressure from rising world energy demand on the one hand and calls for greenhouse gas emission reductions on the other, creating tension between those wishing to take advantage of the economic boom of high energy prices and those wanting to reduce the use of fossil fuels.

We can also expect globalization to continue to have both positive and negative impacts upon Canadian society and the Canadian economy. While international trade and financial flows has been beneficial to many Canadians and have served to increase Canadian exports

PROFILE 13.1 Canadian Security after September 11

In Canada, the attacks of September 11 created a new set of concerns surrounding an old problem. Successive Canadian governments have faced the challenge of how to engage in political, economic, and security cooperation with the United States while still maintaining Canadian sovereignty and foreign policy independence. Even prior to September 11, U.S. officials were looking with unease at the famously undefended Canada–U.S. border as a possible route for terrorists to enter the United States. After September 11, they began looking at border security with much greater concern, and sought policy changes by the Canadian government to strengthen controls over airport security, immigration, and border management.

The Canadian government was in a difficult position. On the one hand, there were legitimate security concerns shared by both countries that required increased security cooperation. On the other hand, initial talk in the United States of "harmonizing" national regulations and building a "perimeter" around the border of North America made many Canadians very nervous. Fearing unilateral U.S. action that could have damaged Canada's access to U.S. markets, the Canadian government did increase the resources spent on a variety of security measures and entered into a new border management agreement with the United States. The U.S. government also created the Office of Homeland Security (now the Department of Homeland Security), and established a new military command known as "Northern Command" responsible for North America. While there was very little vocal objection to Canada's participation in the war in Afghanistan, the uncertain prospects for success and increasing casualties created growing doubts in the Canadian public. More pronounced was Canadian official opposition to the invasion of Iraq in 2003. The Canadian debate that ensued ran along familiar lines, with one political party urging the Canadian government to commit troops to show solidarity with the United States and others opposed because of a lack of Canadian national interest and/or an ethical stance against what was considered by many an unjust war. Nevertheless, disagreements over the U.S. foreign policy are unlikely to compel future Canadian governments to chart a new course away from Canada's most important political and economic partner.

FOR AN INTERESTING CRITICAL TREATMENT OF THE NORTH AMERICAN BORDERS AND POST-9/11 SECURITY, SEE M. B. SPARKE, "A NEOLIBERAL NEXUS: ECONOMY, SECURITY, AND THE BIOPOLITICS OF CITIZENSHIP ON THE BORDER," *POLITICAL GEOGRAPHY* 25, NO. 2 (2006), 151–180.

and facilitate foreign investment, many workers and lower-income Canadians have not seen these benefits in their own lives. Tensions between the obligation to establish laws and regulations consistent with international trade and financial agreements and calls to protect workers, the environment and natural resources, culture, and social programs are likely to continue and even intensify as global economic conditions take a turn for the worse. Canadians have been hit by credit and stock market shocks in the international financial system, and although the fundamentals of the Canadian banking system remain sound, Canada has not been immune to the effects of the global recession. The collapse of the Doha Round of WTO negotiations may prove to be a temporary stumbling block in the path of continued international trade liberalization, but there is a chance that Doha could be a turning point and we will see the rise of protectionism worldwide. This would lower Canada's access to North American and global markets, hurting the Canadian economy and Canadian firms and workers.

Canada's relationship with the United States will continue to be a priority for Canadian governments. While the Obama administration adopted new policies and new rhetoric, the substance of many Canada–U.S. issues are likely to remain unchanged. With a new U.S. President in place, Canada will as always seek a positive relationship with America, trying to preserve access to U.S. markets and cooperate with the United States on North American security, while at the same time preserving Canadian autonomy and sovereignty. Growing protectionist sentiment in America may place pressure on the U.S. government to renegotiate the NAFTA agreement, while continued U.S. concerns over border security and the threat of terrorism will place pressure on Canada to cooperate even more closely on North American security (see Profile 13.1). The Canada–U.S. relationship will also be characterized by conflict and cooperation over issues such as energy policy, climate change and pollution, immigration and refugee policy reform, and trade disputes. The future of Canada's distinctiveness in the face of U.S. cultural influences—especially in the film, television, and Internet mediums—is likely to remain an ongoing concern. Internationally, Canada will also continue to balance its commitments as an ally of the United States with a desire to chart an independent course on many topics, as it has in the past over land mines, the Kyoto protocol, the ICC and the Iraq War. In short, a new administration in the United States and any changes in the government of the day in Canada will have to address a familiar agenda and manage their foreign policy differences.

CONCLUSION: ON THE THEME OF INEVITABILITY

Many of the topics we have covered in this book elicit despair. As we warned in the introduction, the complexity of global politics is overwhelming, and the challenges we face seem insurmountable. Global structures and processes are driven by forces beyond our individual control. Much of the ideological fixations of the past and present, from the recourse to violent conflict throughout history to the tide of globalization, seem as inevitable as changes in the weather. Yet change is the result of human actions, decisions, fears, courage, and other inherently intangible factors. We are all actors on the global stage, and we cannot absent ourselves from the judgments of history. In this light, we all have an obligation to be as informed as possible, and to think beyond our immediate self-interests and desires.

This would, we think, include the need to reflect upon history itself. To even attempt to understand the global politics of the present and future, we need a firm grounding in the past. This grounding will of necessity be formed within our own perspectives on the world, shaped by our experiences and what we have learned through socialization and intellectual inquiry. Yet sensitivity to the past is vital. For example, the word *crusade* has a strong connotation for many people because it evokes an era when Christian forces strove to force their worldview on others, including Muslims and Jews. George W. Bush's initial use of the term after September 11 was quickly rescinded, but it spoke volumes about the general historical ignorance that threatens to make the "clash of civilizations" thesis become an all-consuming reality. This does not in any way justify the use of terrorism, but implies that responses to terrorism, and all of the challenges we will face in the future, need to be cautious and grounded in a sound knowledge and sensitivity to the contemporary implications of history.

The changing nature of global politics suggests that the nature of the global economy, the future of the state, climate change and environmental degradation, and the widening gulf between rich and poor countries and peoples may produce tensions that lead to increased interstate and intrastate violence and war in the 21st century. Increasing our understanding of these dynamic and interrelated factors, and thus our ability to prevent episodic violent conflict, remains the principal task of students of global politics today. We have suggested further, however, that threats to planetary and human security are just as important in this day and age, and that the extreme divisions between the wealthy and the marginalized are themselves a source of instability. Further, while there are strengths and weaknesses to all the theoretical perspectives introduced in this text, new and exciting syntheses are emerging, and the normative questions about the ethical implications of our actions are as important as the analytical models and theorems designed to enhance our explanatory prowess.

It is our hope that this textbook has provided you with a foundation for understanding the world in which we live, and that your interest in global politics will not end here. This is only the beginning of a lifelong attentiveness to the challenges we will all face in the future. Again, it is tempting to look back at the collective experience of global politics with resignation, and capitulate to the depressing state of human relations and the immense problems involved in achieving international cooperation on the vital issues we face today and in the near future. Yet our perspective must change in spite of (and indeed because of) what appears to be the increasing parochialism of humanity. Given the continuing threats we collectively face—from poverty to terrorism, from war to planetary environmental degradation—it is clear that decision makers and citizens alike must think as globally as possible. The construction of the international equivalent of gated communities, built on ultimately unsustainable foundations, is no long-term answer. States and peoples cannot deal with the increasingly transnational global agenda in a unilateral or isolationist fashion. Our very survival will depend on our capacity for cooperation. States with extensive multilateral ties, such as Canada, have a vital role to play. But more to the point, we all do. The first step toward solving such problems is learning about them, and we hope this text has provided a challenging introduction to, as well as encouraged further exploration of, the complex world of global politics.

Endnotes

1. A. N. Whitehead, *Science and the Modern World* (New York: New American Library, 1953), 208.
2. P. Allott, "The Concept of International Law," in M. Byers, ed., *The Role of Law in International Politics* (Oxford: Oxford University Press, 2001), 69–89, 70.
3. "Transcript: Inaugural Address of Barack Obama," *The Washington Post*, January 20, 2009, http://media.washingtonpost.com/wp-srv/politics/documents/Obama_Inaugural_Address_012009.html (accessed March 31, 2009).
4. N. Rescher, *Predicting the Future: An Introduction to the Theory of Forecasting* (New York: SUNY Press, 1998), 2. See also the well-regarded journal, *Futures: The Journal of Policy, Planning, and Futures Studies.*
5. G. Friedman and M. Lebard, *The Coming War with Japan* (New York: St. Martin's Press, 1991).
6. D. J. Staley, *History and Future: Using Historical Thinking to Imagine the Future* (Lanham, MD: Lexington Books, 2007).
7. See the excellent introduction by M. Cox to a reprint of Carr's classic, *The Twenty Years' Crisis 1919 to 1939: An Introduction to the Study of International Relations* (London: Palgrave, 2001). See also M. Cox, ed., *E. H. Carr: A Critical Reappraisal* (London: Palgrave Macmillan, 2000), and R. Falk, "The Critical Realist Tradition and the Demystification of Power," in S. Gill and J. Mittleman, eds., *Innovation and Transformation in International Studies* (Cambridge, UK: Cambridge University Press, 1997).
8. See C. Escude, *Foreign Policy Theory in Menem's Argentina* (Gainesville: University of Florida Press, 1997); on neoclassical realism, see S. Lobell, N. Ripsman, and J. Taliaferro, *Neoclassical Realism, the State, and Foreign Policy* (Cambridge: Cambridge University Press, 2009).
9. See J. Ann Tickner, "Identity in International Relations Theory: Feminist Perspectives," in Y. Lapid and F. Kratochwil, eds., *The Return of Culture and Identity in IR Theory* (Boulder, CO: Lynne Rienner, 1997), 147–62; and C. Enloe, *The Morning After: Sexual Politics at the End of the Cold War* (Berkeley: California University Press, 1993).

10. See O. Young, "Rights, Rules, and Resources in World Affairs," in O. Young, ed., *Global Governance: Drawing Insights from the Environmental Experience* (Cambridge, MA: MIT Press, 1997), 1–23; and A. Hasenclever, P. Mayer, and V. Rittbeuger, "Integrating Theories of International Regimes," *Review of International Studies* 26, no. 1 (2000), 3–33.

11. See D. Deudney, "Bringing Nature Back In: Geopolitical Theory from the Greeks to the Global Era," in D. Deudney and R. Matthew, eds., *Contested Grounds: Security and Conflict in the New Environmental Politics* (Albany: SUNY Press, 1999), 25–57. See also E. Laferrière and P. Stoett, *IR Theory and Ecological Thought: Toward a Synthesis* (London: Routledge, 1999).

12. See A. Jokic, ed., *Humanitarian Intervention: Moral and Philosophical Issues* (Toronto: Broadview Press, 2003).

13. This is not to argue, however, that the familiar trichotomy is not inherently useful, or cannot be used to great effect. See, for example, M. Doyle, *Ways of War and Peace: Realism, Liberalism, and Socialism* (New York: W.W. Norton, 1997).

14. This explanation is offered by Steve Smith, "Reflectivist and Constructivist Approaches to International Theory," in S. Smith and J. Baylis, eds., *The Globalization of World Politics: An Introduction to International Relations*, 2nd ed. (Oxford: Oxford University Press, 2001), 224–49. Ken Booth offers a fascinating critical survey of theoretical linkages in his *Theory of World Security* (Cambridge: Cambridge University Press, 2007).

15. C. Brown, *International Relations Theory: New Normative Approaches* (Hemel Hempstead, Hertfordshire, UK: Harvester Wheatsheaf, 1992), 3–4. For an example of normative analysis, see R. Irwin, ed., *Ethics and Security in Canadian Foreign Policy* (Vancouver: UBC Press, 2001). Environmental issues have raised the further question of intergenerational ethics: see E. B. Weiss, "Intergenerational Equity: Toward an International Legal Framework," in N. Choucri, ed., *Global Accord: Environmental Challenges and International Responses* (Cambridge, MA: MIT Press, 1993).

16. This is also important for understanding the past and could be a key contribution of the constructivist approach. As N. Inayatullah and D. Blaney write, a "commitment to a constructivist IR theory requires … a comparative and historical analysis of how cultures conceptualize others"; see "Knowing Encounters: Beyond Parochialism in IR Theory," in Y. Lapid and F. Kratochwil, eds., *The Return of Culture and Identity in IR Theory* (Boulder, CO: Lynne Rienner, 1997), 65–84, 82.

17. R. Little, *The Balance of Power in International Relations: Metaphors, Myths, and Models* (Cambridge: Cambridge University Press, 2007), 3.

18. National Intelligence Council, *Mapping the Global Future: Report of the National Intelligence Council's 2020 Project* (Washington, DC: US Government Printing Office, 2004), 47.

19. P. Khanna, *The Second World: Empires and Influence in the New World Order* (New York: Random House, 2008), xiv.

20. F. Zakaria, *The Post-American World* (New York: W. W. Norton and Company, Inc., 2008).

21. R. Kagan, *The Return of History and the End of Dreams* (New York: Alfred A. Knopf, 2008).

22. R. Haas, "The Age of Nonpolarity," *Foreign Affairs* 87, no. 3 (May/June 2008), 44–56.

23. H. J. Morgenthau, *Politics Among Nations: The Struggle for Power and Peace*, 5th ed. (New York: Alfred A. Knopf, 1978), 46.

24. R. K. Betts, "Wealth, Power, and Instability: East Asia and the United States after the Cold War," *International Security* 18 (Winter 1993/94), 55.

25. A. I. Johnston, "Is China a Status Quo Power?," *International Security* 27 (Spring 2003), 6.

26. See C. Constantin and B. Job, "China's Strategic Vision," in B. MacDonald, ed., *Canadians and Asia-Pacific Security*, Vimy Paper 2008 (Ottawa: Conference of Defence Associations Institute, 2008), 28–41.

27. C. Layne, "China's Challenge to US Hegemony," *Current History* 107, no. 705 (January 2008), 13–18.

28. M. Brawley, "The Political Economy of Balance of Power Theory," in T. V. Paul, J. J. Wirtz, and M. Fortman, *Balance of Power: Theory and Practice in the Twenty-First Century* (Stanford, CA: Stanford University Press, 2004), 110–111.

29. See "Angry China," *The Economist* 387, no. 8578 (May 2008), 13.

30. G. John Ikenberry, "The Rise of China and the Future of the West," *Foreign Affairs* 87, no. 1 (January/February 2008), 23–37.

31. See S. Gänzle and A. G. Sens, eds., *The Changing Politics of European Security: Europe Alone?* (New York: Palgrave Macmillan, 2007).

32. S. Serfaty, ed., *A Recast Partnership? Institutional Dimensions of Transatlantic Relations* (Washington, DC: Center for Strategic and International Studies, 2008).

33. E. B. Rumer, *Russian Foreign Policy Beyond Putin*, Adelphi Paper 390 (London: Routledge and the International Institute of Strategic Studies, 2007), 8.

34. See International Institute for Strategic Studies, "Russia/Eurasia," *Strategic Survey 2007* (New York: Routledge, 2007), 188.

35. E. Lucas, *The New Cold War: Putin's Russia and the Threat to the West* (New York: Palgrave Macmillan, 2008).

36. See S. F. Cohen, "The New American Cold War," *The Nation*, July 10, 2006.

37. See M. MacKinnon, *The New Cold War: Revolutions, Rigged Elections, and Pipeline Politics in the Former Soviet Union* (Toronto: Random House Canada, 2008).

38. See "Russia Resurgent," *The Economist*, August 16, 2008, 11.

39. See R. Sakwa, "'New Cold War' or Twenty Years' Crisis? Russia and International Politics," *International Affairs* 84, no. 2 (March 2008), 241–267.

40. GDP data from the International Monetary Fund World Economic Outlook Database, http://www.imf.org/external/pubs/ft/weo/2008/01/weodata/index.aspx (accessed May 27, 2008).

41. O. Antonenko, "Medvedev's Choice," *Survival* 50, no. 2 (April/May 2008), 25–31.

42. G. John Ikenberry, "The End of the Neo-Conservative Moment," *Survival* 46 (Spring 2004), 7.

43. R. Kagan, "America's Crisis of Legitimacy," *Foreign Affairs* 83 (March/April 2004), 65.

44. G. Soros, *The Bubble of American Supremacy: Correcting the Misuse of American Power* (New York: Public Affairs, 2004).

45. J. S. Nye Jr., *Soft Power: The Means to Success in World Politics* (New York: Public Affairs, 2004), 5.

46. Ibid., xii. Of course, even the hard-power victory was a short-lived one as the harsh realities of occupying a country amidst fierce resistance took hold.

47. B. Posen, "Command of the Commons: The Military Foundations of U.S. Hegemony," *International Security* 28 (Summer 2003), 6.

48. N. Fergusson, *Colossus: The Price of America's Empire* (New York: The Penguin Press, 2004), 29.

49. J. S. Nye Jr., "Recovering American Leadership," *Survival* 50, no. 1 (February/March 2008), 55–68.

50. A. Chua, *Day of Empire: How Hyperpowers Rise to Global Dominance—and Why They Fail* (New York: Doubleday, 2007).

51. See J. Joffe, *The Imperial Temptation of America* (New York: W. W. Norton and Company Inc., 2006); and J. Sweig, *Friendly Fire: Losing Friends and Making Enemies in the Anti-American Century* (New York: Public Affairs, 2006).

52. C. Layne, *The Peace of Illusions: American Grand Strategy from 1940 to the Present* (Ithaca, NY: Cornell University Press, 2006), 6.

53. C. Layne, "The Unipolar Illusion Revisited: The Coming End of the United States' Unipolar Moment," *International Security* 31, no. 2 (Fall 2006), 37.

54. S. P. Huntington, "The Clash of Civilizations?," *Foreign Affairs* 72, no. 3 (Summer 1993), 22.

55. Ibid., 23–24.

56. K. Mahbubani, "The West and the Rest," *The National Interest*, Summer 1992, 3–13.

57. W. Laqueur, *No End to War: Terrorism in the Twenty-First Century* (New York: Continuum, 2003).

58. N. Podhoretz, *World War IV: The Long Struggle Against Islamofascism* (New York: Doubleday, 2007).

59. A. Pagden, *Worlds at War: The 2,500-year Struggle Between East and West* (New York: Random House, 2008), 538.

60. S. Gill, "New Constitutionalism, Democratisation and Global Political Economy," in *Pacifica Review* 10, no. 1 (February 1998), 23–38.

61. G. Soros, *The Crisis of Global Capitalism: Open Society Endangered* (New York: Public Affairs, 1998), xxix.

62. E. Luttwak, *Turbo-Capitalism: Winners and Losers in the Global Economy* (New York: HarperCollins, 1999); see also his "Power Relations in the New Economy," *Survival* 44 (Summer 2002), 7–17.

63. *2008 World Development Indicators* (Washington, DC: The World Bank, 2008), 193.

64. Ibid., 44.

65. Ibid., 28.

66. A. Balakrishnan, "Daily Currency Trades Equal to Germany's Annual Output," *The Guardian*, September 26, 2007.

67. J. A. Frieden, *Global Capitalism: Its Fall and Rise in the Twentieth Century* (New York: W. W. Norton and Company, 2006), xvi.

68. See in particular M. de Villiers, *Water* (Toronto: Stoddart, 2000); and M. Barlow and T. Clarke, *Blue Gold: The Battle Against Corporate Theft of the World's Water* (Toronto: Stoddart, 2002), from whom we steal

this lovely quote by Michael Parfit (p. xi): "Watersheds come in families; nested levels of intimacy. On the grandest scale the hydrologic web is like all humanity—Serbs, Russians, Koyukon Indians, Amish, the billion lives in the People's Republic of China—it's broadly troubled, but it's hard to know how to help. As you work upstream toward home, you're more closely related. The big river is like your nation, a little out of hand. The lake is your cousin. The creek is your sister. The pond is her child. And, for better or worse, in sickness and in health, you're married to your kitchen sink."

69. J. Sachs, "Disruptions and Potential in the Global Economy," *Current History* 107, no. 705 (January 2008), 21.

70. See H. Weber, *The Politics of Microcredit: Global Governance and Poverty Reduction* (London: Pluto, 2001).

71. W. J. Bernstein, *A Splendid Exchange: How Trade Shaped the World* (New York: Atlantic Monthly Press, 2008), 18.

72. "CSI: Credit Crunch: A Special Report on the World Economy," *The Economist*, October 20, 2007, 4.

73. See International Monetary Fund, *Global Financial Stability Report Market Update*, January 28, 2009, 1, http://www.imf.org/external/pubs/ft/fmu/eng/2009/01/index.htm (accessed April 2, 2009).

74. "What Went Wrong: Wall Street's Crisis," *The Economist*, March 22, 2008, 79.

75. N. Roubini, "The Coming Financial Pandemic," *Foreign Policy* 165 (March/April 2008), 44–48.

76. International Monetary Fund, *The World Economic Outlook Update*, January 28, 2009, 1, http://www.imf.org/external/pubs/ft/weo/2009/update/01/index.htm (accessed April 2, 2009).

77. See D. Archibugi and I. Young, "Envisioning a Global Rule of Law," in J. Sterba, ed., *Terrorism and International Justice* (Oxford: Oxford University Press, 2003), 158–70.

78. For a collection of sophisticated discussions on international law, see M. Byers, ed., *The Role of Law in International Politics* (Oxford: Oxford University Press, 2001).

79. See S. Raymond, "Foreign Assistance in an Aging World," *Foreign Affairs*, March/April 2003, 91–105.

80. M. Byers, *Intent for Nation: What Is Canada For?* (Vancouver: Douglas and McIntyre, 2007), 4. For an analysis asserting Canada's strengths within the context of its close ties with the United States, see M. Hart, *From Pride to Influence: Toward a New Canadian Foreign Policy* (Vancouver: UBC Press, 2008).

81. A. Cohen, *While Canada Slept: How We Lost our Place in the World* (Toronto: McClelland and Stewart Ltd., 2003), 2.

82. J. Welsh, *At Home in the World: Canada's Global Vision for the 21st Century* (Toronto: Harper Collins, 2004), 23.

83. Byers, *Intent for Nation*, 5.

84. S. K. Holloway, *Canadian Foreign Policy: Defining the National Interest* (Peterborough, ON: Broadview Press, 2006), 2.

85. See C. T. Sjolander, H. A. Smith, and D. Stienstra, eds., *Feminist Perspectives on Canadian Foreign Policy* (Don Mills, ON: Oxford University Press, 2003).

Glossary

This glossary contains very brief descriptions of important terms used in the textbook. It has been compiled using a number of sources, including the "Historical Glossary" found in Hans J. Morgenthau, *Politics Among Nations: The Struggle for Power and Peace*, brief ed., rev. K. Thompson (New York: McGraw-Hill, 1993); Cathal Nolan's *The Longman Guide to World Affairs* (White Plains, NY: Longman, 1995); and our own general knowledge. We gratefully acknowledge the suggestions of an anonymous reviewer of an earlier draft of this manuscript as well.

ABM   See *antiballistic missile.*

absolute advantage   Adam Smith's principle that free trade will benefit all states because they will specialize in those goods they produce most efficiently and trade with other states for those goods they do not produce efficiently. The result is a more efficient use of resources, more goods for consumption, and the political benefits of increased cooperation.

absolute gains   Gains (such as economic wealth) that occur when all members of a set or sample of countries or other actors experience an increase in capacity.

absolute poverty   The condition of being unable to meet basic human subsistence needs, defined by the United Nations as food, safe drinking water, sanitation facilities, health, education, information, and shelter.

acid rain   Sulphur dioxide and nitrogen oxide combined with precipitation. Caused by atmospheric emissions of industry, automobiles, and power plants. Acid rain harms and in some cases destroys the ecosystems of forests and lakes.

ACP   See *African, Caribbean, and Pacific states.*

acquired immune deficiency syndrome (AIDS)   A fatal disease that destroys the body's immune system; spread mainly through sexual contact or injection with infected blood.

adjudication   Deciding a legal issue through the courts or some other third party that can make a binding decision.

advisory opinion   An ICJ (International Court of Justice) nonbinding legal opinion provided by request from the United Nations or a specialized agency.

African, Caribbean, and Pacific (ACP) states   An organization of 79 states established in 1975 to promote development and trade cooperation between its members and the European Union.

African National Congress (ANC)   A South African political party, founded in 1912, that for years opposed apartheid but is now governing that state. Its leader, Nelson Mandela, was released from prison in 1990 and served as South Africa's first president.

African Union (AU)   A regional international organization founded in July 1999 (formerly the Organization for African Unity or OAU) to promote development, sovereignty, and cooperation among independent African states.

agricultural revolution   Large-scale shifts in prevailing food production methods that have an impact on the whole of society.

AIDS   See *acquired immune deficiency syndrome.*

Alexander III   See *Alexander the Great.*

Alexander the Great (Alexander III)   (356–323 B.C.E.) King of Macedon, 336–323 B.C.E. Conquered Thrace, Illyria, and Egypt; invaded Persia and northern India; virtual leader of Mediterranean centre of civilization.

alliance   A group of actors who pool their resources for a common cause, usually in relation to national defence against a specific external threat.

alliance cohesion   The degree to which the members of an alliance hold common goals and coordinate policy.

American Civil War   (1861–65) War between the United States of America (Union) and the secessionist Southern Confederate States of America (Confederacy). The war destroyed the Confederacy and ended the institution of slavery in the United States.

anarchy   In its most basic form, the absence of central government in a society. A prominent part of the realist perspective's ontology. More generally, it refers to lawlessness.

ANC   See *African National Congress.*

Angell, Norman   (1874–1967) Famous British pacifist who wrote *The Great Illusion*, 1910. In international relations theory, he was somewhere between an idealist and a liberal.

Antarctic Treaty System (ATS)   A set of negotiated agreements based on the Antarctic Treaty, signed in 1959 by 12 so-called consultative parties with claims on and able to demonstrate a substantial scientific interest in Antarctica. Established the area as a demilitarized zone; various subsequent agreements have been added on conservation and environmental protection.

antiballistic missile   A missile designed to intercept and destroy incoming ballistic missiles. The development and deployment of ABMs had been restricted for 30 years by the 1972 ABM Treaty, which was abrogated by the United States in 2002.

anticipatory compliance   A phenomenon in governmental or nongovernmental organizations in which junior officials, trying to anticipate what their superiors want to hear, will omit or deemphasize information that contrasts with the views of senior officials and leaders.

anti-Semitism   Prejudice, discrimination, or persecution against Jewish people.

apartheid   Racial separation policy in South Africa until the early 1990s.

appeasement   An attempt to satisfy a potential aggressor by making territorial or other concessions to it. Most famously, this technique failed to satisfy Adolf Hitler and prevent World War II.

Arab League   A voluntary association of 22 Arab states, founded March 1945.

armistice   In the general sense, a negotiated peace; most often used to describe the end of World War I.

arms control   Any diplomatic effort designed to regulate levels or types of arms (bilaterally or multilaterally, with conventional or nuclear arms).

ASEAN   See *Association of Southeast Asian Nations.*

Asian Development Bank   A multilateral bank similar to the World Bank with a regional focus; headquarters established in 1966 in Manila, Philippines.

Association of Southeast Asian Nations (ASEAN)   International organization formed by the Bangkok Declaration in 1967, that now includes Indonesia, Malaysia, the Philippines, Singapore, Thailand, Brunei, Myanmar, Vietnam, Cambodia, and Laos.

Atlantic Charter   Statement of general principles, signed by Roosevelt and Churchill in August 1941, related to postwar order, including principles of national self-determination, opposition to aggression, disarmament, and equal access to trade and raw materials.

atomic bomb   A weapon based on the rapid splitting of fissionable materials, inducing an explosion with deadly blast, heat, and radiation impact; more commonly referred to as a *nuclear weapon.*

ATS   See *Antarctic Treaty System.*

AU   See *African Union.*

authoritarianism   A political system in which individual freedom is subordinate to the power of the state, which is concentrated in one leader or group not accountable to the people.

automation   The replacement of human workers with machines. See *robotics.*

balance of payments   The net flow of money into, and out of, a state. Encompasses trade, tourist expenditures, sales of services, foreign aid, debt payments, profits, etc.

balance of power   The condition that exists within a contemporary or historical system (regional or global) in which no one state has the power to dominate all the others.

balance of trade   The relationship between exports and imports.

ballistic missile   A missile using a ballistic guidance system influenced by gravity and friction and employing no thrust after its initial boost phase. Some such missiles travel 300 metres; others can travel halfway around the world.

basic human needs   Adequate food intake (calories, vitamins, protein, minerals, etc.), disease-free and toxin-free drinking water, minimum clothing and shelter, literacy, sanitation, health care, employment, and dignity.

Bay of Pigs   A part of the Cuban coastline where in 1961 a group of Cuban refugees staged a failed invasion under American auspices.

beggar-thy-neighbour   An economic policy of states that attempts to alter their balance of trade by devaluing currency and raising barriers to imports. This strategy is associated with mercantilism.

Berlin Wall   A wall erected in 1961 by East Germany to prevent people from fleeing East Germany into the West. It encircled West Berlin, which was controlled by the Western allies during the Cold War, and became a symbol of the East–West division until it was dismantled in 1989 as the Cold War ended.

biodiversity   Greatly varied flora and fauna in a habitat, a condition that is under threat in many areas of the world.

biosphere   Life and living processes at or near the earth's surface, extending from the oceans' floors and the lithosphere to about 75 kilometres into the atmosphere.

bipolar/bipolarity Global political system with two competing poles of great power, such as during the U.S.–U.S.S.R. Cold War era.

bipolycentrism A distribution of power in which there are two main poles of power as well as a number of other less powerful, but still significant, power centres.

Bolsheviks Members of the radical minority in the Russian Social Democratic Party (1903–17), led by Vladimir Lenin. Carried out the Communist revolution of 1917.

bounded rationality The argument that rational-actor decisions are seldom made under ideal conditions due to time constraints, incomplete information, and limited individual capacity.

bourgeoisie An originally French term for the middle or merchant class. It became a derogatory term with its adoption by Karl Marx and Friedrich Engels to represent the owners of the means of production and the class enemy of the proletariat (workers).

boycott The refusal of a country to import goods and services from another country; done for punitive reasons.

Bretton Woods system The post–World War II international monetary order, named after the 1944 conference held at Bretton Woods, New Hampshire. the main institutions in the system were the IMF, IBRD, and GATT.

bureaucratic politics model An approach to the study of foreign policy that focuses on bargaining and compromises among governmental organizations and agencies pursuing their own interests.

Camp David A mountain retreat for the U.S. president in Maryland, and site of the famous Camp David accords signed in 1978 by President Anwar el-Sadat of Egypt and Prime Minister Menachem Begin of Israel.

Canadian International Development Agency (CIDA) Agency of the Canadian government responsible for planning and implementing Canada's development programs.

capital mobility Ability of international investors to invest in foreign countries with minimal constraints.

capitalism An economic system based on the private ownership of property and commercial enterprise, competition for profits, and limited government interference in the marketplace.

cartel An international agreement among producers of a commodity that attempts to control the production and pricing of that commodity. See *Organization of the Petroleum Exporting Countries*.

Catherine II See *Catherine the Great.*

Catherine the Great (Catherine II) (1729–96) Tsarina of Russia, 1762–96. Expanded and strengthened the Russian Empire, chiefly at the expense of Turkey.

CCAMLR See *Convention on the Conservation of Antarctic Marine Living Resources.*

CFCs See *chlorofluorocarbons.*

chlorofluorocarbons (CFCs) Gaseous compounds found in aerosols and refrigeration chemicals, and used in the manufacture of plastics; thought to be largely responsible for ozone-layer depletion.

Churchill, Winston (1874–1965) British prime minister (1940–45, 1951–55), naval officer, and author.

CIDA See *Canadian International Development Agency.*

CIS See *Commonwealth of Independent States.*

CITES See *Convention on International Trade in Endangered Species of Wild Fauna and Flora.*

classical liberals   Liberals such as Adam Smith and David Ricardo who established the principles of modern liberal economic theory, based on free trade and minimal government interference in the operation of the market.

client states   States highly dependent on great powers for military or economic aid.

Cold War   The ideological, economic, and geopolitical hostility between the United States and the U.S.S.R. in the bipolar era (roughly 1947–90).

collective defence   An effort by two or more states to defend their territory or their interests against a common threat or enemy. Collective defence arrangements are generally called alliances.

collective security   Mutual multilateral consent to an agreement that declares that aggression by one state on any other is an attack on the whole; the primary security mechanism created by the UN Charter in Chapter VII.

commodity speculation   The purchase of a commodity with an aim to sell it when, and if, its value increases. Commodity speculation can drive up prices and can distort government efforts to manage the economy.

Commonwealth of Independent States (CIS)   Arrangement among many of the former republics of the U.S.S.R., formed in December 1991. Includes Armenia, Azerbaijan, Byelorussia (Belarus), Kazakhstan, Kirghizia (Kyrgyzstan), Moldavia (Moldova), Russia, Tadzhikistan (Tajikistan), Turkmenistan, Ukraine, Uzbekistan, and Georgia.

commonwealth   Voluntary association of former dominions, colonies, and other overseas territories of Britain. Forty-nine states belong; annual meeting of heads of state generates some attention.

communal conflicts   Conflicts between communal groups, primarily racial and ethnic groups. The roots of communal conflicts are local, including competing claims to power, autonomy or independence based upon asserted differences of ethnicity, nationality, religion, language, or social class.

comparative advantage   David Ricardo's concept that states will still benefit from free trade even if they do not have an absolute advantage in any good. Such states will still have a comparative advantage with respect to trading partners because they will still produce some goods comparatively more efficiently than others do. That comparative advantage is enough for them to benefit from trade.

complex interdependence   Developed by Robert Keohane and Joseph Nye, a framework that refers to the complex transnational connections between states and societies. The main argument is that the decline of military force as a policy tool and the increased importance of economic and other actors should increase the probability of cooperation among states. It is considered as a synthesis of elements of realist and liberal thought.

comprador   A native and/or citizen of a colonized country who acts as the agent of the colonizer. In postcolonial Central and South America, the comprador class refers to the local elites whose interests are intertwined with the wealthy classes in the United States.

Concert of Europe   A system of consultation established among the European powers after the defeat of Napoleon (1815). The aim of the concert was to maintain the peace and manage the balance of power in Europe, which it did with considerable success until the outbreak of the Crimean War (1854–56).

Congress of Vienna   (1814–15) Peace conference following the Napoleonic Wars at which the great powers—Austria, Russia, Prussia, Great Britain, and France—agreed on territorial and political terms of settlement.

conscription   A policy requiring all men of a certain age to serve in the military, during peace or war. Also referred to as "the draft"; conscription is very controversial in Canada and the United States but more accepted in most other countries of the world.

constructive engagement   The attempt to influence a state's domestic policies by maintaining trade and diplomatic ties, as opposed to the use of sanctions.

constructivism   One of the dominant paradigms/critical theories of international relations discipline, suggesting that the social construction of dominant ideas, including anarchy and conflict, has a decisive role in the outcome of events. May be associated with a liberal or a radical/critical perspective.

containment   The United States' grand strategy during the Cold War, designed to contain the perceived military, political, and ideological threat of the U.S.S.R.

Convention on International Trade in Endangered Species of Wild Fauna and Flora (CITES)
Multilateral accord (1973) that regulates export, transit, and importation of endangered animal and plant species. Meets biannually to determine species' status.

Convention on the Conservation of Antarctic Marine Living Resources (CCAMLR)   Promulgated in 1980 by consultative parties to the Antarctic Treaty System to protect the environment and resources of the Antarctic seas region.

corporate social responsibilities   Perceived ethical obligations of the private sector toward the people and ecology affected by its operations, often expressed in voluntary behavioural codes.

Council of Europe   International body created in 1949 by representatives of Great Britain, France, Belgium, the Netherlands, Luxembourg, Norway, Sweden, Denmark, Ireland, and Italy; joined by Greece and Turkey in 1950; aimed toward a European federation.

Crimean War   (1854–56) France, Great Britain, and Turkey allied against Russia and fought a bitter war on the Crimean peninsula.

crimes against humanity   Genocide, enslavement, rape, deportation, imprisonment, murder, torture, or persecutions on political, racial, or religious grounds committed against any civilian population.

crimes against peace   Generally, planning, preparing, initiating, or waging a war of aggression and participating in a common plan or conspiracy for the accomplishment of war crimes.

cruise missile   A missile, guided remotely (from satellites in some cases), that can fly low enough to escape radar detection, and can deliver conventional or nuclear warheads.

cultural imperialism   Imposition of values on one society by another by direct administrative means (such as education) or more subtle means (such as television commercials).

currency speculation   Purchasing of foreign currency with an aim to sell it when, and if, its value increases. Currency speculation can drive up the value of currencies and can distort government efforts to manage the economy.

customs union   An agreement among a group of states establishing a common external tariff applicable to all imports from outside the member states. As a complementary measure, internal barriers to trade are removed. Different from a free trade area, in which internal barriers are removed but external tariff barriers remain set by individual states.

deficit   The amount by which a government's spending exceeds its revenues in any fiscal year.

demographic transition   A theory that argues that the decline in the industrialized states' birth rates is a direct consequence of social and economic development, and that with time other states will follow.

dependency theory   Contends that advanced capitalist states have created a neo-colonial relationship with poor countries, which are dependent on capital, technology, and the market demands of rich states. Dependency theory originated in Central and South America in the work of critical theorists, especially neo-Marxists.

desertification   Process in which potentially productive land is transformed into arid, desert-like territory. A severe form of land erosion.

détente   A relaxation of tensions or a decrease in the level of hostility between the superpowers during the Cold War.

deterrence   Persuading an opponent not to attack by making sure it is aware that a counterattack would follow. Pertains especially to the nuclear strategy of the superpowers during the Cold War.

disinformation   Spreading of false propaganda or forged documents to confuse counterintelligence or create political confusion, unrest, and scandal. Some would argue that governments do this with their own citizens as well.

doves   Informal term used to describe political figures or commentators who advocate less hard-line or confrontational approaches to their countries' enemies.

dumping   The practice of exporting a good to another country and selling that good at a price below the cost of production. This will make the product attractive to purchase, gaining a large market share for the seller and at the same time putting competing producers out of business. The price of the product will then be raised to achieve a profit. Dumping is illegal in most international trade agreements, although accusations of dumping remain common.

duty   Special tax applied to imported goods, based on tariff rates and schedules.

ecocide   Deliberate destruction of the environment for military purposes. Can also refer to other forms of environmental destruction.

ecofeminists   Feminists who regard gender discrimination and environmental degradation as parts of a social structure that simultaneously devalues both women and nature. They suggest that gender equality may influence the environmental behaviour of states. In other words, states with greater gender equality are more likely to protect the environment.

Economic and Social Council (ECOSOC)   Established under the UN Charter as the principal organ to coordinate economic, social, and related work of the 14 UN specialized agencies, UN functional commissions, and five UN regional commissions.

Economic Community of West African States (ECOWAS)   Founded in 1975 to promote cooperation in West Africa. ECOWAS currently has 15 members.

ECOSOC   See *Economic and Social Council.*

ECOWAS   See *Economic Community of West African States.*

EEZ See *exclusive economic zone.*

electronic numerical integrator and computer (ENIAC)   The first computer. It was so large that it filled a 9-by-17-metre room.

embargo   The refusal of one country or a group of countries to export goods to another, for punitive reasons. One famous example is the American embargo on Cuba.

emigration   Leaving one's home country to live in another.

English school realists   A group of realist scholars (mainly Charles Manning, Martin Wight, and Hedley Bull) in International Relations who had a common academic understanding of global politics, and contributed the idea of an "international society" or a "society of states."

ENIAC   See *electronic numerical integrator and computer.*

epistemic community   A global network of knowledge-based professionals in scientific and technological areas that often have an impact on policy decisions.

EPZs   See *export processing zones.*

ethnic cleansing   The forced removal of an ethnic group from their area of residence using tactics that include executions, the destruction of homes, and rape to instill fear in the target population. In its ultimate form, ethnic cleansing constitutes genocide.

ethnic conflicts   Conflicts between ethnic groups often as a result of intergroup differences, ancient hatreds and century-old feuds, collective fear of the future, ethnic security dilemmas, and/or ethnic nationalism.

EU   See *European Union.*

euro   The common currency of European Union states, introduced gradually in the late 1990s and now in use in 12 EU states.

European Monetary System   Established in 1979 as the first major step toward the establishment of a common currency in the European Union. System collapsed in 1993, but was revived.

European Union (EU)   Previously the European Economic Community, established by the Treaty of Rome, signed on March 25, 1957, and further cemented by the Maastricht Treaty (though it was rejected by some members) of 1991. After a series of enlargements, now includes 27 states that have coordinated policies in a number of areas, such as migration and currency, but have fallen short of a common security and foreign policy.

exchange rate   The values of two currencies relative to each other. For example, one Canadian dollar may be worth 70 cents of an American dollar.

exclusive economic zone (EEZ)   The 200-nautical-mile or 370-kilometre area in which coastal states have jurisdiction over the resources of the sea and the seabed (that is, beyond their 12-mile or 19-kilometre territory) but not territorial rights. Accepted as customary law.

export processing zones (EPZs)   Industrial zones within a state in which imported materials undergo some degree of processing before being re-exported. EPZs have special regulations and other incentives established by governments to attract foreign investors, free trade zones, special economic zones, bonded warehouses, free ports, and customs zones are also considered export processing zones.

exports   Products shipped or otherwise transferred to foreign states.

extraterritoriality   In diplomatic practice, the tradition that visiting diplomats are exempt from local legal jurisdiction.

FAO   See *Food and Agriculture Organization of the UN.*

fascism   An authoritarian ideology that subsumes individuals before the state; popular in Italy, Spain, and Germany in the period leading up to World War II.

FDI   See *foreign direct investment.*

first strike   The opening attack in a hypothetical nuclear war, launched by an aggressor state in hopes that it will destroy the attacked nation's capacity to retaliate.

Food and Agriculture Organization of the UN (FAO)   Formed in 1945 as a UN specialized agency to deal with food production; based in Rome.

foreign direct investment (FDI)   Buying stock, real estate, industry, mines, or other assets in a foreign country with the aim of gaining a controlling interest (usually over 50 percent) in that asset. Differs from portfolio investment, which involves investment solely to gain capital appreciation through market fluctuations.

Fourteen Points   U.S. President Woodrow Wilson's formulation of Allied war aims and of a general peace program, delivered to Congress on January 8, 1918.

Fourth World   An expression referring to peoples living nomadic or pastoral lifestyles outside the industrialized norm and/or stateless and marginalized peoples (especially indigenous peoples).

free trade   International movement of goods completely or relatively unrestricted by tariffs or nontariff barriers.

functionalism   International cooperation in largely technical areas (communications, travel, trade, environmental protection) and related theories about possibly resultant political integration.

futurologists   People who attempt to predict the future on the basis of present trends. (Some claim they are scientists, others do not.)

G-7   See *Group of Seven.*

G-8   See *Group of Eight.*

G-77   See *Group of 77.*

game theory   A mathematical approach to modelling political behaviour. It is used by international relations scholars to evaluate decision-making patterns among two or more actors under certain prescribed conditions.

GATS   See *General Agreement on Trade in Services.*

GATT   See *General Agreement on Tariffs and Trade.*

GDP   See *gross domestic product.*

General Agreement on Tariffs and Trade (GATT)   Concluded in 1948, followed by successive rounds of negotiations culminating in the establishment of the World Trade Organization in 1995. General aim is to facilitate expanded international trade with the reduction of trade barriers.

General Agreement on Trade in Services (GATS)   An agreement first reached in GATT (and which now is part of the WTO) that seeks trade liberalization in the service sector.

General Assembly   The democratic core of the UN, in which all 192 member states are equally represented.

Generalized System of Preferences (GSP)   A system approved by GATT in 1971 that authorizes developed countries to give preferential tariff treatment to less-developed countries.

genetic engineering   Biotechnological process by which the natural genetic code of an organism is altered, producing genetically modified organisms. A contentious ethical and trade issue today.

genetically modified organisms (GMOs)   Plants and animals genetically altered by adding, subtracting, or otherwise changing their genetic code.

geopolitics   A form of foreign policy analysis that emphasizes the link between geographic variables (such as location, resources, and topography) and political behaviour. Political action is seen as largely determined by geography.

glasnost   The Soviet policy of increased openness, developed and implemented under the leadership of Mikhail Gorbachev in the late 1980s.

global civil society   Voluntary associations, movements, parties, unions, and individuals that promote social change, and engage in efforts to resist a perceived attack on life and democracy by the institutions advancing the neoliberal economic policy agenda of privatization and deregulation and the elimination of social safety nets and economic borders.

global commons   Elements of the earth and atmosphere (oceans, seabed, atmosphere, outer space) that are the property of no one nation or individual but are deemed to be the property of all.

global governance   The regulation of interdependent relations between and among states, markets, citizens, organizations and other nonstate transnational actors through the development of institutions, law, and other formal or informal mechanisms of cooperation.

globalization   Term used to describe the increasing interconnection between states, economies, and societies through telecommunications technology, trade, and travel such that events in one part of the world have repercussions in other parts of the world.

GMOs   See *genetically modified organisms.*

GNP   See *gross national product.*

Golan Heights   Contested territory adjacent to Israel, which has occupied it since the 1967 war.

good offices   Services, roles, and functions provided by a third party in an effort to resolve a dispute.

Great Depression   Severe unemployment and financial collapse of the early 1930s; international in scope.

great powers   The most powerful political units in a system (usually states).

Green Revolution   The increase in agricultural production in many developing countries in the 1950s and 1960s, made possible by genetically engineered grains, fertilizers, and more efficient use of land.

gross domestic product (GDP)   A measure of national income that excludes foreign earnings.

gross national product (GNP)   The sum of all the goods and services produced by a state's nationals, whether in that state or abroad.

Group of Seven (G-7)   The seven economically largest free-market states: Canada, France, United Kingdom, Italy, Japan, the United States, and Germany. Russia is now a participant in what are now referred to as G-8 conferences.

Group of Eight (G-8)   The eight largest economies (the United States, Japan, Germany, France, Russia, Italy, the United Kingdom, and Canada); government representatives meet often to coordinate monetary policies.

Group of 77 (G-77)   The 77 Third World states that co-sponsored the Joint Declaration of Developing Countries in 1963 calling for greater equity in North–South trade. Currently includes 130 members.

groupthink   The tendency of decision makers to develop, in groups, a common perception of an issue or problem and exclude those with different opinions or ideas.

GSP   See *Generalized System of Preferences.*

Hapsburg   Ruling house of Austria, 1282–1918; provided the emperors of the Holy Roman Empire from 1438 to 1806.

hard power   A reference to traditional measures of power, such as economic capability, population, and especially military strength.

hawks   An informal term for political figures or commentators who advocate more uncompromising or confrontational policies toward their country's enemies.

head of state   An individual who represents the sovereignty of a state. In many cases, this individual is different from the head of government (for example, the British monarch and the British prime minister; the Queen of Canada, represented by the Governor-General; and the prime minister of Canada); in the United States, the president assumes both roles.

hegemonic power/hegemon   A dominant state that uses its military and economic power to establish global rules and institutions in accord with its interests.

hegemonic stability   Theory that a leading state can provide the public good of stability in the global political system, on the condition that it maintain its contested hegemonic status.

hegemony   Political dominance; either undisputed leadership in politics or dominance in the realm of ideas.

HIV   Human immunodeficiency virus, which can lead to AIDS. See *acquired immune deficiency syndrome.*

Hobson, John   (1858–1940) English economist who wrote on imperialism.

Holy Roman Empire   (962–1806 C.E.) Western European political entity claiming to be successor to the Roman Empire (suspended in 476 C.E.); a European commonwealth; lost importance after Thirty Years' War (1618–48).

homogenization   Any process in which different entities become increasingly similar; the diminishment of diversity.

human security   A framework that focuses on vulnerable individuals, rather than states, as the reference point for security policy. Freedom from want and freedom from fear are the cornerstones of the human security agenda. The governments of Canada and Norway were once the most vocal state advocates of human security.

IAEA   See *International Atomic Energy Agency.*

IBRD   See *International Bank for Reconstruction and Development.*

ICAO   See *International Civil Aviation Organization.*

ICBM   See *intercontinental ballistic missile.*

ICC   See *International Criminal Court.*

ICISS   See *International Commission on Intervention and State Sovereignty.*

ICJ   See *International Court of Justice.*

ICRC   See *International Committee of the Red Cross.*

IDA   See *International Development Association.*

IDPs   See *internally displaced persons.*

IFC   See *International Finance Corporation.*

IFIs   See *International Financial Institutions.*

IGOs   See *intergovernmental organizations.*

IJC   See *International Joint Commission.*

IMF   See *International Monetary Fund.*

immigration   The arrival of foreigners in a country for the purpose of taking up residence. A vital source of economic production.

imperialism   A policy of establishing political and economic control over foreign territories and all the intellectual accompaniments. At times used to refer to the spread of Western capitalism and the current processes of globalization.

industrial espionage   The use of human or electronic means to covertly acquire industrial secrets.

Industrial Revolution   The mechanization of industry and associated changes in social and economic patterns in Europe (and especially Great Britain) in the late 18th and early 19th centuries.

infanticide   The deliberate killing of infants.

intercontinental ballistic missile (ICBM)   A ballistic missile capable of flying from one continent to another, but especially one capable of flight between North America and Eurasia. Ballistic missiles were a central feature of nuclear deterrence during the Cold War.

interdependence   A state of affairs in which states and societies are increasingly connected by trade, finance, travel, and communication to the point they become mutually sensitive and responsive to events and policy changes. Interdependence is considered (especially by liberals) a characteristic of contemporary relations between nation-states.

intergovernmental organizations (IGOs)   International organizations created by and composed of member states.

internally displaced persons (IDPs)   Individuals or groups fleeing war or human and/or natural disasters who have not crossed an internationally recognized state border.

International Atomic Energy Agency (IAEA)   A United Nations agency that inspects nuclear power plants (and carries out other periodic inspections) to ensure compliance with the Non-Proliferation Treaty; it also promotes the development of nuclear energy.

International Bank for Reconstruction and Development (IBRD)   Development-based lending agency affiliated with the UN; commonly referred to as the World Bank.

International Civil Aviation Organization (ICAO)   A specialized agency of the UN, organized in 1947; formed to expand international air trade and promote safety. Headquarters are in Montreal.

International Commission on Intervention and State Sovereignty (ICISS)   An international panel of experts convened to explore the issue of when intervention in a state was justifiable in order to protect human security. The commission's final report was titled *The Responsibility to Protect*.

International Committee of the Red Cross (ICRC)   A neutral humanitarian relief organization, founded in 1859 and based in Switzerland, that cares for wounded during battle and observes the treatment of prisoners of war. Its counterpart in Muslim countries is the International Committee of the Red Crescent.

International Court of Justice (ICJ)   The World Court, which sits in The Hague, Netherlands, with 15 judges.

International Criminal Court (ICC)   Created in 1998 by the 120 signatories to the Rome Statute. The Rome Statute entered into force on July 1, 2002. The 18 judges of the ICC were elected in February 2003, and the ICC was formally inaugurated in March 2003.

International Development Association (IDA)   An affiliate of the World Bank (IBRD) that provides interest-free, long-term loans to developing states.

International Finance Corporation (IFC)   Created in 1956 to finance overseas investments by private companies without necessarily requiring government guarantees; borrows from the World Bank.

International Financial Institutions (IFIs)   International organizations created to manage and create rules for the conduct of international financial transactions and macro-level initiatives for development and crisis response.

International Joint Commission (IJC)   Canada–U.S. body established by the Boundary Waters Treaty of 1909 to deal mainly with transborder water resource questions. Consists of three Canadian and three American commissioners. Provides analysis and rulings related to transborder environmental issues, such as Great Lakes pollution.

International Monetary Fund (IMF)   Autonomous but affiliated with the UN since 1947; designed to facilitate international trade, reduce inequities in exchange, and stabilize currencies.

International Office of Weights and Measures   Intergovernmental organization established in 1875 to standardize weights and measures, affiliated with the UN since 1949.

International Organization for Migration (IOM)   International organization established in 1951 and dedicated to the promotion of orderly and humane human migration.

International Telecommunication Union (ITU)   An amalgamation of the International Telegraph Union (established 1865) and the International Radiotelegraph Union (established 1906). Established in 1932 under the title of International Telecommunication Convention; renamed the International Telecommunication Union in 1934.

International Union for Conservation of Nature (IUCN)   Promotes sustainable development and preservation of nature; involves both governments and NGOs; based in Gland, Switzerland.

Internet   An information network of computers that enables users to communicate and access information from all linked computers. Originated in a U.S. military communications project.

intifada   A series of clashes between Palestinian youths and Israeli security forces in the occupied territories that escalated into a full-scale revolt in December 1987. The El-Aqsa Intifada began in 2000.

IOM   See *International Organization for Migration.*

Iron Age   The historical epoch characterized by the widespread use of iron in tools and weapons.

isolationism   A foreign-policy approach emphasizing self-reliance and limited economic or political interaction with the international system.

ITU   See *International Telecommunication Union.*

IUCN   See *International Union for Conservation of Nature.*

jus ad bellum   Principles used to decide whether a war is just.

jus in bello   Principles used to decide what types of violence are permissible in war.

Kellogg–Briand Pact   Pact signed in 1928 by 44 states, renouncing war and promoting peaceful dispute settlement; named after U.S. Secretary of State Frank Kellogg and French Foreign Minister Aristide Briand.

Kennan, George   (1904–2005) American diplomat and historian; ambassador to the U.S.S.R., 1952.

Keynesian liberalism   An approach to liberal economics that calls for higher levels of government intervention and regulation in the market than envisioned by classical liberals. Named after the influential liberal economist John Maynard Keynes.

Khmer Rouge (Red Cambodians)   Communist rulers of Kampuchea, 1975–79, under Pol Pot and Leng Saray.

Korean War   North Korea attacked South Korea in June 1950; UN forces under American command joined in late June; Chinese communists joined North Korea in November 1950; armistice concluded in July 1953. Korea remains what many would consider to be the last Cold War front.

La Francophonie   Group of French-speaking states that meets to coordinate development policies.

LDCs   See *less-developed countries.*

League of Nations   The international organization that existed, without American membership, between the end of World War I and the end of World War II.

Lenin, Vladimir I.   (1870–1924) Russian revolutionist and statesman; founder of Bolshevism, the Third International, and the Soviet Union.

less-developed countries (LDCs)   Those states with the lowest levels of socioeconomic development as defined by the UN in terms of income (less that US$750 per capita GNP), human resource weakness, and economic vulnerability.

liberal feminists   Thinkers who argue that women have unequal opportunities to contribute to society, and that this form of discrimination holds back the development of society as a whole. They do not seek to eliminate institutions but to change them through women's participation.

liberal institutionalism   A branch of liberal theory that emphasizes the leading role played by international organizations and regimes in world politics, especially in economic affairs.

Liberal International Economic Order (LIEO)   The theoretical principles and institutional structures that managed the world economy after World War II.

liberal realists   Thinkers who emphasize the interaction between the international system, international society, and world society. They argue that despite the underlying condition of anarchy, a society of states does in fact exist. Often referred to as English school realists.

LIEO   See *Liberal International Economic Order.*

Lomé Convention   Agreement concluded between the EU and over 70 African, Caribbean, and Pacific (ACP) countries, allowing the latter preferential trade relations and greater economic and technical assistance. Superseded by the Cotonou Agreement of 2003.

long cycles   The theory that hegemons rise and decline in regular patterns, which in turn influence the international economy and the outbreak of hegemonic wars.

Luxemburg, Rosa   (1870–1919) German Marxist. Founded Spartacus Party during World War I; wrote on imperialism.

Maastricht Treaty   Signed by European Community on February 7, 1992, outlining steps toward further integration. See *European Union.*

MAD   See *mutual assured destruction.*

MAI   See *Multilateral Agreement on Investment.*

malnutrition   Results from inadequate or unbalanced diet, usually deficient in protein, vitamins, or minerals.

marketization   Movement away from state-controlled economy toward private property rights, open competition, trade liberalization, open investment, and floating currency.

Marshall Plan   U.S. Secretary of State George Marshall's 1947 plan to aid the reconstruction of European industry after World War II.

Marx, Karl   (1818–83) German economist and historian. Founder of the ideology of communism; proponent of historical materialism.

megacities   Generally this refers to cities (usually including their immediate municipalities) with over 10 million inhabitants.

mercantilism   The perspective holding that international trade should be regulated by the state to maximize national income. Also known as economic nationalism and neomercantilism.

Mercosur   A trade agreement linking Argentina, Brazil, Paraguay, and Uruguay.

middle powers   Countries that do not possess the power attributes of the great powers but that can have a significant impact on international politics in certain specific regions or in certain specific issue-areas. Canada is often described as a middle power, though some call it a satellite of the United States.

MNC   See *multinational corporation.*

modernization   A special paradigm of development, largely discredited today, evoking a progressive accumulation of social changes with a developmental sequence of industrialization, urbanization, education, communication, mobilization, and political participation.

multilateral   Involving three or more states; usually connotes cooperative action.

Multilateral Agreement on Investment (MAI)   Originally an OECD-coordinated effort to protect foreign investors from governmental intrusion; disbanded but still on the larger WTO agenda.

multilateralism   See *multilateral.*

multinational corporation (MNC)   A profit-seeking enterprise with operations in at least two states. Powerful actors in global politics today.

multipolarity   A distribution of power in which there are a number of poles, or great powers, in the system. This was characteristic of the pre–World War I era, and some analysts believe it can lead to instability.

mutual assured destruction (MAD)   The underlying nature of the nuclear stalemate between the superpowers during the Cold War. Both the United States and the Soviet Union possessed such large and capable arsenals that each side knew that if it attempted to attack the other with nuclear weapons, it would receive a devastating nuclear blow in return. As a result, both sides were deterred from using nuclear weapons against each other.

NAFO   See *Northwest Atlantic Fisheries Organization.*

NAFTA   See *North American Free Trade Agreement.*

NAM   See *Nonaligned Movement.*

Napoleon Bonaparte (Napoleon I)   (1769–1821) Emperor of France, 1804–15. Famous military general and political leader.

Napoleon I   See *Napoleon Bonaparte.*

Napoleonic Wars   (1796–1815) Waged by France under the French Revolution and later under Napoleon against England, Austria, Prussia, Russia, and most of the other countries of Europe. Ended with France's defeat at Waterloo.

nationalism   A sense of shared identity among a group of people, especially with respect to an ideology of attachment to a nation and to its shared interests.

nationalization   A government's assumption of the ownership of property, often previously owned by citizens from another state. Famous cases include the nationalization of the Suez Canal, and Cuban and Iranian appropriation of American commercial property.

NATO   See *North Atlantic Treaty Organization.*

natural law   A system of law binding on individuals by virtue of their nature as rational human beings. Natural law is considered universal across the human experience.

neo-Malthusian   Argument that resources will be outstripped by population growth in the modern era; has led to calls for strict population control.

neo-Marxist   Scholar who amends and/or extends Marxist ideas in order to explain contemporary global politics and economic conditions. Neo-Marxists developed theories such as "dependency" and "the world system" to illustrate how neoliberal capitalism hindered development and brought increased inequality between states and peoples in the global economy.

New International Economic Order (NIEO)   Statement of priorities adopted at the Sixth Special Session of the UN General Assembly in 1974, calling for equal participation of LDCs in the North–South dialogue.

NGOs   See *nongovernmental organizations.*

NIEO   See *New International Economic Order.*

Nonaligned Movement (NAM)   An effort begun in 1955 by developing countries to cooperate on issues of joint interest, especially decolonization, neutrality in the Cold War, and a more favourable international economic environment for their products. The NAM is largely moribund today.

nondiscrimination   A principle of free trade that requires any member of a trade organization or agreement (such as the WTO) to treat all imports entering the country in the same way. In other words, states cannot discriminate against some members of a trade agreement by imposing higher tariffs on a good coming from one country while lowering the tariff on the same good coming from another country. The tariff must be the same for both countries, provided both countries are members of the trade agreement.

nongovernmental organizations (NGOs)   Groups of individuals that do not represent the views of governments; usually operating for the purpose of charity or value propagation.

Non-Proliferation Treaty   Treaty signed in 1968 and in force in 1970, aimed at preventing the spread of nuclear weapons to more states.

nontariff barriers   Erected by a government to discourage imports, usually consisting of formal and voluntary quotas, prohibitions of certain imports, discriminatory restrictions, and licensing requirements. Now the main way governments restrict international trade and engage in protectionism.

NORAD   See *North American Air Defence Agreement.*

normative theory   Normative theory focuses on values and value preferences. It is primarily concerned with explaining what ought to be, rather than what is. Propositions in normative theory typically do not require empirical testing as a means of establishing their validity.

North American Air Defence Agreement (NORAD)   Signed on May 12, 1958 by the United States and Canada, creating a continental air defence (and later ballistic missile defence) warning and surveillance system in response to Cold War fears of an airborne attack by the former Soviet Union. In 1981 it was renamed the North American Aerospace Defence Agreement.

North American Free Trade Agreement (NAFTA)   Trilateral economic agreement reducing barriers on trade between Canada, the United States, and Mexico; contains side agreements on labour rights and environmental protection.

North Atlantic Treaty Organization (NATO)   Collective defence alliance and international organization created in 1949 to prevent the U.S.S.R. from attaining political influence or territorial conquests in Europe. Composed of 28 states in 2009, the alliance has restructured itself after the Cold War and admitted many new members. NATO Headquarters is in Brussels.

Northwest Atlantic Fisheries Organization (NAFO)   International organization of 11 members established to regulate fishing in the northwest Atlantic.

Nuremberg war crimes trials   1945–49. Trials of Nazis for war crimes by an international military tribunal; several were subsequently executed. See *war crimes trials*.

OAS   See *Organization of American States.*

OECD   See *Organisation for Economic Co-operation and Development.*

omnicide   Literally, the killing of all life, as might result from a nuclear war.

OPEC   See *Organization of the Petroleum Exporting Countries.*

Organisation for Economic Co-operation and Development (OECD)   An organization of 30 industrialized states organized around the principles of representative democracy and free market economics.

Organization for Security and Co-operation in Europe (OSCE)   A multilateral forum for discussing a wide range of political questions in Europe; includes Canada, the United States, Russia, and all of the European states. Established in 1995 to give permanent staff and headquarters to the Council on Security and Co-operation in Europe (CSCE).

Organization of American States (OAS)   Intergovernmental organization of 35 states of North and South America established in 1948 as a forum for political dialogue. Canada joined in 1990.

Organization of the Petroleum Exporting Countries (OPEC)   Producers' cartel setting price floors and production ceilings of crude petroleum; its members are the Arab oil producers (Saudi Arabia, Kuwait, the United Arab Emirates, Qatar, Iran, Iraq, Algeria, and Libya), Nigeria, Venezuela, and Indonesia.

OSCE   See *Organization for Security and Co-operation in Europe.*

peace movement   A social movement composed of various organizations and groups mobilized around the cause of peace, either in general terms or with respect to a certain war (that is, Vietnam, Iraq) or a possible war (Cold War). Peace movements advocate a number of strategies, including pacifism, nonviolent resistance, boycotts, diplomacy, the support of antiwar political candidates, and peaceful demonstrations.

per capita   Per person; when aggregate statistical information, such as GNP, is put into per-person form, it is expressed as so many units per capita.

perestroika   Economic reform policies instituted by Mikhail Gorbachev in the Soviet Union in the late 1980s.

Peter I   See *Peter the Great.*

Peter the Great (Peter I)   (1672–1725) Czar of Russia, 1682–1725. Founder of the modern Russian state.

polarity   The number of poles, or concentrations of power, in a region or in the international system. Systems with one dominant concentration of power are called unipolar, those with two bipolar, and those with many multipolar.

Politburo   The supreme decision-making body of the Soviet Union during the Cold War.

pooled sovereignty   The voluntary sharing or ceding of some sovereign decision-making powers by states to a cooperative, institutional framework. The European Union is often cited as an example of pooled sovereignty.

postcolonial feminists   Postcolonial feminists emphasize the experiences and perspectives of post-colonial women. Their philosophy is based on the experiences of racism and colonialism in postcolonial economic, political, and cultural contexts.

Prisoner's Dilemma   In game theory, a model that demonstrates how two actors can make self-interested decisions based on distrust and isolation from one another that leave them worse off than if they had trusted one another and cooperated instead.

proletariat   The ancient Roman word for those so poor that they could only give birth to children for military service. Karl Marx and Friedrich Engels used the term to represent the working-class elements in society.

protectionism   Using tariffs and nontariff barriers to control or restrict the flow of imports into a state in order to protect domestic industry; usually associated with neomercantilism.

proxy wars   Wars, usually in the South, in which the great powers are indirectly involved.

public good   Publicly funded and regulated services or infrastructure, open to use by all members of a society; in the international sense, the provision of political, military, and economic stability by a hegemon.

quota   A quantitative limitation imposed by government, usually applied to inflows of goods or migrants.

radical feminists   Radical feminists emphasize the patriarchal roots of inequality between men and women, or more specifically the social dominance of women by men. They view patriarchy as dividing rights, privileges, and power primarily by gender, and as a result oppressing women and privileging men. They are skeptical of political action within the current system, and instead support broader and more transformational social changes to eliminate patriarchy.

ratification   Official state approval of an international treaty, achieved when a state legislature approves (ratifies) a treaty by passing the necessary laws to align domestic law and regulation with treaty obliga-tions. International treaties enter into force (that is, are activated) only when a certain number of signa-tory states ratify the treaty.

rational actor model   A theory of decision making based on rational actors making decisions in a rational choice process, designed to maximize their desired outcomes.

realpolitik   A German word meaning practical politics, but generally employed as a synonym for power politics in the realist tradition.

recession   Rise in unemployment, decline of investment and growth; usually a period of less than a year. Recessions in important markets cause international concern.

reciprocity   The principle that a state should reciprocate when another state grants it trade conces-sions. This reciprocity should come in the form of trade concessions equivalent in value to the conces-sions granted to it by its trading partners.

Red Cambodians   See *Khmer Rouge.*

refugee   A person who has fled outside the borders of his or her country of origin because of fear of persecution, discrimination, or political oppression.

regime   Rules, principles, and decision-making procedures governing international behaviour in certain issue-areas.

regime theory   A theory, grounded in the liberal tradition, that argues that international institutions or regimes affect the behaviour of states through rules, principles, and decision-making procedures.

relative gains   The difference between actors experiencing a different rate of increase in some measure of capacity (such as economic wealth). If one actor is gaining capacity relative to the other actors, it is experiencing a relative gain with respect to the others.

repatriation   The resettlement by a refugee in his or her home state.

reprisal   A hostile, illegal act rendered legal when carried out in response to a previous illegal act.

resolution   Formal decision of an international organization, usually either registering a widely held or consensus opinion and/or recommending some sort of action (for example, a UN Security Council Resolution).

Revolution in Military Affairs (RMA)   The idea that military history has developed in a series of dramatic shifts in military capability, based on technological and social developments. The current RMA is based on computers and the information age.

RMA   See *Revolution in Military Affairs.*

robotics   Use of highly complex machines to perform complicated manufacturing tasks. See *automation.*

Rousseau, Jean Jacques   1712–78. French philosopher, author of *The Social Contract.* Influenced the concept of popular sovereignty.

SALT   Strategic Arms Limitation Treaties between United States and U.S.S.R.; treaties signed 1972 and 1979.

SAPs   See *structural adjustment programs.*

SARS   See *severe acute respiratory syndrome.*

satisficing   Propensity of decision makers to select an alternative or option that meets minimally acceptable standards at that moment.

Schlieffen Plan   The German military strategy for the conquest of France, put into action in WWI. The plan called for German armies to sweep through neutral Belgium and envelop Paris.

Secretariat   The administrative organ of the UN, headed by the Secretary-General; more generally, the administrative branch of any international organization.

secretary-general   Chief administrative officer of the UN who also plays an important, if often controversial, diplomatic role.

Security Council   Fifteen states (five permanent members) sit on this chief collective security organ of the UN.

security dilemma   A product of international anarchy in which states seek to rely on their own means to ensure their security by developing their military forces. In doing so, they inspire fear and distrust in their neighbours, who also arm. This reaction starts an arms race in which none of the participants is any more secure (and may in fact be less secure) than it was initially.

self-determination   The claim that people have the right to self-rule and (should they desire it) statehood.

severe acute respiratory syndrome (SARS)   Deadly form of pneumonia, which emerged from China in November 2002 and infected many people in other countries, including Canada.

Shiite Islam   The smaller of the two major branches of Islam, consisting of those who regard Ali, son-in-law of Muhammad, as the prophet's legitimate successor.

SLBM   See *submarine-launched ballistic missile.*

small states   Term used to identify those states that are the weakest in terms of power in a regional or global context.

socialist or Marxist feminists   Focus on the links between capitalism and patriarchy as the fundamental cause of women's oppression and identify "class" rather than "sex" as the ultimate cause of women's oppression.

soft power   Elements of state power—such as ideological attractiveness, culture, information capacity, and education—that have traditionally been disregarded (especially by realists) in favour of military or economic strength.

Solidarity   Self-governing trade union movement in Poland that began in 1980 and eventually played a major role in changes there; led by Lech Walesa, elected president of Poland in December 1990.

sovereignty   A government's ability to manage internal affairs and independently represent itself externally. A principle securing noninterference from other states, the keystone of the Charter of the UN.

START   See *Strategic Arms Reduction Treaty.*

state   A political entity possessing determined territory, permanent population, active government, and sovereign recognition by other states. Can also refer to the governing element of society with a monopoly on legitimate coercive violence or the instrument of the ruling economic classes.

state terrorism   The use of state power to terrorize civilians into compliance.

state-sponsored terrorism   Government support for terrorist individuals or groups acting abroad.

Strategic Arms Reduction Treaty (START)   Two treaties, START I and START II, reached between the United States and the U.S.S.R./Russia that made deep cuts in the nuclear arsenals of both countries.

structural adjustment programs (SAPs)   Economic policies established as conditions for IMF or World Bank loans to developing countries, usually requiring such countries to limit their spending, eliminate subsidies, and promote trade liberalization.

structural realists   Structural realists consider anarchy (absence of global government) as the central organizing principle of the international system; this structure forces states to pursue power for their own survival. Contemporary structural realists such as Kenneth Waltz, John Mearsheimer, and Robert Jervis are also often known as neorealists.

submarine-launched ballistic missile (SLBM)   A ballistic missile launched from a nuclear-capable submarine.

subsidies   Government programs that extend direct financial support, tax exemptions, or low-interest credit to certain firms engaged in the research or production of goods with considerable economic potential. Subsidies are used by governments to assist certain economic sectors to ensure their growth or survival.

Sunni Islam   The larger of the two major branches of Islam, consisting of those who regard the first four caliphs as the legitimate successors of Muhammad.

superpowers   The former U.S.S.R. and the United States during the Cold War era.

synthesis   An idea formed by a combination of other ideas.

tariff   A tax levied on imports. Free traders aim to eliminate them.

Thirty Years' War   (1618–48) General European war fought mainly in Germany; petty German princes and foreign powers (France, Sweden, Denmark, England) against the Holy Roman Empire (Hapsburgs in Austria, Germany, Italy, the Netherlands, and Spain); also a religious war of Protestants against Catholics. Ended with the Treaty of Westphalia.

tied aid   Foreign aid extended to recipient countries on the condition that at least part of the aid will be used to purchase goods and services from the donor country.

torture   Deliberate inflicting of pain, physical or psychological. Often state-directed.

trade   Exchanges of products, services, or money between states.

trade-related intellectual property rights (TRIPs)   An issue in international trade law and GATT/WTO negotiations concerning the protection of patent and copyright holders from piracy and copyright infringement.

trilateral   Said of an agreement or arrangement between three states or groups of states, such as NAFTA or the Trilateral Commission (United States, Western Europe, and Japan).

Trilateral Commission   A commission, formed in 1973 by private citizens from the United States, Europe, and Japan, that produces advice for governments and others regarding the management of the global economy.

TRIPs   See *trade-related intellectual property rights.*

Truman Doctrine   Outlined to Congress by U.S. President Truman in March 1947 in support of the Greek–Turkish aid bill; calls for the containment of communism by giving aid to like-minded governments.

trusteeship Council   Originally one of the main organs of the UN, authorized to examine and discuss the political, economic, social, and educational advancement of the peoples of Trust Territories, the Council is now defunct.

UN Children's Fund (UNICEF)   UN agency established in 1946 to provide food and health care to children after World War II; now provides humanitarian and development assistance to millions of mothers and children worldwide.

UN Conference on Trade and Development (UNCTAD)   A coalition of Southern or developing states that began meeting in 1964.

UN Development Programme (UNDP)   Coordinates and supports UN development projects.

UN Educational, Scientific and Cultural Organization (UNESCO)   Founded in 1945 as a specialized UN agency. It develops ideas and establishes standards on education, culture, and communication.

UN High Commissioner for Refugees (UNHCR)   Established in 1950 by the UN General Assembly to safeguard the rights and well-being of refugees and to lead and coordinate international action to protect refugees and resolve refugee problems worldwide.

unacceptable damage   The prospective costs of fighting a war (number of casualties and/or level of destruction) considered sufficient to deter an aggressor from starting a war. In deterrence theory, the ability of a state to retaliate after a nuclear attack and inflict unacceptable damage on the attacking state will deter such an attack. During the Cold War there were various formulas as to what constituted unacceptable damage, including the ability of each side to kill 50 percent of the other's population.

UNCTAD   See *UN Conference on Trade and Development.*

UNDP   See *UN Development Programme.*

UNESCO   See *UN Educational, Scientific and Cultural Organization.*

UNHCR   See *UN High Commissioner for Refugees.*

UNICEF   See *UN Children's Fund.*

unilateral   One-sided; said of the actions of a state taken without consultation or approval of others.

unipolarity   A region or international system in which there is one dominant actor. Some argue that the current international system is a unipolar one, with the United States as the one remaining superpower.

Universal Postal Union (UPU)   Established in 1874 with headquarters in Bern, Switzerland; became a specialized agency of the UN in 1947.

UPU   See *Universal Postal Union.*

urbanization   The process of growth, often rapid, of cities.

USAID   American foreign-aid department.

verification   Process of determining that all sides of an international agreement are in compliance.

Versailles Treaty   The principal treaty terminating World War I.

veto   The right to prohibit certain actions. The permanent members of the Security Council have a veto over the Council's substantive actions.

war crimes   Includes perpetrating mass murder; ill-treatment, deportation, or forced labour of prisoners; killing hostages; plunder; and wanton destruction with no military necessity.

war crimes trials   Prosecution of war criminals by an international tribunal, following World War II at Nuremberg and Tokyo, and presently at The Hague. May also take place within domestic jurisdiction of states.

Warsaw Pact   A treaty signed by the Soviet bloc states in 1955 pledging mutual military allegiance to the Soviet Union; dissolved in 1991.

weighted voting   A system of voting, such as that used in the IBRD, where the value of a member's vote is determined by the contribution (usually financial) the member makes.

Weimar Republic   (1919–33) German state established under a democratic federal constitution passed by a constitutional assembly in the city of Weimar.

WHO   See *World Health Organization.*

Wilson, Woodrow   (1856–1924) Twenty-seventh president of the United States, 1913–21; known for his internationalism.

World Bank   This institution, which was formally known as the International Bank for Reconstruction and Development and includes the International Development Agency, is a leading lender of money for development purposes. The World Bank Group includes the World Bank and three other agencies: the International Finance Corporation (IFC); the Multilateral Investment Guarantee Agency (MIGA); and the International Centre for Settlement of Investment Disputes (ICSID).

World Health Organization (WHO)   A specialized agency of the UN, headquartered in Geneva, founded in 1948 to promote and assist global health programs, including children's immunization.

World Trade Organization (WTO)   International organization established in 1995 as the successor to the GATT. Headquartered in Geneva, it has 153 member states and is the central forum for international negotiations on world trade.

world-system theory   A theoretical approach that emphasizes the global character of capitalism as the organizing principle of international politics.

WTO   See *World Trade Organization.*

xenophobia   A strong dislike, fear, or suspicion of other groups or nationalities.

Yalta Conference   A February 1945 summit meeting of Franklin Roosevelt, Josef Stalin, and Winston Churchill at which major postwar issues were discussed, such as the status of Central and Eastern Europe and voting arrangements in the UN.

zero-sum game   A relationship in which a gain for one actor entails a loss for another actor. Realists saw the Cold War as a zero-sum game.

Index